China's Strategic Seapower

China's Strategic Seapower

The Politics of Force Modernization in the Nuclear Age

John Wilson Lewis
and Xue Litai

STANFORD UNIVERSITY PRESS

Stanford, California

Studies in International Security and Arms Control

David J. Holloway, Michael M. May, and John W. Lewis, *General Editors*
Sponsored by the Center for International Security and Arms Control
Stanford University

Sources of photographs:
Except for photograph 5, which was reproduced by permission of
Jane's Information Group, all photographs were generously provided by
Chinese organizations whose cooperation is gratefully acknowledged.

Stanford University Press
Stanford, California
Printed in the United States of America
CIP data appear at the end of the book

Stanford University Press publications are distributed exclusively by
Stanford University Press within the United States, Canada, and Mexico;
they are distributed exclusively by Cambridge University Press
throughout the rest of the world.

FOR

CYNTHIA, STEPHEN, AND AMY

AND

LIU YING

Preface

This study is not the ordinary fare of China scholars. Submarines, nuclear power, ballistic missiles, and strategic doctrines touch a variety of cultures, disciplines, and specialties. This is not even the study we intended when we completed our history of Beijing's early nuclear weapons program (*China Builds the Bomb*; 1988). We then planned to write a companion volume on the strategic missile program. Though we did complete that study ("China's Ballistic Missile Program," 1992), the situation had changed immeasurably in a few short years.

With China's near-total shift to solid-propellant rockets and the tight linkage of the sea-based and new mobile ballistic missiles, it was clear that the main story belonged to the submarine-launched ballistic missile (SLBM) and the nuclear-powered submarine. That story, moreover, allowed us to carry forward our history of the strategic weapons complex and its fate during the tumultuous decades after the explosion of China's first atomic bomb in October 1964 and its multistage thermonuclear weapon in June 1967. As our subtitle puts it, this is an examination of the politics of strategic force modernization in the decades of the 1960s through the 1980s, China's nuclear era. That era ranged from the politics of the Great Leap Forward begun in 1958 to the economic reforms of Deng Xiaoping in the years after the Tiananmen crisis of 1989.

The tale of China's political development cannot be completed without a detailed understanding of its strategic and defense policies. The men and women who brought the Communist revolution to the Middle Kingdom were first and foremost soldiers, and they perceived a world of enemies and military threats. We have attempted to examine that pre-nuclear world in *Uncertain Partners* (1993), the book we coauthored with Sergei Goncharov on the creation of the Sino-Soviet alliance and the origins of the Korean War. Mao Zedong's world began in war and assumed the inevitability of future conflicts. That worldview shaped his politics and his policies, and served as a constant even as he shifted between compromise and conflict in his effort to determine China's future.

When we started this study, we realized how much we had to learn. Building a nuclear-powered submarine and an SLBM demands far greater technological-industrial knowledge and capacity than building nuclear weapons. From metallurgy to reactors, from solid rocket propellants to advanced guidance technology, we stretched our quest for understanding. We devoured materials in English and Chinese on welding, electronics, underwater launch systems, missile controls, chemicals, and submarine systems. Chinese designers and engineers, we came to understand, had gone through a much more demanding quest on the same types of materials, and in their search they gradually absorbed and embraced a concept found in Western sea-based strategic programs: survivable deterrence. That concept informed their thinking as they struggled for their own survival during the disastrous years of the Cultural Revolution.

Our research has depended to a significant extent on the technical assistance of a number of key specialists. One of these, Bob Dietz, spent hours with us discussing the details of missile guidance and missile development; we could not have completed this work without the knowledge he so kindly shared over several years. Mark Sakitt and Victor Li made critical contributions to the manuscript, and we also wish to thank John J. Engelhardt, John Harvey, Hua Di, and Jon Jenny. Several other American specialists were of major assistance but asked to remain anonymous. We respect their request but acknowledge their significant contributions with thanks.

We faced the challenge that comes from deciding on what must seem trivial matters. All things Chinese are cited and spelled in many different ways. The official spelling systems in the People's Republic of China and Taiwan are quite different but take on a certain political significance. Even from the academic perspective, no spelling system is truly adequate, and the several "standard" orthographies all posed problems. With some misgivings and an exception for the names of some well-known figures and place-names (for example, Chiang Kai-shek, Quemoy, and Yangtze) and Chinese people and places under the jurisdiction of Taiwan, we have used standard pinyin and, for Chinese place-names and boundaries, the pinyin gazetteer in *Zhonghua Renmin Gongheguo Fen Sheng Dituji* (Collection of Provincial Maps of the People's Republic of China; Beijing, 1983).

Our combined labors could not have succeeded without the aid of dedicated editors, cartographers, proofreaders, and manuscript preparers. Here we especially wish to thank the staffs of the Stanford University Press, and of the Hoover Institution's East Asian Collection. A special word of appreciation goes to Gerry Bowman, Carole Hyde, Douglas Peckler, Anca Ruhlen, and Danyune Zhang of the Stanford Center for International Security and Arms Control; each significantly helped us complete this book. During the years of research and writing, our Center colleagues Coit Blacker, Lynn Eden, and William Perry unfailingly provided encouragement and support, and Jacquelyn Lewis shared in the toil of polishing drafts and in countless other ways made this book possible.

The generous help that supported our research and writing came from several important sources. We wish to thank the Carnegie Corporation of New York, the Columbia Foundation, Dr. Marjorie Kiewit, the Peter Kiewit Foundation, the Henry Luce Foundation, the William and Flora Hewlett Foundation, the John D. and Catherine T. MacArthur Foundation, and the Walter H. Shorenstein Family Fund. We must add the obvious disclaimer that we alone bear the responsibility for this volume.

This book represents the last in a series of books and articles intended to understand the scope and evolution of Chinese security policy. Here we have examined that policy from the perspective of Beijing's changing strategic interests and weapons decisions. Our study of the Chinese nuclear weapons program focused on one part of the military-industrial system during the system's formative years, 1955–1967. By dealing with the development of the nuclear-powered submarine and the SLBM, this volume expands the horizon to encompass the broader political events and industrial decisions of the years 1958 to 1993.

We end the book by describing not only the evolution of Chinese strategy but also a 35-year pattern of interaction between politics and technology. An understanding of that pattern, we believe, creates a more accurate framework for the study of Chinese political-economic development during the first 44 years of the People's Republic.

J. W. L.
X. L. T.

August 1, 1993

Contents

Maps and Figures

People's Republic of China

China's Strategic Seapower

ONE

Technology and Self-Reliance in the Great Leap Era

In the late spring of 1958, the Communist Party and military leadership of China met in almost continuous session over a two-month period. First the Party and then the People's Liberation Army hammered out the details for a dramatic shift in national direction.[1] In announcing the results of their deliberations, Mao Zedong and his colleagues proclaimed the "general line of socialist construction" and set in motion policies that disavowed paced, planned modernization in favor of mass-based, political-economic radicalism. Within months, vast teams of workers, unfurling Mao's red banners, launched nationwide water conservation projects, built countless backyard steel furnaces, and restructured their villages into people's communes. The Great Leap Forward had begun.[2]

The social and economic ramifications of the new line were staggering, though not unanticipated.[3] Already at a conference in Nanning in January 1958, Mao had advocated a "rash advance," and in response, political activists were enjoined to mobilize China's millions to "transform the country after three years of hard struggle."[4] Mao later declared that though the rural people's communes emerged in April, the movement toward them had not been foreseen at the Chengdu Conference of March.[5] From all evidence, however, Mao had not only foreseen the communes by then but had formulated the sequence of actions for their creation and for the Great Leap.

Once this radical eruption gained momentum, Mao convoked Party and state meetings to give the movement its bearings, or, as he put it, to break superstitions, galvanize his forces, and energize the country.[6] "During the meetings," he said, "brains started to work and eight years' experience [since the founding of the People's Republic] was summed up."[7] In his many talks to the participants, the Chairman nagged, berated, and generally harangued his colleagues. These were far-ranging seminars on the grand sweep of concerns that had played on his mind for months: bureaucracy; ideology; dependency, both foreign and domestic; development and military preparedness; and creativity. His stated goal was to "catch up with Great Britain" by harnessing the energy potential of the populace.[8] He compared that potential to a uranium atom: "After the fission of the atomic nucleus of our nation, thermal energy will be released which becomes so formidable that we will be able to do what was beyond our ability before."[9]

Mao even hinted that progress on atomic fission in China was being thwarted by experts and technocrats, and in any event only "the masses" could succeed in tapping the nation's developmental energy. He labeled his associates who supported expertise over ideology "mindless politicians divorced from reality."[10] Earlier, he had noted that "our status quo faction is too large."[11]

The Communist leader signaled his contempt for conservative technocrats by comparing them to useless academics. The Party had been terrified of professors, he noted, "ever since we came into the towns" during the later civil war years.[12] Yet the scholars proved not to be innovators. "Ever since ancient times," he said, "the people who founded new schools of thought were all young people without too much learning."[13]

Mao opened the second session of the Eighth Party Congress in May with an all-out assault on superstition. He urged Party leaders not to be afraid of professors and not to be reluctant to become professors, reiterated his reflections on the creativity of the young and untutored, and then presented a roster of history's most inventive minds to prove his point. Stalin was wrong to insist that "technology decides everything," Mao said, for if this was so, he asked, "then what about politics?" The fact was, he declared, the nonprofessional Party politician was much more important than the professional expert and, in all cases, should lead that expert.[14]

Mao's themes and conclusions immediately defined the agenda for the two-month meeting of the Central Military Commission that opened on May 27.[15] From the published speeches that have found their way into print outside China over the past years, Mao appears to have here advocated less dogmatism in following Soviet rules and experience and less reliance on Soviet technology.[16] Indeed, whereas he had simply belittled atomic weapons in comparison with the deadly swords of yesterday's warriors at the second session of the Party congress a few weeks before the military commission's first meeting, he now extended his censure of dependence on the weapons themselves to include the rote adoption of Soviet offensive plans and thinking.[17]

Specifically, Mao referred to a resolution concerning the problem of technological reform passed two years earlier at a Party congress. He now deemed this resolution incorrect because "it overly emphasized Soviet help." Though China was in need of Soviet aid, he said, "what is of primary importance is self-help. If we should unduly stress reliance upon Soviet aid, let us ask on whom the Soviet Union depended for its help?"[18] Given the thrust of Mao's recorded remarks, one might reasonably conclude that Mao's admonitions against "blind faith in foreigners" extended to blind faith in technology, especially foreign technology, and to a rejection of Soviet defense aid in favor of military self-reliance.[19]

Recently published materials from China, however, call that conclusion into question for, as we now know, 1958 was a turning point in Beijing's quest to obtain maximum military-technical aid from Moscow. The direction was toward more, not less. In Mao's mind, it seems clear, his comrades had to distinguish between the unambiguous need for Soviet aid and the unwanted imitation of Soviet ideas and regulations that ran against China's cherished revolutionary traditions, especially the hallowed doctrine of People's War. Mao defined that doctrine as "man over weapons," revolutionary self-reliance, and grass-roots participation in and support for righteous conflicts.

As was usual for him, Mao personalized his critique of "erroneous ideas," in this case ideas about People's War, and identified them with Marshal Liu Bocheng, whose leadership of the Military Academy had given him increasing influence over the military educational system and the thinking of younger military officers.[20] Thus Mao used the occasion of the military commission meeting in the summer of 1958 to order Marshal Liu to attend and subject himself to criticism. Accused at the meeting of "carrying out the bourgeois military line," Liu suffered rebuke after rebuke in "extremely abnormal ways." Several hours later, the already ailing marshal was rushed to the hospital for emergency treatment, and soon after he was "forced to stand aside." In addition, Mao used the platform to berate Chief of the General Staff Su Yu and two vice-ministers of defense allegedly associated with Liu, and they and many other senior officers were dismissed.[21]

Mao's worry about historic Russian efforts to dominate China also informed the logic of a policy that separated the quest for more Soviet aid from the blind acceptance of all things Soviet to the detriment of the nation's sovereignty.[22] In March 1958, when Nikita Khrushchev replaced Nikolai Bulganin as Soviet premier, Mao concluded that Khrushchev would try to intensify his control over China once he had consolidated his position in the Kremlin.[23] Again Mao personalized the matter. His own relations with Khrushchev had long been strained, and the Chairman translated dislike into political mistrust.[24] For Mao, each decision was a balancing act between competing alternatives, as well as a means of retaliating against individuals, both Chinese and foreigners, who had fallen from his favor.

In sum, his bias toward self-reliance was meant to limit only the political and doctrinal effects of Soviet aid, not its volume. When coupled with the bold vision of the Great Leap, Mao's confident expectation that Moscow's aid would increase apparently helped banish any doubts he might have harbored about the most pressing decision then before the Chinese military: whether to attempt the building of a nuclear-powered submarine and its ballistic missile.

The 09 Decision

Shortly after the opening of the Central Military Commission conference in May 1958, Marshal Nie Rongzhen, the leader of weapons research and development, convened a separate symposium to explore the potential for R&D on a nuclear-powered missile submarine.[25] Present at this June meeting were senior figures from the navy, the Chinese Academy of Sciences, the First and Second Ministries of Machine Building, and the Fifth Academy (responsible for missile R&D).[26] Nie had prepared well for the meeting, and within days the participants concurred on the fundamental operational principles, proposed rate of progress, division of tasks, organizational systems, and requirements for plant construction for the new programs.

Let it be noted that, beyond the long presumed but largely unstated commitments to defense modernization and to reducing the American threat to China, Nie's group did not discuss or appear to consider relevant how these programs, if successful, would fit any new strategic concept or contradict the assumptions of People's War. The members of Nie's group did not explicate the underlying strategic rationale for the program, and no one asked them to do so.

This decision-making process should be viewed within the spirit of the times. At this point, Beijing's leaders embraced without question a torrent of utopian slogans and schemes. To cite only one example, in the space of nine months, from November 1957 to July 1958, Mao first called for surpassing Great Britain within 15 years, then seven years, and finally two years.[27] Yet no one dared express skepticism, let alone ridicule. In such an atmosphere, wildly exaggerated optimism inevitably penetrated the military high command, whose members soon called for the development of "what others have" and the creation of a "small but all-inclusive" arsenal.[28] Possibilities now became certainties.

By this time, driven by the unchallenged quest for advanced weapon technologies, the navy's research-and-development system was already taking shape. As early as 1956, Nie had stressed the military aspects of the Twelve-Year Plan for the Development of Science and Technology and had given priority to building a nuclear power plant for submarines.[29] In the following year, Vice-Admiral Luo Shunchu, one of the navy's deputy commanders, had begun organizing the naval scientific system, and by 1958 he had established six research institutes—on warship design, underwater weapons, navigation, underwater acoustics, engineering design, and medical science and service—under the administration of a new service branch, the Naval Science and Technology Research Department.[30] At the same time, Defense Minister Peng Dehuai, then in charge of daily affairs of the Central Military Commission, had approved the building of a large-scale research facility for the development of naval missiles.[31]

Thus, the navy's fundamental R&D administration was already in place when, on June 27, 1958, during the military commission conference, Nie Rongzhen submitted his formal recommendation for commencing the nuclear submarine and SLBM programs to Mao and the central leadership via Minister of Defense Peng and Premier Zhou Enlai.[32] In his "Report on the Problem of Designing and Trial-Manufacturing an Atomic Submarine on a Self-Reliant Basis," Nie noted that with an experimental nuclear reactor already in operation, the Scientific Planning Commission believed the time had come to consider possible military applications.[33]

Nie's proposal to develop both submarine and payload simultaneously was unprecedented. The American Polaris missile program was not given the go-ahead until 1956, when the U.S. navy had solved the mysteries of nuclear propulsion.[34] The Soviet engineers, convinced that concentrating on the twin challenges of nuclear propulsion and sea-launched ballistic missiles in parallel would incur great risks, had likewise elected to proceed sequentially. The first Soviet missile submarine operated on diesel power.

Having gleaned some information about these foreign programs, Nie's first recommendation was to advance gradually and systematically, and to this end, he focused on the program's basic organizational requirements. He advocated the appointment of the vaguely named Four-Person Leading Group headed by Luo Shunchu and Zhang Liankui to conceptualize the steps to be taken in building the nuclear-powered submarine.[35] (We have already met Admiral Luo as the man who earlier in the year had created the navy's research institutes.) Zhang was the vice-minister of the First Ministry of Machine Building, which was then responsible for general civilian and military industry. They, along with representatives from the Second Ministry of Machine Building (nuclear industry) and the Fifth Academy (missile development), would investigate competing design approaches for the submarine and its weapons and would outline the planning, organizational, and manufacturing requirements for the long-term program.[36]

Even though the military high command was meeting in almost daily session in late June 1958, Zhou Enlai gave Nie's report priority attention and quickly passed it through channels to Deng Xiaoping's General Secretariat for referral to the Politburo's Standing Committee. Deng appended a note to his transmittal letter endorsing the proposed project, and a few days later, taking note of the chain of endorsements, the Standing Committee unanimously decided to proceed. There is no record of any debate or moves to delay, let alone any worry expressed about the People's War concept of "man over weapons," self-reliance, or Soviet help. One senior official remarked that the committee's "examination and approval of [Nie's] report was even faster than had been expected." In July, Mao signed the directive authorizing the commencement of the nuclear-powered submarine project and the formation of the Four-Person Leading Group under Luo Shunchu and Zhang Liankui.[37] The code name was Project 09.

With Mao's blessing in hand, the Central Military Commission on July 28, just six days after adjourning its landmark conference on self-reliance, passed the "Resolution on the Construction of the Navy." The document gave priority to the submarine service and to the SLBM (code-named Project JL) and the power plant for the first-generation nuclear submarines. Over the next two months, the Luo-Zhang group worked out the procedural details, and by October 1958, research on the nuclear power plant and on solid propellants for the submarine missile had gotten under way.[38]

Despite the highly publicized emphasis in the Great Leap Forward on mass movements and popular participation in science and technology, Project 09 and its associated missile project proved relatively free from any outside interference during the start-up years. In our earlier study of the nuclear weapons program (Project 02), we showed how that effort was undermined by the zealotry of Mao's followers in this period. Since 02 had very high priority, too, we can only speculate on why the submarine project was able to escape the same fate. It may simply be that the navy's small and isolated initial research facilities on protected military bases remained invisible to hypercritical Party cadres and activists and thus could be insulated bureaucratically from penetration in ways that uranium mining and the construction of the large nuclear weapons industrial facilities could not.[39]

A more likely explanation is that the navy's participation shielded the program. The central role of a military service in an advanced research-and-development program was unprecedented and in fact has not been repeated since. Though the shipbuilding ministry, the Sixth Ministry of Machine Building, would eventually be spun off from the First and the follow-on Third Ministry, and the navy would share some of its project-related authority with this state organ, the navy continued to play a central directing role in the development of both the submarine and the SLBM throughout. In defining this role, it is worth noting, the Chinese consciously studied the bureaucratic powers and techniques of the U.S. Navy's Special Projects Office in connection with the Polaris program.[40] They liked not only the methodology but the relative freedom from outside interference that the U.S. program appeared to enjoy.

The Start-Up Organization

In his report of June 27, 1958, Nie Rongzhen had stressed the importance to the project's future of an effective bureaucratic infrastructure, and following the creation of the Luo-Zhang group, other organizations were set in place. That August, in a directive entitled "On the Development of New Naval Submarine Technologies," the Central Committee put the Second Ministry in charge of the "research-and-design tasks on the reactor of the nuclear-powered submarine and on related control systems and protective equipment."[41] At the same time, the navy and the First Ministry were ordered to prepare a comprehensive design plan for the first boat.[42]

Nie Rongzhen's report of June 27 also set in motion the initial planning and research tasks on Project 09 at the Institute of Atomic Energy (IAE). The Second Ministry had already created some of the building blocks for nuclear energy research at the institute and since January 1955 had, in secret, taken the first steps toward the atomic bomb.[43]

Now, in September, it ordered the IAE's Reactor Engineering Research Section (code-named Section 12) to complete preliminary studies of a submarine nuclear power plant and to form its own Submarine Reactor Design Group.* The principal research thrust on the reactor started in Section 12, as well as in several sister labs and organs, including the Reactor Component and Materials Research Section and the Metal Physics Research Section, both of which worked on reactor components.[44]

The work environment for so ambitious a program was terrible. Section 12's researchers were crammed into a barely refurbished building that had little heat and lighting. The ministry had assigned young and inexperienced technical personnel to the section and left them to their own devices, without any data, experimental equipment, or computers. The section's files

---

*In 1964, the Beijing-based section was enlarged, made more autonomous, and renamed the Reactor Engineering and Technology Institute (Institute 194). Four years later, elements of 194 moved to Sichuan Province to become the Southwest Reactor Engineering Research and Design Academy (First Academy). Li Jue et al., 295, 365, 385.

contained only general pictures of the configurations of foreign nuclear-powered submarines and sketchy details on two marine power plants. As the youthful designers saw it, they were not much better off than the general populace would have been, had it been charted to come up with a workable design entirely on the basis of self-reliance.[45]

Also in September, having checked with the Four-Person Leading Group, the navy and the First Ministry jointly formed the Nuclear-Powered Submarine Overall Design Section, with individual teams assigned to work on the vessel's overall design, power plant, weapons and equipment, and electronics.[46] At the same time, the navy set up its own Shipbuilding Technology Research Section to determine the technical specifications for the sub.[47]

As noted, the designers, even though they saw their own efforts as fully in accord with the can-do spirit of the times, had the good fortune of escaping the most destructive consequences of the Great Leap. By the time they set to work, in the fall of 1958, the mass movements were already beginning to take a toll on the other defense programs.[48] Ordinary workers in key military organs now claimed to know more than advanced experts and, rejecting Soviet advice and blueprints, attempted to modify or develop sophisticated weapons systems on their own. The result was sheer chaos.[49]

Nie Rongzhen, in the meantime, was bringing the submarine program into even better order. In October, right after the studies on the design of the power plant commenced, he submitted yet another report to the military commission, proposing that all strategic weapons programs be brought under unified command, and that the Second Ministry be reorganized within that new command. In response, the commission established the Defense Science and Technology Commission with Nie as director (see Fig. 1) and merged the Aviation Industrial Commission and the Division for Scientific and Technological Research of the General Staff's Equipment Planning Department into the new body.[50] In April 1959, the Fifth Department (responsible for managing missile development) was also merged into the new commission.[51] With its expanded authority and reach, Nie's commission could oversee the development of nuclear weapons and strategic launch vehicles, and shared responsibility with the navy for conducting research and development on the nuclear sub.

Over the next months, as Nie's organization gained experience, a major debate erupted within the elite over the most disruptive Great Leap policies, and one casualty of the struggle was Defense Minister Peng Dehuai.[52] Following the ouster of Peng and Chief of the General Staff Huang Kecheng at a Party plenum in August 1959, other senior military leaders moved up in a general reshuffling. Lin Biao replaced Peng as defense minister, and he,

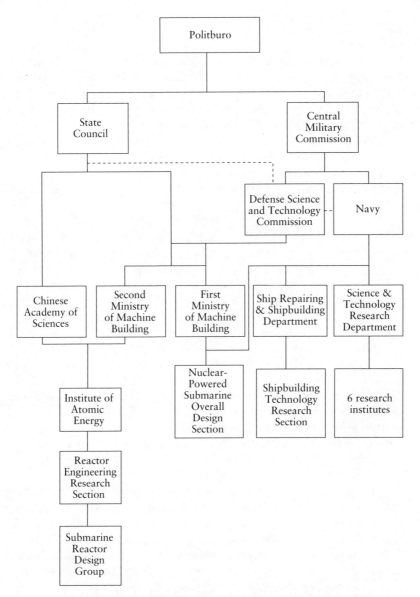

Fig. 1. Initial organization of Project 09 (after Oct. 1958). In this and the subsequent figures charting the changes in the project's command structure, a solid line shows the control and reporting channels and a dotted line shows coordination among the indicated bodies.

Nie Rongzhen, and He Long were made vice-chairmen (under Mao Zedong) of the Central Military Commission.[53] Nie was the only one of the
three not then on the Politburo.

Lin Biao, in turn, recommended to Mao that Minister of Public Security
Luo Ruiqing be appointed chief of the General Staff, but Luo remembers
that within two years after he returned to the army, he "became not so
obedient" in Lin's eyes.[54] As Mao moved people around, their personal animosities and rival networks grew. We shall return many times to the story
of these rivalries, for it was in this chaotic political and personally contentious climate that the Chinese conducted the nuclear-powered submarine
project in its pioneering and most challenging years. Yet the project progressed, and Beijing's leaders looked to Moscow to guarantee its success.

The Quest for Soviet Aid

In our earlier study of the Chinese nuclear weapons program, we reviewed briefly Soviet nuclear assistance to China over the years 1956–58.
Here we want to focus principally on developments related to the navy.
Our purpose is to examine just how the Chinese sought maximum military
aid from the Soviet Union at the moment Mao Zedong was expounding
the virtues of national self-reliance. For the nuclear submarine project
(Project 09), as we shall see, that quest proved futile. Nevertheless, before
self-reliance became an unwanted reality, Moscow helped the Chinese define and make progress on some of the fundamental technologies involved,
including nuclear reactors.

The beginnings of Sino-Soviet cooperation were auspicious. In August
and December 1956, the Soviet Union agreed to help support China's nuclear industries and research facilities and its prospecting for uranium under less restrictive conditions than those negotiated in 1955,[55] though it
was still unwilling to provide assistance on the nuclear weapons themselves. According to Chinese sources, Khrushchev at this time was soliciting political backing to recover from the disastrous aftermath of the Hun-
garian uprising in October 1956 and the anti-Communist and anti-Soviet
movement in Poland, and so was impelled to become "more flexible on the
matter of giving sophisticated technical aid to China."[56]

Not the least of Khrushchev's problems in the wake of these policy failures was a rising opposition to his rule within his own leadership group,
a predicament that gave the Chinese reason to hope that they might exploit
his troubles for their own ends. Beijing's ambassador to Moscow, Liu Xiao,
was quick to alert them to the situation, reporting that, "in order to convince the Chinese [Communist] Party to support his position in the polit-

ical struggle within the CPSU, Khrushchev needs to indicate some manifestation of his friendship toward our country."[57] It was a point that did not escape Nie Rongzhen, who did not delay in recommending to Zhou Enlai that the Chinese "seize the opportunity" and use their political leverage to get greater military assistance. Responding with alacrity, Zhou gave him permission to initiate discussions with Ivan V. Arkhipov, the Soviet adviser in charge of aid to China.[58]

Yet just as the Chinese were coming to sense the possibility of capitalizing on the Soviet power struggle, Khrushchev was beginning to defeat his domestic rivals, and a decisive episode in his favor came in June 1957.[59] Toward the end of the month, the political crisis in the Kremlin, as George Kennan has put it, "culminated in the sudden, unprecedented, and dramatic removal" of Presidium members V. M. Molotov, G. M. Malenkov, L. M. Kaganovich, and other top leaders.[60]

The interesting question for our story is: To what degree, if any, did this victory remove the pressure on Khrushchev to increase military assistance to China? The Chinese were fully aware of the results of the June plenum of the CPSU Central Committee, which ratified the actions against the "anti-Party" group. They also knew that Nikolai Bulganin, who appeared to them to be a friend of China, remained premier even though he had been implicated as a backer of the group. It was not until the following spring that Khrushchev could conclude the affair (on March 27, the Supreme Soviet ousted Bulganin and appointed Khrushchev premier), and in the intervening months, Bulganin is known to have advocated giving a prototype nuclear weapon to Beijing, perhaps merely to curry favor with the Chinese.[61]

For most of this period, at least through the end of 1957, as the Soviet specialist Carl Linden notes, Khrushchev continued to benefit from "Chinese support or, more precisely, acquiescence to his leadership." Further, he was in need of "tranquility in the bloc," and his strongest supporter there continued to be the Chinese.[62] Despite Khrushchev's June victory, Beijing concluded that China's importance to the Kremlin leader remained undiminished.

For a time, this judgment seemed to be vindicated. After contacting his government, Arkhipov on July 20, 1957, told Nie Rongzhen that Moscow would consider additional defense support, and two months later, Nie led a small negotiating team to the Soviet Union. Under the terms of the resulting New Defense Technical Accord, signed on October 15, Moscow agreed to supply China a prototype atomic bomb, some missiles, and major industrial equipment related to China's nuclear weapons and missile programs. But no data on Soviet nuclear-powered submarines would be forthcoming; the Kremlin turned down China's explicit request for technical assistance on its future nuclear-sub program.[63]

Very soon thereafter, the Soviets reneged on their promise to ship a prototype bomb to China, and the ties of comradeship began to unravel. As a further complication, Khrushchev, by now greatly strengthened, regarded cooperation as a two-way street more than at any time since his rise to power, and it was this view that sparked an increasingly divergent dialogue—perhaps parallel monologues would be a better term—between the two nations.[64] This was also a time when a singular emphasis on the submarine in Soviet naval doctrine was being felt.[65] Khrushchev recalls in his memoirs that "once we began to produce diesel and nuclear-powered submarines, our navy suggested that we request of the Chinese government permission to build a [long-wave] radio station in China so that we could maintain communications with our submarine fleet operating in the Pacific." Khrushchev fully anticipated that the Chinese would cooperate.[66]

Beijing, however, was just lifting the opening curtain on the Great Leap Forward, and Mao's admonitions about Soviet influence translated into political paranoia. After Bulganin's ouster in March, the Chinese concluded that Khrushchev would use his strong internal position "to strengthen his control over fraternal parties and fraternal nations."[67] As one of that number, China would not be spared. By one account, Mao and his colleagues were convinced that "Khrushchev thought it appropriate to gain control of China [now that] he had gained a firm foothold [inside the Kremlin hierarchy]," and had decided that 1958 was the "time to deal with China."[68]

Curiously, Beijing did not grasp the incongruity between this conclusion and its quest for increased military assistance. With the main agreement on strategic weapons behind them, the Chinese, apparently not appreciating the shifting political sands beneath their feet, added to their list of demands for aid in modernizing their armed forces. The Chinese position becomes more understandable, however, when considered in the light of Moscow's response during the first half of 1958. Simply put, the Soviets appeared to comply with China's demands. Soviet naval officers were instructed to provide their Chinese counterparts with limited information on Soviet advances in submarine technology. The officers suggested that China should place orders for additional naval equipment from the Soviet Union.[69]

Taking these suggestions as tantamount to a much broader Soviet offer to assist China's naval modernization, Zhou Enlai on June 28, 1958 (the day after Nie Rongzhen submitted his report on the nuclear submarine and

SLBM programs), dictated a letter to Moscow specifically requesting the Soviet Union to supply China the designs for new-type submarines (including nuclear-powered submarines) and to teach it how to build them.[70] Conceivably, Zhou did not need the spur of the officers' suggestions, for the week before he sent his letter, Mao had taken the commission platform to say, "Besides sustained efforts to strengthen the construction of the army and air force, we must go all out to develop the shipbuilding industry."[71] Zhou would almost certainly have interpreted Mao's statement as mandating a new approach to Moscow.

The Soviets for their part read the developments in the first half of 1958 as a sure sign of Beijing's willingness to defer to their wishes in the matter of the China-based radio relay center. As early as April 18, Soviet Defense Minister Radion Ia. Malinovskii approached Peng Dehuai with a proposal for a joint Sino-Soviet effort to build a long-wave radio transmission center (as well as a radio-receiving installation) between 1958 and 1962.[72] The Soviet Union would supply 70 percent of the funds for the two installations. Not fully appreciating how important the long-wave installation in China was to Soviet submarines operating in the Pacific, Beijing dismissed Malinovskii's proposal as an effort to "control our country's intelligence and classified communications."[73]

For the Chinese, the issue was one of ownership and sovereignty. Peng thus informed the Soviet Ministry of Defense on June 12 that China agreed to build these facilities but would do so at its own expense using Soviet technical aid. On July 11, Moscow fired off a draft accord that called for the joint administration of the facilities with the Soviets paying the full cost. Beijing then drastically amended the draft and mailed it back to Moscow: the Chinese would build and own the station and would place orders only for equipment and matériel that they could not manufacture.

As the tensions rose and draft met counterdraft, neither Khrushchev nor Mao Zedong was able to demonstrate finesse or sensitivity. To make matters worse, the Soviet Union chose this moment to make an additional proposal in the way of naval cooperation. Zhou Enlai's letter of June 28 requesting greater technical assistance for the navy led Moscow to assume that the Chinese were ready to deal, and that it had only to devise a compromise. In July, Soviet Ambassador Yudin met with Liu Shaoqi to review China's request for help on Project 09, and he took the occasion to float the idea of a joint submarine flotilla.

Some days later, on July 21, at the moment of maximum misperception and miscommunication, Yudin called on Mao.[74] Invoking Khrushchev's name, Yudin broached the notion to the Chairman himself.[75] Mao responded by asking, "First of all, we should determine the guiding principle.

[Do you mean that] we should create [such a submarine flotilla] with your aid . . . or you won't give us aid?" At this point, Peng Dehuai, who was present at the meeting, shifted the subject to repeat China's continued opposition to the radio station, saying, "the ownership should belong to us; otherwise it is politically unacceptable." Mao added that it was surely "inappropriate to organize a military 'cooperative.' "[76]

The following day, Yudin and Mao met again. The Chinese leader preempted the conversation and told the Soviet ambassador that he was rescinding Zhou Enlai's request for Soviet technical assistance to the navy. He reiterated his opposition to the long-wave radio station and said that "the creation of a joint submarine flotilla is a political problem that involves [China's] sovereignty." Looking directly at Yudin, Mao exclaimed: "On political [grounds], even half a finger is out of the question. . . . You can say that I am a nationalist. . . . If you say so, I will have to say that you have expanded Russian nationalism to the Chinese seacoast." In his cable to Khrushchev after the meeting, Yudin stated that when the Soviet proposals were presented, "Mao [had] shouted, 'How dare you suggest such a thing! This proposal is an insult to our national pride and our sovereignty!' "[77]

Here again the timing of the Chinese position is curious, for this confrontation with Moscow came just as the Politburo was deliberating Nie Rongzhen's recommendation to commence Project 09. It was on July 28 that the Central Military Commission issued the authorizing edict. At the instant of decision, the Chinese leaders were clearly basing their action on the hope of getting full-scale Soviet technical assistance, and the commission's approval prompted Beijing in the next few days to make yet another formal request for help on the nuclear submarine project.[78]

Imposed Self-Reliance

Beijing's request was made during Khrushchev's second visit to China, from July 31 to August 3, 1958.[79] Khrushchev had elected to fly to the People's Republic after receiving Yudin's cable concerning the July 21–22 meetings. The Presidium of the Soviet Central Committee had met in urgent session, and at the end of its deliberations, Khrushchev and other senior leaders decided to make a secret visit to China as soon as it could be managed. The Soviet leader was beginning to grasp that the issue was shifting from the implementation of cooperation to the preservation of the alliance itself.[80]

The Chinese, needing assistance on the submarine project now more than ever, agreed to the visit. They expected Khrushchev to press for the long-wave radio station and the joint submarine flotilla but hoped he had come to deal.[81] And, by his own account, the Soviet leader did want to negotiate. Nevertheless, Khrushchev would not budge on providing direct support to the nuclear submarine project and dismissed the whole idea with a wave of his hand. His stated reason was that China would not be able to complete the project because of its backward industrial technologies and scientific base.[82] Though insulted, Mao responded with feigned indifference: "If we don't agree [with your proposal for a joint flotilla] then we won't have a nuclear submarine. I don't care [*meiyou guanxi*]."[83]

Although Mao had failed to change Khrushchev's mind, the Soviet leader still hoped to move Mao and kept talking. On the subject of the radio station, Khrushchev said that Moscow had no intention of violating China's sovereignty. He blamed his defense minister for failing to get instructions from the Central Committee. Mao said that what he wanted was credits, and Khrushchev, agreeing, said he could also supply technical advice and equipment. China would build the station with Soviet help, and the matter was settled.[84]

On the question of a joint flotilla, Khrushchev accused his ambassador of making mistakes in transmitting official messages.[85] Here Khrushchev's memoirs are misleading. He says only that "our navy wanted to refuel our submarines and to give our crews shore leave at the ports along the Chinese coast."[86] The two leaders in fact argued about a reciprocal arrangement proposed by Khrushchev under which Chinese subs could be based at Soviet Arctic Ocean facilities, and the Soviet Union would be allowed to lease the navy base at Lüshun and the city of Dalian for its subs.[87] Mao summarily dismissed this proposal, and Khrushchev notes that he "couldn't object too strenuously to Mao's reaction. Perhaps we'd been a bit hasty in suggesting that he give us a submarine base in China."[88]

The Taiwan Strait crisis a few weeks later cast still another shadow over Sino-Soviet relations and further confused the dispute on naval cooperation.[89] Even before his July visit, Khrushchev had gotten wind of Beijing's preparations for an attack on the offshore islands controlled by Taiwan.[90] Thus, during the visit, he shifted the conversation from naval matters to a probing of China's intentions toward the Nationalists. He especially wanted Mao to tell him what means might be taken to solve the Taiwan issue and reportedly asked him: "When will Taiwan be put under the jurisdiction of China?"[91] Mao evaded the question but, Khrushchev records, asked for "considerable military aid . . . in order to stage a military operation against Chiang Kai-shek." Khrushchev adds that he gave the Chinese what they asked for in the belief they were planning a decisive action against Taiwan, and that he "made no move to try to restrain our Chinese comrades."[92] Chinese sources do not dispute this Soviet account but emphasize that Khrushchev worried about a possible Soviet-U.S. nuclear confrontation in the event of a Sino-U.S. showdown. By his own admission, Mao did misjudge the possibility of a forceful American response as the PLA buildup opposite Taiwan began in August.[93]

Despite the directness of their conversations on Taiwan, the Chinese in fact did mislead their guests and did not inform the Soviet delegation of their decision to shell Quemoy on August 23, 1958, just three weeks after the delegation departed.[94] When, in September, Foreign Minister Andrei Gromyko flew to Beijing to find out firsthand what was happening, the Chinese somewhat disingenuously told him the Soviet Ministry of Defense should have received the full facts through its advisers at the Chinese ministry. They added that China itself would bear responsibility for the consequences in case of an all-out war with the United States, and that the Soviet Union need not be involved even if the United States employed tactical nuclear weapons against China.[95] Gromyko many years later recalled Mao's recommendation if the crisis should lead to an American invasion of China. U.S. forces should be lured deep into the mainland, he allegedly said, and then Soviet nuclear weapons could be used to annihilate them ("Only when the Americans are right in the central provinces should you give them everything you've got").[96] However, official Soviet documents discredit Gromyko's account.[97]

By most Chinese (and Western) accounts, it was only after Khrushchev's fears of war had been set to rest that, on September 7, 1958, he warned Washington that an attack on China would be tantamount to one on the Soviet Union.[98] Although the sequence of events in the crisis appears to confirm the widely held view that Khrushchev was timid under fire, the facts appear to speak otherwise and in support of Khrushchev's own account. Ambassador Liu Xiao, a leading Chinese official who witnessed these events, notes that he was summoned to an interview with Khrushchev on September 16. By this time, the shelling of Quemoy had gone on for more than three weeks, and though the intensity of the bombardment had waned, the Soviet leader apparently thought the preparations for a Chinese invasion were still on track. Though the massive U.S. response that followed clearly forced Mao to scrap his plans, he apparently thought that this was none of Khrushchev's concern. Thus, Khrushchev contends that he had been tricked into providing "aircraft, long-range artillery, and air force advisors" for a projected invasion of Nationalist-held islands in the Taiwan Strait that the Chinese had no intention of carrying out.[99]

That the Soviet leader was indeed in the dark on Mao's change of heart seems obvious from his offer to Liu to send China air support (newly developed Tu-16 bombers, according to Liu; "interceptor squadrons," according to Khrushchev). These planes, manned by Soviet pilots, would be fully armed with missiles "in order to gain air domination over the Taiwan Strait." Ten days later, when Mao refused the proposal to station these planes at Chinese airfields, Khrushchev was astounded.[100] He wrote: "When we offered to station our interceptor squadrons on their territory, [the Chinese] reacted in an extremely odd way. They made it clear that our offer had offended them."[101]

Yet the following month, the Kremlin decided to renew its program of conventional naval assistance, still hoping that the era of cooperation would continue. The two governments concluded a major agreement in February whereby Moscow would license the building of five types of warships and two types of naval weapons. The five types of warships would be conventional-powered ballistic missile submarines, medium-sized attack submarines, two sizes of missile craft, and hydrofoil torpedo boats. The weapons were a submarine-to-surface missile and a ship-to-ship missile.[102] This was the last and most important naval agreement between the two countries, and most of the current Chinese fleet is still based on ships built under its terms. The imported technologies, though not specifically related to Project 09, gave the Chinese valuable hardware and knowledge on missile propulsion and guidance and aspects of missile submarine construction.

On his third visit to Beijing a year later, in October 1959, Khrushchev could see nothing to show for his "generosity," and his anger at the Chinese over the 1958 events had grown. Four months before, on June 20, 1959, it should be noted, Moscow had informed China of its two-year suspension of assistance on nuclear weapons, thereby reversing its promise to supply a prototype atomic bomb and related technical data.[103] Now, in a seven-hour face-to-face talk with Mao Zedong, Khrushchev blamed him for the "Soviet troubles" caused by the Chinese decision to shell Quemoy and Matsu and then to back down without notifying Moscow.[104] Their exchanges were angry, even insulting.[105]

Worst of all, from Khrushchev's point of view, his public bravado followed by his inaction was certain to compromise his credibility in future Soviet-American confrontations. Khrushchev told Mao that the Taiwan events the year before had "created a tense atmosphere indicating that an all-out war was imminent" but, he implied, had gained nothing and weakened Moscow's position.[106] An official history of Chinese foreign affairs notes that "facts occurring thereafter indicate that Khrushchev took to heart the Chinese behavior [before and during the 1958 Taiwan Strait crisis]."[107]

Developments by October 1959 should have communicated Khrushchev's real message to the Chinese, but apparently it never got through. The message was: we can trust you with conventional but not nuclear weapons. He rebuffed Chinese requests for further help on strategic nuclear forces, and none was forthcoming thereafter.

The combination of Moscow's refusal to provide help on Project 09 and its earlier generosity on less sophisticated and shorter-range arms should have made its position on aid amply clear. Moreover, in October 1958, when the head of the Chinese delegation, the navy's political commissar, asked to visit a Soviet nuclear submarine, the Kremlin turned him down and thereby signaled the distinction that it was trying to draw between long- and short-range delivery systems, especially those that could carry nuclear weapons. The point was lost on the commissar, however, and only later did the Chinese finally accept the reality and abandon their dream of Soviet assistance on Project 09.[108]

Thus, even after the showdown between Mao and Khrushchev in July and the Taiwan Strait debacle in August 1958, the possibility of Soviet assistance on the project was not completely foreclosed in the Chinese mind, and during Khrushchev's visit in October 1959, China, for the last time, again pressed for Moscow's help. And this time Khrushchev's grounds for refusal were even more offensive than before. In a meeting with Zhou Enlai and senior military officials he said, "I don't consider that you are able to develop such complicated technologies as those required for a nuclear submarine. You don't have to spend so much money [to develop this project]. Once the Soviet Union has nuclear submarines you will already have them. We can create a joint [submarine] flotilla." When Mao learned of Khrushchev's rejection, he grew indignant: "We will have to build nuclear submarines even if it takes us 10,000 years!"[109]

For Mao, the illusion of Soviet assistance had finally evaporated, even though some on both sides, especially in the Kremlin, hoped to restore relations as late as 1962.[110] His only path for Project 09 was one of self-reliance.

The Search for Reality

We have reviewed the naval decisions of 1958 and 1959, both in Beijing and within the Sino-Soviet alliance, in order to establish the context within which the nuclear-powered submarine program began. At a time of intense political activism and anti-intellectual, anti-technological dogmatism, the leadership that launched the Great Leap Forward authorized this new strategic weapons project and the acceleration of several others.

By early 1960, the nuclear submarine and missile projects had gained solid political backing and organizational underpinning. The transfer of technology from the Soviet Union, though selective and ultimately contentious, had raised the levels of competence and consciousness in a variety of sophisticated disciplines and in the high command. The imports had much to build on: the government's financial commitment to the enterprise, significant military industrial development, the mobilization of scientists and staff, and valuable first-step experiments. Critical hardware and knowledge had arrived from Moscow, the nuclear warhead project was already five years old and four years from initial success, shipyards had been refurbished and set to work, and the liabilities of dependency had been cast aside. On a scale of one to ten, the baseline for the projects, which was one or two in July 1958, had moved up a notch or so. The political hurricane in progress, with worse to come, was not buffeting a fragile undertaking.

The emphasis in the research-based submarine project was technological and professional, and this priority was to shape a broad spectrum of future efforts toward defense development and industrial modernization. From the perspective of these efforts, the mass campaigns that have dominated our view of the rest of the Mao era from the second half of 1958 through the next two decades recede into the background. Another image of Chinese political-strategic realities in these formative years begins to emerge as we explore the nation's quest for one of the world's most modern technologies.

This is a story of politics and technology in collision.[111] China's quest for strategic seapower coincided with the decades of turmoil during which Mao Zedong assumed that politics could change both society and technology and thereby integrate and activate them. At the same time, he made selected institutions in that society responsible for creating the strategic weapons systems, and it was the fruits of that labor, not the misery inflicted in the name of high politics, that symbolized the more permanent direction of the Chinese nation.

We focus on the nuclear-powered submarine and submarine-launched ballistic missile programs in this study to show how a major high-technology undertaking evolved over the next quarter-century, years of social upheaval and policy vacillation. The decades-long effort illustrates how China experimented with new forms of civil-military relations and industrial organizations, how those relations and institutions evolved over time, how teams of military-technical experts pursued highly complex programs of industrial and weapons development despite intense ideological opposition, and how this process influenced the evolution of the navy and its strategies.

An understanding of those strategies, which we discuss in the final chap-

ters, would help make sense of the progress of the two projects and their
maneuvers to dodge ever dangerous political quicksands. We have deferred
that discussion to the last on the grounds that China's current strategic doctrines are the product, not the cause, of the projects' political-technical evolution. Some readers may prefer to turn to the concluding chapters next in
order to have something of a road map through the maze of programs,
people, organizations, and events that follow.

For those who choose this course, however, we offer a word of caution:
none of the participants had this road map, and many lost their way. The
strategic doctrines did not shape the projects nor provide a coherent context for them. For the players, the history that follows was complex and
often confusing both because there were so many unknowns and because
the context was forever oscillating between dedication and disaster. The
drama provided the lucky ones moments of exhilaration and lasting personal satisfaction, even though some now find it hard to relate to the ending. In this story, the sufferers and deliverers often changed places, and
reading the last two chapters may provide little insight into the villains and
heroes.

The doctrines emerged as a response to domestic dilemmas even as the
projects proceeded in fits and starts and sometimes stopped altogether. But
proceed they did, and in the final analysis, they modernized an entire sector
of the country's industrial base, increased the leadership's confidence in its
security policies, and outlasted and helped discredit political adventurism
within an entire generation of China's best minds.

We shall argue that the technical world of the strategic weapons programs, while interacting with politics, achieved two major successes. At
great cost, it built the country's underlying military industrial base and a
progressive series of advanced weapons. That was its first achievement.
But, within the strategic weapons programs, alternative organizations and
a quite different global view arose to replace them. At one level, as we shall
see, these programs became a world apart, secret bastions in a world gone
mad. Yet their domain was simply too large and demanding to disengage
entirely. In the end, the programs helped define the limits of politics and
the nation's objectives even as they catapulted China into the nuclear age.
That was their second and perhaps more fundamental achievement.

PART I

The Submarine

TWO

Nuclear Propulsion

As work on Project 09 commenced at the Institute of Atomic Energy in 1958, the Chinese were faced with the most challenging technological task ever undertaken by the nation. Most of the skills, data, and equipment needed to begin the project were scattered throughout the country, and virtually no one involved knew what was required or where to find it.

With the populace caught up in the Great Leap Forward and its aftermath, talent and resources were in increasingly short supply or simply beyond the institute's reach. The development of technology on the contemplated scale forced vast sectors of the industrial base to respond to priorities that were at odds, or at least seemed so to many Party stalwarts, with the Great Leap's "general line," and set in motion a political dynamic that was to shape the future of China's modernization.

The Early Hard Years of the Power Plant Program

Investigating the existing technologies was, of course, the first step as the project began. The Chinese knew that Soviet and American engineers had equipped their pioneering nuclear submarines with pressurized water reactors (PWR). Early on in their planning, the Chinese decided to construct this type of propulsion system for their own boats, though with a much lower level of enriched fuels than the Americans used.[1]

In the reactor known to them, water acts as coolant, moderator, and heat-transfer agent. The reactor's fuel is uranium dioxide pellets enriched, in the Chinese case, to about 3 percent U^{235} and clad in a special zirconium alloy. The pressure vessel encasing the reactor core has to be especially strong in order to withstand high pressures, temperatures, and radiation levels. In contrast to a boiling-water reactor, the heat generated in the PWR core is transferred to a secondary loop, where a heat exchanger produces the steam to drive the submarine's propulsion and auxiliary machinery.[2]

The submarine's primary and secondary loop systems are close in design to those found in the PWRs in electrical power plants, but the submarine's must be smaller, safer, more reliable, and more flexible. It must also be capable of surviving in a combat situation, which is to say, be collision-, shock-, and sway-resistant, so as to withstand acute angle changes, especially when surfacing in emergencies. These requirements presented formidable design and engineering problems, as the Chinese quickly learned from Western and Soviet sources of information.[3]

They decided almost from the beginning to build a loop-type reactor using low-enriched uranium fuel, light water as a neutron moderator, and a standard system of control rods to regulate the chain reaction and heat output. Their original plan, to use silver-indium-cadmium rods, was eventually dropped in favor of hafnium rods.[4] Designing the other parts of the loop system also proved harder than the planners had anticipated. The water in the primary loop system (including part of the heat exchangers, circulating pumps, and piping) is highly radioactive. The secondary loop that drives the turbine must not be radioactive, but the Chinese had serious problems devising a safe exchange system between the two loops. Early on, they felt the iron fist of Murphy's Law.

The rest of the propulsion proved somewhat less difficult in the design phase but equally formidable in the engineering and construction stages. In Chinese subs, the steam in the secondary loop connects to twin propellers via the turbines and gearboxes. After the steam in the secondary loop releases its energy to the propulsion system, it passes through condensers, and circulating pumps return the resulting water to the heat exchangers (steam generators). For emergency power, the Chinese decided to equip their 09 submarines with two auxiliary diesel-electric generators.[5]

The designers wrote specifications for a robust power plant whose output could vary over a wide range within a brief space of time. This requirement imposed the need for high flexibility and reliability for the control rods' servo drives. Meeting it turned out to be the main technical obstacle to the success of the power plant program.[6]

In October 1958, within weeks after receiving the directive to build a nuclear-powered submarine with these requirements, the IAE created the Reactor Engineering Research Section and launched the first studies on the propulsion system.[7] The timing seemed unpromising, coinciding as it did with the dramatic upsurge of the Great Leap Forward. The fundamental contradictions between the objectives of the Great Leap and Project 09 might have been rationalized away in the inaugural meetings in Beijing, but they could not be so easily dismissed at the IAE's working levels. Many members of the institute had by then succumbed to the society's political fever, strongly undermining serious research.

Nevertheless, most of the project's experts, even while closely monitoring the political winds swirling through the institute, felt personally insulated by the project and used its high priority to protect their technical work from the mass hysteria of the moment. Their goal was to move from basic research to the building of a full-scale prototype power plant on land; all else was secondary. The prototype would be used to conduct simulations, as well as to train qualified designers. IAE Deputy Director Li Yi and two technical specialists assumed oversight responsibility for the reactor research section's program,[8] and the three authorized preliminary studies on reactor theory and the prototype's design. By the end of the year, during the most chaotic months of the Great Leap, they managed to recruit 200 scientists and technicians, many of them recent college graduates, and ordered them to begin writing plans for the components of the proposed reactor prototype and related equipment.[9]

Most of the research section's specialists spent the first six months of 1959 poring over fragmentary information from foreign textbooks, reports, and periodicals. They then spent a year hammering out the detailed specifications for the plant. The result, "Design Plan for the Nuclear Power Plant of the Submarine (Draft)," was submitted to the Defense Science and Technology Commission under Nie Rongzhen for review and action in June 1960.[10] Though by then the political situation had gone from bad to worse—the imposition of the rural commune system and other politically motivated schemes had by now brought the national economy to the brink of collapse, and Soviet advisers were getting ready to pull out of all strategic weapons facilities, including the institute itself[11]—the commission readily approved the document and took note of the other achievements in the program.

To get the project moving, it then organized a scientific cooperation network (*keyan xiezuo wang*) composed of many research institutes and organs of higher learning. These bodies were assigned to start full-scale explorations on the main subjects related to the reactor program: nuclear physics, hydraulics, reactor construction and engineering, pressure vessels, manufacturing materials, automatic controls, steam turbines, condensers, and water pumps. Various industrial departments accepted a supplementary round of assignments to test-manufacture key items of reactor equipment, other special materials, and instruments. In theory, the networking would help pull all of the project's pieces together into a coherent whole.

But Nie's commission unintentionally undercut its good intentions by pursuing a big-budget policy of creating redundant research-and-development organizations to multiply the chances for success. Under commission pressure, the Second Ministry of Machine Building had already sponsored discussions on the construction of the prototype power plant and conducted a survey of possible locations for a related research base; formed ties with several additional scientific research institutes and other organs under the Chinese Academy of Sciences and universities and encouraged them to begin exploratory studies on reactor physics and engineering; and ordered its industrial departments to learn how to produce the equipment, materials, and instruments required for the prototype's construction.

Over the next months, this cumbersome and costly system could boast some progress, but the redundant organizations refused to cooperate in practice and vied for scarce personnel, matériel, and money at a time of increasing political and economic distress. In a period later to be dubbed the three hard years, most institutes were experiencing severe food shortages, drastic funding cutbacks, and the drying up of technical data from the Soviet Union. The need for consolidation and streamlining was becoming painfully evident. For this reason, right after the cutoff of Soviet technical assistance in August 1960, Nie's commission decided to consolidate some of its facilities and to try to shield them from further disruption.

For example, at the time the IAE had begun its exploratory research on the power plant's fuel components, the Metals Research Institute in Shenyang, Liaoning Province, had also formed a section for studying reactor fuel rods. Initially headed by Zhang Peilin, a key scientist in the nuclear program, this section pioneered in designing the first 09 rods.[12] Zhang's staff had come from a variety of disciplines, including reactor physics, hydraulics, metallurgy, nuclear fuels, machining, and chemical engineering.[13] But personnel from these disciplines were in short supply, and in both Shenyang and Beijing, the researchers were dangerously exposed to the political pressures being directed against all experts. To deflect these pressures, Nie's commission had the relevant groups from the IAE's Metal Physics Research Section transferred to the Second Ministry's jurisdiction in the late summer of 1960 and removed to the ministry's partially completed Nuclear Fuel Component Plant (Plant 202) in Baotou, Inner Mongolia. After the plant established its own Component Research Section in March 1961, it took over all research and development on the fuel rod from the Shenyang institute and absorbed the institute's personnel.[14] Secluded in the Gobi Desert, the plant could give unimpeded attention and greater coherence to work on the reactor components.

The Baotou plant's research section was assigned to manufacture and test various types of fuel and control components and to investigate a series of technological processes such as uranium chemistry and uranium smelting.[15] Over the years, the Chinese encountered endless obstacles in the fabrication of the reactor components, and Plant 202 cooperated with an array of other institutes throughout the nation to overcome them. The mechanisms of cooperation in the main did the job, though not without the kind of conflict and foot-dragging that is common among institutions in competing "systems."[16]

Other difficulties also stood in the way. At that time, because China had no high-powered computers, most of the scientific calculations were done by hand. It usually took over a month for several technicians working on desk-top calculators to complete the computations for one program. For example, they had to calculate the power distribution coefficients for the entire-life fuel components under conditions of full- and reduced-power operations, and this batch of computations took many weeks to complete.[17] Each of the tests led to new batches of preliminary blueprints for the power plant, and changes piled on changes.

As a further complication, the various research organs were tasked to formulate design plans for both the land-based prototype power plant and the submarine power plant itself simultaneously. After these organs had prepared the necessary plans, China's nuclear instrument and equipment manufacturing system under the Second Ministry was assigned to provide all the components required for making the power plants. Tough as it was to manufacture the equipment and parts for the plutonium-production reactor in Gansu, the two power plants presented an even greater challenge, Chinese specialists assert.[18]

Suspension of Project 09

The Chinese authorities had not attached much importance to developing a strong support system for the nuclear industry in the 1950s. Because Soviet industrial assistance, including the provision of advanced machines and instruments, appeared substantial and dependable, they focused most of their efforts on constructing production facilities and installing the Soviet-supplied nuclear equipment in them. In this way, the Second Ministry acquired the Soviet-designed Dalian Machinery Plant, which for years was the only large-scale plant under its jurisdiction capable of fabricating heavy-duty nuclear industrial equipment.[19] The ministry also had at its disposal the Shanghai Electronic Instrument Factory and the Jian'an Instrument Factory in Sichuan Province, which manufactured military radiation indicators and nuclear testing instruments. None of these facilities was equipped to handle the special needs of Project 09 on its own.

Facing the collapse of its relations with the Soviet Union, Beijing immediately identified the problem of instrumentation as one of the most serious bottlenecks in the power plant program. On July 16, 1961, the Party Central Committee issued a document entitled "Resolution on Certain Questions to Strengthen the Construction of Atomic Energy Industry," which concentrated on just such bottlenecks. In response, the Second Ministry held meetings to consider every conceivable means for upgrading the nuclear instrument and equipment manufacturing system and, soon thereafter, created its own Equipment Manufacturing Bureau. By 1963, this bureau had assumed jurisdiction over a dozen or more industrial facilities, including the Shanghai Electronic Instrument Factory and the Jian'an Instrument Factory.[20]

All this reorganization effort, however, had a high price tag at a time of great economic hardship. The crisis of the three hard years had deepened after the Soviet withdrawal in mid-1960, and the economy continued its downward spiral.[21] In that year, compared with 1957, the total value of agricultural output decreased by 30 percent, and grain output dropped by 26 percent (over 51 million tons).[22] On September 30, 1960, the Central Committee approved the "Report on Controlled Quotas for the National Economic Plan of 1961," which advanced the "eight-character" principles of "readjustment, consolidation, reinforcement, and improvement" for the revitalization of the national economy.[23] The committee's Ninth Plenum, meeting the following January, reaffirmed these austerity principles.[24]

From July 18 to August 14, 1961, following up on the plenum's edicts, the National Defense Industrial Commission (NDIC) held an emergency meeting at the resort town of Beidaihe, Hebei Province, one of a series of gatherings to discuss the impact of the crisis on all strategic programs.[25] The principal agenda item for this Defense Industry Conference and its chairman, NDIC Director He Long, quickly became how to prioritize all major defense projects and to justify or minimize their costs. Strong voices were heard in support of modernizing the nation's conventional forces and shelving the strategic programs.[26] Nie Rongzhen, an ardent advocate of strategic weapons, joined the argument in August and relayed Lin Biao's earlier directive giving priority to developing the atomic bomb and guided missiles. On August 20, Nie submitted his own report to Mao.[27]

At the end of a sharp but inconclusive argument, the participants remained committed to their preexisting institutional priorities until Mao announced his own decision: to press forward on the strategic weapons programs, or work on "sophisticated technologies" as he put it. At this, the delegates promptly endorsed a directive to "shorten the battle line, plan tasks in order of priority, and ensure key projects" (*suoduan zhanxian, renwu paidui, quebao zhongdian*) as their guideline for defense science, technology, and industry.[28] In subsequent conferences, the leadership gave precedence to making the atomic bomb and strategic missiles and post-poned other major weapons projects in order "to shorten the battle line."[29]

Backed up by He Long, Luo Ruiqing, the chief of the General Staff and head of the National Defense Industry Office (NDIO), took the lead in de-manding a halt to Project 09.[30] Also reacting, the navy proposed to focus on building and incrementally improving Soviet-designed conventional submarines.[31] The debate on the 09 project raged for more than a year, with Mao holding out for its continuation. By November 1962, however, Mao, Zhou Enlai, and other members of the leadership found the recommen-dations for downsizing the project more persuasive.[32] At a showdown meeting held about this time, the leaders were told: "In view of the pro-tracted nature of scientific research, you should preserve a smaller but im-proved core of [technical] strength in order to continue research on key projects." This change would allow the project to capitalize on "the sci-entific results already achieved and make preparations for the next phase of research once [Project 09] is restarted." The change was not universally favored, however. Politburo member (and Foreign Minister) Chen Yi, for one, opposed the proposed cutbacks in Project 09. Arguing with Chen, Luo Ruiqing asked, "At the moment we can't even assemble a conventional submarine with home-made components. Is there any point to our contin-uing the nuclear submarine project?" Chen responded: "It is true that our country is very poor. But even a poor man needs a stick to drive away a dog." He thought the program should be pursued "no matter whether it will take us eight years, ten years, or twelve years."[33] In the end, Mao of course prevailed. Smaller but still alive, Project 09 continued.

An immediate result of the decision to curtail the project was an im-mediate and sharp cut in the size of the design groups assigned to the power plant program. Many related research efforts were indefinitely postponed or canceled outright, though some well-advanced research on essential technologies and materials was kept alive. In view of the long lead times for developing and manufacturing some of the vital equipment and ma-terials for the power plant, Beijing directed the pertinent but now smaller facilities to continue R&D on the design of the power plant and the reactor fuel rods and to be ready for the full-scale resumption of Project 09 on short notice.[34]

As a result, even as the project remained in limbo, the Second Ministry kept a 50-person research section at work on the nuclear power plant.[35] The ministry paid particular attention to research on the system's high-pressure structural mechanics, including the pressure vessel, the main heat exchanger, the main pumps, stabilizers, fuel rod channels, and high-pressure valves. Engineers labored to understand the safety factors and reliability coefficients of these main reactor components and undertook detailed analyses and testing of the reactor stress points. At the order of Nie's commission, the section's efforts were supplemented by studies at the Chinese Academy of Sciences' Harbin Civil Construction Institute (later renamed the Harbin Engineering Mechanics Institute) and Institute of Mechanics, the IAE's Reactor Engineering Research Section, the Harbin Institute of Mechanics, and the Second Ministry's Design Bureau.[36]

By early 1965, the economic situation in China had stabilized, and Beijing felt confident enough to rescind the austerity regulations of the three hard years.[37] After repeated discussions, the navy, the Second Ministry, and the Seventh Academy of the Sixth Ministry of Machine Building (responsible for warship design) decided that conditions were ripe for a full-scale resumption of the nuclear-powered submarine project.[38]

The Politics of Competing Reactor Designs

By the time work recommenced on Project 09, the IAE's reactor engineering section had been reorganized as the Second Ministry's Reactor Engineering and Technology Institute (Institute 194).[39] As work was proceeding along one path at 194, the ministry turned for assistance to another research organization then working actively on marine reactor studies, the Qinghua University Institute of Nuclear Energy Technology. This institute had been collecting information on the nuclear power plants being built abroad and had settled on the type of system then being planned by the West German firm Gesellschaft für Kernenergieverwertung in Schiffbau und Schiffahrt mbH (GKSS) as its special interest.[40]

Located in Hamburg, GKSS had begun building a 15,000-ton ore carrier and research vessel, the *Otto Hahn*.[41] The ship was to be powered by a pressurized water reactor of 38 megawatts (thermal) and was designed to steam 180,000 miles at 15 knots per reactor core. Although some of the GKSS studies available to the Chinese concluded that the *Otto Hahn* would be "both too slow and too small to be profitable," the Qinghua experts believed the GKSS system had definite advantages for submarine propulsion. They theorized that a submarine outfitted with that system would be more robust under wartime conditions and would require far less shielding than would alternative designs. The information division of the Qinghua institute had gleaned enough clues from publications on the *Otto Hahn* to design their own submarine plant.

While the Qinghua engineers were reaching this decision in 1965, however, specialists in the navy and ministry institutes, including Institute 194, had come to a quite different conclusion. These experts had compiled some details on the nuclear reactors installed on the Soviet icebreaker *Lenin*.[42] Then the largest nuclear ship in the world, the converted *Lenin* had been launched in 1957, and its designers had emphasized the reliability of the various components under Arctic conditions over their size and weight. The conventional wisdom of the time was that this type of power plant would be cheaper and probably easier to build.

The issue was whether the *Lenin* system could be adapted for use in submarines. In an icebreaker, the level of noise is not a serious concern, and the added weight of the pumps, shielding, and reactors is deemed to be an advantage. But these factors could constitute major liabilities for a submarine. Placing the primary pumps outside the main containment vessel would increase the danger of steam and radiation leakage should any of the pumps fail and would require very heavy shielding for safety.

The arguments for and against the two systems galvanized into a "struggle between the two designs." The champions of each could see institutional power and money at stake, and those in favor of the *Lenin* model had the tactical advantages of their location within the Second Ministry and the prestige of a Soviet design. More important, perhaps, they had Peng Shilu, a man with considerable pull at the top, on their side. Peng's father was Peng Pai, a peasant martyr who had led some famous but abortive uprisings in Guangdong Province in the 1920s, and whose exploits had greatly impressed Mao. His son, Shilu, had gone to the Soviet Union after 1949 to complete advanced studies in nuclear science, and then returned to take up a senior post in Institute 715 of the Seventh Academy (Warship Research and Design Academy), where he conducted research on the submarine nuclear power plant. Thanks to his father's ties to Zhou Enlai, Peng Shilu was able to keep close connections with the man who headed the powerful Central Special Commission, a body that had been created in November 1962 to foster coordination and cooperation among competing elements of the nuclear industry.[43]

For all the prestige Qinghua University's Institute of Nuclear Energy Technology had gained as the result of its contributions to the plutonium separation program, it had little official clout.[44] With the first-level decision resting with the Second Ministry's Party committee, its endorsement of the *Lenin*-type reactor in late 1965 came as no surprise. Most of the people involved in the reactor programs surmised that Peng Pai's son had swung the balance in favor of that design. The Qinghua institute, with no formal standing in the military industrial system, could press the matter no further.

Nevertheless, Jiang Naixiang, head of the Ministry of Education and president of Qinghua University, believed that the institute still had a role to play in the business of research on nuclear power and authorized the funds for a continuation of its GKSS program. A large reactor pressure vessel was purchased from a Harbin factory, and step by step the institute began to build an alternative prototype to the officially approved system. By the time the Cultural Revolution brought a complete halt to all research, its design effort was virtually completed, but it had managed to make only the barest start on constructing a model.[45]

Resumption of the Program

When the submarine project was at last revived, all control of the program was brought within the regular channels of the military industrial system. On March 13, 1965, the leading Party groups of the Second and Sixth ministries sent Zhou Enlai's Central Special Commission a two-part proposal for reorganizing the entire project. The Party leaders wanted, first of all, to expand the Nuclear-Powered Submarine Overall Design Section of the shipbuilding ministry's Seventh Academy into an institute of the same name (Institute 719), with administrative jurisdiction over the entire submarine design plan.[46]

They also wanted to consolidate research on the submarine nuclear power plant then vested in both Institute 194 of the Second Ministry and Institute 715 of the Sixth Ministry.[47] (Institute 715, a somewhat murky organization that we encountered in our discussion of Peng Shilu, was located in Beijing and reported to the Seventh Academy.) The Party leaders proposed to move Institute 715 (later code-named 15) to the Second Ministry.[48] As this suggests, constant administrative shuffling, renaming, and renumbering characterized all organizational life within Project 09.

The Central Special Commission approved both proposals at its eleventh meeting (March 20, 1965). It also ordered the Second Ministry to present a concrete plan on the construction of the land-based prototype power plant by the end of the year and to complete the actual construction by 1970.[49]

In the next several months, the commission mulled over proposals from the Second and Sixth ministries on what type of nuclear-powered submarine to build and where to construct the land-based plant. Finally, on August 15, at its thirteenth meeting, it officially restarted Project 09. It also unwittingly started a new dispute when it adopted three principles suggested by the ministries. Two were innocuous enough: to carry out coordination and cooperation in all project work and to build the first submarine for experimental as well as for combat use. But the third raised, for the first time, the possibility of concentrating on one vessel at a time, and suggested working on the attack boat before proceeding to the missile submarine. Not everyone agreed on that order of precedence, and the debate on which type of sub to develop first continued among senior officials until December 1966, when Nie Rongzhen's Defense Science and Technology Commission formally took over the NDIO's responsibility for supervising the strategic weapons development programs in December 1966 and endorsed the Central Special Commission's proposal. Work on the attack submarine (09-1) program would come first.

The Central Special Commission also approved the Second Ministry's choice of a plant site for the land-based prototype at its thirteenth meeting, and groundbreaking began at Jiajiang, Sichuan, the following month. Three years later, the Jiajiang Institute (by then called the Southwest Reactor Engineering Research and Design Academy, or First Academy) would be China's largest base for the nuclear power plant program.[50]

With this site finally approved, the various departments concerned submitted reports on the creation or expansion of a series of related projects.[51] The Central Special Commission endorsed the choice of the Bohai Shipyard (Plant 431 in Huludao, Liaoning Province) for building the nuclear-powered submarine, and a workshop attached to Plant 202 in Baotou, Inner Mongolia, for producing the reactor fuel rods.[52] It also picked the places for the submarine operating bases, for processing the cladding metals, for manufacturing the torpedoes, missiles, sonar, and navigation and communication systems, and for testing torpedoes and missiles. These locations settled, Premier Zhou and the special commission approved their listing as high priority projects. The funds, materials, and equipment required for finishing them would now become available.[53]

After years of delay, the project was back in business. But it was a troubled start, for at just that moment in late 1965, a grand power struggle began in Beijing. For Project 09, the struggle's decisive episode proved to be the ouster of Luo Ruiqing.

The Purge of Luo Ruiqing

We turn the clock back to the three hard years for an understanding of this episode. At that time of national crisis, it will be recalled, as military priorities were reassessed, new bureaucracies were formed, and others abandoned. When the Fifteen-Member Special Commission was created in November 1962, leaders associated with Luo Ruiqing won additional powers; Luo himself was appointed the commission's powerful office director. His National Defense Industry Office (NDIO), which had been organized in November 1961,[54] had strong links to the Central Military Commission (where Luo was the secretary general) and to the General Staff (which Luo headed), and it now took command of the Second and Third ministries and the Fifth Academy (in charge of the missile program). In the bureaucratic reshuffling, the NDIO gained authority at Nie Rongzhen's expense.

Below the bureaucratic shifts lay a deeper issue, the fate of specialists in the Chinese political-military system. From 1949 to the 1960s, the Party's twin policies of indoctrinating and exploiting China's scientists and engineers had resulted in cyclical periods of "anti-rightist" repression and "blooming and contending" relaxation.[55] During the opening period of the strategic weapons programs in the mid-1950s, an anti-rightist campaign had preceded the early phases of the Great Leap Forward and then intensified. In general, the combination of repression and economic disaster swiftly demoralized China's defense experts, among others, and directly hampered their performance in the strategic programs.[56]

In the winter of 1961, Nie Rongzhen joined other leaders, notably Zhou Enlai and Liu Shaoqi, in promoting yet another cycle of relaxation. It is Nie's part of the story that interests us here. From late 1960 on, Nie had been pressing the Politburo to acknowledge and restrict the adverse influence of ideological campaigns and outright repression on the advanced weapons effort.[57] Swamped by political meetings and denounced by Party activists, defense scientists and engineers were devoting less than half their day to professional work. Many in the atomic and missile programs received the brunt of the anti-intellectual criticism, and Nie, recognizing the seriousness of the experts' demoralization, visited the Fifth Academy and various defense-related institutes of the Chinese Academy of Sciences to see what he could do about it.[58] His investigation resulted in a report to the Central Committee entitled "Fourteen Suggestions on the Present Work of the Research Institutes of Natural Sciences (Draft)." These so-called 14 articles and a companion paper, "Draft Provisional Regulations for Work in the Institutions of Higher Learning Directly Under the Ministry of Education" (or, by another source, "Sixty Articles on Work in Institutions of Higher Learning"), became the pivotal documents in his campaign to ease the pressures on intellectuals and experts.[59]

More than a decade later, Deng Xiaoping would note that though Mao had issued many instructions related to education and intellectuals before the Cultural Revolution that "were essentially meant to be encouraging and stimulating," he had gone "overboard in some of his remarks" after 1957 and had only recouped when he endorsed Nie's two sets of articles.[60] In July 1961, in notifying the Party faithful of its approval of the first set, the Central Committee admitted that "quite a few comrades" had "adopted a one-sided approach to knowledge and the intellectuals, and the handling of related matters in an oversimplified and crude way also [had] become more widespread." The 14 articles, as a remedy, stressed the importance of achieving positive research results and "maintaining stability in scientific research work and ensuring adequate time for it."[61]

Nie regarded the leadership's approval of the 14 articles as only a first step in protecting the integrity of China's scientists and engineers. Early the next year, in February 1962, he joined Premier Zhou Enlai and Chen Yi in a National Conference on Scientific and Technological Work in Guangzhou, and the participants, taking a leaf from Mao's writings about friends and enemies, proclaimed that China's intellectuals belonged to the non-enemy working class, a category of prestige and relative safety.[62] All the main speakers praised the intellectuals for their contributions to the nation, but in his own address, Nie went even further, urging the country's experts to give free voice to their grievances and throw themselves selflessly into their scientific endeavors and criticizing the exaggerations of the Party's propaganda machinery during the Great Leap Forward and its unrealistic call for instant success.[63]

Although the scientists appreciated the message, they remained skeptical. They had been victimized by promises of support before and could not fail to notice Mao's ever-more urgent calls for "revolutionization," class struggle, and self-reliance. The intellectuals, not surprisingly, feared the wrath of Mao more than they believed the exhortations of Zhou, Chen Yi, and Nie, and they did not have long to wait before Mao struck back. In 1963, the Chairman began his counterattack by calling on the nation's intellectuals to attack Soviet "revisionism" and to join his campaign to foster "new-born forces" among the younger generation.[64]

As Mao saw it, only the more ideological units of the People's Liberation Army (PLA) under Lin Biao seemed to grasp the need for "revolutionization," and in return for Lin's support, Mao called on his countrymen to learn from and emulate the PLA. During this period of the early 1960s, the strategic units under Nie Rongzhen had successfully tested first-generation missiles and, in October 1964, the atomic bomb. But Lin's lieutenants recognized that, however close China was to having enough retaliatory capability to deprive the superpowers of their blackmail potential, it was still precariously vulnerable. They thus made a virtue of necessity and wholeheartedly endorsed Mao's traditional military thinking with its stress on the importance of People's War.

Lin Biao publicly embraced the concept of People's War in a landmark essay on September 3, 1965.[65] Even though China was by then risking a confrontation with the United States by supplying substantial aid to North Vietnam in its fight against South Vietnam, Lin self-consciously echoed

Mao's views on the need for protracted, self-reliant struggle, and in the months that followed he found an ally in Nie Rongzhen.[66]

Chief Lin (*Lin zong*), as he was called, had staked out the ground to begin his assault on his own adversaries, and his initial target was Luo Ruiqing. Luo had aligned himself with Liu Shaoqi, China's president and titular commander-in-chief, and kept close ties with Party General-Secretary Deng Xiaoping and Marshal He Long—all opponents of Mao's radicalism. But Lin's grudge against Luo was more personal than ideological.[67] As we have seen, after Luo became chief of the General Staff, he began to bypass Lin in the chain of command and to report directly to Mao, Zhou Enlai, and He Long. Though he later claimed he acted on Mao's advice because Lin in 1959 was in failing health, the practice continued long after Lin had recovered and deeply offended him.[68]

In Lin's eyes, Luo's transgressions went beyond mere insubordination. Part of Luo's responsibilities as secretary-general of the Central Military Commission under He Long's stewardship was the granting of ranks.[69] To his later misfortune, when Lin Biao's wife, Ye Qun, came forward to request the rank of senior colonel, Luo refused and appointed her to a lower rank instead.[70] Ultimately, it was the human side of Luo's policies that proved his Achilles' heel and made him the first prey for Mao and Lin Biao.

In November 1965, when Mao first revealed to his Politburo colleagues his plans for a campaign to revolutionize the society, several of the top leaders, notably Liu Shaoqi, Deng Xiaoping, and Peng Zhen, consorted to stop or at least circumvent him. They protested what they regarded as the Chinese leader's intent to unleash societal chaos once again, but Mao regarded their behavior as "rebelling while kneeling" (that is, appearing to support him but actually opposing him). Angered at this disloyalty and searching for a way to retaliate, Mao invited a number of his close friends to his home in Hangzhou in East China. The idea that most attracted him, as it turned out, was put forward by none other than Lin Biao's wife, Ye Qun.[71]

Ye submitted a letter from her husband that set forth damning accusations against Luo Ruiqing.[72] Although Mao apparently did not suspect Luo's loyalty, he did take into account Luo's influence over the military and the fact that he was close to Liu Shaoqi and Deng Xiaoping but far less popular than Liu or Deng. In addition to the hostility prompted by Luo's undermining of both Lin Biao and Nie Rongzhen, many feared him because his influence over the intelligence and internal security services had carried over from his days as head of public security. Purging Luo, while dangerous, would weaken Mao's rivals and would be met with a sigh of relief by many of the elite in the capital. Mao's political instincts led him to take Ye's charges at face value and to acquiesce in the moves against Luo. Mao's wife, Jiang Qing, injecting herself in the plot, phoned Lin Biao and told him to come to Mao's residence for a private chat with the Chairman.

Although the published record of the ensuing conversation is somewhat suspect, its general outline coincides with what we know of Mao's personality and behavior. Mao's real goal was to banish Politburo member Peng Zhen, thereby isolating Liu Shaoqi and Deng Xiaoping and eliminating for all practical purposes any further resistance to the planned political campaign. Mao hinted as much to Lin and warned him to pay heed to his control over the army. Lin replied, "You can rest assured, Chairman. However, I have my own problem." Mao said, "Just let me know. I will help you solve [the problem]." Lin with some emotion said, "It is Luo Ruiqing. I can't guarantee his obedience. He always tries to put on a rival show in the army so as to seize power. I really can't trust him." Then the deal was struck. Mao would condone the purge of Luo, and Lin would support the upcoming Cultural Revolution and the elimination of Peng.

A high-level meeting to oust Luo, an enlarged meeting of the Politburo's Standing Committee, was convened in Shanghai on December 8, 1965, and lasted a week.[73] Mao, always the Machiavellian, put Peng Zhen in charge of the case against Luo to prevent Peng from getting any hint of the plot brewing against him.[74] Orders to attend the conference reached Luo only on the 10th, and Liu Shaoqi and He Long were given only minimal details on the agenda. Upon his arrival in Shanghai, Liu asked He what was going on, and the latter replied, "It is strange. Even you don't know."[75] Peng Zhen, quite unaware that he himself was the real target, evasively told Luo when he left Kunming, "Just go [to Shanghai]. Once you attend the conference, you will know [the purpose]." Luo arrived at the Shanghai airport with his wife on the afternoon of the 11th. Guards put the couple under house arrest as soon as they entered the guest compound at West Jianguo Road.[76]

Denied access to the conference itself, Luo could get only a few hints of what was happening. But he did quickly learn that three allegations were being leveled against him—opposition to Lin Biao; opposition to putting politics in command; and an arrogation of power—for Zhou Enlai and Deng Xiaoping visited him on the very day he arrived, December 11. During that call, and another on the 16th, they instructed Luo to engage in self-criticism, and told him that Mao believed this was something Luo should do even though he might be innocent. Zhou then added a charge of his own—that Luo had failed to show proper respect for China's top military figures, "the marshals," when implementing his decisions. According to Luo's wife, Zhou was vague about which of the ten marshals felt slighted.

Meanwhile, Lin Biao detailed Luo's "wrongdoings" to the assembled leaders, and then promptly circulated the meeting's proceedings. On December 17, two days after the conference ended, Luo and his wife were driven under guard to the western suburbs of Beijing, where Luo, still under arrest, wrote out his confession. In it, Luo resigned from all his posts in the Central Military Commission, the Central Special Commission, the NDIO, the General Staff, and all other bodies on which he had served. His career was at an end.

Mao's next step was to escalate the campaign with a thorough excoriation of the victim. So it was that the matter of Luo's "mistakes" dominated a meeting of the Central Military Commission held during the period March 4–April 8, 1966. By this time, Peng Zhen was heading a seven-person work group to handle the charges against Luo. Luo again confessed to errors during these proceedings, which were interrupted by his attempted suicide. On May 16, the Central Committee released the Peng group's report, and so set the emerging Cultural Revolution on the path to an all-out power struggle.[77] The message was conveyed to all concerned in a Central Committee circular issued the same day. Calling for vigilance against "representatives of the bourgeoisie who have sneaked into the Party, the government, the army and various cultural circles," the committee sealed the fate of these representatives when it damned them as "counter-revolutionary revisionists."[78]

The work group's report, which was transmitted to all high-level Party and army cadres, detailed Luo's alleged transgressions against Mao and his doctrines. These sins purportedly included Luo's opposition to Mao's views on People's War and on augmenting the militia's role within a reorganized PLA. Of special relevance to this study, the Central Committee focused on Luo's actions during the preceding year that had brought him into direct opposition with Nie Rongzhen, as well as Lin Biao.[79]

Luo was accused of opposing and refusing to implement "a series of guidelines and policies concerning the question of establishing the national defense industry, national defense science, and technology work," and of denying "the important achievements" of the Defense Science and Technology Commission under Nie. Indeed, even after China had detonated its first atomic bomb in October 1964, he had "frantically attacked our national defense scientific research work as going from data to data, from design to design, without ever completing anything." Moreover, Lin Biao and Nie had quite rightly disagreed with Luo's "assertion that the system of military representatives [set up in 1950 and extended in 1964] should be quickly abolished in national defense industry."[80] Ignoring their warning that "changing the system of military representatives should be thought over carefully," Luo had expressed his willingness to "take that risk."

Although Nie Rongzhen may have had his own reservations about that system, any risk-taking on his part would have jeopardized his defense programs, not just himself. Having won a measure of protection for the scientific establishment and his defense objectives with his 14 articles, Nie would now have to switch tactics to keep what he had gained. He would have to compromise with Lin Biao and the fast-rising leftists. This meant aligning himself with Mao and Lin in the early stages of the Cultural Revolution so as to buy time. With Luo Ruiqing out of the way, Nie Rongzhen once again dominated the strategic weapons programs.

The purge of Luo Ruiqing and the restoration of Nie's authority in the programs directly affected Project 09, which had been restarted by the end of 1965. The following May, the Party committee of the navy held a meeting to denounce "bourgeois representative figures." After a sharp conflict between two groups of senior naval officers, the radical group—led by Li Zuopeng, Wang Hongkun, and Zhang Xiuchuan—gained control of the service and branded Xiao Jinguang and Su Zhenhua, the commander and political commissar of the navy, respectively, and others "Luo Ruiqing's followers."[81] Among the more than 3,800 naval officers who fell victim to the subsequent investigation and purge, many had worked in the naval weapons development programs. For a time, Project 09, so recently restarted, was once again nearly paralyzed.

The Power Plant Program in the Cultural Revolution

Thanks to the disruptions of the Cultural Revolution, work at the Jiajiang facility slowed to a snail's pace. In 1967, a full two years after the groundbreaking, only the earthwork for the main workshop of the prototype power plant on land was completed. None of the 14 principal laboratories of the associated research base had yet been built.[82]

Other parts of the program made some headway, but in the main the gains were fragmentary and minimal. For example, in early 1966, Plant 202 at Baotou managed to produce the first batch of experimental fuel rods that met the required technical standards, and in May, those rods were inserted in a research reactor for tests. These achievements in turn enabled 202's experts to deal with other technical details and control limits and thus helped solve some of the problems in the making of the rods. However, the intermittent production of experimental fuel components in laboratories was still a far cry from their full-scale manufacture.[83] From late 1966 through 1967, "political turmoil across the nation in the form of seizing power, violent clashes, and suspension of production spread to the nuclear industrial community."[84] Under the circumstances, routine and regular output of the rods was out of the question.

We have noted in our history of the nuclear weapons program how the Second Ministry's rigid discipline collapsed in January 1967. Three rival factions organized against each other, called denunciation rallies, and vilified hated opponents. Verbal hyperbole and lurid propaganda soon gave way to fists and clubs, and by the time one of the factions had won, the struggle had spread throughout the nuclear industry.[85] According to one official history, though research in the nuclear weapons programs "continued without letup," the quality of that research "was impaired because the initiative of many scientists and technicians was gravely constrained by repeated [political] examinations as well as criticism and denunciations."[86]

Some attempts were made to reimpose discipline within the highest priority defense programs, but these met with only marginal success. As a result, on March 11, 1967, Nie Rongzhen submitted a report to Mao recommending that the military take over all defense-related research facilities. Mao agreed, and in April Nie's commission wrested direct control of these facilities from the faction-ridden defense industrial ministries.[87] On May 15, the Central Military Commission ordered military units to occupy the Second Ministry, and there they remained until July 1973.[88]

In order to accelerate the manufacture of the submarine reactor equipment, Nie's commission encouraged greater communication among specialists in different industrial, military, and academic systems. He approved the holding of a national professional conference to solve the most pressing technical problems related to manufacturing the reactor's equipment and instruments. Over 300 people from 70 factories, academies, and research institutes attended.[89] Following up, the commission helped organize several professional meetings, including one in Heilongjiang Province (where the main reactor parts were being built) and another in Wuhan City, Hubei Province (where the pressure vessel was being built).[90]

Not content with these steps, on August 30, 1967, Nie signed a special official letter. The first of its kind ever issued by the Central Military Commission, the letter exhorted participants in the nuclear-powered submarine project to carry out vigorous cooperation and coordination so as to accelerate the tempo of the project and successfully complete the mission entrusted to them by the state.[91]

At one critical juncture, the central leaders themselves went to some lengths to protect the nuclear industry. In the months between March and November 1967, for example, Mao Zedong, Zhou Enlai, Ye Jianying, and

Nie Rongzhen signed and sent 22 telegrams to key plants, research institutes, and construction sites. Zhou personally signed half of them. All emphatically stated: "No seizure of power," "No suspension of production," "No traveling from place to place to exchange experiences," "No violent clashes," and "Guarantee the absolute safety of plants and stable production in plants." Additionally, between late June and mid-August of that year, the central leadership sent three fact-finding missions to the Jiuquan Atomic Energy Complex (Plant 404, which was engaged in nuclear weapons manufacture) and the Ninth Academy in Qinghai (nuclear weapons design) to assess the damage and restore order.[92]

In the end, none of these stabilization measures made much difference, and some backfired. In many cases, the military control committees joined the radicals, the coordinating meetings were transformed into accusation sessions, and the discontented mainly listened to the other messages of Mao and Lin urging the rebels on. During 1967 and 1968, to cite just one example, violent clashes among opposing factions erupted several times in the Baotou Nuclear Fuel Component Plant (Plant 202), bringing production to a halt and interrupting research on the submarine reactor fuel rods.[93] Nie was fighting a losing battle.

Behind the drama of factional warfare, moreover, a systematic destruction of the knowledge base was occurring. By 1969 a number of schools under the Second Ministry had been either disbanded or transferred to the administration of local governments. School buildings were occupied by youthful zealots and ransacked. Large quantities of instruments, equipment, and books and data were destroyed. Over 2,000 teachers were forced to leave for manual jobs in the countryside, and most universities had to abandon the kinds of courses that were relevant to the study of atomic energy.

The staff and workers of every major facility connected to the nuclear submarine project were caught up in the melee. Hardest hit were the Ninth Academy, the Lanzhou Gaseous Diffusion Plant (Plant 504), and Baotou's Plant 202, and the most savage persecution began in November 1969. Over the next two years, 80 percent of the cadres at and above section (*ke*) and workshop (*chejian*) levels, and 90 percent of the senior and middle-level scientific and technical personnel of the Ninth Academy, for example, were victimized in one way or another; the more unfortunate were subjected to physical abuse. During the same period, 60 percent of the staff and workers of the Lanzhou plant were criticized, denounced, and forced to confess their "crimes."

As bad as the first years of the Cultural Revolution had been, things got worse in Lin Bao's heyday. From November 1969 until the winter of 1971, the minister of defense turned on defense officials and specialists with a vengeance in a ruthless campaign to "purify the class ranks." The Red terror made a shambles of the nuclear industry, though some of the stabilization measures and individual heroics permitted isolated pockets to continue operating.[94]

Another source of disruption for all strategic weapons programs resulted from the massive shift of national investment and construction to China's mountainous and less vulnerable interior Third-Line, or *sanxian*, region. We shall discuss the development of this region in detail in Chapter 4. Suffice it to say here that when Mao ordered the shift of strategic facilities to the Third Line, the nuclear ministry's bureaus mobilized their forces for a major building program in these provinces. Yet many must have known that the program initiated by the Central Military Commission in 1964 to build duplicate plutonium, reactor fuel rod, and gaseous diffusion plants and nuclear weapon research facilities in Sichuan Province was already in deep trouble. The plans called for many of the plants to be constructed in caves or underground, but in not a few places, this expensive, ill-planned, and wasteful building effort had come to a halt for lack of tunnel-digging equipment.[95] Nevertheless, Mao and his chosen heir, Lin Biao, relentlessly insisted that the effort continue.

The nuclear industry got its marching orders on July 2, 1969. At the *sanbei* conference (that is, the North China, Northeast China, and Northwest China conference) then in progress, Lin Biao directed the Second Ministry to move Plants 202, 404, and 504 to the Southwest.[96] What is more, this was to be a crash program: the ministry was to see that "all the atomic energy plants [were fully removed] from Jiuquan and Baotou" to places deep inside China by 1970.[97] On July 28, the Second Ministry called an emergency meeting in Beijing to discuss Lin's order.[98]

Some of Lin Biao's allies presided over the meeting at the Beijing Hotel. The nuclear specialists from the northern provinces, such as Jiang Shengjie from Plant 404, made the case against the move to the Third Line. They held that the nuclear fuel plants, especially the plutonium-production reactor, could not be transported without destroying them. The production of nuclear fuels would end, they asserted, if the old nuclear facilities were moved before the construction of new nuclear plants in the Third Line was completed. Under such conditions, the country's nuclear industry would suffer heavy losses. But members of the military were resolutely on Lin's side. As the commander of the air force, Wu Faxian, put it: "You have to move [the plants] even it is necessary to blow them up with dynamite!" Only later were the leaders of the nuclear weapons program able to induce Premier Zhou Enlai to intervene and nullify Lin's order.

In August 1970, Lin created further problems for the program. In a meeting to discuss the formulation of the next five-year plan for defense industrial development (1971–75), Lin called for "ferreting out capitalist-roaders who had escaped unpunished" and for "catching up with advanced world levels in the first three years and then surpassing them in the next two years." He reaffirmed the importance of shifting large-scale capital construction to the Third Line, and as a consequence, the cost of this construction skyrocketed in the ensuing years. With most of the funding going to buildings in remote provinces, little money was available for direct use on weapons research and development.[99]

Completion of the Power Plant

Fortunately for the officials dedicated to the submarine project, Lin's heavy-handed intervention came late in the game. The tentative design plan for the prototype power plant was completed by late 1967, and two years later the entire working drawings for the plant were done.[100] During this period, Peng Shilu, a favorite of Mao's as we have seen, and Zhao Ren-kai headed the Beijing-based group from Institutes 715 and 194. The group oversaw the power plant design and had the final say on all technical questions and their resolution.[101] Having decided on the *Lenin*-type loop system, for example, Peng had to determine the maximum pressure for the reactor's primary loop.[102]

Foreign sources had reported that pressure to be 200 atmospheres, but Peng thought the number too high. He calculated that 200 atmospheres could damage the fuel components and result in serious accidents. His final judgment was that the primary loop should be designed for a peak pressure of 140 to 150 atmospheres. The manufacture of the primary-loop main pump also posed challenges for Peng's group because of the reactor's high pressures and temperatures. The engineers encountered particular difficulties in fabricating the reactor's low-noise, hermetically sealed pump and in meeting the safety standards for its automatic controls.

While Peng's group was designing the power plant, experts on uranium metallurgy labored on the reactor fuel rods.[103] Soon after the August 1967 decision to accelerate Project 09, the Second Ministry instructed Plant 202 to set up a workshop for manufacturing the rods and assigned Zhang Pei-lin, a metallurgist and chief engineer in the ministry's Fuels Production Bureau, to create a rod design team composed of chemists, metallurgists, and other engineers.[104] The organization of the system for running the power plant development is set forth in Figure 2.

The Second Ministry initially assigned a plant in Baoji, Shaanxi Province, to fabricate the cladding material for the rods. The plant created

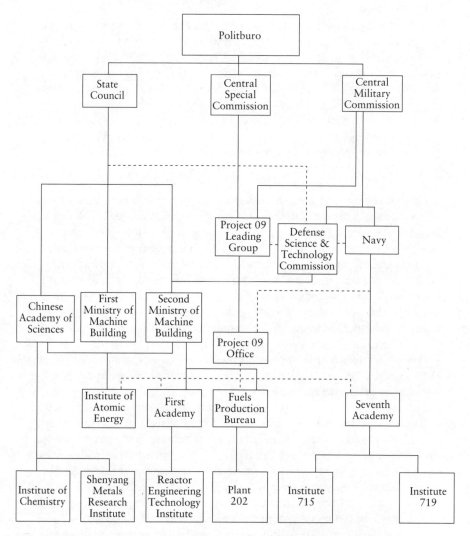

Fig. 2. Organization of the submarine power plant program, 1970

workshops to separate zirconium from hafnium, refine the zirconium alloy, and manufacture the cladding tubes. But when the Baoji plant ran into difficulties in the final stage, the Fuels Production Bureau sent Chief Engineer Chen Guozhen to a plant in Chongqing and put him in charge of the processing task. There he met a new problem: the leftists then running the Chongqing plant had no interest in his mission until he showed them Nie Rongzhen's special official letter on the letterhead of the Central Military Commission. Six months later, the tubes were done.[105]

With the cladding ready, the Second Ministry dispatched Zhang Peilin to Plant 202 to begin production on the complete fuel rods. (He immediately created a minor tempest when he moved into a small room in one of the dormitories. Two staff members living next door promptly moved out because they feared possible exposure to radioactivity and only returned after Zhang explained the physics of radiation.) Under Zhang's leadership, nuclear chemists and physicists stepped up preparations for the trial production of the rods. Some minor problems plagued the effort, but step by step the work proceeded.[106] The plant began manufacturing the fuel components for the prototype reactor by the summer of 1970 and for the submarine reactor by the end of the year.[107]

Meanwhile, in Sichuan, work continued on the land-based prototype nuclear power plant. In March 1968, the Second Ministry and the Seventh Academy created a Construction Site Headquarters at Jiajiang to supervise the erection of the plant and formed the Southwest Reactor Engineering Research and Design Academy (First Academy). The ministry appointed He Qian as headquarters' director to provide unified leadership over the construction of the base. Peng Shilu, now Institute 15's acting director, was in charge of the technical wing.[108]

On July 18, 1968, Mao Zedong ordered PLA troops sent to Jiajiang to join the construction effort, and with this added help, the tempo of the work accelerated.[109] By the end of 1969, the main workshop and most of the 14 labs affiliated with the First Academy had been built.[110] On April 18, 1970, engineers finished assembling the land-based power plant, and on May 1, it began test operation.[111]

In early July, the Nuclear-Powered Submarine Project Leading Group held a meeting to check the preparations for increasing the reactor's power, and on the 15th, the Central Special Commission met to assess the group's report.[112] There Peng Shilu, on hand as the chief designer, asked Zhou Enlai for permission to raise the power on July 18 in commemoration of Mao Zedong's directive two years earlier sending troops to Jiajiang. When a commission member suggested that the equipment be inspected one more time, Peng replied, "We have already carried out an inspection. It is unnecessary to do it once again." Zhou Enlai reproved him, "You should listen to the opinion of others." The additional inspection was ordered.

The commission underscored its continuing concern when it met the following day and decided to send a team of experts to help the plant's regular test unit solve any problems that might arise.[113] These precautions taken, Zhou then consented to the proposal for increasing the reactor power on July 18, though he warned: "You said that you had undertaken four tests on the design, installation, adjustment, and [test] operation [of the reactor]. You still should pay close attention [to raising the power]. Don't be indifferent [to accidents]. You must under no circumstances take this lightly. Accidents might arise at any time from your negligence!" Peng's popularity with Mao did not exempt him from Zhou Enlai's insistence on strict discipline.

Right after this meeting, the coterie of experts and officials left for Jiajiang on Zhou's private airplane.[114] At 2:00 A.M., July 17, the engineers began increasing the water temperature and steam pressure and, at 6:00 P.M. on the 18th, they started raising the power level.[115] All went well until the 19th, when the engineers discovered problems in the testing and measuring instruments and shut down the reactor for emergency repairs. They found leaks in the pulse tubes and defective valves in the secondary-loop system.[116] Zhou Enlai's concerns proved to be well founded.

Later experiments revealed other flaws. The engineers had designed the plant to shut down under nine types of abnormal conditions. But the cutoffs proved to be too sensitive, and the test operations were frequently suspended for no apparent reason.[117] Zhou learned of these difficulties and phoned the test unit several times with words of encouragement but with orders to cease plant operations until all the problems were resolved.[118]

Several days later, on July 23, the plant recommenced the test run, and by the end of August, it reached its full-rated power of 48 megawatts (thermal).[119] Peng Shilu reportedly hoped that, when installed, the submarine reactor would be as close to this output as possible, thus giving the power supply unit a shaft power of 12,000 hp (6,000 per propeller) for its designed efficiency of about 18 percent. Peng's hope, however, was somebody else's headache. The prototype plant was up and operating.

1. Chinese delegation headed by Peng Dehuai (third from right) visiting a Soviet destroyer stationed at Lüshun, Feb. 1955

2. Nikita Khrushchev in Beijing, accompanied by (from left to right) Zhou Enlai, Zhu De, Liu Shaoqi, and Mao Zedong reviewing a guard of honor, Sept. 30, 1959

3. Khrushchev and Mao at state banquet in Beijing, Sept. 30, 1959, celebrating PRC's National Day

4. Marshal He Long (right), former director of the National Defense Industrial Commission, with Premier Zhou Enlai in the late 1950s

5. The Golf-class submarine China bought from the Soviet Union

6. A 39-class submarine carrying anti-ship missiles

7. General Liu Huaqing, vice-chairman of the Central Military Commission, former deputy director of the National Defense Science and Technology Commission, and former commander of the PLA Navy

8. From right to left: Huang Xuhua, chief designer of the 09 nuclear submarine; Huang Weilu, chief designer of the JL-1 missile; and nuclear power plant chief designers Peng Shilu and Zhao Renkai

9. Ship Science Research Center (Institute 702), located on the shore of Lake Tai, Wuxi, Jiangsu Province

10. Wave-making water tank at Institute 702

11. Land-based nuclear power plant in Jiajiang, Sichuan Province

12. The 09-1 nuclear attack submarine, No. 402

13. An 09-1 nuclear attack submarine

14. The 09-2 nuclear missile submarine, No. 406

15. The nuclear missile submarine under way

THREE

Designing

Between 1945 and 1950, the Communist revolutionaries had struggled to gain control of the Chinese mainland mostly from bases in the interior. In time, however, they reached the sea where they faced an unfamiliar threat. Most of Mao Zedong's men and women had never seen the ocean before and had no naval capability to block his enemy's flight by ship to the south and eventually to the island of Taiwan. Herein lay the origins of Mao's dream that China could one day become a major seapower.

A high priority in his plans was to train naval personnel as the cadre for manning the ships of the future.[1] In April 1951, when success on the battlefield in Korea still seemed possible, the PRC began to lay the foundation for an expanded and more modern naval service, assigning 275 officers and sailors to train in the Soviet submarine flotilla at the Lüshun Naval Base and arranging for the training of others in the Soviet Union; over the next two years 166 officers were sent to study at Soviet military academies.[2] The aged Jiangnan Shipyard in Shanghai turned to the task of making small gunboats, and plans went forward for new facilities.[3] In May 1952, China began constructing its first submarine base at Qingdao, Shandong Province.[4]

Despite some incipient efforts to build a submarine fleet in the years after the Revolution, the demands of the Korean War in time put a temporary halt to most naval construction projects. Thus, it was not until 1953 that the Central Military Commission once again felt ready to accelerate the development of the navy.[5] This judgment was based in part on a prior decision to end the war in Korea and in part on the successful conclusion of negotiations with Moscow for substantial naval assistance. The agreement with Moscow, reached on June 4, 1953, would provide 32 warships and complete sets of technical data, parts, and equipment for assembling 49 others in China's shipyards. The Soviet Union also agreed to sell China the licenses to build five types of warships, including an 03-class submarine (designated Whiskey in the West).[6] Based on this accord, China produced 21 submarines of Soviet design in the next decade.[7]

Though only a small component of the total shipbuilding effort in this period (116 vessels were produced under these Soviet licenses, including 4 frigates, 63 torpedo boats, 14 submarine chasers, and 14 minesweepers; 170 in all were turned out by Chinese shipyards), the submarine was restored to its high place on the military priority list almost immediately after the cease-fire in July 1953.[8] (Indeed, in some sense, it had retained its priority, as evidenced by the fact that more than a year earlier, well after the Chinese People's Volunteers began to suffer huge losses, China began constructing the submarine base at Qingdao.) In August, the Submarine School was formally started in Qingdao, under the leadership of Fu Jize, head of the Lüshun Submarine Study Team.[9] The following year, China received its first operational submarines from the Soviet Union, two S-class boats in June and two M-15-class boats in July.[10]

At the end of November 1954, the two S-boats participated in various tactical exercises as part of their initial shakedown cruises and then began regular patrols along the East China coast.[11] Satisfied with these start-up programs, Mao and Premier Zhou Enlai endorsed a proposal to select more than 100 military men who had graduated from colleges or high schools to organize China's first independent submarine group.[12] (In 1951, Zhou had become director of a new Central Ordnance Commission, whose task was to manage the importing of this defense equipment and to create a broad national network of plants and other facilities for China's own military industry.[13])

In the years following the Korean War, Soviet shipbuilding experts helped upgrade the facilities at the Jiangnan Shipyard in Shanghai, where, beginning in the winter of 1955–56, the first Soviet-designed submarines were built. On January 10, 1956, Mao Zedong visited the yard to inspect the inaugural 03-class boat under construction. After examining the yard's equipment and learning that it was made in China, the Chinese leader murmured "Good! Good!" and nodded with approval.[14] Despite Mao's delight at seeing the Chinese equipment at the Jiangnan Shipyard, it was clear that the navy could not fulfill the five-year plan it had adopted in October 1953 without heavy dollops of Soviet aid.[15] Furthermore, Mao must have known that the Soviet-designed 03-class submarine was being assembled in the main from parts shipped from the Soviet Union and that the navy had yet to sign off on plans for its own Institute of Shipbuilding in Shanghai. The first Chinese-built 03 was not commissioned until June 27, 1957.[16]

Whatever Mao's worries about China's dependence on the Soviet Union, he continued to look to it for assistance. In February 1959, on the basis of an agreement reached the previous October, China placed orders for Soviet design plans, technical data, and relevant equipment for five more advanced types of warships and two types of naval missiles, among them a Romeo-class attack submarine (33-class), a Golf-class ballistic-missile submarine (31-class), and an R-11FM submarine-launched ballistic missile (1060 type, without its nuclear warhead).[17] The Soviets agreed to provide special assistance on the Golf and Romeo submarines, and this help was critical in laying the groundwork for the present-day submarine force, including the strategic submarines.[18] New Soviet naval doctrine emphasized the strategic underwater navy, and the Chinese incorporated this emphasis into their own military thinking.[19]

The Learning Curve

When, in August 1958, the Party Central Committee authorized the commencement of the nuclear submarine project, Project 09, it did so in a document entitled "On the Development of New Naval Submarine Technologies."[20] Neither this nor any other contemporary document set forth the precise missions of the submarine, what its costs should be, or what operational or tactical requirements would have to be met. No revised naval doctrine justified the effort. All these matters would have to be postulated or guessed at by the sub's architects.

Instead the thrust was principally on general technological requirements. The chief designer of Project 09, Huang Xuhua, has recalled that at this time the nation's shipbuilders were ordered to conduct a prestudy on alternative designs for the nuclear submarine.[21] Almost immediately, Huang's engineers concluded that it would be necessary to undertake research and development on the submarine's nuclear power plant before making any serious effort to design the submarine itself.[22] In October, prospective specialists were chosen and assigned to begin the exploratory research on the plant.[23]

Despite the precedence given to the power plant, some preliminary thought was devoted to the overall design of the nuclear attack submarine itself. But with very spotty information then available on the submarine programs of other nations, the early designers were left pretty much to come up with schemes of their own.[24] One idea (which had also been considered by the Canadians) was to cut a conventional-powered submarine in half, install the nuclear power plant in a new compartment between the two halves, and weld the three sections together.[25] Only later did the Chinese decide that their nuclear-powered submarine must be an entirely different craft from a conventional-powered one. Some of the learning underlying this decision came from pictures and published academic papers, but others, it seems, came from less weighty sources. For example, Huang Xuhua's design group by chance located a toy model of an American Polaris submarine. The excited designers repeatedly assembled and disassembled the small, coffee-colored scale model and took copious notes on it.[26] The model, it might be noted, was not a good replica or even based on good guesswork; much better data had already been published. This curious episode simply illustrates the somewhat unreal world in which the pioneer Chinese designers operated.

Although the situation of inadequate sources was to change quickly in the early 1960s, few useful published sources on the American and Soviet nuclear-powered submarines reached China during the late 1950s, and the Chinese by this time had become more skeptical about the data they were acquiring. Since they had difficulty interpreting much of the information collected by their intelligence agents—such as a research paper on the requirements for assuring the submarine's stability—they concluded, probably incorrectly, that most of the published foreign data was deliberately leaked misinformation to fool the defense scientists in other countries.[27]

The designers with experience working on the Soviet-designed conventional attack submarines were especially sensitive to some of the complex problems that had to be solved. When the reality of having to design a nuclear boat on their own began to sink in, they compiled lists of unknowns and put up wall charts detailing the main hurdles that lay before them. These charts enumerated the hundreds of items to be accomplished under several general headings:

Optimal displacement
Dimensions and general configuration
Designs for the propeller, hydroplane, fin, and pressure and outer hulls (including the calculation of hull strength and failure points, and hull oscillation and fatigue strength)
Requirements for the nuclear power plant, electronic equipment, communications and navigation, and control systems
Concealment measures needed to reduce the boat's noise and other telltale emissions[28]

Decisions on each of these items, they recognized, were interrelated and interactive. The optimal design for the submarine would have to provide for a comprehensive and functional equilibrium of all the principal systems for propulsion, control, concealment and detection, and weapons.[29]

The design would have to optimize the balance between the weight and volume displaced by the pressure hull and other impenetrable parts of the boat under various conditions. Weight displacement and constant buoyant volume are tightly coupled and directly affect the submarine's list and trim. The sub's center of gravity, which the Chinese engineers well understood in theory but found troublesome to calculate, is a significant determinant of underwater stability.[30] The Chinese, by studying the standard texts on submarine design and through experimentation, adopted a method for placing the center of gravity well below the center of buoyancy; that is, putting ballast as near the sub's datum line as possible and laying the ballast keel near that line.[31]

The designers also conducted experiments to measure the trade-offs between maneuverability and stability. All seacraft gain both maneuverability and stability as they increase speed up to a certain point, though at different rates. The Chinese by pencil and paper computations estimated as best they could the minimal requirements for stability and maximum maneuverability.[32] They also stressed the speed of the attack submarine. Speed would be particularly important for an attack submarine but much less so for the missile sub. Nevertheless, the designers became preoccupied with speed for all future nuclear boats, and thereby insinuated the bias of one project into the design specifications for the next. The engineers later had to design that bias out of the missile submarine.

The designers also recognized that the boat's underwater performance—maneuverability and speed—would be affected to an important degree by the ratio between its length and beam diameter (L/D). When L/D falls below 16, the total underwater resistance decreases progressively until the number falls to six; at figures lower than that resistance increases. Submarines with long and thin shapes have greater stability but less maneuverability than boats with short, thick shapes in either their horizontal or their vertical planes.[33] A significant effect on the stability, particularly during rapid turns, is the size and placement of the conning tower (or the sail, as it is now usually called). The sail can cause a "snap-roll" effect that can be quite dramatic. By studying pictures of American and Soviet nuclear subs, the Chinese deduced that a range of from seven to twelve probably constituted the best L/D for their proposed submarines.[34] They eventually settled on an optimal L/D of 8.5–10.5 for nuclear attack submarines, 11.5–13 for nuclear-powered ballistic-missile submarines, and 7.5–9.5 for conventional submarines.[35]

The sub's planners realized from the very beginning that the missile-bearing craft, the second-generation nuclear submarine that would be based on the attack submarine, would be a prime target in time of war, and they found themselves worrying about incorporating features needed for the missile boat into the prototype attack submarine. For example, the naval architects from the start assumed that a double-hull boat had greater combat survivability than a single-hull one. The real challenge, then, would be the inner hull, for the outer, or false one in fact, would be comparatively thin, and so easier to weld, fit out, and smooth.[36] The Soviet Union's conventional 33-class (Romeo) and 31-class (Golf) submarines had double-hull construction, and the designers almost without debate adopted the same construction for their nuclear-powered boats.[37]

During the earliest stages of their work, they spent weeks debating the various requirements for the sub's survivability before settling on "the ability to maintain combat capacity and cruising performance during normal navigation and in the course of combat," and "to carry out normal operations under unfavorable natural conditions, such as sway caused by wind and waves, vibration, corrosion, and operational wear on mechanical parts." Combat survivability obviously would be determined by "the submarine's ability to protect itself from serious damage in performing combat duties."[38]

The designers decided to define both a radius of safety and a radius of danger. The radius of safety was "the shortest distance from the center of an explosion of an antisubmarine weapon to the submarine's body and its mechanical equipment so that the effects of the explosion will not harm the main combat capacities defined by tactical technical data." The danger, or critical, radius was "the shortest distance from the center of the explosion of an antisubmarine weapon to the point at which the damage inflicted upon the submarine's body, machinery, and crew causes the submarine to lose its combat capacity, but the submarine can still float on the surface." For the Chinese, then and now, the safety radius and danger radius are the major specifications for ensuring the survivability of a submarine under attack. These specifications imply rigid requirements for increasing hull strength, hardening equipment against shock, and improving the damage control systems.[39]

The Chinese designed their boat's pressure hull to withstand large hydrostatic pressures and wanted to deal with the dynamic pressures caused by underwater explosions.[40] However, like other submarine designers the world over, they found the latter requirement impossible to meet. Despite all their creative calculations and inventive answers, at best they could only marginally improve the chances for surviving an explosion at fixed depths.

Concentrating on other measures to make the sub combat-safe, the engineers looked for ways to lower the level of radiated noise. Their battery of experiments showed that, under some conditions, cutting the level of radiated noise by ten decibels can reduce the effective operational distance of enemy sonar by at least 50 percent.[41] But approaching this and similar obstacles to survivability, they often discovered additional requirements while grappling with the problems at hand. They learned almost by accident, for example, to attach special importance to the noise caused by their own sonar equipment.[42]

The rate at which the propellers produce air bubbles relates directly to radiated noise, and this too they found out the hard way. Air bubbles not only reduce both survivability and operational performance but also induce corrosion. Engineers from Institutes 702 and 725 adopted what they believed were the standard measures to lower the bubble rate: decreasing the angular velocity of the propellers (to 125–200 revolutions per minute), increasing the number of propeller blades from three to five or seven (an odd number to eliminate the thumping of a propeller having an even number of blades), enlarging the diameter of the propeller, improving the machining on the propeller blades, and applying sound-absorbing materials.[43] They also manufactured noise-reducing materials for the blades.[44]

Submarines have two other well-known sources of serious underwater noise: the vibration of machinery, and the rush of water over the skin coating of the hull. Both sounds intensify in proportion to speed, but the deeper a submarine dives, the less the noise emitted by its propellers and the greater the operating range of its sonar. From experiments, the Chinese experts discovered that they could reduce vibration and radiated noise by placing the machinery and piping on specially designed pedestals and cladding them in soundproof materials. And so the list of requirements grew: reducing noise levels of fluids flowing through hydraulic pressure systems and reactor pumps, increasing the efficiency of the reduction gearboxes and various pumps or even replacing the gearboxes with more advanced systems, and limiting the number of openings in the outer hull. As we shall see, the Chinese understood that the submarine's configuration also affected noise, but it took them years to settle on a water-drop hull shape (*shuidi xianxing*).

During the 1960s, Chinese intelligence uncovered clues to an infrared detection device that could detect heat radiation from the diesel exhaust, yet another source of vulnerability. These clues suggested optimal depths for snorkeling under diesel power and ideas for putting anti-radar coating on the submarine's snorkel and periscope to limit detectability.[45] They added demagnetization to their list when they grasped the perils of airborne magnetic detectors and magnetic mines.[46]

From their close reading of the increasing number of publications on the American Polaris program, the Chinese also decided to pay added attention to the on-board oxygen and radiation protection systems and the living and working environments so as to maintain the crew's effectiveness over extended periods at sea.[47] Finally, they had to allow for the unknown extras by estimating and setting aside weight for them (which could be compensated by adding lead if the actual additions proved too light) and to specify and fabricate hundreds of high-strength, weldable steel alloys for each major component of the pressure hull, with the weakest component capable of withstanding hydrostatic pressures at depths up to 300 meters.[48]

Digging into Western and Soviet sources and their own engineering texts, the Chinese unearthed an endless menu of commonsense approaches to the internal configuring of the submarine: the underwater acoustic detectors should be put in the bow; the command and control console, electronic equipment, navigational console, living cabins, and storage batteries should be installed in or just forward of the central section. Generally speaking, the reactor of a nuclear-powered attack boat must be placed at or just aft of amidships so as to balance the longitudinal static moment caused by the reactor's massive weight. The designers refused to take any of these placements for granted, and one by one each permutation was tested and retested before approval.[49]

The list of technical jobs to be accomplished was staggering and seemed to expand geometrically with each passing month, and to accomplish them, some of China's top minds were assigned to Project 09.[50] These included physicists and experts in shipbuilding, nuclear reactors, and rocketry; most were to remain anonymous to the very end of their careers.[51] When they joined the project in 1958, the majority were young enthusiasts; when the first nuclear attack submarine was commissioned in 1974, they were seasoned veterans who had overcome both design and engineering obstacles, as well as political insults and injury, during the Cultural Revolution.[52]

They now recount the story of a dance held by a group of engineers who joined Project 09 in the early years. One handsome young man stopped dancing suddenly and with high emotion announced to his comrades: "I won't get married until the nuclear-powered submarine is launched." He kept his word and was wed only after the first attack submarine (09-1) was commissioned—16 years later. When he took off his hat and nodded a greeting to the guests at the wedding ceremony, all reportedly felt sad for their colleague. He looked old and was completely bald. The same kind of dedication we found in the nuclear weapons program permeated Project 09, especially among those who joined at the beginning.

Debates on the Type and Shape of the Nuclear Submarine

When Project 09 was cut back in 1961 and then suspended in 1962, most of the engineers were temporarily shifted to other jobs.[53] But a core group was retained to work on subsystems that require long research lead times, and some of its members continued, on an informal basis, to probe the principal design problems of the nuclear sub. These men, Chief Designer Huang Xuhua and his assistants in the Nuclear-Powered Submarine Over-all Design Section of the Seventh Academy,* kept on working on drafting the general plans for what Huang assumed would be the ballistic-missile sub.[54] Deciding on an appropriate configuration for the submarine and which type of missile ejection system should be adopted kept Huang and a few of his colleagues busy for most of the next few years.[55] The principal raison d'être of their activity was to stay ready for the day when the project would be restarted.

That day came in August 1965. But as we have seen, when the Central Special Commission finally did resurrect the project, it also shifted the project's direction, giving clear precedence to the attack submarine. Zhou Enlai declared the project's guiding principle to be *liangbu zou* (go in two steps) and authorized a timetable that, if met, would see the attack submarine launched by 1972.[56]

As we have also seen, the formal decision did not end the policy debate, and much time was wasted on other meetings until December 7, 1966, when Nie Rongzhen, who had the final say on the matter, told the participants in yet another meeting: "You [should] just follow the decision approved by the [Central] Special Commission [in August 1965] to develop the nuclear-powered attack submarine first. However, the Seventh Ministry of Machine Building [missile] also should accelerate the research and development on the missile [that can be launched from a submerged submarine]." In China, as elsewhere, consensus-building required both compromise and ambiguity.

From the outset, Chief Designer Huang Xuhua had argued for the immediate adoption of the water-drop design then in use in the most advanced of the world's nuclear fleets.[57] Huang and his associates were convinced that the linear shape (*xianxing*) routinely used for conventional subs would be unsuitable for nuclear-powered boats operating at high speeds and at depths up to 300m. Because each tangent plane of the hull is round in the streamlined water-drop or "whale" shape, they contended, the boat would be subject to minimum friction or drag and have good stability at great depths. Although the water-drop-shaped submarine maneuvered poorly on the surface, it was incomparably better than traditional boats underwater, or so the Chinese concluded.

---

*The Warship Research and Design Academy (Seventh Academy) was established in June 1961 with the merger of the six research institutes under the Naval Science and Technology Research Department and some research facilities attached to the Third Ministry of Machine Building (conventional weapons).

For Huang's antagonists, the question was not really whether but when to adopt the water-drop configuration. What impressed them, and indeed most of the designers, was the American example, whereby program managers had chosen to proceed in three steps, first building a conventional sub with a water-drop shape, then installing nuclear power plants on submarines with a linear shape, and finally applying the water-drop shape to the nuclear-powered submarine. The other leader in the field, the Soviet Union, had pursued an even more circuitous path to this end. Was it possible, the advocates of the staged approach asked, for China, a nation that lacked advanced industrial technologies and sufficient qualified technical personnel, to use this advanced design in its very first nuclear submarine?

Huang's answer was an unqualified yes. He later explained his decision this way: "The feasibility of adopting the water-drop shape for configuring nuclear-powered submarines was proved [by foreign countries] before we undertook the project. What was the point for us to follow a three-step course?"

Nevertheless, a major dispute erupted on the issue, and Huang's reasoning proved unpersuasive. As he recollects it, heated debates occurred right after his institute began formulating the design plans. The dominant group thought it better to adopt the standard linear shape for the first nuclear submarine and then make the transition to the water-drop model. Some also worried about the factors affecting stability in the water-drop sub. Huang held his ground, but given the charged political climate against "academic authorities" in the early days of the Cultural Revolution, he had to move cautiously.

He started by organizing his scientific and technical personnel to make scale-model hydrodynamic experiments. Most of the tests were performed at Institute 702 located on Lake Tai in Jiangsu Province. Created in 1958, 702 boasted the biggest ship-testing pools in China, including the largest wave tank in its Seaworthiness Laboratory. The tank could simulate any sea state. An experimental minisub was built to test the water-drop shape at low speeds.[58] Some experiments on fluid mechanics were also carried out at the hydrodynamic water tanks at several universities and colleges. Of those smaller experimental water tanks, the Hydrodynamic Laboratory at Jiaotong University in Shanghai was the most modern by the late 1960s.[59]

The scale-model experiments repeatedly verified the overall superiority of the more revolutionary water-drop shape, but the tests left unresolved several questions about the maneuverability and stability of a submerged submarine so configured. With such mixed results, Huang conceded the debate to the traditionalists. All the while, the Nuclear Powered Submarine Overall Design Institute (Institute 719) had been busy drawing up a full set of plans for the attack submarine (an assignment it had started in June 1965, even before Project 09 was officially revived), and in November 1966, when it submitted its first draft, the plan called for a conventional linear shape.[60] That decision lasted about a month.

Here again, Nie stepped in to settle the matter. On taking over Project 09, his commission had quickly become aware of the experts' disagreements over the sub's shape. After due consideration, Nie acted decisively. At the same meeting of December 7 where he decreed that work must proceed first on the attack sub, he rejected the institute's proposal in no uncertain terms: "Don't adopt the linear shape of conventional-powered submarines. You should redesign [the submarine]. Otherwise, it will become nondescript, neither conventional nor nuclear-powered." Quietly the arguments died, and the draft plan was rewritten accordingly.[61]

Three days later, in the follow-up talks at the Beijing Hotel, Nie ordered senior specialists to inspect the revised design plans one last time before he transmitted them to the central authorities. Wisely not challenging Nie Rongzhen's declarations on the type and shape of the boat, the experts concentrated in a somewhat pro forma way on technical matters related to the new design plans and returned the draft to their boss. Nie then submitted his report to the Central Military Commission and the Central Special Commission. On December 16, the special commission approved both of Nie's decisions and issued this directive: "The Defense Science and Technology Commission and the National Defense Industry Office should help the Sixth and Second Ministries of Machine Building make better arrangements for the solution of problems relevant to coordination and cooperation among various scientific research facilities as well as the manufacture of equipment and so on."

Attempted Coordination in the Period of Turmoil

No sooner had the type and shape of the nuclear attack submarine been officially approved than the project fell victim to the Cultural Revolution. The nationwide social and political crisis, as we noted in the previous chapter, disrupted all phases of Project 09, which remained somewhat immune to high-level measures adopted to restore order. Yet even in the throes of the national upheaval, most of the survivors tried to complete their tasks and press on with the job. In addition to the chaotic world around them, the professionals now had to find ways to coordinate their activities and weave them into a whole. We turn to this part of their story.

Once the Central Special Commission decided to restart Project 09, building the sub was labeled a "key" program. Zhou Enlai went even further, stipulating that supplying the program with all the required "funds, materials, and equipment should claim precedence over all others."[62] To speed things along, the Seventh Academy now sought and got Zhou's permission to recruit more shipbuilding specialists. In addition, at Zhou's direction, the Ministry of Education assigned 1,500 college graduates to the academy over the next three years. All that helped, but there was a more pressing need, for the program had already progressed to the point where the problems to be solved cut across many disciplines, some quite new to the Chinese. Since most of the best specialists in these disciplines worked in institutes scattered across China and in facilities beyond the Sixth Ministry's direct control, the Seventh Academy needed to identify the appropriate personnel and then persuade them to become involved. To this end, the Seventh Academy promoted academic exchanges among various research facilities, and after the opening of the power plant research base in Jiajiang, Sichuan Province, it set out to create a critical mass of specialists there. Following the arrival of more than 200 technicians from the Seventh Academy, the First Academy of the Second Ministry (Southwest Reactor Engineering Research and Design Academy) at Jiajiang directed them to work together in studying the available professional knowledge on submarine nuclear power supply. This interdisciplinary approach had the added payoff, according to Huang Xuhua, of breaking down disciplinary barriers. To him, the new system was "miraculous."[63]

At the meeting of December 7, 1966, held to determine the type and shape of the submarine, Nie Rongzhen attempted to limit the geographical and organizational fragmentation within Project 09 and to clarify the simplified division of labor in it. He declared: "The Defense Science and Technology Commission and the National Defense Industry Office should jointly supervise [Project 09]. The Sixth Ministry of Machine Building is in charge of building the submarine. The Second Ministry of Machine Building is responsible for constructing [the submarine] nuclear power plants. The navy should help various industrial ministries and research academies promote the project."[64] On paper, Nie's proposal appeared feasible.

But the problems created by the social turmoil of the Cultural Revolution proved far too intractable to be overcome by standard organizational remedies or edicts. In January 1967, officially egged on by Mao Zedong and Lin Biao, radical activists began seizing power from officials at all levels, and by the summer violent clashes spread throughout the nation.[65] The organs of the project did not escape.

For example, political unrest engulfed Institute 719, which was responsible for administering the nuclear submarine project. One target was Qian Lingbai, who had made the "mistake" of studying in the Soviet Union.[66] As a section director at the institute, Qian was busily working on submarine designs when the Cultural Revolution erupted in his office. Forcing their way in, squads of youthful rebels focused on his Soviet training and expertise, and as part of his punishment for having professional credentials, he was isolated from the project. It was not until his colleagues at the institute were unable to solve a critical formula for calculating the submarine's total weight that Qian was "liberated" and told to bail them out. As of 1990, Qian still worked at Institute 719.

Even before Qian came under attack, the chief designer of Project 09 himself, Huang Xuhua, had felt the Red Guards' wrath. In 1966, while he was presiding over a project coordination conference held in Beijing, revolutionary rebels from Institute 719 rushed into the meeting and hauled him back to Huludao. There he was denounced and "sentenced" to raising pigs.[67] Over the next months, the rebels tried and retried his case as a public spectacle. In one of these grotesque episodes, the following dialogue occurred between Huang and a member of the military control team that had taken over the institute:[68]

Military representative: "You said you weren't an enemy agent assigned to worm your way into the underground Party organization at Jiaotong University [where Huang had studied]. Is this possible? You come from a bourgeois landlord family. How could you have risked joining the underground Party? That would have meant that you had forsaken your class origins. Is it possible for something so unusual as this to have occurred?"

Huang Xuhua: "A few leading comrades of the central authorities also come from landlord and capitalist families. Why did they rebel against their own class to carry out revolution?"

Military representative: "You dare to compare yourself to the leading comrades in the Center! You are guilty of a crime for which even death cannot atone. To which kind of people do leading comrades in the Center belong? To which kind of people do you belong?"

Huang Xuhua: "We are all human beings! We are all Party members!"

Military representative: "You said that you were not an enemy agent. Then you should confess who stood at your right side and left side each time you went onto the streets and demonstrated [as a Jiaotong student]?"

Huang Xuhua: "Can you yourself remember who stood at your right and left sides when you did physical exercises more than twenty years ago?"

Military representative: "You are an agent who only deserves to be given two peanuts [bullets]!"

At about this time, one of Huang Xuhua's supervisors at the institute was driven insane by such threats, but reportedly "Huang was lucky enough not to be given . . . 'peanuts' because the nuclear-powered submarine project needed him." At the express order of Zhou Enlai, he had been put under "special protection" and restored to duty, though the radical factions continued to assail him.

In the hope of preventing further damage to the project, Nie Rongzhen decided to hold a conference and invite some central leaders who might rein in the radicals. Further, in the notices he dispatched to the participating units, issued in the name of the Central Military Commission, he stipulated that anyone who received an invitation must be permitted to attend the conference even if he or she was being criticized and denounced at public meetings.[69] Hundreds of directors, secretaries of Party committees, and chief engineers/designers in charge of developing the 09-1's subsystems gathered at the Nationalities Hotel in Beijing on June 20, 1967. The conference, which ran over several days, was presided over by Liu Huaqing, deputy director of Nie's commission.

Nie himself, trying to stay in the background so as not to lay himself open to attack, merely called for the promotion of the project "as scheduled" in his brief address to his colleagues.

But by now no second-echelon official alone could halt the spread of anarchism throughout the project's industrial and scientific network. Thus, about this time, at its eighteenth meeting, the Central Special Commission tried its hand at restoring order and discipline. Under Zhou Enlai's guidance, it decided: "The State Planning Commission, the Ministry of Materials, and other departments concerned are responsible for providing the equipment and matériel most needed by the various departments concerned with promoting research and development on the nuclear-powered submarine. Similar problems that arise hereafter should be resolved in a timely way by the departments concerned [using the same method]."[70] Following up, on August 30, Liu Huaqing recommended that the Central Military Commission issue an official letter as an emergency measure for promoting Project 09. We briefly mentioned this letter, which was signed by Nie Rongzhen, in the previous chapter.

The letter reaffirmed that the nuclear submarine program was crucial to the building of China's national defense and stressed that no interruption of research or production would escape punishment. In response to the letter and Mao's follow-up directives, the PLA ordered its trucks, warships, and aircraft to deliver urgently needed equipment. The industrial ministries sent propaganda teams to hundreds of plants and institutes connected to the project, this time with the restoration of order on their minds. They stressed that their mission had been approved by Mao Zedong himself and was vital to China's security. Labeling disruptions and delays a crime against Mao, the teams threatened harsh reprisals for any further outbursts.

Yet even these drastic moves proved only partially successful. The groups working on the prototype power plant in Jiajiang were able to complete their assignments, but those working on the general submarine design found their efforts frustrated by the need to have every forward step scrutinized and accepted by warring factions. In desperation, the design team leaders turned for relief to outside specialists uncontaminated by previous clashes. They invited Deng Sanrui to be their chief adviser for the overall design plan, for example, and one of his main tasks was interpersonal mediation, even individual therapy.[71]

Sometimes it was unclear who was helping whom. The Seventh Academy, for instance, wanted Qian Lingxi, a professor at the Dalian Institute of Technology and an authority on structural mechanics to analyze the submarine's design plans, but Qian at the moment was being criticized and denounced at public meetings as an "academic authority," and the label rendered him untouchable. Powerless to pry Qian loose from the Dalian institute, Chen Youming, then deputy director of the academy, asked Zhou Enlai for approval to have Qian examine the submarine's structural designs and to formulate the standard specifications for those designs. Zhou approved Chen's request, but cautioned him not to transfer the professor formally to Project 09 and to solicit his help only in general terms.[72] From this and numerous other cases, it was becoming painfully clear that a much more authoritative administrative body was needed to oversee the ongoing work of the project.

Evolution of the Command Structure

Qian's case made clear the urgent need for a new project command center separate from the Defense Science and Technology Commission, the Second Ministry, the Sixth Ministry, and the navy, and directly subordinate to the Central Special Commission. Nie's commission decided that the way to handle this and similar problems was to create an interagency administrative body to handle the project's day-to-day affairs. In February 1968, it set up the Nuclear-Powered Submarine Project Office (He Qianting Gongcheng Bangongshi), with Chen Youming as director. For convenience and secrecy, the office was usually referred to as the 09 Office or Lingjiuban.[73]

In his early career, Chen had commanded a torpedo boat flotilla operating out of Hainan Island, but after 1954, he was involved primarily in R&D administration, first as director of the Seventh Academy's Institute 701 (general warship design), and then as the academy's deputy director.[74] Chen's Lingjiuban was put under the administration of the Defense Science and Technology Commission, and was composed of officials from that body, the navy, the NDIO, and the Sixth Ministry.

The following year, the commander of the navy, Xiao Jinguang, enters the story of Project 09 for the first time.[75] On October 9, 1969, Xiao presided over a fact-finding conference to audit the progress of the nuclear attack submarine or 09-1 program. Ranking cadres from the State Planning Commission, the NDIO, the Defense Science and Technology Commission, the Second and Sixth ministries, and the First and Seventh academies attended.[76] After a recounting of the dreary list of horror stories about factions and failures, the delegates recommended that the State Council and the Central Military Commission establish a new body at a level above the Lingjiuban in order to enforce cooperation among the project's units.

Agreeing, the council and the commission jointly appointed the Nuclear-Powered Submarine Project Leading Group (He Qianting Gongcheng Lingdao Xiaozu) and made the first political commissar of the navy, Li Zuopeng, the group's head.[77] The new organization, usually called simply the Leading Group, reported to both the Central Special Commission and the Central Military Commission.[78] With this change, the Lingjiuban came under the Leading Group, only to be moved again to the purview of the navy headquarters in 1970, as 09's main activities shifted from the R&D institutes to the naval shipyards.[79]

In retrospect, the Lingjiuban probably played a more critical role in Project 09 than the Leading Group, but both were important. The Leading Group exercised substantial power for about a year, but after the decline of its radical boss, Li Zuopeng, in late 1970, it steadily lost influence. The Lingjiuban handled the project's daily affairs, and in so doing, kept closer connections with Zhou's special commission and played a more direct role in managing the project than the Leading Group.

The changing power configurations over the years, a snapshot of which is given in Figure 3 for October 1969, reflected the center's continuing quest for organizational solutions in Project 09, as well as in other strategic weapons programs. After the resumption of the project in August 1965, the Central Military Commission and the Central Special Commission kept adjusting 09's command structure, entrusting leadership first to the NDIO and the Defense Science and Technology Commission jointly, and then successively to the commission alone (1966–69); the Leading Group (1969–70); the navy (1970–78); and the commission again (1978–82). Since 1982, the project leaders have reported to the Commission of Science, Technology, and Industry for National Defense (COSTIND).[80]

Still, it took more than a change in the command system to produce significant results, even though the project's high political profile technically ensured its access to restricted equipment and materials until the early 1970s. After Chen Youming reported that unyielding obstacles still plagued the project at a meeting of Zhou Enlai's special commission on

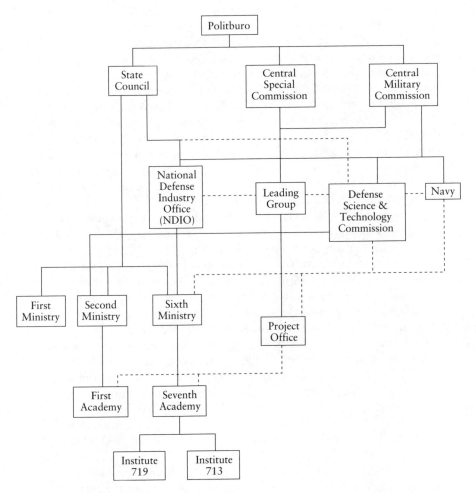

Fig. 3. Organization of Project 09, Oct. 1969

July 15, 1970, Zhou put his own prestige on the line. When the meeting reconvened the following day, he introduced Chen to officials in a position to ease his way,[81] and made it plain he expected their full cooperation, saying: "Yesterday Comrade Chen Youming said that several problems concerning the nuclear-powered submarine project still remain to be solved. Please help him solve these problems. Comrade Chen Youming, hereafter you should negotiate directly with them as soon as you meet problems. Don't ask the special commission for instructions on everything because this will delay [the progress of the whole project]." Zhou's personal clout more than Chen's decreed task made the difference, and from then on the project experienced few serious delays for want of equipment or materials.

At a time of great shortages, that clout was essential to carrying out a project of 09's magnitude. From the outset, Mao and Zhou regarded the project as larger in scale and more complex than the ones on nuclear weapons (Project 02) and strategic guided missiles (Project 05).[82] For example, almost twice as many plants, research institutes, and colleges and universities were reportedly involved in Project 09 as in Project 02 (2,000 spread out in 27 different localities vs. 1,000 in 20).[83] The two leaders thus understood that Project 09 needed the most authoritative attention and demanding systems management, and somehow had to be freed from the constant political interference and bureaucratic red tape.

For example, on the night of October 10, 1969, Zhou Enlai summoned Luo Shunchu (deputy director of Nie's commission), the Second Ministry's Vice-Minister Liu Xiyao,[84] Chen Youming, and several electronics specialists to his office to discuss the progress on the sub's atomic clock and radio navigation equipment. After hearing their briefing, Zhou Enlai pointed out: "Just as you have told me, [developing these instruments] is very complicated in terms of technology. The nuclear-powered submarine project is very complicated, even more complicated than *liangdan* [the strategic missile and nuclear warhead projects]. The nuclear-powered submarine itself includes *liangdan*." So why, Zhou was implying, were his calls for unity and coordination in the project meeting such indifference or resistance?

Completion of the Nuclear Attack Submarine's Design

Within the ever-changing command system, the groups under Huang Xuhua doggedly pressed ahead on solving the remaining puzzles in their design work. At this stage in formulating the overall plans for the first submarine, Huang concentrated on the interior atmospheric and environmental systems, inertial navigation, sonar, and long-distance communications equipment and insisted on his engineers using the latest methodologies of systems engineering in their design.[85]

He also exhorted his designers to study other nuclear submarine programs carefully as information on them became public or was obtained through intelligence. Admonishing his specialists "to derive nourishment from others' experiences," he told them, "You can get twice the result with half the effort if you know how to pick others' brains," the more so, since today's "sophisticated [scientific] results are usually made up of conventional [scientific] results. Don't make a mystery of the most advanced branches of science. . . . Most of the advanced branches of science adopted for the American Polaris and Apollo programs were based on an appropriate synthesis of existing technologies. Synthesis is truly creativity. . . . What counts is how to synthesize [existing technologies]."[86]

Huang's point proved well-taken in every case where the designers faced unexplored technical territory. An example was the high pressure air tanks for ballast control.[87] According to foreign sources, modern submarines required compressed air at pressures as great as $400kg/cm^2$ (or about 400 atmospheres; that is, many times the pressure at maximum test depth), which far exceeded Chinese capabilities at the time.[88] Huang ordered his associates to solve the problem by improving the air tanks then available, not by trying to invent new types.[89] Huang believed in the motto of the times: "When the conditions exist, go ahead; when they don't, create them and go ahead." In each case, evaluating the conditions began with a rigorous mining of all the available foreign literature.

Sometimes solving a problem depended more on hands-on management than engineering science. Case in point: correctly calculating the sub's total weight and center of gravity. Both factors are crucial to the vessel's stability; failing to account for thousands of items of equipment in its small hull would plainly mean disaster. The designers first tried to compute the boat's ideal stability but had trouble deciding on the figures for its reserve weight and other specifics.[90] They had to calculate and adjust for the weights and location of each item of on-board equipment, a simple problem to solve in theory but baffling to work out in practice. As part of the solution, Huang told every engineer responsible for designing a given piece of equipment to go to the factories where it was manufactured and measure its precise weight and center of gravity.[91]

In this way, Huang adopted a method of designing while manufacturing the 09-1 boat's subsystems. His decision to do both at once reflected the urgency attached to the project but simultaneously magnified the chances of error. The general design plans could only be finalized at the end of the equipment manufacturing process, and when the moment of truth arrived, the gross weight far exceeded the engineers' initial estimates.[92] Further-more, the method introduced errors in both the design and test-manufacturing stages. For a time the process of trial and error favored error. As the engineers were completing the overall design plans, they discovered to their dismay that increasing the total weight of the submarine had caused a shift in the balance of the various on-board subsystems. None of the manuals told them how to restore the balance, so Huang Xuhua after some hasty meetings made his best educated guess and settled on the final interior arrangements by fiat.[93]

In an attempt to forestall even greater inaccuracies, a careful record was kept of the weight of each item before it was installed on the full-scale wood-and-steel model of the 09-1 Huang had his workers build at the shipyard. Once an item was installed, the weight of any leftover bits and pieces, as well as superfluous pipeline and electrical cable, was deducted from its original weight on coming aboard.[94] Based on these sums and using trial and error throughout the building phase, the designers were able to assemble accurate data for measuring the submarine's weight and center of gravity, and then proceed on to calculate the boat's ideal operating stability.[95]

In November 1968, engineers and workers started building the submarine's double hulls at the Bohai Shipyard (Plant 431), even though the interior design had not yet been finalized.[96] The problem was that the design depended on the manufacture of the interior equipment, and the manufacturing process, caught up in the Cultural Revolution, was proceeding badly. None of the internal systems referred to at the beginning of this section was ready. Without them, as one Chinese writer has noted, the 09-1 would be a "bastard" submarine with a "sophisticated" father (nuclear power) and a "backward" mother (outdated weapons and systems).[97]

The torpedo ejection system was ready and waiting, but the torpedo design was causing enormous headaches, and, indeed, the Chinese continued to wrestle with the problems long after the first 09 sub was launched. Once the designers settled on a ring-shaped layout for the placement of the torpedo tubes, the Seventh Academy, in 1965, without demur assigned Institute 705 to design the ejection system, and four years later, the Wuhan Auxiliary Engine Plant (Plant 461) built the system for the 09-1.[98]

There was no such consensus on the torpedo itself. The engineers had set their sights on developing a revolutionary deep-water homing torpedo,[99] but they had a long way to go and few supporters. At the outset, in the early 1960s, Liu Huaqing, then director of the Seventh Academy, pressed Institute 705 to copy a Soviet-model torpedo for missions against surface targets.[100] Although Liu's experts understood that the principal prey for the torpedoes of the future would be submarines, not surface ships, they accepted the assignment and made it one of their top priorities.[101]

In 1966, when the navy began building two torpedo testing ranges in Qinghai and Yunnan provinces,[102] organs of Liu's academy had already built a gas-powered torpedo, code-named Yu-1. Meanwhile, other research bodies had started working on a copy of a Soviet rocket-assisted aerial torpedo, the Yu-2.[103] But all concerned recognized that neither the Yu-1 nor the Yu-2 would close the technological gap with the Soviet Union and the United States, and in that year, experts started designing two electric homing torpedoes. Using a Soviet model, they designed acoustic homing devices for the new torpedoes, a passive one for the Yu-4A and an active/passive one for the Yu-4B.[104] Neither, however, was suitable for the 09-1.

Also in 1966, the Defense Science and Technology Commission finally specified the mission for nuclear attack submarines, and over the next decade Institute 705, now in its new home in Kunming, worked on a torpedo to attack enemy submarines in deep water.[105] As part of the construction in the Third-Line region, many technicians were transferred from other institutes and plants to Kunming to work on acoustic homing torpedoes.[106] In 1983, this heterogenous group began the final tests on an electric passive-homing prototype, code-named Yu-3, and readied the first batch for deployment within a year.

The noise level of Yu-3 remained high, however, and the effectiveness of its homing systems was still low compared with Western torpedoes. They could not be used on attack submarines operating at great depths.[107] Thus, in 1983 the navy started a six-year effort on an advanced small-sized homing torpedo for attacking submarines at great depth.[108] Technicians at the China Naval Research Center's Torpedo Research Section initiated R&D on improved homing mechanisms.[109] In 1985, the Seventh Academy directed Institute 705 and two plants to design an active/passive-homing device and other subsystems for the advanced torpedo; this project alone cost three million yuan over the next three years.[110] By 1989, these organs, in cooperation with Plant 5002, had succeeded in producing the more sophisticated Yu-3, now called China Sturgeon No. 2. The designers believed the Sturgeon approached the highest international standard.[111]

Other key items of the on-board subsystems primarily related to electronics. With the help of the research facilities attached to the Fourth Ministry of Machine Building (electronics), institutes under the Seventh Academy labored on each of these subsystems throughout the years of the Cultural Revolution. Despite the near chaos surrounding them, the workers at

Institute 707 in Tianjin made progress on the inertial navigation system, and other institutes met similar successes on their assigned items.[112] An entire sector of China's industry focused on the project, and by August 1974, when the 09-1 submarine was commissioned, most of the subsystems had been installed. The schedule had been met, but hidden in many of these systems were defects that were to continue to plague the 09 boats into the mid-1980s.[113]

Completion of the 09-2 Design

Well before the 09-1 entered the final stages, work had begun on the nuclear-powered ballistic-missile submarine, the 09-2,[114] and by October 1967, the first draft of the general design plans was completed. Thereupon, Nie Rongzhen's Defense Science and Technology Commission and the navy convened a meeting and officially restarted the missile submarine program under Project 09.[115] The meeting ended in a decision to set 1973 as the target year for launching 09-2.[116]

According to Huang Xuhua, the chief designer of the 09-2 as well as the 09-1, the Chinese knew that the French had built a small, low-speed, nuclear missile submarine, and that the low speed reduced its noise emissions and made it less susceptible to detection. Huang and his designers found this trade-off between noise and speed in the French design well worthwhile, since to their minds, the first priority ought to be given to 09-2's concealability. Huang is quoted as arguing that missile submarines "are regarded as having a second-strike capability; that is, having the capability to survive a first nuclear strike. . . . There is no point in increasing its speed. . . . For example, a poisonous snake has venom fangs . . . and captures its prey more by concealment than by speed. Accordingly, a poisonous snake creeps much slower than a nonpoisonous one."[117] In practice, this would mean undoing the bias toward speed in the 09-1 program.

Indeed, many of the technical principles adopted for the 09-2 program at the 1967 meeting reflected the prior development of 09-1.[118] Some parts of the 09-1 design could be transferred, some could not. Both, for example, would use the same kind of pressurized water reactor. Much later, when adapting this reactor to the missile submarine, the designers could tap the plant's additional potential by up to 20 percent. The plant, they decided, would have to be installed aft of the missile tubes.[119]

Huang put his chief assistant, Xu Junlie, in charge of formulating the missile sub's overall design plans.[120] The main difference between the attack and missile submarines, of course, was the addition of the missile launch tubes and missile ejection systems. These additions again involved unknowns on which no body of literature was available to the Chinese. Xu and his colleagues had learned a little about how to launch a missile from a submarine when they were assembling the Golf diesel-electric missile submarine (31-class) under Soviet license at the Dalian Shipyard. But since that sub launched its missiles from the surface, their experience proved of marginal utility in working out 09-2's underwater-launch system.[121]

Chief Designer Huang and his colleagues believed the ejection system posed the main technical problem in the design of 09-2, and as it turned out, all other problems paled by comparison. They learned from Western sources that an underwater-to-surface missile was usually launched from a submarine operating at a muzzle depth of less than 30m. They guessed that the timing of missile ignition in Western SLBMs varied, usually according to a preset distance traveled.[122]

The missile launch tube involved less guesswork, for in this case the essentials were known from the sources in hand. Each missile rests within the inner of two tubes, and several U-shaped backup rings and airtight seals are installed between the tubes to maintain their concentricity as well as to keep the ejection blast out of the space between them. Automatic air conditioning attached to the launch tubes protects the missile's sensitive electronic equipment by maintaining the temperature at about 20°C and the humidity at about 70 percent. Special adapters (*shipei qi*) located between the missile and the case of the inner tube form part of the launch-assistance system discussed below; they help keep the missile positioned in the tube correctly during the launch by moving with the missile to the top of the tube.[123]

The hydrostatic pressure at the tube muzzle is about three atmospheres at a muzzle depth of about 30m, and the lid of the outer tube can only be opened with the assistance of a pressure-balance system. Before missile ejection, water is injected into the space between the lid of the outer tube and a watertight film at the mouth of the inner tube; at the same time, the inner tube must be filled with air to balance the exterior and interior pressures. The film resists small pressure differences but not the ejection itself. Step by step, the pressures outside the submarine and inside the tubes are brought into relative balance. Prior to launch, the missile's guidance system, engines, and warhead instrumentation can be monitored electronically from outside the tubes. The cabling for this monitoring detaches automatically just before liftoff.[124]

To achieve the required high accuracy of the missile, the designers had to ensure that the submarine remained stable at the moment of ejection. A slight change occurs in the boat's center of gravity as the missile clears it, because the water entering the launch tube weighs more than the missile. Missile-weight compensation water tanks must, therefore, be added to blow out the excess and keep the submarine in balance.[125]

The 09-2's missile launch system also incorporated a number of safety design features. Special equipment was installed to set off an alarm should water enter the missile tube before launch and to monitor any abnormal changes in pressure, temperature, or humidity. The designers provided for an emergency ejection system to protect the sub from a missile accident and for equipment to pump out seawater and pump in fresh water for cleaning the missile tubes.[126]

The job of working out all these features fell to Institute 713, in Zhengzhou, Henan Province.[127] In selecting people for this assignment in mid-1965, Huang had hoped to draw on the experience of the technicians who had helped assemble the Golf-class submarine's missile launch tube and ejection systems, but the transfer of knowledge, as we have remarked, was minimal, and the institute had to start almost from scratch. The 713 technicians converted a rundown greenhouse into their laboratory and built a simple pool by welding several gasoline tanks together. Using a paint-spraying compressor as their power source, they started performing 1:25 model-scale ejection tests from the pool. Following the incremental trial-and-error method as the only one available to them, they completed the preliminary research work on the ejection system design and some key technical items by the end of the year.[128]

With this done, the next step was to choose an energy source for the system. Huang learned that the Americans had initially used compressed air to eject the missile but had then switched to a chemical propellant (the propellant produces steam when exhausted into a tank of water, and the steam creates the required pressure below the missile).[129] Using a propellant made maintenance simpler but produced a column of water that exposed the sub's location.[130] The Chinese puzzled over this trade-off and wondered whether they too should follow a staged approach beginning with the compressed air. If not, how would they meet the rigorous and risky requirements for propellant-fueled ejection?

In such an ejection system, the propellant would have to produce enough steam to boost the missile to a speed of several meters per second (usually about 45m per second or less in submarines submerged to depths of 30m). At the same time, the engineers had to design a system that would expose the missile to pressures of less than ten atmospheres.[131] Huang believed such a design was possible and recommended skipping the compressed-air stage.[132] As we shall see, he commissioned research chemists in two industrial institutes to develop a suitable explosive propellant.

Having decided in principle on this course, the designers next had to choose between a gas system and a gas-steam system. They chose the latter. The gas-steam ejection system is composed mainly of a gas generator, a gas-cooling apparatus, a gas-steam pipeline, a compression chamber, and airtight seals. Once the propellant in the gas generator is ignited, the gas enters the water-filled gas-cooling apparatus, producing a gas-steam mixture. The mixture moves through the pipeline to the compression chamber in the launch tube and rapidly increases pressure there. The chamber is the space between the bottom of the missile or launch-assistance device (discussed below) and the bottom of the launch tube. Seals, whose location can vary within the launch tube, ensure that the full force of the pressure wave comes at the base of the missile.

Another critical decision involved the operating speed of the sub at firing time. In the Soviet system, in which missiles were usually launched from a moving submarine maintaining speeds up to five knots, the motion of the boat helps preserve maneuverability and stability at the critical moment of launch. U.S. subs, by contrast, fire when they are making little or no headway, never faster than 0.5 knot. For a dead-in-the-water boat to maintain its depth during launch, it must have large pumps to move great volumes of ballast water quickly and accurately. A moving submarine, while easier to control, creates a separate set of technical problems. The force created by the water at speeds above 0.5 knot tends to tip the missile away from vertical as it emerges from the launch tube. If this torque cannot be corrected, the missile may scrape the side of the tube and be damaged or become a horizonal torpedo.[133]

The Chinese came down in favor of a Soviet-type method for launching their missiles from submerged submarines moving at two to four knots.[134] They designed a relatively simple launch-assistance system, including the adapters installed in the inner tube, to guide the missile out of the tube during the launch. In this system, the missile basically sits on a launch-assistance device (LAD) and is connected to the adapters, which serve as rails within the tubes. As the LAD and missile move up the launch tube, the system counteracts the force of the water and keeps the missile vertical. The device, which takes the brunt of the ejection blast, moves to the top of the launch tube before separating from the underway missile. A thermal shield under the missile forms part of the LAD; it protects the missile from the heat of the blast and bears the impact of the initial thrust. The LAD separates from the missile at the top of the tube and returns to the bottom.[135]

All this was quite straightforward engineering if the missile was going to be launched from a depth of less than 30m. Otherwise the challenge was enormous. The designers took the easy way out and went for a shallow launch. The JL-1 missile does not ignite until it reaches a height of about 10–15m above the surface.[136]

In 1966, after the navy approved Huang's recommendations for the ejection system, specialists from the Seventh Academy's Institutes 713 and 719 made preparations for conducting 1:5 scale-model underwater ejection tests. They built a larger test pool, 6.5m deep and 2.5m in diameter, and a landing impact pit. Over the next two years, they conducted dozens of tests on the gas-steam system and listed 18 major technical problems to be solved in perfecting the system. One by one they resolved these problems and confirmed the feasibility of the gas-steam system. These tests verified the necessity of installing special adapters between the missile and the case of the inner launch tube and identified various design mistakes to be rectified.[137]

Meanwhile, research proceeded slowly on the chemistry of the explosives. As late as 1968, no investigation in China had begun on fast-burning double-base powders, the compounds presumed to be appropriate for the ejection system. Research then under way on fast-burning composite explosives provided some clues for making double-base powders but convinced Huang's group that much more needed to be done.[138] Dong Jinrong, an engineer in the group, heard of a college professor conducting research on such composite powders.[139] But radicals had labeled the professor "a bourgeois reactionary academic authority," and he was being paraded before public denunciation meetings.

With the professor in disgrace and beyond reach, the military had assigned a factory in Taiyuan, Shanxi Province, to continue working on the professor's special formulas.[140] Learning of this turn of events, Dong set off for Taiyuan, only to discover that an accidental explosion had occurred at the factory shortly before his arrival, and few workers were ready to rush back to the mixing vats. Dong sensed, however, that fear could be transformed into heroics once the workers learned of Mao's high interest in the project, and he used that interest to persuade the factory technicians to return to work. Continuing the professor's line of inquiry, they joined forces with the Lanzhou Institute of Chemistry and Physics and Institute 3 in Xi'an, two institutes that specialized in high explosives.[141] The first full-scale rocket launched from a Golf-class sub in September 1972 was testimony to their ingenuity and perseverance.

With the matter of the propellant lagging behind the design of the ejection system, Beijing issued an order in late 1969 to accelerate the research in that domain, and specialists from the Xi'an and Lanzhou institutes spent the next several years producing the first practical fast-burning double-base powder. After further testing and redesigning of the ejection system, they used the powder on a land-based model of the gas-steam ejector in 1975 and for the test of several full-scale model rockets from a submerged Golf sub in 1979.[142]

Two more questions puzzled the Chinese: what would be the maximum sea state for safely launching a missile from a submerged submarine and what should be the minimum depth for the launch? Sea state indexes the level of potential turbulence that could throw the missile off vertical; sea depth, limiting keel and muzzle depth, affects both the sub and the missile during launch. From experiments, the engineers calculated that the maximum sea state must be less than grade 5 with an underwater current velocity of under two knots, and that the depth of the water at launch command must exceed 80m.[143]

All this work culminated in the JL-1's first successful test flight from a Golf sub on October 12, 1982.[144] By then, the engineers had also resolved the remaining technical questions about the 09-2 design, none of which approached the ejection system in complexity. The final step in designing a nuclear ballistic missile submarine had been taken.[145]

FOUR

Military Industry

The story of the building of the nuclear-powered submarine, the subject of the next chapter, must begin with the history of China's military industry. That history will show how a major strategic weapons project not only depended on the formation of a broad industrial base geared to defense production but also spurred and shaped its development from the late 1950s until a change of policy in the early 1980s turned the nation's resources to civilian production. By 1989, as measured by total value of output, two-thirds of the military industry had been converted.[1]

Generally speaking, the People's Liberation Army (PLA) defined and implemented China's technological advancement for the first 40 years of the People's Republic, and the nation's strategic weapons programs determined the essential composition and pace of that modernization effort. Up to the 1980s, a large share of China's total industrial production was organized under the military and controlled in secret by it. The military sector, moreover, virtually monopolized the most technologically advanced parts of China's industry and absorbed its best talent and scarce resources. The military dominated large plant construction, mineral and chemical processing from mines to finished product, the manufacture of fine machine tools and optics, the entire electronics and instrumentation industry, all aviation, most shipbuilding, most of the automotive industry, and virtually all research (including that in the Chinese Academy of Sciences) that had any military significance.[2]

From the 1950s on, military specialists ran large, technically demanding projects—everything from fabricating missiles and nuclear-powered submarines to producing computers and space-age plastics. Many received training abroad, knew and worked with foreigners, and grasped the significance of the technological age. Even though many of these specialists were forced to pursue their careers in the rustic hinterland, most managed to stay in close touch with powerful mentors in Beijing. The pervasive and enduring personal and institutional networks they fashioned remain relevant to this day. By examining the building of the Project 09 submarines, we thus illuminate the maturing not only of a critical sector of the defense industry—its size, quality, industrial networking, leadership, and development—but also of its political power and professional outlook.

The Creation of the Defense Industry

With the proclamation of the People's Republic on October 1, 1949, the new government assumed formal control of 68 munitions plants.[3] Before the year was out, it reorganized these plants, as well as the PLA's own defense facilities in the former revolutionary base areas, and set up what was first called the Ordnance Industry Office and then (in May 1950) the General Ordnance Bureau under the Ministry of Heavy Industry to run them.[4] In October 1950, soon after Beijing's decision to enter the Korean War (which lasted until July 1953), the central leadership convened a national ordnance conference in order to expedite arms production, and the following January, the Central Ordnance Commission (1951–54) was established to manage the assimilation of Soviet weaponry and the building of the nation's own defense industry.[5]

In the next years, a bewildering array of bureaucratic organs entered and vanished from the scene. The General Ordnance Bureau, for example, was first put under the joint jurisdiction of the Ministry of Heavy Industry and the Central Ordnance Commission in 1951 and then replaced, in August 1952, by the newly created Second Ministry of Machine Building.[6] (The body then called the Second Ministry was in charge of the development of conventional weapons. It is not to be confused with the Second Ministry familiar to us from earlier chapters. With a reorganization in 1958, the nomenclature changed, with the old Second Ministry becoming the First, and the Third, overseer of the nuclear industry, becoming the Second.) Zhao Erlu, a man with extensive experience in logistical work in the Red Army, was the logical first choice to run the ministry.[7]

With the concurrence of the Central Military Commission's armaments department, Zhao listed aeronautics and electronics as the two "weakest links" to be fortified in order to wage the Korean War and meet the nation's long-term defense requirements. Determined to build a base for China's own arms industry, his ministry gave precedence to creating basic research institutes in electronics, optics, aeronautics, and special materials.[8] Zhao launched this enterprise with a barebones number of technicians, fewer than 1,000 all told. At the same time, Zhao drafted an ambitious plan that called for refurbishing the existing defense plants within a two-year period and for organizing an interlocking network of facilities capable of meeting the three-to-five-year production goals in aircraft, military electronics, tanks, and heavy artillery.

Zhao's plan rested on the assumption of substantial Soviet aid. And indeed, in a Sino-Soviet accord concluded in 1953, 41 of the 156 key industrial facilities the Kremlin agreed to help assemble were directly connected to the output of conventional weapons.[9] (A mere six of these, we may note, were navy-related, since the Korean War had by then forced the Chinese leaders to assign priority to building the air force.[10]) Soviet financial assistance figured even more importantly in the efforts of Zhou and others to build a modern defense industry. According to one senior Soviet adviser, most of the nearly $2 billion in Soviet credits to China from 1950 to 1959 was used to pay for war equipment, machinery for munitions plants, and other big military enterprises. Thirty percent of the roughly 250 industrial facilities eventually outfitted by the Soviet Union were in the defense sector.[11]

When the Second Ministry and the Ministry of Electrical Industry were merged into the First Ministry of Machine Building in 1958, Zhao Erlu remained on as minister of the reorganized body. His job of constructing a modern defense industrial system was not made the easier by the fact that Mao Zedong had now decreed a new "general line" promoting mass-based projects and the communization of the countryside.[12] Nevertheless, defense-related missions continued to receive a green light, and these missions included R&D on strategic weapons. It was at this point that the central scientific and industrial organs in our story—the Fifth Academy responsible for the strategic missile project, the (new) Second Ministry of Machine Building, and the body that administered and supervised it, Nie Rongzhen's Defense Science and Technology Commission—were set up.[13]

The pursuit of these missions already diverted immense sums of money from the state budget to the military and complicated the implementation of civilian programs by the time Nie's commission took charge. For this reason, Mao Zedong had acted as early as April 1956 to settle the appropriate relationship between the civilian and defense sectors. In his report "On the Ten Major Relationships," he declared that precedence should be given to constructing the overall economy, for "only with the faster growth of economic construction can there be greater progress in defense construction." As Mao saw it, the defense industry was a component of the national economy and had to serve the needs of civilian economic development as well as of defense.[14] Nonetheless, when Chinese scholars in the mid-1970s analyzed how Mao's somewhat confusing military-civilian formula had been carried out over the previous decade, they concluded that the defense sector had continued to "possess considerable independence and initiative." This sector, one article said, had capitalized on the "latest scientific and technical achievements" and "continued to put forth demands on other industries."[15] In fact, Mao's formula favoring civilian construction had been ignored.

For the military, then, the concern was not a loss of resources to civilian industries, but improving their own supply system by integrating research, trial manufacture, and series production into a coherent R&D process for both conventional and strategic weapons.[16] To this end, in December 1959, roughly a year after the Central Military Commission had formed Nie Rongzhen's commission, it authorized yet another body, the National Defense Industrial Commission (NDIC).[17] Nine months later, still another ministry of machine building, the Third, was spun off from the First as a separate organ under the NDIC to be in overall charge of conventional arms and military equipment production.[18] The unending search for organizational panaceas reflected both a resolve to stay apace of the evolving R&D process and the politics of high technology in the People's Republic.[19]

The constantly shifting organizational map mirrored the course of those politics in the decade that followed. We discussed these shifts in our study of the making of the atomic bomb and thus will recount only the points most relevant to this discussion. The NDIC lasted until September 1963, when it was merged into the National Defense Industry Office (NDIO); the NDIO had been created in November 1961 to coordinate relations between the NDIC and Nie's commission. Marshal He Long headed the NDIC until its demise, while Chief of the General Staff Luo Ruiqing led the NDIO.[20] Both He Long and Luo, who had close ties, were on the Politburo; Nie Rongzhen was not.[21]

From 1961 to 1963, Nie has told us, "The functions and powers of the [principal] organizations were as follows: the Defense Science and Technology Commission was in charge of scientific research on weaponry and military equipment; the National Defense Industrial Commission was in charge of the production of weaponry and military equipment; and the National Defense Industry Office was in charge of coordinating and maintaining relations between the scientific research and production of weaponry and military equipment."[22] Because the Soviet Union had supplied most of the nation's next-generation conventional arms and related technologies, the NDIC-led Third Ministry opened a few facilities for research and development but focused for the most part on modifying Soviet-supplied weapons instead of creating new ones. As a result of this focus, the task of developing strategic weapons was effectively left at first to scientists and engineers under Nie Rongzhen's command.

That primacy gave way in 1962, when the central leadership authorized Luo Ruiqing to take command of a considerable part of the strategic weapons development from Nie's commission.[23] In response, NDIC/NDIO officials, with the political muscle of He Long and Luo Ruiqing to back them up, gained control of R&D for virtually all arms. A fierce turf battle between the two powerful networks led by Nie and by He Long and Luo Ruiqing ensued.[24] The expanded reach of the NDIC/NDIO, however, enlarged the base of political support for the strategic weapons programs just as many leaders were beginning to question them.

Power Politics and the Integration of Research and Production

In Chapter 2, we discussed the personal aspects of this rivalry and its disastrous results for Luo Ruiqing on the eve of the Cultural Revolution; here we focus primarily on the impact of the feuding on the defense industry. We recall that the domestic crises following the rupture of relations with Moscow and the collapse of the Great Leap Forward intensified the wrangling between the two networks even as all concurred on the goals of national unity and overall military preparedness. Throughout the early 1960s, the NDIC/NDIO group, on the one side, and Nie and his colleagues at the Defense Science and Technology Commission, on the other, quarreled incessantly as funds and resources dried up and as the prospect of large-scale fighting in India and Indochina increased.

In many cases, the functions and powers of the three organs were vague and overlapping. Moreover, the three did not have the last word. Although personal interests and bureaucratic rivalries often inflamed the policy debates on how to bolster the defense effort, in the final analysis Mao alone determined the outcome. Until he intervened decisively, the dissension among the three principal organizations festered. The top military elite was thus sundered at a time when military threats and the disarray of central programs in the aftermath of the post-Leap crises made genuine harmony throughout the military industry imperative.

Many top Politburo leaders were themselves closely bound to one or other of the two rival networks and predictably took sides in the contest. Mao simply vacillated or remained aloof. For months, no real effort was made to reconcile the personal and ideological animosities dividing the military, but in October 1962, Luo Ruiqing saw an opportunity to take action. He submitted a report to Mao Zedong suggesting the creation of a high-level coordinating body that ostensibly would reconcile the opposing positions. His proposed organizational solution would erase the persistent inequities in funding the conventional programs while ensuring that the nuclear weapons project would receive the support it needed from the

NDIC and the NDIO. It also would fortify his own commanding position. He advocated that "a special leading body should be set up to take charge of China's defense scientific and technological program." Mao approved Luo's report on November 3.[25] At a Politburo meeting convened to consider ways to implement it, Liu Shaoqi stressed, "Only if Premier Zhou [Enlai] handles the matter can the problem be solved." The Politburo agreed.[26]

So it was that on November 17, 1962, the Politburo created the body usually known in its first years as the Fifteen-Member Special Commission. Most vice-premiers and top leaders of the military industrial bureaucracy joined the original roster. Zhou became its head, and Luo Ruiqing (as powerful office director) and Zhao Erlu (Luo's deputy at the NDIO) were made responsible for the commission's day-to-day business.[27] "Afterward," Nie Rongzhen says, "every important test and all existing problems we encountered in the development of the *liangdan* projects [for nuclear weapons and strategic missiles] would be submitted to the special commission for discussion and settlement."[28] Nie does not mention that the commission also assumed control over the even more secret Project 09 when it was restarted in 1965.

The commission, which reportedly had only a small permanent staff, did not attempt to play a direct role in that project's operations. For this, it heavily relied on the administrative personnel of the NDIO.[29] But the commission had sweeping decision-making powers, which it exercised in periodic plenary meetings, and it was given a more imposing name, the Central Special Commission, in March 1965, when the Politburo extended its assignments to include the strategic missile project.[30]

Many Chinese believe that the creation of this coordinating body put Nie at a disadvantage in the competition with He Long and Luo Ruiqing. However, it is clear that whatever additional power He and Luo may have gained by the reorganization was balanced by the increasing authority of Lin Biao, who not only served as minister of defense but was also moving to affect all decision making within the Central Military Commission. Lin was no friend of He Long and Luo, and by the mid-1960s, Lin more than any other official was extending his influence over the Chinese military apparatus.

Still, the balance of political power was not all that clear to the participants at the time, and none could have predicted Lin's ultimate fate. As we have noted in our study of the nuclear weapons project, the merger of the NDIC into the NDIO in 1963 allowed the NDIO to enlarge its role in the defense industry because it could now control the Fifth Academy's strategic missile development, as well as the Second Ministry's production of

nuclear fuels, plant construction, and industrial production. Nie's authority in the defense industrial arena was thus confined to research on strategic
weaponry.[31]

Parallel to the changes in the defense industry was the evolution of the
defense science organs. By 1964, four academies formed the core of those
organs: the Fifth (missile), Sixth (aviation), Seventh (warship), and Tenth
(radio electronics); the most important for this study is the Seventh Academy. Though the four academies were formally subordinate to the Ministry of National Defense, in practice they reported to Nie Rongzhen's Defense Science and Technology Commission, since the ministry was no more
than a facade.[32] Conflicts often occurred between these organs of basic research and the industrial plants designated to execute their designs, leading
to serious interruptions in the development of military hardware.[33]

Faced with a situation in which plant officials all too often resisted what
they saw as intrusive assignments outside their normal annual plans and
in case after case fought the academies over such jurisdictional questions
as job allocations and standard setting, Chinese leaders looked for a way
to resolve these conflicts. One way open to them was to emulate the Soviet
military industrial structure and connect the plants chosen for trial production to the pertinent research institutes. But the Central Military Commission believed that the backwardness of China's economy precluded this
option. The search for a solution led to another idea: perhaps close ties
could be forged between research organs and industrial facilities by attaching the four academies to the relevant ministries. The military commission tested this last option in the nuclear weapons program as the most
promising solution for all the strategic weapons projects, and mirabile
dictu it seemed to work.

In organizing the nuclear weapons effort, the military commission
moved the Northwest Nuclear Weapons Research and Design Academy
(usually referred to by its code-name, the Ninth Academy) to the control
of the Second Ministry. After tinkering with the details of this merger over
several years, the commission in November 1964 adopted Luo Ruiqing's
proposal to extend the practice to all the other projects. In a brief, eight-
character directive—*buyuan jiehe, changsuo guagou* (Merge academies
into the ministries, couple the factories and research institutes)—it integrated the four core academies (the Fifth, Sixth, Seventh, and Tenth) into
their related ministries and ordered a general augmenting of the ties between all other research institutes and factories.

Mao Zedong assigned Luo Ruiqing to carry out the directive. Luo in
turn placed his own prestige on the line with the bold claim that the change
would benefit both research and production over the long term. In January

1965, the Fifth Academy and several factories from the Third, Fourth, and Fifth ministries became the Seventh Ministry of Machine Building, in charge of the missile program.[34] Later in the year, several other academies (the Sixth, Seventh, Tenth, and Artillery) were brought into their relevant ministries.[35] With the six military industrial ministries (Second through Seventh), as well as their newly affiliated academies, now under the jurisdiction of Luo's NDIO, the role of Nie's commission in the strategic weapons programs was further diminished, restricted to formulating guidelines for defense science-and-technology development and for running various weapons test bases.

By August 1965, Luo had apparently emerged the victor in his political competition with Nie Rongzhen, and the open controversies between the NDIO and the Defense Science and Technology Commission momentarily subsided. The legacy of earlier encounters would not be overcome so easily, however, and the hidden antagonism between the two groups simmered and then steadily intensified as the nation moved toward the Cultural Revolution.[36] It was in this climate that the Chinese restarted the nuclear-powered submarine project.

Shipbuilding Within the Industrial and Scientific Systems

The shipbuilding industry followed its own tortuous organizational path through the years, culminating in the China State Shipbuilding Corporation, which has been in charge of most of the large shipyards since 1982.[37] This ministry/corporation had its beginnings in the Shipbuilding Industry Bureau, which started life in 1950 under the Ministry of Heavy Industry and then was moved in 1952 to the administration of the First Ministry.[38] The following year, upon the Soviet Union's agreement to sell China the licenses to build five types of warships and the wherewithal for them, the bureau began enlarging the country's principal shipyards. Later, in 1959, Moscow approved the sale to China of design plans, technical data, and relevant equipment for additional warships and naval missiles.[39] But the program stalled before it got properly started, with the Soviet Union's decision the next year to cease supplying the requisite data, equipment, and components.[40]

In the spring of 1960, as the rift with Moscow was growing, an enlarged meeting of the Central Military Commission decided to give priority to assembling the Golf class (diesel-powered missile) and Romeo class (diesel-powered attack) submarines from the remaining Soviet equipment and components. By then the Chinese had expanded the Dalian (in Liaoning Province) and Huangpu (near Guangzhou) yards and constructed the Bohai yard near Huludao, Liaoning. The 1960 decision caused yet another round of heavy investment in the three shipyards as the nation perforce moved toward self-reliance.⁴¹

After some further organizational changes, the Shipbuilding Industry Bureau (Ninth Bureau) was handed over to the Third Ministry, which had been established in September 1960 to oversee the self-reliant development of conventional weapons. Three years later, the bureau split off from the Third Ministry to become the Sixth Ministry of Machine Building.⁴² Closely affiliated with the navy, the Sixth Ministry then began to exercise the major role in fashioning the industrial network for shipbuilding.

In 1961, the navy created the Warship Research and Design Academy (Seventh Academy) out of the six research institutes under its Science and Technology Research Department and some research facilities that had been attached to the Third Ministry. By the end of the year, the navy had these various institutes at work on warship design, warship power plants, underwater weapons, navigation, special auxiliary engines, acoustics, electronics, materials, and technology.⁴³ When the Sixth Ministry acquired the Seventh Academy in 1965, it had at its command a comprehensive array of organizations devoted to shipbuilding.⁴⁴

The Central Military Commission's decisions in the spring of 1960 also prompted the formation of a high-level experts' committee to give advice on shipbuilding. Specifically, the navy and the relevant industrial departments jointly founded a senior scientific research group for grappling with the key technical problems they faced in copying Soviet warships, including the Golf and Romeo submarines, now that Moscow's support was coming to an end. The military commission also charged the navy with developing indigenous naval weapons and equipment. In 1969, as part of the changes wrought during the Cultural Revolution, the commission and the State Council replaced the expert-dominated research group with the Shipbuilding Industry Leading Group under Li Zuopeng, first political commissar of the navy. As a government apparatus above the ministry but under the State Council, Li's group, composed of cadres from the General Staff, the navy, the Defense Science and Technology Commission, the NDIO, the Sixth Ministry, and other military industrial ministries, had more power than its predecessor to direct research and development on warship construction. The navy's deputy commander, Zhou Xihan, ran the group's daily affairs.⁴⁵

Other organizations also took shape within the highest echelons of the navy in the 1950s and 1960s. For example, it created a shipbuilding organ in the winter of 1950 that two years later became the Ship Repairing and Shipbuilding Department. This body, which after a number of subsequent reorganizations, became the Naval Equipment Department in 1963, set the procedures and management regulations for all navy shipyards, dock facilities, and factories.[46]

In the Cultural Revolution, all departments involved in the procurement and maintenance of warships and naval weapons fell victim to the national confusion. The Naval Equipment Department collapsed and was only resurrected (as the Naval Equipment and Technology Department) in 1974.[47] This department thereafter was made responsible for determining the technical specifications for all Project 09 submarines.[48]

Evolution of the Industrial and Scientific Systems

Just as the shipbuilding network was coming together in the mid-1960s, the Cultural Revolution destroyed the power of Luo Ruiqing and He Long and ruptured the system that had been recently installed to run China's overall defense industry. For a brief moment, it was Nie Rongzhen's turn to gain control of the industry for his organization, though given the danger to all "authorities" in these years, his motives were more defensive than opportunistic. He sought to insulate the industry from the upheaval, and because of the collapse of the high command, not just the removal of his rivals, Nie acted to take the defense research academies, including the Seventh, away from the various embattled ministries.[49]

On March 20, 1967, Mao accepted Nie's suggestion to put research under military rule, and authorized Nie's commission to take charge of the Sixth, Seventh, Ninth, Tenth, and Twentieth (ordnance) academies, along with four design academies (strategic and tactical missiles) under the Seventh Ministry. The commission later assumed control of several other military research academies and of the research organs under the Chinese Academy of Sciences' New Technological Bureau. Its leader and main units removed, the NDIO's authority evaporated.

In response to Mao's March 20 decision, Zhou Enlai announced at a high-level meeting in April that military control committees would be dispatched to the six military industrial ministries (Second–Seventh). Within two months, all the rest of the ministries were placed under direct military rule.[50] The navy not only took charge of the Sixth Ministry, but sent out hundreds of military teams to oversee all naval research institutes, shipyards, and shipbuilding facilities.

On October 25, 1967, Mao approved Nie Rongzhen's proposal to consolidate the defense science system into 18 research and design academies under his Defense Science and Technology Commission. Four months later, in line with another of Nie's proposals, the Central Military Commission conferred new code numbers on these 18 academies.[51] By early 1968, Nie's mandate covered 133,000 technicians and workers in more than 100 research institutes and more than ten trial-production plants attached to them.[52] Nie had reached the zenith of his administrative career.

His preeminence was short-lived. Nie's remarkable success in expanding his domain was regarded by others in the elite as too aggressive and personally threatening, and they now acted against him. In February, Mao criticized the Defense Science and Technology Commission for using a wrong slogan ("support the correct leadership of the Party Committee of the Defense Science and Technology Commission with comrade Nie Rongzhen as its core") and thus by inference damned Nie.[53] On March 23, 1968, Yang Chengwu, acting chief of the General Staff, and two assistants were arrested, and Lin Biao and Jiang Qing ordered their cohorts to search out Yang's "black backer." Everyone in the top command immediately knew that this order constituted a not-so-disguised dagger pointed at Nie, Yang's former army boss and presumed political "backer." Mao as usual remained passive in response to the accusations made by Lin and Jiang; he did so even when his close comrades of yesteryear were the targets.[54] By not shielding Nie but letting the Lin-Jiang order stand, Mao sealed Nie's fate, and in April Nie was virtually stripped of his powers.[55]

Thereafter, the radicals launched struggle campaigns throughout the defense science apparatus and assailed Nie for his advocacy of "a major buildup of the defense science system."[56] In addition, Mao's elder daughter, Li Min, a senior cadre in Nie's commission, and her band of zealots accused Nie of attempting to "set up an impregnable 'independent kingdom,' " and to "foster in a big way a 'mountain stronghold' " with himself as the core.[57] Nie was paying the price for his gains following the ouster of Luo Ruiqing.

After Nie's fall, the leadership structure at the Defense Science and Technology Commission simply dissolved. A few months later, Mao assigned Wang Bingzhang, minister of the Seventh Ministry, to take over as acting head of the commission and to try to restore order to it.[58] That assignment was part of a design, reflected in a series of Politburo decisions, to readjust the defense industrial and scientific networks from top to bottom. But before these decisions could be implemented, war drums began to beat across the land. As the year wore on, the relations between China and the Soviet Union steadily deteriorated, and in March 1969, fighting erupted along their common border. A war between them appeared imminent, or so Mao believed, with the result that the nation's defense budget jumped a full 34 percent that year.[59]

Whatever plans the central leadership had for a rationalization of the defense industry now went by the boards as the country geared up for war. In April 1969, after the conclusion of the Ninth Party Congress, the Central

Committee directed the Administrative Group (Banshi Zu) of the Central Military Commission to take over the conventional weapons sector from the Defense Science and Technology Commission.[60] In August, the Central Military Commission appointed four leading groups headed by deputy chiefs of the General Staff to oversee the crash development of conventional arms needed for a major conflict with the Soviet Union: the Aviation Industry Leading Group under Wu Faxian; the Shipbuilding Industry and Scientific Research Leading Group and the Telecommunication Industry Leading Group, both under Li Zuopeng; and the Conventional Ordnance Leading Group under Qiu Huizuo.[61] As the war fever intensified, so did the dictatorship mentality within the nation's defense industry and science academies.

On December 22, the military commission created the National Defense Industry Leading Group (Guofang Gongye Lingdao Xiaozu), with Qiu Huizuo, an associate of Lin Biao, as head. De facto, the group replaced the long defunct NDIO, and the commission charged Qiu with carrying out the NDIO's coordinating work in conventional weapons development. The group quickly asserted its jurisdiction over the Third, Fourth, Fifth, and Sixth ministries and the academies attached to them.[62]

By 1970, several other academies responsible for R&D on conventional armaments were transferred from the Defense Science and Technology Commission to either the industrial ministries or the military services. That spring, as noted, the military commission once more merged academies into the ministries and factories with research institutes, restoring what it had done six years earlier but what had been undone in the Cultural Revolution. The Defense Science and Technology Commission's authority was once again limited to monitoring the strategic weapons programs.[63] The commission thereafter was in charge of only the Second Ministry (including the Ninth Academy), the Seventh Ministry and its four academies, and three weapons test bases—Base 20 (strategic missile), Base 21 (nuclear weapons), and Base 22 (tactical missile).[64] If one had trouble keeping track of the labyrinthine bureaucracy before, the task now became hopeless. Figure 4 provides a somewhat simplified road map.

Wang Bingzhang was soon to pay an even dearer price than his predecessor for his affiliation with the Lin Biao "clique." In the wake of Lin's death in September 1971, Mao launched a purge of military officers associated with him, and Wang was listed as one of Lin's "sworn followers" and summarily imprisoned.[65] The following February, the central leadership ordered a seven-man study team under Gao Weisong and Liu Xiyao to root out any of "Lin's followers" still operating in the commission and its subordinate bodies.[66] With the backing of firebrands such as Li Min, the

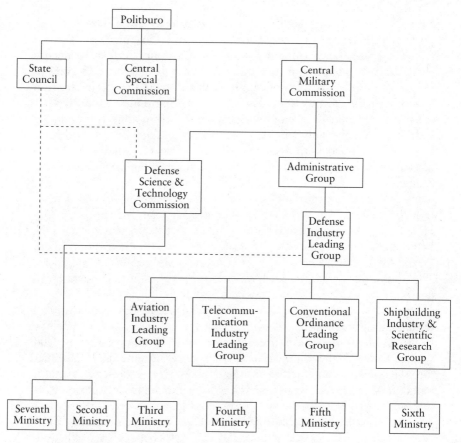

Fig. 4. Organization of the defense industry, Dec. 1969

team members conducted a frenzied search for likely scapegoats, many of whom were publicly vilified and dismissed. The list of possible successor leaders at the commission steadily dwindled.

The purge of Lin Biao's clique and other elements in 1971 represented the readjustment process gone amok, and few in the bowels of the "system" any longer understood the authority structure, had any faith in it, or much cared. In September 1973, the military commission and the State Council restored the NDIO with Fang Qiang as director to replace the National Defense Industry Leading Group, and charged it with overseeing the conventional weapons programs, including the shipbuilding industry and other weapons programs.[67] Via the Sixth Ministry, the resurrected NDIO issued new directives to the various shipyards and plants that manufactured equipment and components for warships, but there was little incentive to heed these orders, which had a half-life of a few weeks at best.

In 1974, Mao made matters worse when he unleashed a movement to criticize Lin Biao and Confucius. Neither was in fact his real target, however. The political campaign was actually aimed at Zhou Enlai, whose power was sharply diminished from then to the end of his life, in January 1976. The terminally ill Zhou simply could no longer protect whatever remained of the small island of sanity in the Politburo. Mao's wife, Jiang Qing, and her extremist associates were secretly pleased and used the movement to gain ascendancy over the Defense Science and Technology Commission and the defense bodies under it.[68] Their disciples started wresting power from officers at all levels on the pretext of "developing the movement in depth."[69]

Despite the relentless hunt for political scapegoats, the formal table of organization at the top, as shown in Figure 4, remained relatively unchanged, if largely irrelevant, for the next several years. The leaders of the defense industrial bureaucracy were mostly engaged in a holding operation and made only a few modifications in their organizational charts. One of these found the principal ship design body, the Seventh Academy, which had reported to the navy since 1970, shifted to the joint control of the weakened NDIO and Sixth Ministry in 1975.[70]

But like the others, this was a mere paper move, and the Central Military Commission did not make any important changes in the structure of the defense industrial bureaucracy until July 29, 1982, when the NDIO, the Defense Science and Technology Commission, and the office of the Science and Technology Equipment Committee of the Central Military Commission were amalgamated into the Commission of Science, Technology, and Industry for National Defense (COSTIND).[71] Under the leadership of Chen Bin, COSTIND soon assumed dominion over the Second, Third,

Fifth, and Seventh ministries and related research academies. It has been in overall command of all weapons programs.[72]

Despite the monumental absurdity of political life in China from 1965 to 1976, the pieces of the shipbuilding "system" were eventually up and running, though far behind schedule and more or less on their own. As of 1987, the system embraced 528 shipyards with 540,000 staff and workers, 162 factories, and over 80 research institutes.[73] It is these organs that manufactured and assembled the components for the Project 09 submarines.

War Preparedness in the Third Line

One additional event heavily influenced that production process: the creation of the Third Line.[74] During the Third (1966–70) and Fourth (1971–75) Five-Year Plans, China carried out a massive program of industrial construction in its remote interior.[75] The program constituted a "strategic shift in China's economic distribution" toward the counties south of the Great Wall and west of the Beijing-Guangzhou Railway. The effort was concentrated first in Sichuan, Guizhou, Shaanxi, Yunnan, and Gansu, and then expanded to the western parts of Henan, Hubei, and Hunan and to Qinghai and Ningxia.[76]

Historians may see in Mao's Third-Line policy reflections of the profound dualism in China's recent past. Mao, the man from the interior, belonged in spirit to what he regarded as the nation's rustic heartland and detested the Western-oriented coastal centers. The treaty ports along the coasts and banks of the major rivers had served as points of foreign contact, modest industrialization, and revolutionary ferment, to be sure, but they had also constituted a world apart. That foreign world, as the geographer Rhoads Murphey has written, had a "profound impact on the Chinese mind" and "hurt China psychologically more than it helped her economically, at least up to 1949." Mao, after his rise to power, could not remove the treaty-port "cancers on the Chinese body," but he could attempt to stem their growth by shifting the locus of modernization to the Third Line.[77] Although we shall concentrate on the military strategic aspects of the Third Line, we suspect that Mao's attachment to it lay deeper in his soul.

Chinese scholars trace the origins of this strategic shift to Mao's speech "On the Ten Major Relationships," delivered in April 1956. At that point, fully 70 percent of China's industry was located in the coastal regions. Mao declared that "a period of peace for a decade or more" probably lay ahead and implied that a window existed to repair this imbalance. "The notion that the atomic bomb is already overhead and about to fall on us in a matter of seconds is a calculation at variance with reality." Thus, industrial construction could continue in the coastal areas, he said, but "without doubt, the greater part of the new industry should be located in the interior."[78] Though his true concerns lay elsewhere as he began to lay the groundwork for the Great Leap Forward, Mao's message was clear, but his ministers could read the tea leaves in Mao's unsteady cup and ignored him; they kept right on constructing plants in the coastal provinces.

There the matter rested until 1964, when escalating U.S. involvement in Vietnam and Mao's mounting fears of an imminent war led him to once again fasten on the interior.[79] At a work conference of the Party Central Committee in May and June, he first linked the drafting of the Third Five-Year Plan to preparations for the "inevitable" military conflict and then issued one of his well-known calls: "You should speed up the construction of Panzhihua [in Sichuan]. Only when you complete the construction of Panzhihua can I sleep well." "The outcome of war," he added, "will be decided not by the atomic bomb, but by conventional weapons."[80] His conclusion: "As long as imperialism exists, there is always the danger of war. We must build up the strategic rear."[81] This time he would not be defied.

A few days later, he summoned local Party committees to pay heed to military affairs and to get ready to fight a nuclear war: "When war begins, it will be necessary to depend upon China to hold on."[82] It is more accurate, then, to date Mao's shift in policy from the 1964 conference, not from the earlier speech. This was where he decided that "getting ready to fight a war" meant "giving priority to determining the strategic [industrial] distribution and strengthening the construction in the Third-Line region while formulating long-term plans."[83] This was where we first find him defining a plan for promoting "the vast strategic rear region" of the Third Line. And he was doing so "in preparation for the possibility of war."[84]

As shown on the map on page 90, Mao and his supporters conceived the nation as consisting of three zones, with the First Line composing the coastal and border regions, the Third Line the strategic rear, and the Second Line the ambiguous territory between the two. The American actions in Vietnam, not economic principles, dominated the definition of the Third Line and planning for it. In this formulation, Chinese policy makers were guided in large part by the Soviet Union's construction of an emergency strategic rear area east of the Ural Mountains during the height of the German offensive.[85]

On August 5, in the aftermath of the Tonkin Gulf incident, the U.S. air force began bombing North Vietnam. Worried about the possible spread of the conflict to China, Mao pressed his colleagues on August 17 and again on the 20th to gear up for a probable war. He ordered industrial and research facilities to leave the coastal provinces for the Third Line in antic-

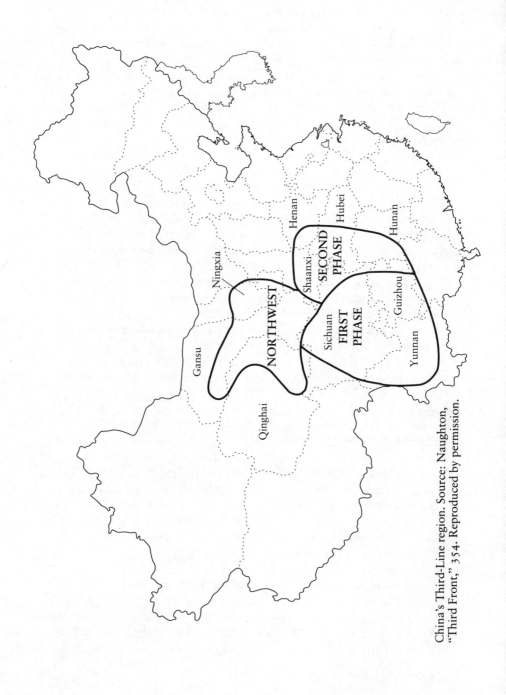

China's Third-Line region. Source: Naughton, "Third Front," 354. Reproduced by permission.

ipation of an "imperialist invasion." Support for construction in the Third Line, he said, would be a litmus test of "whether you are a revolutionary."[86]

A few days later, the State Council held a meeting to study how to implement Mao's order. Luo Ruiqing, head of the NDIO, also convened a national defense industry conference attended by senior officials from the six defense-related industrial ministries to consider how to start large-scale industrial construction in the Third Line.[87] Premier Zhou Enlai and Party General Secretary Deng Xiaoping took charge of this effort, and no other national program received higher priority.[88] The State Council later in the year set up a new body, the Minor State Planning Commission (Xiao Jiwei), to plan the construction,[89] and dispatched "several massive work teams" to survey the Third-Line territories for plant sites as other groups set to work on housing, logistics, and communications. By early 1965, a comprehensive plan for the construction of the Third Line had been prepared, and from a glance at the draft, it is obvious that the planners had deliberately chosen some of China's most mountainous and inaccessible regions for their factory and institute sites. They proudly reminded themselves that "the roads in Sichuan are more difficult than going to Heaven."[90] If they could not travel these roads easily, neither could an invading army.

Early 1965 also saw the first of a succession of oversight groups established, with the creation of the Southwest Third-Line Construction Committee in February. Then, in April, the resurrected State Construction Commission was charged with overseeing construction there and in all other parts of the Third Line. Expansion brought another area-specific body, the Northwest Third-Line Construction Committee in January 1966. Still later, provincial-level command organs were established for on-site authority in the Southwest and Northwest.[91]

In August 1965, the State Construction Commission convened a National Relocation Work Meeting, which reaffirmed Mao's call to base the nationwide relocation on preparations for "an early war, an all-out war, and a nuclear war."[92] It also promulgated the Third-Line's guiding principle: "decentralization, closeness to mountains, and concealment" (*fensan, kaoshan, yinbi*).[93] Two months later, the priority for the Third Line appeared in the new five-year plan: "Defense construction claims precedence over all other construction; construction in the Third Line should be augmented to gradually change [our country's] industrial distribution."[94]

Then the westward tide began. That winter, in what was seen as a race against time, Beijing transferred 1.6 million workers to the interior, and by February, the need to manage this huge migration and the logistics for it led to the creation of the Capital Construction Engineering Corps.[95] The initial priority, consequently, went to making roads and rail lines.[96]

In the next ten years, Beijing sent thousands of its best and brightest off to the Third Line in secret. (Even the term Third Line was classified.) Key industrial colleges (such as the China University of Science and Technology, the Tangshan Institute of Technology, the Harbin Military Engineering Institute, and the Naval Engineering Institute) and top technical personnel began moving to the west, and most of the university graduates in the mobilization decade ended up in the region.[97] By the 1970s, the ratio of engineers and technicians to total staff members and workers was 200–300 percent higher in the Third-Line research and industrial facilities than in the coastal areas.[98] The movement of so many educated personnel to these technology-intensive posts created such an extraordinary congregation of talent that the Chinese started referring to them as their "tigers hidden in the remote mountains."[99]

For the critical defense industries, including those associated with Project 09, duplicate plants were built in the strategic rear with little thought given to cost. Only large-scale redundancy, it was believed, could assure China's survival in a nuclear war: "To deal with the possible outbreak of war, industries in the Third-Line regions were distributed in self-contained systems with all supporting facilities provided. Thus energy, raw and semifinished materials, machine-building, electronics, chemical, and defense industries formed their own fiefs. The coastal areas and the Third-Line region had separate industrial systems."[100] The Third Line would serve as a secure base capable of supplying the weapons for a protracted global conflict.

The Second Wave of Third-Line Development

The Third-Line building process ran in cycles. The promising start of 1964–66 rapidly subsided under the onslaught of the Cultural Revolution. Third-Line construction was mostly halted in the next few years, but when violent clashes broke out on the Sino-Soviet frontier in March 1969, the "second high tide in construction of the Third-Line regions" began.[101] Mao convened an emergency meeting on July 2 to discuss China's response to the impending Sino-Soviet military showdown, and the Third Line was his answer.[102]

Beijing's leaders again accelerated the transfer of strategic facilities to the Third Line in preparation for war.[103] In March 1970, the State Council instructed the industrial ministries to put a provincial-level construction program in place large enough to build ten self-contained defense industrial bases by 1972.[104] In an attempt to ensure the fulfillment of the strategic weapons programs as scheduled, the Central Military Commission and the State Council adopted a resolution to put all the "key" defense projects and principal research bases, including those in Project 09, under military control.[105] From 1969 to 1971, China drastically increased its investment in defense construction, and much of this went to the Third Line.[106]

The investment placed a heavy burden on an already sagging economy. In 1971, China faced "three breaking points" (*san ge tupo*): the state had undertaken to employ more than 50 million people in government-run enterprises and agencies; it had to pay these people over 30 billion yuan; and it had to provide more than 40 billion kilograms of grain to urban dwellers. One result was inflation, and Zhou Enlai especially decried the rising money supply.[107] Mao recognized the burden of the Third Line, and the prospect of improving his relations with the United States appeared to provide a way out.

Only when Mao reassessed the Soviet threat in the context of Sino-U.S. relations did the Third-Line crusade lose momentum.[108] That reassessment was reflected in the nation's annual economic plan for fiscal 1972, which returned to the principle that defense construction must fit the total needs of the national economy and have a lower priority than agriculture and light industry.[109] In early 1973, Mao and Zhou Enlai approved the importing of $430 million worth of Western industrial equipment, all of which was to be installed in the coastal areas.[110] That decision marked the beginning of the end for the Third-Line policy.[111] From 1973 on, Third-Line construction was principally confined to either winding up key projects or rejuvenating established industrial units in order to manufacture complete sets of equipment. Defense budgets fell.[112]

The Result of the Third-Line Policy

At best, this ten-year effort was a mixed blessing for China. The building of the Third-Line industries and institutes during the Third and Fourth Five-Year Plans, 1966–75, cost over 200 billion yuan (or roughly $80 billion at the then current rate of exchange). About 140 billion yuan went to new factories, out of a total industrial construction budget of 275 billion yuan for the years 1966–80.[113] Over the 14 years between 1965 and 1979, Third-Line investment accounted for 43.4 percent of the national total, and produced more than 2,200 medium- and large-sized enterprises, for a 48 percent share.[114] Some of the sectoral figures are even more impressive. Most of the money invested in the aviation industry, for example, was poured into the Third Line (93.4 percent of the total in 1966–70, 83.2 percent in 1971–75).[115]

About one-fifth of the Third-Line budget—some 28 billion yuan (1965–

80)—went to the defense industry alone, fashioning a military industrial complex composed of 483 manufacturing plants and 92 research academies and institutes.[116] The new facilities included a large conventional weapons production base in Chongqing, Sichuan Province, some nuclear research and industrial bases in Sichuan, two electronics industrial bases in Sichuan and Guizhou provinces, two strategic missile research and industrial bases in Sichuan and Shaanxi provinces, three aviation industrial bases in Guizhou and Shaanxi provinces and the western part of Hubei Province, and several shipbuilding bases in Sichuan and Hubei provinces. By 1975, the ordnance factories in the region could manufacture almost half of the nation's conventional weapons, the aircraft plants two-thirds of the nation's military planes.[117] By the late 1980s, these facilities could produce half of the nation's military hardware.[118] In terms of productive capacity, number of technical experts, and level of equipment, the Third-Line defense industry now surpasses the whole of the industry in the rest of the country.[119]

As impressive as all these developments may seem at first glance, Mao's decision to build the strategic Third Line led to staggering waste and uncertain results. On balance, the building of comparable facilities in the coastal areas would have cost far less.[120] Official investigations conducted in Sichuan and Shaanxi by 1989 revealed that almost half the enterprises operated below capacity or had not even begun production. More than 18 percent of the Third-Line investment between 1966 and 1978, totaling over 30 billion yuan, was reportedly squandered.[121]

Mao's fear of war and especially of air or missile strikes led to his policy of "decentralization, closeness to mountains, and concealment," and this policy resulted in near fatal drawbacks in practice.[122] A significant number of research and industrial facilities were constructed in caves and underground, and in several places, this expensive, ill-planned, and wasteful effort halted for sheer lack of tunnel digging equipment.[123] For example, the Sixth Ministry decided to construct a marine machinery production base in Wulong, Sichuan Province, but later abandoned the site after having spent millions on the tunnels.[124]

Moreover, maintaining all the new facilities was a horrendous problem, placing a maximum burden on China's east-west transportation system. Dead-end rail lines and trunks had to be built or significantly upgraded to reach the mountain bases, and the excessive dispersal and inaccessibility of those facilities caused endless administrative confusion and a resulting misallocation of personnel and matériel.[125]

The emphasis on speed and output precluded concern for the people involved. The "livelihood of workers and staff members was not taken into account," Chinese sources later admitted, and the policy of "decentralization, closeness to mountains, and concealment" in practice meant deprivation and boring isolation. The people in the relocated defense industries were supposed to create their own support infrastructure, including kindergartens, schools, hospitals, shops, cinemas, and bus companies, but these always came second on the list of priorities.[126] Factory and institute managers became the de facto mayors of their communities and had to set up organs to oversee the employment of family members.[127]

In the end, these organs fell far short, and the managers had to introduce measures to counteract the repeated and unauthorized brain drain from the Third Line back to the coastal areas. All these measures failed. Thousands of professionals in the Northwest and in the Southwest slipped eastward to new jobs.[128] In an attempt to staunch the flow and extricate the Third-Line enterprises from their downward spiral, the State Council in 1983 set up an office to readjust the distribution of the nation's industries and shift the focus to the coast again.[129]

Carrying out the policy of "unleashing fierce tigers out of remote mountains," the office worked along several lines: reconceptualizing the distribution of the entire industrial network, moving people and plants from the interior and reorganizing hundreds of enterprises in the Third Line, transferring technologies to civilian industry and shifting production from military hardware to a mixture of civilian and military products, and developing economic and technological cooperation between the interior and the coastal areas.[130] In the course of this "readjustment," 121 of the 2,000 large and medium-sized enterprises in remote mountain areas were removed to the coastal provinces in the years 1986–89.[131] All the major facilities connected to Project 09, however, were kept in place.

Shipbuilding in the Third Line

This huge industrial system had a dramatic impact on China's strategic weapons. Our principal concern here is with the creation of the shipbuilding bases in the Third-Line regions, but we should keep in mind that the rush to the Third Line shaped the development of all defense industries.

At the time Mao issued his edict in 1964, the navy was under instructions to modernize China's fleet, and plans for four large parts plants were on the drawing board.[132] With the promulgation of the new policy, the Central Military Commission decided that three of these plants—which were scheduled to manufacture diesel engines and marine auxiliary engines—would be built in the Third Line.[133]

Obedient to the slogan "Make haste," the Sixth Ministry (shipbuilding) sent teams to survey the Third Line for appropriate sites in 1966, then set its three design and research organs to drawing up the plans for an array of yards and other facilities in the selected sites. Construction began right after the completion of the design drawings.[134] This was the start of a program that by 1980 brought 39 shipbuilding bases and 43 related research institutes to the interior.[135]

The earliest and most important of these bases were in Sichuan, Hubei, and Jiangxi. The Sichuan base was the first to be constructed and became the largest, with three autonomous components: shipyards in Chongqing and Fuling; eight factories and associated research institutes near the city of Wanxian for the manufacture of navigation instruments; and seven diesel engine and machinery factories with associated research institutes in Jiangjin, Yongchuan, and Chongqing.[136]

The Jiangxi base, the next to follow, was already under construction before the Sichuan base was finished in the late 1960s. The Jiujiang Instrument and Meter Plant there played a central role in developing the instrumentation for the early 09 submarines.[137] Work also began on the Hubei base at Yichang and Yidu before the Sichuan base was completed. This complex, made up of three research institutes for developing underwater weapons, on-board electro-optical devices, infrared sensitive systems, and electronic instruments, and four plants for manufacturing diesel engines and on-board instrumentation, was also central to Project 09.[138] The Third-Line policy also produced, among others, three medium-sized shipyards in the Guangxi Zhuang Autonomous Region, a large base near Lake Kunming, Yunnan Province, for conducting research on torpedoes and mines, and an expansion of the existing plant in Taiyuan (Plant 884) and an attached facility near Houma, Shanxi Province, for developing mines and torpedoes.[139]

In 1976, while construction in the Third Line region was still under way but winding down, General George Brown reported to the U.S. Congress that China had created defense programs with "long-range implications such as the construction of . . . impressive new facilities for producing large quantities of nuclear material, solid propellant missiles; [and] R&D initiatives addressing advanced airframes and sophisticated engines."[140] According to a U.S. air force study, a single plant in China would often design, manufacture, and test launch vehicle components or major subsystems, "which results in the duplication of research effort and training facilities."[141] About the same time, U.S. intelligence also noted a commitment in the missile field to work on high-temperature materials, structural materials and design, nuclear warhead design, electronic components, and aerodynamic test facilities.[142] What U.S. intelligence was watching was the miracle—or debacle—of the Third Line. How to evaluate that accomplishment, which most experts in China unequivocally denigrated, very much depended on whose eye was doing the beholding.

The Hidden Hazards in the Minor Third Line

Building the Third Line was only part of Mao's plan. In 1964, he also called for the construction of defense-related industrial facilities in the "minor Third Line" (*xiao sanxian*).[143] This region constituted designated "rear areas" for provinces, autonomous regions, and centrally governed cities in the First and Second Line in the Northeast and along the coast; some sources suggest that the *xiao sanxian* order also applied to provincial-level organs in the Third Line itself. Thus instructed by Beijing, the governments at this level in the next decade created bases in remote areas for the production of light arms.[144]

The origins of Mao's thinking about the minor Third Line can be traced to his ideas about the multiple roles of rural people's communes, one of which was to turn the peasants into soldiers. As early as June 1958, he told an enlarged meeting of the Central Military Commission: "I am in favor of producing more light weapons to arm [our] broad-based militia [in the communes]." Two months later, he reiterated that various provinces should construct ordnance factories to produce rifles, submachine guns, light and heavy machine guns, mortars, bullets, and explosives. The next year, he endorsed the construction of defense industry in rear bases: "Proceeding from the necessity of training and combat readiness, various provinces should construct factories to produce weapons and ammunition for the militia." Some provinces did comply and put up munitions plants.[145]

When Mao hit on the term "minor Third Line" in July 1964, he once again demanded that the provincial-level authorities build their own ordnance factories, first for arms repairs and then their manufacture.[146] At a meeting of the Central Secretariat in August, Mao mentioned the need for defense industries in the minor Third Line.[147] More talk and more planning followed, until the State Council in March 1965 ordered local authorities to commence the program.[148] In November, Mao exhorted officials in East China to accelerate the effort and said, "If war breaks out, you shouldn't count on the Center for help. You should depend on yourselves. You should strive for a speed-up of the construction of your rear areas and achieve success within three to five years. . . . You yourselves should produce steel and weapons."[149]

The motives that impelled Mao to initiate the minor Third-Line construction were more complex than this suggests. In these years, he worried most about the possible emergence of a "revisionist group" in the central leadership and then about a foreign invasion. His decision derived from his thinking about the impending grand struggle for power in what became the Cultural Revolution, as well as from his ideas about war.[150] His manifest motive, of course, was to expand the capacity for ordnance production of each locality in support of Chinese troops retreating from an invasion force moving inland.[151] But his hidden intention was to create widely dispersed armed bands of loyalists who could counterbalance and, if necessary, defeat his opponents in the central leadership should they move against him.

As early as June 8, 1964, Mao cautioned provincial-level authorities that "a province might rebel and declare independence" if "revisionists" assumed power in the central leadership.[152] By 1965, on the eve of the Cultural Revolution, Mao apparently considered it unlikely that his revolutionary strategy would be realized in the coming showdown against his domestic foes unless he made his real intentions even more explicit. On October 10, he told the first secretaries of the Party committees of the Central Committee's six regional bureaus,

You should make a success of the minor Third-Line construction. . . . If the revisionists assume power in the central leadership, you may revolt against them. You will be able to rebel once you have [defense-industry bases in] the Third Line. . . . You should pay attention so that from now on, you may refuse to carry out incorrect directives even from the central leadership.[153]

This call apparently anticipated the Cultural Revolution and the struggle against Liu Shaoqi and Deng Xiaoping.

With Mao's endorsement, Beijing put forward a three-year plan (1966–68) for a defense industrial network in the minor Third Line.[154] In the next years, the local governments responded, and the *xiao sanxian* industry began taking shape in 17 provinces and autonomous regions. Thirty percent of the enterprises were defense-related. Provincial-level civilian and military officials jointly ran these enterprises, most of which produced small arms.[155] But many projects succumbed to the rising turmoil toward the end of the plan period, and a special conference was called to approve the investment of 800 million yuan and to extend the timetable to 1969.[156] Thereafter, local ordnance factories spread throughout the nation.

As Mao predicted, the creation of the minor Third Line did toughen the local radicals, though not in the way he envisioned or wanted.* In most cases, these elements ended up using the arms against each other in fac-

---

*In the fall of 1976, right after Mao's death, the associates of the Jiang Qing clique in Shanghai used the munitions from factories under their control in the minor Third Line and Shanghai to support an abortive armed insurrection. For details, see Cao Zhang et al.; Li Zhongshi and He Wannan; and "Last-Ditch Struggle," 127–28.

tional battles rather than in support of Mao's revolutionary mission. Many if not most of the armed clashes occurred where the ordnance industry had been built up on a local basis and thus where guns could be seized by the rival groups.[157]

Along with the "second high tide" in defense construction after the border conflicts on the Sino-Soviet frontier in 1969, Mao pressed for a speed-up of minor Third-Line defense construction. Beijing also directed the defense industrial ministries to take control of most of the minor Third-Line munitions factories as an emergency means to cope with a possible Sino-Soviet war.[158] Construction funds flowed from Beijing until August 1973, when the crisis had subsided and control could be returned to the provincial-level officials.[159]

By 1980, 268 ordnance factories had been built in minor Third-Line localities to manufacture light arms. They employed 280,000 workers and technicians, and at a cost of 3.2 billion yuan, had manufactured 6 million guns, 100,000 artillery pieces, and huge quantities of ammunition.[160] Small defense industrial bases had sprouted in most provinces and autonomous regions.[161] China had become a nation of tiny armed bastions readying themselves for a war that never came.

Turning Point

The eastward shift away from the Third Line after the Cultural Revolution was accompanied by a major re-evaluation of China's modernization that affected the status of the defense industry and altered the strategic environment for Project 09 in the 1980s. In the 1970s, vast problems were uncovered in both the civilian industrial sector and the defense industrial sector.[162]

In May 1975, Deng Xiaoping, who was momentarily rehabilitated before another banishment, revealed the critical difficulties underlying the iron and steel industry. He blamed what he called sluggish production on the industry's "weak, lazy, and lax leadership." His solution was for the Party to "try to find and recruit into the leading groups cadres who are not afraid of losing their jobs" and for a struggle against factionalism in the plants. Deng also called on the cadres to implement Party policies more conscientiously and to establish "essential rules and regulations."[163]

Deng was determined to straighten out the chaos in the defense industrial system. That same month, he said, "the two diametrically opposed factions of the Seventh Ministry of Machine Building do not even have patriotism, let alone socialism." He imposed a deadline for solving the factional strife within one month and ordered the Defense Science and Technology Commission to reorganize the leadership of the ministry.[164]

Some months later, Deng told a conference of defense industry leaders that they too needed "to establish bold leadership," to improve the quality of production, and to attend to the welfare of the workers, especially in the Third-Line factories.[165] At about the same time, he reaffirmed the soundness of the "Seventy Articles on Industrial Work" that had been adopted in 1961 but ignored and then repudiated in the Cultural Revolution. Adherence to the articles, he argued, would have helped stabilize the defense industries.[166] He labeled the most common problems poor management and equipment lying in disrepair, and he apparently included the defense industrial system in his condemnation.[167] The revelation of the poor management in that system prompted Deng to instruct the NDIO to convene a defense industry conference to discuss how to revitalize the leading bodies in the main defense enterprises and to rectify the whole military industrial front.[168]

When Deng returned to power once again after the death of Mao, this time for good, he attacked these deficiencies with full force and called for the implementation of the eight-character guiding principle of "adjustment, reform, consolidation, and improvement" throughout the national economy. As Deng's program for demilitarization of the national economy moved into high gear, starting in 1979 and continuing into 1982, the nation's defense industries experienced a sharp reduction in orders for military hardware. Half of the military industrial enterprises had either to operate far below capacity or to cease production altogether. Almost all of those that survived limped along, hard hit by a lack of funds and an accumulation of unallocated military products.[169]

The defense industrial system confronted one more drastic readjustment, thanks to a fundamental change in the Chinese leadership's estimation of war possibilities in the early 1980s. In 1980, Deng Xiaoping twice pointed out that no major war was likely to erupt in the next five years. He later amended this, first to state that it was possible to delay an all-out war between China and the Soviet Union for at least ten years, and then at an enlarged meeting of the Central Military Commission in June 1985, to extend the deadline beyond the year 2000.[170] The military commission meeting thereupon agreed to cut the army by one million and to shift from war preparedness to peacetime development. (Later that year, an even more optimistic Deng predicted that China could focus on economic construction in a peaceful environment for the next 50 years.[171])

The shift of the army's mission resulted in continued sharp reductions in the nation's defense budget. Between 1950 and 1985, the military's share in the annual state budget averaged about 16.9 percent. From a high point of 18.5 percent in 1979, the figure dropped over the next decade, to reach about 8 percent in 1989.[172] There the shrinkage ended, perhaps only temporarily, in the wake of the Tiananmen incident of June 4, 1989.[173] In 1991, in presenting the economic plan for the coming decade, Premier Li Peng said that China "should appropriately increase the outlay on national defence and work hard to develop defence science and technology, focusing on research in and manufacture of new weapons and equipment," but added that a concomitant emphasis should be on "converting military industrial production capacity to manufacture of civilian products."[174] Thus after the mid-1980s, in contrast to the start-up years, Project 09 had to compete for drastically limited defense funds and for critical equipment and talent in time of peace.

These shifting priorities can be summarized as follows. In the early 1980s, the line-up for funds for weapons and equipment put the army first, followed by the air force, and then the navy. The army stressed the development of anti-tank weapons and field air defense systems. From the mid-1980s to early 1991, the navy went to the head of the list, but the Gulf War prompted another review of the nation's preparedness.[175] Since 1991, the military has demanded more money for upgrading air defense and early warning systems for both ground and naval forces, anti-submarine technologies, advanced aircraft, and an oceangoing fleet.[176] The military commission told COSTIND to get ready for an electronic war.[177] The result was a lowered priority for Project 09.

Like all the military, the project leaders had to adjust to the revamped weapons procurement policies. They now took a new guiding principle: defense scientific research should go ahead of mass-production of military hardware (*keyan xianxing*), and quality should come first (*zhiliang diyi*).[178] Following the guiding principle, the military formulated a sixteen-character weapons procurement policy to replace the previous one: *duo yanzhi, shao zhuangbei, xinlao bingcun, zhubu gengxin*. Loosely translated, this new policy assigned first importance to research and development and settled for supplying combat units with less up-to-date military hardware; old weapons would be maintained alongside new ones and would only be replaced gradually.[179] Almost lost in the policy shift was the notion of a special status for Project 09.

Limited by insufficient funds, even the research facilities for defense were steadily downgraded and operated below capacity. In the mid-1980s, for example, Institute 719, now renamed the Wuhan Second Ship Design and Research Institute, suffered a radical cut in its research budget. To make enough money for themselves, many experts on submarine design had to take on outside contract work, and some who had worked on Project 09 were shifted to designing automobile ferries and fishing vessels. The result was a growing feeling of insecurity at the institute, and the most qualified technicians started job-hunting for higher pay or for greater job security and career opportunities. Director Huang Xuhua asked: "Do the technical personnel engaged in sophisticated defense projects [in the United States, France, and Britain] need to work in sideline production or to raise funds by themselves?"[180]

The years after 1982 must have been disheartening indeed for the director. The project to which he had devoted his career was in trouble. The development of the new SSBN/SLBM systems encountered many political, financial, and technical difficulties after 1982, and it was only the successful launch of the JL-1 in September 1988 that made the difference; that is, rescued the project. Without that success, Project 09 would probably have remained an orphan or been indefinitely suspended.

In the 1950s and 1960s, revolutionary idealism and patriotism brought the nation's best minds into the strategic weapons programs, and Project 09 was a beneficiary. After the mid-1980s, personal gain and opportunism began to replace idealism and patriotism, and more and more college graduates refused their job assignments in defense-related work, especially at facilities located in remote areas such as the Third Line.[181] The pool of qualified successors to carry on long-term projects was steadily eroding. Leading defense scientists warned their leaders that without a policy change, the "best qualified technical personnel would scatter within three to five years!"[182]

Yet the potential of the defense industry remained high as the decade of the 1980s ended. It "ranked among the world's largest"; by 1989, more than 3,000,000 personnel were engaged in weapons programs at about 2,000 defense plants and institutes, and more than 1,000 other enterprises supported the defense production effort.[183] As of this writing, the fate of the defense industrial structure built over the past four decades hangs in the balance.

FIVE

Building and Deployment

As the network of military-run industries evolved in the post–Great Leap decades, the Central Military Commission gained mastery over substantial parts of the nation's economic resources and exerted ever greater influence over the state budget.[1] Factories, design institutes, and scientific centers proliferated as material resources and money became available to military planners. The commission set the agenda and priorities for all of these defense institutions, tracked their capabilities, and in time, predicting success, authorized the construction program for the nuclear submarines. It is this program to which we now turn.

Following the Sino-Soviet agreement of February 1959, the Soviet Union undertook to help China build two modern shipyards, the Bohai Shipyard, later formally named the Nuclear-Powered Submarine General Assembly Plant (Plant 431), in Huludao, Liaoning Province, and the Huangpu Shipyard (Plant 201), in Guangzhou, Guangdong Province.[2] The First Ministry of Machine Building (later to be divided into several machine building ministries, including the Sixth for shipbuilding) planned both yards for submarine construction.[3] It assigned the Bohai yard to build nuclear submarines, and the Huangpu yard to build conventional submarines.[4] The two yards pioneered the use of indoor horizontal floating drydocks and lured the nation's most skilled builders to their work force.

In 1965, the Central Special Commission reviewed the order from the high command to begin construction on the nuclear boat and decided that Bohai would install the nuclear reactor on the submarine only after the land-based prototype power plant had attained initial criticality. The yard would not be allowed to launch the nuclear attack submarine until the plant had reached its full rated power.[5] As we have seen, the first of these requirements was met in August 1970.

In the intervening years, 1965–70, the special commission had directed that all affected institutes expedite research on the materials and equipment needed for building the nuclear attack boat. By the end of the period, a variety of facilities in the military industrial system had received production orders related to Project 09, and despite setbacks caused by the Cultural Revolution, these orders were being met, though usually far behind schedule.

Special high-strength structural alloy steels for the pressure hull, for example, were trial-cast by the Steel and Iron Research Academy in Beijing. For quality control, each steel plate, designed for a yield limit of 60kg/mm² (85,700lb/in²) or higher, had to carry a signed inspection certificate attesting to its proven properties; steels of this moderately high strength are rated HY80 and used for modern submarine construction in the West.[6] Meanwhile, a battery plant in Zibo, Shandong Province, as another example, had begun manufacturing special lead-acid storage batteries, and other plants were manufacturing marine anti-fouling paints.[7] As these products were being developed, the Bohai Shipyard laid the keel and began assembling the first nuclear attack submarine, code named 09-1, in November 1968.[8]

Construction of the Nuclear Attack Submarine (09-1)

Welding the plates of the pressure hull together posed the first major challenge to the shipbuilders.[9] The size, thickness, and complex shapes of 09's hull plates, the requirement to attach stiffening ribs and launch tubes, and the need to reduce the high stresses within the metal exceeded the competence of all but the most advanced welders. The sheer size of the hull made it impossible to heat-treat the whole hull, and cracks appeared in the welds when the necessary heat treatment was administered section by section. Over time, 95 percent of fatigue failures in Chinese submarines resulted from defective welds.[10]

The designers had stipulated that each weld should be capable of withstanding temperatures down to −40°C and should have a yield limit rating (elasticity) of 70–80kg/mm² at critical points and 56kg/mm² at all other seams on the hull. Because automatic welding had not yet attained the high quality and accuracy (or high speeds) found in modern nozzle-control systems, they set the ratio of automatic to manual welds at 50:50, in contrast to 60:40 for conventional submarines. Manual welds would be used on each irregular shape, and to a large extent 09-1 was hand-welded.[11]

The Chinese, like the American and Soviet shipbuilders before them, had to devise a special welding rod or electrode, as well as novel techniques for welding the bulky pressure hull. The composition of the manual arc electrode has a powerful effect on the way metal is transferred to the metal pool in the seam between the plates. For the alloy steels resistant to low temperatures and high pressures, the welding engineers needed to fabricate special rods composed of a variety of metals, such as nickel and chromium. They also had to practice how to affix pieces of zinc alloy to the most exposed hull plates as a corrosion preventative measure and how to add thicker steel plates where the launch tube base and muzzle meet the pressure hull.[12]

By following foreign texts, they were able to formulate the required processes for welding the thick plates of the pressure hull, but as it turned out, nothing quite went according to the book. The engineers determined, for example, that these steel-alloy plates had to be heated to very high temperatures before any welding was done, but it proved difficult to determine exactly how high a temperature was needed for this process. As in the development of most techniques, only after the yard workers conducted endless experiments did they come up with a solution.[13]

Theory proved to be an especially inadequate guide for welding hull plates that were up to 40mm thick and would be cut with more than 1,000 openings.[14] The welds in plates of such thickness and configuration suffered a high incidence of both cold and hot cracks from a variety of causes, such as an uneven distribution of heat, improper welding speeds and low current density, the dilution of the weld metal, and the unpredictability of temperature change in the preheating process itself.[15] The shipbuilders found that some cracks in the welds would occasionally appear when the plates were reheated, and that the welding of stiffening ribs to reinforce the pressure hull could actually fracture the existing seam welds.[16] Several master welders were brought in from other yards to help solve the baffling technical difficulties involved, but in the end trial and error marked the slow path of welding the hull of the first attack boat.[17]

Step by step, each welded seam in the pressure hull underwent repeated X-ray inspection and pressure tests to detect flaws, procedures well advanced in the West but relatively unknown or untried in China. The navy drew up detailed methods for checking and certifying each assembled hull component and set what it considered to be exacting standards for parts that would bear the heaviest pressures at maximum depth.[18] All exterior pipes, valves, and accessories at these pressure points were repeatedly tested until they passed muster, and the Chinese quickly discovered how time-consuming the testing process could be and how difficult it was to enforce rigid standards with confidence among the first-generation shipbuilders at Bohai.[19] Nevertheless, everything finally tested out, and the hull and outer shell were completed on December 26, 1970, Mao Zedong's birthday.

As the Bohai workers began putting the finishing touches on the basic hull structure, technicians dispatched by the Second Ministry's First Academy (Southwest Reactor Engineering Design and Research Academy in Jiajiang, Sichuan) had been standing by at Huludao to guide the assembly, installation, and test operation of 09-1's power plant. That job began in early 1971.[20]

With the power plant and its shielding (80mm-thick lead plates each weighing 200kg) coming together in the boat's hull, the installation of the other myriad subsystems loomed as the most complicated engineering challenge ever to face China's shipbuilders. Tens of thousands of instruments, meters, and equipment began arriving at the pier, and no one knew precisely where to put them, let alone how to fit them into a whole with the thousands of feet of electric cables and pipelines. The possible permutations seemed infinite, and personnel trained to find the right combinations were in short supply.[21]

As we noted in our discussion of the submarine's design, to determine the optimal placement of the subsystems inside the sub's limited space, the Bohai Shipyard had fabricated a full-sized steel-and-wood model to use for trial assemblies. In each permutation, the engineers had to calculate weight distribution, safety, noise levels, and operational effectiveness and determine how each variable interacted with the others, often in unpredictable ways. After repeated on-site revisions of design plans and assembly techniques, the yard engineers eventually settled on their best-guess arrangement of the sub's equipment and support systems, as well as the exact location for the more than 1,000 openings on the pressure hull. Chief designer Huang Xuhua argued that the use of the model, while time-consuming, had saved time and avoided costly mistakes in the long run in completing the interior architecture and outfitting.[22]

With the model as their guide, the technicians spent the first months of 1971 placing the power plant and many of the subsystems inside the pressure hull. By April, this operation had been fine tuned to the satisfaction of the First Academy and yard personnel. Only the loading of the nuclear fuel rods in the power plant remained to be done.[23]

In June 1971, the workers finished loading the reactor and brought it to initial criticality. The powerful plant was ready for a full test. The Project 09 Leading Group reported this success to the Central Special Commission and the Central Military Commission and submitted a recommended schedule of dockside tests and sea trials. Zhou Enlai received the report on June 20, and, not wanting to rush the go-ahead decision, drafted the following instruction: "The experimental plan on starting test operation of the [submarine nuclear] power plant won't be authorized until the special commission holds a meeting on June 25."[24] Attempting an engineering feat of this magnitude once more had activated the high command.

On the night of the 25th, accompanied by the vice-chairman of the Central Military Commission, Ye Jianying, and Vice-Premiers Li Xiannian and Yu Qiuli, Zhou Enlai met in the Great Hall of the People next to Tiananmen Square. Chen Youming, head of the Project 09 Office, briefed the assembled dignitaries on the leading group's schedule. The meeting then recessed, and by the time it resumed the following day, Zhou was ready with a directive. 09-1 would be tested in four phases:

The first phase is a complete test of the submarine berthed at the pier; the second phase is a maiden voyage of the submarine on the surface; the third phase is a submerged trial run in shallow water; and the fourth phase is a submerged trial run in deep water. No trial run is to be carried out until the navy and the Central Military Commission have approved a written report [on the previous one]. You should pay particular attention to safety. Don't rush through your tasks.

The premier seemed most at ease when making the obvious seem significant, but the value of just his imprimatur during this period of political uncertainty is not to be underestimated.

Zhou also took this occasion to remind Vice-Minister Bian Jiang where his ministry's responsibilities lay:

The Sixth Ministry of Machine Building is in charge of the integral test of the submarine tied up to the pier. Bian Jiang, you are responsible! You must not think that things will go off without a hitch once the submarine is launched. You may not turn over the submarine [to the navy] until you have completed the four-phase trials.

Zhou gave the officials of the Second Ministry the same stern reminder: they continued to be responsible for the power plant and must "send people [to the pier] to help carry out one more inspection. All of you are responsible for the project."[25]

A week later, on July 1, everything seemed to be proceeding according to schedule. The supervising technicians issued the order to bring the 09-1 reactor on line, and two months later, the first-phase test was successfully conducted on the submarine at the main pier of the Bohai Shipyard.[26] With step one out of the way, the Nuclear-Powered Submarine Project Leading Group, as instructed, requested authorization to set the date for the sub's maiden voyage.[27] Optimism ran high throughout the project that the end was in sight. On August 23, the 09-1 power plant achieved complete operational status, and the submarine cast off.[28]

But the years of chaos and inattention to technical quality control had taken their toll, and numerous "abnormal phenomena" came to light during the cruise. When word of the several technical mishaps reached him, Zhou Enlai issued the following directive:

Several problems have already occurred in the maiden voyage of the nuclear-powered submarine. Other problems will probably appear hereafter. You should sum up experiences at all times so as to avoid accidents, especially any major accident that would result in the death of crew members or the destruction of the submarine.[29]

The tenor of Zhou's message suggests just how bad things were during the initial sea trial.

But again power politics intervened. With Lin Biao's alleged failed coup attempt and death on September 13, all military projects came to a temporary halt. In the purge that followed, Project 09 came under sharp attack. Accused of being a sworn follower of Lin Biao, Li Zuopeng was dismissed from his post as head of the Project 09 Leading Group. Some senior officers went so far as to associate Li's efforts to develop the project with his attempt to participate in Lin Biao's plot to usurp the supreme Party leadership and state power. A few described 09 as a "black project." The leading group's approval of the phased tests was rescinded, leaving 09-1 in limbo.[30]

Fortunately for those who had invested their all in the project, several rapid changes in high-level personnel rescued it before much damage could be inflicted. Even before the September incident, Marshal Ye Jianying, in his capacity as vice-chairman of the Central Military Commission, had quietly begun lessening the influence of Lin Biao over the Chinese military, and a few days after Lin's death, the Politburo began reassigning the staff of the Central Military Commission to Ye. Before formalizing its personnel decisions, the commission created an organ called the Administrative Meeting (Bangong Huiyi) under Ye to oversee the commission's routine procedures, replacing the Administrative Group (Banshi Zu) that had been dominated by Lin Biao. Using the Bangong Huiyi, Ye Jianying assumed full control of the commission's daily affairs by early October.[31]

Meanwhile, upon Li Zuopeng's ouster, his deputy, Zhou Xihan, who till then had been responsible for the daily affairs of the project and concentrated mainly on technical matters, had taken over by default. In his new circumstances, Zhou briefed Marshal Ye on the postponement of the 09-1's test program and asked that the hold on it be lifted.[32]

At about the same time, Zhou Enlai instructed Ye to call a meeting of the Politburo to discuss how to address 09's political problems, and Ye took the occasion to go on the offensive. With some anger, the marshal told his colleagues, "Premier Zhou himself was in charge of the nuclear-powered submarine project. It is a red project. Who says it is a black project?" With so much going on in the aftermath of the Lin disaster, no one was prepared to contradict Ye, and Mao nodded his assent. Ye then instructed the commander of the navy, Xiao Jinguang, who attended the meeting, to give more active backing to the project. After the session, Ye ordered Zhou Xihan to press ahead with the 09-1 program and simply to ignore the gibes of its opponents.

So, with a measure of calm restored, the project moved ahead. Twenty more sea trials were conducted from 1972 to 1974, and all experienced misfortunes of varying (and still secret) degrees. Many years later, a senior navy official disclosed that the crew members who served during these and later trials immediately showed the ill-effects of overexposure to radioactivity: "The white blood cells of officers and sailors who had directly or indirectly been engaged in radioactive jobs were found after physical examination to be universally lower than those of normal people." The official reported to the National People's Congress that the crews of these vessels were demoralized and needed help to "stabilize their thinking."[33]

The news of the plight of the 09-1 crewmen could not be contained. As word of the potential danger spread throughout the fleet, other sailors resisted assignment to the nuclear navy. Some sailors dreaded the "nuclear terror," one source reported, and "are full of concern because they equate the [operation of a submarine's] reactor with the explosion of an atomic bomb."[34] Many alleged that large numbers of dead fish could be seen floating in the wake of 09-1's operations.[35]

Though the dangers to humans and marine life sometimes took years to be known and may well have been exaggerated in the telling, most of the more mundane technical problems were discovered and dealt with at once. There were a few, however, that stubbornly resisted solution. In one of the sea trials, for example, the crew found corrosion at stress points in the heat exchanger's piping and repeatedly detected radioactivity in the boat's drainage pipes.[36] Although radioactive elements are normal in the primary loop pipes, the engineers could not figure out how radioactivity had moved from this supposedly hermetically sealed loop to the second-loop drainage system. They also could not solve the leakage of valves in the primary loop. Some Chinese specialists say these and similar problems have yet to be fully resolved.* Reports of these deficiencies were flashed to the Project 09 Office, and Zhou Enlai immediately ordered Ye Jianying and Vice-Premier Li Xiannian to personally monitor the repairs and again called on the tech-

*In at least one nuclear sub, the condenser and major valves leaked high-pressure steam, intensifying the crew's fear of accidents. Liu Shengdong and Zhang Weixing; Guo Xiangxing et al.; Jia Yuping and Sun Yongan, 14–15; Jiang Rubiao and Xiang Xin.

nicians and 09-1 crew to consider all possible ways to avoid accidents that could result in death or the loss of the submarine.

In response, engineers from the Sixth Ministry and technical officers from the navy joined ranks to perform almost 200 tests in more than 20 additional sea trials on the boat. In the process of rounding off all four phases of the test sequence, 09-1 traveled more than 6,000 nautical miles. Finally, Zhou was satisfied that the nation's first nuclear submarine was safe and authorized the navy to take it over from the Sixth Ministry. On August 1, 1974, the Central Military Commission issued an instruction to name the craft Long March No. 1 and to add it to the battle order of the navy.[37]

The completion of the four-phase functional test laid the foundation for the series construction of China's first generation of nuclear attack submarines.[38] The navy assigned the first 09-1 the hull number 401. After some delay for minor design modifications, 402 was commissioned in 1977.[39]

Both boats continued to be plagued with endless technical problems (including corrosion and leakage of the steam generator and defective pumps, condensers, and main reductions gear). What is more, the institutes under the Seventh Academy and the Fourth Ministry had made little headway in their efforts to develop sonar systems, long-distance communications, the inertial navigation system, and a deep-water homing torpedo. These electronic components and weapons could still not meet the required standards and thus were not installed on either sub. For this reason, these early models were sometimes characterized as "sharks without teeth."[40]

Nevertheless, in July 1978, the navy recommended that the construction of the 09-1 boats continue. On the 20th, Deng Xiaoping agreed to the proposal "in principle" but added, "the cost of such things is very high. You must ensure the solution of all technical problems before you start follow-on series construction."[41] The month before, Deng had told the military industrial ministries to start a fresh round of attempts to solve the quality problems of all naval weapons systems. He ordered the navy to refuse any substandard ships from the Sixth Ministry. As a result of his prodding, the Chinese began equipping their nuclear boats with acceptable subsystems by the mid-1980s.[42] By 1991, the navy had commissioned four more nuclear attack submarines of the 09-1 class, bringing the total to six.[43]

Retrofitting the 31-Class Submarine

Before the completion of the first 09-1, the navy had set in motion plans to transform the design for the attack boat into a design for a ballistic-missile submarine and to translate the engineering designs for the missile-launch mechanisms from the drafting table into an operational system for the new craft. For the latter task, it decided to retrofit its single Soviet-designed conventional-powered ballistic-missile submarine.

Although the designing of the nuclear missile submarine, code-named the 09-2, and the research and development on the missile ejection system in the Soviet-model submarine proceeded in parallel, the latter had to be completed first in order to determine the final design of the 09-2. Accordingly, we turn first to the story of the retrofitting of that boat and the perfecting of its ejection system as a prelude to understanding how the 09-2 was built.

As we have seen, in compliance with its agreement of February 1959, the Soviet Union sold China the equipment, components, and technical data required for assembling a Golf-class submarine and an outdated naval missile, the R-11FM. (Both designations are the ones used in the West; the Chinese counterparts are 31-class and missile 1060.)[44] The navy selected the Dalian yard for building the submarine.[45] By the time the job was completed, the yard had become the nation's largest and one of at least six constructing submarines.[46] Working with Soviet designs and equipment, Dalian built a special shipway and then, in 1961, began assembling the boat from Soviet-supplied components. The submarine was launched in 1964 but was not ready for training missions for two more years.[47]

In November 1967, about a year after the launching, the Defense Science and Technology Commission and the navy held a joint meeting to examine and approve the design plans for a two-stage solid-propellant ballistic missile for launch from a submerged submarine.[48] This missile, the *Julang* 1 (JL-1) will be discussed in the following chapter.

As originally built, however, the 31-class submarine could not launch this missile. In the first place, its ejection system was designed for surface, not underwater, launch.[49] Moreover, its missile tubes, located in the conning tower of the sub, were designed for the smaller R-11FMs (1060) and could not accommodate the JL-1: the JL-1 was 10.7m in length and 1.4m in diameter; the R-11FM missile measured 9.5 by 0.88m.[50]

By this time, the Seventh Academy's Institute 713 had made considerable progress on the JL-1 missile's ejection system, and in 1968, the navy and the Defense Science and Technology Commission gave final approval for rebuilding the Golf to the specifications of the new missile.[51] Soon afterward, the navy set up Office 931 for the daily management of 31's retrofitting and transferred officers from the Naval Equipment Department to man it.[52]

The rebuilding process principally meant changing the structure of the conning tower and installing the advanced missile ejection system in it. Under the administration of Office 931, technicians from Institutes 713 and 719 and other research facilities teamed up to plan the ship work and quickly concluded that they should concentrate first on perfecting the ejection system.

To do this, they began conducting land-based ejection tests of model rockets of varying sizes but quickly decided that any ejection system had to be tailor-made to fit each specific missile.[53] Thus, the technicians designed two full-sized reusable models filled with water in rubber bags with JL-1's exact weight.[54] They made "model one" for ejection from a silo and "model two" for launch from the yet-to-be retrofitted submarine. In 1970, the team began conducting ejection tests of model one from a semi-buried silo at the Naval Test Base (Base 23) in Huludao.[55] Over the next years, they conducted hundreds of these tests and incrementally modified the system.

Accidents during these tests were not common, but when they happened, they left a lasting impression on the witnesses. On one occasion, for example, after the technicians ignited the gas-steam generator, the powerful mixture ejected the missile improperly, shattering part of the generator and causing a rupture in the silo wall. One steel fragment from the silo was hurled tens of meters and smashed the roof of a car. Those safely lodged in shelters stared in shock, and one of the observers, later to become captain of a missile boat, remained acutely aware throughout the rest of his career that a similar accident in his submarine would destroy it and him.

This experience led the team members to devise a test to assure themselves that the sub would survive even if the missile failed. They decided to drop model-two dummy missiles from a height of several meters to calculate various safety parameters. During several nights in August 1970, JL-1's chief designer, Huang Weilu, took his team and the simulators to the Changjiang Bridge in Nanjing, Jiangsu Province. There they dropped the dummies from the bridge into the river to determine the probable damage to a real missile and theoretically to the submarine and its crew. They conducted these drop tests from different angles and finally convinced themselves that the missile was safe for testing.[56]

With the tests on the silo-based system nearing completion, the navy and the Defense Science and Technology Commission met on June 21, 1971, to plan the next phase, tests from the sub. But at that point, the officials could only approve the plan in principle, for the Dalian yard had not yet completed work on the conning tower.[57] In anticipation of that day, the navy went forward with its planning for a test program. To guarantee the safety of submariners even in case of serious breakdowns, it selected a shallow area as the test site and ordered Xu Junlie to form a team to evaluate defects in the conduct of the forthcoming test series.[58]

The test was put on hold for more than a year as the task of modifying work on the conning tower went slowly at the Dalian yard. The work was finally concluded toward the end of the summer of 1972, but the first outing and test, on September 15, flopped. Only two months later, on November 23, could the navy declare success.[59] It approved the basic design of the system and then ordered follow-up tests to assess each subcomponent.

Accidents again plagued the test program during this follow-up phase. In one case, the gas generator ignited prematurely, and the model rocket was ejected from its tube improperly, causing the missile to fall perilously close to the submarine itself. The submariners could only guess their fate if a live JL-1 had hit the boat.[60] As one might expect, this and other accidents had the effect of forcing a close review of every step necessary for conducting each test, and this requirement was translated into continuous bureaucratic intervention and red tape. By 1975, as can be seen in Figure 5, the construction effort had produced still more bureaucratic layers.

Months were to go by before the navy and the commission, in May 1973, were willing to give the central authorities their best estimate of the steps essential to the test process in a report entitled the "Summary of the Coordination Conference on the Second-Phase Retrofitting of the 31-Class Submarine." On May 13, 1973, the State Council and the Central Military Commission approved the document and in principle called for the completion of the second-phase refitting and the resumption of tests with the model two by 1975.[61]

The work of the defense scientists, however, could not escape the particularly intense turmoil that was to last until the death of Mao in September 1976, and the completion of the second phase was thus delayed until late in the decade. Yet slowly and haltingly, with their engineering work mixed with political struggle, the technicians installed the last of the sub's 140 new instruments in its missile launcher compartment and readied the JL-1 for its inaugural underwater firing.[62]

Between May 7 and November 20, 1979, when all was ready on the submarine, the navy conducted six more ejection tests with a modified version of the model-two simulator. The engineers used the "comparatively complete technical data" from these tests to further refine the design of the JL-1 itself and to adjust their test operations in accordance with actual sea conditions.[63] After 14 years (1965–79) of halting progress, the ejection system for an underwater launch was ready, and at other bases the work on the missile was being frantically pressed forward. The missile engineers con-

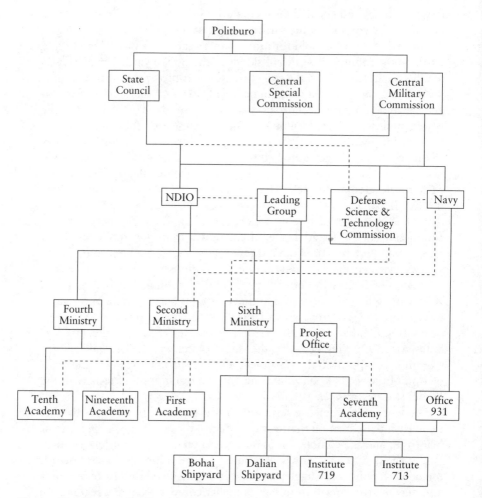

Fig. 5. Organization for the construction of the 09 submarines, 1975

ducted land-based flight tests of the JL-1 missiles from a launching pad in June 1981 and from a test launch tube the following January and April to verify the performance of the ejection system. Finally, on October 12, 1982, the first JL-1 flew from the submerged 31-class submarine and ignited just after breaking the surface to begin a perfect trajectory.[64]

Construction of the 09-2 Submarine

As the work on the 31-class submarine and its missile-launch mechanisms moved fitfully forward, the Project 09 planners kept pushing back the schedule for designing and building 09-2, the nuclear missile submarine that would use the 09-1's power plant but be reconfigured for launching 12 JL-1s. Nevertheless, as early as 1967, when the 09-2 program was officially started, the design engineers could make some assumptions about the pace of the 31's retrofitting and begin drafting at least tentative plans for the construction of the missile sub.

By the fall of 1967, they had completed the first version of these plans, and in October Nie Rongzhen's commission and the navy convened yet another round of meetings to examine and approve the final procedures for 09-2 and its missile. A flow chart laying out the interrelated steps for both programs, including the retrofitting of submarine 31, was reviewed and adopted. When the Central Special Commission put its chop on all these plans, it also decided to use a single 09-1-type reactor in the missile boat.[65]

The two reactors would nevertheless differ in some respects. The 09-2's would have 20 percent more power, for a rated output of about 58 megawatts (thermal) against 48 for the 09-1, yielding a shaft power of 14,400hp vs. 12,000hp, a power efficiency of about 18 percent, the same as 09-1. The 09-2 would also displace more tons (up to 4,000 vs. up to 3,000), and be slightly slower (with a maximum submerged speed of 22 knots vs. 26).[66] Both boats would have pressure-hull plates of the same thickness, 40mm, but the 09-2's pressure hull would be of larger diameter (10m vs. 9m).[67] It would also be able to stay submerged for a longer period (90 days vs. 60 days).[68] Like 09-1, it would be capable of withstanding hydrostatic pressures at depths of up to 300m, and would be equipped with advanced wire-guided or acoustic homing torpedoes capable of attacking submarines.[69] Figure 6 is an artist's synthesis depicting the two submarines.

Since the Bohai yard's technicians and workers had already built a nuclear boat, the navy decided, without much deliberation, to construct 09-2 there. Any other decision would have caused major delays and greatly increased costs. The work started in 1971, at about the time 09-1 embarked on its maiden surface voyage.[70] Originally scheduled for launching

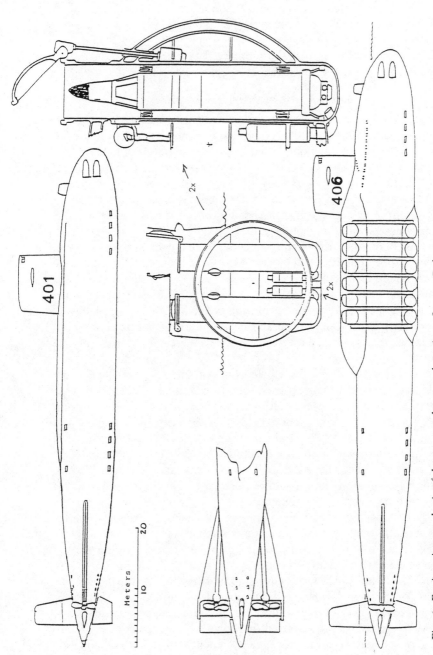

Fig. 6. Engineering synthesis of the 09-1 and 09-2 submarines. Source: Bob Dietz, an American SLBM expert.

in 1973, the missile sub did not slip down the way at Bohai until 1981.[71] Not a little of this delay was due to the ceaseless political turmoil in the wake of the Lin Biao affair.

From 1973 to 1976, the radicals refused to relent or tolerate a return to business as usual, and like other key strategic weapons programs, Project 09-2 lay in shambles. Zhang Aiping tried but failed to revive it when he became director of the Defense Science and Technology Commission in March 1975, but only the arrest of the radical leaders—the infamous Gang of Four headed by Mao's wife—after Mao's death in the fall of 1976 opened the way for construction of the 09-2 to get moving again.[72]

Still, politics accounts for only part of the delay. Technological obstacles also plagued the developers. For years, the research facilities under the Tenth Academy (radio electronics), the Seventh Academy (shipbuilding), and the Nineteenth Academy (telecommunications) had tried to make the 09-2's electronic components, and though the cooperation among the three units was apparently quite good, they repeatedly failed in their efforts to perfect the 09-2's subsystems.[73]

The 09-2 plans called for multiple sonar devices, each to a different end: navigation, reconnaissance, warning, search and tracking, fire control, attack, and underwater communication. Most of these sonars would depend on hydrophones (passive sonar) mounted in a large unit in the bow and in secondary arrays near the bow, amidships, and the stern for total defensive coverage.* These passive systems proved relatively easy to develop, and the experts were especially proud of their anti-interference innovations.[74] Fabricating the active systems for navigation, communication, and attack, however, turned out to be far harder, as did the development of the integrated sonar command-and-control systems. Not until the early 1980s did Institute 706 (with help from the Tenth Academy and the Academy of Sciences, as well as industrial enterprises) achieve success on these technologies.[75]

Long-distance communication posed perhaps the greatest hurdle the navy faced in meeting its new requirement to ensure strict command and control of strategic units built to cruise freely in remote sea areas. Its existing stations at Qingdao, Ningbo, and Zhanjiang, built in the 1950's with Soviet equipment, could not provide assured communications with any boats at long remove. Effective command and control of the wide-ranging

---

*Sonar technology is critical to the success of most submarine missions and often leads to compromises in hull configurations. For example, the large bow sonars that are extremely sensitive for detecting other submarines often preclude the use of straightforward torpedo tubes and require skewed placement. Information from an American specialist, 1991.

09s thus became the single highest priority.[76] The problem of long-range communications with submarines, once so much on Nikita Khrushchev's mind, was now to plague Mao's heirs.

Given the state of Chinese knowledge, the trade-off the communication engineers had to make was between effective control and the submarine's safety. The research institutes had already made substantial progress in mastering communications using very low frequencies (VLF: 3–30KHz), but like their counterparts across the world, they were stumped by extremely low frequencies (ELF: 30–300Hz). The problem is that VLF radio can penetrate only a few meters below the surface, whereas ELF radio can reach 100 or more. A submerged submarine that is dependent on VLF as its primary means of communication must thus deploy its antennas and patrol near the surface, thereby risking detection. These technical realities complicated command and control. More compact electronic vocabularies had to be invented for speed of transmission, and the engineers had to draw on an old branch of Chinese learning, cryptography, for ensuring the authenticity of messages sent in those vocabularies.[77]

The long-forgotten agreement with Moscow now became important as the Chinese investigated long-distance communications with submarines. As part of the disastrous negotiations on naval cooperation, the defense ministers of China and the Soviet Union, on August 3, 1958, had signed an agreement for constructing a high-power, long-wave radio station. The Soviets had thereupon sold the Chinese the required equipment and began to provide technical assistance on the station. But the project had come to a halt two years later with the termination of all such assistance.[78] In 1961, when defense programs had begun to recover from the blow of the Soviet withdrawal, Zhou Enlai instructed the navy to establish a special committee to continue the construction of the long-wave radio station with the assistance of the relevant industrial departments. Over the next years, the work on the station proceeded on schedule, and in August 1965, it began routine communications with the expanding submarine fleet.[79]

This system was only the prelude to the one that would be needed for the missile sub then on the drawing boards. In 1969, Mao Zedong approved the construction of an extremely high-power VLF station as part of Project 09, and for 13 years, until September 1982, research, design, and then construction proceeded, driven more by political than technological imperatives.[80] The completion date coincided with the scheduling, for October, of the launch of the first JL-1 from the 31-class submarine. Meanwhile, as the work on the land-based station was under way, Institute 722 (communications) in Wuhan and other research organs under the Tenth and Seventh academies made progress on developing a shipboard myriametric-wave receiver.[81] By 1982, the navy felt confident that its head-quarters could communicate by VLF with its strategic submarines in all proposed operating zones.

But this still did not solve the problem of how a submarine could communicate safely with its home base. The Chinese knew that Western surveillance systems required only about a few seconds to detect and locate the transmissions of all but the most modern submarines. The best defense against such intercepts, they understood, was to develop technologies for so-called instantaneous communications for both transmission and reception. Institute 1019 in Shijiazhuang, Hebei Province, worked out these technologies, and then developed a high-power microwave system that could communicate via space satellites.[82] In completing this system, other institutes concentrated on making and improving specialized communication satellites, five of which were launched between 1984 and 1990.[83] The military was awarded control of the majority of the satellite channels, with priority given to the General Staff and the navy.[84] With the installation of these systems, the leadership considered the matter of full and reliable command, control, and communications settled—at least for the time being.[85]

The electronics specialists also worked closely with specialists on modern navigation aids. In the late 1970s, the navy had started work on three high-power radio navigation stations in South China; they came on line in 1989. The year before, the navy had broken ground for another three stations located in the north and the east.[86] But none of these facilities had the capacity to service submarines operating far from China's coasts.

The Chinese approach to this problem, as we have noted, was to develop an inertial navigation system for 09-1. The engineers at Institute 707 knew that in such systems the error rate increased with the range cruised and that they would have to find ways to offset these errors.[87] By 1979, engineers at 707 had made two workable systems, and in the next decade, the institute developed an even more advanced system.[88]

Meanwhile, other engineers were working on a stellar system, and by the mid-1980s, Institute 20 in Xi'an and Institute 707 had developed a more modern integrated inertial navigational system linked to the U.S. NavStar and Omega (VLF) systems, as well as to on-board optics (for astronomical sightings) and computers.[89] The Chinese apparently were willing to take the risk that the United States might deny them access to its systems in wartime. Although the Chinese recognize that their present system is not as accurate and certainly not as invulnerable as the one used by U.S. missile submarines, they consider it adequate for 09-2's current missions.[90]

Thus the electronics work proceeded one component at a time. When the last item on the list, the improved radar, was completed,[91] the Chinese developers congratulated themselves on designing, fabricating, and testing thousands of instruments, controls, and hardware. They regard themselves as the unsung heroes of Project 09.

Most of 09-2's subcomponents were now ready for installation and testing.[92] In the first half of 1983, the engineers and navy technicians began various performance tests in preparation for the boat's trial voyages.[93] Again, problems surfaced, but none were as serious as those that plagued the 09-1 at this stage. New equipment and interior designs, for example, created such sharp "climatic" variations that the crew members in the instrument compartment had to wear wool overcoats while their fellows in the engine room were forced to work in sleeveless undershirts. One visitor compared the environmental differences throughout the boat to "the changes of the four annual seasons."[94]

The noise level also proved too high in the early trials. Another visitor described the noise as "unbearable" and quoted a sailor as saying that "the rumble of the machinery made him lie awake all night." He added, "Some sailors figured out a way to fall asleep quickly by singing repeatedly a small song they composed: '[The sound of] lung lung lung, peng peng peng accompanies you and makes you go off to dreamland.'" He and his comrades feared that the peng, peng, peng also might reach the ears of an eavesdropping enemy.

This and other early problems were quickly fixed, with the result that 09-2 rapidly moved through its sea trials. In August 1983, the Central Military Commission added the missile submarine to the navy's battle order; it joined the fleet as hull number 406.[95] Years later, senior officers were quoted as saying that the missile submarine assured China the capability "of staging a counterattack even after being subjected to a surprise nuclear attack."[96] Their confidence rested on the capability of 406 and its future sister ships to attack targets at ranges up to 1,700km with 12 400-kiloton warheads.

The sister ships were already under development when 406 joined the fleet. The Sixth Ministry had designated the Huangpu Shipyard near Guangzhou to build the next missile submarines, the 09-3 and 09-4.[97] The navy had started upgrading the aging shipbuilding facility in 1953, and it had become reasonably modernized by the late 1970s.[98] It was chosen over Bohai mainly because of the severe problem of cracking that occurs when welding is done at relatively low temperatures. The warmer climate of South China weighed heavily in favor of the shift to Huangpu.[99]

Equipped with an 09-2 nuclear reactor and 12 JL-1 missiles, the 09-3 sub was to be an improved version of the 09-2. In the late 1960s, the engineers designing the 09-3 planned to install the most advanced equipment and to outfit the sub with a new variable speed propeller drive.[100] The Nuclear-Powered Submarine Project Office (Lingjiuban) assigned Jiaotong University in Shanghai to develop a hydraulic coupler, about which we know little other than that it would replace the propeller shaft gearbox and dramatically reduce the noise radiated from the shaft. At the yard, Director Wang Jinlong took charge of the construction project.[101] Yet, by the early 1980s, Deng Xiaoping had moved to curb defense spending and to shift the priority to civilian modernization. With the change of priority, the construction of 09-3 was delayed and then indefinitely suspended.[102]

By this time, however, 09-4 was already in the works, and with the 09-3 out of the way the engineers could become ever more daring in their attempts to apply the latest technologies to the craft. In 1985, the Naval Equipment and Technology Department and the Beijing Steel and Iron Research Academy experimented with stealth technology, for example, after studying the foreign literature and intelligence reports on the subject. They recognized that the main problems lay in the shape and exterior material for the boat's periscope. In time, they developed an anti-radar coating and redesigned the periscope, thereby greatly reducing detectability.[103] In 1987, the navy and the China State Shipbuilding Corporation also gave priority to upgrading the reactors, electronics equipment, and weapon systems for the future subs and to retrofitting the 09-2.[104] The 09-4 reactor would be a more powerful and reliable loop-type system.[105]

Politics intertwined with technology in the development of 09-4, whose history dates back to the prestudy phase in 1974. On September 8 of that year, the Nuclear-Powered Submarine Project Leading Group held a meeting to discuss how to formulate the general design plans for the boat.[106] The 09-4 would not only be a more advanced submarine, it would also carry a totally new missile, the JL-2. At the multidisciplinary meeting, specialists exchanged points of view on the sub's dimensions, the missile ejection system, and the SLBM's general performance characteristics. The main parameters of the JL-2 missile also were tentatively determined at the meeting. The goal was to build a submarine carrying 20 8,000km missiles with 400-kiloton warheads.[107]

In 1976, the State Council and the military commission approved the commencement of Program JL-2. However, repeated debates on the missile's range caused a lag in the JL-2's overall design plan and thereby delayed plans for the 09-4. In response to a navy report in 1978 suggesting a speed-up in Project 09, Deng Xiaoping obliquely called instead for a postponement. "In terms of nuclear-powered submarines," he said, "you should give priority to the quality rather than the quantity. You should place ever greater stress on enhancing the quality." In plain language, Deng meant to check the momentum of the 09-4/JL-2 project, which did not resume until the mid-1980s.

In December 1984, the Ministry of Astronautics Industry (successor to the Seventh Ministry) began a feasibility study of the new, longer-range SLBM.[108] In March 1986, the ministry decided to complete research and development on the land-based DF-31 missile before installing a redesigned sea-based version, the JL-2, on the 09-4 submarine.[109] The next month, the ministry submitted a report on its decision to the Commission of Science, Technology, and Industry for National Defense for approval. At this writing, both the sub and its missile are still under development.

Deployment

Long before the missile submarine joined the fleet, the navy had ordered the Submarine Institute to open special courses for training officers and sailors to man the nation's nuclear boats.[110] The navy set the most rigid requirements for selecting and educating these elite submariners.

Virtually all of these future members of the nuclear navy had previously served on conventional-powered submarines, and most of the candidates for commanding officer had already commanded a submarine.[111] Moreover, most trainees had better-than-average educations, and by the early 1990s, 95 percent of the officers assigned to the nuclear subs had graduated from universities or colleges, including Qinghua University and the Beijing Institute of Technology. The educational level of the nuclear submarine crew members exceeds that of all other PLA combat units.[112]

Created in 1953 and located in Qingdao, Shandong Province, the Submarine Institute is one of four naval colleges that prepares officers for command.[113] At any given time, the institute has an enrollment of about 2,000 studying more than 40 courses, including not just the requisite technical subjects, but also such electives as psychology, ethics, Western philosophy, and Western economics.[114] Because the school trains all the men slated for submarine duty and deep-water rescue vehicles from the lowest sailor up, it is known as the "blue cradle."[115] None of the men go to their assignments without a strong understanding of safety procedures.[116]

Crew training at the institute is organized at four levels: for captains, department heads, noncommissioned officers, and ordinary sailors.[117] The institute assigns the highest importance to training department heads. In the early years, these officers majored in separate specialties, navigation, weaponry, or observation and communication (*guantong*). But this specialized training clearly hurt a man's chances for promotion to more gen-

eral positions, especially as a commanding officer or a shore-based administrator, and since 1979, the course for prospective department heads has
embraced all three fields.[118]

In recent years, the institute's faculty and technical support staff have
developed computer-aided simulators, giving it the finest facilities for
audio-visual education of all the naval colleges.[119] The simulators are designed not only to help the sailors learn all aspects of operating nuclear-
power plants and missile mechanisms but also to take them through mock
runs.[120]

In preparation for the 09 deployments, the navy added base construction
to its seeming endless list of requirements. In February 1966, Mao, ever
concerned to protect the country's defenses from air raids, urged the navy
to "build more shelters" for its ships in man-made caves. "In building
[such] shelters, you do not have to adopt underwater operations," he
wrote. "You can begin by digging a vertical shaft just like the miners do.
Then dig through the rock horizontally to let seawater in. After that, add
a hardened cover over the shaft." At this, the navy embarked on a search
for a place where the nation might "shelter" its submarines.[121]

About two years later, Mao approved the navy's choice of an inlet near
Qingdao and ordered the building to commence.[122] The navy immediately
transferred several engineering regiments to work on the project's first
phase, and they proceeded to remove 810,000 cubic meters of rock and to
pour 200,000 cubic meters of concrete. The gigantic sea cave completed,
construction crews then installed 17,000 pieces of equipment and laid
220km of pipeline, much of it related to maintaining nuclear power plants.
By the mid-1970s, the concealed base was camouflaged and hardened
against attack and made ready to receive the first nuclear boat, no. 401.[123]
In 1975, the navy authorized the North China Sea Fleet to form the Nuclear Submarine Flotilla.

The base comprises multiple shelters, each of which has a number of
facilities to load and unload nuclear fuel rods, move supplies, monitor the
performance of various subsystems, repair breakdowns, and conduct demagnetization.[124] The cavernous shelter where the boats are docked is as
high as a 12-story building. Large-sized cranes in this shelter can load or
off-load the JL-1 missiles.[125] Partially protected against nuclear or chemical
attack as well as conventional air raids, the shelters can maintain communication and independent operations under combat conditions. The
base commander can conduct effective command and control of his submarines for extended periods even when cut off from all outside support.[126]

Given the small number of nuclear subs and their vulnerability to attack
when in port, the navy created a Nuclear Submarine Repair Team and

charged it with keeping the subs in a high state of readiness. The base took command of the team and filled its ranks with the most qualified master technicians. The navy credits the team with preventing serious accidents to any of its nuclear boats, and submariners have dubbed it "China's No. 1 Submarine Repair Team."[127]

Operating from this base, the 09 boats have provisions for extended sea duty, and special attention is given to the safety and well-being of the crews. The navy provides 13 types of protective clothing for the sailors in hazardous jobs (in addition to 36 types of work clothes for the technicians on the base).[128] It also awards a special monthly allowance to the crews and tends to their medical needs in a facility specially built for them, Convalescent Hospital 409.[129]

Beginning in the late 1980s, all military men suffered declining living standards because of the government's repeated budget cuts, and the nuclear submariners did not escape.[130] Many of them, especially the technical and noncommissioned officers, refused to reenlist in the hope of finding better jobs in the coastal cities. Accordingly, the navy adopted a variety of means to placate or at least retain those submariners with legitimate grievances, including conferring professional posts on technical officers, extending the terms of service of captains and technical officers, and housing their families on the base.[131] The navy has also tried to make the service more attractive by recommending exemplary sailors for admission to the Submarine Institute.[132] It even allowed the institute to recruit local high school graduates who were in good health but had relatively low examination scores.[133]

These new recruits are entering a system of training that has been much strengthened over the years. The navy appraises its level of combat preparedness by the number of category 1 fighting ships (qualified for the round-the-clock alert). In 1982, fewer than ten vessels were able to pass the qualifying tests.[134] To repair the situation, the navy's commander, Liu Huaqing, began enforcing an unprecedentedly rigid training system in 1983, with the result that four years later, half the nation's combat ships were able to pass the tests. In 1988, in order to increase the number of category 1 ships still further, the military commission approved the navy's proposal to create a Combat Ship Training Center at each of its three fleet headquarters. The fruits of these efforts have allowed the navy to shorten the training time for its ready-alert submarines from one-and-a-half years to one year and have brought more and more of them into category 1 status.[135]

The operational command structure for the nuclear navy has also changed considerably over the years. Initially, all nuclear submarines, like all conventional ones, came directly under the dual jurisdiction of the Submarine Corps and the Qingdao naval base.[136] But as the missions of these subs became clearer the Central Military Commission reassigned them first to a separate service arm (*bingzhong*) and, soon afterward, to a wholly new body, the Nuclear Submarine Corps, both under naval headquarters.[137] The navy appointed Yang Xi, the first captain of the 401, to command the new corps.[138] His foremost duty was to keep the missile submarine, a grade 1 boat, at "first-degree combat readiness," and to see that the technicians followed through on their charge to check the status of the sub's missile ejection systems and nuclear power plants every half hour.[139]

The small number of 09 boats and the JL-1's low accuracy have limited their combat assignment to launching retaliatory strikes against an enemy's cities and other "soft" targets.[140] By decree of the military commission, they are under the same strict release rules that are applied to other nuclear weapons. The chain of command runs up from the Nuclear Submarine Corps to navy headquarters, to the General Staff, to the military commission. Only the chairman of the commission has the authority to commit China to nuclear war.[141]

PART II

The Missile

SIX

Solid Propulsion and the End of an Era

The Chinese passion for explosives transformed warfare in East Asia centuries before the West gave up the sword and the bow. The bamboo firecrackers that marked joyous celebrations in the Middle Kingdom as early as 200 B.C. also accompanied the charge of ancient warriors. Gunpowder was augmenting the lethality of fire arrows by the tenth century; a military commander by the name of Zhao Xie reportedly amassed an arsenal of 250,000 gunpowder arrows for the siege of one hapless city in that era. Over the centuries, the Chinese fashioned an astonishing collection of bombs that would kill, expose, or bring terror to their adversaries.[1]

The solid rocket came next. The Chinese made their first contraption sometime after 1150. They launched an arrow smeared with poison and with an iron balance to hold down the feathered end of the rocket-arrow. The science historian Joseph Needham cites a passage that describes how Chinese had learned to bore an internal cavity in the rocket propellant for more efficient burning: "If the hole is straight-sided (i.e. parallel with the walls of the tube) the arrow will fly straight; if it is slanting the arrow will go off at a tangent. . . . The shaft has to be absolutely straight, and the rocket-tube and [end-weight of] the arrow must balance perfectly."[2]

By the year 1300, the Chinese had further refined their rockets by constricting the orifice of the rocket-tube. This discovery of the Venturi-tube effect (some 500 years before the principle was formulated by Giovanni Venturi) underlies all modern-day designs of rocket nozzles. Soon thereafter, the Chinese fashioned stabilizing devices to their rockets, giving them the appearance of a medieval V-2, the German rocket that wrought havoc in wartime Britain.

Perhaps most revolutionary of all, Chinese rocket makers hit on the idea of multistage weapons sometime in the fourteenth century. One such projectile, a forerunner of the modern-day Exocet anti-ship missile, was made of two large tubes placed behind a carved dragon head. The fuel near the head of the apparatus would burn first, lighting the second stage just as the first-stage burn terminated. It would "fly 3 or 4 ft. above the water. . . . At a distance it really looks like a flying dragon coming out of the water."[3]

Thereafter, the Chinese inexplicably ceased their exploration into rocketry even as their inventions in this field were being transmitted to the West. The writer Wen Xing laments that many of his countrymen "with lofty ideals devoted their efforts to the development of China's space technology, but they made very little progress because of the limitations of various objective conditions."[4]

Soviet Assistance on the Submarine-Launched Missile

Despite some intriguing antecedents, China's modern missile enterprise cannot truly be traced to any ancient triumphs in rocketry but dates more unpretentiously from the mid-1950s. This chapter and the next two treat the history of China's first submarine-launched ballistic missile, the Julang-1, that was begun in that decade.

One year after the January 1955 decision to inaugurate the nuclear weapons program (Project 02), Mao Zedong directed research and development to start on aircraft and missile delivery systems for the future strategic warheads. A central figure in Mao's plan was the missile engineer Qian Xuesen, who had served as an officer in the U.S. army and had held professorships at both MIT and the California Institute of Technology. In February 1956, shortly after Qian's return to China from the Jet Propulsion Laboratory in California, he submitted a report on defense aviation to the Central Military Commission. Two months later, the commission accepted Qian's main recommendations and organized the Aviation Industrial Commission under Marshal Nie Rongzhen to manage the programs for guided missiles and military aircraft.[5]

In May, Nie signed off on a proposal to create an inaugural unit for developing surface-to-surface strategic missiles. Mao agreed in principle but, as was true of the later atomic bomb and nuclear submarine projects, he assumed the need for maximum Soviet technical assistance in the quest for modern missiles and ordered his negotiators to Moscow.[6] With the Soviet commitment of September 13 to provide that assistance, the Central Military Commission the next month formed the Fifth Academy under the Ministry of National Defense. Qian Xuesen was made director a few weeks later.[7]

Assigned to manage the missile program, the academy quickly organized specialized subordinate units to do the job: the First Subacademy (rocket engines), the Second Subacademy (control systems), an aerodynamic range, and a training unit for missileers.[8] By 1960, the Chinese authorities had transferred 100 experts and 4,000 college graduates to these units. In addition, the military sent the academy more than 1,000 senior and intermediate-level officers, mostly for the purpose of buttressing various political sections.[9]

Even as the engineers of the Fifth Academy were initiating the military-run missile program, their counterparts at the Chinese Academy of Sciences were ordered to conduct parallel work on missile technologies. In 1957, the academy designated its Institute of Mechanics to coordinate this work and transferred several experts on power engineering there from Shanghai and other parts of the nation.[10] Under the supervision of Qian Xuesen, who held the concurrent post of institute director, these experts set about investigating ideas for designing the first-generation sounding rockets.[11]

As one might expect, the engineers at the Fifth Academy initially dedicated their R&D efforts to surface-to-surface missiles powered by liquid-fueled engines, for by 1957 this was a domain in which there had already been a substantial transfer of Soviet technology. Though a small solid-propellant rocket program existed, it received much lower priority, and here Soviet assistance was negligible.[12] The decision taken shortly after to develop a modern navy was eventually to trigger stepped-up research on solid propellants.

In line with that decision, it will be recalled, China began pressing Moscow for assistance in its naval program, and Moscow, after backing and filling, finally agreed, in early 1959, to sell China the designs, technical data, and relevant equipment for (among other things) an R-11FM, a liquid-fueled SLBM (Chinese code name 1060).*

Though the R-11FM could only be fired from a surfaced submarine, it had been successfully flight-tested just four years earlier and was the best SLBM in the Soviet inventory at the time.[13] The Fifth Academy in due course received a complete set of design drawings and one prototype, immediately assigned its best Russian-speaking technicians to translate the drawings into Chinese, set a goal of two years for building its own version, the 1060, and began farming out the appropriate work assignments.[14]

Yet the 1060 was not at the top of the missile priority list. As a single-stage missile that had a maximum range of 162km and could deliver a 800-kilogram nuclear or conventional warhead,[15] it made a great deal of sense

---

* The Soviet specialist Mikhail Turetsky states that the Soviet Union supplied an R-13 (SS-N-4). This is incorrect. As the FM designation (*flotskaia modifikatsiia*; fleet model) indicates, R-11FM, was a navy version of an army missile (probably the SS-1B). For a description of the R-11FM, see Turetsky, 65–72.

for Soviet strategists seeking a quick-fix retaliatory weapon to offset the striking power of U.S. long-range bombers and European-based nuclear-armed systems. But the Chinese military soon decided that the 1060 did not have much strategic relevance for a country whose navy was charged wholly with "coastal defense" (*jinhai fangyu*).[16] With no prospects for expanding its naval reach soon, the high command had little interest in adopting a sea-based strategic posture. The missile submarine program, even if substantial Soviet aid was forthcoming, was many years away from completion, and military wisdom dictated that China for the immediate future concentrate on procuring a land-based strategic force. As a result, the Fifth Academy downgraded the 1060 and turned its development over to the navy. It transferred about 100 of the less-qualified missile experts to the naval units and made them responsible for working on the Soviet-supplied SLBM.[17]

Domestic events also weighed against the 1060. Some years before, in December 1957, the Soviet Union had delivered two land-based, liquid-fueled R-2 missiles to China.[18] The Chinese gave them the code name 1059, and it was these that now became the prime focus of the Fifth Academy's attention. The timing proved unlucky, however, for the decision to work on the R-2's development soon coincided with the high tide of the Great Leap Forward, when technology and reality fell victim to mob politics. As a result, both the 1059 and the 1060 programs lapsed, and when the time came to reactivate them, economic conditions made it imperative to choose between the two. It was an unequal contest after Lin Biao took over as minister of defense in 1959. The land-based missile program was to be awarded the highest priority, one even greater than the nuclear weapons program. In the words of his oral directive to all services on September 1960: "Give priority to missiles and nuclear bombs; [but compared with the atomic bomb,] give priority to missiles. Between surface-to-surface and surface-to-air missiles, give priority to surface-to-surface missiles" (*liangdan weizhu, daodan diyi; didi dikong, didi diyi*).[19] At a time when the entire nation was in retreat from the Great Leap Forward, and seeking ways to survive the "three hard years," Lin's new mandate had the effect of scrapping the 1060 project.

Had the Soviets been more forthcoming in their assistance to the missile submarine program, Lin might conceivably have been less categorical in defining his priorities. They were not. So with no apparent incentive or support to continue the 1060 project, no Chinese specialist was prepared to appeal for its retention, though the missile designers did dismantle the prototype for engineering clues and thereby gained some knowledge that later proved useful in the design of the first missiles for underwater launch.[20]

Besides, many of the designers at the Fifth Academy had already come to favor solid propellants from their study of the American Polaris program.* As a consequence, the Chinese put forward a formal request for Soviet aid on solid propulsion during Khrushchev's third visit to Beijing, September 30 to October 4, 1959.[21] At the low point in the exchanges, after Khrushchev had already refused to grant assistance on the nuclear submarine, Zhou Enlai mentioned his hope of obtaining SLBM technologies from the Soviet Union.[22] Both Nie Rongzhen and Luo Ruiqing sat in on this discussion to represent the military's position, but the conversation did not go well and allowed them no opening to state their case. Khrushchev rudely waved aside Zhou's request by implying that the Chinese would never be able to master the complicated technologies involved. He joked: "Aha, you had better manufacture [the missile] yourselves. We will order it after you have achieved success." Mao, it appears, had expected good news from the Zhou-Khrushchev meeting and became quite indignant after Zhou recounted the gist of the conversation.[23] All doubts were now erased. China would go it alone on the submarine missile.

Research on Solid-Propulsion Technologies

Though the Fifth Academy mustered most of its forces for the development of a liquid-fueled missile, it did not totally ignore the matter of solid propellants. Within months of the academy's creation in October 1956, it had formed ten research sections, each headed by a senior scientist.[24] With no apparent reference to any future submarine missile, one of these, Section 6, contained a three-person group to study solid propellants. From this modest beginning the Solid Propellant Research Group grew to include more than 70 people in 1960, and it was principally these researchers who denigrated the 1060's liquid-fueled engine for use in the nation's missile subs.[25]

As in the nuclear weapons program, the top specialists paid principal attention to the U.S. program, for as Mao once remarked, "What the enemy has, we must have." The Chinese quickly learned that the Americans

*The decision to go ahead with solid-propellant motors for the Polaris missile program would be made only when the nuclear specialists could promise to produce a warhead of less than 1,000 lbs that was capable of 1nm accuracy (circular error probable); when a guidance concept that would accommodate solid propulsion and a launch mode for a submerged but stopped submarine had been developed; and when the navy had managed to extricate itself from the army-led Jupiter program. This decision was reached in December 1956. Information from an American specialist, 1990.

had decided on solid-propellant motors for their submarine missile, and at the time they had no idea what type of engines the Soviet SLBMs would possess.[26] The Chinese did know that liquid engines might be best suited to steering the missile after an underway launch, that compared with solid rockets, the guidance system for liquid-fueled missiles was easier to build, that the range/payload ratio per volume was better for liquids, and that attitude vectoring and thrust termination would be simpler on liquids. By the time they had figured out the directions of the Soviet SLBM program and the advantages of the liquid engine, the Chinese were far too committed to the development of solid motors to alter course.

At first, the research group's technicians, all recent college graduates, knew little about missiles beyond elementary definitions and basic physics. They possessed no knowledge of the structure of solid propulsion and only minimal linguistic skills to tackle the mountain of foreign publications on these motors that had preceded them to the office of the Solid Propellant Research Group. After reading these publications as best they could, they were able to recite the formal meaning of such concepts as "composite propellants," "case-bonded grain," and "star-shaped internal hole," but any true understanding would be years in the making. They did recognize right away, however, that the project would be demanding and dangerous and had a high probability of failure. In their worst nightmares, they could imagine an unpleasant moment some years down the road when Mao's high priority nuclear submarine would be set to sail without his high priority solid-propellant SLBM aboard.

After intensive study of the foreign writings over many more months, the engineers of the Solid Propellant Research Group gradually came to grasp the general principles differentiating the structure of a solid-propellant motor from that of a liquid-fueled engine and had tested some of those principles in the laboratory. They recognized the need to produce a propellant that, when cast as a single, uniform solid or "grain," would be sealed to the rocket's steel jacket, or "case bonded," and that to prevent a burn-through of the jacket, a heat-insulating material would have to be installed between the case-bonded grain and the rocket casing. The grain, insulation, and motor casing thus would be an integrated whole. The center of the grain would have to have a hollow core, probably star-shaped, to yield a neutral burn; that is, a nearly constant thrust during the entire burn time.[27]

The engineers also studied various chemical mixtures of solid propellants and through reading and experimentation decided to concentrate their efforts at the outset on so-called composite propellants made by combining an oxidizer and an adhesive fuel. In general, solid propellants fall into two broad types (and a third that combines the two).[28] The first type, called double-base, constitutes "a homogeneous propellant grain, usually a nitrocellulose type of gunpowder dissolved in nitroglycerin plus minor percentages of additives. Both the major ingredients are explosives and function as a combined fuel, oxidizer, and binder." Composite propellants, by contrast, "form a heterogeneous propellant grain with the oxidizer crystals [usually ammonium perchlorate] and a powdered fuel (usually aluminum) held together in a matrix of synthetic rubber (or plastic) binder [which is also fuel]. . . . Composite propellants are less hazardous to manufacture and handle than double-based propellants." In the third type, the composite modified double-base propellant, the percentage of double-base materials is usually smaller.[29]

Foreign source materials had told the specialists in the research group that the oxidizer in the composite propellants could be either ammonium perchlorate or potassium perchlorate but had provided only minimal information on the adhesive for binding the oxidizer into a solid or grain. When one of the young technicians ran across an article published in the 1940s about the use of polysulfides as both liquids and solids, he and his colleagues surmised that they might fabricate one of these polysulfides for the adhesive binder.[30] They had made a good guess.

In an attempt to reach a breakthrough in grain casting, the group's technicians started experimenting on a variety of composite propellants. They ordered potassium perchlorate at first from the Harbin Military Engineering Institute and later from a plant in Dalian, Liaoning Province; a chemical plant in Shanghai provided the first batches of ammonium perchlorate. Through years of testing, the motor designers gradually settled on ammonium perchlorate as the best oxidizer, and by the mid-1960s, the Dalian plant was producing this compound at the standards required for the planned submarine missile.[31] With respect to the adhesive fuel, the Institute of Applied Chemistry was directed to manufacture liquefied polysulfide, which it succeeded in synthesizing in the spring of 1958.[32] Thereafter, the Academy of Chemical Engineering in Jinxi, Liaoning Province, took over the production of the polysulfide binder and joined a growing list of facilities in the Northeast assigned to the nascent solid-rocket program.

With the first run of oxidizers and binders in hand, members of the Solid Propellant Research Group started exploring the casting of propellant grains in their somewhat primitive laboratory. They immediately encountered severe problems. The high viscosity of the liquefied polysulfide ruined one casting after another, with the result that by October 1958, after months of wearisome effort, only one small grain the size of a fountain pen had been made. What was needed was a single uniform grain the size of the rocket motor itself.

The next year, the group sent technicians to Institute 3 (a facility we encountered in our earlier discussion of the missile ejection system) and Plant 845 in Xi'an to perfect the grain-casting techniques.[33] The technicians concentrated on ways to increase the fluidity of the liquefied polysulfides and over many months conquered the viscosity barrier. In 1960, at roughly the same time the 1060 project was being abandoned, they cast a grain for an experimental motor with a diameter of 65mm and conducted a successful test firing. The Fifth Academy finally had the evidence for staying with solid composite propellants.

In January 1961, in the course of a meeting called by the Defense Science and Technology Commission to debate ways to promote R&D on all missile propellants, the participants formulated a three-year plan of research on solid composite propellants. Recognizing the value of specialization, the next year the commission directed the Fifth Academy to make the Solid Propellant Research Group an independent body and to transfer the specialists working on solid propellants from Institute 3 to the group's new facility at Hohhot, Inner Mongolia. It was there that real progress would be made on grain-casting techniques.

Research on the Solid Motor

Impressed by that progress and by what he perceived to be the trend toward the use of solid propellants in all U.S. missiles, Nie Rongzhen at the Defense Science and Technology Commission, in May 1962, directed the Fifth Academy to attach greater importance to the solid-rocket program. In transmitting Nie's instruction to his colleagues, Qian Xuesen, then deputy director of the academy, reinforced Nie's decision by stressing the superior operational utility of solid over liquid-fueled missiles. The next month, the academy elevated the status of the Solid Propellant Research Group and ordered a speed up in the transfer of Institute 3's technicians to the staff of the director of what was now the Solid Rocket Motor Institute.[34]

The new institute's first assignment was to design a 300mm-diameter rocket motor with the proven solid composite propellant.[35] The purpose of a motor of this size would be propellant development, and the case, case bonding, and nozzles would have little to do with the final design of the JL-1 motor (except to define the propellant characteristics). In the autumn of 1962, Plant 845 in Xi'an helped install a large mixer and related equipment for test-casting a propellant grain of this dimension at the institute.

In the next few months, the missile case was manufactured and its insulator installed, and the propellant ingredients for the motor were cast in the mixer. After completing the casting process and fitting the nozzles to the case, the technicians demonstrated the motor at the nearby static test stand.

This quick success tragically led the workers to underestimate the perils of composite propellants, and their haste resulted in a fatal accident on December 6. While casting grains for the 300mm-diameter solid motors, 200kg of polysulfide caught fire in the mixer and exploded, causing heavy casualties, including four deaths. As a result of this and other setbacks, work on the motor slowed, and recurring debates erupted among the frightened technicians on how to proceed safely.

In the spring of 1963, Zhang Aiping, Nie's chief deputy at the Defense Science and Technology Commission, visited the institute to break the impasse. Zhang told the personnel there to work patiently on the fundamentals of the solid rocket and then to try to improve its quality a step at a time. The visit from Beijing appeared to calm the contentious and nervous atmosphere at the institute, and an orderly development process resumed.[36]

A year later, Zhou Enlai added his voice to the arguments about the conduct and value of the SLBM program by declaring, incorrectly it would seem, that solid rockets had better maneuverability and stability than liquid rockets.* At a meeting of the Fifteen-Member Special Commission, he said, "If we vigorously carry out coordination and cooperation among several units, we'll surely achieve success [in building solid rockets]."[37] This pronouncement had the effect of ending speculation that the solid-rocket program might be terminated and galvanized the defense industry's leadership to think ahead on the requirements for China's future SLBM.

The commission hinted, but did not make explicit, that the submarine missile would have the projected solid-propellant motor and opened the way for first thoughts about what a long-term SLBM program might require. In March 1964, the General Staff and Nie's commission jointly gave the projected missile its code name, *julong yihao* ("giant dragon no. 1") thereafter abbreviated as JL-1.[38] (Eight years later, Nie's commission changed *julong* to *julang*, or "giant wave," allowing the designator JL-1 to be retained.[39])

---

*Solid-propellant missiles have better operational readiness and are believed to be safer to store, though this is debatable. But they are not more stable over the long run and are not more reliable. Presumably, Zhou Enlai had received the conventional wisdom about the overall superiority of solid-propellant missiles and, because of his belief that the Americans would only adopt the most advanced system, chose to accept that wisdom at face value.

Two organizational changes over the next several months reflected the ever-greater weight given to work on solid propulsion systems. First, in April, the Solid Rocket Motor Institute was expanded to become the Solid Rocket Motor Subacademy (Fourth Subacademy) of the Fifth Academy. Then, in January 1965, in the reorganization that saw the Fifth Academy become the Seventh Ministry of Machine Building, the unit became a full-fledged academy. Drawing together a number of small units from other parts of the country, the new Solid Rocket Motor Academy (Fourth Academy) received authorization from Zhou Enlai to procure scarce building materials for enlarging its research complex in Hohhot.[40]

Compared with their counterparts in other academies of the missile ministry, all of which were located in Beijing, the technicians at the Fourth Academy in the Inner Mongolian desert lived under especially sparse conditions. They slept in adobe dormitories and existed on a diet of steamed corn, sorghum bread, and salted vegetables. The dormitories could not even accommodate a visiting spouse, and during the few times set aside for family get-togethers, the nearby fields had to serve as conjugal beds. A bitter-sweet memory of those who spent their married lives at Hohhot is one of fields dotted with colored handkerchiefs on bamboo poles that had been placed to warn off intruders during moments of intimacy.[41]

That same year, 1965, the Seventh Ministry completed work on an ambitious long-term program, the Eight-Year Plan for the Development of Rocket Technology.[42] It set as one goal the production of four kinds of land-based missiles by the year 1972.[43] In March 1965, the Central Special Commission approved this "four missiles in eight years" (*banian sidan*) plan and ordered its implementation.[44] The plan also "called for success ahead of schedule on a solid rocket" to be designed for launch from a submarine. The *julong/julang* was no longer just a dream of a few designers, though the project was still two years away from receiving a formal go-ahead.

Later in 1965, as the organizational system was coming together for both the nuclear-powered submarine and the SLBM, the technicians at the Fourth Academy achieved a breakthrough on the twin problems of unstable propellant burning and low levels of energy release by adding tiny (10μ to 100μ) aluminum spheres to the propellant grain.[45] Next, they found a way to cast larger propellant grains evenly within the casing without producing fissures. Within months, they had fabricated 28 300mm-diameter solid motors and conducted repeated experiments to test their operational characteristics and response to storage, shock, and vibration. By late August 1965, hot tests had been run on six of the motors minus their controls.[46] The propellant development was finally making enough progress to provide the data, and the incentive, to undertake R&D on the full-sized motor.

Once the researchers reached this stage, the ministry escalated its preparations for the JL-1 program. Several items were singled out for special attention: developing a new-type adhesive binder (polybutadiene), an ultra-high-strength steel for the motor casing, glass-fiber reinforced plastics, nozzles, and a nozzle lining; mastering the technologies for conducting thrust termination and thrust-vector control; and providing facilities for conducting static tests on larger missiles. To hasten this work, the ministry was authorized to turn for help to any plant or institute in the nation.[47]

Project JL-1

In late 1965, the technicians at the Fourth Academy, in collaboration with the nuclear submarine designers, started building a 654mm-diameter solid motor; this would be a little less than half the size of the projected JL-1 missile. They accepted polybutadiene as the best and now proven binder and stepped up research and development on the prototype solid-propellant motor, giving special attention to the requirements for casting case-bonded grains.[48] The R&D on experimental solid motors with diameters of 300mm and 654mm reportedly laid a basis for further improvements in solid propulsion technologies.[49]

During a three-day meeting of the special commission at the end of December, Zhou Enlai nudged the missile ministry to expedite work on all classes of missiles, and the word went out to the academy to make still greater efforts on Project JL-1.[50] The research facilities connected to the project thereafter underwent a bewildering series of reorganizations, ostensibly to remove various impediments to their work. That no single structure was stuck with for long testifies to Beijing's penchant for adopting tailor-made organizational solutions to all manner of specific problems and the myriad crises plaguing the society. Throughout the missile program, moreover, the leaders could seldom find the right persons for the job, and usually the reorganizations had been poorly thought through.[51] More often than not the results were disruptive not only for the individuals involved, but for the research effort as a whole.

In 1965, the Fourth Academy launched into a two-year course of preliminary studies on the most important technical problems. In 1967, with the results in hand, the special commission reviewed the academy's progress and tentatively approved the start-up of the project.[52] On the assumption that many of the liquid rocket technologies would have to be adapted to the solid missile, the ministry assigned the First Academy (Carrier Rocket

Research Academy) to manage the full project. Twelve years later, in 1979, the Second Academy (surface-to-air missile) was put in charge so the First could concentrate on the *dongfeng* (DF) series of land-based missiles and satellite launchers.[53] As the command structure shifted, the Fourth Academy adjusted its lines of operation to fit.

In making these bureaucratic changes, the Chinese paid close attention to publications on the U.S. Polaris project's Program Evaluation Review Technique (PERT), little realizing that this much-heralded management system disguised a something less than well-organized effort.[54] They were also attempting to copy, to the extent possible for their very different industrial system, the American method of having a general weapons system manager over multiple subcontractors with direct development and production responsibilities. Just as the TRW Corporation, for example, was awarded the general management contract for several of the U.S. Air Force's important missile programs, so the Seventh Ministry played the role of system manager in the Chinese scheme of things. It moved the management of program development from the Fourth to the First Academy because in 1967 the First was a much more competent body to complete the comprehensive design and on-board guidance and attitude controls for the JL-1. Then, in 1979, it moved the JL-1 project again, because, with the abandoning of the antiballistic program, the Second Academy had little to do and could relieve the First of the heavy JL-1 burden, allowing the First to concentrate on building the DF-5 ICBM.

At the outset, in 1965, three organs under the Fourth Academy had been given the most important tasks. The Solid Motor Strategic Missile Overall Design Department (Department 4) was in charge of conceptualizing the general configuration of the JL-1; the Solid Rocket Control System Institute (Institute 43) had the assignment of producing the JL-1's guidance and attitude control systems; and the Solid Rocket Motor Institute (Institute 41) was responsible for developing solid propulsion technologies. Of the three, only Institute 41 remained in Hohhot as the core body that continued perfecting solid-propellant technologies over the coming decades.

Both Department 4 and Institute 43 underwent many bureaucratic transformations in the succeeding years, and because of their importance to Project JL-1, we will pause to briefly review their history. The Fourth Academy had established Department 4 in August 1965. Two years later, after the ministry had granted broad authority for the project to the First Academy, the department, still in Hohhot, reported to its new academy boss in Beijing. By the end of the 1960s, the department had grown to about 400 technicians, and in May 1970, the ministry moved it to Beijing and appointed Huang Weilu the department head. In April 1979, it was moved to the Second Academy and put in charge of formulating and implementing the missile's design plans, including providing technical specifications to the various research units and coordinating these units. Its authority increased a few months later, when it absorbed Second's Institute 26, which had direct responsibility for China's antiballistic missile program.*

Immediately after Department 4 was created in 1965, it formed two units for the purpose of completing preparatory studies of the on-board missile guidance and attitude control systems. In order to bolster research on these systems, the ministry in May 1967 told the Fourth Academy to create the Solid Rocket Control System Institute (Institute 43) by amalgamating Institute 7 (an internal security organ) with those two units.[55] Six months later, the ministry moved the new institute from Hohhot to Beijing and placed it under the First Academy, which redesignated it Institute 17. Under Director Chen Deren, a leading specialist on missile control systems, technicians at Institute 17 completed the guidance and attitude control systems for the JL-1. In 1979, when Project JL-1 was assigned to the Second Academy, Institute 17 went with it. Figure 7 shows where these organizations fit in the general bureaucratic structure with that change.

In late 1965, Department 4, envisaging that the first and second stages of the JL-1 missile would be equipped with a 1,400mm-diameter motor, added research on a motor of the size to the scheduled development of the 654mm prototype. All the R&D work on the two new motors would extend the findings from the tests of the 300mm motor. Though the engineers worked on both the 654mm and 1,400mm motors, the latter quickly took precedence and eclipsed the effort on the smaller prototype.[56]

By 1966, the ministry and its counterparts masterminding the missile submarine felt confident enough of this preliminary development work to assign the Xinguang Machine Building Factory in Shenyang and the Carrier Rocket General Assembly Plant (Plant 211) in Beijing to attempt the manufacture of the 1,400mm casing. Almost immediately, the two plants

---

*In February 1964, Mao said, "The spear and shield [missile and antimissile missile] exist side by side. . . . We will spend ten years [to build the antimissile missile], if five years are not enough. We will even spend fifteen years, if ten years are not enough." Sixteen months later, the Second Academy set up Institute 26 and made it responsible for Project 640, the code name for the nation's antimissile missile project. The project consisted of five items: 640-1 (an antimissile missile), 640-2 (a secret "superweapon"), 640-3 (a laser weapon), 640-4 (an early warning system), and 650-5 (target discrimination). Several research facilities participated in the project. Reportedly, a prototype antimissile missile was successfully flight-tested in the late 1970s. In 1980, the Seventh Ministry formally abandoned the project. Gu Mainan, 14–16; Chen Bin et al., 102; Liu Congjun, *Hangtian . . . Yuanshi*, 167–69, 194.

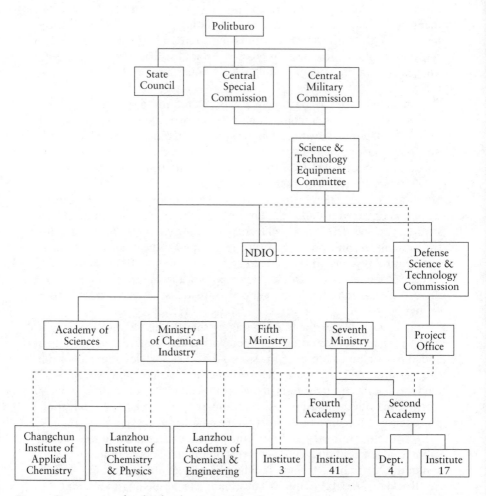

Fig. 7. Organization for the development of the JL-1 missile, 1979

encountered the same obstacle. Their furnaces were simply too small to temper (*cuihuo*) a casing of this size. Given the time pressures and financial constraints, there was only one solution: the casing would have to be worked in pieces, and then welded into a single rocket jacket. It was about this same time that the Fourth Academy overcame the casting difficulties, and in the late fall, the first case-bonded grain was cast with a diameter of 1,400mm and a star-shaped hollow core. On December 1, 1966, the first full static test of the motor was run at Hohhot.[57]

With this evidence of headway on the missile's controls, the Defense Science and Technology Commission in March 1967 received permission to continue Project JL-1. Meanwhile, the Chinese high command was closely watching the evolution of space technologies in the Soviet Union and the United States and was deeply impressed by their first-generation satellite reconnaissance systems.[58] The reconnaissance satellites of these two hostile nations, Beijing concluded, could locate and target all China's fixed land-based missiles, including those to be based in underground silos.[59] The Chinese leaders followed the literature on improvements in missile accuracy and even before their counterparts in Moscow and Washington reached similar conclusions, determined that China's projected strategic missiles and aircraft would soon be hopelessly exposed to a preemptive strike. For a time, Beijing joined the superpowers in flirting with antiballistic missile protection for its silos, but it eventually recognized the folly of this course, and abandoned the effort.[60]

In the next several months after the March go-ahead, the Chinese strategists pondered how to overcome the vulnerability of their nation's retaliatory forces. The only answer, they decided, was to abandon fixed systems and base China's strategic warheads on nuclear-powered submarines and on a new generation of mobile land-based missiles. In October 1967, armed with these findings, the Defense Science and Technology Commission and the navy convened a conference to examine the final comprehensive design plan for the JL-1. The next month, right in the midst of the chaos of the Cultural Revolution, the Central Military Commission officially ordered the final planning for Project JL-1 accelerated.[61]

For the first few months thereafter, as we have remarked, the burden for formulating a full plan fell on the Fourth Academy. But its personnel were clearly out of their depth. The engineers in Department 4 had trouble with one technical unknown after the other, as the questions tumbled in on them in seemingly endless profusion. How could the volume and weight of the missile be reduced? How could the safety and reliability of the missile and its associated equipment be assured? How could the missile be protected from sea water before launch and be ignited and go through stage separation after launch? How could the missile's flight path be corrected if it ignited sharply off-vertical? How could yaw deviations be controlled after launch? What would be the best way to connect the missile guidance systems to the shipboard target selection, navigational, guidance, and testing equipment?[62] To the extent that the sources are forthcoming, we shall try to indicate how the Department 4 engineers addressed these questions.

We do know that the technicians in the department, who were working directly with and under the prestigious First Academy in Beijing, spent seven months providing enough answers to these questions to complete JL-1's final plans. As concerns for solid propulsion technologies, they stipulated the following: the two stages of the missile would be 1,400mm-diameter solid-propellant motors; the motors would be equipped with a new kind of igniter and special safety components; a unique composite propellant would be cast with an oxidizer of ammonium perchlorate and a polybutadiene binder containing several additives; and the motor casing would be made of an ultra-high-strength steel. The plan further stipulated that a type of strapdown compensation system then being used in the land-based *dongfeng* missiles would be adapted to the JL-1, and that the second stage would be outfitted with an advanced type of thrust termination. The plan adopted several technologies for attitude control: an on-board gyroscope would serve as an inertial measurement device, thrust vectoring would be done by four first-stage rotating nozzles made of special metals, and a secondary liquid injection system would be added to the second-stage nozzles.[63]

The designers decided that the methodology for the test-launch should also be made part of the missile's comprehensive design plan. They recognized that SLBM test-launch procedures in other nations could be quite complicated—and expensive. Foreign missile builders had not test-launched their missiles from submerged submarines until they had completed a series of intermediate tests from various land-based and then fixed sea-based platforms, and this was the course contemplated in their plan as originally finalized and approved.[64]

Constructing the required facilities would require a substantial investment, money that the Chinese in the troubled years of the Cultural Revolution simply did not have. With state revenues for 1967 and 1968 off by 25 and 35 percent, respectively, from 1966,[65] defense research funds had to be slashed, and the Seventh Ministry accordingly telescoped the requirements for the test program. Just as the Fourth Academy was breaking ground near Hohhot for a large land-based laboratory for testing the missile's seaworthiness, word came down to place the construction on hold.

Department 4 then proposed a three-step test plan as a substitute for the now-aborted one. The missile would be test-launched from a submerged converted Golf-class submarine after trials first from land-based launching pads and then from land-based launch tubes. With the Central Military Commission's approval of the proposal in May 1970, construction of the seaworthiness laboratory was permanently shelved, for an eventual savings of nearly 100 million yuan and many months of intermediate testing.

But the test schedule was essentially all that changed. The fundamental structure of the design and building operations set forth in the original October 1967 blueprint remained more or less intact in the volatile years to come, as did the basic areas of responsibility it staked out: the Defense Science and Technology Commission would be generally responsible for decision making on all R&D plans, as well as for experiments on the missile ejection system; the Seventh Ministry would supervise work on the missile itself; and the navy would be in charge of the test launches.[66]

Turning the modified October 1967 designs into reality was something else again. Countless technical obstacles had to be overcome even as the political turmoil heightened tensions throughout the Seventh Ministry and its academies. The production of the motors alone involved manufacturing 91 types of materials with all sorts of variations in their individual specifications. To get the work done, the ministry had call on some 55 units working under other ministries in the fields of chemistry, metallurgy, ordnance, engineering, and petroleum. Along the way, the Chinese had to probe the scientific and engineering mysteries in disciplines that were not only still in their infancy in China but under assault. The military connection helped these fields mature intellectually and survive politically during the Cultural Revolution, though the going became increasingly rough.[67]

Early on in the project the engineers began wind-tunnel experiments at the ministry's Institute of Aerodynamics (Institute 701), in Yungang, 25 km southwest of Beijing, to verify the aerodynamic properties of different missile and reentry vehicle configurations.[68] The facilities available to them by then permitted tests at simulated speeds from low to hypersonic.[69] By trial and error, these experiments inched the project forward, confirming the optimal configuration for JL-1, and especially for its reentry vehicle.

The Impact of the Cultural Revolution

So far, we have suggested that the Cultural Revolution had a serious but not shattering effect on Project JL-1, and this was true to a large degree through early 1967. In retrospect, the survivors of the "decade of turmoil" begun by Mao in the summer of 1966 record that the principal impact of the orgy of "power seizures," denunciations, and mass demonstrations fell on the Defense Science and Technology Commission and the Seventh Ministry within the strategic weapons programs.[70] A superficial analysis seems to bear them out—to suggest that it was mainly the men in the top echelons who suffered under the onslaught, and that the system for developing the weapons, though battered, endured and recuperated more or less intact. To leave the matter there, however, would be quite misleading.

The system did not endure. In response to Mao's call to hunt down "reactionary leading academic figures," radicalized technicians and workers in the research organs under the commission berated, persecuted, and then sundered the relations between senior scientists and leadership cadres, between the technical community and the policy makers. In one "struggle meeting" after another, the bond of trust between higher and lower levels was shattered even as the ties of comradeship at each level gave way to personal vendettas and long-plotted campaigns of revenge. Fear for one's survival among the commission's staff reflected not only a concern for personal safety but a collapse of the broad social order.[71]

In his capacity as head of the commission, Marshal Nie Rongzhen was deeply troubled about the influence of the mass movement on the strategic weapons programs. Although he himself was never in serious physical (as opposed to political) danger, Nie did seek help from Fu Chongbi, commander of the Beijing Garrison, to defend the staff of those programs. He told Fu, "Now the rebels are charging the specialists [working] on the atomic bomb and missiles with being 'reactionary leading academic figures' and are eager to expose them. Could we have detonated our atomic bomb without the [specialists'] efforts? . . . Can you figure out a way to allow them to continue their research?" Fu said he could and promptly dispatched guards to shield the defense scientists. But he could do nothing to redeem the vision to which they had devoted their lives or to restore order to the chaos around them.[72]

In fact, the disaster was only staved off a bit longer in the missile ministry than elsewhere. The splintering into warring factions spread swiftly there after late 1967, with most of the administrative staff and junior and intermediate-level officials joining the September 15 Rebellion Corps, and virtually all the engineers and technical workers joining the September 16 Rebellion Corps. Ye Ying, Lin Biao's sister-in-law, was the behind-the-scenes leader of the first corps, which denounced followers of the deposed Luo Ruiqing and members of the National Defense Industry Office (NDIO), including Zhao Erlu; the September 16 corps, which is to say, the scientific community, backed the NDIO and assailed Nie Rongzhen and his Defense Science and Technology Commission.[73]

Violence repeatedly exploded between these two diametrically opposed organizations. One of the most famous clashes broke out on June 8, 1968, at the ministry's First Academy, which had only months before taken over the assignment of developing Project JL-1 from the Fourth Academy. A mob of thousands of self-appointed young Maoists joined the fray, contributing more than their share to the casualties. Among those killed was the Director of Institute 703, Yao Tongbin. One of the leading experts of his day, Yao was then heading a team to conduct intensive tests on materials required for the JL-1 missile. His death was a major blow to the project.

Alarmed by Yao's death, Zhou Enlai immediately ordered Su Yu, the head of the NDIO's military control committee and himself a target of the September 15 corps, to conduct a thorough investigation into the causes of the incident and issued a directive forbidding further assaults on the defense scientists for any reason.[74] Zhou afterward directed the control committee to draw up a list of the scientists who were indispensable to the weapons programs and to place them under special protective custody.[75]

Isolation did not protect JL-1's test bases any more than it did the other remote strategic weapons bases, though serious violence did not occur again until 1974. For years the bases could not escape the society-wide anarchy.[76] On one occasion, for example, Huang Weilu and his team set out for a missile test base to conduct an ejection test, only to be balked by warring factions of railway workers.[77] Absorbed in struggle meetings, the workers simply shunted the team's train onto a siding far from food and water. When an urgent message for help finally reached the ministry, its cadres, too, were preoccupied with the campaign slogans of the moment, and when they refused to act, the plans for the test had to be junked. A woman technician on the team thereupon burst into tears and told Huang: "We devote every effort to prepare for the test and haven't made any mistakes. Why do they deliberately make things difficult for us? I would rather quit the job!" Huang had no reassuring reply. His despair was even greater than hers, for he realized that the cohesion and drive long sustaining the weapons effort had evaporated.

Indeed, Project JL-1 engineers found themselves constantly flirting with disaster. A "red terror" reigned at the First Academy for years, some say for the entire period from early 1968 to the end of 1971. More than 1,300 staff members were publicly criticized and harried to make confessions. By 1970 alone, the academy's military control committee had accused 746 technicians of having made serious errors and had rallied hundreds of "mass dictatorship" groups to scrutinize their cases. In the process of these examinations, three of the technicians committed suicide, and others became seriously disturbed mentally.[78]

The persecution of defense scientists endlessly delighted their revengeful tormentors, and it reached its high tide in the radicals' campaign to purify the class ranks, designed to sow fear and destroy self-esteem.[79] Petty "offenses" could elicit the most damning allegations, as one technician discovered who had an imported typewriter. Ignorant security officers accused him of "having a transceiver used by a special agent," an accusation that could carry the death penalty. Another technician noticed that one of the multitude of Mao statues being erected was off balance, and he unthinkingly commented, "It looks like it's falling." Security officers accused him of implying that Mao "looks like he is coming to grief" and arrested the hapless engineer. And so the atrocities multiplied.[80]

The case of the senior missile guidance specialist Song Jian illustrates the kinds of abuses to which intellectuals were typically subjected. He felt the rebels' wrath in June 1968, when they ransacked his home and confiscated his property.[81] Trained in Moscow, Song had been in charge of planning the first generation of surface-to-air missiles and had established himself as a top expert on missile controls.[82] At the time of the Red Guards' invasion of his home, Song was deputy director of Institute 26, in charge of the technical side of the anti-ballistic missile project. Alarmed by the attack on such a pivotal scientist, Zhou Enlai immediately added Song to the list of those to be protected and transferred him to a base far from Beijing for his personal safety.[83] Those not so prominent were less fortunate.

Zhou finally acted to squelch the open warfare between the two factions at the Seventh Ministry and its academies. He orchestrated some 20 meetings of the leaders of the two rebellion corps with senior ministry officials.[84] Threatening punishment and playing on their patriotism, he finally brought emotions under control and forced an end to the most crippling demonstrations. Under Zhou's prodding, the two factions temporarily receded into the background, their leaders awaiting later opportunities for revenge.

The truce did seem to buy time, but in the autumn of 1969, just as preparations for launching the nation's first satellite were nearing completion, tempers again flared and fights erupted. On August 9, Zhou convened yet another urgent meeting to assure himself that nothing would interrupt the satellite launch. He charged Yang Guoyu, deputy head of the ministry's military control committee, with guaranteeing the safety of the scientists engaged in the project. When Zhou received the names of scientists needing protection, he approved the list and issued a directive to the control committee: "You may resort to force to protect them if anyone attempts to inflict physical abuse on them or to kidnap them. In short, your task is to do whatever you can to protect them from being disturbed or punished."[85] At the time, Huang Weilu, the specialist on missile guidance whom we encountered during the train incident, was doing forced manual labor, found his name on the list and, with some trepidation, returned to his office. The next year, the ministry put him in charge of the comprehensive design plan for Project JL-1.[86]

The project also could not avoid the disruptive consequences of the massive shift to the Third Line. Responding to Mao's somewhat frenzied renewal of his call for that shift in 1969, Zhou Enlai ordered the Seventh Ministry to rush the building of Third-Line bases for the strategic missile programs, even if those programs themselves were harmed. The ministry had started construction on a large-scale research facility in Lantian, Shaanxi Province, in 1966, and regarded it as a rear base of the Fourth Academy in Hohhot, Inner Mongolia, some 750km to the north.[87] Following Mao's call, the Central Special Commission selected this site for the design of equipment for casting large case-bonded grains for solid motors,[88] and the ministry accelerated the construction at Lantian. The design, manufacture, and assembly of this equipment were farmed out among roughly 100 research institutes and plants under ten ministry-level departments.[89]

The geographical scattering of Project JL-1 tended to exaggerate the system's human and professional disintegration. On balance, over the ten-year period of social turmoil, R&D on the JL-1 came to a virtual standstill. The flight test of the missile was postponed, and development took years longer than originally scheduled.[90] And the selfless and purposeful drive that brought so many triumphs in the strategic weapons arena had largely vanished, never to return to its earlier pinnacle.

In looking back at the damage wrought by the Cultural Revolution, Nie Rongzhen lamented that the "scientific research core" of the defense establishment had been decimated. Extremists had persecuted, even killed, leading scientists and administrators; programs had been stopped and equipment destroyed.[91] Equally distressing, projects like JL-1 had become the spoils in an endless power game, not the means of attaining China's cherished global status and security. Gradually, the lofty vision of building a militarily strong China had been pushed aside and with it, the spirit of personal sacrifice.

For the JL-1 project in particular, the change was fundamental. No longer could the engineers at the First Academy, for example, unquestioningly trust their national leaders, let alone their fellow workers. Everyone knew that Mao's authority had withered and been subverted to preposterous, often monstrous, ends. Building a modern submarine missile had now become a technical job, not a crusade, and in subtle ways, the First's engineers succumbed to the sins of their brothers in civilian industry: indolence, indiscipline, and incompetence. In 1975, Deng Xiaoping was to denounce such sins as endemic in the military, but before the Cultural Revolution, the strategic programs would have been exempted from Deng's indictments, as he himself was to stress.[92]

The total system failure of the years of turmoil had taken these programs out of their predicted orbits. Strategic doctrines and explicit strategies had been unnecessary before then because the programs' goals seemed so self-evident and so intimately linked to the leadership networks. By the early 1970s, all that had changed. The Central Military Commission had dissolved into a propaganda machine issuing inane directives, the major organs of the defense industry—the National Defense Industry Office and the Defense Science and Technology Commission—had become locked into an orgy of perpetual revenge with their leaders in disgrace, the navy and the Seventh Ministry had split into hostile factions, and the First Academy was in a state of shock. As Deng Xiaoping returned to power in 1977, the best he could do was to accent the need for adherence to regulations, for reorganization of the leading bodies, and for the cleansing of the military's top brass of evil and hated men.[93] He could not put the military Humpty Dumpty back together again.

When China entered the race for strategic weapons in the 1950s, there was a defiant, almost arrogant quality to its quest. Following the missile and nuclear tests of the early to mid-1960s, the grand overseer of the program, Nie Rongzhen, not only could herald the string of technological victories but also could forecast unabated advances toward parity with the great powers. The first atomic test, he said, "marked the bankruptcy of the imperialists' policy of nuclear monopoly and nuclear blackmail, and frustrated the attempts to pressure the Chinese people into submission." To Nie, it was obvious that the strategic programs had produced more than "missiles and nuclear bombs by concerted attacks on the key problems." They had "stimulated the development of many new materials, meters and instruments, and heavy equipment needed for economic construction and promoted the establishment and development of many new production departments and branches of science."[94] He was implying that the military industry was the pacesetter for all modernization in China.

Despite Mao's demand in 1956 for spending more on civilian economic construction and less on the military, the reverse had been true for a quarter century. The economic disaster that accompanied the Cultural Revolution restored the general economic imperative, and after Lin Biao's demise, the leadership began lowering the military's budget and its power over the nation's industry. The decline of the military industrial system was evident to all.

When Deng Xiaoping spoke on military power to the Central Military Commission in 1977, the mood of confidence had shrunk to a plea for buying time. No more could Deng share Nie's self-assurance. Instead he had to resort to the dogma of People's War to save China over the long run because "even if we gain 10 or 20 years in which to modernize our army's equipment, it will still be inferior to the enemy's." He could not foresee a time when this situation would be "completely changed."[95]

Moreover, Deng gave no special credit to the military for major scientific and technical contributions to the nation's economic development. In a national meeting on science in 1978, he praised scientists in general for producing instruments and creating new industries, "including high-polymer synthesis, atomic energy, electronic computers, semiconductors, astronautics, and lasers" without mentioning that all these and many more had been developed in defense programs such as Project 09.[96]

In short, the dynamic synergy that had linked high politics and strategic programs had all but disappeared. What the Cultural Revolution had done was to smash the bonds between Mao's worldview and the worldview of the strategic weaponeers. The two views had overlapped in important ways, mostly as they focused on the role of military power in achieving national goals. Earlier, we described the different but closely connected emphases expressed at the 1958 meeting of the Central Military Commission that launched Project 09. A decade later, these differences had become bitter, personal, and antithetical.

Regaining the Momentum

As one political campaign followed another in the Cultural Revolution, the best the JL-1 builders could do was to try to insulate themselves as much as possible and concentrate on their own seemingly endless technical difficulties. By early 1970, technicians at the Changchun Institute of Applied Chemistry and the Lanzhou Academy of Chemical Engineering were able to supply Institute 41 with a polybutadiene binder.[97] The other materials and components for the motor had already arrived, and the engineers at Plant 692 in Luzhou, Sichuan Province, and elsewhere had answered the principal questions on the solid-propellant igniters and the missile rivets.[98] In April 1970, the technicians at Institute 41 built a prototype solid motor with a diameter of 1,400mm and conducted a complete-process test, with positive results. But they could not repeat the results and concluded that they had been a fluke.[99]

Moreover, a series of mishaps occurred at a grain-casting plant attached to the institute because of the inadequacy of the directions given to replacement workers for producing the propellant. In the worst accident, on

March 16, 1974, Wang Lin, the deputy leader of the workshop where the propellant compound was being mixed, was killed when his crew started an experiment without taking the proper precautions, and the mixer exploded, blowing a protective door off its hinges and full force onto Wang.[100]

For a while nothing seemed to go well. Overcoming the main technical obstacles in casting the large case-bonded grains appeared to be relatively easy and straightforward in one test, only to elude the researchers in the next. The worst headaches came from failures in bonding the propellant to the motor casing, in achieving the specifications for hermetic sealing, and in ensuring the casing's structural strength.[101]

In tackling all of these problems, the missile engineers lacked the necessary detectors to locate the flaws in the large-sized grains, and test operations on each problem proceeded by trial and error—mostly by error. The survivors of this ordeal recall that the fabrication of the JL-1 motor at this late stage constituted the most important but most difficult achievement in the entire SLBM program. It is not a happy memory.

A team formed earlier by the Fourth Academy in Hohhot and headed by Cui Guoliang bore the main brunt in removing the endless technical obstacles. Cui, a top expert on solid propulsion technologies, had completed graduate work in the Soviet Union and, since 1961, had worked exclusively in that field.[102]

Cui urged his colleagues to read systematically the few reference materials in the academy's library on mechanics, materials, chemistry, dynamics, and grain-processing techniques and to draw as many ideas as possible from the general literature. Between this and what they could learn from soliciting the help of research organs and industrial plants across the country, the team hoped to turn his research findings into a workable motor. But the responses from the outside were slow in coming and often flawed.

The Fourth Academy, likewise, looked for outside help, requesting the Steel and Iron Research Academy in Beijing to fabricate and cast a new kind of steel alloy for the rocket casing, and Institute 17 to work on the rotating nozzles for thrust vector control on the first stage.[103] All these parts and the heat-insulating material to be installed between the grain and the casing required important advances in alloys, plastics, and bonding processes.[104] They, too, were slow in coming.

After years of tedious labor, the industrial facilities under the Ministry of Metallurgy, in cooperation with the iron and steel academy, finally cast the steel casings and nozzles and developed special metals for the nozzle lining.[105] They devised techniques to isolate the rare elements contaminating the alloys and remove them.[106] The learning curve began to scale upward.

And in time the political uproar subsided, though it did not disappear entirely and could recur without warning. The fact that the missile builders found a friend in the new director of the Defense Science and Technology Commission, Zhang Aiping, certainly helped.[107] Zhang attached great importance to Project JL-1, and soon after his appointment in March 1975, he visited the First and Fourth academies and exhorted them to redouble their efforts in coordinating and promoting the project. He encouraged Chief Designer Huang Weilu, Cui Guoliang, Xiao Gan, and other specialists to accelerate their work on solid propulsion technologies and promised them greater protection from the continuing struggle outside their gates. Nonetheless, given the larger events in China, Zhang's words still had a hollow ring, and in any case, his influence over the defense science system faded toward the end of the year with the resurrection of the radicals, led by the Gang of Four.[108]

It was not until the fall of the Gang in October 1976 that an acceptable tempo returned to Project JL-1. Zhang Aiping then staged a comeback as commission head and marked the conclusion of the Cultural Revolution by breathing life into Project 09.[109] Almost a year later, in September 1977, Zhang submitted a report to the Central Military Commission on the development of the nation's strategic strike forces, including the DF-5 ICBM and the JL-1 SLBM. The commission promptly approved the report and urged the Seventh Ministry to speed up the research and development on both.[110]

Promoted to director of Institute 41, Cui Guoliang had the duty of translating these orders into a realizable schedule. By early 1978, the Changchun Institute of Applied Chemistry and the Lanzhou Academy of Chemical Engineering had improved the quality of the polybutadiene binder;[111] technicians at Plant 692 had developed workable solid-propellant igniters; and Plant 5334 had made special rivets for the missile. A team at Institute 41 conducted a complete-process test on the first-stage motor of the JL-1, and by May, the team had built a prototype first-stage that basically reached the acceptable standard.[112] Cui was appointed deputy chief designer of the JL-1 project the following April, and as a first priority, he started rebuilding some of the broken ties within the Fourth Academy.[113]

Cui's institute then conducted complete-process static ground tests on more than ten complete motors consisting of both stages of the missile and achieved satisfactory results.[114] By late 1980, the performance of the JL-1 motors had reached the design specifications set by Department 4. The institute promptly delivered eight of them to the department, and the ministry could celebrate the end of the 13-year quest for dependable SLBM propulsion. For obvious reasons, the celebration was muted.

SEVEN

Guidance and Flight Control

On that unlikely day when nuclear warheads rain down on China, senior members of the Central Military Commission will order a retaliatory strike. From the underground command center at Yuquanshan Mountain in the Western Hills outside Beijing, the order is flashed to the Operations Department of the General Staff: destroy enemy cities A, B, and C.[1] The department's officers, not a computer, decide that A and B can only be reached by the land-based missiles located in Qinghai Province, but that ballistic-missile submarine 406 at its assigned station at sea can use two of its missiles to attack target C. The operations officer confirms the command and communicates the target order to the navy headquarters special operations officer with the proper authentication codes. The officer tells the radioman to send the firing command to 406 in digital code. On board the sub, the captain receives the command, confirms it, and inserts it in the target data computer memory. The horn sounds, and the crew goes to general quarters. Step one in the fire control sequence is complete. There is no special key system, only years of discipline and a stern political officer who authenticates the order as the countdown begins. For 406, nuclear war has begun.

Such was the scenario that planners could imagine in the 1960s. To realize the mission, the builders of the submarine had to devise reliable navigational and fire control systems. The first would provide continuing updates to fix the boat's position, velocity, and azimuth reference at the moment of firing, and the second would convert the target coordinates, adjusted for the earth's rotation during time of flight, to the required direction and velocity of the missile at the moment of thrust termination. The mission of the missile builders was to make sure that the missile could hit its target with reasonable accuracy.

Concepts of Missile Guidance and Flight Control

Contemporary missile forces require sophisticated engineering for stabilizing and directing weapons through outer space to preselected destinations.[2] Their guidance and flight control systems, a triumph of modern industrial technologies, have three functions. The first is to maintain missile stability or attitude. The second is to turn or "pitch" the missile onto a proper target heading in the boost phase of the flight. The final function is engine thrust shutdown.[3] Missile guidance and flight control utilize the most advanced concepts of mechanical engineering, electronics, and navigation.

The system, shown schematically in Figure 8, executes the stabilization or attitude control function by sending signals from a stabilized platform to the flight control subsystem, which converts the signals into commands to the thrust vector servos for execution; the outputs of the accelerometers, also part of the stable platform, are sent to the guidance inflight computer and are used to track boost-phase velocity. That subsystem determines flight-path commands for the missile flight controls and fixes the moment of shutdown.[4] In organizing their missile design groups, Chinese engineers divided the missile control systems into two closely connected subsystems: attitude control and guidance. The first subsystem ensures stability by keeping the missile from tumbling and properly pointed (function 1); the second determines the missile's range and accuracy (functions 2 and 3).[5]

Corrections to the missile's attitude (function 1) require the detection of angular accelerations with respect to its three axes: right or left along the vertical or yaw axis; rotational along the longitudinal or roll axis; and up and down along the lateral pitch axis. The forces along any one of these axes or vectors are introduced by changing the thrust in the direction of one or more of them, and together their control is called thrust-vector control. The attitude-control subsystem measures the missile's attitude with respect to the three axes and issues the gimbal-angle commands to the thrust-vector control servo mechanisms in the missile flight controls.

Four events size thrust-vector control during the boost phase. The first of these is called launch recovery and occurs when the SLBM breaks the surface. At this point, the missile can be as much as 60° off-vertical. A rapid thrust must be introduced to keep it from tipping over entirely and to point it on its powered-flight trajectory. The next two events come at the times of maximum aerodynamic pressure, or "max q," and stage separation (when there is a small delay in second-stage ignition), and the fourth is caused by shifts in the missile's center of gravity as the propellant is expended. Keeping a missile stable is sometimes compared to balancing a

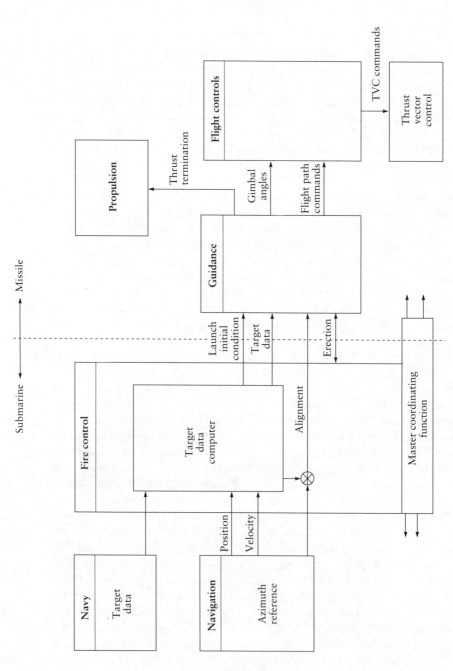

Fig. 8. A missile's guidance and flight control systems. Source: Bob Dietz.

pencil in the air on the tip of one's finger, but in this case the shape and composition of the "pencil" are more supple, the aerodynamic pressures on it are far greater, and the mass and center of gravity are constantly changing.

During the experimental years of missile development, engineers in many countries fashioned devices to carry out the thrust-vector control commands for maintaining missile stability. They installed graphite jet vanes, vernier engines, swivelling motors, and several types of nozzles. After early experiments with other types of mechanisms, a type of rotating nozzle and a fluid-injection nozzle became the mainstays for achieving stability on the solid-fueled missiles in most foreign programs at the time China was designing its first-generation *julang* missiles.[6] The Chinese studied these programs and incorporated what they learned in their own planning.[7]

Prior to launch, the crew uses optical beams from the navigational system to fix the missile's position. The guidance subsystem also receives data on the target and the initial launch condition via the fire control computers. The data include information on alignment (where is north) and erection (where is up). After the missile is launched, guidance subsystem computers compare data from the accelerometers to the preset "correlated velocity" in order to calculate commands to both the flight-control and engine-shutdown mechanisms. Corrections can also be introduced after launch for the missile's drift off course.[8] The U.S. and Soviet designers initially used so-called implicit inertial guidance systems.* In the 1970s, Western engineers added stellar inflight correction to improve the accuracy of missiles launched from undersea platforms.[9]

Comprehensive Design of JL-1's Guidance Flight Controls

As work proceeded on the JL-1's two-stage engine, other crews were working on the missile's guidance and flight controls. The initial burden fell on the design department (Department 4) of the Seventh Ministry's Fourth Academy (Solid Rocket Motor Academy), which was preparing the comprehensive design plan. By October 1967, when the academy submitted the document, the department engineers had convinced their superiors that the missile's guidance and flight control subsystems should be more

---

*There are a number of different guidance concepts. The early V-2 type missiles used mixed inertial and radio guidance (where a ground-based station keeps the missile in its "equisignal" plane), whereas the Soviet liquid-fueled missiles adopted fly-the-wire guidance (where the missile flies a preprogrammed acceleration profile). Implicit inertial guidance employs the concept of correlated velocity, in which velocity is modified in flight by compensation coefficients or "Qs." There are several other inertial or inertial-aided concepts in use.

advanced than any then installed on the land-based ballistic missiles. The next month, the Defense Science and Technology Commission and the navy approved the recommendation in principle.[10]

The engineers understood from easily available literature on missile controls that there were fewer options for thrust-vector control in solid rockets than in liquid-fueled missiles.[11] Gimbaling the main thrust chamber, for example, was impractical in a solid-propellant missile because the engine was bonded to the missile casing.[12] Drawing on their analysis of Western sources, Beijing's designers chose two technologies to develop for thrust-vector control: modified rotating nozzles for the first-stage engine and liquid-injection nozzles for the second stage.[13] Neither of these two types of nozzles had yet been used in the land-based strategic missiles, DF-2 through 4.[14]

The principal types of rotating nozzles tested by the Chinese for the first-stage engine could force a maximum angular change between 12° and 20°. In one type, a concentric ring made of high-strength metals and layered elastics connects the fixed and flexible parts of the nozzle, and commands from the guidance subsystem to the thrust-vector control servos and thence to the nozzles cause changes in the nozzle angles. The main technical problems confronting the Chinese were devising techniques for making fine adjustments in the control torque and protecting the hermetic seals in the concentric rings during first-stage engine burn.[15]

The injection technology for the four second-stage nozzles could have used liquid or gas as the high-pressure fluid for follow-on thrust-vector control after first-stage separation. The JL-1 nozzle was relatively simple to design but, like all rocket nozzles, it was difficult to fabricate because of the problems of bonding different materials for the housing, heat sink, insulator, and flame barrier.[16] In some Western missiles, the second-stage nozzles use liquid freon, which is injected through four servo-activated injectors; the Chinese used freon and also hydrogen peroxide.[17] When injected into the exit cones, the freon or hydrogen peroxide deflects the flow of exhaust gases, changing the thrust direction.

In 1967, JL-1's guidance-system designers decided to copy foreign models as best they could and to use an inertial guidance subsystem composed of gyroscopes, accelerometers, computers, and servo mechanisms for control and shutdown. The ministry's First Academy (Carrier Rocket Research Academy) had already adopted inertial guidance for use in the land-based DF ballistic missiles, and the Department 4 engineers held that they could successfully adapt that guidance system to their first-generation submarine-launched missile.[18]

Inertial control is self-contained and requires no external energy or radiation source to determine its operation. It emits no signal, and it does not depend on ground equipment to operate it once the missile is launched. The control operations make use of Newton's second law of motion, which states: "The rate of change in the momentum of a body is proportional to the force acting on the body and is in the direction of the force."[19] An unbalanced force acting on a body causes it to accelerate in the direction of the force, and the acceleration is directly proportional to the unbalanced force and inversely proportional to the mass of the body.

The inertial guidance used in all early missiles, including China's, worked only during the boost phase or up to completion of the fuel burn. Missilemen would feed in precise information that correlates to the predicted target information and the initial launch condition. The system alters the early flight path to compensate for undesired changes in missile acceleration. The course corrections can offset differences in speed and direction caused by the wind, atmospheric conditions, and variances in the missile configuration and engine performance. Although corrections can be introduced during the ballistic or free-fall part of the trajectory in some advanced guidance systems, no Chinese missiles have this capacity so far as is known.

The Chinese considered using either a strapdown or a stabilized platform guidance system. The rate gyros and accelerometers in an ideal strapdown type are fixed to the missile body, with pickoffs sent to a very high speed orientation computer.[20] The system has the advantages of a simple structure and high reliability. However, the accelerometers measure only the missile body-oriented accelerations, and the real accelerations of the rocket must be computed taking into account the missile's real-time attitude in space. The real numbers are then used to calculate true velocity or true range from time of launch. When the velocity or range is equal to the precalculated or theoretical one, the system shuts off engine thrust, thereby controlling the rocket's final range.[21] For accuracy, the pure strapdown system requires high-speed and high-capacity computers. In theory, the Chinese might have sidestepped the need for such computers by creating a hybrid strapdown system, which would put the gyros on a stable platform but have the accelerometers attached to the missile frame, but they did not. In the early DF-2 series, they simply could not solve the problems involved in building any type of stable platform.* As a result they stayed with the strapdown system for the DF-3 and DF-4.

---

*Accelerometers measure linear accelerations in all three perpendicular directions along the pitch, roll, and yaw axes. Gyroscopes detect changes in the missile's angular orientation about the three axes. This type of system puts both the gyros and the accelerometers on a stabilized platform. It includes stabilizing and pickoff circuits and

The First Academy directed the Department 4 designers to make full use of the knowledge of flight controls gained during the development of the DF liquid-propellant missiles. Accordingly, they adapted the DF-3 and -4 strapdown compensation system then being deployed in their original plan. The term "compensation" simply referred to Chinese-invented formulas containing compensation coefficients to increase the missile's accuracy.[22] The formulas constituted a major technical breakthrough and had brought a state science prize to their inventor. They made it possible to make calculations directionally on the apparent accelerations and did not require transformation into real accelerations. Moreover, the designers argued that since it was unnecessary to make real-time calculations during the boost phase, only a simple calculating device rather than a sophisticated computer would have to be installed on the missile.

Department 4 specialists had made only a bare start on the redesign of the DF inertial guidance for the JL-1 when, in October 1968, the Seventh Ministry decided to replace the strapdown compensation system with a more advanced platform system.[23] Many of the designers, however, considered the platform system a step backward, and a raging debate ensued. At this moment, it will be recalled, the entire missile program, like the nation around it, was embroiled in political struggle, and no debate could be conducted on purely technical grounds. Opponents of the change argued that the platform type had yet to be perfected, while the strapdown compensation type had been rigorously tested in the deployed DF missiles.

The advocates, while acknowledging the risks of the platform system, offered extensive calculations showing that the strapdown system, however advanced, could not provide the required maneuverability for an SLBM launched in turbulent seas. What sealed their case, though, was the argument that the JL-1 with the platform system would be the first Chinese missile to employ the recently developed floated-gyro inertial components, putting Mao's missile program on a par with the world's best. In the Cultural Revolution, even an implied endorsement by China's Chairman could settle the technical debates, and the platform system won the day.

That decision behind them, the designers went to work on the platform system, but they now faced a new difficulty, one in which they had no DF experience to draw on. In contrast to a liquid-propellant rocket, where

gimbals that allow the inertial components to remain stable in their predetermined launch position and independent from the missile's movement. The accelerations measured by this type of inertial mechanism are real. Gao Keren and Yu Huijie, 178; Zou Jiahua, 169; Ying Zhe, 7. The gimbaled platform makes sensor operations easier and lowers the requirements for gyro accuracy and for computer capacity and speed in comparison to the strapdown type. But it also has a more complicated structure, is more expensive, and is of lower reliability than the strapdown system.

thrust is terminated simply by shutting off the flow of fuel, the thrust in a solid-propellant rocket continues until the fuel is exhausted and can only be neutralized by one of several methods: "rapid depressurization, reversal of thrust direction, inert liquid quenching, or a combination of these."[24] After investigating each of these methods, all of which had been listed in the 1967 design plan, the engineers decided to apply reverse nozzle technology to the missile's second-stage engine.[25]

Electronic Quality Control and the Technical Foundations of Doctrine

One thing JL-1's designers were sure of from the start: the electronic elements of the flight control system would clearly tax their engineering skills even more than the design of the mechanical components. Most of them had been repeatedly frustrated by electronic mysteries in the DF program, and solving those mysteries for a new guidance system and missile operating in an entirely unknown underwater medium gave them moments of painful anxiety.[26] Understandably, they put off as long as possible confronting the even more distressing problems associated with the hardening of electronics against nuclear radiation.[27]

The task of building compact, high-performance electronics equipment for all military programs fell to the Fourth Ministry of Machine Building, which commanded an impressive empire of some 2,450 factories and 100 research institutes, as well as training academies and administrative or liaison organs. For the ministry and its provincial affiliates, the assignment could not have come at a worse time. It was bad enough to work in a global jungle governed by severe restraints on technology transfer. Now they were being summoned to fill the needs of the high-priority JL-1 program in a world gone mad. Little wonder that the electronics specialists greeted their assignment with mixed feelings.[28]

The ministry had been an early target of the Cultural Revolution. In May 1967, the Central Military Commission had sent a military control committee to wrest power from the senior officials there.[29] All technically illiterate newcomers, the committee leaders immediately declared that political campaigns should take precedence over technical programs, adding insult to injury by insisting that the technology effort could only prosper as a result. Politics thus overturned normal operations in the name of unparalleled progress. It was this fantasy land that received the most exacting JL-1 orders.

When armed conflicts erupted on the Sino-Soviet border in March 1969 and war appeared imminent, the working environment for experts at the ministry deteriorated even further. In August 1969, the Central Military

Commission set up four leading groups to tighten control over selected industrial sectors. As head of the Telecommunication Industry Leading Group, Li Zuopeng, the navy's first political commissar and a zealot affiliated with Lin Biao, was detailed to oversee the electronics industry.[30] Driven by Mao's fear of impending war, the four leading groups in April 1970 decided to wrest 32 key enterprises away from the Fourth Ministry and to place them under the jurisdiction of other ministries.[31] For programmatic reasons, especially those related to the SLBM, the reassignment made no sense, but the logic of the times was to destroy the system in order to save it for vague "higher purposes."[32]

Throughout the early 1970s, military-led radicalism snarled the work of the entire industry and brought a steady deterioration to all R&D on military hardware. Few electronic components produced during these years met the SLBM program's standards. Of notoriously low reliability, instability, and short shelf-life, most proved unacceptable even for first-generation conventional weapons.[33]

The decline in quality became apparent to even the most resolute radical by 1972, when much of the electronics industry's stock of parts—80 million semiconductors and 230 million other components—had to be scrapped.[34] The Fourth Ministry later cited three reasons for these deficiencies. First, the entire quality control system had been abandoned shortly after the outbreak of the Cultural Revolution. Next, the industry, in chaos, became frozen in time and thus dependent on backward technologies and obsolete equipment for processing electronic parts. And finally, the supplies of raw materials required for manufacturing the new components had been cut off because of domestic shutdowns or foreign embargoes.[35] The missile engineers would have imputed their string of test failures less to defective parts than to faulty workmanship. A high percentage of the failures could be traced to a loose nut, a broken wire, or a "cold" weld or solder point.[36]

No doubt both bad parts and bad workmanship played a role. At any rate, according to one official source, defective electronic components accounted for fully 40 percent of the failures in missile flight tests from September 1971 to January 1978. The damage was incalculable, entailing not just the loss of the missiles and test data, but the wasted time and salaries of thousands of technicians and soldiers at the test sites.[37]

In December 1973, the Fourth Ministry convened a meeting to discuss ways to improve the quality of the electronic parts for military use and to draw up a list of measures for restoring quality control. But the times and funds were not right for instituting rigorous and expensive organizational remedies, and little progress was made during most of the 1970s. For these years, for example, semiconductors fabricated for military use received a low rating of either 3 or 4 (where a 3 would have one-tenth the operating life of a grade 4 device) on a scale of 10.[38]

As late as April 1978, the First Academy of the Seventh Ministry, then responsible for Project JL-1 (as well as the DF programs), asked the Defense Science and Technology Commission for immediate assistance in fixing over 400 serious defects in the missile electronic components. Minister Song Renqiong added the Seventh Ministry's weight to this request by visiting his counterpart, Wang Zhen, at the Fourth Ministry. The two ministers met several times to consider steps for spurring the electronics industry to initiate effective controls. Zhang Aiping, director of the commission, deemed the question of component reliability vital to guaranteeing further progress in the missile programs and prodded Wang Zhen to action in terms of "wiping out a humiliation."[39]

By the end of the year, Wang's ministry had given the task of rectifying quality control to his Military Electronic Components Academy (Fourteenth Academy) and its associated manufacturing plants. As was typical in these cases, he demanded that they bolster their "cooperation and coordination" but offered little practical guidance on how to do so.[40] Finally, Wang put his seal on an urgent directive requiring speedy movement on the quality front and promulgating "seven special measures" for production-and-acceptance tests for all electronic components needed for strategic weapons.[41] By the mid-1980s, the ministry, crediting the special measures, could cite statistics showing a dramatic turnaround from the dismal record of the previous two decades.[42]

This crusade for higher quality standards coincided with the military's growing concern with the survivability of China's strategic forces. We noted that in 1967 the leadership had elevated the priority of submarine and land-mobile arms even while recommitting the nation to a no-first-use policy and to the development of a limited nuclear arsenal. Almost immediately, the experts at the Fourth Ministry applied the concept of vulnerability in the atomic age to the electronic components, and as they wrestled with the problem of quality control, they tackled the seemingly hopeless task of having to protect those components from radiation and related electromagnetic damage. In a small and somewhat desultory way, they had begun research on this matter as early as the mid-1960s, but now the high command had given that research added salience. By the mid-1980s, they had reportedly achieved success in enhancing the antinuclear radiation capabilities of on-board electronic components.[43] The prodding, it seems, had worked.

During the 1980s, the recurring campaigns to enforce quality standards also led to steady improvements in the reliability of these components.[44] In the course of this quest for reliability, the Chinese by repeated experimentation had worked out a generalized approach to design and innovation. That approach was characterized by five principles:

Single out simple designs and use as few components as possible
Use standard, proven components in preference to untested components and electric circuits
Build in redundancy, employing as many duplicate circuits as feasible
Use components whose power requirements are much lower than the rated output of any given component part
Carry out a double-check system to guarantee the proper fit of connected parts

Chief Designer Huang Weilu contends that this approach to component design, production, and installation proved itself in the demonstrated dependability of the JL-1 systems.[45]

Looking back to the origins of this success in the 1960s, we can see a pattern emerging where technological and military-strategic arguments found in Western deterrence theories were beginning to be used to shape China's strategic weapons programs. We saw the most explicit expression of these arguments coming from JL-1 flight control experts when they embraced the importance of accuracy even though accuracy as such had rated relatively low in the specifications for the first three DF missiles.[46] Failures in the DF program, we have noted, made more critical the matter of electronics reliability and hardening against nuclear effects, but it was Project JL-1 that began to impose these technical requirements on the entire missile effort by connecting reliability and hardening to the need for survivable retaliatory forces.

There were fundamental reasons for this change, and we should review them briefly. One reason surely was that the sea-based missile program, JL-1, was a latecomer in China's quest for strategic delivery systems. In applying the Great Leap "general line" *duo, kuai, hao, sheng* (more, faster, better, and more economical results) to the DF missile effort, the Seventh Ministry stressed kuai; better and more economical took second place. The slogan was *kuai zi dang tou, duo zai qi zhong* (If faster is in the lead, quantity will naturally follow).

On the other hand, the submarine imposed a different logic on the development engineers. The SLBM and its warhead would be smaller, and thus missile accuracy weighed much more heavily in the requirements for the JL-1. Concerns for accuracy easily combined with attention to penetrability and, in light of the emerging antiballistic missile programs of the West in the late 1960s, to the survivability of electronic components in a nuclear environment. The failures and accidents in the DF program had taken a certain toll, of course, but they could be tolerated in the Gansu test facility at Shuangchengzi or the empty target zones of the Xinjiang desert. They were quite another matter, however, when considered in the light of a few expensive nuclear submarines carrying multiple missiles. No failures, no accidents—that was essential. Thus the JL-1 engineers had to draw on all the DF experience and their own talent to ensure safety, and safety in the strategic context equated to reliability.

We do not know whether the high command or the engineers were the first to embrace these concepts of accuracy, penetrability, survivability, and reliability, and in the final analysis, it does not matter. The point is that at the very time the grand coalition forged for the early strategic programs was disintegrating and the Party's rationales for those programs appeared less and less relevant, the JL-1 engineers and some of their bosses and associates were almost unconsciously replacing Maoist principles and assumptions with foreign technical arguments and strategic doctrines. For the first time—ironically coming during the high tide of the political furor and ideological torment of the Cultural Revolution—technology and Western military concepts had begun to displace politics and ideology as the underpinning of China's military policies. Almost by accident, the Chinese in the JL-1 program were making explicit the foundations for the modern strategic doctrines that we will discuss in the concluding chapters.

Evolution of the DF Series Guidance Systems

Most of the working-level engineers involved in the program, of course, gave no thought to grand strategy. For them, survival mostly meant avoiding in-house political fanatics. Their answer to what seemed perpetual disturbances was to bury themselves in their work at their desks and drafting tables. The JL-1 flight-control engineers made the translation of DF strapdown-type inertial guidance to their missile their daily preoccupation, if not their personal means of escape. That dedication, for whatever reason, brought a steady string of mini-breakthroughs, and the development of the control and guidance subsystems moved forward.

Following its usual practice, the Central Military Commission authorized the creation of an intricate bureaucratic structure to push forward this development. In January 1965, as part of the reorganization of the Fifth Academy into the Seventh Ministry, the First and Fourth design departments of its second subacademy were transferred to the Seventh's First Academy as Institute 12 (Control System Institute) and Institute 13 (Inertial Component Institute), respectively. The two institutes joined forces to create the guidance system required for the DF missiles, and we will briefly review the history of those efforts here because it helps explain the corpus of knowledge on which the JL-1 designers could draw.[47]

In the early phase of developing the DF guidance mechanisms, the Chinese copied and slightly modified the instruments in the two R-2s they had received from Moscow in the late 1950s. They installed the R-2's guidance system, which provided a combination of inertial and radio guidance, on the first-generation DF-2 missile. Prior to lift-off, the launch team had to insert preset information in the form of electrical charges to an electrolytic integrator and to install a special ground-based radio station for making lateral corrections. In the first successful test flight of the DF-2 missile on June 29, 1964, the team members described the station as a "big tail"; the station had to "tail" many kilometers behind the missile in the same target plane and had to be relocated whenever the target direction was changed.[48]

The "big tail" rendered the DF-2 missile dependent on good radio reception, and that imperative made it virtually impossible to deploy the DF-2 in mountainous areas where it would be most protected if attacked.[49] Moreover, the inertial part of the guidance system could not make corrections for variations in wind direction and thrust. The system, similar to the one used on the German V-2, could compensate for deviations in engine thrust at lift-off weight, so the Chinese described it as a "single compensation" inertial guidance system.[50] In the fall of 1964, Zhou Enlai told the Fifth Academy to modify the missile and replace the R-2 guidance system with a fully inertial guidance system. Although the replacement system would add to the missile's accuracy, the principal purpose of Zhou's order was to allow for greater flexibility in deployment.

This system could compensate for both lateral and linear deviations. Inertial guidance could overcome lateral wind and thrust deviations by incorporating a coordinate conversion device. To offset any errors from the engine thrust in the longitudinal direction, the engineers had to invent additional compensation formulas and thus changed the adjective describing the system to "dual compensation." In November 1965, the engineers conducted flight tests of the missile, which had been retrofitted with the new guidance system and redesigned engines, and redesignated it the DF-2A.[51] The missile had shed its "tail."

The next missile to come on line, the DF-3, was successfully flight-tested in December 1966; the DF-4 followed in January 1970.[52] These two missiles constituted the main strategic launch vehicles assigned to the Second Artillery Corps in the 1970s and 1980s.[53] Their more advanced guidance system had replaced the primitive V-2 electrolytic integrator with a gyro-

16. Qian Xuesen (center), one of China's leading missile experts and former director of the Fifth Academy

17. Nie Rongzhen at the launching of the DF-1 missile, Nov. 5, 1960

18. Launching site of the DF-2 medium-range missile

19. The DF-3 intermediate-range missile being erected

20. Gyroscope used for the DF-3 missile's guidance system

21. Launching site of the DF-4 limited-range intercontinental missile

22. The DF-5 intercontinental ballistic missile (ICBM)

23. Vertical test of a DF-5 missile

24. The launch squadron ready for carrying out the DF-5's first flight test

25. Marshal Nie Rongzhen, left, former director of the Defense Science and Technology Commission, and Deng Xiaoping at the Command Post in Beijing watching telecast of the DF-5 ICBM test, May 18, 1980

26. Helicopter taking off from a salvage ship for the DF-5's warhead impact point in the South Pacific, May 18, 1980

27. Plant 845 technicians carrying a 300mm-diameter solid engine for a hot test in 1962

28. Experimental rocket with a 300mm-diameter solid engine being flight-tested in Aug. 1968

29. The first 1.4m-diameter solid engine, designed by the Fourth Academy and designated for JL-1, at its test stand, Dec. 1966

30. The first 1.4m-diameter solid engine being lifted onto a test stand, Dec. 1966

31. Test of the two-stage JL-1 missile's stage separation

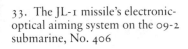

32. Full-scale model rocket (Model II) for testing the JL-1's gas-steam ejector

33. The JL-1 missile's electronic-optical aiming system on the 09-2 submarine, No. 406

34. The JL-1 missile's first flight test from a submerged 31-class (Golf) submarine, Oct. 12, 1982

35. *Distant Observer*, an oceangoing instrumentation ship

36. The JL-1 missile on parade, Tian'anmen Square, Oct. 1984

37. The JL-1 missile being lowered into the 09-2 nuclear missile submarine, No. 406

38. The DF-21 missile, a land-based version of the JL-1

39. The DF-21 missile being erected

40. The DF-21 missile being ejected from a launch tube

scopic integrator that could compensate for errors in measuring apparent velocity along the longitudinal axis and that copied the instrument in the Soviet-supplied 1060 missile. The DF-3 engineers also copied the 1060's device for making lateral corrections. They dubbed the guidance a "complete compensation" system.[54]

Compared with the DF-2, several innovations in this system represented important technological accomplishments for the Chinese. These included in-flight calculators, air-bearing gyros, and air-suspension gyro-accelerometers. The last two components used the vacuum-cleaner principle of air-in/air-out to achieve near frictionless suspension. With these advances, the Chinese, by the early 1970s, had substantially mastered the technologies for strapdown inertial guidance.[55]

In 1965, the Chinese began developing the DF-5, a two-stage, full-range ICBM capable of delivering a multimegaton warhead to Hawaii and the continental United States—and the western Soviet Union.[56] A key problem for the DF-5's guidance engineers was how to improve the performance of the strapdown system used in the previous *dongfeng* missiles. At the time, China could not manufacture either the high-quality inertial components or the high-speed, huge-capacity computers needed to do the job. As a result, as we have noted, the engineers turned to the platform-type system.[57]

Overseen by the First Academy, Institute 12 established a team to design the DF-5 inertial guidance. Under Liang Sili's leadership, the team members figured out a workable design plan for the inertial guidance platform.[58] While the computational requirements would be less exacting, the missile would still have to have a sturdy on-board computer of medium speed and capacity; the DF-5 was China's first missile with an in-flight computer. Despite these fairly modest requirements, some further improvements in the nation's computers would be necessary for making the precise calculations needed to control the direction and velocity of the moving rocket and to time engine cutoff more precisely for the DF-5's long voyage. Though pinpoint accuracy was not a paramount consideration, any reasonable accuracy for a missile traveling up to 12,500km would require highly dependable computers that would meet four rigorous specifications: small size, high reliability, low power consumption, and long life.[59]

In 1965, computer engineers at the Chinese Academy of Sciences began an intensive year-long research effort to develop the DF-5 computer. Their labors resulted in a somewhat jerry-rigged instrument assembled from newly designed integrated circuits. The Seventh Ministry took one look and rejected it as too complicated and unreliable.[60] But if the nation's most skilled computer makers had done their best, who could do better? A substitute had to be found, and the design staff began studying other approaches to on-board computation.

The solution, they first believed, had to be in the computer software, where substantial progress did occur at the theoretical level. The engineers from Institute 12 devised a concept called "incremental computation." Instead of computing the entire family of ballistic equations throughout the boost phase, incremental computation would skip most of the boost phase, which had little to do with thrust termination, and deal only with the period just before shutdown. Moreover, they discovered that only the difference between the actual flight data and the preset parameters needed to be computed. The new method simplified the shutdown equation and reduced the requirement for computer speed and memory.[61]

The method opened up fresh possibilities for hardware innovations. To promote research on integrated circuits and minicomputers, the ministry in the mid-1960s set up the Lishan Microelectronics Institute (Institute 771) in Lintong, east of Xi'an, Shaanxi Province.[62] Following the tried-and-true method of trial and error, technicians at the institute doggedly set out to develop the minicomputer for the DF-5.[63] By 1974, they succeeded by incorporating incremental digital computation and using the most advanced components then available.[64]

In 1965, when the years-long effort on the minicomputer was just starting, the Defense Science and Technology Commission also had to deal with other inertial components. It ordered two institutes of the Chinese Academy of Sciences, the Automation Institute and the Changchun Institute of Optical and Fine Mechanics, to develop both liquid-floated and air-bearing integrating rate gyros for the DF-5, and code-named their work Project 157.[65] Two years later, in 1967, the commission adopted the model using air-bearing gyroscopes and air-suspension pendulum-type accelerometers on the grounds that they had to meet lower requirements for environmental purity in the assembly shops than the liquid-floated ones.[66] (The commission, however, later chose the liquid-floated model for the JL-1 missile because of its higher accuracy over long operational periods.)*

The First Academy then charged its own Institute 13 with designing the complete DF-5 inertial guidance platform and relieved the two Chinese Academy of Sciences' institutes of this job. In 1974, technicians at Plant 230, a facility for the manufacture of inertial components in the western suburbs of Beijing, assembled several prototype platforms.[67] The test platform met its most exacting test when the DF-5 was used to launch a re-

---

*The liquid-floated gyroscope is more accurately called an IRIG, or inertial rate-integrating gyroscope. The IRIG uses the rate gyro concept but replaces that gyro's spring with a viscous fluid.

coverable satellite on November 26, 1975, but 230's technicians continued trying to perfect the platform. In September and October 1979, they conducted over 100 experiments on 29 platforms to acquire data on how to set the platforms' optimum rate of airflow for the gyros and accelerometers.[68] That effort not only guaranteed the needed accuracy for China's first ICBM but also instilled a necessary confidence in the guidance design team designated to tackle the JL-1.

Developing the JL-1's Guidance Subsystem

From the outset, the man in charge of developing the JL-1's guidance system, Chen Deren, director of the Seventh Ministry's Institute 17, saw his biggest challenge in the 1967 plan's requirement for abovewater ignition.[69] For Chen, the puzzle that had to be solved was how to stabilize the missile after ejection and achieve the preset guidance trajectory even if the rocket ignited at an angle significantly off-vertical.

Chen decided that accuracy and reliability would, in the first instance, depend on the inertial guidance system, and especially on the system's minicomputer and gyros. Once the ministry approved the computer-based inertial guidance platform for development, he set the specifications for and closely followed work on the minicomputer at the Lishan Microelectronics Institute but had his own Institute 17 spend most of its time working with Institute 13 on designs for the liquid-floated gyroscopes, the instrument proposed for the JL-1. Chen's mission was principally one of design and specification setting; the other institutes had the job of translating No. 17's designs into finished products. For these tasks, Chen enjoyed the support of Huang Weilu, his boss and an expert on missile controls. As head of Department 4, Huang was responsible for carrying out coordination and cooperation among various units involved in Project JL-1.[70]

The Chinese set out the most severe requirements for the on-board minicomputer. The computer for a long-range missile, they calculated, had to have a memory capacity of 15,000 characters and be capable of accomplishing 15,000 instructions per second.[71] The Lishan Institute had already built such a minicomputer for the DF-5, but the JL-1's computer, like its other electronic equipment, had to be much smaller in size. The major requirement, then, was for further miniaturization with the same or higher output and with much higher reliability.[72] Because this task potentially involved so many units outside the Fourth Department, the Defense Science and Technology Commission in 1970 assumed overall responsibility for coordinating the miniaturization effort, though the indispensable liaison remained that between Chen's Institute 17 and the microelectronics institute at Lishan.

Starting in October 1968, Engineer Shen Xubang headed the work on the JL-1 minicomputer at the Lishan institute. He introduced integrated circuits in the computer and together with an engineer named Wang, worked out the definitive relationships between hardware design and quality control. Their main contribution was the improvement of quality screening and test systems. With the help of an army of Shens and Wangs, the Lishan institute finished a prototype incremental digital minicomputer first with MOS integrated circuits and then, by the end of the 1970s, with the more advanced medium- to small-scale CMOS integrated circuits.[73] The team quickly demonstrated the superiority of its minicomputer over the DF-5 version.[74]

As usual everything was going on at once, and pursuant to the 1967 comprehensive plan, the Defense Science and Technology Commission ordered Institute 13 to work on the SLBM's inertial guidance platform. The need was for a platform stabilized by three rate-integrating gyros (floated gyros) using fluorocarbon oil or silicon oil and capable of angular measurement to an accuracy of one angular second (1/3600°); three accelerometers on the platform would have to measure acceleration to 0.0001g.[75] These requirements put the maximum burden on China's infant machine tool-and-die industry and its capacity to cooperate with electronics specialists. In the early 1970s, the Seventh Ministry settled on Plant 171 (Second Inertial Component Plant) near the town of Huangniupu, about 50km southwest of Baoji City, Shaanxi Province, to manufacture the gyros and assemble the platform components from Institute 13's design plans.[76]

Situated in a mountainous area, Plant 171 was one of the main industrial facilities attached to Base 067, a missile R&D complex established in the post-1965 rush to build facilities in the Third Line and manned by transfers from the Seventh Ministry's First Academy and the New Technological Bureau of the Chinese Academy of Sciences.[77] Following the guidelines for Third-Line construction, the First Academy had dispersed Base 067's facilities into two zones, one near Fengzhou and the other at Huangniupu.[78] Plant 171 in the second zone was geographically close to a local branch of Institute 13 and Plant 107 (First Inertial Component Plant) and affiliated with the Beijing-based Institute 13 and Plant 230, which we encountered in our discussion of the DF gyro fabrication.[79] By 1970, Base 067 was operating as a central part of the First Academy's development-and-production network in the Third Line.[80]

Plant 171's surroundings, typical of the Third Line, were hardly conducive to meticulous work. The "transport facilities were poor, the workshop and industrial equipment were simple and crude, and the production and living conditions were extremely poor." Nevertheless, the ministry still insisted that the plant meet high standards, and 171's technicians began studying how to fabricate the special JL-1 gyros with the inadequate materials and library at hand. True to the spirit of the times, they rushed to assemble the first prototype by the end of 1971, and predictably, the result was a flop.

Reaching out to people he could trust in the chaotic aftermath of the Lin Biao affair, the head of the First Academy looked for an engineer who could truly meet the high standards and resist the temptation to be swept along with the ever-shifting political currents. He chose for the job the deputy director of the plant, Ding Henggao, whose wife, Nie Li, was the only daughter of Nie Rongzhen, the erstwhile head of the Defense Science and Technology Commission. Clearly, family networks were involved in the selection, but Ding was also highly qualified. A graduate of the Leningrad Institute of Fine Mechanics and Optics, he had served successfully as the deputy director of Institute 13 before he checked in at Plant 171.[81]

In his assignments, Ding came to rely heavily on a young specialist named Lü Yingxiang. Lü, who is now generally credited with having made the greatest contribution to the manufacture and installation of the gyros on the JL-1 guidance platform, had earned a master's degree in the Soviet Union and then won his political spurs by volunteering for the Third Line. But his solid engineering skills quickly dispelled whatever doubts Ding may have had that Lü was simply a political enthusiast. Night after night, Lü delved into books and articles on guidance and inertial components, and his growing expertise persuaded his boss to assign him to run the gyro research program. After six years, Lü's research paid off, and in 1976, Plant 171 used his results to make four operational platforms. These were then delivered to Plant 284 (Coordinate Display Equipment Plant) in Beijing. Three were for installation on the first three JL-1 missiles, and one was for a backup spare.[82]

In the next years, Lü and his colleagues continued making improvements on the platform and built incrementally more complex copies. So arduous was the effort that Lü succumbed to Ménière's syndrome; and his health may be counted as one of the JL-1 program's costs. But the dedication had produced the desired results. In the fall of 1981, Plant 284 received three more platforms, all capable of providing near-perfect accuracy. On October 12, 1982, one of these platforms guided the first submarine-launched JL-1. In the post-test euphoria, the Chinese hailed the JL-1's platform as having "turned a new page" in the development of the nation's inertial guidance technology.[83]

One more task for the propulsion engineers to complete was thrust termination, a principal determinant in missile accuracy. With the decision to use reverse nozzle technology for this mission, the trick was to install several nozzles symmetrically at the front end of the second-stage engine and to equip them with opening mechanisms that would activate the nozzles simultaneously. The flight-control computer would issue the opening command when the missile had reached a preset speed.[84] Though the work on the nozzles, which began in 1963, proceeded slowly at Institute 41 (Solid Rocket Motor Institute) in Hohhot, the problems were principally ones of fine machining and installation, not of engineering science. Given the wealth of Western and Soviet literature on the subject, the principles of thrust termination and reverse nozzle operation were well understood. The technicians drew on assistance from several sister institutes, including No. 17, and basically finished the job in 1970. Only a few tasks in the missile program had the aura of heroic adventures. Most were dull and slow, and building the reverse nozzle was part of this majority.

Flight Stability and Underwater Launch

As work on the guidance subsystem proceeded, technicians in Beijing struggled with JL-1's attitude controls, which had to function far more rapidly than its guidance parts.[85] All modern missiles are inherently unstable during their boost phase, principally because the center of aerodynamic pressure lies ahead of the center of gravity. Various types of thrust vector controls have proved effective in maintaining a missile's attitude, but for the first three DF missiles, Chinese engineers relied mainly on graphite jet vanes for attitude control. The jet vanes alone, however, proved inadequate to fully stabilize the DF-1, so the designers added fixed tail fins. These fins, which act much like the feathers at the end of an arrow, proved adequate in the DF-2 through DF-4. But for the DF-5 ICBMs, which were designed for launch from silos and thus could not have external fins, the Chinese had to develop engine-swivelling technology for adequate thrust-vector control.*

Though most of this development experience had little relevance to the JL-1, the Seventh Ministry had accumulated substantial knowledge on such basic control components as nozzles, servos, and circuitry. Because of the very limited volume of a submarine launch tube, the designers had

---

*The first-stage rocket of the DF-5 was equipped with four swivelling motors to control thrust vector, and the attitude-control system of the second-stage rocket was composed of a vernier engine consisting of one turbopump and four gimbaled thrust chambers. Zhang Jun, 176, 182. The DF-5 vernier chambers were copied from a U.S. Thor-Able-Star rocket that landed accidentally in Cuba in Dec. 1962. Premier Fidel Castro personally authorized an auction of the missile parts. The Soviets bought the engine, and the Chinese purchased the chambers. "Rocket Fragments Fell on Cuba," *New York Times*, Dec. 2, 1960; picture in *Miami Herald*, Jan. 4, 1961.

to abandon any thought of equipping the SLBM with fixed tail fins. The comprehensive design plan of 1967 had called for the development of four rotating nozzles for the first-stage engine and liquid injection technology for the second stage, and in 1968 Institute 17 began work on the first-stage nozzle technology.[86] Some of these technologies were well understood, at least in theory.

No. 17's task was to design servomechanisms that would move the nozzles tangentially during engine operation. The first nozzles were sized for the 300mm rocket engine, and by the end of 1968, three tests on the nozzle had been conducted with unexpected ease. The tests revealed no fundamental flaws in the nozzle design. Yet later, when fitted to the 1,400mm JL-1 engine (which had already survived its first full static test in late 1966), the tests on the experimental designs based on the 1968 data led to one failure after another.[87]

From extensive reviews of those data, Chen Deren concluded that the problem lay in the links between the attitude control subsystem and solid propulsion. He arranged for Institute 41 to assist in constructing a laboratory that could run cold tests on a variety of nozzle designs. For the next decade, engineers at the lab conducted hundreds of tests on 15 first-stage engines to try to discover a possible solution. It was not until September 1979 that "a series of complicated technical problems affecting control momentum and hermetic seals were eventually solved," but many of the participants in the tests remember mostly the agony of their defeats over so long a period. Unlike the engineers in the guidance program, who were witnessing the success of their new strategies and could envision broader purposes to their drudgery, the control subsystem engineers could find little satisfaction in higher theory or their own progress.

During this same decade, other engineers designed and tested possible liquid injection technologies for the JL-1's second-stage engine. The Fourth Academy had assigned a team to start research on these technologies in 1963, but Institute 17 subsequently took over this assignment. Most of the effort was very technical and endlessly tedious. For example, the team members discovered that the injected liquid freon or hydrogen peroxide could deflect the exhaust gas flow within angles of less than $\pm 4°$, an angle somewhat larger than in the U.S. Polaris A-3. Step by step, they experimented with different gases, angles, and gas-flow rates and perfected their models for the engine controls. Starting in 1979, the engineers conducted five high-altitude tests of the second-stage engine and confirmed a design that potentially would work. The tests further verified the theoretical specifications for the mechanisms to control counteryawing.

By this time, to the dismay of Chen Deren and his colleagues at Institute

17, the results of underwater tests now indicated that their biggest problem for attitude control would come not from the shock of ignition, but from the shock of underwater launch. Both the movement of the submarine and the resulting torque forces on the missile emerging from the launch tube would move it far off-vertical before it cleared the surface. So the problem now facing the engineers was how to stabilize a missile already significantly askew before ignition.[88]

The designers of the submarine's missile ejection system, as we have seen, were also well aware of the difficulties of launch from a submerged underway boat. Both the submarine designers and the missile designers knew that the need for attitude control of an ejected missile probably would become extreme even before the attitude control subsystem could become operational following ignition. Designing missile controls for submarine launch thus presented much greater obstacles than designing them for ground launch. For the Chinese, the problem proved particularly intractable because the missile would be ejected from a moving boat.

To begin with, the sub's motion in all dimensions would make it difficult to fix the missile's initial position for calculating its alignment and using the attitude control system to move it to the programmed flight path after ignition. According to the 1967 plan for the JL-1, an alignment system was to be developed for the base calculation of the azimuth, but both the movement and the flexure of the hull of the submerged submarine worked against the alignment subsystem's reliability and accuracy.[89] Here, finally, were challenges that could stimulate the adrenaline.

Chen Deren approached these difficulties with almost no concrete knowledge to draw upon. Practically speaking, the available Western literature was a total blank on the subject; this part of the U.S. and Soviet programs remained classified or at least hidden away in the libraries of defense plants and design labs.* So Chen was forced to start at a very elementary level. His team began an open-ended series of scale-model tests in 1968 with little more than hope for its guide, and only after four years' work did it succeed in tracing the problem to an insufficient allowance for the rotation of the gimbaled gyro-platform.[90] The team engineers guessed that a solution would come if they could more accurately compute the relationship between the platform's angular rotation and the overall opera-

---

*The Chinese engineers found Soviet textbooks the most useful for designing the JL-1. Most of these texts were strong on mathematics and theory but weak in engineering. What U.S. texts there were, according to the Chinese, were much too elementary, though some American aerospace journals and patent reports did provide helpful photographs and data. The upgrading of the guidance systems for the U.S. fleet's ballistic missiles is expertly reviewed in MacKenzie, Chap. 5.

tion of the controls. To this end, Chen asked and was granted permission to conduct scale-model ejection tests.[91]

Not unexpectedly, almost all the initial tests proved little, but before the missiles crashed, they had sent back some useful telemetry that guided the designers in making incremental adjustments. They also had to concentrate on the missile ejection system to make sure that a missile launched from the underway submarine would not break the surface at an angle greater than 60° from vertical; otherwise no amount of thrust-vector control could save the missile. After years of research and testing, the designers finally "figured out the various unfavorable combinations relating to the allowable maximum extent of the angular rotation of the platform" along each axis. The designers later completed the battery of calculations for both underwater and surfaced conditions and incorporated them as specific changes in the attitude control subsystem, the internal-control platform, and their connecting parts. By the end of 1978, they had basically perfected the operations of the subsystem, including azimuth computation.

In March 1979, in preparation for the assembling of the flight-control subsystems for eight JL-1 prototype missiles, Plant 284 sent a group of technicians to Institute 17 to learn about its experiences with assembling control mechanisms and dispatched purchasing agents to buy the advanced equipment to do the job. The equipment was installed at a special assembly line in the plant's Workshop 63, where 500,000 electronic components and 110,000 meters of conducting wire awaited the assemblers.[92]

Despite the apparent go-ahead for the workshop, Chief Designer Huang Weilu expressed reservations about the quality of the attitude control subsystem completed in 1978, and in June 1980, he called a meeting in Beijing to discuss whether even with all the adjustments, the subsystem was good enough to guarantee the absolute safety of the forthcoming tests. His worry and the meeting's agenda concentrated on ways to control the JL-1's flight attitude more effectively. Convinced of the necessity for even further improvements, the participants returned to the plant to make still more adjustments in the controls. More time was lost, but by the second half of the year, the technicians at Plant 284 had finished the redesigned control mechanisms and delivered them to Plant 307 in Nanjing, Jiangsu Province.[93] It was now up to 307 to install the attitude control and guidance subsystems on the missiles and to ready them for flight-testing.

EIGHT

Success

As work on the JL-1's solid propulsion, guidance, and flight controls proceeded, the engineers gradually narrowed the list of unknowns and began to devise the timetable for manufacturing, assembling, and testing the missile, including its warhead. Numerous technical details remained unresolved, and, of these, stage separation and the protection of the reentry vehicle (RV) proved the most perplexing.[1] As this chapter will show, none of these final puzzles proved as difficult to untangle as those encountered in developing the technologies for the missile's propulsion and control systems.

Developing the Warhead

The three critical technologies in building the SLBM were solid propulsion, a compatible missile guidance set, and a small, potent warhead.[2] The physicist Edward Teller's assurance that a 1,000-pound warhead could be designed for the Polaris was crucial to the first American SLBM program, and the Chinese, too, had to downscale their thermonuclear devices to fit their pioneering JL-1.[3]

All nuclear weapons nations closely guard the secrets of their warhead development, and it is not surprising that the Chinese have revealed little on the subject. Most of what we have learned comes from published Chinese materials. Here we sketch what is known about China's missile warhead program because it forms a crucial part of the story of the nation's quest for strategic seapower.

Nuclear scientists and missile engineers began designing warheads for the DF missiles in 1967, and four years later, the Seventh Ministry of Machine Building's First Academy (Carrier Rocket Research Academy) created the Institute of Warheads (Institute 14) specifically for this work. In the next decade, the guideline for the institute's effort was *xiaoxing, ji-*

dong, tufang, anquan, kekao (small size, quick maneuverability, great penetrability, improved safety, and high reliability).[4]

By the end of the 1970s, China had deployed its first-generation nuclear missiles, and all of these liquid-fueled launchers were designed to carry heavy warheads. The DF-3, for example, was capable of carrying a 2,150kg payload over 2,650km. The DF-4 would use the DF-3 as the first stage and carry a 2,200kg payload over 4,750km; it would have the same warhead as the DF-3 but, as we discuss below, with more heat-insulation material for higher reentry speeds.

Following the success of China's first thermonuclear test with a three-megaton yield in June 1967, the First Academy argued that in case of a tug-of-war over resources, work on the DF-4 should give way to the DF-5 because the thermonuclear warhead was too heavy for the DF-4. The DF-5 was designed to carry a 3,200kg payload, as against the DF-4's 2,200kg.

On January 4, 1966, Qian Xuesen advocated the development of an advanced DF-5 warhead with penetration aids. In December, the First Academy completed the preliminary design of the missile's reentry vehicle. It would be equipped with light exoatmospheric decoys and with electronic countermeasures even though these would be ineffective after reentry. Endoatmospheric decoys with the same aerodynamic characteristics as real nuclear warheads were deemed too heavy for the DF-5.

The first successful DF-5 flight test was conducted in 1971, and with this, the goals for all the first-generation missiles had been met. The time had come to plan for the new generation, and the designers decided to shift from fixed-based to mobile systems. Engineer Li Xu'e led Institute 14's design of the JL-1 warhead and, with help from the Ninth Academy (nuclear weapons), built the nation's first small-sized warheads.[5] Two technological achievements justified their decision: the miniaturization of nuclear warheads as part of the SLBM system and the computerization of the DF-5's missile-control system.

According to the general design plans, the payload of the JL-1/DF-21 would be about 600kg (more than double the original Polaris W-47 warhead) and would be designed to deliver a 400-kiloton or higher yield. The Chinese originally planned to put the same nuclear device on the follow-on DF-31/JL-2 and DF-41, and warheads of these missiles would differ only in their thermal insulation and technologies for penetration. However, in nuclear tests conducted in the 1990s, the Chinese sought to develop a new warhead with a much higher yield-to-weight ratio and with a capability of further miniaturization.

At first, the Chinese were unable to miniaturize their thermonuclear warheads. They had installed a mechanical neutron initiator in the center of the weapon to cause the primary chain reaction, a necessary change that had complicated efforts to downsize the warhead. The early nuclear weapons had used a polonium-beryllium initiator, which because of polonium's short half-life is unsuitable for a large, mature weapons program.[6] But once they discovered how to redesign the warhead in ways that would boost its yield, the door was opened for the Chinese to reduce the size of their nuclear weapons.

Remaining Technical Problems: Stage Separation and Heat Protection

Successful stage separation in a two-stage missile requires precise engineering and delicate timing. Unless there is a clean break, the forward stage will be damaged or at least deflected. The original plans for the JL-1 called for the use of explosive bolts for executing separation in one of two ways: "hot" or "cold," based on the timing of second-stage ignition.[7] In the hot process, the upper-stage engine would ignite an instant before the detonation of the explosive bolts and pull away from the first stage. Cold separation would delay ignition until after the detonation of the bolts. A booster rocket on the upper stage would ignite simultaneously with the ignition of two reverse-thrust rockets on the lower stage. The main second-stage engine would remain idle until full separation had been achieved.[8]

Chinese design crews decided to investigate both separation paths during the initial R&D years, and both led to failures, virtually all of which stemmed from mistakes in timing or from erroneous estimates of aerodynamic pressures. Eventually, the engineers tried replacing the explosive bolts with more advanced linear-shaped charges, but the failures persisted. Their close reading of the increasingly abundant foreign publications helped little, and in the doldrums of the Cultural Revolution, few experts felt optimistic about finding a solution any time soon.[9]

In 1975, after hundreds of tests on hand-made linear-shaped charge explosives and four years of trial and error, the engineers performed the first separation tests on real rocket casings. Over the next years, the design on the linear-shaped charges improved somewhat, and in 1980, the engineers carried out both cold and hot ground tests at Institute 41 (Solid Rocket Motor Institute) in Hohhot. After analyzing the test results, Chief Designer Huang Weilu, head of Department 4 (Solid Motor Strategic Missile Overall Design Department), decided on the hot method for the first JL-1 flight test, which was successfully conducted in mid-1981.

The other major worry was heat protection for the reentry vehicle. The reentry speed of an RV varies between 5,000 and 8,000m/sec; the longer a missile's range, the greater the reentry speed and the higher the temperature of the RV's nose cone. In the reentry phase, the temperature of an

ICBM's RV ranges between 8,000°C and 12,000°C. Without effective heat protection, the warheads burn up or break apart.[10]

Research on heat protection for the JL-1's RV required a superior understanding of aerodynamics, thermodynamics, and special materials, and the designers had to draw on all available knowledge from the DF land-based missile program to make an effective protection system for the SLBM. They knew that in the 1960s Western scientists started coating their RVs with an ablative material that would absorb a significant amount of heat as it burned off and slough it into the slipstream. Early on, they used veneers of inorganic fibers and synthetic resins, forming a composite material. The fibers were made from asbestos, glass, silicon, carbon, and boron; synthetic resins were made from phenolic, epoxy, and polyamide resins. Phenolic resin-coated silica and carbon-coated quartz fibers later became the ablative materials of choice.

Achieving nose-cone protection long eluded the Chinese. Though the engineers understood the need for heat protection as early as 1964, they could not fabricate effective ablative materials. Their failures caused repeated setbacks in the DF program. In the same year, Institute 703 (Institute of Materials and Technology), the Academy of Building Materials in Beijing, and the Harbin Institute of Architectural Engineering began combined efforts to produce a fiberglass-reinforced plastic for the DF-2, and when this proved practicable, it was approved for use on the DF-3s and 4s.[11] The approval was premature. The greater reentry speeds caused higher temperatures and the incineration of the DF-3; two of its dummy warheads were destroyed during reentry tests in September and October 1969. Similar failures plagued the DF-4.

The following March, the Seventh Ministry approved the installation of equipment at Plant 211 (Carrier Rocket General Assembly Plant) for pressurizing and solidifying reinforced inorganic fibers.[12] The plant also imported foreign equipment for processing new types of protective coating. A year later, the ministry's First Academy ordered Institute 14 to redesign the warhead. Technicians at this institute and Institute 703 eventually combined forces to solve the problems of the DF-3's heat protection, but it was not until 1971 that they found the formula for a suitable coating and the DF-3 could be certified for combat deployment.[13]

The same material (phenolic resin-coated silica fiber) was adapted to the DF-4 missile, though successive changes were made in the coating throughout the decade. But because the reentry speed of the intercontinental DF-5 would be much greater than the DF-4's, that coating would not do. Some Chinese specialists anticipated the unusual requirements of the DF-5. As early as June 1967, the First Academy submitted a report on the missile's comprehensive design plan, recommending that the ministry approve phenolic resin-coated silica fibers for the RV. After the successes with the DF-3 and DF-4 protective coating, the engineers began investigating more arcane ablative materials.

In October 1973, technicians from Institutes 14 and 703 and Plant 211 formed a Beijing-based team to study possible materials.[14] Engineers at the Institute of Aerodynamics (Institute 701) and the Academy of Sciences' Institute of Mechanics later joined the team when it became obvious that the selection of materials in part depended on the warhead's stability and angle of reentry.[15] With little progress being made in the midst of the Gang of Four's political campaigns, the Seventh Ministry, in September 1975, formed two competitive teams in Shanghai to study the problem. The teams focused on carbon-coated quartz fibers and finally devised a satisfactory substance for the DF-5.[16] Over the next decade, other institutes across the nation improved on the Shanghai formula and imported the equipment for manufacturing the fibers. The Chinese now claim to have reached the "international level" for warhead heat protection.[17]

These developments had a direct bearing on the heat protection for the JL-1's reentry vehicle. A research organ under the Fourth Academy (Solid Rocket Motor Academy) had started research on the problem even before the formal inauguration of the project, and at the end of 1967, the Seventh Ministry shifted this research to its First Academy. Starting in 1968 and continuing into the next decade, a few engineers at Institutes 14 and 703 were assigned to work on coatings for the JL-1, and in the main, they took their lead from the DF program, selecting first phenolic resin-coated silica fibers and then the DF-5's carbon-coated quartz fibers for the submarine missile RV.

When, in mid-1979, the missile engineers had completed research on the JL-1 warhead, Chief Designer Huang Weilu ordered full functional tests carried out on the SLBM warhead using the DF-3 as the launch vehicle. Four such tests were conducted at Base 25 on June 3 and 15, August 21, and September 4. These tests turned out to be successful and indirectly confirmed the heat protection system for the JL-1.

Speedups and Slowdowns

In February 1974, with Project JL-1 clearly lagging far behind schedule and behind the progress being made in Project 09, the Seventh Ministry convened a meeting to discuss how to accelerate work on the missile. Although the specialists contended that they could not finish the design of the JL-1 before 1979, the participants passed a resolution calling for the elimination of all bottlenecks at a faster pace.[18] Such resolutions are commonplace in the Chinese political and military systems and seldom have the desired effect. In response to the document, the First Academy began drawing up a plan to develop not just the JL-1 but three other solid-propellant missiles over the next ten years: the DF-21 (a land-based mobile version of the JL-1), the DF-21A (an extended-range DF-21), and the follow-on JL-2.

More than a year passed with little progress. In April 1975, the academy held its own round of meetings to investigate delays in Project JL-1 and forwarded the findings to the Defense Science and Technology Commission. The next month, the commission worked out a comprehensive report on the development of the nation's strategic missiles and submitted it to Mao Zedong for approval. The report anticipated having the JL-1 completed and deployed on the 09-2 submarine by 1980.[19]

Only a few months before, it will be recalled, Deng Xiaoping had returned from political oblivion to become vice-chairman of the Central Military Commission and chief of the General Staff and to breathe fresh life into the most important military programs.[20] With Mao's endorsement of the Defense Science and Technology Commission's report, Deng ordered a speedup in research and development on the nation's strategic weapons and urged the Seventh Ministry in particular to attach greater weight to the JL-1, DF-5, and satellite programs.[21]

At about this time, Zhang Aiping, also recently rehabilitated and the newly appointed director of the Defense Science and Technology Commission, set out to stiffen discipline in the defense science system. Like Deng, he assigned high priority to Project JL-1 and other strategic weapons programs, and although still in ill-health from his ordeal during the Cultural Revolution, he visited the First Academy several times, believing it important to hold face-to-face, all-day discussions with specialists such as Huang Weilu and to give them personal encouragement. Zhang put the full force of the commission behind the scientists' efforts to solve the technical problems in the project.[22]

Unfortunately, the attempt to restore order in the system did not last long. Some months later, Mao (and his surrogates) initiated a full-fledged political campaign for the purpose of precluding any attempts to negate the Cultural Revolution after his death. Deng and Zhang once again faced dismissal and disgrace, and with the upsurge of radicalism in the spring of 1976, Project JL-1 was brought to a halt. Mao's death in September 1976 and the arrest of his wife and her radical associates the following month momentarily accentuated the turmoil, but very rapidly order and direction returned to the program.[23]

In July 1977, Deng Xiaoping staged his final comeback and put his personal prestige behind the project.[24] As a consequence, the Defense Science and Technology Commission in a special report asked the Central Military Commission to give precedence to the development of the JL-1 missile (plus the DF-5 and the communication satellite).[25] In September, the military commission approved the report's recommendations and ordered their implementation by the nation's defense scientific and industrial establishment.

In respect specifically to Project JL-1, the commission said: "Characterized by great maneuverability and concealability, the JL-1 is the first submarine-launched solid-propellant missile [of our country]. Furthermore, the development of solid missiles is the proper course for us, and technical breakthroughs in solid propulsion should be made as soon as possible." In December, in response to that statement, the State Planning Commission directed all municipalities and provinces to assign maximum priority to supplying the equipment and materials required for the project.

The following month, the military commission set a firm deadline for the SLBM: the JL-1's design plan would have to be finalized by the first half of the 1980s. The order reflected a change in the Chinese leaders' thinking, which eventually would constrain the deployment of the silo-based DF-5 intercontinental missile.[26] They had begun to worry about the survivability of the nation's strategic missiles and bombers and were becoming convinced that the highest priority should be given to the sea-based deterrent.

With the deadline in hand, the Defense Science and Technology Commission and the Seventh Ministry set about readjusting schedules for the strategic weapons programs. In June 1978, Deng Xiaoping and other Chinese leaders attended a session of the Central Special Commission and reached a conclusion consistent with the American doctrine of mutual assured destruction: "Offense is the best defense. We should concentrate our forces on accelerating research and development on offensive nuclear weapons." In addition, they directed the ministry's Second Academy to stretch out its work on costly antimissile and antisatellite weapons (Project 640) and to shift to developing offensive weapons, including the JL-1.

Speed was the order of the day, and that order was formalized by the military commission in December.[27] Specialists at the Seventh Ministry began studying just how to accomplish the speedup, but after repeated delays and mistakes, they could only guess at the pitfalls that lay ahead. The ministry's experts estimated the earliest reasonable dates for readying the rocket engine, guidance mechanism, warhead, and other components and posted revised schedules for the completion of each stage for every component.

Hoping they had it right this time, the experts understood that the principal problems stemmed from organizational disarray and the myriad personal traumas carried over from the Cultural Revolution. Early the next year, Deng Xiaoping, now at the height of his powers,[28] told Zhang Aiping to reissue the directive that Deng had dispatched to the makers of the atomic bomb in the 1950s: "The relevant line, principle, and policy have been decided. Now it depends on [your] work. Just go ahead boldly with your work. You can claim all the credit for yourselves if you achieve success, and you can ascribe your errors to us if you commit mistakes."[29]

Once acceleration had been mandated, the Defense Science and Technology Commission had to adopt a high-risk approach in order to quicken the pace. As recounted in an earlier chapter, they thoroughly reorganized the missile program, entrusting the development of surface-to-air and antitank missiles to a new ministry, the Eighth Ministry of Machine Building, and putting the Seventh's Second Academy in charge of a crash program for the JL-1.[30] The latter decision, taken on December 17, 1978, also placed Department 4 and Institute 17 (Solid Rocket Control System Institute) under the academy's jurisdiction, a move that took until the following September to accomplish. R&D on the JL-1's solid propulsion remained under the Fourth Academy.[31]

Toward the end of 1978, the ministry also began importing Western machines and instruments for manufacturing and testing its missiles. These technologies were needed to run various tests, to design software for the control systems, to manufacture the carbon-coated quartz fibers for RV protection, to conduct precision fabrication, and to manage the flow of data. From 1978 to 1983, the ministry purchased 19 major pieces of equipment from the United States, Great Britain, West Germany, Sweden, and Holland.

During this period, the Chinese once again, as in the 1950s, equated bureaucratic administration with operational efficiency. In April 1979, in "a series of organizational measures to push the project forward,"[32] the ministry appointed Huang Weilu chief designer of the project and made Chen Deren, Dai Shizheng, and Cui Guoliang his deputies.[33] While granting Huang added powers for control of the technical parts of the project, it put Vice-Minister Cheng Lianchang in overall charge and Chai Zhi, the Second Academy's head, in administrative charge.[34]

One year later, in April 1980, as the process of bureaucratization continued, the ministry approved the Second Academy's proposal to create the Chief Designer's Office to increase the staff support for Huang. Under the office, Department 4 was assigned to supervise the implementation of the comprehensive design plan and directed to apply the methods of systems engineering to its work. Although all subordinate units were supposed to obey his orders on technical matters, Huang augmented his staff (and paperwork) to enforce compliance. The ministry also kept close to the action and used the office to manage the links between the technical and administrative arenas and to monitor the support coming from the scientific community and other state organs. The operation of Huang's Chief Designer's Office was to become a model for other strategic projects.

Final Assembly

It took years for the Seventh Ministry to settle on a plant for the final assembly of the JL-1. In March 1970, the ministry handed the assignment to Rocket Engine Test Stand 101 because of its previous experience in fabricating models of the missile.[35] Three years later, with little headway to show, the ministry picked Plant 307 (Solid Rocket General Assembly Plant) in Nanjing to do the task.[36] Caught up in the political crisis, the Central Military Commission delayed its approval of the request until 1976, when it ordered Department 4 and Institute 17 to move to Nanjing to form an R&D center alongside Plant 307.* Then, the minister, in a reversal so characteristic of the Chinese bureaucracy in those years, changed his mind and ordered the JL-1 missile assembled at Plant 211.[37] Located in Nanyuan, 15km south of Beijing, that plant had assembled most of the nation's land-based strategic missiles before other rocket assembly centers were constructed in the Third-Line region and Shanghai.[38] The matter was finally settled in March 1977, when the ministry decided that Plant 211 was too overburdened with its assignments on the DF missiles, and that Plant 307 should do the job after all, since it already possessed the necessary equipment. The Party's line of "seeking truth through facts" was beginning to make a practical difference at the working levels.

The arrangements for the JL-1's final assembly and production were pinned to a predetermined testing schedule. In February 1979, the Defense Science and Technology Commission convened a meeting to examine and adjust one more time the JL-1's technical specifications, and in March the Second Academy delivered two prototypes to Plant 307 for vibration and

*By 1979, the principal R&D centers working on the JL-1 missile were in four locations. Under the Fourth Academy (solid propulsion), Institute 41 (Solid Rocket Motor Institute) in Hohhot, Inner Mongolia, was responsible for developing the JL-1's two-stage engine; the Fourth Academy and Institute 41 had a large R&D base in Lantian, Shaanxi Province, working on solid propulsion for the JL-1 engine and other solid motors; under the Second Academy, Department 4 and Institute 17 in Beijing were in charge of supervising the implementation of the comprehensive design plan and fabricating the on-board guidance and flight control systems, respectively; and Plant 307 in Nanjing was assigned to conduct the final assembly of the missile. Note that these assignments apply only to Project JL-1. In 1986, the First Academy assumed the job of developing the three-stage JL-2 missile.

experimental flight tests. Department 4 had carried out six months of vibration tests on a prototype JL-1 missile on roads in western Liaoning Province in 1976, and these had uncovered defects that Plant 307 corrected and validated in the prototypes delivered three years later.

At the February meeting, the commission decided to flight-test the prototype JL-1s and its land-based mobile version, the DF-21, in two batches. Batch 01 was to test JL-1s that ignited after breaking the surface; the prototypes in 02 would be designed for underwater ignition. The batches would also serve different purposes: 01 would test the comprehensive design plan and the missile's subsystems; 02 would test the missile's range and accuracy. The general plan for 02 called for extending the missile's maximum range and reducing its minimum range. The goal was enhanced force flexibility in line with emerging strategic doctrines.[39]

In August 1979, Huang Weilu led an enlarged conference that decided on the test schedule for Batch 01. That batch, consisting of eight telemetry missiles (*yaoce dan*), was to be assembled by Plant 307 by the end of 1980. More meetings followed that concentrated on the remaining problems. As we have noted, defective electronic components resulted in 40 percent of the failures in missile flight tests from September 1971 to January 1978. These failures usually could be traced to sloppy workmanship. The JL-1 missile consisted of more than 10,000 parts. The Chinese learned the hard way that flaws in almost any component could cause the missile to fail.

In the first half of 1980, engineers at Plant 307 busily hammered out the details for the final assembly of the eight missiles, and their planning was affected by an incident at Plant 211. In April, as 211's technicians were dismantling a DF-5, they found a shoestring near the igniter valve of the first-stage engine. The Seventh Ministry promptly listed this as a serious "error caused by negligence," and in follow-up memos ordered the Second Academy to implement a stringent set of regulations for quality control in the final assembly at Plant 307.

These regulations consisted principally of four items. First, engineers and master workers in the assembly shop had to guarantee the exact number of required components and parts, down to the last wire and nut. Next, they had to bring their tools to a designated storeroom and confirm that each tool was back in storage after hours. Third, they had to follow a double-check system for all steps in the final assembly, and for some a triple-check. In the latter, one technician performed the task, one oversaw it, and a third checked it over. Finally, a rule of "no admittance except on authorized business" was enforced. These four rules, the Chinese say, guaranteed quality control during the final missile assembly.[40]

On October 27, 1980, technicians at Plant 307 checked out the first te-

lemetry missile (Yao-1) at Base 25 but missed a design flaw in the inertial
guidance platform. The missile, which was launched in January 1981, flew
erratically after lift-off, and the range safety officer destroyed it. The same
month, Huang's Chief Designer's Office held a meeting on the failure,
which the designer ascribed to defects in the missile's pitch-control system,
and worked out guidelines for equipping the second missile (Yao-2) with
an improved design and advanced parts.[41]

Workers then moved the assembled Yao-2 to the final inspection workshop, and scientists, engineers, and technicians put it through a final check.
After having conducted over 30 preflight tests, the plant shipped the missile
to Base 25 in April 1981.

Satisfied with their quality review, the technicians conducted inspections
of the remaining six missiles in Batch 01: Yao-3, November 1981; Yao-4,
February 1982; Yao-6, May 1982; Yao-7, June 1982; Yao-8, July 1982;
and Yao-5, June 1983. Some of these were shipped to Base 25, others to
Base 23, both of which will be described below. One (Yao-5) was sent to
a storage cave to determine the JL-1's active shelf life.[42] Like Yao-1, Yao-2
was launched from a pad at Base 25. The others were flight-tested from
launch tubes (Yao-3, 4, and 8) at Base 25 and from the Golf submarine
(Yao-6 and 7).

Although the JL-1's design work still had some loose ends, the years of
development work were coming to an end. The research and development
on the missile had reportedly involved 68 plants and research institutes,
ten industrial ministries, and 19 provinces, municipalities, and autonomous regions.[43] All these units had created ties to comparable bodies working on the nuclear submarines. The 68 units involved in the manufacture
of subsystems or individual components of the missile had met the rigorous
specifications for each part and put it through exhaustive testing. A vast
network of factories, bureaucratic organs, and military systems had
formed and proven its competence. It comprised the heart of China's military industrial complex.

Beijing soon recognized that this complex needed a major overhauling
and streamlining. On July 29, 1982, the Central Military Commission
amalgamated the Defense Science and Technology Commission, the National Defense Industry Office, and the office of the Science and Technology
Equipment Committee of the Central Military Commission into the Commission of Science, Technology, and Industry for National Defense (COS-
TIND), with Chen Bin as head. In his capacity as deputy secretary-general
of the military commission, Zhang Aiping continued to oversee the nation's defense science and industry systems until his retirement in 1988.[44]

Even as Plant 307 was going over the Batch 01 prototypes, the Second

Academy began working out a preliminary plan for Batch 02. As we have noted, that batch would be used to ascertain JL-1's maximum range and accuracy, as well as to improve its performance. In February 1982, the academy met to review 02's technical data, testing schedule, number of prototypes, and developmental procedures, and two months later, it called for the dispatch of 02's blueprints to the relevant factories and institutes by the end of the year. Other meetings followed, the most important of which was an academy conference in November that settled on 02's technical requirements and warhead design.[45]

The next month, Zhang Aiping, speaking for the Central Military Commission at a gathering in Dalian, noted that there was a worldwide trend toward solid-propellant missiles and called for a comprehensive development of these rockets in China. The commission's decision spurred the academy to step up work on Batch 02. By the end of the year, Department 4 had finalized Batch 02's comprehensive design plan as well as its test scheduling, and the academy had farmed out the remaining assignments.

But the endless round of meetings and directives was hardly over. A session called by the Chief Designer's Office in January 1983 rehearsed the details for reaching the test goals and reactivated some of the research units to revise the design plans yet again.[46] The same happened in July, and in November, COSTIND finally met to implement the design plans and settle on the number of missiles in the batch. Again, some of the 11 JL-1 and DF-21 prototypes were to be launched from land-based launch tubes, some from launching vehicles, and some from the 09-2 submarine. Two (Yao-5 and 8) were placed in reserve.

Several innovations were made in the second batch in an effort to improve the missiles' performance, including reducing the quantity of freon carried for thrust vectoring in the second-stage rocket's nozzle, installing rate gyro units on the flight control system to measure the angles of the rocket in flight (see Fig. 8, p. 156), redesigning the on-board computer, replacing the mechanical device in the self-destruct system with an electronic one, installing an air-escape valve on the instrument module, and updating the telemetry system. Some newly manufactured components replaced older ones.

The Chief Designer's Office laid down additional quality-control rules, the so-called four not's and one guarantee (*sibu yibaozhen*): (1) research institutes must not send industrial departments any blueprints containing deficiencies; (2) the manufacturer must not produce any faulty products; (3) technicians must not start final assembly until they had eliminated any flaws in the components; (4) the flight engineers must not carry out any test until they had eliminated defects in all subsystems; and (5) all research and industrial units must do their best to guarantee the predetermined technical requirements.

In the winter of 1983–84, technicians at Plant 307 vowed to obey the *sibu yibaozhen* rules and delayed the assembly process until further checks on the Batch 02 missiles had been made. The process was tedious and time-consuming, and it was not until April 10, 1984, that Plant 307 could ship Yao-1 and 2 to Base 25; Yao-6 and 7 followed several months later. These four missiles were to be flight-tested from submarine-type launch tubes. By January 1985, the plant had delivered Yao-3 and 4 to the base for testing from DF-21 transport-erector-launching vehicles. In the summer, the plant shipped the last three 02 prototypes (Yao-9, Yao-10, Yao-11) to Base 23 for flight-testing from the 09-2 submarine.

As we shall see, virtually all of the tests of 02's land-based missiles (DF-21) succeeded, but most tests of the JL-1 failed. Those that were designed to ignite above water worked well, but the version for underwater ignition was a disaster. One more test batch would be needed, and again the new batch, 03, would have a sea-launched and a land-based version. Department 4 assigned a group of designers to start formulating technical specifications for the new batch.[47]

After considerable debate, the designers simply abandoned the plans for underwater ignition. They gave all their attention instead to extending the missile's range while keeping the size of the missile constant. To increase the missile's thrust and reduce the weight of its second stage, they changed the composition of the propellant and used a new material for the casing. In addition, a group of engineers from Institute 215 joined the Department 4 designers in improving the second-stage thrust-vector control to enhance roll control.[48]

This process was completed in 1986. Institutes 41 and 17 then tinkered with the missile's subsystems for months, delaying the assembling of the batch at Plant 307 until the first half of 1988. By the summer, the plant had finished the check-out procedures on three of the 03s and shipped them to Base 25 for flight-testing from launch tubes. Other military units had long been making preparations for Batch 03's flight-testing at Base 23. Three missiles arrived in August, and the next month, flight tests of this sea-launched version began.

Bases 23 and 25

As soon as Project JL-1 started in the 1960s, plans were put in motion for testing the missile. In October 1967, the Defense Science and Technology Commission and the navy met to examine the comprehensive design plan for the JL-1 and agreed on a division of assignments for the test phase: the commission would run the ground tests, and the navy the sea tests. The Central Military Commission designated Bases 25 and 23 to conduct the testing program, the former for the land tests and the latter for tests from the submerged Golf submarine.[49]

Base 23 had its origins in the New Defense Technical Accord signed by Marshal Nie Rongzhen and Marshal I. S. Konev in Moscow on October 15, 1957, which committed the Soviet Union to help China develop strategic and tactical weapons, including help in crew training and the construction of plants, research facilities, and missile test ranges.[50] In January and February 1958, four Soviet specialists, along with a group of Chinese naval officers, began searching for sites to test two Soviet antiship missiles.[51] They wanted a test range close to rail and air communications and to a bay whose topography would conceal the tests from spying and would serve as a baffle to radio frequencies used in the tests. Three possible sites were located (two in Liaoning Province and one in Shandong Province), and in due course Defense Minister Peng Dehuai chose Huludao, Liaoning Province, for the Antiship Missile Test Range (Base 23).[52]

On October 20, 1958, the navy appointed Zheng Guozhong and Yang Guoyu base commander and deputy commander of this top secret base. Two months later, engineering units began groundbreaking, and hundreds of technicians arrived to erect the test facilities. The technicians were isolated on the base and forbidden all outside contact. Wives remember their husbands "suddenly disappearing before their eyes."[53] In March 1959, seven Soviet specialists joined the base force to help finish the layout and rush the completion of the initial phase by June. The first test was conducted on June 12, but to the obvious dismay of the specialists, the antiship missile missed the target by 280m. Despite this unfortunate start, the base had begun operating, and by the mid-1960s, its personnel had acquired the basic skills needed for the *julang* project.

In August 1967, the Defense Science and Technology Commission directed Base 23 to organize an office to oversee the construction of an SLBM test range. Three months later, the office submitted two reports on the location and layout of the range to the commission, and in response, the commission and the navy set out to locate an impact zone in the Gobi Desert.[54] In early 1968, Bing Ye, then the base deputy commander, headed a prospecting team to investigate potential sites near the main *dongfeng* test facility, Base 20, later called the Jiuquan Satellite Launch Center, at Shuangchengzi, Gansu Province, as well as other areas.[55] After two-and-a-half months of aerial surveys, Bing recommended shifting the search to the coast, and the General Staff approved.

Given the constantly shifting priorities of the Cultural Revolution years, the search proceeded in fits and starts, and only years later did Beijing finally designate a sea zone west of Dalian, Liaoning Province, as the place for the SLBM sea trials and a zone about 325km off the Zhejiang coast as the impact zone.[56] In May 1976, the Base 23 commander created the Ballistic Missile Test Department to oversee these tests, the construction of the test range, the emplacement of the measurement instruments, and the formulation of procedures and safety regulations. Full-scale construction of the range then commenced.*

Chinese missile test ranges principally consist of centers for command and control, communications, and data processing, plus a timing system for the precise synchronization of all electronic equipment. They also embrace various stations for flight measurement and control, most of which contain telemetry systems to receive signals indicating the flight status of the missile, optical tracking equipment (including cinetheodolites, tracking telescopes, and laser range finders), a radio tracking system (including pulse and continuous-wave radars), and a system to control the missile during the boost phase.[57]

The main range for testing the JL-1 was Test Range 2, and hundreds of pieces of monitoring equipment were installed along the coast and on islands situated within its boundaries. As of the mid-1970s, some of the required equipment had not yet arrived or even been developed.[58] The principal difficulty came in fabricating a triggering radar that could lock on to the missile as it broke the surface of the sea and deliver information to a computer for initiating the operation of all other tracking and measurement equipment. For years, the Tenth Academy (Military Radio and Electronics Academy) of the Fourth or Electronics Industry Ministry failed in its attempts to complete the radar, rendering all other monitoring systems inoperable.[59] A specialist named Gu Shouren finally did the job.[60] In 1977, the Ballistic Missile Test Department, predecessor of Test Range 2, assigned Gu to design the radar and dispatched him and a 12-member design team to the Chang'an Machine-Building General Plant in Lu'an, Anhui Province.[61] Some of the 12 despised the hard life of the Anhui mountains, a minor Third-Line area, and quickly invented excuses to return to Base 23. Within a very short period, only three assistants remained with Gu to continue the project, and it took until 1980 to refine the design drawings for the radar.[62]

The Ballistic Missile Test Department also needed equipment capable of

---

*Over time, Base 23 acquired more responsibilities and, in the late 1970s, with the addition of two new departments to the three it had, one for testing electronic countermeasures equipment and radar (May 1978) and one for testing depth charges (April 1978), it was renamed the Naval Test Base. In May 1981, the General Staff reorganized the five departments into four test ranges in the Huludao-Lüshun area and gave them different assignments: Test Range 1 for antiship missiles, guns, and navigational equipment; Test Range 2 for SLBMs, torpedoes, and mines; Test Range 3 for electronic countermeasures equipment and radar; and Test Range 4 for depth charges.

precisely measuring JL-1's ballistics during the boost phase and requested permission to import it. Premier Zhou Enlai approved the request, and in early 1975, the Defense Science and Technology Commission began negotiating with a French firm. The sticking point was price: the French wanted $10 million for each set of equipment, and the Chinese would go only as high as $7.5 million. No amount of bargaining, it seemed, could break the impasse. But the French negotiators, stuck in Beijing, eventually capitulated and, on December 31, agreed to the Chinese price.[63]

The tracking and measurement equipment began to arrive from France that summer, and the technicians faced the task of assembling the more than 400 pieces of equipment into an integrated system. Gu Shouren once again undertook the assignment and headed a 30-person group that worked around the clock until the summer of 1981. System tests consumed the next few months, and by the end of the year, the equipment appeared ready for the first missile test.[64]

The JL-1's other test site, Base 25, also dated back to the 1960s. Spread across Kelan-Wuzhai-Xingxian counties, in northern Shanxi Province, it had been built for the testing of the DF-3 intermediate missile.[65]

Paradoxically, far from impeding the development of this base, the general turmoil of the Cultural Revolution had caused the military to accelerate work on it. By the spring of 1967, Base 20 in Shuangchengzi had already attracted the attention of the radicals, and the Defense Science and Technology Commission desperately sought a way to continue missile testing insulated from them. Construction of the DF-3 test range in Kelan had only just started on a small scale and had not yet been disrupted by political rallies. In addition, it was relatively close to Beijing, so that the commission could easily oversee the entire project. Thus, in April 1967, Nie Rongzhen, still functioning as the commission's director, ordered the immediate construction of a base headquarters.[66]

The commission assigned one of the institutes at Base 20 to help integrate the myriad electronics and optical equipment for the new base's missile tracking and monitoring system.[67] With the system finally in place, Base 25 conducted its first successful test of a DF-3 in December 1968, and by the early 1980s, it had become a large test complex for the DF program and even contained a silo for launching the DF-5.[68] In 1977, the commission made the base the locale for testing the JL-1 from launch pads and tubes and an area in Inner Mongolia the impact zone.[69]

The Instrumentation Fleet

Before the full testing program could begin, one more unit had to be completed, the ship-based telemetry system. The Chinese had begun installing tracking equipment at Base 20 and along a full test range in the

Northwest in the late 1950s. This was mostly optical tracking equipment, imported from the Soviet Union and suitable only for short-range missiles. When all Soviet military assistance halted in the summer of 1960, the Chinese were forced to build telemetry systems on their own, especially those for longer-range missiles.[70]

In most test programs, telemetry systems (for monitoring accelerations along the missile's three axes and other information) are supplemented by optical tracking equipment (for measuring some angles with high precision).[71] In May 1963, the Tenth Academy (radio electronics) assigned the Southwest Institute of Electronic Technology (Institute 1010) to study alternative tracking systems. Located in Chengdu, Sichuan Province, and attached to the Tenth Academy, the institute had long been the premier body for creating both tracking and telecommunication systems and is credited with most of the work done on these systems for the DF program.[72]

In June 1965, the Defense Science and Technology Commission ordered the Fourth Ministry to develop a workable telemetry system for the DF series missile tests. The commission approved the ministry's suggestion to proceed in two steps: first developing a system for the DF-3 and DF-4, and then developing a system with a longer operating range for the intercontinental DF-5. The ministry then ordered several institutes (including 1010) to carry out these steps. By April 1968, they had built tracking systems required for the various telemetry networks and achieved medium accuracies in measurement for the first two missiles.

As part of the efforts to prepare for the DF-5 flight tests, one of the institutes (1014) started work on a new telemetry system with much higher precision and longer operating ranges. The most important component of the system, a radar code-named 180, proved the main stumbling block, and no progress on the 180 could be reported after years of frustrating failure. In 1978, the Tenth Academy ordered the Electronic Engineering Institute (Institute 1028) in Nanjing, a radar research organ, to provide technical assistance to the project. No. 1028 assigned its senior engineer, Liu Xing, to help out.[73] Together, this array of institutes completed a working model of the 180 and by the end of the decade perfected its operation.

Meanwhile, other institutes hurried to finish the optical tracking equipment. The commission assigned the Changchun Institute of Optical and Fine Mechanics to the task, which was code-named Project 150.[74] A cine-theodolite with a maximum operating range of 150km was listed as the key component of the system.[75] This is a special surveying theodolite in which motion picture cameras take precise time-correlated pictures of the missiles (or other space objects) in flight. The institute not only built a cine-theodolite that exceeded the minimum requirements but also, in the 1980s, developed a laser range finder, extended its detection range to hundreds of kilometers with a measurement error in percentage terms of less than 10^{-5}, and integrated it into the cinetheodolite. This laser cinetheodolite could rapidly compute the position of a spacecraft from either a ground- or a ship-based platform.[76] In 1978, technicians at the Institute of Photoelectric Technology in Chengdu also investigated how to apply photoelectricity to the tracking system, and by 1985, they had developed a sophisticated system capable of photographing very small objects miles away.[77]

In addition to the land-based tracking and monitoring equipment, the navy had to construct instrumentation ships and stations for monitoring the down-range reentry of nose cones over the sea.[78] The United States and the Soviet Union had designed special ships for this purpose in the 1950s, and in the 1970s, France retrofitted an oil tanker to that end.[79] China identified its need for the ships during the planning phase on the DF-5, and Zhou Enlai called for their construction at the thirteenth meeting of the Central Special Commission, in August 1965. The commission charged the Defense Science and Technology Commission with conducting feasibility studies, which it did the following year.[80]

After prolonged research, Nie Rongzhen's commission concluded that a modern sea-based telemetry system should include instrumentation ships, auxiliary ships, and destroyers for convoying the task force. In two reports submitted to the Central Military Commission in July and August 1967, it recommended the creation of this fleet (subsequently code-named Project 718).[81] In September, the military commission approved the reports and told Nie's commission to work out the details and report back. Again the Cultural Revolution intervened; Nie was ousted a few months later, and little progress was made over the next three years. In December 1970, the Central Special Commission met to assess the state of Project 718 and quickly became embroiled in controversy.

Zhang Chunqiao, a Politburo member with special influence in Shanghai, the nation's principal shipbuilding industrial base, was vehemently opposed to the project. "Is the Seventh Academy capable of designing these ships?" he asked. "I still doubt whether it is necessary to drain off huge sums to build so many ships. I am in favor of land forces. We should depend on the army to fight a war." His opinions echoed sentiments associated with Mao's traditional military thinking and forced a series of delicate compromises. The special commission, for example, overrode Zhang and approved the project, but gave him something of a sop by creating a Project 718 Leading Group headed by one of his associates, the radical Li Zuopeng.[82] Zhou Enlai, for his part, appointed the expert Chen Youming as director of the Project 718 Office and imbued the office with genuine powers.[83] Calling for the fulfillment of the project by the end of 1972 as part of the quest to complete the DF-5, the commission delineated each organ's authority and assignment: the Defense Science and Technology Commission would take overall charge of research on the instrumentation ships' subsystems for measurement, control, communication, and meteorology; and the Sixth Ministry of Machine Building (shipbuilding) would conduct research on other subsystems and prepare the ships' comprehensive design plans.

Mao Zedong, always an enthusiast for modern weapons, approved the special commission's decision, and the State Council and the Central Military Commission reaffirmed the priority status of Project 718, declaring that it "should take precedence over others" in the supply of materials. Despite Mao's endorsement, the affected units in Shanghai were not pleased and moved to sabotage the effort. When Qiu Huizuo, then the Politburo member in charge of logistic supplies, joined the project's opponents, the obstacles mounted.[84] At that time, Qiu and Li Zuopeng were vying for Lin Biao's favor, and Qiu told Li, "What do you mean special case? You cannot settle this matter until you have consulted me!" With the elephants fighting, the mice scurried for cover. The project ground to a halt and was shelved until 1972.

At that point, Qian Xuesen, an adviser to the nation's missile program, warned, "In order to conduct full-range flight tests of our intercontinental ballistic missiles [for verifying their accuracy], we have to build oceangoing instrumentation ships."[85] In response, Zhou Enlai, then seriously ill, told Marshal Ye Jianying to review the project, and on April 8, 1972, Ye convened a conference for this purpose.[86] Zhang Chunqiao attended this Central Military Commission meeting and again expressed opposition, adding, "It will be very difficult for Shanghai to undertake the assignment even if you decide to start the project." Ye Jianying flared in anger: "Since the approval of the Premier, we have let almost eight years slip by without accomplishing anything. Can we wage one more War of Resistance Against Japan [a war that also lasted eight years]?" Outraged by Zhang's objection and unwilling to waste eight more years, Ye Jianying preemptively announced that the project would be restarted. The goal was 13 ships of five types: instrumentation ships, survey ships, salvage vessels, support ships, and rescue tugboats. Six ships were to be built in phase one: two instrumentation ships, and one each of the others.

From April to September 1972, the Project 718 Leading Group held six meetings to settle the technical specifications for the five types of ships, the largest of which would displace over 12,000 tons. The group determined that the instrumentation ship and its equipment would be the most difficult to design and build. The measurement equipment, possibly operating in heavy seas, would have to track an incoming missile with high precision, and the navigation system would have to establish the ship's position accurately. Precise measurement would require all instruments to operate according to a common baseline in these same unpredictable seas; the instruments would have to negate the interference from vibration, noise, and electromagnetic waves; and the main command and engine controls would need advanced automation and communications.

The job of meeting these requirements fell to Institute 708 in Shanghai, and specifically to the 70 members of Work Team 64, headed by Xu Xueyan. Formulating the design plans for the instrumentation ship took two years.[87] In September 1974, the Project 718 Leading Group approved the design plans, and the nation's defense science and industry establishment launched a shipbuilding crusade. Thirty-five ministries and commissions under the State Council mobilized over 1,180 organizations in Shanghai, Beijing, Tianjin, and 21 provinces to complete the project.[88]

But the crusade quickly mired down, further delaying the full-range flight test of the DF-5. In November 1976, following the death of Mao and the arrest of the Gang of Four, the Central Military Commission and the State Council disbanded the Project 718 Leading Group and ordered the Defense Science and Technology Commission to take over its assignments. Zhang Aiping issued a ritual speedup edict, and indeed the Jiangnan Shipyard did launch two instrumentation ships in August and October 1977. Nevertheless, slow progress on the inertial navigation system, the central computer, and the missile-range-instrumentation radar impeded the outfitting of the two vessels, and the deadline for their completion slipped again, this time to December 31, 1979.[89]

At this point, in September 1977, Zhang warned that senior officials would be punished if their departments failed to fulfill their assignments by the deadline. Three tardy programs received special attention, and Zhang ordered three institutes to take control of them:[90]

Institute 707 in Tianjin, to develop the inertial navigation system.[91]
The North China Computation Institute in Beijing, to build the central computer (DJS-260).[92]
Institute 1014 in Nanjing, to make the missile-range-instrumentation radar (code-named 180).[93]

Under these units, the tempo of the three programs quickened.

More meetings followed, and by December, all equipment had been installed on the two instrumentation ships, *Distant Observer* Nos. 1 and 2. Institute 1028 sent specialists to integrate the telemetry system's tracking and monitoring equipment, and on December 16, the system was put into test operation.[94] A new base in Jiangyin, Jiangsu Province, became the measurement fleet's home port.[95] In the next few months, the rest of the ships were outfitted,[96] and on May 1, 1980, the fleet set out with a convoy of six destroyers to monitor the first full-range flight test of the DF-5 missile on May 18.[97] The fleet was ready for the flight tests of the JL-1.

Flight-Testing Batch 01

Once the bases and instrumentation ships were readied, the preparations for the upcoming flight tests focused on endless small details. Surveyors had to precisely determine the locations of the launch pads or tubes in relation to each observation station. They had to calculate how the gravitational force increased as latitude increased. Each new figure had to be entered into the launch coefficients.[98]

Among the thousands of civilian and military topographers who took on the job, the General Staff relied most on its Mapping Brigade No. 1.[99] The brigade had earned its reputation for having made seminal contributions to the strategic weapons program, and its specialties were astronomical geodesy, including the measurement of gravity anomalies.[100] In 1970, Zhou Enlai extended the brigade's mission to the Qinghai-Tibet plateau, telling them to map the best sites for launch complexes and observation stations on the "roof of the world." In 1978, the General Staff assigned two helicopters and two air transports to the brigade as part of the DF-5 and JL-1 testing programs, and the brigade completed the geodetic work on these programs three years later. For the JL-1 tests, it concentrated its surveys at the launch sites at Bases 23 and 25 and the impact zones in Inner Mongolia and off the Zhejiang coast.[101]

As the topographic work proceeded, the eight telemetry missiles from Batch 01 began to arrive at the two test bases. After the failure of the first test on January 2, 1981, Chief Designer Huang Weilu and his specially formed test team took extra pains on the second missile, which was shipped in April. A special train was assigned to the missile, and during the trip, the team repeatedly checked its instrumentation. Huang and his coworkers had spent nearly 5,000 days in developing the various subsystems and overseeing the final assembly of Yao-2, and they kept reassuring themselves that this time the bird would fly.[102]

The flight test on June 17, 1981, became a textbook for all future tests. Huang roused his crew at four in the morning and headed for the launch pad. Rain was falling, but the base weathermen assured Huang that the storm would clear, providing a launch window between 0800 and 0900. Everything seemed to go on schedule until T minus 5 minutes. In the underground command post, Huang was notified that the voltmeter needle in the first-stage servomechanism was flickering. Huang knew that the missile was highly sensitive "to a blast of wind or a very slight earth tremor" and assumed that the proximity of test crews on the ground had jolted the voltmeter. Nevertheless, he asked for a judgment on whether the problem indicated a possible failure of the inertial guidance platform and, when given a firm negative, ordered the countdown to resume. The lift-off brought a roar from the bunker, which was repeated on news that the dummy warhead had landed on target in Inner Mongolia.[103] The base commander grabbed Huang by the hand and congratulated him. Now crying, Huang took a deep breath and murmured, "This has taken us 14 years [1967–81]."

The next two tests, in January and April 1982, were made from silo-based launch tubes.[104] The second of these was designed to test the JL-1's ability to achieve its proper attitude if ignited significantly off-vertical. Engineers installed a miniature rocket engine at the base of the missile to produce a lateral thrust comparable to an actual launch condition at sea. The test verified the performance of the SLBM's autostabilization system, and the Defense Science and Technology Commission declared that its success "had prepared the ground" for flight-testing the JL-1 from the Golf submarine at Test Range 2, Base 23.

As early as March 1980, the commission and the navy had formed a joint headquarters for flight-testing at sea. Under the supervision of Zhang Aiping, this organ oversaw the mobilization and deployment of all test personnel (including 899 technicians from 23 naval units) and ships, the safety of the relevant shipping lanes, and inspection of the observation stations.[105] From April to August 1981, the Ocean Measurement Brigade of the North China Sea Fleet undertook a complete sonar mapping of the ocean bottom under the test range in order to pinpoint obstacles that might imperil the operation of the Golf submarine. The brigade also surveyed and charted the impact zone and measured gravity anomalies along the test flight path. It completed this operation by the end of the year.[106]

In January 1982, Zhang Aiping ordered the completion of all preparations for the test, code-named 9182, by August 31. In March, his headquarters set up a command post at Test Range 2, with Tian Zuocheng as head and Huang Weilu and Huang Xuhua as deputies, and a command post at the impact zone under Tian Zhenhuan.[107] In the summer, Plant 307 shipped three missiles (Yao-6, 7, 8) to the base.[108]

Zhou Ganlin, director of a research institute attached to Test Range 2, and his engineers then ran through an item-by-item check list of all parts and instruments on the missiles. They found 74 defective components, such as a faulty electrical control cable, and sent them back to the factories for replacement. Welders and installers from two shipyards spent one night testing the control cable on the submarine. For some, the work had personal as well as professional meaning; during these long hours "some young men and women got acquainted, fell in love with each other, and got married." One couple, however, had to postpone their wedding day three times in order to make preparations for the launch.

Details piled on details. The central computer's software bedeviled the specialists right up to the last minute. As early as 1978, Test Range 2 had assigned Li Fucai, head of Institute 230's Mathematics Programming Research Section, to develop a program for processing and displaying all of the incoming data during the flight.[109] His work involved a dozen or so disciplines, including geophysics, geodesy, cybernetics, flight mechanics, and applied mathematics, and the job was not wrapped up until the autumn of 1982.

Other technicians spent long hours on the raft-carried antenna that would ensure unimpeded communications between the submarine and the command post and mark the boat's location.[110] Another 80 people, including two women, were ordered to undergo survival training, which included donning heavy diving gear and being ejected through one of the torpedo tubes.[111]

Meantime, the navy ordered the North China Sea Fleet to send the Golf submarine to Test Range 2 for "precombat" training, and the fleet commander directed a submarine flotilla stationed at Lüshun to join the training.[112] From January 15 to September 7, 1982, Captain Shi Zongli took the Golf to sea on 37 runs, which included both on-board tests and ship-to-shore drills (using aircraft to simulate the SLBM in tuning all communications and telemetry) as well as survival training.[113] During the tests, various "failures" were fed into the missile launch system to test the crew's readiness for emergencies.

On September 20, Zhang Aiping, still not satisfied, ordered a full dress rehearsal to be conducted by the end of the month. Three days later, a test involving all units was carried out, and on October 1, the Beijing news agency announced that between October 7 and October 26, China would launch missiles into a circular ocean area with a radius of 35 nautical miles, centered at 28 degrees, 13 minutes north latitude and 123 degrees, 53 minutes east longitude.[114]

On October 4, three days before the first missile was scheduled to go off, Zhang called for special weather and sea-state reports on the launch and impact zones. He further asked the navy to prepare for support and rescue at the test range, the splashdown area of the first-stage rocket, and the impact zone for the second stage and RV; 73 warships and 19 planes were dispatched to the three areas. The two instrumentation ships (one of which was to serve as a command post) and two rescue tugboats set sail for the impact zone, and some 320 engineers and officers from 40 units assembled at Test Range 2 as part of the grand mobilization.[115]

One incident underscored the high drama of the moment. Senior officials came from Beijing to give the crew a send-off party, and during the banquet on the day of the test, October 7, they asked the crew whether they had any last words for their families. The officials deliberately accentuated the risks facing the submarine and urged the married crew members to leave notes for their spouses telling them not to remain single if the test ended in disaster.[116]

On this less than encouraging note, the crew boarded the submarine and cast off. Arriving at the test range, they quickly submerged and, upon receiving confirming orders, they launched Yao-6 at 1514 hours. The first-stage engine ignited normally after breaking the surface, but then acted erratically. The range safety officer pressed the destruct button, and the missile disintegrated. The time: 4.2 seconds after ignition.

That night, a discouraged Huang Weilu looked at the telemetry data and concluded that the failure had resulted from a disconnected stage-separation plug, blocking commands to the first-stage servos.[117] Relieved that the problem was so simple, he ordered corrective measures and recommended that the tests continue. COSTIND agreed, and preparations for the next flight test resumed.[118]

On October 9, the weathermen predicted good test conditions in three days, and on the morning of the 12th, Huang received an emergency call from Zhang Aiping's command center in Beijing.[119] The caller, a senior official, tactfully "suggested" a postponement of the test, and Huang found himself in a quandary. At the time, the weather was marginal, cloudy with light rain, but the base weathermen assured him that the afternoon would be clear. Recognizing the gamble, Huang called the command center and recommended against the postponement. The official relented and gave his consent.

Again escorted by surface warships and observation vessels, the Golf submarine put to sea. The procedures of the earlier test were repeated, and on station, the submarine dove to launch depth and awaited the message to fire. Captain Shi Zongli was in command. With the boat on the right course and speed at T minus 5 minutes, he ordered the opening of the hatch on the launch tube. Clocks on rafts on the surface indicated the time remaining, and red dyes marked the missile's point of exit from the sea.[120]

"Open the firing pin safety!" "Disconnect the test plug!" The final two console lights showed green, and Li Guiren, head of the launch control center, began the countdown.[121] Technicians updated the missile guidance computer with precise data on position, depth, and angles of gradient. At 1500, Li gave the order to fire, and Yao-7 burst out of the water.

Observers on board the closest vessel, a kilometer away, watched the first stage ignite and the missile roar into space. The optical equipment monitoring the rocket transmitted the success to the large screen at the test range command post. The entire down-range system came alive and began to process the incoming data. An image on an electronic map plotted the missile's progress to the target. The thrill of the moment, the Chinese who were present believe, must have matched that at the Kennedy Space Center when the first manned mission to the moon lifted off.

By this point, computers had told the two instrumentation ships at the impact zone to prepare for reentry. The tracking and monitoring system had only about 30 seconds to lock on to the RV and activate the full monitoring and RV recovery systems.[122] It worked. A "fireball" soon emerged from the clouds and careened into the sea, sending up a column of water. A coloring agent from the RV turned the water emerald green. Super Frelon helicopters imported from France had already taken off from the two tugboats to photograph the splashdown and recover the capsule.[123] The photographs and telemetry proved crucial because by all indications the data in the RV capsule were lost.[124]

But this was minor. The commander at the impact zone reported to his counterpart at Test Range 2 that the test was a complete success. A wave of self-congratulations descended on the command post and engulfed Huang Weilu, who once again burst into tears.[125] The mood in Beijing that evening, October 12, 1982, was euphoric.[126]

Flight-Testing Batch 02

The Second Academy had originally meant to use one of Batch 02's telemetry missiles to test the range and accuracy of the JL-1. But following the test of Yao-7 on October 12, it ordered the engineers to retrofit Batch 01's Yao-8 for launching from a ground tube at Base 25, and on May 1, the test went off on schedule. The JL-1's maximum range was reportedly 1,700km and its circular error was probably less than 3km.[127]

The main purpose of 02's sea-based version, it will be recalled, was to test underwater ignition. These tests would be used to finalize the design of the missile before it was put into serial production. In addition, this version would be fired from the nuclear submarine, boat 406. The Chinese therefore attached the highest importance to the 02 tests.

The new round of testing required additional equipment and the precise synchronization of all the electronics in the network.[128] To this end, the

Fourth Ministry had two 2,000kw long-wave pulse transmitters installed at the Shaanxi Astronomical Observatory to increase the precision of the timing signal from milliseconds to microseconds.[129] Furthermore, in the Yao-7 test, the difference between the computer-calculated splashdown point and the actual one had been 5km; the base engineers set out to reduce the difference to 1km.[130]

By this time, 1984, the Chinese had begun flight-testing Batch 02's land-based version (DF-21) from launch tubes at Base 25. The first two of these (Yao-1, 2) were successfully launched on August 12 and 22, but a defect in the inertial guidance platform forced the destruction of a third missile (Yao-6), launched on November 22. Analysis pointed the way to easy corrections, and the next test (Yao-7), on December 28, went off without a hitch. These tests led the way to follow-on tests of the DF-21 (Yao-3, 4) from the erector-launcher the following spring.[131] With the success of these tests, the emphasis shifted back to sea and the JL-1.

As early as August 1983, the navy convened a meeting of specialists to discuss the proposed tests from the 09-2 nuclear-powered submarine. In response, COSTIND made the Second Academy responsible for the submarine's safety and authorized the academy to build four dummy missiles to double-check the sub's missile ejection and fire-control systems. These were ejected from the submerged 406 the following March and April without incident. Later in the year, the academy assigned Department 4 to perform ejection tests on small-scale model rockets to study the effects of underwater ignition. These too were successful, and all concerned were now convinced of the feasibility of their project.

Thereafter, the navy quickened preparations for the sea tests, code-named Test 9185. In an effort to bolster "precombat" training, the joint headquarters directed the crew of the 406 and the missile engineers to conduct a series of on-board tests from January to June 1985. In August, Plant 307 shipped three telemetry missiles to Base 23 for launch from the submarine to verify the underwater ignition techniques. The first of these, launched on September 28 (Yao-10), ejected normally but then became erratic and was destroyed. On October 7 and 15, the next two missiles (Yao-9, 11) suffered the same fate.

In November, a group of specialists began summing up the experiences acquired in Test 9185. After analyzing the data, Huang Weilu attributed the failures to the poor adaptability of the flight controls to underwater ignition. He believed that the basic design of the JL-1 was correct and should be adhered to despite the failures. He stressed that the JL-1 was functional if it was ignited above the ocean surface but acknowledged that the three failures would delay the final design decisions. In April 1986,

COSTIND and the navy set the end of 1987 as the deadline for finalizing the JL-1 design and ordered one more batch of test missiles.

The 1985 flight-testing also exposed serious defects in the two instrumentation ships. On both, the fresh-water distillation plant broke down, and on one, the supply of water to the main boiler was totally cut off.[132] A main radar transmitter on the other failed even before it lifted anchor, and emergency repairs caused a delay of several hours.[133] Other defective electronics needed replacement, the command-and-control communications turned out to have inadequate range and capacity, and the cost of each test proved to be prohibitive. The list of deficiencies seemed endless.[134]

Flight-Testing of Batch 03

From April 1986 to October 1987, over 70 research and industrial facilities were involved in replacing or upgrading 300 items of equipment and 100 special compartments that housed them in the measurement ships.[135] Meanwhile, work went forward on Batch 03, and by the summer of 1988, Plant 307 had shipped three land-based prototypes to Base 25. Again the ground-based tests there went well, and attention shifted back to the sea experiments.[136]

By then, however, the Chinese military faced new problems. Starting in the mid-1980s, Chinese leaders put unprecedented stress on making economic and social reforms. One result was a slackening of social discipline, and in some areas, the local citizens began stealing materials from military bases for their personal use. Half of the nation's communications depended on lines the military had built in the two previous decades in aid of the strategic weapons tests, but now the theft of electrical cable and equipment threatened to cripple the military's capacity to provide communication support for the JL-1 sea trials.[137]

Governed by the principle of maintaining good army-people relations, the military could not employ force to halt the thefts, and the lawlessness, which even reached Bases 23 and 25, grew steadily worse. Some bases were virtually looted.[138] Since the ordinary security police had fewer inhibitions in the use of force, the military and the Ministry of Public Security decided in 1987 to set up police substations at the affected installations, and the situation gradually improved.[139] The losses, however, put a severe crimp in the plans for upgrading the communications system at Test Range 2 and throughout the test complex.[140]

Another problem plagued the military. Previously, strict secrecy had enshrouded all strategic weapons tests. On the eve of the first nuclear test, for example, Zhou Enlai repeatedly warned the high command to guard the nuclear secret with vigilance. He tolerated no leaks and did not even mention the forthcoming test to his wife, herself a senior official.[141] By the late 1980s, however, knowledge of the JL-1's test program had spread throughout the country and even reached foreigners.[142] Testing over the ocean areas would reveal still more about the missile's capabilities and potential limitations. In planning the next sequence of JL-1 launches, the military thus had to contend with a quite unexpected consequence of China's turn to a policy of greater openness.[143]

Finally, the organizational changes of the 1980s had taken their toll, as had the deaths and retirements of the veterans of the building years.[144] COSTIND was no Central Special Commission. It had less power than the now defunct commission to manage the vast network of defense ministries, industrial and research agencies, and military departments, where indifference, rejection, and graft now too often replaced innovation, responsibility, and ungrudging compliance. Increasingly, the understaffed Central Military Commission had to intervene to break deadlocks and to calm emotions that would not have arisen in earlier years. Bureaucratism had infected the strategic weapons organizations as never before, and the commission had to monitor the most mundane details as it set the JL-1 test process in motion in the summer of 1988.

Most of the attention, of course, focused on the sub and missiles chosen for the test.[145] In March 1988, Du Yongguo, aged 36, had taken command of the 406 after completing an advanced course at the Submarine Institute for prospective captains of nuclear-powered submarines.[146] That June, the Nuclear Submarine Repair Team at Qingdao sent a 24-man force to Base 23 to double-check 406's subsystems, make repairs, and serve as on-board troubleshooters during the launch series.[147]

The arrival of the three Batch 03 prototypes at Base 23 in August touched off a feverish round of test-range inspections and missile checks. Other specialists from the Second and Seventh academies worked with the 406 crew to go through a long checklist of possible emergencies and failures. On September 7, 1988, the official news agency broadcast that between September 14 and October 3, China would launch rockets into the same circular sea area as the 1982 test.[148] The countdown began.

Gunboats and aircraft moved to patrol Test Range 2. Naval units, the Lüshun Bureau of Public Security, and the local armed police headquarters augmented the forces guarding the areas near the port of Lüshun.[149] Other units manned posts along the Dalian-Lüshun highway and around Test Range 2. Thousands of militiamen were moved into position to protect every installation, including every electrical pole, connected to the test; one militiaman stood every 50m along the communication lines to guard the cables. Security was especially tight at Test Range 2. Everyone had to carry a numbered pass, which was coded for the locales and levels of his or her authorized access.[150]

The crew of the 406 buckled down to its "precombat" regimen and gave the boat a thorough going over. The technical officers concentrated on each missile launcher compartment and the nuclear power plant. Captain Du ordered ten of the officers to check the main components of the missile ejection system every half hour.[151]

At 0900, September 15, 1988, with a south wind providing good visibility, submarine 406 and its accompanying fleet set sail from Lüshun for the test range.[152] At 1230, the range command post went to full-alert status as the post commander, Wang Huique, announced "Minus two hours has been reached!"[153] This was the order for 406 to dive and begin its underwater maneuvers. At T minus five minutes, the monitoring equipment at the test range began recording the signals from the submarine. Wang: "Minus one minute has been reached!" When the countdown clock indicated 30 seconds, Liu Yueming, the 30-year-old chief of the missile launcher compartment on the 406, began to call out the remaining seconds, and the safeties were released. At 1430, Liu's deputy pushed the red button. Crew members recall hearing a rumbling noise and heaving a collective sigh of relief as the missile ejected. The submarine shuddered slightly.

The watchers at the command post caught a glimpse of the missile as it broke surface, ignited, and rocketed upward. The camera caught the rising projectile and filmed it disappearing into the heavens. In a few seconds, it was gone, leaving behind a vapor trail of white smoke. At the tracking and control center, an automatic logger began showing the missile's progress. It followed closely the precalculated theoretical path. The words flowed: "Rocket flying normally!" "First-stage engine cutoff. Second-stage engine ignition!" "Second-stage engine cutoff!" The down-range tracking center issued equally positive messages. The instrumentation ships reported in: "The *Distant Observer* ships have located RV. Flying normally!" "Reentry vehicle splashed down. On target at the designated point!" All ships in unison sounded their sirens in victory.

The high command rejoiced. Encouraged by this unqualified success, it decided to test one more JL-1 rocket to acquire complete flight data. The range command post studied the weather reports, including data from special weather balloons, and proposed September 27 as the launch date.[154] The joint headquarters in Beijing gave the okay.

On the afternoon of the scheduled day, about 100 technicians and sailors boarded the 406 and embarked for the test range. Escorted by several vessels, the submarine put out to Test Range 2. This second test wrote the textbook on forecasting the actual splashdown point, tracking and measuring, and recovering the flight data.[155]

Commander Wang Huique told the press soon thereafter that the two tests marked "one more leap forward for China's national defense modernization" and, compared to those launched from the Golf submarine in 1982, had "made great technical breakthroughs." Huang Xuhua, the chief designer of the 406, was even more effusive, observing: "Some subsystems of Chinese-built nuclear-powered submarines have approached or attained advanced world levels."[156] The navy simply noted that China had acquired a sea-based retaliatory capability.[157]

PART III

Strategy

NINE

Strategic Uncertainty

Although China has built one of the most weapons-oriented military forces in the world, Western sources continue to quote Mao's dictum "man over weapons" and mock its quaintness.[1] But as we have seen, the message Mao imparted to his inner circle and to those who built the nation's retaliatory forces was far different: whatever they have, we must have. His avowal of "man over weapons," Chinese even now say, "boosted the morale" of the people from the 1950s to the 1970s.[2] That he spoke in other terms to his poverty-stricken people is not surprising, but he believed that they would grasp his secret intentions once the missiles and nuclear submarines stood guard. He was not wrong.

Mao's more extreme communications to his people did spawn an era of great upheaval. He wanted it both ways: strategic power and revolutionary conversion. As a consequence, experts and builders became the ministers of progress and the victims of extremism. Those quartered in safe military and industrial havens embraced Mao's call to arm and welded it to their own special brand of national pride and scientific zeal.[3] Their insularity, organizational flexibility, and the innovative leadership of the Beijing military industrial complex coincided with the high drama of the atomic weapons program, and the high adventure overcame or simply outlasted Mao's inquisitions against them. The next generation of missile and nuclear submarine builders were not so fortunate.

In the atomic program, few worried about the inconsistencies between explicit propaganda and implicit program guidelines. Mao's worldview dominated overt doctrinal formulations and precluded a legitimate search for strategic explanations more compatible with military realities and weapons plans. The path of action obscured the anomalies of official ideology.

It could be argued that Mao's theory of People's War merely made a virtue out of necessity and would be treated as such by the architects of the strategic weapons enterprise. That may be true to a degree, but his precepts crippled creative policy making and became a club against the generation who dedicated their lives to projects like 09 and JL-1. Until the early 1980s, the leadership disallowed the systematic search for paradigms that would give coherence and meaning to these projects and would justify the effort in the national consciousness. Even then, as this part will show, the concept of People's War continued to shape the reformulation of doctrine.

This book has examined this collision of ideological and technological imperatives. We have seen how the Cultural Revolution ripped apart the fundamental consensus that had governed the military elite and its institutions and, within the strategic programs, forced officers, engineers, and scientists to search within themselves for reasons to sacrifice so much. Neither the central government nor the society at large fortified their understanding of their mission or their personal dedication. Just the opposite. The participants in the programs found their comfort, if not refuge, in technology, and their motivation in unraveling its nagging mysteries. Many paid a high price for living in technological fortresses in a land of Luddites, but the irrationality of it all bolstered their faith in the inherent sanity of machines and scientific knowledge.

Yet the surviving scientists and engineers of Projects 09 and JL-1 were more iconoclasts than ascetics. Their crusade to fashion the complex institutions capable of producing missiles and nuclear submarines put them in touch with approaches and concepts from the West, and these proved as magnetic as the technologies themselves. The experts drew comfort from the notions of survivable and penetrable nuclear forces. The realists among the projects' high command, and there were many, recognized that a process of doctrinal osmosis was occurring, and they let it happen. They knew that the system was being strangled by outmoded ideas, and while their subordinates were perfecting technologies, they were exploring alternative ways of thinking.

The coincidence of a system disabled and ideas discovered is not unusual in the global scheme of things. The outcome, however, reveals a very different history of contemporary China than the one to which we have become accustomed. Technology and science defined and then helped preserve a significant strand of the nation's life and politics. The social patterns fashioned in the weapons-building process were enduring and transferrable, its participants competent and self-assured. In the technologically oriented navy, professionalism began early in the People's Republic, was seldom an issue, and carried into Projects 09 and JL-1.[4]

Once the bond between ideas and technologies was understood, nothing could stop the hunt for mature doctrines and scientific disciplines. The strategic projects, if not the entire weapons complex, had to find their proper place in domestic and foreign policies. The meaning of security in the nuclear age fascinated the rational minds of the engineers and scientists. Some, of course, looked to China's past for strategic wisdom and found it in the classics, but the mandated starting point for their quest was People's War.[5] In the pages that follow, we first trace what happened to that doctrine as the People's Liberation Army (PLA) entered the modern age and then examine how naval and nuclear weapons doctrines evolved thereafter.

The Transformation of People's War

At the heart of the People's War doctrine is the concept of "active defense" (*jiji fangyu*). From the earliest days of the revolution, Mao and his successors regularly studied the likely character of future conflicts and the potential weaknesses and strengths of the enemy and embraced a concept of active defense that, when stretched out over time, became "protracted warfare."[6]

At the onset of the revolution in the 1920s and 1930s, the Communist guerrillas repeatedly faced the possibility of annihilation. Their strategy depended on mobile retreat, good intelligence provided by a supportive population, and the "luring of the enemy deep." Luring deep was defined as causing the foe "to move in the direction we want, leading the enemy to battlefields prepared and organized in advance."[7] As the retreat continued and the war dragged on, the enemy would overextend his forces, commit mistakes, and expose or create strategic weaknesses by his own actions. The strategic retreat in the face of a previously strong, threatening adversary could then become transformed into a strategic offensive against a vulnerable one.

At the right moment for a counterattack, popular support, good intelligence, surprise, mobility, and locally superior firepower would guarantee victory. Chairman Mao reminded his troops: "When we say, 'Pit one against ten, pit ten against a hundred,' we are speaking of strategy, of the whole war and the over-all balance of forces. . . . However, we are not speaking of campaigns and tactics, and in this sphere we must never do such a thing."[8] At moments of tactical superiority, Mao called for pitting ten against one and, at the decisive instant, for the retreat to be transformed into a counteroffensive.

After the establishment of the People's Republic, Mao's military writings assumed a Biblical quality. Up until his death in 1976, any heretic who attempted to challenge Mao's revolutionary-era thought was summarily

removed from power.[9] A critic of the Chairman's stifling influence on innovation once noted that "military theoretical study to a very large extent
went no further than explaining a certain article or speech of the leader,
and certain theories themselves became a kind of religious dogma."[10]

The Korean War challenged that dogma. It brought Chinese troops face-
to-face with the devastating lethality of modern air and naval power. The
threats by the United States to use nuclear weapons in Korea and against
China itself during the war and subsequent crises activated Mao's ambi-
tion to make China forever immune to such intimidation. Despite the apparent perpetuation of People's War as scripture, Beijing secretly started
Projects 02 (nuclear weapons), 05 (ballistic missiles), and 09.[11] It strengthened its conventional forces and updated its views on military intelligence,
mobility, and troop concentration.[12] Revolution's theories and modern
practice began to diverge, though the term "People's War" could never be
questioned.

From 1955 on, China's military planners placed an ever greater emphasis on the role of weaponry in future warfare. They inaugurated programs
of preparedness ranging from upgrading the people's militia to practicing
combined service operations in nuclear and chemical environments.[13]
Gradually reality modified theory, and in 1959 the military was able ever
so quietly to call these modifications "People's War under modern conditions."[14]

The revision of the concept depended on three assumptions. First, the
military concluded that a future war would be large-scale and employ sophisticated weapons. Second, the war would inevitably escalate, making
China a main battlefield. Finally, at the beginning of the war, the enemy
would possess superior arms.[15] The war would be prolonged and costly, but
in the end "the people" would prevail. These assumptions and the revised
concept of People's War continued in force until the late 1970s.[16]

Still, another principle came into play in the mid-1960's. Once the PLA
was able to put bombers armed with nuclear weapons in the air, minimum
deterrence became China's unspoken strategic doctrine. That was all fine
in theory, but the reality was, as Mao saw clearly when Sino-Soviet tensions
mounted in 1969, the nation was not yet ready to compete against modern
arms as an equal or to embrace a world without People's War. In the face
of what promised to be "an early war, an all-out war, and a nuclear war,"
he held, China's cities and coastal areas would be destroyed, but the arms
factories in the Third Line would survive and provide the means for the
people's army to prevail.

The exploration of alternative military theories speeded up after Mao's
death in 1976. (It was not until then, in fact, that the words "limited retaliation" were even breathed out loud.[17]) Marshal Ye Jianying, vice-

chairman in charge of the daily affairs of the Central Military Commission, helped trigger the process by declaring that the development of military theory was the prerequisite for a reliable national defense. "Even if we have mastered modern military hardware," he pointed out, "we still will be unable to cope with an enemy in a modern war, or at least will pay a greater price [for a victory] if we do not have a correct military theory as a guideline."[18]

For a time, the search for theory and the quest for technologically advanced hardware went arm in arm. The higher priority given to preparedness for a nuclear war became particularly evident when combined-operations units staged a massive military exercise in North China in September 1981.[19] Deng Xiaoping stated that this exercise had given "us an opportunity to assess our achievements in building modern, regularized armed forces, and have simulated modern warfare fairly well."[20] Thus, even while some of Mao's basic ideas continued to find expression at the level of general wisdom, the tools of contemporary warfare took precedence and pushed his ideas to one side or caused their reformulation.

By this time, the military was pushing for a greater reliance on scientific technologies and modern methods of combat, and the central leaders were ready to respond. After all, missiles and nuclear weapons were now flowing to the Second Artillery in numbers large enough to buoy them with high confidence in the country's defensive capabilities.* Moreover, with the steady improvement in U.S.-China relations after the withdrawal of U.S. troops from Indochina in 1973, and the Soviet Union bogged down in protracted war in Afghanistan, the threat of war on either front had receded. The time had come for another revision of strategic doctrine.[21]

In 1980, Deng Xiaoping enunciated his basic premise. In effect pronouncing the huge standing army inherited from the 1960s a white elephant in this day and age, he declared: "Our principle is to use more money to renew equipment by cutting the number of troops."[22] Over the next few years, he became more and more convinced that China could stay clear of a full-scale war for at least several decades, and that the nation could safely start downsizing its military and concentrating on economic and social reforms.[23] The "new stage," as it was called, would give the armed services the strategic framework to "coordinate with each other in combat, react

---

*Although the Second Artillery (*dier paobing*) is usually referred to in English as the Second Artillery Corps, technically this is incorrect. Unlike other PLA combat units, it is organized into "bases" (*jidi*, equivalent to the corps, *jun* level), brigades (*lü*), and battalions (*ying*, the basic combat unit). The most appropriate translation would be Second Artillery Army; however, the term corps has become too well established to drop. Based on Guo Qingsheng, "Visit," 99; Shi Yan, "Creation," 49; and Li Fumin and Li Dunsong, 51, 52.

quickly, counter electronic surveillance, ensure logistical supply, and survive in the field."[24] By the mid-1980s, Deng was ready to carry through on
the notion of reducing the army and basing the nation's security instead on
the threat of nuclear retaliation and the force of its diplomacy. For a brief
moment, he considered and then, as tensions with Moscow eased, dismissed the need for a broad "united front" with the United States against
the Soviet Union.[25]

At a landmark meeting in May–June 1985, the Central Military Commission approved Deng's call for a phased reduction of one million troops
and the use of the resulting savings for economic development.[26] The military understood that, as one Chinese officer put it, the proposed reforms,
which included the reorganization of all major commands, as well as troop
reductions, was essentially a shift in the balance of domestic power. The
policy, he said, "would certainly meet resistance, even relatively great resistance."[27] Deng anticipated that resistance but worked to neutralize and
then break it. In the end, he had his way, and the planned reduction was
completed in 1988.[28]

With the reform under way, the commission decided to abandon the
state of combat readiness for "an early war, an all-out war, and a nuclear
war" and decreed that a condition of peacetime construction existed for
building up national defense. The chief of the General Staff, Yang Dezhi,
later noted that the policy decision to pursue a "peacetime strategy" had
been reached by Deng himself "in the light of the international situation
that has brought an important strategic change in the guiding ideology for
our army building and the buildup of our national defense as a whole."
Yang declared, "We urgently need to find a road to developing national
defense faster and better."[29]

By the late 1980s, therefore, the People's Liberation Army was exhibit-
ing a greater responsiveness to unprecedented realities and concepts. For
many years, Mao's stress on People's War seemed immutable and increasingly unrelated to China's actual defense programs. In our study of Chinese
defense programs from 1955 to the 1970s, we have been struck by the rigid
adherence to Mao's earlier formulations even as the Chinese, with Mao's
blessing, advanced into the nuclear age. The adoption of a "peacetime
strategy" removed some of that burden, but before considering that strategy, we must digress briefly to consider how the changes in the People's War
concept affected its central element, active defense.

The Evolution of Active Defense and the Emergence of Doctrine

Active defense is still listed as the nation's military strategy. Its basic
principle, as first enunciated by Mao in the 1930s, is *houfa zhiren*: Gain

mastery by striking only after the enemy has struck first. But in the subsequent decades, only this simple statement of principle remained unaltered. Mao in fact repeatedly shifted strategic gears, so to speak. Before the Chinese People's Volunteers (CPV) entered the Korean War, for example, he devised a plan to wage positional warfare to check the United Nations advance. Shortly thereafter, before putting the plan into effect, he changed his mind and decided to engage the enemy in mobile warfare. In June 1951, he again reversed himself, returning to the idea of wearing down the enemy in positional warfare.[30] In the war, active defense, which was used to characterize each of Mao's policies, was more a slogan than anything else and certainly not a consistent strategy.

After the Korean armistice in 1953, Mao and the high command made a number of significant changes in the main content of the active defense strategy.[31] The process began with Mao's order to Peng Dehuai, the vice-chairman in charge of the daily affairs of the Central Military Commission, to accentuate research on the impact of a modern war on the established military strategy.[32] In the winter of 1953–54, at a high-level military conference, Peng and his fellow officers, in an attempt to adjust their forces to the coming age of intercontinental warfare, made a series of decisions on creating a regularized and modern army.[33] They clung closely to Soviet experience and advice and bought Soviet weapons.

The army was reorganized largely along Soviet lines. With an eye to strengthening the leadership of the Party in military affairs, the Politburo, in September 1954, adopted a resolution to redefine the military commission's authority and its relations with top-level Party organizations. It put the commission under the Politburo and the Central Secretariat.[34] Thereafter, the commission expedited the overhauling of military strategy.

From March 6 to March 15, 1956, the commission members met to debate a range of issues on strategy and the buildup of national defense.[35] They affirmed the traditional active defense strategy but rewrote its substance. Preoccupied by the lessons of Korea, Peng Dehuai told the gathering that the "combination of positional defensive warfare with mobile offensive warfare" would become the PLA's main operational doctrine.[36] The participants further reinterpreted the PLA's guiding principle in future wars. After the outbreak of a war, Chinese troops would check the enemy's advance in prepared fortified zones and so thwart his plan for a quick victory. The initial battles would buy time to stabilize the battlefield and convert the national economy to a wartime footing. After forcing the enemy into a protracted struggle, the army would move from active defense to the strategic offensive.[37] This new strategy had obvious implications for "luring deep," and in 1962, in anticipation of a possible Nationalist invasion from Taiwan, the commission ordered the PLA to stand ready to resist all landing operations.[38]

In the spring of 1969, the rapidly escalating Sino-Soviet border conflicts prompted Chinese leaders to adjust their guidelines for waging war once again. Mao, anticipating a full-scale Soviet invasion, now pointed out, "I stand for giving up land in an all-out war."[39] With the nation facing a showdown with the Soviet Army, Mao returned to the revolutionary-period notions of "luring the enemy deep" and mobile warfare. Mao's statements greatly influenced the adjustment of the PLA's strategic guide-line, which was reaffirmed after his death. In 1977, on behalf of the Central Military Commission, Ye Jianying announced that the PLA's new eight-character guiding principle would be *jiji fangyu, youdi shengru* (active de-fense and luring the enemy deep). This principle, simplified into a short slogan and invariably referred to by the number of characters, was to con-tinue in force throughout the rest of the decade.

Under Deng Xiaoping, the meaning of active defense underwent another mutation. In the autumn of 1980, the military commission resurrected the 1956 concept of having front-line troops hold off the enemy from prepared fortifications until the nation could be put on a wartime footing.[40] Aban-doning Mao's idea of luring the enemy deep, the new guideline placed po-sitional warfare at the forefront of Chinese strategy.

Before long, however, PLA theorists and planners began thinking in terms of sudden attacks from multiple directions and at targets deep inside China.[41] They identified four possible scenarios: small wars (presumably at the frontiers), medium-sized conventional wars, full-scale conventional wars under the condition of nuclear deterrence, and nuclear war.[42] Deng Xiaoping's adoption of a peacetime strategy in 1985 was based on the premise that neither of the last two would occur in this century, and thus investments in forces for "limited retaliation" against a nuclear first strike could be lowered and the people's militia (for a People's War) substantially reduced.[43]

The debate about strategy accordingly converged on scenarios one and two, small- and medium-sized conventional wars.[44] PLA analysts worried about the optimal approaches to winning local wars between China and its neighbors.[45] They deemed Vietnam and India to be their most probable future adversaries.[46] A new 12-character phrase captured the approved pol-icy toward these regional conflicts: *lizheng zhizhi, quebao dasheng, jian-hao jiushou* (adopt every diplomatic means to check the outbreak of war; ensure victory if war is inevitable; and end the war on favorable terms after the predetermined goals have been achieved).[47]

Despite the decision and the thousands of pages of detail (all classified) on the policy, some Chinese strategists still voiced concern about the danger of a lightning or surgical strike against strategic targets in China during escalating crises.[48] Twenty years hence, they said, the United States or another superpower, even Japan, might pose such a threat. The strategists weighed the chances of a superpower surprise attack on the country's coastal areas and proposed an integrated response in which the navy's role would be indispensable.[49] They mostly put the possibility of such a U.S. attack in the context of a future confrontation between the PRC and Taiwan. Some apparently assigned a greater probability to future hostilities with the United States after the deterioration of U.S.-China relations in June 1989.[50]

As China's search for more appropriate strategic concepts continues in the 1990s, the emphasis falls on developing advanced technologies that will lessen both the threats to the nation and its weaknesses. Yang Shangkun, China's president and a senior leader on the Central Military Commission, told colleagues in late 1986: "The principal contradiction in our army building is the contradiction between the objective requirements of modern warfare and the low level of modernization of our army." To resolve the contradiction, the leadership has determined that "army building should be aimed at promoting the modernization of equipment and man. Particular attention should be paid to . . . the modernization of defense science and technology, the modernization of weapons and equipment, the modernization of management, and the modernization of military thinking."[51]

The military began formalizing its views on strategy in the late 1980s. In army-wide symposia that ran from 1986 to early 1990, experts systematized military terminology and worked out the principles of the PLA's own military science (*junshi kexue*) on the nature and laws of war and how to prepare for and conduct it.[52] While some aspects of this science are unique to China, the Chinese make no claim to originality.

Specifically, the high command, taking its lead from Mao, called for research in three realms: defense strategy, operations or campaigns, and tactics. In a directive issued in about 1986, it quoted Mao as saying:

The science of strategy deals with the laws that govern the war situation as a whole. The science of campaigns deals with the laws that govern campaigns and is applied in directing campaigns. The science of tactics deals with the laws that govern battles and is applied in directing battles.[53]

In concrete terms, strategy was defined as encompassing the use of forces at the front and included what Western and Soviet military specialists call theater operations. It would deal with the operations of forces ranging from corps (*jun*) and army (*bingtuan*) levels up to the level of the field army (*yezhanjun*). Tactics in turn would focus on military units at or below divisions, down to the platoon.[54] The Chinese held that the philosophical foundations for their perspectives on strategy were laid down in ancient military treatises, particularly those of Sun Zi, Wu Qi, and Sun Bin.[55]

Meanwhile, the Politburo charged the State Council and the Central Military Commission with responsibility for formulating national defense policy.[56] They complied by directing the strategists in various institutes to delineate the new policy within four basic parameters: the state's overall goals, military theories based on Mao's military thought, the status of China's power, and an assessment of foreign threats. They were told to set a definite timeframe for implementing each strategy; ten years was to be considered normal for a short-term strategy. The actual time limit set would define the period required for mobilizing the nation to meet any major potential threat.[57]

For some, like Yang Shangkun, vice-chairman of the military commission, ten years seemed overambitious. In December 1986, he thought it would be the year 2050 before "the modernization of our country's national defense and military equipment will have approached that of the world first-class powers" enough to solidify China's international position as a world power. Technology thus would define the time horizon for fundamental national strategy. The setting of such a distant time limit for achieving parity in weaponry would necessarily force a reconsideration of the short- and medium-term strategies. In 1986, the military considered 1986–95 and 1996–2005 as its principal frames of reference for short- and medium-term policies. The strategists judged it feasible for the PLA to modernize its armory sufficiently by 2005 to reach the level of military sophistication of the United States and the Soviet Union in the 1990s.[58]

Having defined the relevant time periods, the strategists concentrated on the contents of a short-term defense strategy. They endeavored to work out a consensus on the goals for the buildup of national defense and on ways to achieve them. The agreed goals were general: "The country should possess powerful defensive capabilities and counterattack capabilities that should be able to deter enemy states, should play an important role in maintaining global equilibrium, and should ensure the implementation of our independent and peaceful foreign policy."[59]

PLA planners then captured the means to achieve these goals in a new set of eight Chinese characters (not to be confused with the eight-character principle noted earlier): *zongti fanqwei, zhongdian fazhan* (strengthen overall national power for defending security, emphasize the main points of defense science and technology). In a word, the current short-term defense strategy is to accelerate the modernization of China's war potential and its capacity to mobilize from peacetime to wartime in emergencies.[60] Allocations and additions in recent Chinese military budgets reflect these changes.

The World of Naval Strategy

The Chinese navy long pursued a coastal defense (*jinhai fangyu*) strategy, and the revision of military thinking appears to have developed slowly in the naval field.[61] The navy's strategy began as a child of People's War and active defense and changed in step with its parents. Active defense and coastal defense have thus evolved together. Both have direct links to Mao's ideas on People's War. The analysis of the shifts in general strategic policies raises two questions: How does naval strategy fit those policies, and how has it altered over time?

Earlier, we referred to the leadership's rude awakening about the importance of seapower when Chiang Kai-shek's ships successfully evacuated retreating troops from the Northeast and from Shanghai. Even with the major defections of ships and crews to the Communist side, the PLA could not inflict a coup de grace on the Nationalists as their remnant armies fled the continent. On October 3, 1949, five battalions of the PLA's 61st Division began an assault on Nationalist-held Dengbu Island. But even with their crushing superiority, the PLA units could not prevent the introduction of enemy reinforcements by sea, and after suffering 1,490 casualties, the Communist troops retreated in defeat. Later the same month, the PLA Tenth Army attacked the island of Quemoy, and again lost the battle at sea. It could not reinforce the initial invasion force. Taking more than 9,000 casualties, the stranded force perished, and ever after its defeat for lack of sea and air support constituted an oft-repeated "bloody lesson."[62]

Turning to China's past, Mao and his generals looked beyond these painful memories and recognized the historical threat from the sea.[63] As he wrote in 1949, "We must build a navy capable of defending our coastal areas and effectively guarding against possible aggression by the imperialists."[64] The Chinese leader some years later, in 1953, reminded his countrymen that "most imperialist aggression against China came from the sea," and he spoke eloquently and often about building a strong navy to thwart such aggression in the future.[65] For Mao, the United States constituted the main potential threat, one that issued from the Pacific Ocean.

To meet it, China's naval leaders reconsidered People's War and its main component, active defense. The essence of People's War on land, they decided, applied equally to naval warfare. But the military regarded naval warfare as dependent on the land campaign, and the navy as merely a force to limit the invader's options and provide support for ground operations. Practically speaking, moreover, the country could not afford modern naval vessels. For all these reasons, the Chinese high command adopted a doctrine of coastal defense; it did not import the doctrine from Moscow. That coastal defense echoed early Soviet naval thinking was a coincidence, an extra bonus, not a conscious choice.[66]

In August 1950, shortly after the establishment of the navy headquarters of the PLA, 23 senior military officers met in Beijing to work out the "concrete guiding principle" for building the navy. They acknowledged the relevance of the Soviet experience but sought a principle grounded in China's actual circumstances. They adopted the concept of a "modern coastal, small-sized naval combat force" that would balance offense and defense. It would make the most of existing ships as the foundation on which "to develop a new fighting capacity such as torpedo boats, submarines, and the naval air force" and "gradually to build up the country's powerful navy."[67]

The Chinese held to this *jinhai fangyu* principle throughout the Korean War and for most of the next three decades. Consistent with it, on December 4, 1953, the navy's first five-year plan was presented to the Politburo, where Mao Zedong emphasized the objectives of ending coastal piracy, ensuring maritime safety, preparing for the takeover of Taiwan, and defense against invasion.[68]

Yet linking coastal defense to People's War limited just how powerful the navy could become. For example, the ground-minded military equated large ships to the forces of imperialist aggression and, in any case, well beyond China's means. As Mao studied the navy's five-year plan in 1953, he remarked: "We must gradually build up a powerful navy in a planned way based on the [country's] industrial development and financial situation."[69] As another example, a few years later, the Central Military Commission sanctified the primacy of the army and air force, giving second place to the navy.[70] The commission limited the development of the navy and told it to concentrate on building an air force, submarines, and fast attack craft.

For the first decade of Communist rule, the high command interpreted *jinhai fangyu* to mean that the navy should operate primarily at the behest of the army's coastal divisions. Operationally, the military stipulated that the navy should retreat in the face of a superior force, while inflicting as heavy a toll as possible on the enemy. These guerrilla-type attacks would disrupt the enemy's sea lanes of supply and isolate the attacking force so that the ground troops could destroy them with relative impunity.

While the navy accepted these constraints, many of its officers believed that it could still develop an independent and winning strategy of its own.

They rejected the idea that China had always been weak at sea, having concluded that the real weakness lay in leadership. They argued that foreign nations had bullied China in the Qing Dynasty (1644–1911) because of the regime's erroneous strategy and tactics. By the last years of the Qing, they asserted, China had built a navy more powerful than America's and an equal of Japan's. Unlike the Japanese government, however, the Qing regime pursued obsolete policies in the buildup of the country's naval capacity, and its faulty maritime strategy resulted in the destruction of China's imperial fleet.[71] "Even after the Sino-Japanese sea battle [of September 1894], the North China Sea Fleet still maintained considerable fighting capability. Yet the remaining ships holed up in a passive position at Weihai, and they were thus destroyed [by the Japanese]."[72] Because many modern naval strategists found clear analogies between these historical failures and current shortcomings, commentaries on Qing naval policy, to a certain extent, may be taken as surrogates for critiques of People's War as applied to Mao's navy.

Despite all these doctrinal changes and debates, the offshore islands posed the acid test of the navy's primary missions throughout the first years of Communist rule.* The legacy of the "bloody lessons" and the dream of national reunification made the liberation of these islands central to naval planning. The Korean War delayed all plans for the seizure of the islands from mid-1950 to mid-1952, but the goal was never abandoned.[73]

The preparations for the invasion of the offshore islands, including those opposite Taiwan in Fujian Province, resumed and accelerated in July 1952, when the East China Military Region Command directed its chief of staff, Zhang Aiping, to work up detailed assault plans. Mao quickly approved the plans, and the Central Military Commission elevated Zhang to oversee the unified command for the assault. With the signing of the Korean armistice the following year, the commission decided that the change in the international climate would permit the army to "extend [China's] strength forward" and approved large increases in the navy's budget. Concerned about an American response, however, it limited the extension to moves

---

*On August 28, 1949, Mao, Zhu De, and Zhou Enlai told Zhang Aiping, the commander of the navy of the East China Military Region, that the navy should join with the army and air force in preparations for Taiwan's liberation, and these preparations started. In June 1950, however, President Harry Truman dispatched units of the Seventh Fleet to the Taiwan Strait, effectively ending any possibility of a successful invasion. The military then changed the priority to "reopening the Changjiang River, eliminating remnants of bandits on the coastal islands off Jiangsu and Zhejiang provinces, occupying the [Nationalist-held] Zhoushan Islands [off the Zhejiang coast], and building naval bases there." Yang Guoyu, *Dangdai*, 40–41, 84–85; Hu Shihong, "Description," 39. The quotation is from Yang Guoyu, *Dangdai*, 41.

against the coastal islands off Zhejiang and ordered Zhang's forces to "occupy the coastal islands one by one from small to large and from north to south." These operations, the commission stated, would "create the conditions for liberating Jinmen [Quemoy] and Mazu [Matsu]." Zhang Aiping's units completed the Zhejiang phase of the offensive on February 26, 1955.

The fight for control of the coastal region of the East China Sea and of China's shipping lanes coincided with the battle for the offshore islands. Nationalist forces had tightened a blockade of the mainland by harassing China-bound shipping and Chinese fishing vessels. Throughout the 1950s and 1960s, the contest over the coastal seas continued, and as Beijing put it, "the military struggle on land was transformed into the battle for the sea." In these years, the navy adhered to the guiding principle of extending the ocean operations zone from the coastal areas to the more distant seas and building ever larger ships.[74] It also adhered to the combat tactics of People's War because of the superiority of Nationalist sea and air units. The naval high command ordered its captains to employ hit-and-run surprise tactics and the "pitting of ten against one." Typically, they hid attacking torpedo boats behind fishing craft or reefs as they waited in ambush.[75]

Doctrinally speaking, nothing much happened until the mid-1960s, despite China's quest to construct its conventional navy with Soviet aid and the strategic navy on its own. When the Cultural Revolution erupted in 1966, senior officials sparked a debate on the role of modern technologies and how they affected fundamental military strategies.[76] An early indication of this debate surfaced in a September 1967 article denouncing Luo Ruiqing. Most of the article was an unsubstantiated diatribe written to justify the policies and ambitions of Lin Biao, but it did make clear that the development of advanced weapons had become a political issue. Luo had allegedly argued that with modern technical equipment, "any invading enemy can be annihilated at sea, in the air, or at the bases from which it launches its attack." In effect, the article claimed, this would negate Mao's tenets on active defense and reduce China's strategy to one of passive resistance. "Acting according to this incorrect policy would inevitably lead to the building of defensive works everywhere and the wide dispersal of forces to man them. In that way, we would always be in a passive position." Luo's strategy would allegedly lead to a massing of forces and their destruction by the imperialists.[77] We know little of what happened in this debate thereafter, though our discussion in earlier chapters has made clear how badly the navy projects fared during the years of struggle that followed.

Throughout the era of the Gang of Four in the first half of the 1970s, the gang made the leaders who had advocated a major buildup of the navy the target of its attacks.[78] Its message, moreover, suggests that the historical issue of maritime-versus-continentalist strategies had continued to fester and had now resurfaced.[79] The specific issue this time was fueled by the decision of whether or not to build a fleet of 14 vessels for monitoring the long-range tests of China's ICBM, the DF-5.[80] Following the death of Lin Biao in 1971, the Central Military Commission, on April 8, 1972, met to review the project, and Premier Zhou Enlai, now seriously ill, turned the matter over to Marshal Ye Jianying, who had assumed control of the commission's day-to-day work.[81]

One of the Gang of Four, Zhang Chunqiao, attended this meeting as a member of the commission's Administrative Meeting. The radical leader listened to a senior naval officer's opening remarks on the need for the missile-test monitoring fleet but then cut him short. "You don't have to continue your report," he said. "All of us can read. . . . I have told the people in charge of the shipbuilding industry that I am for land forces." Ye, sensing the danger, kept silent, but the leader of the missile program, Qian Xuesen, spoke up: "We have conducted the high-low ballistic tests [over a partial range] on our ICBMs, as well as many simulated tests. However, we can't monitor the entire performance of our ICBMs unless we conduct full-range tests. [For this,] we need oceangoing measurement ships."[82] Despite backing from the State Planning Commission and the General Staff for the Ye-Qian position, Zhang was adamant. Insisting that "the assignment given to Shanghai [where Zhang was the mayor] is too onerous," he stated. "I still doubt whether it is necessary to continue the project."

Going further at this and subsequent meetings, Zhang staked out a continentalist position. "We are continentalists," he said. "Now the guided missiles are well developed. Installed on shore, they can hit any target, and there is no need to build a big navy."[83] Others in the Gang of Four camp also reportedly supported a "continentalist view" of the navy and said warships should be built only for convoy duty and as a "reserve force." Building a larger navy, they believed, wasted money and manpower, and contradicted Mao's emphasis on ground forces and People's War.[84]

When the members of the Gang of Four were arrested in October 1976, the strict constructionists of continentalism vanished with them. Hua Guofeng, first as premier and then as Party chairman, quietly abandoned the concept and unequivocally affirmed the navy's strategic mission in deterring nuclear war. Convinced of the real possibility of a major conflict with the Soviet Union, Hua pressed for the acceleration of the nuclear-powered

Evolution of the Navy's Strategic Guideline

Period	Policy	Comments
1950–1975	Coastal defense with continental bias	Though the navy possessed aircraft units, submarines, and fast attack craft by the early 1970s, it was still not in a position to conduct effective sea-based coastal defense.
1976–1982	Sea-based coastal defense	This capacity was achieved with the addition of 33-class submarines, 051-class destroyers, and 053H-class escort vessels, in series production from 1969, 1972, and 1976, respectively, all using domestic systems and equipment.
1983–2000	Sea-based coastal defense under the condition of limited nuclear retaliation	With the successful flight-testing of the JL-1 SLBM in 1982, the navy entered the era of limited nuclear retaliation. The JL-1 could be launched in extreme emergencies in that year, but its design was not finally validated until the test from an 09-2 class submarine in 1988.
2000–	Integrated sea-based nuclear deterrence	The 09-4, China's second-generation missile sub, is expected to be completed by about the year 2000. The sub will have greater survivability than the 09-2 boat and will be equipped with JL-2 missiles of an 8,000km range.

ballistic-missile submarine program, as well as the completion of the DF-5 long-range tests.[85] This priority on the strategic navy lasted until the consolidation of power by Deng Xiaoping and Zhao Ziyang.

Deng, coming close to a continentalist position, thereupon downgraded the navy's strategic mission and, in April 1979, reasserted its role as a coastal defense force: "Our navy should conduct coastal operations. It is a defensive force. Everything in the construction of the navy must accord with this guiding principle."[86] That principle resurrected the strategy of coastal defense and reaffirmed the direction of China's naval policy up to the mid-1980s. By 1987, Beijing's leaders had further defined China's naval strategy as "active defense, coastal operations" (*jiji fangyu, jinhai zuo-zhan*).[87]

This review of the evolution of China's naval strategy, summarized in the accompanying table, shows that it has changed at a pace and in a direction that, while reflecting the navy's special character, mostly mirrored the nation's general strategy. For decades, the emphasis fell on coastal defense with a continental bias, just as the general strategy stressed conventional ground operations plus People's War. The navy moved to a sea-based coastal defense posture only in the mid-1970s and by the early 1990s was calling for preparedness to fight a conventional war under the condition of limited nuclear retaliation. This strategy and the need for an effective sea-based nuclear deterrent remain high on the navy's agenda.

Current Naval Strategy

Having treated the evolution of general guidelines, we now turn to the contemporary strategic themes related to the buildup of naval forces for conventional war under the condition of limited nuclear retaliation and long-term preparations for deterring nuclear war. These themes delimit and define the small doctrinal domain of China's nuclear navy.

When Deng Xiaoping proclaimed a peacetime strategy in 1985, he rejected the idea that a world war or an all-out war between China and either of the superpowers would break out by the end of the century. He believed that as long as the two superpowers were preoccupied with each other, they could not or would not attack China. Rather, each would try to win China over to its side or at least nudge it toward neutrality. The Chinese leader, however, did not exclude the possibility in the medium term of territorial conflicts, including tensions over Taiwan and the islands in the South China Sea, erupting into localized armed confrontations.

Many such conflicts could engage China's conventional navy in the medium to long term. The concern is the traditional one: China has a coastline of about 18,000km and covers more than 3,000,000 sq. km of territorial waters that are rich in resources.[88] Chinese strategists argue:

The strategic position of our coastal areas is extremely vital [to our national interest]. Numerous key cities, industrial bases, foreign trade ports, and naval and air force bases . . . are scattered along our coastal areas. [These areas play] an extremely important role in our efforts to check the hegemonists' . . . expansion in Southeast and Northeast Asia. In view of this, surprise attacks launched by the enemy against our coastal areas might achieve greater results than those against our landlocked borders.[89]

Here again, as in the nineteenth century, we witness China's fears for the safety of its vulnerable coast and islands.[90] The sea-borne threat had come from the United States in the 1950s, the Soviet Union in the 1960s and 1970s, and Vietnam in the 1980s. What changed was a growing sense that China could cope with the challenge with its navy rather than from the land alone. The opponents of a narrow interpretation of continental coastal defense, so derided by the Gang of Four, had won, at least temporarily, despite the apparent opposition from some senior commanders.

In 1987, the official navy history recast the strategy of coastal defense, though it stressed that the premises underlying this strategy—opposition to aggression and defense of the homeland—remained firm. It said: "This doesn't mean in any way that our navy should only cruise the coastal seas, and that the imperialist countries alone [have the right to] build up their navies as 'strategic armed services' for the purpose of seeking hegemony in waters far away from their countries. . . . China, of course, needs to build a navy powerful enough to match its international standing."[91]

Even earlier, Liu Huaqing, then commander of the navy, noted that the world had entered a new stage in the exploitation of the seas as a result of technological advances. "The military value of the seas will be greatly increased," he said, "and the struggle for [mastery of] the seas between the superpowers will become more acute. . . . Accordingly, the pending strategic assignments given to the construction of our national defense are to accelerate the building of a powerful modern navy capable of frustrating any invasion from the sea and to safeguard [our] national marine rights and interests."[92] China was beginning to think like a strategic seapower, though its capabilities still fell far short of its aspirations.

At this writing, China is engaged in disputes with ten of its regional neighbors over sea resources, the delimitation of sea areas, territorial sovereignty, and the ownership of certain islands. These disputes could easily lead to armed clashes, which, the Chinese say, would be "characterized by sudden outbreaks, a quick conclusion, a broad theater of war, long distances from the land, and much greater requirements for the capabilities to stage combined operations by the three armed services."[93]

Anticipating future conventional warfare, the Central Military Commission, during Liu Huaqing's tenure as navy commander (1982–88), ordered his service to prepare actively for two high-probability missions in the near-to-medium term, as well as for two longer-term missions, the prevention of a large-scale invasion and the deterrence of a nuclear attack. The clear demarcation between coastal defense and strategic seapower was becoming increasingly blurred as the Chinese peered into the twenty-first century.[94]

We list the navy's four principal missions, beginning with the most immediate and ending with the long-term contingencies:

To safeguard China's territorial integrity
To conduct a possible blockade of Taiwan
To defeat a sea-based invasion
To make ready survivable nuclear retaliatory forces

Liu Huaqing ordered naval theorists to study these missions and make recommendations on their implementation, and by the end of the 1980s, they had prepared a report on the "systematic" principles required for carrying them out.[95]

In respect to the first mission, safeguarding Chinese territory and economic assets, including those under the seabed, the theorists thought it highly likely that disputes between China and its neighbors would result in armed conflicts at sea.[96] They recalled that the Chinese and Vietnamese navies had fought a fierce battle for control of the Nansha Islands (Spratlys) on March 14, 1988, and noted the vulnerability of these and other islands in the South China Sea.[97] Although units of the Soviet Union (now Commonwealth of Independent States) were sharply reduced in the early 1990s, the Chinese could not be sure when and how CIS forces might be augmented and come to the aid of the Vietnamese in any future crisis.[98] Even after the rapprochement of Vietnam and China in late 1991 and early 1992, the PLA navy continued to count the combined Vietnamese-CIS naval presence as a potential threat.[99]

The Chinese recognized the great difficulty in providing air cover for naval operations far from protected air bases.[100] As stated in one official article, "Without the control of the air, there will be no mastery of the sea."[101] The navy improved the avionics and armaments on its planes, but only its main bomber, the Hong-6D (B-6D), could reach the Nansha Islands and return.[102]

The Chinese cannot maintain continuous control of the air over the Nansha Islands because they have neither aircraft carriers nor in-flight refueling capability. The ongoing debates within the military on the need for aircraft carriers reflects its dread of air inferiority.[103] As a stopgap measure, in the late 1980s, Beijing ordered the Ministry of Aerospace Industry to accelerate the DF-25 missile program. Conventionally armed, the DF-25 could reach targets as far away as 1,700km.[104] Despite improvements in Sino-Vietnamese relations in late 1991 and early 1992, the Chinese have reportedly kept alive contingency plans to recapture the islands in the Nansha group still under Vietnamese control in amphibious operations, with the DF-25 held in reserve as a last resort.

The navy has apparently overcome its past difficulties in provisioning ships operating in the South China Sea. In the late 1970s, Beijing ordered the construction of multipurpose auxiliary and underway replenishment ships, and within a decade the total tonnage of service ships jumped by almost 200 percent.[105] The commander of a combined warship group claims that the navy now has the capability to engage in combined operations in distant oceans.[106]

Preventing Taiwan's move toward independence is the navy's second principal mission. Only when Taiwan submits to Beijing's sovereignty will the current generation of Chinese leaders consider their dream of national reunification and the restoration of China's rights to have been realized. While monitoring each step in Taiwan's political development, they thus repeatedly express fierce opposition to any moves toward an independent Taiwan and keep up on the preparations to defeat them.[107]

Deng Xiaoping himself has taken a personal interest in the Taiwan issue and its impact on relations with the United States and on China's future military posture. American responses to political changes on Taiwan could lead to an "eruption" in U.S.-Chinese relations, Deng said in 1984, when he told Defense Secretary Caspar Weinberger: "China does not now have the military forces to invade or occupy Taiwan, but we have the military power to blockade" the Taiwan Strait. The following year, when answering questions on a possible blockade of Taiwan, Hu Yaobang, then head of the Chinese Communist Party, rated the feasibility of such a blockade as low and concluded that China would not have sufficient forces to accomplish it for at least eight years. But he went on to say: "Once we decide to enforce the blockade of Taiwan, we do not believe it will be difficult to deal with Taiwan itself," even though China would have to take into account the possible armed intervention of foreign countries.[108]

Unquestionably, the Chinese navy of the 1990s has built the forces needed to determine Taiwan's fate, if called on to do so. Should Taiwan declare its independence, however, Chinese leaders would face a stark choice. Their entire worldview would find the declaration abhorrent, but their modernization goals and their understanding of the costs of another "civil war" would give them pause. On balance, they estimate that a blockade of the island would constitute a minimal reaction to any move toward Taiwanese independence.[109] Partly against this eventuality, the Central Military Commission has ordered the navy to continue constructing submarines and has given "the development of submarines . . . precedence over all other [construction]."[110] If another Taiwan Strait crisis should occur, these submarines would represent the front-line force.

So far as the navy's third principal mission is concerned, Beijing now considers the probability of an attack from the sea low and likely to remain so for decades. Nevertheless, in the late 1980s, China conducted several large-scale, anti-landing exercises, continuing a practice that had begun in the 1950s.[111] From the 1970s to the demise of the Soviet Union in late 1991, the Chinese assumed that any invasion from the sea would be secondary to an all-out land invasion.

Before the breakup of the Soviet Union, Chinese military analysts worked out the responses to a number of possible Soviet battle scenarios. They posited, for example, the following sequence. A Soviet aerial bombardment would precede landings by naval infantry and paratroops and immediately thereafter by a motorized infantry. PLA ground units would counterattack, while the Chinese navy concentrated on cutting the Soviet sea lanes of supply. The Soviet navy would then conduct operations against China's ports, or seize a coastal position bypassed in the Soviet ground offensive, and perhaps also stage a major amphibious landing on the Liaodong Peninsula near the port of Dalian, thereby reducing the Soviet Army's logistical problems in occupying the Northeast.[112] Though tensions between the two countries greatly diminished after the mid-1980s, the Chinese military continues to develop arms to defeat an amphibious assault on China's coast from that quarter, and preparations have been postulated on the need for them into the next century. In 1992, the PLA, like the military in other countries, began to assess the consequences of the collapse of the Soviet Union on national security.

The navy's contingency planning also contemplates surprise attacks against strategic points along China's coast under as yet unforeseen conditions, and some naval officers have recommended a "general guiding principle to cope with this main threat and its grave consequences." They propose to put the armed services under a centralized, unified command, thereby enabling ground, naval, and air forces to come together in a fully coordinated counterattack. Other planners, struck by China's experience in recent conflicts, would have immediate improvements in early warning and theater-wide mobilization capabilities and in training for quick reaction to surprise attack and support of counteroffensives on land.[113]

PLA strategists estimate that China will face a real danger of surprise attacks from the East and South China Seas early in the next century. Paradoxically, the increased emphasis on the country's economic development has increased the fear of attack because so much of that development is concentrated along the coast. The dangers would come within the sea area bounded by what the military calls *diyi daolian*, the first chain of islands (the Japanese home islands, the Ryukyu Islands, Taiwan, the Philippines, and Borneo).[114] The introduction of such systems as sea-launched cruise missiles in the U.S. and other large fleets has forced the Chinese to extend the depth of their defenses and begin to examine a coastal defense strategy that might encompass the second island chain (*dier daolian*), including the Marianas, Guam, and the Carolines.[115]

Since the late 1980s, navy planners have called for changing from a coastal defense (*jinhai fangyu*) strategy to an offshore defense (*jinyang fangyu*) strategy. They would extend the defense perimeter to between 200nm and 400nm from the coast, and even more in the case of the South China Sea islands.[116] The navy hopes to have a so-called offshore navy on patrol by the year 2000 and a blue-water navy (*yuanyang haijun*) operating by 2050.[117] In 1988, the commander of the navy, Zhang Lianzhong, hailed the development of three systems that would permit continuous offshore deployments: underway replenishment ships, a long-distance communication system, and a global navigation system. In response to foreign comments on the increasing number of underway training days for the navy, Zhang said, "The high seas are open to all of us!"[118]

Until such time as these hopes are realized, the navy's concrete policy for defeating any large-scale invasion from the sea before the end of the century is centered on a multilayered defense perimeter:

The exterior defense perimeter is conceived as encompassing the seas out to the first chain of islands. This region will be defended by attack submarines (including 33/35/K3-class conventional submarines as well as 39-class subs armed with antiship missiles and 09-1 nuclear submarines), naval medium-range aircraft, and surface warships. The submarines will play a dynamic role to ensure defense in depth, including the laying of mines in the enemy's sea lanes of communication.

The middle defense perimeter extends 150nm from the coast and comes within, but in most cases does not reach, the first line of islands. Antiship planes, 051-class destroyers, 053H-class escort vessels, and missile craft will carry the main burden in this area.

The interior defense perimeter extends to 60nm from the coast. This will be the theater of operations for the main naval air force, fast attack boats, and land-based antiship missile units.[119]

The force requirements for these three zones have determined the priorities for naval spending in the near term.[120]

Since the successful flight test of the first ballistic missiles from a nuclear submarine, the navy's conception of sea combat goes beyond operations at sea to launching nuclear attacks deep inside an enemy's territory. Liu Huaqing, the former commander, has predicted that fewer than 10 percent of China's land-based missiles would survive a large-scale nuclear first strike and has said that the less vulnerable SLBMs would "preserve our nuclear counterattack capabilities." Thus, he added, these missiles "can really play a role in deterrence and containment."[121] His statement reflects the current intention of the Chinese high command: to give sustained impetus to the development of strategic forces at sea for the long term.

TEN

Rationale and Reason in the Nuclear Era

Many PLA strategists turn to ancient Chinese military treatises for an authentic national perspective on deterrence. They single out the writings of Sun Zi as especially relevant to the present situation. Twenty-five hundred years ago, they hold, Sun Zi stated in *The Art of War*: "Forcing the other party to resign to our will without fighting a battle" and "Attacking the [enemy's] strategy [are] superior to engaging in diplomatic negotiations; engaging in diplomatic negotiations is superior to waging field operations; and waging field operations is superior to attacking fortifications."[1] Here, Chinese strategists say, is quintessential deterrence theory.

Chinese views on deterrence also draw on Mao's Theory of People's War.[2] During the precarious early years of the revolution, Mao worried most about sheer survival and saw a dialectical relationship between threats and capabilities. His ideas about contradictions made him concentrate on how threats to the revolutionary fighters on the battlefield could be transformed into the enemy's strategic weaknesses, and he wrote in 1948: "While we correctly point out that, strategically, with regard to the whole, we should take the enemy lightly, we must never take the enemy lightly in any part, in any specific struggle."[3]

The Making of a Strategic Concept

Mao's first approach to nuclear weapons was consistent with his dictum that "political power grows out of the barrel of a gun."[4] As the shadow of U.S. nuclear bombs loomed large in the mid-1950s, Mao pointed out, "If we are not to be bullied in the present-day world, we cannot do without the [atomic] bomb."[5] Mao taught his colleagues to adopt an appropriate attitude toward nuclear bombs: "We are afraid of atomic weapons and at the same time we are not afraid of them. . . . We do not fear them because they cannot fundamentally decide the outcome of a war; we fear them because they really are mass-destruction weapons. Accordingly, we have to handle them with a scientific attitude."[6]

During these formative years, leaders in the strategic weapons program saw the building of a nuclear deterrent as one element, but not the decisive element, of the PLA's comprehensive deterrence posture. According to Nie Rongzhen, the head of the program, the initial development of strategic retaliatory forces only enabled the country "to own the minimal means to stage a counterattack in case our country suffered a surprise nuclear attack by the imperialists."[7] PLA strategists long maintained that there had to be a balance between People's War to deter or repel conventional attacks and small nuclear forces to deter a nuclear attack.[8] An explicit and operational nuclear strategy, however, remained to be formulated for the nation.

Having launched the atomic bomb program in early 1955, Mao over the next decade issued various statements on the bomb that came to be regarded as a comprehensive set of guidelines for the nuclear weapons program. Typical Maoisms were: China's nuclear weapons "will not be numerous even if we succeed [in the strategic weapons program]." "A few atomic bombs are enough [for China]. Six are enough." "The success [of our strategic weapons program] will boost our courage and scare others." "In any case, we won't build more atomic bombs and missiles than others." "Build a few [nuclear weapons], keep the number small, make the quality high [*you yidian, shao yidian, hao yidian*]."[9] By the mid-1960s, Mao's instructions justified the lasting need for a strategic weapons program and set the boundaries for the projected nuclear arsenal.[10]

His one-sentence maxims and brief instructions provided grist for the mill of all future planners and training commands, which dutifully issued their own statements, both secret and open. Seven principles can be derived from the numerous official statements in the 1960s through the 1970s, and most remain valid to this day:[11]

1. No first use. In line with active defense and recognizing China's inherent vulnerability to a preemptive attack, the Chinese government declared this principle on the day of its first nuclear detonation, October 16, 1964: "At no time and under no circumstances will China be the first to use nuclear weapons."[12] This precludes "launch on warning," but China would see a nuclear attack of any size, including a so-called "surgical strike," as justifying nuclear retaliation.[13]

2. No tactical nuclear weapons. In the first three decades of the atomic program, Mao decided to build only strategic nuclear weapons and to forgo tactical nuclear weapons.[14] Because of the small number and low accuracy of the early weapons, the military principally built thermonuclear warheads.[15] This principle eroded in the 1980s.

3. "Small but better" (*shao er jing*). Mao sought to create a limited but reliable force that could inflict heavy damage on any prospective enemy's principal population centers. Such a force, he believed, would dissuade any enemy from attacking

first.[16] To dissuade the United States, China's ICBMs would have to reach New York and Washington; against the Russians, they would have to be able to hit Moscow.

4. "Small but inclusive" (*xiao er quan*). Mao saw the need to develop many types of strategic nuclear weapons in his small armory.[17] In 1983, Deng Xiaoping said, "We will continue to develop nuclear weapons in one way or another, but, in any case, on a limited scale."[18]

5. "Minimum retaliation" (*qima de huanji*). China began its nuclear weapons explicitly to break the American nuclear monopoly and frustrate nuclear blackmail.[19] Its leaders held that a minimal retaliatory capability would deter others from initiating a first strike and guarantee China's security. That guarantee would produce a nuclear stalemate and create the basis for global nuclear disarmament.[20] This now is called "limited nuclear retaliation" (*youxian he baofu*).

6. Quick recovery. Mao believed that China would survive a nuclear war better than more advanced nations because of its large population, geographic size, and underdevelopment.[21] Echoing Mao's views three decades later, Deng Xiaoping said, "It is impossible to exterminate the human race by using nuclear weapons. Now there are more than four billion people in the world. If the worst came to the worst and more than two billion people died, the other more than two billion people would remain. More than two billion people would live on the globe just the same."[22] He advocated what Westerners would call a policy of damage limitation and pushed for both active and civil defenses, including the hardening of command and control systems.[23]

7. Soft-target kill capability. The limited accuracies of the DF missiles forced the Chinese military to embrace a retaliatory policy akin to massive retaliation. The missiles could only destroy urban areas or "soft" military targets in a second strike.[24]

The nuclear arsenal built over the decades increased the Chinese leaders' confidence in the chances of preventing a nuclear attack against the nation and their faith in the seven principles.[25] In the late 1970s, these principles provided the basis for advancing the current strategy, "limited nuclear deterrence" (*youxian he weishe*).[26]

Beginning about 1979, a few brave souls in various military organs wrote some general think pieces on the subject of nuclear strategy, and some of these reached the top command a couple of years later. In 1983, Deng Xiaoping declared that Beijing's nuclear arms "had forced the superpowers not to use" nuclear weapons against China, and he added, "China only wants to adhere to [this] principle: we [must] have what others have, and anyone who wants to destroy us will be subject to retaliation."[27] In about 1985, the government circulated a new draft document on nuclear strategy throughout China, and a year later, Defense Minister Zhang Aiping said, "We have built a powerful national defense and possess a nuclear strike capability. The enemy no longer dares to strike [the first blow] or to underestimate us."[28]

Freed from the shackles of People's War's more primitive ideas, strategists then began a systematic elaboration of "China's concept" of deterrence. They avidly read the literature of the West, paying special attention to works on medium-sized nuclear powers, especially France, and to discussions of the unpredictable and imagined world of nuclear war.[29] We have already seen how the guidance engineers in Project JL-1 embraced the concepts of survivability, penetrability, and accuracy during the black hours of the late 1960s, and how the impact of technology on doctrine reinforced the systematization of their thinking on nuclear strategy.

Xiao er quan (small but inclusive), when translated into force procurement policies, supported the development of a strategic triad. "Inclusive" appeared to call for a wide range of weapons systems within a relatively limited arsenal. China's leaders long ago understood the linkage of warning time to the basing of forces on different types of delivery systems and were especially impressed by the need for effective command and control of their strategic arsenal. It did not take a close reading of the Western and Soviet literature on different survival modes to convince them, but it helped.

The Chinese typically defined diversity as providing both survivability and flexibility, and they developed a strategic force consisting of land-based missiles, submarine-launched missiles, and bombers. Moreover, within each leg of the triad, they planned to build weapons of different ranges, capabilities, and survival potential in order to compete in or deter a variety of possible conflicts.[30] All weapons systems, of course, could actually be used should deterrence fail, and against this contingency, the Central Military Commission steadily improved its command-and-control systems.[31] It also ordered the building of a large number of high-yield warheads for the nation's first- and second-generation stockpiles.[32]

China's nuclear bombers, mainly retrofitted H-5s, H-6s, and Q-5s, constituted the original leg of the triad but were considered by many its weak link.[33] Because of their relatively short operating ranges and poor penetrability, these planes, once the mainstay of the retaliatory forces, are now assigned mainly to tactical missions or to roles of last resort. The rapid development of anti-aircraft weapons systems, particularly those used by the United States in the 1991 Gulf War, made questionable the penetrability of any bomber weapons without very advanced avionics, stealth, and stand-off missiles. Some PLA planners currently dismiss the listing of China's antiquated bombers as a viable leg of the triad.[34]

They reached the opposite conclusion about tactical missiles. The Chinese did not attach great importance to tactical nuclear weapons until the early 1980s, when they concluded that these weapons in the hands of the superpowers could only be deterred with tactical nuclear weapons of their own. The familiar arguments of NATO planners about confidence, matching the opponent's weaponry, and having a range of nuclear options found a welcome ear in China. Like their counterparts in London and Washington, the Chinese wished to avoid a Solomonic choice, "either to use strategic nuclear weapons prematurely or to remain paralyzed."[35]

In 1984, Chinese scientists made critical breakthroughs in theoretical designs for nuclear weapons "with special [destructive] effectiveness"; that is, neutron bombs.[36] Over the next years, they achieved success in testing these and other low-yield weapons.[37] With the 600km-range DF-15/M-9 missile ready for first-line service, they had the capability of employing nuclear weapons in theater operations by the end of the decade.[38] China, by its own lights, thereby made its deterrent more flexible and robust.

The mobile solid-propellant missiles, the subject of this book, fit this pattern. Here is the notable place of the submarine-launched JL-1 and its sister missile, the land-mobile DF-21. Mobility translates into enhanced survivability but characteristically degrades the missile's accuracy and reliability. It is the requirement for mobility that drove Project 09 and the engineers' preoccupation with accuracy and reliability,[39] and all the industrial, bureaucratic, and military complex built up in the missile and submarine projects owe their origins to these and other very basic requirements. That Mao did not fully grasp or embrace the strategic concepts underlying those requirements does not gainsay the fact they were absolutely fundamental to the genesis and evolution of the projects.[40]

As of this writing (August 1993), China's first generation land-based strategic missiles—the liquid-propellant DF-3, DF-3A (a range-extended DF-3), DF-4, and DF-5 missiles—remain in service.[41] The DF missiles have a reasonable soft-target kill capability and are still regarded as the backbone of China's strategic strike forces. However, their slow response, vulnerable basing vis-à-vis a surprise counterforce attack, large radar cross-sections, and poor accuracies render them increasingly obsolete.[42] For these reasons, the Central Military Commission decided to replace them with the solid-propellant DF-21, DF-31, and DF-41 missiles.[43] Like the Americans and the Russians, the Chinese were wedded to the idea of land-based missiles in their triad.

Nevertheless, the process of shifting a large fraction of the force from land-based to submarine-based launchers has been accelerated. Many Chinese strategists, again echoing foreign sentiments and arguments, regard the SLBM as the best second-strike weapon. Most of them appear to believe that by the early years of the next century, the JL-1 and its successor should constitute a considerable fraction of their strategic missile force.[44]

The balance in choosing between SLBMs and ICBMs will be tilted according to judgments about the survivability and penetrability of the two systems. The wild card in the current state of play is the potential deployment of Western and possibly other anti-ballistic-missile systems. No other country has paid greater attention to the U.S. strategic defense initiative (SDI) in the 1980s than China. SDI, which some saw as having an offensive as well as a defensive potential, alone caused the Second Artillery repeatedly to urge the missile designers to concentrate on missile survivability and penetrability in future decades.[45]

China has stressed two main actions to ensure the survivability of its retaliatory forces, round-the-clock alerts and decentralization and concealment. The first has been a set policy since 1984, when the Central Military Commission ordered the Second Artillery to establish such a system.[46] The deployment of DF-21s and JL-1s in 1988 strengthened the link between alert status and force responsiveness. The second has a much longer history, dating back to Mao's emphasis on guerrilla-like dispersal and mobility.[47] In the 1980s, as Deng Xiaoping weighed the pros and cons of SLBMs over ICBMs, he promoted the idea of "conducting guerrilla warfare with modern weapons" in order to increase DF survivability. The military noted that the principle was to install missiles "either under the sea or in caves (*xiahai rudong*)." Some DF-5s were deployed in fixed silos, but the emphasis soon shifted to mobile land-based and sea-based launching platforms.[48] Extending the operating area for the mobile systems would also help, and to this end, the missile experts successfully extended the DF-21's range and code-named it the DF-21A. Consistent with these principles, the Second Artillery ordered its combat units to practice under all weather conditions, randomly rotate all mobile nuclear-armed missiles among launch sites, launch missiles from trains, move missiles along different land routes, and maximize the use of camouflage and night operations.[49]

These principles also have figured heavily in debates on the future of the SLBM program. There is strong opposition in military and political circles to the development of the second-generation nuclear submarine (Project 09-4) and its missile, the JL-2. Some PLA planners deplore the costs of the submarine system, as compared with mobile land-based missiles like the follow-on DF-31. They argue that the coastal defense strategy does not sanction deploying missile submarines in distant oceans and question the long-term survivability of the 09-4, given advances in anti-submarine warfare. These continuing debates account in large measure for the on-again, off-again character of the 09-4's development.[50]

The navy and the veterans of the 09 and JL projects, of course, have used the logic of deterrence to reach just the opposite conclusion. For them, "possessing sea-based nuclear strike forces signifies that the navy is a 'strategic armed service.'"[51] They invoke survivability, maneuverability, and penetrability to oppose any effort to abandon the submarine projects in favor of a total reliance on mobile land-based missiles.[52] They argue that the cruising range of the submarine transforms the 8,000km SLBM into a 13,000km missile, making it highly cost effective.[53]

Moreover, China's active defense strategies, they insist, require building sea-based strategic units. The uncertainties of China's future security needs and the revolution in global power relations are also cited as evidence for the superiority of sea-based over land-based strategic missiles. For a combination of reasons relating to the forcefulness of these arguments and the power of the individuals making them, the sea-based programs survive, sometimes even flourish. Their continuation and the future of deterrent seapower seem assured.[54]

The Changing World of the Missile Engineer

In concluding our study of the nuclear-powered submarine and its weapons, let us look behind this impressive engineering enterprise and consider what it all meant. A search for meaning leads us back to the origins of the 09 project. As we have seen, the Soviet Union and the United States built their nuclear retaliatory forces years before commencing work on their ballistic-missile submarines. For them, going to sea added significant options for nuclear retaliation, ensured the ultimate survivability of their nuclear weapons, and thereby enhanced deterrence. But Project 09 was driven by an altogether different strategic logic. Beijing set out to acquire a nuclear fleet even before it possessed nuclear weapons, let alone long-range bombers or missiles. Trying to escape the trap of future obsolescence, China sought to create the most advanced retaliatory system long before it could build the most rudimentary ones.

Moreover, when the United States and the Soviet Union began their programs, they had in place a modern scientific and industrial base. China did not. For Beijing's leaders, the submarine and other strategic weapons projects provided one additional way to organize, create, and finance that base. Their long-term goal was as much scientific and industrial excellence and ranking as ensuring national security.

Mao embraced the weapons projects as a way to rebuild the Middle Kingdom's power and status. Nothing could shake his dream of retrieving China's proper place in the world. The alliance with the Soviet Union was only one building block toward establishing China's rightful place in the world. So, too, were strategic weapons a means to this political end.

The management of the sea-based weapons projects passed through several different stages determined by the evolution of the Sino-Soviet alliance. The Chinese first expected to move through the stages of dependence, interdependence, and then independence or self-reliance that characterized the evolution of their nuclear weapons effort.[55] They would have gladly settled for the kind of collaboration that existed between Britain and the United States, whereby the British designed and built four nuclear submarines with substantially their own equipment and the United States supplied Polaris missiles carrying British reentry vehicles and warheads. The Soviets would never go this far. Soviet assistance was limited to providing a Golf-class submarine and some missiles for it. After years of foot-dragging by Khrushchev and then the collapse of Sino-Soviet relations, Beijing was eventually forced to depend almost entirely on its own efforts to complete the submarine and SLBM programs.

In the formative years, the assessment of the American threat, the shortage of critical resources and capabilities, and the demanding negotiations with the Kremlin prompted the senior leaders in Beijing to work together. The leadership, including Mao Zedong, endorsed the initial plans for the submarine and SLBM programs and picked the managers and systems to implement them. In setting the tone for the undertaking, these leaders and organizations played a vital and positive role in them.

As they coped with programs of such magnitude, China's leaders and administrators, engineers, and scientists slowly moved forward. In the formative years, 1958–62, they set up the needed scientific and industrial facilities, conducted feasibility studies, and drafted general designs. But first the "three hard years" (1960–62) forced Beijing to put most of 09 on hold till 1965 even as it forged ahead on the atomic bomb.

The economic disaster made all strategic programs vulnerable to critics. Opponents, long silenced, questioned 09's privileged organizations and priority allocations of money and talent. In 1962, after forcing the suspensions of the project, Mao had to intervene to create the Fifteen-Member Special Commission and impose a working consensus on this and other strategic weapons projects.

By the time the Politburo decided to resurrect Project 09 in 1965, the breakdown of Sino-Soviet relations was complete and the threat of U.S. military intervention in Indochina was mounting. At this point, the Politburo as a body could regulate the top echelons of the nation's military industrial network but could no longer easily micromanage the intellectual resources so crucial to the project's success. It fell to senior program officials like Nie Rongzhen and Luo Ruiqing, backed by Zhou Enlai, to mold a special defense scientific system capable of energizing the wounded system.

These senior leaders became sufficiently immersed in the substance of the program to try to bridge the gap between their own powerful but ill-equipped realms and the lower-level research, production, and test facilities. To an unusual degree for the political system of the 1960s, these leaders allowed the lower-level bodies greater autonomy and protected them as best they could from the excesses of the coming decade. The Defense Science and Technology Commission, under Nie Rongzhen's leadership, provided much of the genius for constructing the organizational system that was to survive the numerous extreme tests ahead.

This was the context in which the specialists seemed to gain greater authority even as Mao unleashed the Cultural Revolution. The illusion and even the reality of their power increased when military and political leaders declared war on each other. In this stage, the engineers and scientists overcame one obstacle after the other as chaos or anarchy gripped the nation. The reasons why they could quicken the tempo of the project during an unprecedented period of political instability deserve special comment.

One important reason was that the domestic crisis coincided with the perceived dual threat of American and Soviet aggression. Mao fueled this perception and personally approved the transfer of PLA units to finish the key 09 and JL-1 facilities. In the war fever that fed the Third-Line mentality, all civilian projects and less critical defense programs gave way to the strategic weapons programs. In the face of Mao's decrees, who would voice objections to the submarine and SLBM programs, especially when their forward progress seemed to vindicate Mao's strategic wisdom? Even the radicals could not openly oppose the programs that Mao assigned such high priority.

The personal standing of Zhou Enlai also played a major role. Drawing on Zhou's immense prestige, Nie Rongzhen could compensate for his own wavering authority in the realm of defense science and industry and largely neutralize the hidden pressures from the radicals. Because that realm did not impinge on the most sensitive points of the domestic power structure, especially in the initial years of the Cultural Revolution, the radicals mostly directed their attacks against Party, state, and military organs in other spheres. Despite Nie's own troubles, he had created a more decentralized and viable system that either remained stable and outside the main fray or that, when caught up in the struggle, could sufficiently safeguard the main centers for research and development to allow them to continue working. Cut off and thus somewhat protected, these centers began to change fundamentally. This brings us to the world of the missile engineer.

As the engineers, technicians, factory personnel, and political officials of Project JL-1 gradually, almost imperceptibly, entered and to a degree shaped a new world of technology and politics, they underwent what might be called a paradigm shift.

They were leaving behind a paradigm that had emerged in the nuclear weapons program and had spread to other strategic weapons projects, including Projects 09 and JL-1. In 1958, the pioneers in Project 09, like their comrades in similar super-secret, top-priority military undertakings, had participated in an action universe unified by high purpose, strong political networks, and unyielding commitment. Created and sustained by the elite's revolutionary aims and by foreign threats, that universe seemed to rise above the giddy cycles of campaign hysteria and Soviet-style officiousness. As the keystone of all military industry, whose sophistication and competence (not to mention budgets) outdistanced all other modern economic activities in China, the strategic weapons programs of the 1950s and early 1960s seemed to need no more strategic rationale than Mao's occasional quips and aphorisms, his "great calls." Appeals to People's War and against American imperialism silenced any would-be critics, and the spirit of high scientific and technological adventure brought astonishing dedication despite hardships, repeated failures, and Red Guard harassment.

The disintegration of this protected and somewhat privileged world in the Cultural Revolution forced a realignment of individual and institutional arrangements, as we have seen. As people at all levels sought alternative ties and activated sub rosa personal networks, unfamiliar ideas penetrated the organs of the Seventh Ministry that justified technical decisions for Project JL-1 and that began to define a non-Maoist strategic framework.[56] Especially for the guidance engineers, the designers and more senior technicians and cadres communicated in the vocabulary of strategic specialists in Moscow and Washington, though without the taboo labels of deterrence and stability. For the moment, the vocabulary of accuracy, survivability, and reliability would do; the full exploration of nuclear doctrines would only come later.

The diffusion of the new language had a hit-and-miss aspect to it. At the middle and higher levels within the ministry and its elite bodies, such as the First Academy, the still unfamiliar terms, always carefully circumscribed by Mao's slogans, were used as engineering, not strategic or political, concepts. Their currency derived from their technical applicability; anything more would have triggered (and occasionally did trigger) the wrath of the radicals. The flag carriers of the Cultural Revolution in which the JL-1 newspeak emerged would not have tolerated any effort to consciously disseminate it.

Those who missed the change were on the margins of the program or at too low a level to know or care about alternative rationalizations of their work. For most factory officials, junior technicians, and ordinary workers, the Cultural Revolution, after its moment of exhilarating drama and will-o'-the-wisp passions, ruined the extraordinary solidarity that had given their work meaning and left them as mere drudges.

The differences between the guidance engineer and the factory hand building the inertial control platforms, for example, were thus far more than those engendered by educational background and professional status. These two levels of men and women were literally traveling in detached mental universes and gave little if any thought to making a common journey. Thus the Cultural Revolution not only redefined the relationship between high-level politics and leading experts; it also ruptured the ties between the experts and their lower-level colleagues. Even more important, it widened the gulf between the risk-taking, independently motivated experts in the military industrial system and the politically dominated officials in the civilian sector.

When Deng Xiaoping returned to power momentarily in 1975, he quickly recognized the symptoms of the change: organizational indiscipline, lack of leadership, sloppy workmanship, organizational separateness, and indifference to regulations.[57] What Deng missed when he spoke of transforming the military industrial system several years later were the underlying causes of these symptoms and the transforming role that military industrial experts would play in changing China.

The surviving pioneers of the strategic weapons program knew what he did not appear to know. More than making atomic weapons, missiles, and nuclear submarines, these experts had designed and overseen the creation of China's modern engineering and manufacturing sectors. They remember how it was, and they had the foresight to pass on their knowledge and their standards to their successors. Their memory was not only of an arsenal created but of a world that must not be lost. The wealth of data underlying this book suggests that they want the memory kept alive and vital in today's China.

They thus looked to the future even while trumpeting past triumphs. These engineers and scientists had studied international science and technology, learned foreign languages, traveled abroad, and done their homework. They set about creating networks of excellence and a successor generation capable of getting things done.

When, in the early 1980s, Deng ordered the military industrial system to convert to civilian production, it responded. In January 1982, he issued a sixteen-word edict to "combine military with civilian production, join peacetime and wartime efforts, and with the military as the priority let the civilian nurture the military sector."[58] By 1985, the military had begun to energize the modernization of all other sectors of the society. Within a decade almost 70 percent of the output value of that system was converted to commercial production. Many of the key players also moved into leadership positions in state economic and educational organizations and into high-level Party positions. More than just entering the civilian market, the converting military industries helped create the market. Transformed from an earlier era, many military industrial experts donned civilian hats, entered business, and sparked competition.

Much of the answer to why China could shed the legacy of past political upheavals and move so decisively into the modern age lies in the history of the nation's military industry. Our story of Projects 09 and JL-1 coincides with the nuclearization and finale of the Cold War. The swords of war have not dulled, but many of their makers now hammer out plowshares and pruning hooks. Perhaps in time the nuclear era itself may come to a close, and China's modern warriors may heed the call of an ancient writer to "put the weapons back in storage and let the war-horses pasture on Zhongnan Mountain."[59]

Appendix

Key Figures in China's Nuclear-Powered Submarine Project, 1958-1992

Political Figures

CHEN YI 陈毅 (1901–72)

Vice-premier (1954–68), member of the Politburo (1956–68), minister of Foreign Affairs (1958–68), vice-chairman of the Chinese Communist Party (CCP) Central Military Commission (1966–72). Repeatedly appealed to the Politburo to give priority to the strategic weapons program as a way to improve China's international status.

DENG XIAOPING 邓小平 (1904–)

Vice-premier (1954–66, 1973–76, 1977–80), member of the Standing Committee of the Politburo (1956–66, 1975–76, 1977–87), general-secretary of the CCP Central Committee (1956–66), vice-chairman of the CCP Central Committee (1975–76, 1977–82), chief of the General Staff (1975–76, 1977–80), deputy director of the Central Special Commission (1977), vice-chairman (1975–76, 1977–81) and then chairman (1981–89) of the CCP Central Military Commission. Twice purged (1966, 1976) and rehabilitated (1973, 1977). In 1981, assumed China's supreme power with the final say on all Party and state affairs.

HE LONG 贺龙 (1896–1969)

Member of the Politburo (1956–67), vice-chairman of the Central Military Commission (1959–67), in charge of the commission's daily affairs in 1964, director of the National Defense Industrial Commission (1959–63), vice-premier (1954–67), member of the Fifteen-Member Special Commission (renamed the Central Special Commission in 1965) (1962–67). In charge of the production of weaponry and military equipment.

LIN BIAO 林彪 (1906–71)

Vice-chairman of the CCP Central Committee (1958–71), vice-chairman in charge of the daily affairs of the Central Military Commission (temporarily retired in 1964) and defense minister (1959–71). Died while fleeing the country in 1971.

LUO RUIQING　罗瑞卿　(1906–78)

Chief of the General Staff and secretary-general of the Central Military Commission (1959–66), director of the National Defense Industry Office (1961–66), member of the Central Secretariat and office director in charge of the daily affairs of the Fifteen-Member Special Commission (1962–66). In charge of coordinating the research on weaponry and military equipment with production. Officially removed from all offices in 1966.

MAO ZEDONG　毛泽东　(1893–1976)

Chairman of the CCP Central Committee and Central Military Commission. Until his death in 1976, had final authority in all strategic weapons decisions.

NIE RONGZHEN　聂荣臻　(1899–1992)

Director of the Defense Science and Technology Commission (1958–74) and of the State Science and Technology Commission, vice-premier, member of the Fifteen-Member Special Commission. Vice-chairman of the Central Military Commission (1959–87). After 1958, headed the overall scientific part of the strategic weapons program.

ZHOU ENLAI　周恩来　(1898–1976)

Member of the Politburo (1949–56), premier (1949–76) and minister of foreign affairs (1949–57), member of the Standing Committee of the Politburo (1956–76), director of the Fifteen-Member Special Commission (1962–76). Participated in original decision to develop strategic weapons in the mid-1950s and later, as commission director, had principal responsibility for implementing weapons policies and coordinating all strategic weapons organizations.

Scientists

CHEN DEREN　陈德仁　(1922–)

Deputy director of Institute 12 of the First Academy of the Seventh Ministry (missile), director of Institute 17 of the ministry's Second Academy, deputy director of the Second Academy, deputy chief designer of the JL-1 project. Specialty guidance and flight controls.

CUI GUOLIANG　崔国良　(1931–)

Director of Institute 41 of the Fourth Academy of the Seventh Ministry and deputy chief designer of the JL-1 project. Specialty solid propulsion. After retirement from active service, held the post of secretary-general of the ministry's Science and Technology Committee.

HUANG WEILU　黄纬禄　(1916–)

Director of Institute 12 of the First Academy of the Seventh Ministry, deputy director of the Second Academy. As Project JL-1's chief designer, in overall charge of the missile's comprehensive design, greatly contributed to China's first generation of submarine-launched ballistic missile.

HUANG XUHUA 黄旭华 (1926–)

Deputy director and then director of Institute 719 of the Seventh Academy of the Sixth Ministry (shipbuilding). In his capacity as Project 09's chief designer, in charge of the 09 boats' comprehensive designs, greatly contributed to China's first and second generations of nuclear-powered submarines.

PENG SHILU 彭士禄 (1925–)

Acting director of Institute 715 of the navy's Seventh Academy and later head of Institute 15 (successor of Institute 715) of the First Academy of the Second Ministry (nuclear), vice-minister of the Sixth Ministry. As deputy chief designer of Project 09, greatly contributed to the submarine nuclear power plant program.

SONG JIAN 宋健 (1931–)

Deputy director of the Second Academy of the missile ministry, vice-minister of the ministry, director of the State Science and Technology Commission, state councillor. Specialty astronautics. As Project JL-1's first deputy chief designer, helped Huang Weilu supervise the progress of the missile's various subsystems.

XU JUNLIE 许君烈 (dates unknown)

Deputy chief engineer of Institute 719 of the Seventh Academy of the Sixth Ministry and Huang Xuhua's chief assistant responsible for formulating the 09-2's overall design plans. Also greatly contributed to the successful underwater test launch of the JL-1 missile from the 31-class (Golf) submarine.

ZHAO RENKAI 赵仁凯 (1923–)

Chief engineer of Institute 194 of the Second Ministry and later deputy head of Institute 15 of the ministry's First Academy. As deputy chief designer of Project 09, contributed to the submarine nuclear power plant program.

Administrative Officials

CHEN BIN 陈彬 (1919–)

Deputy director of the Defense Science and Technology Commission and first director of the Commission of Science, Technology, and Industry for National Defense (1982–85).

CHEN YOUMING 陈佑铭 (1922–)

Director of Institute 701 of the navy's Seventh Academy, deputy director of the academy, director of the Project 718 (instrumentation fleet) Office, head of the navy's Naval Equipment and Technology Department. As director of the Nuclear-Powered Submarine Project Office, was directly involved in the administration of the 09 project.

DING HENGGAO 丁衡高 (1931–)

Received candidate degree from the Leningrad Institute of Precision Machinery and Optical Instruments in 1961. Deputy director of Institute 13 of the First Academy of the Seventh Ministry, deputy head of the Department of Science and Technology of the Commission of Science, Technology, and Industry for National Defense, director of the commission (1985–), office director of the Central Special Commission in charge of daily affairs (1989–). As an expert on optical and fine mechanics, helped build the JL-1 missile's inertial platform.

FANG QIANG 方强 (1911–)

Deputy commander of the navy, deputy head and secretary-general of the National Defense Industrial Commission, minister of the Sixth Ministry, director (from 1973) of the National Defense Industry Office in charge of four military industrial ministries (the Third, Fourth, Fifth, and Sixth).

LI ZUOPENG 李作鹏 (1914–)

Member of the Politburo, deputy head of the General Staff, first political commissar of the navy, and head of the Nuclear-Powered Submarine Project Leading Group. In overall charge of the 09 project from 1969 to 1971.

LIU HUAQING 刘华清 (1916–)

Director of the navy's Seventh Academy (1961–65), vice-minister of the Sixth Ministry, deputy director of the Defense Science and Technology Commission, deputy chief of the General Staff. Later, commander of the navy (1982–88), deputy secretary-general of the Central Military Commission (from 1987), deputy director of the Central Special Commission and vice-chairman of the Central Military Commission in charge of its daily affairs (1989–).

LIU JIE 刘杰 (dates unknown)

Member of the Fifteen-Member Special Commission. Vice-minister (1956–60) and minister (1960–66) of the Second Ministry. Oversaw the ministry's day-to-day operations and the initial progress of the 09's nuclear power plant program.

LIU XIYAO 刘西尧 (1916–)

Vice-minister, then minister (from 1975) of the Second Ministry, deputy director of the National Defense Industry Office. During the Cultural Revolution, served as Zhou Enlai's liaison official in the defense science and industrial systems. In 1972, made deputy head of a work team assigned to intensify the purge of "Lin Biao's followers" in the Defense Science and Technology Commission and its subordinate bodies.

WANG BINGZHANG 王秉璋 (1914–)

First deputy commander of the PLA air force, deputy director and then director of the Fifth Academy of the Defense Ministry, minister of the Seventh Ministry, deputy director of the Defense Science and Technology Commission. In charge of China's strategic weapons program from 1968 to 1971. Soon after the "September 13 Incident," purged on the charge of being an associate of Lin Biao.

ZHANG AIPING 张爱萍 (1910–)

Deputy chief of the General Staff, deputy director, then director (from 1975) of the Defense Science and Technology Commission, deputy director of the National Defense Industry Office, member of the Fifteen-Member Special Commission, (from 1977) head of the Science and Technology Equipment Committee of the Central Military Commission and office director of the Central Special Commission, defense minister (1982–88). Oversaw all strategic organs involved in Projects 09 and JL-1 from 1975 until he took over as defense minister.

ZHAO ERLU 赵尔陆 (1905–67)

As minister of the First and Second ministries, in charge of research and development on weaponry and military equipment. Deputy director of the National Defense Industry Office and deputy secretary-general of the Fifteen-Member Special Commission. Helped Luo Ruiqing supervise coordination among various organs in the strategic weapons program.

ZHOU XIHAN 周希汉 (1913–88)

Deputy commander of the navy, deputy head of the Nuclear-Powered Submarine Project Leading Group, of the Shipbuilding Industry and Scientific Research Group, and of the Telecommunication Industry Leading Group. On behalf of the navy and as Li Zuopeng's assistant, for a time was responsible for the daily affairs of the 09 project.

Notes

Notes

For complete authors' names, titles, and publishing data on works cited in short form, see the References Cited Section, pp. 331–75. The *Foreign Broadcast Information Service* is abbreviated as FBIS in these notes.

Chapter One

1. For a description of the main meetings held by the Party and military leadership of China in 1958, see Su Donghai, 709–13; Zhang Hongru et al., 3–5, 205; Party History Research Section, 1987, 288–97; Academy of Military Science, *Zhongguo Renmin Jiefangjun Dashiji*, 356–57; and Academy of Military Science, *Zhongguo Renmin Jiefangjun Liushi Nian Dashiji*, 569–70.

2. For information on the evolution of the campaigns to unleash the Great Leap Forward and people's communes, see Cong Jin, 100–162; and Liu Jizeng and Mao Lei, 518–24.

3. Unless otherwise cited, this paragraph is based on Chen Mingxian et al., 231–41; Zhou Enlai, 219; Chen Xuewei, "Debates"; Chen Rulong, 1: 134–39; Fan Shouxing; and Xiong Huayuan.

4. The Nanning Conference formally endorsed the "rash advance" policy and began preparing public opinion for large-scale construction programs. At the meeting, Mao reportedly began overruling the rest of the Politburo. Jiang Fuyi, 58; Party History Research Section, 1987, 288–89; Fan Shouxing, 15; Mao [9], 140.

5. The Chengdu Conference reaffirmed Mao's radical policies. Pei Di; Party History Research Section, 1987, 289.

6. The sequence of the major meetings in 1958 was Nanning (Jan. 11–22), Beijing (Jan. 25–Feb. 2), Chengdu (March 8–26), Hankou (April 1–6), and Beijing (May 5–23, 25 [Party], May 27–July 22 [PLA]).

7. Mao [2], 98.

8. Mao [10], 10. Some Chinese sources now state that it was Khrushchev's call in Nov. 1957 to catch up with the United States within 15 years that prompted Mao to unleash the Great Leap. See Zhang Xiuying, 85–90; He Jun, 9–13; and Ding Shu, 19–20.

9. Mao [10], 12.

10. Mao [15], 77.

11. *Ibid.*, 79.

12. Mao [12], 116.

13. *Ibid.*, 119.

14. Mao [11], 91–95, 105, 110.

15. The Central Military Commission has undergone a complicated evolution. In Sept. 1954, the Politburo decided to reestablish the commission and place it under the Politburo and the Central Secretariat. For short but authoritative histories of the commission, see Lei Yuanshen, 218–35; Yan Jingtang, 50–59; Zhi Shaozeng, 50–54; and Song Ke, 62–64.

16. Mao [8], 19.

17. Mao [11], 109; Mao [8], 19.

18. Mao [8], 16.

19. See *ibid.*, 18.

20. On Sept. 27, 1955, the Central Military Commission awarded ten senior military leaders—Zhu De, Peng Dehuai, Lin Biao, Liu Bocheng, He Long, Chen Yi, Luo Ronghuan, Xu Xiangqian, Nie Rongzhen, and Ye Jianying—the rank of marshal. No officers have since been appointed to this rank. *Zhongguo Renmin Jiefangjun Jiangshuai*, 1, 2. Unless otherwise cited, this paragraph is based on Zhang Zongxun, 442–55; and Li Pu and Shen Rong, 13, 14.

21. The two purged vice-ministers of defense were Xiao Ke and Li Da. For a discussion of the meeting, see Cong Jin, 274–99; Li Rui, *Lushan*, 238; Xu Xiangqian, *Lishi*, 854–55; Xiao Jinguang, "Mourn," 14; Academy of Military Science, *Zhongguo Renmin Jiefangjun Liushi Nian Dashiji*, 569; Zhang Hongru et al., 205; and Party History Research Section, 1987, 291.

22. For a full discussion of the formation of Mao's view of the Soviet Union, see Goncharov et al.

23. He Chunchao, 269.

24. The feeling was mutual. In his memoirs, Khrushchev writes that as early as his first visit to China in 1954, he had come to distrust Mao, and that he strongly disliked him. The Chinese leader, as he puts it, "played politics with Asiatic cunning, following his own rules of cajolery, treachery, savage vengeance, and deceit." *Khrushchev Remembers*, 462–63.

25. Information in this paragraph is from Zhi Yin, "Inside Stories," 16; and Chen Youming, "Concern (1)," 2.

26. The participants were Navy Political Commissar Su Zhenhua, Navy Deputy Commander Luo Shunchu, Academy of Sciences Vice-President Zhang Jingfu, Second Ministry Vice-Minister Liu Jie, First Ministry Vice-Minister Zhang Liankui, and the president and vice-president of the Fifth Academy, Qian Xuesen and Wang Zheng.

27. Han Xilin and Li Nanqing, 1; Gan Guanshi and Xiao Xiaoqin, 18; Ma Lu et al., 2. See also Shi Qingsheng, 54; and Peng Cheng and Wang Fang, *Lushan*, 31.

28. Deng Sanrui, 167.

29. Nie refers to a nuclear power plant for "military purposes," but it is clear from the context here and in later passages that he was talking about a plant for submarines. *Nie Rongzhen Huiyilu*, 778. On the initial priority given to the submarine nuclear power plant, see also Wang Rongsheng, 385.

30. Unless otherwise cited, this paragraph is based on Chen Fucai, 30; and Yang Guoyu, *Dangdai*, 460, 697. In June 1961, the Naval Science and Technology Research Department was amalgamated with several local research facilities and renamed the Warship Research and Design Academy (Jianting Yanjiu Sheji Yuan). Code-named the Seventh Academy, it was put under the newly established Sixth Ministry in 1965. Yang Guoyu, *Dangdai*, 460, 697.

31. The government began construction on the Naval Missile Test Range (code-named Base 23) near Huludao, Liaoning Province, in early 1958; we return to a discussion of this base in later chapters. Zhang Xinghua et al.; Li Xueyin and Zhang Heng; Yang Guoyu, *Dangdai*, 454–57, 649–55.

32. The details in this paragraph are from Yang Guoyu, *Dangdai*, 243–44; Zhi Yin, "Inside Stories," 16; and Chen Youming, "Concern (1)," 2.

33. The Scientific Planning Commission had been created in March 1956 to formulate a long-term plan for the development of science and technology. The State Technological Commission was established in May of the same year to develop national policies on technology and to manage technical personnel. In Oct. 1958, the two commissions were merged into the State Science and Technology Commission, with Nie Rongzhen as head, to oversee the civilian side of science and technology. On the early evolution of the nation's scientific system for civilian purposes, see Lewis and Xue, *China Builds*, 49–54. Nie's report was approved two days after its submission, on June 29, by Deng Xiaoping, then general-secretary of the CCP Central Committee. Xie Guang, *Dangdai*, 2: 509-11. For information on the reactor and the history of the Chinese nuclear weapons program which was initiated in Jan. 1955, see Lewis and Xue, *China Builds*, 41, 261.

34. The best studies of the Polaris program are Davis; and Miles. For a history of U.S. navy nuclear propulsion, see Hewlett and Duncan, Chaps. 7–9. In the summer of 1955, a committee appointed by President Dwight Eisenhower and chaired by James R. Killian, Jr. of the Massachusetts Institute of Technology recommended that a 1,500nm missile be considered for both land and sea missions. The navy proposed a solid-propellant missile for eventual deployment on surface ships and submarines. The concept had its origins during the Second World War in a pilot German program for firing mortars from partially submerged U-boats, and the U.S. navy had developed plans for adapting the German idea for its own missile force. The navy also proposed the building of a fleet of submarines with missile-launching capabilities. On July 20, 1960, the USS *George Washington* (SSBN-598), while submerged, made history by launching two Polaris missiles off Cape Canaveral. Lockheed Missile and Space Company, A-1 to A-10.

35. Unless otherwise cited, the information in this paragraph is from Chen Fucai, 30; Zhi Yin, "Inside Stories," 16; and Chen Youming, "Concern (1)," 2.

36. In Jan. 1965, the Fifth Academy became the Seventh Ministry of Machine Building. Zhang Jun, 566.

37. Chen Youming, "Concern (1)," 2–3; Zhi Yin, "Inside Stories," 16; Huang Caihong and Cao Guoqiang, "For the Birth (1)"; Yang Guoyu, *Dangdai*, 244; Peng Shilu, 13.

38. Yang Guoyu, *Dangdai*, 694; Li Jue et al., 201, 301; Zhang Jun, 127–28; "Riddle," 7.

39. See Lewis and Xue, *China Builds*, esp. 51–52, 87–88.

40. Huang Xuhua, 397; Zu Wei, 4, 5, 8, 9; Chen Xueren, 32. For a study of the U.S. Polaris program's organization, see Sapolsky.

41. Li Jue et al., 64, 564.

42. Zhi Yin, "Inside Stories," 17, 21; Chen Youming, "Concern (1)," 3, 4.

43. The Institute of Atomic Energy was under the joint leadership of the Second Ministry and the Academy of Sciences. For a discussion of the status of the nuclear weapons program at this time, see Lewis and Xue, *China Builds*, Chap. 3.

44. Peng Shilu and Zhao Renkai; Li Jue et al., 192, 294–95, 365; Chen Youming, "Concern (1)," 3.

45. Huang Caihong and Cao Guoqiang, "For the Birth (1)"; Li Jue et al., 64–65; "Riddle," 7; Zu Wei, 4.

46. Zhi Yin, "Inside Stories," 17, 21; Xie Guang, *Dangdai*, 1: 343; Chen Youming, "Concern (1)," 3, 4; Huang Caihong and Cao Guoqiang, "For the Birth (1)"; Zu Wei, 6.

47. The leaders of the Shipbuilding Technology Research Section were Xue Zonghua and Wang Xinglang. They reported to the navy's Ship Repairing and Shipbuilding Department. Chen Fucai, 30.

48. For recent discussions of the Great Leap's impact on the economy, see Yu Baotang, 55–60; Wu Yuwen, 80–84; Li Xiangqian, 59–67; and Qiao Yimin and Liu Qi, 98–102. Unless otherwise cited, this paragraph is based on Lewis and Xue, *China Builds*, 53–54.

49. The Chinese military, for example, had to return most of the aircraft and tanks produced in 1958–59 to their manufacturers for repairs. Many defense industrial facilities later stopped production and were reorganized. Zheng Hantao and Li Ruhong, 119; Wang Shangrong.

50. Under Zhang Aiping's supervision, the Division for Scientific and Technological Research was originally assigned to manage the conventional weapons programs. Unless otherwise cited, this paragraph is based on *Nie Rongzhen Huiyilu*, 787; and Zhang Aiping, 74. For a discussion of the relevant complicated organizational changes, see Lewis and Xue, *China Builds*, 50, 54, 264.

51. Note that many of the organs designated "Fifth" dealt with missile development. In May 1956, the Central Military Commission ordered its Aviation Industrial Commission to form the Fifth Bureau (Wu Ju) as a "missile management organization" and the Fifth Academy as a missile R&D center. Created in Oct. 1956, the Fifth Bureau was merged into the Fifth Academy in March 1957. On May 19, 1958, the military commission created the Fifth Department (Wu Bu) with Wan Yi as head. Under the Ministry of National Defense, the department was assigned to supervise the missile institute (Fifth Academy; Wu Yuan) and to form special technical units for missile test ranges. On April 27, 1959, the Fifth Department was merged into the Defense Science and Technology Commission. Han Huaizhi and Tan Jingqiao, 2: 93; *Nie Rongzhen Huiyilu*, 787; Zhang Jun, 560, 561.

52. For background on the Peng Dehuai affair, see Peng Dehuai, *Memoirs*, Chap. 15; Peng Dehuai, "Why," 140–42; Li Rui, *Lushan*; Xu Yuandong et al., 161–70; Lin Tianyi, 45–58; Zhao Linsen, 14–20; Liu Ying, 45–48; Li Rui, "Why," 123–44; Li Rui, "Lessons," 5–11; Li Yimin, 190–92; and *Luo Ronghuan*, 903.

53. The Politburo elevated the three on Sept. 26, 1959. Four other famous marshals—Chen Yi, Liu Bocheng, Xu Xiangqian, and Ye Jianying—were not promoted to this position until Jan. 8, 1966. *Zhonggong Dangshi Yanjiu*, 580–85; Zhi Shaozeng, 52; Yan Jingtang, 58.

54. Da Ying, 332, 333, 343; Cong Jin, 630–31; Dian Dian, *Feifan*, 181. Dian Dian is Luo's daughter.

55. Lewis and Xue, *China Builds*, 39–44; Li Jue et al., 19–22.

56. *Nie Rongzhen Huiyilu*, 807.

57. Liu Xiao, "Mission (4)," 10–11, 12.

58. Nie Rongzhen, "On the Science," 61; *Nie Rongzhen Huiyilu*, 807; Liu Xiao, "Mission (4)," 12. Arkhipov worked in China in 1950–51 and 1953–58 as chief economic adviser to the State Council. For his comment on Soviet-Chinese relations, see Arkhipov, 39.

59. The best analyses of this period are Boffa, 99–118; Linden, Chap. 3; Micunovic, Chaps. 21–28; and Pethybridge, esp. Chaps. 4, 5. We thank David Holloway for his assistance in dealing with the events of this period.

60. Kennan, xi.

61. Lewis and Xue, *China Builds*, 61.

62. This is the judgment of Pethybridge, 151. See also Liu Xiao, "Mission (4)," 17. The "tranquility" quote is from Linden, 56.

63. Lewis and Xue, *China Builds*, 60–63; Li Jue et al., 32. The other members of the Chinese delegation were Chen Geng and Song Renqiong. The Soviet negotiating team was headed by Mikhail Pervukhin, who soon thereafter was purged from the Politburo as a member of the "anti-Party group."

64. Liu Xiao, "Mission (5)," 17.

65. In the decade 1954–64, Khrushchev began to downgrade the importance of traditional conventional arms as he weighed the impact of strategic nuclear weapons on future global conflicts. The new naval doctrine emphasized the submarine and held that "other branches of the fleet . . . were 'outmoded' as weapons of war." In 1958, the first nuclear-powered submarines of the November class entered the Soviet navy, and for some years thereafter, the "Party wanted a navy less dependent on surface ships and more dependent on submarines and missiles." Hudson, 279, 282; MccGwire, 139; Moore, *Soviet Navy*, 71. For Khrushchev's views on naval development, see his *Last Testament*, Chaps. 2 ("The Navy") and 3 ("Bombers and Missiles").

66. Khrushchev, *Last Testament*, 258.

67. He Chunchao, 269.

68. He Xiaolu, 171.

69. Unless otherwise noted, the information in this and the next four paragraphs is from Han Nianlong, 112–13; and Cong Jin, 349.

70. See Li Yueran, 168; and Rong Zhi, "On Postwar," 104.

71. Yang Guoyu, *Dangdai*, 694.

72. The Soviet Union wanted to site both facilities in South China. Goncharov, "From Alliance."

73. He Xiaolu, 171.

74. In his memoirs, Khrushchev notes that "it was obvious that Mao had no respect for Yudin at all. . . . As an ambassador, Yudin had been a weak administrator and poor diplomat. . . . When he clashed with Mao on philosophical grounds, he was no good to us." Khrushchev, *Last Testament*, 258.

75. As later disclosed, the proposal to create a joint submarine flotilla comprised several plans. The principal one was to let the Soviet Union lease the Lüshun port (Port Arthur) for its subs and the city of Dalian to give crews shore leave. Liu Xiao, "Mission (6)," 20.

76. The information in this paragraph is from Han Nianlong, 112–14; and Cong Jin, 349, 350. The account of the follow-up meeting is from the same sources.

77. Khrushchev, *Last Testament*, 258.

78. Peng Shilu, 12–13; Peng Shilu and Zhao Renkai, 206; Huang Caihong and

Cao Guoqiang, "For the Birth (1)"; Yang Guoyu, *Dangdai*, 694. Peng Shilu and Zhao Renkai were chief designer and deputy chief designer, respectively, of the nuclear power plant program.

79. On the timing of Khrushchev's visit to China, see *Nie Rongzhen Huiyilu*, 808.

80. Khrushchev, *Last Testament*, 258–59; Han Nianlong, 114.

81. *Nie Rongzhen Huiyilu*, 808. Most of the information in this paragraph and the next is from Han Nianlong, 114; and Khrushchev, *Last Testament*, 258–60.

82. Huang Caihong and Cao Guoqiang, "For the Birth (1)"; Peng Shilu and Zhao Renkai, 206.

83. Cong Jin, 350.

84. The two defense ministers signed the documents authorizing the agreement for the radio station on Aug. 3. Two years later, the Soviets withdrew all their assistance, but by 1965 the Chinese had completed the project, which provided crucial communication for China's rapidly growing submarine force. *Haijun Shi*, 338; Jiang Rubiao and Zhang Ming, "Messages." As Khrushchev puts it: "Nothing ever came of that [agreement] in the end either. . . . Later, we started launching satellites, which are better for maintaining radio contact with submarines anyway." However, the Soviet leader was wrong in saying the "Chinese reneged on their agreement and didn't build the station." Khrushchev, *Last Testament*, 260.

85. Han Nianlong, 114.

86. Khrushchev, *Last Testament*, 259.

87. Liu Xiao, "Mission (6)," 20; Khrushchev, *Last Testament*, 259.

88. Khrushchev, *Last Testament*, 260.

89. Han Nianlong, 114.

90. Among the many publications on the 1958 crisis, the reader might wish to consult Howe; Halperin; Pollack; and Stolper, Chap. 8.

91. Liu Xiao, "Mission (6)," 20.

92. Khrushchev, *Last Testament*, 261–62.

93. For a brief review of these events, see Lewis and Xue, *China Builds*, 63–64.

94. He Di, 61. According to Han Nianlong, 115, "China informed the Soviet Union in advance of the operations that would be conducted," but clearly any such notice was ambiguous and misleading.

95. He Xiaolu, 162; Han Nianlong, 115. The information on Gromyko's visit to China is from these sources. The information on tactical nuclear weapons is from an interview with a Soviet specialist, 1990. Mao went on to say that if the U.S. resorted to strategic nuclear weapons, the Soviet Union should retaliate against the invading American forces.

96. Gromyko, *Pamiatnoe*, 133 (for the English version, see his *Memoirs*, 251–52).

97. Because Gromyko's statements were deemed erroneous and anti-Chinese, his memoirs were removed from Soviet bookstores after the Chinese made a formal protest. Information from a Soviet specialist given access to the relevant official documents, 1990.

98. He Xiaolu, 162; Han Nianlong, 115. In an article that deals with Soviet faintheartedness toward the West in the late 1950s, Fukuyama, 598, argues that Khrushchev sent the letter to Eisenhower only after it was "fairly clear the Chinese had no intention of escalating the crisis after Sept. 6." See also Nye, 340.

99. Khrushchev, *Last Testament*, 261–63.

100. See Duan Zijun, "Premier," 9–10; and Liu Xiao, "Mission (6)," 20–21.

101. Khrushchev, *Last Testament*, 262.

102. The missile submarine was the 31-class Golf, the diesel attack submarine the 33-class Romeo, the 21- and 24-class missile crafts Osa and Komar, and the torpedo boat the 25-class Huchuan. The missiles were the 1060 (R-11FM) and the 544 or SY-1 (SS-N-2A). *Haijun Shi*, 51; Han Huaizhi and Tan Jingqiao, 2: 157; Yang Guoyu, *Dangdai*, 234; Ling Yu, "Chinese," 96–98; Turetsky, 39, 65–79; Moore, *Soviet Navy*, 72, 76.

103. Lewis and Xue, *China Builds*, 64, 71–72.

104. Han Nianlong, 115.

105. Mao's bodyguard has described the bitter quarrel that erupted between Mao and Khrushchev. Quan Yanchi, *Zouxia*, 51.

106. Han Nianlong, 115–16.

107. *Ibid.*, 115.

108. Chen Youming, "Concern (1)," 3; Zhi Yin, "Inside Stories," 17. It was not until 1960 that Beijing's leaders realized that Moscow had consciously limited its technical aid to conventional weapons. See, for example, Nie Rongzhen, *Nie Rongzhen Huiyilu*, 809–12.

109. Nie Rongzhen and Luo Ruiqing attended the negotiations between Zhou Enlai and Khrushchev. The information in this paragraph is from Zhi Yin, "Inside Stories," 17; Chen Youming, "Concern (1)," 3; and Yang Guoyu, *Dangdai*, 243.

110. Liu Xiao, then serving as Chinese ambassador to the Soviet Union, quotes Khrushchev as saying in 1962, "If the Chinese brothers understand and agree with our opinion, the Soviet side will do whatever it can to improve relations between the two countries." Liu Xiao, *Chushi*, 120. Significant conventional equipment continued to flow from the Soviet Union to China until 1962, and Chinese military trainees remained in the Soviet Union until 1964.

111. A comparable story of the relationship of politics and technology is told by MacKenzie. This section reflects some of the ideas expressed in his Chap. 8.

Chapter Two

1. Zhong Xie, 181; Chu Jiakang, 8; Wang Jinzhong, 24; Song Shilun, *Zhongguo*, 2: 846. U.S. submarine reactors use weapons-grade enrichment, about 93% U^{235}. The French use an enrichment of only a little more than 3%, well below weapons grade. This difference in choice has multiple design consequences. For example, the U.S. reactors run for at least a decade without refueling, so no hatches are built into the hull for refueling. Information from an American specialist, 1991.

2. This paragraph is based on Stephenson and Weal, 126; Shu Deqi and Li Chunfang, 62–63; Xie Guang, *Dangdai*, 1: 352–53; Zhong Xie, 182; and Ge Qiguang et al., 323–24.

3. Li Jue et al., 301; information from an American specialist, 1991. On the technological requirements for the submarine's nuclear power plant, see also "Riddle," 7. By 1958, the open literature on PWRs had mushroomed, and under the Atoms for Peace program, the UN had published the proceedings of two major conferences on the peaceful uses of atomic energy with detailed information and bibliographies on PWRs. See esp. United Nations.

4. Unless otherwise cited, this paragraph and the next are based on Zhong Xie,

182–83; Chen Youming, "Concern (1)," 4; and Song Shilun, *Zhongguo*, 2: 846. For further information on the structure and operation of a submarine nuclear power plant, see Zhong Xie, 180–85.

 5. Jiang Rubiao et al., "China's No. 1"; Zhong Xie, 7.

 6. Li Jue et al., 304; "Riddle," 7; Wang Rongsheng, 387.

 7. Zhi Yin, "Inside Stories," 16–17, 21; "Riddle," 7; Li Jue et al., 294–95.

 8. The IAE had two deputy directors named Li Yi (rendered with different characters). The man referred to here (李毅) was in charge of producing uranium hexafluoride (for his role in the nuclear weapons program, see the index entry for him in Lewis and Xue, *China Builds*). The other Li Yi (力一) ran the accelerator. Li Jue et al., 17, 302, 358, 394.

 9. Zu Wei, 8–9; Li Jue et al., 301–2; "Riddle," 7.

 10. This paragraph and the next are based on Peng Shilu and Zhao Renkai, 208; Huang Xuhua, 397; "Riddle," 7; and Li Jue et al., 65, 302–3.

 11. For a discussion of this pullout, see Lewis and Xue, *China Builds*, Chap. 3.

 12. Zhang Peilin was transferred to the Second Ministry in 1963 as chief engineer of its Fuels Production Bureau. Du Chunshi, 103, 108–9; Wu Ming; Li Jue et al., 201.

 13. Peng Shilu and Zhao Renkai, 208.

 14. Li Jue et al., 192, 193, 201; Du Chunshi, 109.

 15. Li Jue et al., 193.

 16. The classic study of this phenomenon in China is Barnett, Part 1.

 17. The information in this paragraph and the next is from "Riddle," 7; and Li Jue et al., 304, 368, 385, 457. For information on Chinese efforts to gather data for the submarine project, see, for example, Li Jue et al., 368–70.

 18. On the plutonium production reactor, see Lewis and Xue, "Chinese Strategic Weapons," 4–14.

 19. The Dalian Machinery Plant was code-named Plant 523. The information in this paragraph and the next is based on Li Jue et al., 440–43.

 20. Among the facilities the bureau took in charge between late 1961 and 1963 were the Hengyang Mining Machinery Plant in Hunan Province, the Tianjin Drilling and Boring Machine Plant, the Suzhou Valve Plant in Jiangsu Province, the Suzhou Optical Instrument Factory in Jiangsu Province, the Beijing Nuclear Instrument Factory (Plant 261), and the Guanghua Instrument and Meter Factory (Plant 264) in Shanghai. Over the years, the central leadership set up additional large plants for manufacturing nuclear instruments and equipment in Xi'an, Wuhan, Nanchang, and other cities.

 21. Yang Bo, 148; Wu Lengxi, 317.

 22. Wu Qungan, 1–2; Hu Sheng, 381; Xue Muqiao et al., 41; Ma Yunfei, 11.

 23. Guo Binwei and Tan Zongji, 199–200; Dao Yin, 40; Wang Yu, 390.

 24. "Eighth Central Committee"; Chen Rulong, 1: 188–89. In Sept. 1963, the Central Committee decided to continue the "eight-character" principles from 1963 to 1965. Wang Yaping, 33–37.

 25. The Chinese military also met at Beidaihe that summer, as it did in the summers of 1960 and 1962, to discuss how to implement a policy readjustment. *He Long Nianpu*, 406, 412, 417.

 26. *Nie Rongzhen Huiyilu*, 814–15. For a full discussion of this meeting and its consequences, see Lewis and Xue, *China Builds*, 121–34.

 27. *Nie Rongzhen Yuanshuai*, 162; Liu Boluo, "Premier Zhou Devoted," 344.

28. On Mao's decision, see Lewis and Xue, *China Builds*, 129–30, 277. Unless otherwise cited, the information in this paragraph and the next is from Zhang Jun, 16; Chen Youming, "Wise Decision," 12–13; Chen Youming, "Concern (1)," 3; and Zhi Yin, "Inside Stories," 17.

29. For information on subsequent conferences, see also Duan Zijun, "Principal Founder," 210; and *He Long Nianpu*, 417.

30. The origins and evolution of the Defense Science and Technology Commission, the NDIC, the NDIO, and other parts of the military industrial bureaucracy will be discussed in Chap. 4.

31. In the first half of the 1960s, the Chinese navy gave priority to the building of 31- and 33-class (Golf and Romeo) submarines. Yang Guoyu, *Dangdai*, 234, 235–36. The code names for these ships are from *ibid.*, 235, 650; and Han Huaizhi and Tan Jingqiao, 2: 157.

32. The decision to suspend work was reportedly reached at a meeting of the Central Special Commission in late 1962. Yang Guoyu, *Dangdai*, 244. The commission was created on Nov. 17, 1962. Li Jue et al., 568.

33. On the statement of Chen Yi, see Shu Deqi and Li Chunfang, 51.

34. *Haijun Shi*, 83, 234; Li Jue et al., 303; Yang Guoyu, *Dangdai*, 244.

35. Zu Wei and Lin Pukai, 55.

36. Li Jue et al., 385. The Nuclear Engineering Research and Design Academy cited in this source seems to be a mistake. That academy was not set up until the mid-1960s. The Design Bureau dated back to the early 1960s, when the Second Ministry merged its Design Bureau with the Design Academy of its Twelfth Bureau. The Design Bureau was charged with completing engineering designs for nuclear industry and with the design and manufacture of nonstandard equipment. The ministry dissolved the bureau in 1965 and eventually reestablished several design academies. *Ibid.*, 417–18.

37. Unless otherwise cited, information in this paragraph is from Chen Youming, "Wise Decision," 13; Chen Youming, "Concern (1)," 4; and Zhi Yin, "Inside Stories," 17.

38. The Seventh Academy, or Warship Research and Design Academy, was shuttled back and forth between the navy (1961–65, 1970–75) and the Sixth (shipbuilding) Ministry (1965–70, 1975–82). Since 1982 it has been part of the China State Shipbuilding Corporation. Yang Guoyu, *Dangdai*, 252, 460. For a detailed description of the academy, see footnote, p. 55, and Chap. 3, note 54.

39. For a useful history of maritime nuclear propulsion in general, see Pocock, Chaps. 1–2. The Reactor Engineering and Technology Institute was an outgrowth of IAE's Reactor Research Department (itself an expansion of what had been the Reactor Engineering Research Section). The Second Ministry took over the department in 1964. Li Jue et al., 295, 364.

40. GKSS was founded in 1956 as a joint venture of the West German Government, the four north German coastal Lander, and 39 enterprises. In 1973, GKSS decided that it had gained enough knowledge from the *Otto Hahn* to begin construction of a lead vessel, a container ship to be used on Asian routes. See Great Britain, Department of Industry, 8, 12, 19.

41. Great Britain, Department of Trade and Industry, esp. 6–7, 40; Fiebig, 111–16.

42. For information on the *Lenin* to which the Chinese would have had access, see Alexandrov et al., 204–19; and Lank and Oakley, 108–37.

43. Peng Shilu, 12–16; Chen Youming, "Concern (1)," 6; Li Jue et al., 574. The commission began life as the Fifteen-Member Special Commission in Nov. 1962 and was in charge of Project 02 (nuclear bomb). In March 1965 the Politburo added seven members to the commission, extended its assignments to include the strategic missile project, and renamed it the Central Special Commission. The commission experienced a number of leadership changes: in April 1977 Hua Guofeng was appointed director with Ye Jianying, Li Xiannian, and Deng Xiaoping as deputies, and in Oct. 1989 Li Peng was appointed director with Yao Yilin and Liu Huaqing as deputies. Academy of Military Science, *Zhongguo Renmin Jiefangjun Liushi Nian Dashiji*, 602; Xie Guang, *Dangdai*, 2: 517, 527, 540.

44. Lewis and Xue, "Chinese Strategic Weapons," 10–11.

45. During the Cultural Revolution, Jiang Naixiang and the head of the institute were imprisoned for "attempting to usurp the power of the navy."

46. The institute's code name is from Yang Guoyu, *Dangdai*, 244. The Nuclear-Powered Submarine Overall Design Section was originally under the dual administration of the navy and defense-related industrial ministries (the First Ministry from 1958 to 1960, the Third Ministry from 1960 to 1963, and the Sixth Ministry from 1963 to 1965). Information in this paragraph is from Chen Youming, "Wise Decision," 13; Chen Youming, "Concern (1)," 4; and Zhi Yin, "Inside Stories," 17.

47. On the assignments of Institute 715, see *Haijun Shi*, 83.

48. Institute 715 was created by the navy in 1963, and then, in 1970, formally brought under the Second Ministry. The ministry later moved it to Jiajiang County, Sichuan Province, and put it under the administration of the Southwest Reactor Engineering Research and Design Academy (First Academy). Most of its experienced technicians were transferred to Jiajiang, though some of them still operated under the institute's name in Beijing. Chen Wang, 392; Peng Shilu, 12–16; Li Jue et al., 65, 309, 574; Chen Youming, "Wise Decision," 13.

49. The information in this paragraph and the next is from Zhi Yin, "Inside Stories," 17, 18; Li Jue et al., 65–66, 303; Chen Youming, "Concern (1)," 4, 5; and Chen Youming, "Wise Decision," 14.

50. Li Jue et al., 65–66, 303–5, 309.

51. Unless otherwise cited, this paragraph is based on Zhi Yin, "Inside Stories," 18; Chen Youming, "Wise Decision," 13–14; and Chen Youming, "Concern (1)," 4.

52. Chen Youming, "Concern (2)," 46–47. We shall discuss the various shipyards related to Project 09 in Chap. 5.

53. In his capacity as vice-chairman of the Central Military Commission, Nie Rongzhen placed the PLA General Logistics Department in charge of supplying materials to all units under the Defense Science and Technology Commission. Wang Lihua and Zhang Jiade, 145.

54. "Evolution"; Li Jue et al., 567.

55. The works on this subject are legion. See, for example, Goldman, *Literary*; MacFarquhar; and Goldman, "Party."

56. *Nie Rongzhen Huiyilu*, esp. 781–82, 827–28, 844–45.

57. Hu Shihong, "National Defense," 20.

58. Dong Kegong et al.; *Nie Rongzhen Huiyilu*, 828.

59. For the sources on these documents, see *Nie Rongzhen Huiyilu*, 827–842; and Deng Xiaoping [5], 62, 401. The text of the 14 articles is in *Nie Rongzhen Huiyilu*, 831–34.

60. Deng Xiaoping [5], 61–62.
61. These quotes are from Deng Xiaoping, *Selected Works*, 401.
62. Dong Kegong et al.; *Nie Rongzhen Huiyilu*, 836–37.
63. "Adopt a Correct Attitude." Immediately following the Guangzhou conference, Zhou Enlai and Chen Yi arranged a special banquet in the Great Hall of the People for several hundred defense scientists, where they exhorted the scientists to press on with the weapons programs. Information from a Chinese specialist who attended the banquet, 1989.
64. See Lewis, "Revolutionary Struggle," 126–47.
65. Lin Biao, 9–30.
66. According to Chinese sources, the PLA had sent a total of 320,000 military personnel to Vietnam by the end of March 1968, with a high of 170,000 in one year alone. Academy of Military Science, *Zhongguo Renmin Jiefangjun Liushi Nian Dashiji*, 616; Su Wenming, 108; Shi Yingfu, 65.
67. In fact, some of Luo Ruiqing's own writings at this time echoed Mao's (and Lin's) calls for People's War. See Luo Ruiqing, *Commemorate*; and Luo, *People*.
68. Zhu Jizhong and Cai Chuandao, 33; Dian Dian, *Feifan*, 181; Da Ying, 332, 333, 343.
69. *Huiyi*, 242; Wang Jianying, 96; *He Long Nianpu*, 163. Mao put He Long in charge of overseeing the commission's affairs in Jan. 1964.
70. Zhu Jizhong and Cai Chuandao, 20, 29, 35; Da Ying, 352.
71. Unless otherwise cited, the information in this paragraph and the next two is based on Shi Dongbing, 14, 15–16; Ye Yonglie, 24; Zhu Jizhong and Cai Chuandao, 45–47; and Dian Dian, *Feifan*, 59.
72. Lin Biao's letter was dated Nov. 30, 1965. Cong Jin, 633.
73. Guan Shan, 163; Zhou Guoquan et al., 511–12; Pang Xianzhi, 80. For supplementary English sources, see "Report."
74. Unless otherwise noted, the information in this paragraph and the next three is from Dian Dian, "Smile," 374; Dian Dian, *Feifan*, 198–216 *passim*; Zhu Jizhong and Cai Chuandao, 6–9, 49–51, 208; and Peng Cheng, 59.
75. At the Shanghai conference, He Long became so nervous about his ties to Luo Ruiqing that he had to be treated for high blood pressure. Wang Ding, "Doctor," 265; Wang Ding, "Marshal," 3. He Long apparently sided with Liu Shaoqi in the power struggle between Mao and Liu and paid a price for it. On July 31, 1966, the day before the 11th session of the 8th Central Committee in which Mao directly attacked Liu, He Long told Zhou Enlai "to be cautious in handling problems involving Liu Shaoqi and to take inner-Party unity into account." *He Long Nianpu*, 445. Two months later, Mao instructed Lin Biao to take measures against He. Wang Nianyi, *1949–1989*, 505.
76. This house, 618 West Jianguo Road, is now the Polish consulate.
77. "Comment of the CCP," 31–32.
78. "Circular," 28.
79. This and the next paragraph are based on "Report," in Ying-mao Kau.
80. Ironically, this system of sending military representatives to ordnance factories was abolished early in the Cultural Revolution. In 1977, the Central Military Commission and the State Council decided to resume the system, and the navy set up eight regional offices to administer military representatives in various industrial facilities. For further information, see Han Huaizhi and Tan Jingqiao, 2: 202–5; Yang Guoyu, *Dangdai*, 442; and *Haijun Shi*, 220.

81. Wang Hongkun was a senior deputy commander of the navy. In June 1962, Lin Biao sent Li Zuopeng and Zhang Xiuchuan to the navy as deputy commander and head of the Political Department, respectively. In addition, Lin put Li in charge of the daily affairs of the navy's Party committee. For information on the power struggle within the navy during the years 1966–67, see "Correctly Handle." This paragraph is based on *Haijun Shi*, 76, 77, 78.

82. Li Jue et al., 65–66.   83. *Ibid.*, 201.

84. *Ibid.*, 74.   85. Lewis and Xue, *China Builds*, 203.

86. Li Jue et al., 77.

87. The full title of Nie's report was "Report on the Military Takeover and Adjustment and Reorganization of Defense Research Facilities." By 1968, Nie's commission controlled eight research and design academies in addition to the Academy of Sciences' New Technological Bureau, including about 133,000 technicians and workers in over 100 research institutes and 10 pilot plants. Han Huaizhi and Tan Jingqiao, 2: 98.

88. Li Jue et al., 74, 572. The takeover had already been decided on on March 17, 1967. Zhang Jun, 567.

89. The guest list would have included, for example, the Beijing Steel and Iron Research Academy, which reportedly cast two special kinds of alloy steel resistant to heat, pressure, and radiation for the pressure vessel and the main heat exchanger. Lu Da, 476.

90. Most of the participants in these professional gatherings came from the research and industrial facilities under the First Ministry of Machine Building. Unless otherwise cited, the information in this paragraph is from Li Jue et al., 456–57; and Chen Ping et al., 165.

91. Yang Guoyu, *Dangdai*, 245. Yang gives the date of the letter as Aug. 28, but we choose to accept the Aug. 30 date given in Chen Youming, "Wise Decision," 15; Chen Youming, "Concern (1)," 6; and Li Jue et al., 573.

92. Li Jue et al., 74, 76; Yang Guoyu, *Dangdai*, 245.

93. Unless otherwise cited, the information in this and the next three paragraphs is from Li Jue et al., 76–77.

94. For a description of the terror that swept China's nuclear industry in the years 1969–71, see Su Fangxue, "National Spirit," 23.

95. Chen Ping, 164–66; Li Jue et al., 70–74, 413–15. Most of the discussion of the Third Line that follows is based on Lewis and Xue, "Chinese Strategic Weapons," 12–14.

96. The purpose of the *sanbei* conference, which was held at the headquarters of the General Staff and presided over by Lin Biao, was to discuss China's military options in the event of a full-scale conflict with the Soviet Union. Zhang Yunsheng, 306.

97. Lin Biao was here merely reiterating Mao's long-held view on the need to locate the nuclear industry in the Third-Line region. As early as 1965, Mao urged Zhou Enlai to make preparations for moving nuclear industrial facilities from the North and Northwest to the Southwest. Zhou persuaded him to give up the idea. Liu Xiyao, 334.

98. Unless otherwise cited, the information in this paragraph and the next two is from Zhang Chunting, "Jiang Shengjie," 6; and Li Jue et al., 74–75.

99. Chen Ping, 164–66; Li Jue et al., 75, 77.

100. Li Jue et al., 303.

101. Zhao Renkai, a senior scientist at Institute 194, was later appointed deputy chief designer of the nuclear power plant program. Huang Caihong and Cao Guoqiang, "For the Birth (2)." In 1986, he and Peng Shilu were awarded the national science-and-technology prize for their contributions to the project. Zu Wei and Lin Pukai, 51.

102. Unless otherwise cited, the information in this and the next paragraph is based on Zu Wei and Lin Pukai, 54, 57; and Peng Shilu and Zhao Renkai, 207, 208.

103. The information in this paragraph is from Du Chunshi, 108–9, 112–14; Wu Ming; Xiao Heng, 203, 207; Li Jue et al., 201–2; and Xie Guang, *Dangdai*, 1: 352–53.

104. The trial and series production of the submarine reactor rods involved Plant 202, a nonferrous metals processing plant in Baoji, a plant in Chongqing, the Beijing Nuclear Engineering Research and Design Academy (the Second Ministry's Second Academy), Institute 401, Institute 5 in Tongxian, the Metals Research Institute in Shenyang, the Nonferrous Metals Research Academy, the Nonferrous Metals Research Institute in Shanghai, the Institute of Chemistry, and the Institute of Applied Chemistry.

105. Xiao Heng, 209–10; Xie Guang, *Dangdai*, 1: 353.

106. Wu Ming; Du Chunshi, 113, 114; Li Jue et al., 194.

107. See Peng Shilu, 13–14; and Li Jue et al., 202, 304–5.

108. Li Jue et al., 66, 304, 572.

109. Mao Zedong and Zhou Enlai ordered the Chengdu and Shenyang Military Region commands to send construction troops to both Jiajiang's First Academy and the Huludao shipyard (Plant 431), where the nuclear submarine would be assembled. Zhi Yin, "Inside Stories," 18; Chen Youming, "Concern (1)," 4; Li Jue et al., 66, 573.

110. Li Jue et al., 66. With the merger of Institute 194 in 1968, the academy developed into China's largest research facility on submarine reactors. Today, it operates at least four research institutes, including Institute 15, the Reactor Engineering and Technology Institute, and the Institute of Materials and Fuel Components (Fourth Institute). At least four reactors were built near Jiajiang: the prototype power plant for Project 09, a high flux experimental reactor, a small experimental reactor using depleted fuel from the high flux one, and a pulse reactor. (A pulse reactor has a high peak output but average low output and is used to test reactor design.) *Ibid.*, 203, 295, 309, 365, 385, 574; Guo Tiejun; Xu Bo, "Operation"; Xu Bo, "Completion"; Fang Ren; Jiao Xinguang; Wan Yuan and Liu Yonghua.

111. The construction of the Jiajiang prototype power plant was completed under the aegis of two Second Ministry organs: the Seventh Architectural Engineering Division and the First Installation Engineering Division of the 23rd Installation Engineering Company. Li Jue et al., 304–5, 415. But over 60 industrial and research facilities were reportedly involved in its construction and installation. Yang Guoyu, *Dangdai*, 245–46.

112. This paragraph and the next are based on Peng Shilu, 12–14; Chen Youming, "Concern (1)," 6–7; Zhu Guangya, 310; Yang Guoyu, *Dangdai*, 246–47; and Li Jue et al., 67. We will discuss the Nuclear-Powered Submarine Project Leading Group and its Project Office in Chap. 3.

113. The work group sent to Jiajiang was composed of officials and experts

from the Second Ministry, the Beijing Nuclear Engineering Research and Design Academy (Second Academy), and Qinghua University.

114. Zhu Guangya, 310; Peng Shilu, 14.

115. Peng Shilu, 14; Li Jue et al., 67, 305; Chen Youming, "Wise Decision," 15; Chen Youming, "Concern (1)," 7. According to Li Jue et al., the engineers started raising the power of the power plant on July 17.

116. Chen Youming, "Concern (1)," 7; Chen Youming, "Wise Decision," 15; Zu Wei and Lin Pukai, 55, 58. The Chinese term for the pulse tubes is *maichong guan*. They form part of the pulse system for automated data sampling and control. *Dianzi*, 2: 20.12.

117. Zu Wei and Lin Pukai, 55.

118. Zhou Jiading, 5; Peng Shilu, 14; Chen Youming, "Wise Decision," 15; Chen Youming, "Concern (1)," 7.

119. Peng Shilu, 14, states that the prototype power plant reached full power on Aug. 30. Chen Youming, "Concern (1)," 7, puts the date a bit earlier, at Aug. 28. And Li Jue et al., 67, 305, says it occurred still earlier, on July 30. Peng served as chief designer of the power plant program, and we use his date. The plant's thermal power is from an interview with a Chinese specialist, 1989.

Chapter Three

1. For a complete discussion of this subject, see Lewis and Xue, *Military Readiness*.

2. Yang Guoyu, *Dangdai*, 49; "First Submarine"; *Haijun Shi*, 46.

3. In March 1951, the first 40-ton gunboat was launched at the Jiangnan Shipyard. The designers had miscalculated the boat's center of gravity, however, and when loaded, it capsized and sank. Xiao Li, 14; Huang Shengtian, 23; *Haijun Shi*, 26; Yang Guoyu, *Dangdai*, 65–66.

4. New China News Agency Reporters, 238–39; Yang Guoyu, *Dangdai*, 53, 688.

5. Zhou Jiading, 2; Yang Guoyu, *Dangdai*, 71, 688.

6. Han Huaizhi and Tan Jingqiao, 2: 109, 155–56.

7. The Hudong (Shanghai) yard was assigned to build the frigate, Wuhu (Anhui Province) the torpedo boat, Jiangnan (Shanghai) the sub, Qiuxin (Shanghai) the submarine chaser, and Wuchang (Wuhan) the minesweeper. Han Huaizhi and Tan Jingqiao, 2: 109, 155–56; Xiao Li, 14; Yang Guoyu, *Dangdai*, 229, 231, 232, 240; Chen Ping et al., 122–23; *Haijun Shi*, 50; Run Bei, 3.

8. On the restoration of the submarine's priority, see Run Bei, 2; Zheng Wenhan, 4; Yang Guoyu, *Dangdai*, 41–42, 689–90; and *Haijun Shi*, 331.

9. The navy's first submarine squadron was formed in Qingdao in June 1954, with Fu Jize as commander. "Liu Huaqing Speaks," K11; *Haijun Shi*, 46; Yang Guoyu, *Dangdai*, 107, 690.

10. Yang Guoyu refers to this Soviet medium-sized S-class submarine by the Cyrillic letter "C" and states that two such submarines, built in 1943, were stationed at Lüshun and were taken over by Chinese crews in June 1954; they were designated "New China" 11 and 12. The two small-sized subs, class M-15, were newer, built in 1950 and 1951; the Chinese took them over in July 1954 and designated them "National Defense" 21 and 22. Yang Guoyu, *Dangdai*, 53–54, 69, 690. Moscow had given China a retired S-class boat for training purposes in 1953. Jin Tao, 5; "First Submarine." By Chinese definition, mini-subs displace tens of tons, small-

sized ones 300 and 500 tons, medium-sized ones 1,000 and 1,500 tons, and large-sized ones above 2,000 tons. Zhong Xie, 4. We are indebted to John Engelhardt for providing a copy of Zhong's book and his own article.

11. Yang Guoyu, *Dangdai*, 53.

12. Shen Shungen, "Description"; Shen Shungen and Zhang Ze'nan, 33; Zhang Ping.

13. Acting Chief of the General Staff Nie Rongzhen and Minister of the Ministry of Heavy Industry Li Fuchun were deputy directors of the Central Military Commission's Ordnance Commission. Zhou Jiading, 4; Han Huaizhi and Tan Jingqiao, 2: 110–11.

14. "Bright Light," E10; Yang Guoyu, *Dangdai*, 692.

15. During the mid-1950s, Soviet military support covered the full range of weapons. For a discussion of Soviet military assistance to the development of Chinese strategic weapons during this period, see Lewis and Xue, *China Builds the Bomb*, Chap. 3.

16. Muller, *China*, 30–31; Yang Guoyu, *Dangdai*, 229–30, 693. This submarine was one of 21 03-type submarines built by 1962 under Soviet license. Han Huaizhi and Tan Jingqiao, 2: 156.

17. For additional information, see Chap. 1, note 102. The Soviet decision in 1960 to stop supplying technical data, equipment, and components caused China to suspend temporarily the building of the five warships and two missiles. Han Huaizhi and Tan Jingqiao, 2: 157; Yang Guoyu, *Dangdai*, 234, 696. The Western designations for the submarines and missiles are from Sharpe, *Jane's Fighting Ships*, 101, 108, 110; Turetsky, 39, 65–79; and More, *The Soviet Navy*, 72, 76. The Soviets designated the Golf-1 submarine, which they supplied to China, the 611 class. Golf and Romeo are the Western code names.

18. Muller, *China*, 30–31, 37–38. In 1966, the Chinese completed the assembly of the Golf submarine from Soviet components at the Dalian yard, and the navy added the boat to its battle order. Yang Han and Wei Naiwen, 405. Three years later, a Romeo submarine for the first time was built with all Chinese-made components, and on June 22, 1969, the boat joined the fleet. Yang Guoyu, *Dangdai*, 235, 236, 704. According to a PRC source, China possessed "more than 20 submarines under three submarine flotillas" by Jan. 1959. *Ibid.*, 600. Most of the subs are believed to have been the S-class built in 1948 and the 03-class built in the latter half of the 1950s. This is based on *ibid.*, 69, 692, 693; and Han Huaizhi and Tan Jingqiao, 2: 156.

19. Hudson, 282.   20. Li Jue et al., 64, 564.

21. Zu Wei, 3, 4.   22. "Riddle," 7.

23. Li Jue et al., 302; "Riddle," 7.

24. At that time, for example, Chinese specialists reportedly had acquired only two pictures of the shapes of foreign nuclear-powered submarines. Xia Yuansheng, 87; Huang Caihong and Cao Guoqiang, "For the Birth (1)"; Xi Qixin, 2; Zu Wei, 4.

25. Canadian designers, in their aborted attempt to develop a nuclear submarine, also sought to modify existing diesel-electric designs (such as those for a 209, or Tr1500-class boat) by putting in a midsection piece containing a small reactor.

26. Zu Wei, 3–4.

27. Huang Xuhua, 397; Zu Wei, 4.

28. Shen Hongyuan, "Structural Design," 55. Shen Hongyuan was an engineer

and a specialist in submarine design at the Institute of Ship System Engineering in Beijing. For his many recent articles on the subject, see the Reference Cited section.

29. Shen Hongyuan, "Structural Design," 55–56. For information on Chinese viewpoints on designing nuclear boats, see Zhong Xie, 27–40, 180–85.

30. Liu Jingzhi, 14; Huang Xuhua, 398; Shen Hongyuan, "Structural Design" 58.

31. Shen Hongyuan, "Structural Design," 58.

32. Zhong Xie, 81.

33. Shen Hongyuan, "Structural Design," 56.

34. Zhong Xie, 64; Shen Hongyuan, "Structural Design," 58; Yu Zhibin, 12.

35. Yi Shaolin, 201.

36. There is typically about a meter of space between a double-hull submarine's outer and inner hulls. Zhong Xie, 6, 103–4. Chinese submariners hold that double-hull construction can protect the water valves in the sub's inner, or pressure, hull from being damaged if the outer hull is hit by a "small" explosive charge. Shen Hongyuan, "Single Hull," 13.

37. By 1959, the Chinese had been provided the Soviet technical data for building the Romeo and Golf submarines. U.S. submarines are single-hull boats that "minimize hull-created noise both radiated and self" and ensure "a least hindrance to listening capability." Phoenix, 15–16, 17.

38. Zhong Xie, 18–19; Engelhardt, 49–50.

39. The quotations in this paragraph are from Engelhardt, 48–49; and Zhong Xie, 16, 18, 19.

40. See, for example, Shen Hongyuan, "Structural Design," 59–60; and Zhong Xie, 18–19, 85–95.

41. A reduction of the detection range depends on many factors. For example, sound decreases by the radius squared at long distances, but by the radius cubed at short distances. This is the effect of the sound channel in the deep ocean.

42. This paragraph is based on Zhong Xie, 8–11; Ge Qiguang et al., 305; Shen Hongyuan, "Self-[Generated] Noise"; and Shen Hongyuan, "Structural Design," 55–60 *passim*.

43. The Seventh Academy's Institute 725 in Luoyang, Henan Province, was set up in 1961 to work on materials and technology. Unless otherwise noted, the information in this and the next two paragraphs is from Xie Guang, *Dangdai*, 1: 365, 2: 272; Li Jie, "Various Means"; Shen Hongyuan, "Self-[Generated] Noise"; Xia Yinshan; Zhong Xie, 8–11, 65, 69–70; Ge Qiguang et al., 359–61; and Shen Hongyuan, "Structural Design," 59–60.

44. By the late 1970s, Chinese engineers had designed new propellers with reduced noise and increased speed. Xie Guang, *Dangdai*, 2: 273.

45. *Haijun Shi*, 236.

46. Demagnetization clearly helps but using nonmagnetic materials is better. Modern airborne systems, called MAD, can detect any disturbance in the earth's magnetic field by the presence of large amounts of magnetic metallic material.

47. Lu Jianxun, 392; Wang Rongsheng, 386, 387; *Rixin Yueyi*, 167; Shen Hongyuan, "Structural Design," 56.

48. Shen Hongyuan, "Structural Design," 56. The maximum submerged depth of the 09-1 and 09-2 subs is inferred from *ibid.*, 60; Li Jie, "Panorama," 35; Li Ke and Hao Shengzhang, 303; and Cheng Wang, 320. The maximum submerged depth of first-generation U.S. and Soviet nuclear-powered submarines varied from

300m to 350m; later models could operate at 400–500m. Depths between 600m and 900m became possible once hull structures of titanium alloys were developed.

49. Shen Hongyuan, "Structural Design," 57; Huang Xuhua, 397.

50. Unless otherwise cited, the information in this and the next paragraph is based on Huang Caihong and Cao Guoqiang, "For the Birth (1)."

51. As of this writing, many of the details on Project 09 remain secret. Even now, the principal scientists and engineers cannot even release their names and pictures without special permission. Premier Zhao Ziyang reportedly told Huang Xuhua, then 09's chief designer: "Propaganda can be conducted on those experts who have rendered outstanding service on other fronts of endeavor so as to let them be known by people. It is not the case, however, for you. You and your colleagues can only remain as unknown heroes." Zu Wei, 2, 11. Later, Huang received high honors, and his role in Project 09 became widely reported.

52. China's first nuclear attack submarine was commissioned on Aug. 1, 1974. *Haijun Shi*, 337; Yang Guoyu, *Dangdai*, 247.

53. Chen Youming, "Concern (1)," 3; Chen Youming, "Wise Decision," 13; Li Jue et al., 65.

54. Now composed of 22 research institutes and their 24 pilot plants, the Seventh Academy has more than 30,000 staff members and technicians and 6,500 workers. Han Huaizhi and Tan Jingqiao, 2: 157; Yang Guoyu, *Dangdai*, 234–35, 460, 697; Chen Ping et al., 127; Lu Jianxun, 391; Zhang Ming and Shen Shungen. A list of its research facilities as of 1992 appears in the table on page 270. According to Zu Wei, 3, Huang Xuhua is the only person who has been on the project since its inception in 1958. By the mid-1960s, Huang had become deputy chief engineer at Institute 719, where he was in charge of doing exploratory research on the overall design for nuclear-powered submarines. Subsequently, he was made chief designer of both the 09-1 (attack) and the 09-2 (missile) subs. Huang Caihong and Cao Guoqiang, "For the Birth (2)"; "Honor Roll," 1986; Yang Guoyu, *Dangdai*, 244. Later still, he became, first, 719's deputy director in charge of the technical wing and then director. Shen Rongjun, 200; Zu Wei, 7.

55. Unless otherwise cited, this paragraph is based on Xi Qixin and Liu Jingzhi; Zhi Yin, "Inside Stories," 17, 21; Zu Wei, 3, 4; and Chen Youming, "Concern (1)," 4. For detailed information on the suspension of Project 09 between 1962 and 1965, see the previous chapter.

56. Work was also to commence on the prototype land-based power plant, the nuclear-powered submarine base, and the pier where the nuclear-powered submarines would be berthed. Additional information on this decision is found in Chap. 2. Unless otherwise cited, the information in this and the next paragraphs is from Wang Rongsheng, 385; Zhi Yin, "Inside Stories," 17–18; Chen Youming, "Concern (1)," 4, 5; and Yang Guoyu, *Dangdai*, 244.

57. Xi Qixin, 2; Xi Qixin and Liu Jingzhi. The information in this paragraph and the next three is from Zu Wei, 5–6; Zhong Xie, 5–7; Liu Jingzhi, 12–13; Zhu Lemin; and Huang Caihong and Cao Guoqiang, "For the Birth (2)."

58. Institute 702 was renamed the Chinese Ship Science Research Center in the late 1970s. Nearly 1,000 technicians worked there. Dong Shitang, 407–9; Zhao Jianhua, 48; Chen Ping et al., 127; Mao Rongfang; Huo Rusu, 2. Unless otherwise cited, this paragraph is based on Dong Shitang, 408; and Zhu Lemin.

59. The Ship Hydrodynamic Laboratory at the Central China Institute of Technology, which is charged with, among other things, deep-water experiments on

TABLE TO NOTE 54
Structure of the Warship Research and Design Academy, 1992

Unit	Specialty	Location
Academy headquarters		Beijing
Ship System Engineering Department[a]		Beijing
Institutes		
701	Overall warship design	Wuhan
702	Hydrodynamic testing	Wuxi
703	Boiler, steam turbine	Harbin
704	Warship auxiliary engine	Shanghai
705	Torpedoes, antisubmarine weapons	Kunming
707	Navigation	Tianjin
708	Overall designs for auxiliary warships and civilian ships	Shanghai
709	Computation	Wuhan
710	Mines, depth charges, demagnetization	Yichang
711	Diesel engine	Wuhan
712	Electric propulsion system, battery	Wuhan
713	Artillery, missile launcher	Zhengzhou
714	Intelligence on technologies	Beijing
715	Sonar and electronics	Hangzhou
716	Fire control, computation	Lianyungang
717	Electro-optical devices	Yichang
718	Antichemical facilities	Handan
719	Overall nuclear boat design	Wuhan
722	Communication engineering	Wuhan
723	Gun-pointing radar, electronics	Yangzhou
724	On-board warning radar	Nanjing
725	Materials technology	Luoyang

SOURCE: Cheng Wang, 69–70, 143, 551.
NOTE: The academy's Institute 706 (acoustic physics) was taken over by the State Ocean Bureau in 1972, and its Institute 720 (radio navigation) was moved to the Tenth Academy in 1975. So far as is known, there is no Institute 721.
[a]Called the Warship Prestudy Department until 1979.

model submarines, is said to be the "biggest one of its kind in China's institutions of higher learning." Located in Wuhan, Hubei Province, the laboratory is composed of four major experimental facilities: an indoor model ship experimental pool, an outdoor controllable pool, a wind tunnel, and a shock-wave pool. Cheng Zhenzhong.

60. At the time China started Project 09, foreign source materials had disclosed very little about the new water-drop configuration in submarine design. Consequently, the Chinese designers had to perform a series of scale-model hydrodynamic experiments to ascertain the feasibility of adopting that shape for 09-1. Huang Xuhua reportedly spent many sleepless nights doing scale-model experiments at hydrodynamic laboratories. This paragraph is based on Liu Jingzhi, 12–13; Huang Caihong and Cao Guoqiang, "For the Birth (2)"; Zhu Lemin; and Chen Youming, "Concern (1)," 5. Institute 719 later moved to Wuhan from Huludao. By 1989, its name had been changed to the Wuhan Second Ship Design and Research Institute. Based on Huang Xuhua, 396.

61. The information in this and the next paragraph is from Chen Youming,

"Wise Decision," 14; Chen Youming, "Concern (1)," 5; and Zhi Yin, "Inside Stories," 18.

62. Zhi Yin, "Inside Stories," 18; Chen Youming, "Wise Decision," 13–14. On the efforts of Beijing's leaders to support the principal defense projects, see Wang Lihua and Zhang Jiade, 145.

63. Zu Wei, 9.

64. Chen Youming, "Wise Decision," 14; Chen Youming, "Concern (1)," 5.

65. An official editorial declared: "It is a strategic task for proletarian revolutionaries to unite in seizing power from the handful of inner-Party capitalist-roaders in this new phase of the Great Proletarian Cultural Revolution. . . . This is the general orientation [of the current struggle]." "On the Struggle."

66. Qian Lingbai was the son of Qian Junrui, a veteran revolutionary who served in a series of senior positions in the PRC. Qian Junrui, 7–8. This paragraph is based on Huang Caihong and Cao Guoqiang, "For the Birth (1)."

67. Unless otherwise cited, the information in this paragraph is from Zu Wei, 3, 5.

68. By a decision taken on March 17, 1967, the central leadership put various defense industrial ministries under military control. Zhang Jun, 567. Huang Xuhua was probably taken into military custody that year. The institutes under the Seventh Academy are believed to have been controlled by teams sent by the navy.

69. Unless otherwise cited, the information in this and the next two paragraphs is from Yang Guoyu, *Dangdai*, 245, 246; Wang Rongsheng, 386; Chen Youming, "Wise Decision," 13, 14, 15; and Chen Youming, "Concern (1)," 4, 5, 6.

70. As early as 1960, the Ministry of Materials set up the Special Materials Bureau to meet the needs of the units under Nie's commission. The bureau opened Special Account No. 3 for those units and gave their requirements the highest priority. It was later merged into the Special Materials Planning Department of the PLA General Logistics Department. Wang Lihua and Zhang Jiade, 145.

71. Deng Sanrui, a graduate of the Naval Mechanics School, was considered one of the leading experts of the day on system engineering and ship design. At this writing, he is the president of the Harbin Ship Engineering Institute. This paragraph is based on *Haijun Shi*, 267; Yang Guoyu, *Dangdai*, 533; and Deng Sanrui, 161–68.

72. Chen Youming, "Concern (2)," 44–45.

73. Unless otherwise cited, the information in this paragraph and the next is from Yang Guoyu, *Dangdai*, 246.

74. Chen Youming played one of the key administrative roles in Project 09. He became director of the Project 09 Office in 1968 and joined the Project 09 Leading Group the following year. He had been made deputy head of the Naval Equipment and Technology Department by 1978, and had become head by 1983. Since his retirement in 1986, he has published three articles on Project 09 and is reportedly now writing a book on it entitled *Huigu yu Sikao* (Review and Thinking). Chen Youming, "New Shipping Line"; Yang Guoyu, *Dangdai*, 246, 249, 438, 444; Shu Deqi and Li Chunfang, 59.

75. Xiao Jinguang commanded the navy for three decades (1950–80). For information on him, see Song Renqiong; Zhang Wei and Jun Qi, 148, 150, 274; Shi Xiaoyan, 192–95; Jin Chuntian, 48, 49, 51; and his own two-volume memoirs, especially 1: 23, 96, 140–42.

76. Unless otherwise cited, the information in this and the next paragraph is from Yang Guoyu, *Dangdai*, 246.

77. The other members were Yu Qiuli, director of the State Planning Commission; Qian Xuesen, Luo Shunchu, and Zhao Qimin, deputy directors of the Defense Science and Technology Commission (Zhao was also a deputy commander of the navy; *Zhongguo Renmin Jiefangjun Jiangshuai*, 382); Zhou Xihan, deputy commander of the navy and deputy head of the Shipbuilding Industry Group ("Farewell Ceremony"; Peng Ziqiang, 3); Rao Zijian, vice-minister of the First Ministry; Liu Wei, vice-minister of the Second Ministry; Bian Jiang, vice-minister of the Sixth Ministry; Zhang Yuanpei, head of the military control team for the NDIO; Li Ruhong, deputy head of the NDIO; Hou Xiangzhi, deputy head of the Naval Equipment Department; and Chen Youming.

78. Chen Bin et al., 103; Chen Youming, "Wise Decision," 16; Chen Youming, "Concern (1)," 7.

79. Yang Guoyu, *Dangdai*, 246. The Lingjiuban remained under the navy until 1978, when the military commission put it under the Defense Science and Technology Commission. Since 1982, it has been an organ of the Commission of Science, Technology, and Industry for National Defense (COSTIND). Chen Bin et al., 103.

80. *Ibid.*; Chen Youming, "Wise Decision," 16; Chen Youming, "Concern (1)," 7.

81. These included Li Shuiqing, Chen Shaokun, Yi Wen, Li Jue, Qian Xuesen, and Zhu Guangya. Li Shuiqing, then head of the military control committee of the First Ministry, became ministry head the following year. His counterpart at the Ministry of Metallurgical Industry, Chen Shaokun, likewise moved up to head his ministry that year. In his capacity as deputy head of the General Logistics Department, Yi Wen was appointed head of the military control committee of the Ministry of Fuel and Chemical Industry. Li Jue was then vice-minister of the Second Ministry. Qian Xuesen and Zhu Guangya were both deputy directors of the Defense Science and Technology Commission. The information in this paragraph is from Chen Youming, "Concern (1)," 4–5.

82. Unless otherwise cited, the information in this paragraph and the next is from Chen Youming, "Concern (2)," 44; and Chen Youming, "Wise Decision," 18–19.

83. Data on 02 from Liu Jie; and "Riddle," 6. Data on 09 from Huo Rusu, 2; Wang Rongsheng, 387; Peng Shilu and Zhao Renkai, 208; Peng Shilu, 15; and Yang Guoyu, *Dangdai*, 245.

84. Liu Xiyao and Liu Qisheng were in charge of the Second Ministry's daily affairs after the outbreak of the Cultural Revolution. Liu Xiyao was appointed minister of the ministry on Jan. 17, 1975. Li Jue et al., 575.

85. Lu Jianxun, 392; Huang Xuhua, 397; Wang Rongsheng, 386; Liu Jingzhi, 14. The missile scientist Qian Xuesen probably ranks as the earliest advocate of the need to introduce scientific management principles into the strategic weapons programs. See, for example, his 1967 article, "Organization."

86. Zu Wei, 5, 8.

87. High pressure air tanks are used for ballast control, not missile ejection, in Chinese submarines. In case of an accident, the maximum depth from which a submarine can surface by itself is to some extent determined by its reserves of compressed air. For information on the on-board compressed air system, see Zhong

Xie, 59, 197–202; Shen Hongyuan, "What Measures," 26; and Shen Hongyuan, "Structural Design," 58. A submarine normally powers to the surface and uses diving planes to give the boat lift. So long as the reactor and controls are working, power is a stronger determinant of depth and attitude than pure buoyancy.

88. Compressed air at pressures of 200kg/cm² is appropriate for most conventional submarines. Zhong Xie, 197. Though physicists consider the use of kg/cm² to express pressures incorrect and use atmospheres, newtons/cm², or pascals instead, that measure is commonly used in the engineering community, and is routine in both Chinese and Soviet reports.

89. Unless otherwise cited, this paragraph is based on Zu Wei, 8.

90. Zhi Yin, "Inside Stories," 18; Liu Jingzhi, 14; Shen Hongyuan, "Structural Design," 56.

91. Huang Xuhua, 398; Zu Wei, 8; Liu Jingzhi, 14.

92. Huang Caihong and Cao Guoqiang, "For the Birth (1)"; Liu Jingzhi, 14.

93. Huang Caihong and Cao Guoqiang, "For the Birth (2)"; Zu Wei, 4.

94. Zhi Yin, "Inside Stories," 18–19; Wang Rongsheng, 386; Liu Jingzhi, 14.

95. Huang Xuhua, 398; Zu Wei, 8.

96. Ling Xiang, 27, 32; Xiao Jun, "Combat Ships," 3; Yang Guoyu, *Dangdai*, 246.

97. Wang Rongsheng, 386.

98. Based on Zhong Xie, 29; Xie Guang, *Dangdai*, 2:255–56; and Cheng Wang, 506.

99. Chinese weapons specialists recognized early on that nuclear attack submarines must be equipped with advanced deep-water homing torpedoes. See, for example, Liu Kun, "Prospect," 22; Tang Yunchang, 2–3; Ge Qiguang et al., 376–77; and Luo Chuanli and Shao Fuling, 82.

100. Huang Xuhua, 397; Lu Jianxun, 390, 391; Cui Xiaonan and Chen Wanjun; Wang Rongsheng, 386; Cheng Wang, 499–500.

101. History Team, 22; Chen Youming, "Wise Decision," 13; Lu Jianxun, 390.

102. Cheng Wang, 503; Xie Guang, *Dangdai*, 2:278.

103. Xie Guang, *Dangdai*, 2:252–53, 255, 281; Cheng Wang, 501–4.

104. Chen Wanjun and Li Kewen; Qiao Tianfu; Cheng Wang, 504–5, 766; Xie Guang, *Dangdai*, 2:254.

105. At that point, a deep-water homing torpedo became one of the 09-1 submarine's seven priority subsystems. Huang Xuhua, 397; Wang Rongsheng, 386; Lu Jianxun, 391.

106. This paragraph is based on Cheng Wang, 502–4, 765; and Xie Guang, *Dangdai*, 2:253–54, 281.

107. Liu Dengrong et al., 282; Zhong Xie, 113–14; Wang Huilin, 137.

108. Si Yanwen, "New-Type Torpedo."

109. The Torpedo Research Section is attached to the Weapons Institute of the China Naval Research Center. Established in 1983, the center has become the navy's principal research facility. Several research organs, including the Warship Institute, the Weapons Institute, the Electronics Institute, and the Special Aircraft Institute, operate under its administration. *Haijun Shi*, 233; Guo Xiangxing, "Visit," 85–89; Guo Xiangxing, "Think Tank"; Shen Shungen, "Prizes"; Li Xueyin and Guo Xiangxing, "Naval Research Center"; Li Xueyin and Guo Xiangxing, "Great Successes."

110. Unless otherwise cited, the information in this paragraph is from Cui

Xiaonan and Chen Wanjun; Xie Guangbin and Huang Zong, 47; Lu Jianxun, 391; Xie Guang, *Dangdai*, 2: 255; and Cheng Wang, 504, 771.

111. The navy apparently started a six-month test program in Jan. 1990 on a wire-guided torpedo (designated C-34) that could be fired at both submarines and surface vessels and was to be deployed on all nuclear attack submarines. Based on "Chinese Communists Are Test-Launching"; and "Surface Warships." Professor Ma Shijie at the Naval Engineering Institute in Wuhan, we believe, made important contributions to the development of the C-34's engine. See Shi Changxue et al.

112. Yang Guoyu, *Dangdai*, 574–75; *Haijun Shi*, 188; Lu Jianxun, 391. On the location of Institute 707, see "Institute 707's Degenerate Party Committee."

113. The Chinese continued to improve the on-board subsystems of their 09-1 nuclear subs in the years 1978–85. Xiao Jun, "Combat Ships," 3; Yang Guoyu, *Dangdai*, 438–41; Han Huaizhi and Tan Jingqiao, 2: 116, 120.

114. Chen Youming, "Concern (1)," 5–6.

115. Liu Congjun, *Hangtian . . . Yuanshi*, 225.

116. Chen Youming, "Concern (2)," 47.

117. Zu Wei, 9.

118. Chen Youming, "Concern (2)," 46, 47.

119. Song Shilun, *Zhongguo*, 2: 845; Shen Hongyuan, "Structural Design," 57.

120. In 1986, Xu Junlie and Huang Xuhua were awarded the national science-and-technology prize for their work on the 09 project. "Twenty-three"; "Great Contributions"; Zu Wei and Lin Pukai, 51. Xu also contributed to the successful underwater test launch of the JL-1 missile from the 31-class (Golf) submarine.

121. As we will discuss in Chap. 5, the Chinese completed the assembly of the Golf-class submarine at the Dalian Shipyard in 1966; some sources set the date at 1964, but Chinese sources give the later date. Unless otherwise cited, this paragraph is based on Yang Han and Wei Naiwen, 405; and Zhi Yin, "Inside Stories," 19.

122. Wang Jinzhong, 26–27; Wang Linchen, "Nuclear-Powered Submarines," 21; Shen Hongyuan, "At Which Depth," 20.

123. Gao Mingkun, 296–306; Wu Wenzheng, 193–95, 214–15; Zhong Xie, 124–25; Wang Linchen, "Nuclear-Powered Submarines," 21; Wang Linchen, "Ejection Technology," 14, 15.

124. Ni Huocai and Li Fangchun, 29; Zhong Xie, 125–26; Gao Mingkun, 302–3; Wang Linchen, "Ejection Technology," 14, 15.

125. Huang Xiaohui, 7; Zhong Xie, 126; Wang Jinzhong, 25–26.

126. Zhong Xie, 125–26.

127. Institute 713 is the Zhengzhou Machinery and Electronics Institute. On its code name, see "Exchange," 17; and Zhang Jun, 142.

128. Unless otherwise cited, the information in this paragraph is from Zhu Lemin; Zhi Yin, "Inside Stories," 19; and Yang Han and Wei Naiwen, 405.

129. The Polaris designers switched away from compressed air with the A-3 model. The most modern Soviet-built subs use gas alone, whereas the U.S. subs use gas with steam. Gunston, 56, 94–95; Wang Linchen, "Ejection Technology," 14–15; Lin Shen, 17.

130. Gao Mingkun, 298.

131. "Glossary," 1989, 24; Wang Jinzhong, 26–27; Zheng He, 18.

132. The information in the rest of this paragraph and the next is from Zhi Yin,

"Inside Stories," 19; Yang Han and Wei Naiwen, 405; Gao Mingkun, 303–6; Wang Linchen, "Ejection Technology," 14–15; and Zhong Xie, 124–26.

133. The information in this paragraph is from interviews with an American specialist, 1988.

134. Based on Zhang Jun, 140; Liu Shaoqiu and Lu Zhen, 5; Liu Xing (2), 34; Gao Mingkun, 297; Xi Qixin, 3; Wang Linchen, "Nuclear-Powered Submarines," 21; and Wang Linchen, "Ejection Technology," 15.

135. Zhong Xie, 124–26; Gao Mingkun, 298–302; Wang Linchen, "Ejection Technology," 15; Ni Huocai and Li Fangchun, 29.

136. The JL-1's first successful flight test was conducted on Oct. 12, 1982. Yang Guoyu, *Dangdai*, 654; *Haijun Shi*, 230. On the pros and cons of igniting a missile before or after it clears the surface, see Shen Hongyuan, "Ignition," 28.

137. Zhi Yin, "Inside Stories," 19; Yang Han and Wei Naiwen, 405.

138. Unless otherwise cited, this paragraph and the next is based on Huang Caihong and Cao Guoqiang, "For the Birth (2)"; Cheng Wang, 485–86; Yang Han and Wei Naiwen, 405; and Zhi Yin, "Inside Stories," 20. The difference between double-base and composite explosives is discussed in Chap. 6.

139. Chinese sources credit Dong Jinrong with having made important contributions to 09-2's missile ejection system. By the late 1980s, he had become Institute 713's director. "Exchange," 17.

140. China constructed several large-scale chemical plants in Taiyuan in the 1950s and 1960s that are now among the nation's top suppliers of chemical explosives. The Jiangyang Chemical Plant and the Xing'an Chemical Material Factory are the largest of these plants. See *Zhongguo Qiye*, 344–45.

141. Institute 3 was attached to the Fifth Ministry of Machine Building (ordnance industry). The Lanzhou Institute of Chemistry and Physics and Institute 3 jointly contributed to the development of the high explosives and detonators for China's first atomic bomb. Zhang Jingfu, 81; Li Yadan, "Man," 77; Li Jue et al., 267; Xiang Dong, 15; "Riddle," 6. As we shall discuss in Chap. 6, Institute 3 also helped make the JL-1 missile's propellant. Zhang Jun, 128–29.

142. Zhi Yin, "Inside Stories," 20; Yang Han and Wei Naiwen, 405–6; Cheng Wang, 486–87, 523–24.

143. Wang Jinzhong, 27; Wang Linchen, "Nuclear-Powered Submarines," 21. Sea state normally is indexed on the Beaufort scale. A Beaufort scale of 5 refers to a fresh breeze 29–38km/hr, which translates into a no. 4 sea disturbance, with moderate waves (1.2–2.4m high) and many white caps. We believe, however, that the Chinese usage (*haiqing*) refers to a no. 5 sea disturbance; at this level, the waves would rise to 2.4–4m high, with white foam and wind-driven spray everywhere and wind speeds to 39–49km/hr. For a definition of *haiqing* (or sometimes *haikuang*), see *Cihai*, 941.

144. When conducting an inspection, Defense Minister Zhang Aiping singled out the design group for special praise. Yang Han and Wei Naiwen, 406.

145. In 1986 the 09-2's overall design plan won the national science-and-technology prize. "Twenty-three."

Chapter Four

1. Yu Zhengdao and Lei Xinlong.

2. For example, the more than 30,000 staff and technicians who worked in

defense-related projects at 47 research institutes under the Academy of Sciences' New Technological Bureau in 1966 constituted more than 50% of the academy's total personnel. Gu Yu, "Reminiscences," 469. These introductory paragraphs are based on Lewis, Hua, and Xue, 99.

3. The largest of these 68 plants were No. 40 in Chongqing, No. 50 in Qingdao, No. 60 in Nanjing, No. 70 in Beiping, and No. 90 in Shenyang. See Zhang Jinke and Zhou Wenbin, 869.

4. Unless otherwise cited, the information in this paragraph is from Jin Zhude et al., 89; and Chen Ping et al., 11–12.

5. Academy of Military Science, *Zhongguo Renmin Jiefangjun Liushi Nian Dashiji*, 503; Jin Zhude et al., 90; Chen Ping et al., 12; Peng Jichao et al., 6.

6. Lai Jinlie, 349; Chen Ping et al., 15; Zheng Hantao and Li Ruhong, 117.

7. Zhao Erlu went to his grave in Feb. 1967 disgraced and alone. Years later, his name cleared, he was remembered for his struggle to build a strong defense industry in post-revolutionary China. Duan Junyi et al.; "Name List," 15. Unless otherwise cited, the information in the next paragraph is from these same sources.

8. By 1953, the ministry had created six research institutes. Jin Zhude et al., 90.

9. Zheng Hantao and Li Ruhong, 118. See also Lin Yunhui et al., 411–12.

10. Cheng Wang, 80; Chen Ping et al., 126. It was not until the autumn of 1953 that the Central Military Commission decided to "extend [China's] strength forward" and speed up the development of the navy. Yang Guoyu, *Dangdai*, 71, 77; Zhou Jiading, 2.

11. Arkhipov, 42–43.

12. Mao [6]; "Resolution on the Adjustment," 33; Zheng Hantao and Li Ruhong, 118.

13. The Central Military Commission created the Fifth Academy to run the strategic missile project on Oct. 8, 1956. For detailed information on the initial efforts to create a scientific and industrial network for developing strategic weapons, see Lewis and Xue, *China Builds*, 47–54.

14. Mao [5], 288.

15. Theoretical Group.

16. Zhang Aiping, 75.

17. Personal communication from Nie Rongzhen, Feb. 15, 1986; Han Huaizhi and Tan Jingqiao, 2: 94; *He Long Nianpu*, 401; Zheng Hantao and Li Ruhong, 118. According to "Brief Introduction," the NDIC was created in Jan. 1960.

18. Zhang Liankui, the first head of the Third Ministry, served only four months before being replaced by Sun Zhiyuan. Duan Zijun, *Dangdai*, 676, 677; Jin Zhude et al., 91; "Appointments." Sun Zhiyuan had been the second secretary of the NDIC's Party committee and chief assistant to He Long, head of the NDIC. Credited as one of the driving forces in China's defense industry, especially the aviation sector, Sun was removed in 1966 and died in disgrace that same year, at the height of the Cultural Revolution. Cheng Zihua and Lü Zhengcao.

19. For example, in Feb. 1963, the Tenth Bureau (electronics) was split off from the Third Ministry to become the Fourth Ministry of Machine Building, and a Fifth and a Sixth were added seven months later, composed, respectively, of the former Fifth (ordnance) and Ninth (shipbuilding) bureaus of the Third Ministry. Liu Yin et al., 653, 654; Duan Zijun, *Dangdai*, 679; Chen Ping, et al., 21; Xu Haofeng, 230.

20. Lewis and Xue, *China Builds*, 59, 126–34.

21. He Long was elected to the Politburo in 1956, and Luo Ruiqing was made an alternate member in 1962. Nie was not elected to the Politburo until 1966. Party History Research Section, 1987, 278; *Zhongguo Gongchandang Jianshi*, 322; *Nie Rongzhen Yuanshuai*, 163.

22. Personal communication from Nie Rongzhen, Feb. 15, 1986.

23. Han Huaizhi and Tan Jingqiao, 2: 94; Zheng Hantao and Li Ruhong, 118; Duan Zijun, *Dangdai*, 678; Li Jue et al., 567.

24. For a discussion of the organizational fights in this period, see Lewis and Xue, *China Builds*, Chap. 5.

25. Mao appended a note to Luo Ruiqing's report: "[All departments concerned] should vigorously carry out coordination and cooperation [*dali xietong*] so as to complete this [strategic] program." Hu Sheng, 417.

26. Unless otherwise cited, the information in this paragraph is from *Monan*, 111–12; Liu Boluo, "Premier Zhou Devoted," 342; and Liu Shuqing and Zhang Jifu, 25.

27. The commission's other deputy office directors were Zhang Aiping, Liu Jie, and Zheng Hantao. Liu Boluo, "Premier Zhou and the CCP," 129; Li Jue et al., 47; Gu Yu, "How to Tackle," 11. Some sources state that the commission was formally set up on Dec. 14, 1962. See, for example, Academy of Military Science, *Zhongguo Renmin Jiefangjun Liushi Nian Dashiji*, 602. According to Gu, both Nie Rongzhen and Luo Ruiqing were in charge of the commission's routine duties.

28. *Nie Rongzhen Huiyilu*, 823. Gu Yu, "How to Tackle," 11, adds that the commission "determined the key programs, the allocation of funds, and the coordination among various departments."

29. The commission's office was located in the NDIO's headquarters. There were only nine people on the office staff, including Liu Boluo, its deputy secretary-general. Liu Boluo, "Premier Zhou and the CCP," 129; Li Jue et al., 47.

30. Academy of Military Science, *Zhongguo Renmin Jiefangjun Liushi Nian Dashiji*, 602. Some sources use other names instead of the prevalent Fifteen-Member (or Central) Special Commission, including the National Defense Industry Special Commission (Gu Yu, "How to Tackle," 11); the Sophisticated Weapons Production Commission (Wu Qungan, 5); and the Central Science and Technology Special Commission (Wang Zhenxian, 17). For a discussion of the commission, see Lewis and Xue, *China Builds*, 126–34.

31. Lewis and Xue, *China Builds*, 126–27; Li Jue et al., 567; Han Huaizhi and Tan Jingqiao, 2: 94; Zheng Hantao and Li Ruhong, 118.

32. The Tenth Academy was formed in Dec. 1960; and the Sixth and Seventh were set up the following June. Zhang Jun, 560; Duan Zijun, *Dangdai*, 66, 677; Liu Yin et al., 317–18, 652; Yang Guoyu, *Dangdai*, 252, 460, 697. On the Ministry of Defense, see Lewis, Hua, and Xue, 88, 90.

33. The information in the rest of this paragraph and the next two is from Zhang Aiping, 75; Han Huaizhi and Tan Jingqiao, 2: 97–98; and Duan Zijun, "Principal Founder," 215.

34. Xie Chu, No. 8, 30; Zhang Jun, 36.

35. In Feb., the Sixth, Seventh, and Tenth academies were brought under the Third, Sixth, and Fourth ministries, respectively. In Aug., the Artillery Academy was merged into the Fifth Ministry's Academy of Precision Machinery (ordnance, code-named the Twentieth Academy). Unless otherwise cited, this paragraph and the next are based on Xie Guang, *Dangdai*, 1: 50; Zhang Aiping, 75; Zheng Han-

tao and Li Ruhong, 118; Li Jue et al., 567; and Han Huaizhi and Tan Jingqiao, 2: 97–98.

36. The merger policy was one of the major grounds for the radicals' attacks on Luo Ruiqing in the Cultural Revolution. For them, research was to be kept separate from the military industrial complex. Liu Boluo, "Premier Zhou Devoted," 347.

37. A committee was established on Sept. 8, 1981, to make preparations for the new corporation. It was formally set up the next year, with the merger of the large-scale shipyards originally under the Sixth Ministry and the Ministry of Communications. As a ministry-level unit under the State Council, the China State Shipbuilding Corporation is in charge of building all naval vessels, as well as almost all large civilian ships. Xie Guang, *Dangdai*, 1: 160, 2: 532; Chen Ping et al., 121.

38. Yang Guoyu, *Dangdai*, 229; Chen Ping et al., 119.

39. Yang Guoyu, *Dangdai*, 229–30, 234, 688, 696; Han Huaizhi and Tan Jingqiao, 2: 157.

40. *Haijun Shi*, 51; Han Huaizhi and Tan Jingqiao, 2: 157; Yang Guoyu, *Dangdai*, 234.

41. Chen Ping et al., 124–25; *Haijun Shi*, 51; Han Huaizhi and Tan Jingqiao, 2: 157.

42. Xu Haofeng, 230; Duan Zijun, *Dangdai*, 679.

43. Lu Jianxun, 390; Yang Guoyu, *Dangdai*, 234–35, 460, 697; Han Huaizhi and Tan Jingqiao, 2: 157. See also the information on the Seventh Academy in Chap. 3.

44. Zhang Aiping, 75; Han Huaizhi and Tan Jingqiao, 2: 97–98.

45. Yang Guoyu, *Dangdai*, 234, 252; Peng Ziqiang, 3; Han Huaizhi and Tan Jingqiao, 2: 116.

46. Unless otherwise cited, the information in this paragraph and the next is based on Yang Guoyu, *Dangdai*, 67, 254.

47. As of 1991, the Naval Equipment and Technology Department remained one of the navy's five main departments. The other four are the Naval Headquarters, the Naval Political Department, the Naval Logistics Department, and the Naval Equipment Repairing Department. See Pei Duan (an unpublished speech delivered by the director of the Naval Research Institute at a ceremony to welcome an American naval delegation).

48. By 1986, the Naval Equipment and Technology Department and the Naval Equipment Repairing Department jointly supervised 34 dockyards. In addition to repairing warships, these enterprises were reportedly able to build over 20 types of ships, including freighters, oilers, tugboats, barges, ferries, and glass-reinforced plastic ships. None of these boats displace over 5,000 tons. "Navy Factories"; Yang Weiyuan, "Promotion."

49. The information in this paragraph and the next is from Han Huaizhi and Tan Jingqiao, 2: 98; Xie Guang, *Dangdai*, 2: 519; and Zhang Aiping, 75.

50. The information in this paragraph is based on Xie Chu, No. 3, 46; Li Jue et al., 572; Duan Zijun, *Dangdai*, 682; Liu Yin et al., 657; and Zhang Jun, 567.

51. Four of the 18 academies had not been formally established. *Nie Rongzhen Huiyilu*, 795–96; Han Huaizhi and Tan Jingqiao, 2: 98; Zhang Aiping, 75; Wang Yongzhi, *Hangtian*, 208. We believe *Nie Rongzhen Nianpu*, 163, is wrong in asserting that Nie made the proposal to consolidate the defense science system in Sept. 1967.

52. Han Huaizhi and Tan Jingqiao, 2: 98.

53. The commission's Party Committee rescinded the slogan on April 4. Wang Nianyi, *1949–1989*, 278.

54. For a discussion of the purge of Yang Chengwu and his associates, one of the key events in the grand struggle for power during the 10-year Cultural Revolution, see Dong Baocun, *Yang Yu Fu*; Ji Xichen, 16–50; and *Nie Rongzhen Huiyilu*, 851–56.

55. As we would say today, Nie was out of the loop after April 1, 1968, taken off the list for documents that were circulated to vice-chairmen of the Central Military Commission and members of the Politburo. *Nie Rongzhen Huiyilu*, 853; Ji Xichen, 41.

56. Nie Rongzhen, "On the Science," 58; *Nie Rongzhen Huiyilu*, 795–96.

57. Li Min et al.; "If Nie Rongzhen."

58. *Zhongguo Renmin Jiefangjun Jiangshuai*, 170; *Nie Rongzhen Huiyilu*, 853–54. Wang Bingzhang's formal position on the commission was deputy director.

59. Mao's continuing fear of war led to substantial increases in the military appropriations for 1970 and 1971, of 15% and 17%, respectively. Zhao Dexin [1], 184; Jin Zhude et al., 93; Chen Xuewei, "On Economic Construction," 172.

60. On July 17, 1967, the military commission had created a so-called Caretaker Group (Kanshou Xiaozu) headed by Yang Chengwu to control the General Political Department and all military units in Beijing that had been paralyzed by internal conflicts. It was later renamed the Administrative Group and made responsible for the commission's daily affairs. The group was under the control of four of Lin Biao's associates—Huang Yongsheng, Wu Faxian, Li Zuopeng, and Qiu Huizuo. Yu Nan, 79; Ma Qibin et al., 308; Jin Chunming et al., 283.

61. Unless otherwise cited, this paragraph is based on Zhao Dexin [2], 184; Han Huaizhi and Tan Jingqiao, 2: 98, 116; and Zhang Aiping, 75.

62. Qiu Huizuo was then deputy chief of the General Staff and head of the General Logistics Department. Unless otherwise cited, the information in this and the next paragraph is from Zhao Dexin [4], 97; Peng Min, 160–62; Han Huaizhi and Tan Jingqiao, 2: 93–95, 98–99; Wen Guang, 79; and Zhang Aiping, 75.

63. For information on the 1970 mergers, see also Zhi Yin, "Chronicle," 19.

64. Base 21 is in Lop Nur, Xinjiang, and Bases 20 and 22 are both in northwestern Gansu Province. The Chinese had started constructing these three test bases in the Northwest in the late 1950s. See, among others, Wang Lihua and Zhang Jiade, 145; and Wang Dinglie, 311–13.

65. Lin Biao died in a mysterious air crash in Outer Mongolia on Sept. 13, 1971, as he was making his escape from China. On the change in his relationship with Mao and the actions of the Lin Biao clique, see Zhang Yunsheng; Yu Gong; Xiong Lei, 29–32; He Li; and Wu Bin. After the "Sept. 13 Incident," Wang Bingzhang, Liang Jun (chief of the staff of the Defense Science and Technology Commission), and countless others were arrested. Chen Youming, "Wise Decision," 18; Xie Guang, *Dangdai*, 2: 520.

66. Xie Guang, *Dangdai*, 2: 522–23.

67. The NDIO replaced the National Defense Industry Leading Group on Sept. 10, 1973, and assumed responsibility for supervising the Third, Fourth, Fifth, and Sixth ministries. The Second and Seventh ministries remained under the Defense Science and Technology Commission. Zhao Dexin [4], 44, 119. Fang Qiang was a former deputy commander of the navy and deputy head of the NDIO. Yang Guoyu,

Dangdai, 284; Li Jue et al., 567. Unless otherwise cited, the information in this and the next paragraph is from Wen Guang, 79; Zhang Aiping, 75; Han Huaizhi and Tan Jingqiao, 2: 93–95, 98–99; Zhao Dexin [4], 97; and Peng Min, 160–62.

68. On Mao's motives in unleashing this mass campaign and its impact, see Peng Cheng and Wang Fang, "Mao's Last Decision," 36–40; Ni Zhongwen, 215–16; Guo Hualun, *Zhonggong Mingci*, 406–7; and Jin Chunming, 236–37.

69. For descriptions of how the "movement to criticize Lin Biao and Confucius" affected the strategic weapons program, see Zheng Chiying, 21; Yang Jianming, 151–53; and Zhou Xiao.

70. Yang Guoyu, *Dangdai*, 460.

71. The Science and Technology Equipment Committee, headed by Zhang Aiping, had been set up in Nov. 1977 to devise guidelines for arms development and acquisition. Han Huaizhi and Tan Jingqiao, 2: 95, 120.

72. Unless otherwise cited, the information in this paragraph is from Academy of Military Science, *Zhongguo Renmin Jiefangjun Liushi Nian Dashiji*, 674, 717; "Resolution of the Standing Committee . . . on the Creation"; and Han Huaizhi and Tan Jingqiao, 2: 96.

73. But reducing the list to the core of the system brings the total to 117 facilities: the 26 major shipyards in Shanghai, Dalian, Tianjin, Guangzhou, Wuhan, Jiujiang, Fuling, and Chongqing, the 64 factories that supply most of the ship components, and the 27 "key" Seventh Academy research organs. Chen Ping et al., 119, 120, 121; Wang Rongsheng, 384; Zhu Jianhong; Xiao Li, 15; Ni Zhongwen, 330.

74. The area covered by the Third Line changed over time, and the variations in the sources reflect these changes. Basically, it covered Sichuan, Guizhou, Yunnan, Shaanxi, Gansu, Qinghai, and Ningxia and the western parts of Henan, Hubei, and Hunan. Zhao Dexin [2], 172–73; Peng Min, 156.

75. Barry Naughton has published extensively on the Third-Line region; see, for example, Naughton, "Third Front"; and Naughton, "Industrial Policy."

76. Yan Fangming, 70; Ma Hong, 386; Lin Xi and Ji Yin; Zhao Dexin [2], 185; Peng Min, 162, 167; Li Yongzeng and Li Shuzhong, 10.

77. Murphey, 66–67. For Mao's attitude toward enemy elements in the port areas, see Mao [1].

78. Mao [5], 287. For a discussion of the official Chinese viewpoint on the relationship between Mao's speech and the Third-Line construction, see Xu Liangchen; and Li Yongzeng and Li Shuzhong, 10.

79. Chen Xuewei, "On Economic Construction," 158. See also Zhao Dexin [2], 15; Zhao Dexin [1], 631; Chen He and Yang Zhibin, 13; and Peng Min, 157.

80. This Central Committee conference, traditionally termed the Beijing Conference in Party histories, was held between May 15 and June 17, 1964. Zhang Hongru et al., 8; Zhao Dexin [3], 522; Peng Min, 157; Party History Research Section, 1987, 333. The iron and steel complex at Panzhihua became one of the most important projects in, and a synonym for, the Third Line. Cheng Zihua, 7, 9.

81. Mao [14], 354. See also Peng Min, 157.

82. Mao [13], 356, 357.

83. Li Yongzeng and Li Shuzhong, 10; Zhang Hongru et al., 8; Zhao Dexin [3], 522.

84. Deng Xiaoping once explained Mao's plan to accelerate industrial construction in the Third Line. See Deng [2], 41, 399.

85. Peng Min, 157; Li Yongzeng and Li Shuzhong, 10; Yan Fangming, 71.

86. Zhao Dexin [2], 172; Peng Min, 157; Zhao Dexin [1], 631; Zhao Dexin [3], 522, 525, 652–53.

87. Lei Xun, 492; Yan Fangming, 71.

88. Gu Mu.

89. Zhao Dexin [1], 181.

90. Li Yongzeng and Li Shuzhong, 10. On the initial determination of the locations for the Third-Line defense facilities in the winter of 1964, see Zhao Dexin [2], 181; Chen Ping et al., 164; and Li Jue et al., 70–71.

91. Zhao Dexin [2], 182–83; Zhao Dexin [4], 181–82; Yan Fangming, 71; Cheng Zihua, 7; Peng Min, 158. Li Jingquan and Liu Lantao, first secretaries of the Central Committee's Southwest and Northwest bureaus, were appointed directors of the two construction committees.

92. Cited in Guo Shouhang, 8. Unless otherwise cited, this paragraph is based on Zhao Dexin [1], 631; and Peng Min, 159.

93. Mao had given his blessing to the six-character formulation earlier, it seems, for He Long, former head of the NDIC, had conveyed it to Li Jingquan, director of the Southwest Third-Line Construction Committee, in an emergency phone call on June 27, 1965. *He Long Nianpu*, 437.

94. A central work conference held in Beijing from Sept. 18 to Oct. 12 determined the guiding principles for the Third Five-Year Plan (1966–70). Hu Guoping, 41; Zhao Dexin [3], 581.

95. Zhao Dexin [3], 657. On the evolution of the corps, see Zhang Hongru et al., 239; and Han Huaizhi and Tan Jingqiao, 2: 38.

96. Peng Min, 157, 164–66; Zhao Dexin [1], 631.

97. Most of the 500 million yuan allocated in the years 1965–75 for the capital construction of universities and colleges was used for their removal and reorganization. Peng Min, 182. On the fate of naval schools and institutes during the Cultural Revolution, see Lewis and Xue, *Military Readiness*, 11–21.

98. Ji Bing, 97; Xu Xing, 485; Xiao Min; Zhao Dexin [2], 183, 189; Li Yongzeng and Li Shuzhong, 11; Lu Peifa and Liu Gang; Li Yadan, "What We Saw."

99. Wu Yirong and Xiao Min; Quan Zong, 13; Li Yongzeng and Li Shuzhong, 11.

100. Li Yongzeng and Li Shuzhong, 10. See also Zhao Dexin [2], 183–84.

101. Chen Xuewei, "On Economic Construction," 172–73; Yan Fangming, 71–72; Peng Min, 159–60; Li Yongzeng and Li Shuzhong, 10; Hu Guoping, 41.

102. The meeting is traditionally termed the *sanbei* conference (that is, North China, Northeast China, and Northwest China conference) in Party histories. Zhang Yunsheng, 306; Li Jue et al., 74. On the subsequent related meetings, see Li Jue et al., 75, 77; Peng Min, 160; Zhao Dexin [2], 184; and Chen Xuewei, "On Economic Construction," 172.

103. See Zhang Yunsheng, 316–17; Peng Min, 160, 192; and Li Jue et al., 74–75.

104. Each of the following had self-contained defense industrial bases: the Southwest, Northwest, Central Plains, South China, East China, North China, and Northeast regions; Shandong Province; Fujian and Jiangxi provinces as a combined base; and the Xinjiang Autonomous Region. Chen Xuewei, "On Economic Construction," 172; Zhao Dexin [4], 46; Zhao Dexin [2], 184; Peng Min, 160.

105. Peng Min, 192. For example, the nuclear power plant R&D base in Jia-jiang (First Academy of the Second Ministry) was immediately put under military control. See Peng Shilu, 12.

106. The annual allocation for capital construction increased from 11.79 bil-lion yuan in 1968 to 20.62 billion yuan in 1969 and 29.84 billion yuan in 1970. The 1969 and 1970 sums accounted for 39.2% and 45.9% of the state budget. In 1971, the capital construction allocation rose even higher, jumping to 34.08 billion yuan. Chen Rulong, 1: 241; Peng Min, 192. The lion's share of total investment went to the defense industry, more than doubling between 1968 and 1969. From 1970 to 1972, defense projects alone got 91.23 billion yuan. Peng Min, 161.

107. Yu Qiuli; Yang Shaoqiao and Zhao Fasheng, 239; Hu Guoping, 22.

108. For the Chinese view of this significant change in the international situa-tion, see Guo Shouhang, 8, 9.

109. The fiscal year 1972 economic plan was passed at the National Planning Conference held in Beijing from Dec. 16, 1971, to Feb. 12, 1972. Zhao Dexin [4], 56.

110. The Chinese used the $430 million to purchase 13 complete sets of equip-ment to produce chemical fertilizers. Unless otherwise cited, the information in the rest of this paragraph is from Yan Fangming, 72; Yu Qiuli; Xia Yuansheng, 85; Zhao Dexin [2], 180; and Wang Yu, 463.

111. In 1973, China still invested roughly the same amount in the Third Line and the coastal areas. But the next two years, investment in the coastal areas greatly exceeded that in the Third Line. Zhao Dexin [2], 185.

112. Between 1972 and 1974, China reduced its military allocations by five bil-lion yuan. Research Section, 29.

113. State Statistical Bureau, 300–301; Fan Gui; Lin Xi and Ji Yin. Of the 140 billion yuan, 126.9 billion yuan were spent during the period 1965–75. Peng Min, 163.

114. Ma Hong, 386; Zhou Zhenhua, 98; Fan Gui; Peng Min, 163. One-third of all medium- and large-scale industrial and research facilities built in China over the past four decades were constructed in the Third Line. Li Yongzeng and Li Shu-zhong, 10; Lin Xi and Ji Yin.

115. Duan Zijun, *Dangdai*, 73.

116. Xiao Min. Most of these facilities—297 industrial enterprises and 42 re-search academies and institutes—were built or expanded in the crisis years 1965–75. Peng Min, 169.

117. Li Jue et al., 68–73, 203; Peng Min, 167, 169.

118. Lin Xi and Ji Yin; Li Yongzeng and Li Shuzhong, 10.

119. Peng Min, 169–70.

120. On average, the Third Line's input-output ratio is about 2.7 times worse than the coastal areas', and the lead time for construction is about 25% longer. Zhao Dexin [2], 194–95. On the poor economic performance in the Third Line, see also Li Yadan, "What We Saw."

121. Yan Fangming, 73.

122. Zhang Pan, 4; Li Yongzeng and Li Shuzhong, 11.

123. Li Jue et al., 71; Yi Jianru, 8.

124. Chen Ping et al., 132.

125. In Sichuan Province, for example, fully 75% of the military industrial en-

terprises were built in remote, mountainous areas. Jin Chunxiang, 491; Li Yongzeng and Li Shuzhong, 11.

126. Ma Hong, 386.

127. Unless otherwise cited, the information in the rest of this paragraph and the next is based on Li Yongzeng and Li Shuzhong, 11; Xiang Bing and Zhao Mingliang; and Yu Qingtian.

128. Liu Fangyu, 5.

129. Lu Dadong was appointed head of this body, the Third-Line Construction Readjustment and Transformation Planning Office. Li Yongzeng and Li Shuzhong, 11; "Stable Implementation"; Ma Hong, 386. Sec. 3, Chap. 20, of the 7th Five-Year Plan (1986–90) dealt with the criteria for and approaches to continuing, upgrading, or closing down enterprises in the Third-Line regions. See *Fourth Session*.

130. Lu Dadong, 115–16; Fan Jun.

131. Li Nanling and Cheng Jian; Hou Jiayin; Fan Jun.

132. In Aug. 1964, Mao called for building shipyards in the Third-Line region. Xie Guang, *Dangdai*, 2: 762.

133. The navy's plan, completed in June 1964, contemplated building 210 submarines and 400 fast attack craft over the next eight years. *Haijun Shi*, 55; Han Huaizhi and Tan Jingqiao, 2: 157. The four plants were to be the Henan Diesel Engine Plant (Plant 407 in Luoyang), the Shaanxi Diesel Engine Plant (Plant 408 in Xi'an), the Wuhan Auxiliary Engine Plant (Plant 461) in Hubei Province, and the Zibo Battery Plant in Shandong Province. China gave priority to developing advanced batteries for submarines and had come up with the Q-1 (Lead-1) battery by the late 1960s. *Haijun Shi*, 67; Yang Guoyu, *Dangdai*, 309. In the next decade, three large battery plants operated in Baoding (Hebei Province), Zibo (Shandong Province), and Yichang (Hubei Province). The Yichang Battery Plant later shut down. Cheng Wang, 80, 453. Unless otherwise cited, this paragraph is based on Chen Ping et al., 126.

134. The three design and research organs were the Ninth Design and Research Academy, the 602nd Design and Research Academy, and the Survey Academy. Unless otherwise cited, this paragraph and the next are based on *ibid.*, 126–33; Cheng Wang, 89–90, 765, 792; and Cui Xiaonan and Zheng Shuyan.

135. From 1966 to 1975, the bulk of the nation's funds for shipbuilding was thrown into this effort, with the Third Line receiving three times as much as the coastal areas. In those 10 years, China allocated half the total amount spent on the shipbuilding industry as a whole in the 1949–65 period for the construction of this Third-Line network. Chen Ping et al., 121, 128, 133.

136. The Chuandong (East Sichuan) Shipyard in Fuling was the largest Third-Line producer of conventional submarines. Plant 405 is the code name for the Jiangjin-Yongchuan complex. For further information on the Sichuan-based shipbuilding industry, see "Increasing Output"; and *Zhongguo Shenzhen*, 87, 90, 91, 92.

137. The Jiangxi shipbuilding base includes the Jiangzhou yard for building submarines. For further information on the base, see Hong Shikun and Li Renli; Wang Zhanyi, 570; Zhang Yuanping; Huang Chaoxing; and *Zhongguo Shenzhen*, 91.

138. For further information on the Hubei shipbuilding industry, see *Zhongguo Shenzhen*, 91.

139. The Yunnan base principally consisted of Institute 705, Plant 5002, and the Southwest Chunguang Machinery Plant in Lufeng County. The Lufeng plant, which produced on-board electronic equipment for torpedoes, was later renamed the Chunguang Equipment Plant. Cui Xiaonan and Chen Wanjun; Liu Yin et al., 614. Plant 884 had started producing contact mines in 1958 and non-contact mines in 1965 based on Soviet models. *Haijun Shi*, 52; Zhu Bin and Chen Ming; and Chen Ping et al., 129.

140. Brown, 46.

141. U.S., Air Force Dept., *Space Systems*, 2.

142. U.S., Defense Intelligence Agency, *Ballistic Missile Payloads*, 126.

143. Chen Ping et al., 25; Peng Min, 157.

144. Zhao Dexin [2], 173; Peng Min, 183; Han Huaizhi, 70, 135.

145. Han Huaizhi, 70, 135.

146. Zhao Dexin [2], 172.

147. Zhao Dexin [1], 631; Zhao Dexin [3], 522; Peng Min, 157.

148. Chen Ping et al., 25, 26. In response to Mao's call, for example, the Shanghai authorities built up a minor Third-Line base in southern Anhui Province. Between 1965 and 1975, they allocated 500 million yuan and sent 50,000 mechanics to construct 80 defense-related enterprises there. Chen Baoshan.

149. Zhao Dexin [3], 525.

150. See, for example, Yan Fangming, 71; and Party History Research Section, 1987, 341.

151. Chen Ping et al., 26—27; Peng Min, 182.

152. Wang Nianyi, "Mao Zedong's Appraisal," 35.

153. Ma Lu et al., 204; Party History Research Section, 1987, 341.

154. Zhao Dexin [4], 179; Zhao Dexin [2], 176.

155. Peng Min, 183.

156. Zhao Dexin [4], 179.

157. Based on *ibid.*; and Theoretical Group.

158. Zhao Dexin [4], 118; Zhao Dexin [2], 45.

159. Zhao Dexin [2], 45, 185; Zhao Dexin [4], 118.

160. Peng Min, 183—84; Chen Ping et al., 26—27.

161. Zhao Dexin [2], 184; Zhao Dexin [4], 189.

162. See, for example, Schurmann, esp. Chap. 4; and Donnithorne, Chap. 7.

163. Deng Xiaoping [6].

164. Zhang Aiping, newly appointed head of the commission, began reorganizing the missile ministry in July and soon afterward initiated changes throughout the entire defense industrial system. Zhang Tuosheng, 113, 115.

165. Deng Xiaoping [2].

166. In a footnote to Deng's *Selected Works*, 399, the editor notes, "Following the Great Leap Forward of 1958, many enterprises failed to implement strict systems of responsibility and neglected business accounting; their wage and reward systems suffered from egalitarianism and their Party committees took all the day-to-day administrative work into their own hands." One of the 70 articles had gone to exactly this point, reaffirming "the system of factory directors assuming overall responsibility under the leadership of Party committees" and calling for the establishment and improvement of the chains of command and rules and regulations. See Zhang Hongru et al., 113.

167. Deng Xiaoping [4].

168. The NDIO convened a defense industry conference in 1974 in the hope of strengthening the leading bodies of military industrial enterprises and improving the quality of military hardware, but this had accomplished nothing. Theoretical Group.

169. Chen Zhiqiang, 14.

170. "Strategic Shift," 20.

171. "Deng Xiaoping Talks Freely," 10. Unless otherwise cited, this paragraph is based on Shi Wenting et al.; Liu Huinian and Yi Jianru, 10; Zhang Qingsheng and Zhang Chunting, 19; and Liu Huinian, "Vital Strategic Decision-Making," 10.

172. The average is based on the figures by periods: 1953–57, 23.4%; 1958–62, 12%; 1963–65, 18.8%; 1966–70, 21.8%; 1971–75, 19.1%; 1976–80, 16.5%; and 1981–84, 13.7%. Chen Rulong, 2: 260. See also Ren Tao and Guo Xiangxing. The year-by-year figures from 1979 to 1987 are as follows: 1979, 18.5%; 1980, 16.9%; 1981, 15.1%; 1982, 15.3%; 1983, 13.8%; 1984, 11.9%; 1985, 10.4%; 1986, 8.7%; and 1987, 8.2%. The military's share continued to shrink at a reported rate of 0.2% in 1988 and 1989. Qi Miyun, 20; Yuan Jiaxin, 10; Zhang Yining.

173. "China's Defense Budget." Most of the increases in the fiscal years of 1990 and 1991 were reportedly used for personnel costs. See "Administrative Expenditures." This was not the case for fiscal 1992. Wudunn; "Annual Increase"; "Increase"; "Foreign Minister."

174. Li Peng, p. XIII.

175. Liao Guoliang et al., 600–601.

176. Chen Weijun, 12.

177. See, for example, Jiang Zemin, 9. On June 6, 1991, Beijing created a ministry-level organ, the China State Electronics Corporation, for an urgent buildup of the industry. "Mainland China Creates." On March 29, 1993, Beijing reestablished the Ministry of Electronics Industry to run the industry. "Order (No. 2)."

178. Chen Xiang'an. Yang Shangkun, then executive vice-chairman of the Central Military Commission, later expanded on the guiding principle: "Scientific research should go ahead, and greater importance should be attached to research and development [on weapon systems] as well as the technological reserve." Yang Shangkun, "Speech."

179. Li Huaixing; Wang Yamin, 51; Jiang Siyi, 35–36.

180. Zu Wei, 11.

181. Jiang Lin; Lu Tianyi. For example, in the 1980s, less than 30% of the more than 100 college graduates who were annually ordered to report for work at the Guizhou Astronautics Industry Corporation ever checked in. Zheng Shuyan and Xu Wenliang.

182. Chen Siyi and Gu Mainan, 5; Li Yadan, "Open"; Ren Xinmin, 266.

183. Xie Guang, "Science," 125; Lei Xinlong; Hu Nianqiu.

Chapter Five

1. The State Council allocates funds to military industries for dual civilian-military use through the regular state plan in the form of unspecified block grants to the Central Military Commission. These funds are to be used for all military

purposes except weapons research, which is separately funded through the Commission of Science, Technology, and Industry for National Defense. Neither the R&D funds nor the dual-use funds are considered part of the defense budget.

2. The construction of the two yards was started in the late 1950s, suspended in the early 1960s, and restarted in 1968. Unless otherwise cited, this paragraph and the next are based on Chen Ping et al., 124–25; and Cheng Wang, 93, 751.

3. Han Huaizhi and Tan Jingqiao, 2: 157; Chen Ping et al., 124–25.

4. Chen Youming, "Concern (2)," 46–47; Niu Guohua.

5. Lu Yingjie, 15; Peng Shilu and Zhao Renkai, 207.

6. Lu Da, 476; Xie Guang, *Dangdai*, 2: 426–27; Zhong Xie, 94–95; Huang Xuhua, 398.

7. The Chinese were not able to produce a suitable battery for their subs until the late 1960s when the Zibo Battery Plant developed the Q-1 (Lead-1) battery. He Long, 577; Cheng Wang, 453; Yang Guoyu, *Dangdai*, 309.

8. *Haijun Shi*, 84; Yang Guoyu, *Dangdai*, 246.

9. We have consulted two texts in the preparation of this section: Davies, 2 vols.; and Houldcroft and Robert. Chinese submariners considered 1m the appropriate distance between the pressure hull and outer shell (false hull) of a submarine. Zhong Xie, 104. For information on the construction of the 09-1 sub, see Ling Xiang, 27, 32; Xiao Jun, "Combat Ships," 3; Yang Guoyu, *Dangdai*, 246, 247; and Chen Youming, "Concern (2)," 46–47. Yang Minqing asserts that the 09-1 submarine was built at the Dalian yard. We believe this is incorrect.

10. Doc. CB/Z124–79 prohibited workers from heat-treating submarine steel plates at all when using weld rods *Shanghan* 59 or *Chuanhan* 395. Chen Xiaoyu, 23–24. For Chinese approaches to solving the problem of welding the pressure hull's plates, see also *ibid.*, 23–45, 117–47; and Chen Chu.

11. Unless otherwise cited, the information in this paragraph and the next two is from Shu Deqi and Li Chunfang, 67–68; and a Chinese specialist now residing in the United States, 1989.

12. China routinely uses zinc alloy plates in its submarines. Yi Xuan, 32. Where the launch tubes meet the pressure hull, heavier steels must be used to offset the greater stresses. Information from an American specialist, 1991.

13. In the late 1980s, of the total, only 25%–30% of the welding in China's shipbuilding was in the high-efficiency category, compared with 60%–70% for Japan. For a general introduction to the application of advanced welding technology to China's shipbuilding, see Hu Maozi, 12, 13.

14. The plates for the outer hull and the main ballast tanks were 10mm thick; the bottom plates were slightly thicker. Unless otherwise cited, this paragraph and the next are based on Cheng Wang, 169; Shu Deqi and Li Chunfang, 67, 68; and Wang Rongsheng, 386.

15. Cracks that occur right after welding are called hot, and those occurring after 24 hours cold. Hot cracking takes place in the weld itself, but cold cracking can occur in either the weld or the adjacent metal. On this general problem, see Davies, 1: 110.

16. Main ribs were usually welded to the inner wall of the hull to reinforce it but could also be welded to the outer wall to save space on the inside. The technical requirements were much stricter when the welding was done on the outer wall. The distance between the two ribs depended on the thickness of the plates of the pres-

sure hull. Chinese engineers held that 600mm–800mm was an appropriate distance in submarines over 2,000 tons. Zhong Xie, 4, 91–92.

17. In total, about 3,000 master workers were transferred to Bohai from other yards to help build the attack submarine (09-1). The welding problems encountered in that project also plagued the builders of the 09-2 missile sub. Xie Guang, *Dangdai*, 1: 344, 347–48.

18. The navy had a Military Representative Section at the Bohai yard composed of 29 naval technical officers and headed by Meng Qingning. Guo Xiangxing, "Outstanding Contributions"; Hu Hongbo.

19. Zhi Yin, "Inside Stories," 18; Huang Xuhua, 398; Peng Shilu and Zhao Renkai, 208.

20. Li Jue et al., 305; "Riddle," 7.

21. The figures for on-board equipment were staggering: 2,600 types for a total of 46,000 items, with 900,000 components. For information on the boat's complicated interior fittings, see Wang Rongsheng, 387; *Haijun Shi*, 84; Yang Guoyu, *Dangdai*, 247; Shu Deqi and Li Chunfang, 69; Zheng He and Long Yunhe, 13; Liu Jingzhi, 14; and "Strengthening (2)."

22. Zhi Yin, "Inside Stories," 18–19; Huang Xuhua, 398; Wang Rongsheng, 386.

23. Yang Guoyu, *Dangdai*, 247; Chen Youming, "Concern (1)," 7.

24. The information in this paragraph and the next is from Peng Shilu, 14; Peng Shilu and Zhao Renkai, 207; Chen Youming, "Concern (1)," 7–8; and Yang Guoyu, *Dangdai*, 247.

25. Chen Youming, "Concern (1)," 8.

26. Peng Shilu, 14; Chen Youming, "Concern (1)," 8.

27. Chen Youming, "Concern (1)," 8.

28. Cheng Wang, 171; Xie Guang, *Dangdai*, 1: 358; Peng Shilu, 14. Li Jue et al., 67, and Chen Youming, "Concern (1)," 8, state that the 09-1 made this first voyage in Sept. 1971. We believe this is incorrect.

29. Peng Shilu, 14.

30. Chen Youming, "Wise Decision," 16; Chen Youming, "Concern (1)," 8.

31. This was the first of a series of organizational changes the military commission made in the administration of its daily affairs. In Feb. 1975, it disbanded the Administrative Meeting and restored its Standing Committee (Changwu Wei-yuanhui), with Ye Jianying as head; in Nov. 1979, it reestablished the Administrative Meeting, with Geng Biao as head, and put it under the Standing Committee; in Sept. 1982, it replaced the Standing Committee with a new body, the Daily Affairs Meeting (Changwu Huiyi), with Yang Shangkun as head. This paragraph is based on Academy of Military Science, *Zhongguo Renmin Jiefangjun Liushi Nian Dashiji*, 648–49, 659, 696, 722.

32. The information in this paragraph and the next is from Chen Youming, "Wise Decision," 16; and Chen Youming, "Concern (1)," 8.

33. "Attach Importance"; Xie Guang, *Dangdai*, 1: 358–59.

34. Li Runshan, 179.

35. Information from a Chinese specialist, 1989.

36. Stress corrosion usually results from an increase in the metal's temperature. This paragraph is based on Chen Youming, "Concern (2)," 45; Xie Guang, *Dangdai*, 1: 358–63; and Cheng Wang, 396.

37. See *Haijun Shi*, 85; Yang Guoyu, *Dangdai*, 247; and Xiao Jun, "Combat Ships," 3.

38. The navy did not conduct a maximum-depth test on the 09-1 until April 1988. Guo Xiangxing, "Outstanding Contributions"; Xie Guang, *Dangdai*, 1: 364–65. On the series construction of the 09-1 boats, see Li Jue et al., 67; Sharpe, 100; Chen Youming, "Wise Decision," 17; Ling Yu, "Strength," 20; and Yang Guoyu, *Dangdai*, 438.

39. See Ling Yu, "Strength," 20.

40. For Deng Xiaoping's similar remarks on the 09 boats, see Xie Guang, *Dangdai*, 1: 148. This paragraph is based on *ibid.*, 359; Cheng Wang, 396; Huang Xuhua, 397; Wang Rongsheng, 386; *Haijun Shi*, 219; and Yang Guoyu, *Dangdai*, 437–40, 574–75.

41. The navy's report was entitled "A Proposal on the Research and Development for and Construction of Nuclear-Powered Submarines." Chen Youming, "Wise Decision," 20.

42. Yang Guoyu, *Dangdai*, 437–40; *Haijun Shi*, 219.

43. The number of boats is from Ling Yu, "Strength," 20; "Military Snub," 11; "Chinese Communists Own"; *Haijun Shi*, 247; and a series of pictures released by various Chinese official sources.

44. Moore, *Jane's Warsaw Pact*, 37; Blake, 483; Turetsky, 39, 65–79; Han Huaizhi and Tan Jingqiao, 2: 157; Yang Guoyu, *Dangdai*, 234, 696; Wang Yongzhi, *Hangtian*, 260; Liu Congjun, *Hangtian . . . Yuanshi*, 33–34.

45. Zhang Minjie and Lan Gongjue, 6; Yang Guoyu, *Dangdai*, 250, 699; Xu Simin, 13–14.

46. The Dalian yard accounted for 25% of the nation's shipbuilding. In 1988, it ranked 18th in world tonnage. For an introduction to the yard, see "Shipbuilding"; Xu Yan'an; Yang Jizhu; Zhang Pingli; and Wang Zhe and Liu Wencai. The other five yards constructing submarines are Jiangnan (Shanghai), Bohai (Huludao), Huangpu (Guangzhou), Wuchang (Wuhan), and Chuandong (Fuling).

47. Cheng Wang, 160, 483; Xie Guang, *Dangdai*, 2: 232; Yang Han and Wei Naiwen, 405.

48. Zhang Jun, 141.

49. Yang Han and Wei Naiwen, 405.

50. On the Golf and R-11FMs, see Moore, *Jane's Warsaw Pact*, 37; Moore, *Jane's Fighting Ships*, 517; Liu Congjun, *Hangtian . . . Yuanshi*, 33–34; and Wang Yongzhi, *Hangtian*, 260. For additional information on the JL-1, see Part 2. Sharpe, 101, states that after retrofitting, the 31's conning tower accommodated two JL-1 missiles (as against three 1060s, in the original design). We have no independent confirmation of this statement; it should be noted that the Soviet Union modified its Golf subs with a single missile launcher for SLBM prototype development.

51. The information in this paragraph is based on Zhi Yin, "Inside Stories," 19–20; Yang Han and Wei Naiwen, 405; *Haijun Shi*, 229; Yang Guoyu, *Dangdai*, 650; and Zhang Jun, 142.

52. The code name 931 combines the 9 of Project 09 and the 31 of the Golf submarine.

53. Over 1,000 ejection tests of different scale-model rockets were conducted from 1969 to 1984. Most of them were land-based. Unless otherwise cited, the

information in this paragraph and the next is from Zhang Xinghua et al., 178–80; and Zhang Jun, 142–43.

54. The two-stage JL-1 missile weighed 14.7 tons. The Seventh Ministry of Machine Building assigned Rocket-Engine Test Stand 101 to fabricate the model rockets for ejection tests. Wang Yongzhi, *Hangtian*, 231, 244; Xie Guang, *Dangdai*, 1: 368, 370.

55. The Naval Test Base was initially created in Huludao, near the city of Jinxi, Liaoning Province, in 1958. A unique facility, it now comprises several research institutes and four test areas located in Huludao, Lüshun, and other places, and is responsible for testing all naval weapons and equipment. Some research facilities in the Zhoushan Islands, Zhejiang Province, in the Changshan Islands, Shandong Province, and in Inner Mongolia are also believed to be under its administration. Both SLBMs and antiship missiles are flight-tested there. Yang Guoyu, *Dangdai*, 454–57; *Haijun Shi*, 227–28.

56. Yang Xuequan; Zhang Xinghua et al., 185; Zhang Jun, 143.

57. Unless otherwise cited, the information in this and the next paragraph is from Wang Yongzhi, *Hangtian*, 248, 255, 256, 260; Zhang Jun, 142–43; and Zhi Yin, "Inside Stories," 20.

58. Xu Junlie, deputy chief engineer at Institute 719 (now the Wuhan Second Ship Design and Research Institute), contributed to the successful test launch of the JL-1 missile from the submerged 31 sub on Oct. 12, 1982. In addition, he greatly contributed to the formulation of the 09-2's overall design plans. "Twenty-three"; Li Derun; "Great Contributions."

59. Zhang Jun, 143, states that a full-sized model rocket was first successfully test-ejected from an experimental submarine in Oct. 1972. We believe that date is incorrect.

60. Zhang Xinghua et al., 206, 210.

61. Wang Yongzhi, *Hangtian*, 260.

62. These instruments alone added 1,000 new items to the crew's operating instructions. Yang Guoyu, *Dangdai*, 651–52. Among the new instruments were an optical aiming system and a fire control computer designed and manufactured by the Changchun Institute of Optical and Fine Mechanics and Institute 716 in Lianyungang, Jiangsu Province, respectively. These and other advanced devices were added to provide complete data on the JL-1's underwater launch performance. Wang Daheng, 472; Cheng Wang, 523.

63. Zhang Jun, 147; Wang Yongzhi, *Hangtian*, 348.

64. Yang Guoyu, *Dangdai*, 654; *Haijun Shi*, 230; Zhang Jun, 148–50. Though the navy still considers the 31 submarine "experimental," it is capable of launching JL-1s in the event of war.

65. Cheng Wang, 396–97.

66. On the 09-1's maximum submerged speed, see Li Ke and Hao Shengzhang, 304; and Cheng Wang, 320. Chief Designer Huang Xuhua disclosed that the 09-1's tonnage approaches that of the first U.S. nuclear submarines. Zu Wei, 9. The first American nuclear submarines had surfaced displacement tonnages of 3,075 (the *Skipjack*-class SSN) and 6,020 (the *George Washington*-class SSBN). However, the two American subs had a broader beam, and the SSBN had four more tubes than the Chinese boat. Correcting for these differences, the Chinese submarines would have to be much smaller.

67. Xue Hanjun, 349.

68. Based on Huang Caihong, "First"; "Strengthening (1)"; and Song Shilun, *Zhongguo*, 2:844.

69. The maximum submerged depth of the 09 boats is inferred from Xie Guang, *Dangdai*, 1:365; Li Ke and Hao Shengzhang, 303; and Chen Wang, 320. For detailed information on China's advanced torpedoes, see Chap. 3.

70. Chen Youming, "Concern (1)," 5; Chen Youming, "Concern (2)," 47. Sharpe, 101, states that the 09-2 sub was "laid down in 1978." Based on Chinese sources, we believe that year is incorrect.

71. Zhang Minjie and Lan Gongjue, 5; Chen Youming, "Concern (2)," 47; Lin Yingguang and Wu Qingyu, 23.

72. Zhang Aiping was appointed on March 8, 1975. Tao Lujia was simultaneously made the commission's political commissar. Chen Bin et al., 101; Chen Youming, "Concern (2)," 47; Xie Guang, *Dangdai*, 2:52. The Gang of Four consisted of Jiang Qing, Wang Hongwen, Zhang Chunqiao, and Yao Wenyuan.

73. Yang Guoyu, *Dangdai*, 437–40, 574–75; *Haijun Shi*, 219; Huang Xuhua, 397; Wang Rongsheng, 386; Liu Jingzhi, 14. The Nineteenth Academy was the code name for the Communications and Computer Academy. The Tenth and Nineteenth academies are the nation's most important research facilities on military electronics. For information on them, see Xie Guang, *Dangdai*, 2:300; Tong Zhipeng, 428; and Wang Shiguang and Zhang Xuedong, 423.

74. Yu Youhua, 24–25; Yang Shi'e, 3; *Dianzi*, 2:31.24, 31.27; Liu Dengrong et al., 389–94.

75. Three machinery plants (named Dongfeng, Jiangning, and Jiangxin), the Great Wall Radio Factory in Beijing, and the 22nd Radio Factory in Shanghai are the five main industrial enterprises assigned to manufacture sonar equipment. To date, the 09 boats' sonars remain substandard. For example, the detection range of their active sonars is 2–3nm, vs. 5–10nm for Western systems. Zheng Ming et al., 4; Cheng Wang, 538–45, 551–52; Xie Guang, *Dangdai*, 2:262.

76. Shu Deqi and Ling Xiang, (7); Jiang Rubiao, "Head"; Jiang Rubiao and Zhang Ming, "Visit," 112.

77. Sun Junren, 1:70–71; Zhang Zhaozhong, 41; Huang Shanhu, 82–86.

78. Han Nianlong, 114; *Haijun Shi*, 69. For further information, see Chap. 1.

79. Li Yunsheng, 172; *Haijun Shi*, 70, 338; Jiang Rubiao and Zhang Ming, "Visit," 112; Shen Shungen, "Description." For a description of the station, see Jiang Rubiao and Zhang Ming, "Visit," 112.

80. This second VLF station, completed in 1982, reportedly had the highest power output in the world at that point. The project won the national science-and-technology prize in 1985. Unless otherwise cited, the information in this paragraph is from Jiang Rubiao, "Progressive Renewal"; Chen Youming, "Wise Decision," 11; *Haijun Shi*, 86–87, 338; Yang Guoyu, *Dangdai*, 320–21; Li Yunsheng, 173; and Jiang Rubiao, "Head."

81. Cheng Wang, 555.

82. Wang Huilin, 194; Lu Jianxun, 391; Wang Shiguang and Zhang Xuedong, 421; Ling Xiang and Gu Han, 24. The submarine can transmit on various frequencies (1–10GHz, 14/11GHz, 30/20 GHz, and 225–400KHz) via satellite. See Sun Junren, 2:758, 824–25; and *Dianzi*, 2:16.2, 16.3.

83. Tong Zhipeng, 427; Wang Shiguang and Zhang Xuedong, 421; Lu Jianxun, 391. The satellite communication system was manufactured in Shaanxi Province.

Liu Yin et al., 509. The five communication satellites were launched in April 1984, Feb. 1986, March and Dec. 1988, and Feb. 1990; some of these had military applications. On the upgrading of satellite communications, see Xie Feng et al., 410–11; Zhang Jinqing; and Liu Chang'an et al..

84. Liu Chen, 9; Li Xiuqing.

85. Zhang Ze'nan, "New Developments," 2; Shen Shungen, "Our Country's Submarine"; Jiang Rubiao, "Progressive Renewal"; Jiang Rubiao, "Head."

86. Han Hong; "Completion of a Long-Distance Radio"; Ji Yanglin; "Our Country Has Built Its First," 24.

87. Shao Dingrong and Gu Weilun, 89–90; Wu Min, 37; Gu Weilun, 40; Mu Pinghe, 37; Sun Junren, 2: 1009.

88. Unless otherwise cited, the information in this paragraph is from Cheng Wang, 568–600; and Xie Guang, *Dangdai*, 1: 293–94.

89. Institute 20 (Radio Navigation Technology Institute) is now under the administration of the Ministry of Electronics Industry and has principal responsibility for developing radio navigation. Institutes 707 and 717 under the Seventh Academy are responsible for developing naval navigational systems. Liu Yin et al., 126–27, 129, 508; Yang Guoyu, *Dangdai*, 573–74; *Haijun Shi*, 187–88. The Lingyun Radio Factory in Baoji, Shaanxi Province, and the Guangzhou Radio Factory in Guangdong Province produce the H/WDCY Satellite/Omega Navigation System; the Baoji plant also manufactures the DY-12M automatic Loran A/C receiver. Liu Yin et al., 126–27, 129, 516; *Zhongguo Dianzi*, 307, 434; Zhang Chunting, "China Displays," 17.

90. Xie Guang, *Dangdai*, 2: 260–61; Cheng Wang, 571. In addition to its own integrated navigation system, China purchased satellite-linking systems from the West in the 1980s, and in 1987, the navy created a center to maintain them. Yang Weiyuan, "Navy"; Shi Gong, 31.

91. By 1986, Institute 724 (shipboard radar) in Nanjing and the Fourth Radio Factory in Shanghai had developed a phased scanning three-dimensional search-attack radar (Sea Eagle) for the 09 boats. Xu Jiling; Wang Jinhe; Yang Biao.

92. Lin Yingguang and Wu Qingyu, 23.

93. Chen Bin et al., 101.

94. This paragraph and the next are based on "Strengthening (3)." The navy set the following environmental standards for the submarine living quarters: temperature to be lower than 30°C and humidity lower than 60%, with inter-compartmental temperature held to between 5°C and 8°C. Zhong Xie, 17.

95. Xie Guang, *Dangdai*, 2: 533. The identification number is based on Huang Caihong, "First"; and "Strengthening (1)."

96. See, for example, Lu Jianxun, 391; and Chen Bin et al., 101.

97. Chen Ping et al., 124; Deng Xiucheng and Zhou Zhiwu; "Chinese Communists Own."

98. *Dalu Zaochuan Gongye Gaikuang*, 48–50; *Dalu Zaochuan Gongye Xianshi*, 163–67. The yard is located close to the famous Huangpu Military School, where most of Chiang Kai-shek's (and some of Mao's) generals completed their preliminary education.

99. Based on Zu Wei, 10.

100. In the 09-2 submarine, the steam turbines apply power to the propeller shafts via a gearbox.

101. Engineer Wang Jinlong was reportedly promoted to director of the Huangpu Shipyard in the 1980s. In the 1950s, he studied in a Soviet university and majored in shipbuilding engineering. Unless otherwise cited, the information in this paragraph is from Chinese specialists now residing in the United States, 1990.

102. Based on Jiang Rubiao et al., "Visit"; and an analysis of the usual practice of the Chinese in the development of Project 09.

103. The development of anti-radar coatings reportedly spurred their use on other weapon systems. *Haijun Shi*, 236.

104. This is based on a statement by a senior official from the China State Shipbuilding Corporation. Chen Ming and Zhou Zongmin.

105. Chen Wang, 396–97. For meeting actual combat specifications, engineers have designed a new-type servo drive with the largest allowable tilt angle of 45° to enhance the feasibility and reliability of the control rod. Wang Chengxuan.

106. Unless otherwise cited, the remainder of this section is based on Huang Caihong, "New Development of Chinese," 4; Wang Yongzhi, *Hangtian*, 275, 327; and "New Breakthrough," 20.

107. Lewis and Hua. The Chinese call the JL-2 a "long-range missile [*yuancheng daodan*]." Judging from their definition of "long-range," the maximum range of the JL-2 missile would be about 8,000km. Zhong Xie, 123; Liu Dengrong et al., 195; Song Shilun, *Zhongguo*, 2: 1219. The number of JL-2 missiles to be installed on the 09-4 boat remains to be confirmed.

108. The dimensions of the three-stage JL-2 missile are different from those of the two-stage JL-1 missile. For example, both the first and second stages of the JL-1 are 1.4m in diameter; both the first and second stages of the JL-2 are 2m in diameter, and the third stage of the JL-2 is 1m in diameter. Wang Yongzhi, *Hangtian*, 275, 327.

109. The Chinese cannot test-launch the large-sized JL-2 missile from the 31-class (Golf) submarine. The Wuchang yard built a fixed underwater launching platform for the JL-2 testing program, and by 1992 COSTIND took it over from the yard. "New Breakthrough," 20. The DF-31 is a solid-propellant, surface-to-surface long-range ballistic missile for strategic operations.

110. The navy disbanded the Submarine Institute in Feb. 1969 and reestablished it in Dec. 1973, eight months before the first nuclear attack submarine was added to the battle order. Yang Guoyu, *Dangdai*, 247, 301, 302. This paragraph is based on Jiang Rubiao et al., "Visit"; and "Strengthening (3)."

111. Based on Jiang Rubiao, "Sketch," 2. For example, Du Yongguo served as captain of a 33-class submarine before the navy assigned him to the Submarine Institute and then appointed him to command boat 406. See *ibid*.

112. Hu Chunhua, 17; Jiang Rubiao et al., "Visit"; "Strengthening (3)."

113. Among the navy's 13 schools, the Submarine Institute, the Dalian Warship Institute, the Guangzhou Warship Institute, and the Nanjing Naval Command Academy are designated for training commanding officers. Most of the other nine schools are in charge of training technical officers and noncommissioned officers. See Lewis and Xue, *Military Readiness*.

114. Shen Shungen, "Description"; Zhang Xinxin, K9, K10; Wu Yundian and Shu Jianping, 14.

115. Shen Lijiang, "Commander," 3; Shen Shungen and Zhang Ze'nan, 29.

116. Wu Yundian and Shu Jianping, 14; Shen Shungen and Zhang Ze'nan, 29;

Yang Jun and Lu Wu. On safety, see Shen Shungen and Wu Yundian; and Wu Yundian and Tang Xun. After a Chinese submarine (hull number 418) sank on Dec. 1, 1959, sending 38 crew members to their death, the navy made safety education a major part of all submarine training. See Li Maoqin, 3, 9–11.

117. Huang Caihong, "Our Country's Submarine," 22; Huang Caihong, "Chinese Submarine," 18–19; Wu Yundian and Shu Jianping, 14.

118. Zhu Yida, "Consideration"; Yang Guoyu, *Dangdai*, 503; *Haijun Shi*, 253.

119. Li Xianying. Partly as a result of budget cuts, the navy has called for the development and use of computer-aided simulators for training since the mid-1980s. Li Xueyin.

120. In 1989, the Submarine Institute had four such simulators. Yang Jun. See also Xiao Hao.

121. Unless otherwise cited, the information in this and the next paragraph is from Yang Guoyu, *Dangdai*, 318, 546–47; *Haijun Shi*, 274; and Li Ke and Hao Shengzhang, 369.

122. The location of China's first nuclear submarine base is based on Shen Lijiang, "U.S. Chief," 7–8; Wang Chuliang, 16–18; and "Strengthening (2)."

123. The navy commenced work on a second nuclear submarine base in 1984. We believe this base is near the naval port of Lüshun, Liaoning Province.

124. Shi Changxue; Shi Changxue and Xia Hongqing; Jiang Ming and Xu Sen, 15; "Our Country's First Warship," 12. For detailed information on Chinese approaches to demagnetizing submarines and surface warships, see Du Zhiying.

125. Unless otherwise cited, this paragraph is based on *Haijun Shi*, 274; and Yang Guoyu, *Dangdai*, 546–47.

126. Beijing set the requirement of self-sufficiency for all strategic command posts. See "Our Country Has Built a Relatively Integrated Defense."

127. Jiang Rubiao et al., "China's No. 1."

128. Yang Guoyu, *Dangdai*, 308; Liu Shengdong and Zhang Weixing; *Haijun Shi*, 67.

129. *Haijun Shi*, 72; Hu Chunhua, 17. Submariners on conventional-powered boats do not receive preferential treatment. For example, during a three-week submerged voyage, the crew of boat 303 (a 33-class sub based at Yulin, Hainan Island) ate only tinned food and were allowed only one cup of drinking water a day. Hu Zhanfan and Peng Baowu, 432, 434, 437, 439.

130. Living standards appear to be a common subject for discussion among submariners. See Sun Jilian.

131. Jiang Rubiao and Yang Jianmin; Hong Liu; Zhang Ming, "Navy."

132. Since 1979, the navy has pursued a policy of promoting sailors to officers after their graduation from the Submarine Institute. Zhu Yida, "Important Link." In 1980, the Central Military Commission issued a regulation forbidding the direct promotion of soldiers to officers unless they had agreed to take advanced courses at military colleges. "This Year."

133. Li Yuliang and Qi Sanping.

134. According to navy regulations, combat ships unable to pass the category 1 qualification tests or undergoing training are assigned to category 2; vessels being overhauled belong to category 3. Zhang Ze'nan, "New Developments," 2.

135. Unless otherwise cited, this paragraph is based on Liu Guohua; and Jiang Rubiao and Deng Haiming.

136. Each of the navy's three fleets (*jiandui*, equivalent to army level, *bingtuan ji*) has three bases (*jidi*, equivalent to corps level, *jun ji*). The fleets do not command the submarine flotillas in combat. The headquarters of the nine bases are located in Qingdao, Lüshun, Yantai, Shanghai, Zhoushan (Dinghai), Fujian (Feiluan), Guangzhou, Yulin, and Zhanjiang. Each base operates as the highest-level combat unit that can independently engage in battle. The Submarine Corps supervises submarine training. Based on Lin Boye et al., 212–13; and *Haijun Shi*, 62, 69.

137. Shu Deqi and Li Chunfang, 73; Xu Jingyue, "Development," 6; Xu Jingyue, "Formation."

138. In 1988, Yang was made a rear admiral. "Strengthening (1)"; "Chinese Communist Nuclear."

139. Jiang Rubiao et al., "Visit." The navy lists its conventional-powered submarines, missile destroyers, missile frigates, oceangoing salvage vessels, training ships, and underway replenishment ships as grade 2 vessels, and minesweepers, minelayers, submarine chasers, and landing ships as grade 3 vessels. Jiang Rubiao and Yang Jianmin.

140. Zhu Yida, "Combat Use," 47–48; Guo Qingsheng, "China," 23, 24.

141. Guo Qingsheng, "China," 24.

Chapter Six

1. Unless otherwise noted, this section is based on Needham, 147–61, 472–525; Temple, 232–41; Wen Xing; and Zhang Jun, 2–4.

2. Needham, 480.

3. *Ibid.*, 508.

4. Wen Xing.

5. Nie Rongzhen, "On the Science," 55.

6. Nie Rongzhen's report, dated May 10, 1956, was titled "My Preliminary Ideas on Initiating Our Country's Missile Research." Unless otherwise cited, the information in this paragraph is from Bao Keming, 260, 261.

7. On Sept. 13, 1956, the Soviet Union agreed to provide two R-1 (the Soviet copy of the German V-2) rocket models for educational purposes and also accepted 50 college students for the study of missile technology. The two R-1 rockets were delivered to China in Dec. Wang Yongzhi, *Hangtian*, 1, 2. Zhang Jun, 9, 561, states that they were delivered in Oct., but we believe this is incorrect. The Fifth Academy was established on Oct. 8. Qian Xuesen was appointed director later in the month. Liu Yalou, commander of the Air Force, replaced Qian as director in April 1960, but Qian later held the post of deputy director. Chen Shiqu, 3; Zhang Jun, 560, 563.

8. The Fifth Academy set up its First and Second subacademies in Nov. 1957. Zhang Jun, 561. The Fifth Academy was equivalent to the army (*bingtuan*) level of the military. The subacademies, research institutes, and research sections, respectively, were equivalent to the corps (*jun*), division (*shi*), and regiment (*tuan*) levels. Nie Rongzhen, "On the Science," 90.

9. Liu Youguang, 91.

10. Many experts were subsequently transferred to continue their research at the Shanghai Rocket Design and Research Academy, the real name for the Shanghai Mechanics and Electricity Design and Research Academy. In Jan. 1963, that academy was placed under the Fifth Academy. Pan Xianjue, 13; Zhang Jun, 565.

11. A sounding or vertical probe rocket flies straight up and is designed to take

atmospheric, ionospheric, and geomagnetic measurements at altitudes from 30km to 200km. Missile designers often build sounding rockets to obtain the data necessary for the development of more advanced missiles and reentry systems. Zou Jiahua, 471.

12. Zhang Jun, 127–28, 140.

13. Yang Han and Wei Naiwen, 405; Zheng He, 18. For an overview history of the Chinese missile program, see Lewis and Hua.

14. By Dec. 1959, the Fifth Academy had received all the 1060s design drawings. Liu Congjun, *Hangtian . . . Yuanshi*, 33–34; Liu Congjun, *Hangtian . . . Dashiji*, 16.

15. We know of no Western source that refers to this Soviet-built SLBM. The 1060's other specifications (based principally on Lewis and Hua) were:

Length: 9.5m-10m	Weight at launch: 6 tons
Diameter: 880mm	Payload: 950kg
Guidance system: Strap-down, fully	Fuel: Kerosene
inertial	Oxidizer: AK-20 (80% nitric acid + 20%
Takeoff thrust: 9 tons	nitrogen tetroxide)

16. For information on the evolution of China's naval strategy, see Yang Guoyu, *Dangdai*, 41–42, 464, 523, 679, 718; and Chap. 9.

17. Liu Congjun, *Hangtian . . . Yuanshi*, 33–34.

18. The R-2 (approximate range 590km) is a modified version of the German V-2. Zhang Jun, 15, 561–62; and "Cradle," 2, state that the first two R-2s were delivered to Beijing in Jan. 1958; we believe the date is incorrect. The Soviet Union delivered six more rockets to Beijing in Oct. 1958 and a final six R-2s in Jan. 1959. Wang Yongzhi, *Hangtian*, 2, 15, 19.

19. This policy had already been articulated to some extent in a document adopted by an enlarged meeting of the Central Military Commission in early 1960: "Give priority to missiles and nuclear bombs; give priority to missiles [over the atomic bomb]; actively develop jet, radio, and electronics technology." Zhi Yin, "Chronicle," 18; Bao Keming, 261; Xie Guang, *Dangdai*, 2: 511; Wang Shiguang and Zhang Xuedong, 423; Liu Boluo, "Premier Zhou Devoted," 344; Wang Yongzhi, *Hangtian*, 56.

20. Yang Han and Wei Naiwen, 405.

21. For information on Khrushchev's third visit to Beijing, see Min Li, 92–99. Unless otherwise cited, the information in this paragraph is from Chen Youming, "Concern (1)," 3; Su Fangxue, "Report," 5; and Zhang Jun, 21.

22. Khrushchev recalls, "The Chinese always delegated Chou [Zhou Enlai] to raise unpleasant matters with us, first, because he was their Prime Minister and, second, because he was a masterful diplomat." Khrushchev, *Last Testament*, 248.

23. Xi Qixin, 2; Su Fangxue, "Report," 5; Gao Xinqing.

24. The 10 sections and the senior scientists who headed them were Ren Xinmin (comprehensive design), Zhuang Fenggan (aerodynamics), Tu Shou'e (missile structures), Liang Shoupan (missile engines), Li Naiji (propellants), Liang Sili (control systems), Zhu Jingren (components), Feng Shizhang (radio telemetry), Zhu Zheng (computation), and Wu Deyu (technical physics). Liu Youguang and Zhang Jun, 251; Zhang Jun, 472.

25. Unless otherwise cited, the information in this paragraph and the next two is from Liu Xing (1), 67; Zhang Jun, 127–28; Liu Shaoqiu and Lu Zhen, 4.

26. See, for example, Xing Qiuheng, 281.

27. Ke Bitian, 22–24; Zhang Jun, 127.

28. Qun Ren, 32–34; Zuo Yang, 14–16; Zhang Jun, 127–28; "Glossary," 1990, 29.

29. Sutton, 292.

30. Liu Xing (1), 67; Zhang Jun, 127–28. In 1944, the Jet Propulsion Laboratory in Pasadena had secretly used a liquid polysulfide rubber adhesive that a U.S. company had developed a year earlier as a propellant adhesive. Li Yiwei, "Evolution," 46.

31. This was the Potassium Perchlorate Production Plant in Dalian, which shifted to the production of ammonium perchlorate. Zhang Jun, 128.

32. Located in Changchun, Jilin Province, the institute provided many types of adhesives for solid composite propellants. Unless otherwise cited, this paragraph and the next three are based on *ibid.*, 128–29.

33. Created in 1952 and located in Xi'an, Institute 3 was responsible for conducting research on explosives. It, along with Plant 845, was later assigned to the Fifth Ministry of Machine Building (ordnance industry). Zhi Yin, "Chronicle," 16; Zhang Jun, 128, 130.

34. Xiao Gan had been the director of Institute 3 in Xi'an. Unless otherwise noted, this paragraph and the next two are based on Xing Qiuheng, 281–82; Liu Shaoqiu and Lu Zhen, 4; and Zhang Jun, 21–22, 129–30.

35. By this time the Chinese had ruled out the use of double-base solid propellant. Sutton, 292.

36. Zhang Jun, 130.

37. Liu Boluo, "Premier Zhou and the CCP," 131–32.

38. Wang Yongzhi, *Hangtian*, 129. In ancient times, a giant dragon symbolized the prosperity of the Chinese Empire.

39. As early as May 1970, Mao worried that *julong* might be considered national chauvinism. It was at his instructions that the commission two years later, on April 29, 1972, formally replaced *julong* with *julang*. Wang Yongzhi, *Hangtian*, 253.

40. Xing Qiuheng, 282; Liu Xing (1), 68; Zhang Jun, 47, 130–31; Liu Boluo, "Premier Zhou Expended," 348. Starting in the late 1960s and continuing into the next decade, the Fourth Academy moved to Lantian, Shaanxi Province, as part of the shift to the Third Line. Xing Qiuheng, 282.

41. Zhou Xiao; *Renmin Ribao* and *Xinhua* Reporters, K10; Xing Qiuheng, 282.

42. The Fifth Academy had started work on this plan in 1964. Unless otherwise cited, this paragraph is based on Zhang Jun, 41, 139, 566.

43. The four missiles were all surface-to-surface missiles: DF-2A (range-extended DF-2, medium-range), DF-3 (intermediate-range), DF-4 (limited-range intercontinental), and DF-5 (intercontinental).

44. On the *banian sidan* plan, see Lewis and Xue, *China Builds*, 211–14.

45. For information on the aluminum's function and its varying ratios to solid composite propellants, see Qun Ren, 34. By 1990, an advanced facility had been built at the Academy of Sciences' Institute of Mechanics to mass-produce a new kind of tiny aluminum sphere. Li Xiguang.

46. Unless otherwise cited, the information in this and the next paragraph is

from Liu Xing (1), 68; Zhang Jun, 131; Xing Qiuheng, 282; and Liu Shaoqiu and Lu Zhen, 4, 5.

47. Thrust termination and thrust vector control are the main activation systems for guidance and attitude control.

48. The Chinese knew from foreign sources that, by the 1960s, the Americans had produced a breakthrough on a series of polybutadiene propellants with comparatively high thrust impulse and density. They could be stored in places of extreme temperatures, "aged" slowly, and could be produced simply and inexpensively. Li Yiwei, "Evolution," 47. For information on the relative advantages of various binders, see Li Yiwei, "Development," 54–56, 38.

49. Zhang Jun, 135.

50. Liu Boluo, "Premier Zhou and the CCP," 130.

51. On this point, see, for example, Zhang Aiping, 75.

52. Unless otherwise cited, this and the next four paragraphs are based on Zhang Jun, 129, 131, 135, 143, 146, 147; Chen Bin et al., 102; Liu Congjun, *Hangtian . . . Yuanshi*, 225–27, 412–16; Liu Congjun, *Hangtian . . . Dashiji*, 161; and Wang Yongzhi, *Hangtian*, 209, 228.

53. The principal assignments of the Seventh Ministry's five academies were: First (surface-to-surface missiles), Second (surface-to-air missiles), Third (antiship missiles), Fourth (solid propulsion technologies), and Fifth (satellites). The largest academy today is the First; in 1990, it had a staff of 26,000, including 7,000 engineers and 10,000 experienced workers. For information on the academy, see Zhang Heping; and "Cradle," 2–3.

54. On PERT and the myth of managerial effectiveness, see Sapolsky, Chap. 4. On the official version of PERT, which was read and imitated by the Chinese, see United States, Dept. of the Navy. On its application to China's strategic missile management system, see Liu Jiyuan and Sun Jiadong, 258–59.

55. Months before Institute 7 became part of the Solid Missile Control System Institute in May 1967, its personnel had been transferred from the Ministry of Public Security to the Defense Science and Technology Commission. The commission put No. 7 under the administration of the Seventh Ministry.

56. This paragraph is based on Zhang Jun, original draft, Chap. 6, 13–14. The Chinese made few changes in wording in the published version of the book. Mentioning the JL-1's diameter, they replaced the "1,400mm-diameter engine" with "a new-type experimental engine with a larger diameter." Zhang Jun, 135.

57. Zhang Jun, 135; Zhang Jun, original draft, Chap. 6, 14; Liu Xing (1), 68; Liu Shaoqiu and Lu Zhen, 4.

58. Unless otherwise cited, this paragraph and the next are based on Lu Jianxun, 391; Huang Caihong, "New Development of Chinese," 4; Huang Caihong and Cao Guoqiang, "For the Birth (1)"; and Chen Shoukang.

59. Jiang Jun, 18; Zou Jiahua, 570–71.

60. Chen Bin et al., 102.

61. Liu Xing (2), 34; Zhang Jun, 141.

62. Zhang Jun, 140; Xi Qixin, 3; Liu Shaoqiu and Lu Zhen, 5; Liu Xing (2), 34.

63. Liu Xing (1), 68; Zhang Jun, original draft, Chap. 6, 14–15, 19; Zhang Jun, 136, 140–41, 143.

64. Unless otherwise cited, the information in this paragraph and the next two

is from Yang Xuequan; Gao Xinqing; Liu Shaoqiu and Lu Zhen, 5; Liu Xing (2), 34; Wang Yongzhi, *Hangtian*, 233; and Zhang Jun, 141.

65. The revenues for fiscal year 1966, 1967, and 1968 were 55.87, 41.94, and 36.12 billion yuan, respectively. Chen Rulong, 1: 241.

66. Zhang Jun, 141.

67. *Ibid.*, 136.

68. The Institute of Aerodynamics was one of the four research facilities attached to the Fifth Academy (missile) that the Chinese started building in 1960. By the time it was completed (in 1965, under the code name Project 8108), the Seventh Ministry had taken over for the academy. Unless otherwise cited, this paragraph is based on Zhuang Fenggan, 11, 13–14.

69. As of 1987, technicians had built more than 10 wind tunnels at the institute. Ren Xinfa and Wang Xingrang.

70. Zhang Aiping, 76.

71. Unless otherwise cited, this paragraph and the next are based on Dong Baocun, "Commander," 29; and Dong Baocun, *Yang Yu Fu*, 51.

72. Fu Chongbi was Nie Rongzhen's subordinate in the late 1940s. Yuan Wei, 279; *Zhongguo Renmin Jiefangjun Fazhan*, 210–11.

73. Most of the information in this paragraph and the next is based on Peng Jieqing; Jiao Yong, 1; Zhou Xiao; and Wang Yongzhi, *Hangtian*, 194–95, 215.

74. Song Shilun, "Illustrious Name," 25; Zhang Jun, 59, 567.

75. Unless otherwise cited, the information in this paragraph is from Zheng Chiying, 15.

76. Mao's wife, Jiang Qing, the most notorious of the Gang members, had already worked considerable damage on the missile program. In March 1974, she and Wang Hongwen had had Li Fuze, commander of the Jiuquan Missile Test Base (Base 20) arrested as an alleged follower of Lin Biao. The testing programs thereafter became disorganized and subject to long delays. *Ibid.*, 21; Yang Jianming, 152–53.

77. Huang Weilu ran the technical side of Project JL-1 for many years before being formally appointed chief designer in April 1979. Unless otherwise cited, this paragraph is based on "Description."

78. Wang Yongzhi, *Hangtian*, 216–17.

79. Zhang Jun, 57; Li Jue et al., 75–77; Duan Zijun, *Dangdai*, 83. Originally, the campaign was directed at the remnants of the "May 16" clique that had attacked Zhou Enlai in 1967. The persecution was extended to virtually all intellectuals of "bad" class backgrounds. Ni Zhongwen, 209.

80. Zhou Xiao.

81. Unless otherwise cited, the information in this paragraph and the next is from Gu Mainan, 14–15; and Liu Congjun, *Hangtian . . . Dashiji*, 94.

82. Born in Shandong Province in 1932, Song joined a Communist army unit in 1946. At one point, he served as a bodyguard to General Luo Ruiqing. After the Communist victory of 1949, Song first studied at a university in Harbin and then at the Bauman Institute of Technology in Moscow. A prize-winning student, he was selected to study under the Soviet cyberneticist A. A. Fel'dbaum and became one of the few Chinese ever invited to give lectures at a Soviet university. In 1960, he returned to China, where he joined the Fifth Academy and worked on missile control systems. He was chief editor of the book *Coordinate Conversion in Missiles' Control* (Daodan Kongzhi zhong de Zuobiao Bianhuan) and in the early 1980s co-

authored a book *Missile Control Theory* (Daodan Kongzhi Lun). Gu Mainan, 14; "Song Jian Appointed"; "Song Jian on Science," K11.

83. Song was repeatedly promoted in the 1980s. Made first deputy chief designer of Project JL-1 in Feb. 1980, he rose to vice-minister of the missile ministry in 1982, to head of the State Science and Technology Commission in 1984, and to state councilor in 1986. Zhang Jun, 572; "Order (No. 19)"; "Song Jian Appointed."

84. Jiao Yong, 1; Zhang Jiayu, "Tentative Study," 4.

85. Yang Guoyu sat on the control committee as a senior naval officer. Yang Guoyu, "Reminiscences," 8, 9; Zhang Jun, 59.

86. Li Yadan, "Description"; Yang Xuequan.

87. Zhang Jun, 139; Xing Qiuheng, 282.

88. The design group was headed by Feng Yaoping, a woman engineer, and comprised specialists from the First (machinery), Third (aviation), Fourth (electronics), and Seventh (missile) ministries of machine building and the Ministry of Chemical Industry. Liu Boluo, "Premier Zhou and the CCP," 131.

89. Xing Qiuheng, 282; Liu Boluo, "True Record," 11; Liu Boluo, "Premier Zhou Devoted," 348.

90. Zhang Jun, 137–38, 141.

91. Nie Rongzhen, *Inside the Red Star*, 729–30.

92. See Deng Xiaoping [2] and [9].

93. Based on Deng Xiaoping [8].

94. Nie Rongzhen, *Inside the Red Star*, 711–12.

95. Deng Xiaoping [8], 93–94.

96. Deng Xiaoping [7], 103.

97. Zhang Jun, 136.

98. The Fifth Ministry had made Plant 5534 responsible for developing igniters for China's strategic missiles, but in Aug. 1971, the Seventh Ministry had Plant 692 take over the assignment. It succeeded in developing a solid-propellant igniter for the JL-1 with help from the Luzhou Chemical Plant. The Luzhou Chemical Plant is a large-scale industrial facility in the Third Line. *Zhongguo Qiye*, 356–57; Cheng Zihua, 9; Wang Yongzhi, *Hangtian*, 249, 253–54.

99. Zhang Jun, 137–38.

100. Xi Qixin, 3; Zhang Jun, 138.

101. The information in this and the next paragraph is from Liu Shaoqiu and Lu Zhen, 5; and Zhang Jun, 137.

102. Cui was born in 1931 in Hebei Province. This paragraph and the next are based on Zhong Yi, 6; and *Renmin Ribao* and *Xinhua* Reporters, K9-K10.

103. Unless otherwise cited, this paragraph and the next are based on Lu Da, 476; and Zhang Jun, 136, 137.

104. Ke Bitian, 22.

105. Rocket nozzles are usually made of high-strength alloy steel or glass-reinforced plastics. In recent years, technicians at the Fourth Academy have preferred the latter. Bai Hande, 26; Ke Bitian, 22. For an introduction to China's use of glass-reinforced plastics, see Dai Lan.

106. Huang Weilu, 276.

107. Unless otherwise cited, this paragraph is based on Wang Zhenxian, 58; and Su Fangxue, "Report," 5.

108. In Nov. 1975, Mao's wife, Jiang Qing, and three associates (the so-called

Gang of Four) unleashed the mass movement to "criticize Deng [Xiaoping] and counterattack against the Right deviationist wind to reverse correct verdicts." Ostensibly approved by Mao, this was to be the last political campaign he ever launched. For information on the movement, see Ni Zhongwen, 219–20; Jin Chunming et al., 228–30; and Party History Research Section, 1981, 208–10.

109. Liu Shaoqiu and Lu Zhen, 5; Chen Bin et al., 101; Zhang Jun, 138.

110. Liu Youguang and Zhang Jun, 253; Chen Bin et al., 102.

111. Zhang Jun, 136. For information on the contributions of the Dalian Institute of Chemistry and Physics, the Xi'an Institute of Modern Chemistry (Institute 3), the Beijing Institute of Chemistry, the Shanghai Institute of Organic Chemistry, and the Lanzhou Institute of Chemistry and Physics to the development of solid and liquid propulsion technologies, see *ibid.*, 129; Jiang Chengwei, 371; Zhang Jingfu, 81; Tao Tao, 479–80; and Li Yadan, "Man," 77–79.

112. Unless otherwise cited, the rest of this paragraph and the next are based on Su Fangxue, "Report," 6; and Zhang Jun, 138.

113. Two other men also became deputy designers, Chen Deren and Dai Shizheng. Chen was charged with developing the on-board systems for guidance and flight attitude control; Dai was responsible for revising and implementing the missile's overall design plans. Liu Congjun, *Hangtian . . . Dashiji*, 159.

114. Shortly after the successful flight test of the JL-1 missile on Oct. 12, 1982, the Seventh Ministry promoted Cui from director of Institute 41 to deputy director of the Fourth Academy. After his retirement in the late 1980s, he became secretary-general of the ministry's Science and Technology Committee. Based on Zhong Yi, 6.

Chapter Seven

1. One of the few articles probably referring to the command system, including Yuquanshan, credits Chinese engineers with "guaranteeing command automation and strategic survivability and . . . strategic nuclear counterattack capability." The writer goes on to say: "The project has a complete set of equipment for communications, water drainage, and power. Even under conditions of being isolated from the outside world, its staff members can survive and conduct command [functions] without interruption for an extended period of time. . . . The post has the capability of protecting itself from nuclear, conventional, and chemical attacks." "Our Country Has Built a Relatively Integrated Defense."

2. Zou Jiahua, 358; "Aerospace," 16.

3. Bi Shiguan, "Missile Guidance Systems: Their Basic Composition," 18; Bi Shiguan, "Missile Guidance Systems (1)," 24; Zou Jiahua, 52, 53, 54; Zhao Shaokui, 4.

4. For a discussion of the flight control subsystems, see Chang Gong, 6: 14–15; and Chang Gong, 7: 11.

5. This paragraph and the next two are based on Chang Gong, 6: 13–15; Chang Gong, 7: 11; "Aerospace," 16; Bi Shiguan, "Missile Guidance Systems: Their Basic Composition," 18–19; and Zou Jiahua, 358–59.

6. Gao Keren and Yu Huijie, 260–62; Gunston, 14; Zou Jiahua, 489. The earliest type of nozzle was the so-called jet-a-vator, which had a mechanical deflector attached to the end of the nozzle.

7. Zhang Jun, 136–37.

8. Based on Zou Jiahua, 408; and Chang Gong, 6: 14.

9. Shen Hongyuan, "On Whether," 31; Tang Zhongfan, 22; Zhao Shaokui, 5; Jiao Yulin, 18–19.

10. Zhang Jun, 136–37, 141; Liu Xing (2), 34.

11. For typical Western works (in addition to hundreds of journal articles) on missile guidance that were available to Chinese designers in the late 1950s and early 1960s, see Clemow; Newman, one of the volumes in a series entitled "Principles of Guided Missile Design"; Puckett and Ramo; and Miles. Some of these books, such as the Emme volume in which the Miles paper appears, contain quite complete bibliographies and references to journal literature indexes. The Soviet Union regularly surveyed these Western publications and published comprehensive compilations of the material. See, for example, Bukalov and Narusbaev, Chap. 7.

12. Zou Jiahua, 489; Chang Gong, 7: 11.

13. Zhang Jun, 136–37; Liu Shaoqiu and Lu Zhen, 4–5.

14. Chinese engineers adopted graphite jet vanes for the DF-2, DF-3, and DF-4 missiles to control thrust vector. They applied a more advanced attitude-control system to the DF-5 missile: the first-stage engine was equipped with four swivelling motors; and the second-stage engine was a vernier engine consisting of one turbopump and four gimbaled thrust chambers. Zhang Jun, 176, 182.

15. Unless otherwise cited, this paragraph and the next are based on Zou Jiahua, 489; Gao Keren and Yu Huijie, 261; Chang Gong, 7: 11; Zhang Jun, 137; and United States, Air Force Dept., *Guided Missiles*, 7.17–7.18.

16. For a brief introduction to nozzle materials, see Sutton, 330–32.

17. Gao Keren and Yu Huijie, 261.

18. Zhang Jun, 140.

19. United States, Air Force Dept., *Guided Missiles*, 9.15. This and the next paragraph are based on *ibid.*, 9.15–9.43.

20. No U.S. or Soviet ballistic missile ever used the pure strapdown system because the gyros are not accurate enough or the computers fast enough. The United States did use the system in some experimental maneuvering reentry vehicles (MARVs). Information from an American specialist, 1990.

21. Unless otherwise cited, this and the next paragraph are based on Zou Jiahua, 169–70, 323; Gao Keren and Yu Huijie, 166–67, 177; Zhang Jun, 115, 165; and *Cihai*, 699.

22. The compensation coefficient accounts for deviations caused by wind and thrust in the longitudinal direction. The system also includes a coordinate conversion device for making lateral course corrections. Liu Congjun, *Hangtian . . . Yuanshi*, 42–47.

23. Unless otherwise cited, this paragraph and the next two are based on Zhang Jun, 140–41, 143–44.

24. Sutton, 330.

25. Zhang Jun, 137; Zou Jiahua, 489. For a description of the comparable American system, see United States, Air Force Dept., *Guided Missiles*, 7.19.

26. Cao Yuhe and Gao Xiangzhu, 445.

27. Chen Xingxin, 443.

28. The original Fourth Ministry followed a tortuous institutional path to the present-day Ministry of Electronics Industry, so named in May 1982. In 1950, the Ministry of Heavy Industry created the Telecommunication Industry Administration for military development. Under the code name Tenth Bureau, the administration was placed under the Second Ministry of Machine Building in 1953, the

First Ministry in 1958, and the Third Ministry in 1960, respectively. In 1963, the Tenth Bureau split off as a separate ministry: the Fourth Ministry. Liu Yin et al., 27, 32, 47, 48, 644, 645, 649, 652, 654, 671. In March 1988, the Ministry of Electronics Industry was merged into the Ministry of Machine Building and Electronics Industry. "Introduction to the Ten New Ministries." On the subsequent changes in the electronics ministry, see Chap. 4, note 177. The information in this paragraph is from Chen Xingxin, 443; Chen Ping et al., 93, 95, 104; and Liu Yin et al., 74, 85.

29. In 1970, the Central Military Commission withdrew the military control committee from the Fourth Ministry. This paragraph is based on Liu Yin et al., 59, 657, 659.

30. For detailed information on the four leading groups, see Chap. 4. The Telecommunication Industry Leading Group was disbanded in May 1974. Liu Yin et al., 59–60, 662.

31. Assigned to manufacture radar systems, telecommunication control and monitoring units, and sonar equipment, these enterprises were placed under the Third (aviation), Fifth (ordnance), and Sixth (shipbuilding) ministries, respectively. They were not restored to the Fourth Ministry until Jan. 1973. *Ibid.*, 59–60, 659, 660.

32. For analyses of the confusion in the nation's electronics industry during the Cultural Revolution, see Chen Ping et al., 97–98; and Han Huaizhi and Tan Jingqiao, 2: 116.

33. Cao Yuhe and Gao Xiangzhu, 445; Liu Yin et al., 73–74. A typical example of poor quality was the Jian-6 (F-6) fighter, a version of the MiG-19 built between the late 1960s and early 1970s. In 1971, the aviation industry built 40 Jian-6 fighters for foreign sale. Seven proved defective, and when Zhou Enlai halted their delivery on Dec. 15, he sent a directive to senior officials warning them about the low quality of military hardware. Zhao Dexin [4], 110.

34. In 1971, China produced 200 million semiconductor devices and one billion electronic components. Liu Yin et al., 64.

35. *Ibid.*, 74.

36. Huang Weilu, 274, 275; Li Yadan et al., "Description," 48; Cao Yuhe and Gao Xiangzhu, 445. On the effect of the defective electronic components and equipment in flight-testing strategic missiles, see Yang Xuequan; Gao Xinqing; and Wang Yongzhi, "Success."

37. Cao Yuhe and Gao Xiangzhu, 445.

38. The information in this paragraph and the next is from Liu Yin et al., 328–30; and Cao Yuhe and Gao Xiangzhu, 445–46.

39. In the early 1980s, in his capacity as vice-minister of the Seventh Ministry, Song Jian even called for the need to "rescue" the communication satellite project because of the serious quality problems of the on-board electronic components.

40. The Fourth Ministry had taken over the Fourteenth Academy from the Defense Science and Technology Commission in 1976. In 1982, the academy was formally renamed the Component Bureau of the Ministry of Electronics Industry. Liu Yin et al., 664, 671; Xie Guang, *Dangdai*, 2: 395.

41. The seven special measures adopted for rigorous quality control related to special master workers, special machines, special raw materials, special batches of devices, special acceptance tests, special screening, and special records. Liu Yin et

al., 330. In 1981, the Fourth and Seventh ministries extended the quality control system to the entire electronics industry. This decision affected 158 production lines at 81 factories and research institutes. By 1984, the Fourth Ministry had established 13,500 quality control teams at key electronics factories. Cao Yuhe and Gao Xiangzhu, 446.

42. For example, the rejection rate of electronic components for the control system of the DF-5 ICBM was 73.1% before the seven special measures were adopted. The new system brought the rate down to 5.5%. *Ibid.*; Zhang Jun, 462–64; Liu Yin et al., 329–30.

43. This paragraph is based on Chen Xingxin, 443. The Lishan Microelectronics Institute in Lintong, Shaanxi Province, developed electronic components resistant to nuclear radiation and related electromagnetic damage. Li Maoju; Wang Shihui and Ying Mingyang.

44. The efforts of Chinese specialists to upgrade the on-board electronic components continued throughout the 1980s. From 1981 to 1985, the electronics industry ministry spent over 100 million yuan on converting 26 production lines and installing the system of seven special measures. To support even more advanced weapons programs, the industry has been working to increase the reliability of the on-board electronic components from grades 5–7 to grades 7–9. Currently, only a few components have been upgraded to grade 7. Cao Yuhe and Gao Xiangzhu, 446–47.

45. Huang Weilu, 274–75. For information on the quest for reliability, see also Zhang Jun, 192.

46. See Lewis and Xue, *China Builds*, 214.

47. This paragraph is based on Zhang Jun, 68, 143, 146, 150, 164–66, 180, 449, 472–95 *passim*; Liu Congjun, *Hangtian . . . Yuanshi*, 7, 130; and Wang Yongzhi, *Hangtian*, 230, 290. For a more detailed review of the history of China's missiles, see Lewis and Hua.

48. Unless otherwise cited, information in this and the next two paragraphs is based on Zhang Jun, 112, 565, 566–67; Academy of Military Science, *Zhongguo Renmin Jiefangjun Liushi Nian Dashiji*, 612; Wang Yongzhi, *Hangtian*, 78, 141, 147, 164, 174, 177, 194, 195, 243; and Liu Congjun, *Hangtian . . . Yuanshi*, 42–47.

49. The Artillery Corps and the First Design Department of the Second Subacademy of the Fifth Academy, predecessor of Institute 12, jointly reached the conclusion on the missile's weaknesses after a detailed investigation conducted from Aug. 1964 to April 1965.

50. With a maximum range of 1,050km, the DF-2 was a medium-short-range rocket (*zhongjincheng huojian* by the Chinese classification). Few of the unmodified DF-2s were ever produced.

51. In Nov. 1964, the Fifth Academy gave the range-extended DF-2 missile the code name DF-2A. In addition to replacing the guidance system, the engineers succeeded in raising the rocket thrust from 40 tons to 45.5 tons and increased the missile's maximum range by 20%. The DF-2A was originally designed to carry a 1,500kg payload and a 20-kiloton fission warhead (before the 1-megaton fusion warhead was available). During a test on Oct. 27, 1966, the missile carried a 12kt warhead. With a maximum range of 1,260km, the DF-2A was categorized by the Chinese as a medium-short-range rocket (*zhongjincheng huojian*). It was the first

Notes to Pages 166–68

strategic missile deployed in China: deliveries to the Second Artillery Corps began on Sept. 15, 1966. In Jan. 1971, the Seventh Ministry stopped manufacturing the missile, and all DF-2As had been decommissioned by the end of 1978.

52. The DF-3 served as the first stage of the DF-4. The two missiles were equipped with control systems based on almost the same principles. With a maximum range of 2,650km, the DF-3 was classified by the Chinese as a medium-range rocket (*zhongcheng huojian*); the DF-4, maximum range 4,750km, was an intermediate-range rocket (*zhongyuancheng huojian*). Lewis and Xue, "Strategic Weapons," 550; Lewis and Hua; Zhang Jun, 567.

53. In 1971 and 1980, the Second Artillery Corps formally started deploying the DF-3 and DF-4 missiles. Academy of Military Sciences, *Zhongguo Renmin Jiefangjun Liushi Nian Dashiji*, 633; Han Huaizhi and Tan Jingqiao, 2: 152, 530.

54. Starting in the early 1960s, Institute 12 assigned Lin Jin and Zong Shaolu to develop a "complete compensation" inertial guidance system. This paragraph and the next are based on Zhang Jun, 165–66; and Liu Congjun, *Hangtian . . . Yuanshi*, 42–47.

55. Generally speaking, ball bearings are applied to low-precision gyroscopes, and air bearings and other floated bearings to high-precision gyroscopes. Feng Chongzhe and Huang Jianyi, 22.

56. For information on the DF-5 development program, see Lewis and Xue, "Strategic Weapons," 551–52. Unless otherwise cited, this paragraph is based on Zhang Jun, 180.

57. As a result of the rapid development of integrated circuits, inertial components, and computers in the 1980s, the Chinese began fitting or retrofitting all their missiles with advanced strapdown inertial guidance. Liu Jianghai.

58. Liang Sili, head of the Fifth Academy's Control System Research Section, had moved to Institute 12 in the reorganization of 1965. In 1970, he succeeded Huang Weilu as the institute's director. Zhang Jun, 140, 180, 472.

59. Wu Baokun and Yuan Youqing (3), 20; Wu Baokun and Yuan Youqing (5), 42; Zhang Jun, 140, 180.

60. Engineering Division 156 of the Academy of Sciences was assigned to develop the DF-5 computer in Aug. 1965. The information in this paragraph and the next is from Zhang Jun, 180–82; and Wang Yongzhi, *Hangtian*, 175, 179.

61. By adopting the concept of "incremental computation," the engineers at the Lishan Microelectronics Institute reduced the number of circuits and components in the DF-5's computer.

62. Xie Guang, *Dangdai*, 1: 372, 2: 335; Zhang Jingfu, 81. Xi'an is one of China's three major centers for electronics-related research. Sun Minqiang; "Rapid Development."

63. An on-board incremental digital minicomputer only calculates the differences between a moving missile's actual velocities, coordinates, and flying times and the preset values. Accordingly, the application of incremental computation helped the Chinese greatly simplify the structure of the DF-5's computer by cutting the circuit components of the original computer in half. Zhang Jun, 181–82.

64. On Nov. 5, 1974, the Chinese used the new minicomputer in a flight test of the DF-5 missile. The test failed because of a broken circuit in another component. See *ibid.*, 192.

65. The Changchun Institute of Optical and Fine Mechanics contributed to the optical instrumentation for both Project 09 and Project JL-1. See Wang Daheng,

470–73. Unless otherwise cited, the information in this paragraph and the next is from Zhang Jun, 166; and Wang Yongzhi, *Hangtian,* 163, 173, 175, 193, 210–11, 218–19, 250, 323, 358.

66. The requirements for assembling a liquid-floated gyroscope are more stringent than for an air-bearing one. If the work is not done in a dust-free environment, the lubricating oil in its motor quickly clogs up. Wang Caiyao, 29.

67. Liu Congjun, *Hangtian . . . Yuanshi,* 130.

68. In May 1980, China successfully conducted a full-range flight test on its ICBM (DF-5). The Second Artillery Corps started deploying the missile the following year. Han Huaizhi and Tan Jingqiao, 2: 152, 530; Academy of Military Sciences, *Zhongguo Renmin Jiefangjun Liushi Nian Dashiji,* 700–701; Wang Yongzhi, *Hangtian,* 378.

69. Yang Guoyu, *Dangdai,* 654; *Haijun Shi,* 230; *Renmin Ribao* Reporters. Chen Deren was born in Jiangsu Province in 1922; in 1945, he graduated from a university in Chongqing, and in 1957, he began work on missile control systems. Before his transfer to Institute 17, Chen was a deputy director at Institute 12. After developing the JL-1's control system, Chen was made one of three deputy chief designers of the project in April 1979; he was promoted to deputy director of the Second Academy in Aug. 1980. Chen, Huang Weilu, and Cui Guoliang won the national science-and-technology prize for their work on JL-l. Zhong Yi, 6; Liu Shaoqiu and Lu Zhen, 5; Zhang Jun, 143–44; "Twenty-three"; Liu Congjun, *Hangtian . . . Dashiji,* 159.

70. Huang Weilu earned his master's degree in electrical engineering at the University of London in the 1940s. He was recruited by the Fifth Academy in 1958 and awarded the rank of colonel. In his capacity as director of Institute 12 from 1965 to 1970, he devoted himself to developing control systems for the DF series missiles. Sun Yinnan et al., K14; Li Yadan, "Description"; Yang Xuequan. In March 1970, Huang was transferred to Department 4 and later put in overall charge of the technical wing of Project JL-1. In April and June 1979, he was appointed the project's chief designer and deputy director of the Second Academy. Gao Xinqing; Li Yadan et al., "Description," 48; Zou Jiahua, 268; Liu Congjun, *Hangtian . . . Dashiji,* 159, 160.

71. Wu Baokun and Yuan Youqing (3), 20.

72. Unless otherwise cited, the rest of this paragraph and the next one are based on Xie Guang, *Dangdai,* 1: 372, 2: 335; Zhang Jun, 145; and Zhu Lemin.

73. CMOS stands for "complementary metal oxide semiconductor." CMOS uses a form of field-effect transistor that is inherently simpler to pack than earlier bipolar transistors. With n-channel (negative-conducting properties) MOS transistors and p-channel MOS transistors on the same chip, CMOS translators have low power dissipation and high density of elements per unit area and are used in digital circuits such as the logic systems of computers. Sun Junren, 1: 388; *Dianzi,* 1: 13.110–11.

74. Zhang Jun, 145. On the manufacture of integrated circuits at the Lishan institute, see Li Maoju; Chen Xiuxian, 34; and Sun Minqiang.

75. On the use of silicon or fluorocarbon oil in the Chinese liquid-floated gyroscopes, see Wang Caiyao, 29; Gao Keren and Yu Huijie, 160; and Feng Chongzhe and Huang Jianyi, 22.

76. Unless otherwise cited, this paragraph is based on Su Fangxue, "Report," 8, 9; Zhang Jun, 140, 144–45; and Wang Yongzhi, *Hangtian,* 210–11, 227.

77. This paragraph and the next two are based on Cui Chengwu and Zhang Quncheng; Su Fangxue, "Report," 8, 9; Zhang Jun, 140, 144–45; Liu Congjun, *Hangtian . . . Yuanshi*, 130; and Wang Yongzhi, *Hangtian*, 227, 257. The quotation is from Zhang Jun, 144.

78. Base 067's first-zone facilities, located near Fengzhou, a Shaanxi town 100km southwest of Baoji City, comprised a local branch of Institute 11, Plant 103 (Liquid Rocket Engine Plant), and Rocket Engine Test Stand 165. These facilities were affiliated with Institute 11 (Liquid Rocket Engine Institute) and Plant 179 (for building liquid rocket engines), both in Beijing.

79. As copies of Plant 230 in the Third-Line region, Plants 107 and 171 were assigned to manufacture accelerometers and gyroscopes, respectively.

80. In addition to Base 067, the First Academy's network in the interior includes Base 062 in northern Sichuan Province, which is composed of a branch of Department 1 (Carrier Rocket Overall Design Department) in Xuanhan County for formulating comprehensive design plans for liquid-propellant missiles, and a branch of Institute 12 in Wanyuan County for developing control systems for liquid engines. By 1972, the academy had transferred 14,000 staff and workers to these two facilities, whose construction cost 340 million yuan.

81. Ding Henggao was later promoted to the post of deputy head of the Science and Technology Department of the Defense Science and Technology Commission. In 1985, he became the head of the Commission of Science, Technology, and Industry for National Defense.

82. Under the administration of the Seventh Ministry's Second Academy, No. 284 was originally assigned to manufacture coordinate data-processing sets for surface-to-air missiles, and now the ministry ordered it to the JL-1. Unless otherwise cited, this and the next paragraph are based on *Renmin Ribao* and *Xinhua* Reporters, K10; and Zhang Jun, 145, 148.

83. In the 1980s, Chinese specialists achieved other successes in developing inertial components, such as liquid-floated gyroscopes, solid-state gyroscopes, and integrating pendulum accelerometers. Liu Jianghai. On comparable Soviet developments on guidance components, see the two works listed under United States, Defense Intelligence Agency.

84. This paragraph is based on Zhang Jun, 137; Zhang Jun, original draft, Chap. 6: 15; and Zou Jiahua, 489.

85. Unless otherwise cited, this paragraph is based on Zou Jiahua, 358–59, 489; and Wang Yongzhi, *Hangtian*, 169, 298–99, 345, 382, 392, 410.

86. Liu Shaoqiu and Lu Zhen, 4; Zhang Jun, 136–37.

87. This and the next two paragraphs are based on Zhang Jun, 135, 136–37; Zhang Jun, original draft, Chap. 6: 13, 14–15; and Gao Keren and Yu Huijie, 261. The quotation is from Zhang Jun, 137.

88. This paragraph and the next are based on Liu Xing (2), 34; and Zhang Jun, 140, 144.

89. Azimuth in this case would be expressed as the angular distance between the direction of a fixed point (such as true north) and the heading of the missile. The information in this paragraph is from Wang Daheng, 472; Gao Keren and Yu Huijie, 170–72; and Zhang Jun, 144.

90. Unless otherwise cited, this and the next paragraph are based on Zhang Jun, 144; Liu Shaoqiu and Lu Zhen, 5; and Liu Xing (2), 34.

91. In their attempts to improve the missile ejection and control systems, the

Chinese reportedly performed almost 1,000 ejection tests on different-sized model rockets between 1969 and 1984, first on land and then at sea. Zhang Jun, 142. These tests were mentioned in Chaps. 3 and 5.

92. This and the next paragraph are based on Zhang Jun, 147; and Wang Yong-zhi, *Hangtian*, 262, 306, 333; Liu Congjun, *Hangtian . . . Yuanshi*, 134, 228, 441–46; and Liu Congjun, *Hangtian . . . Dashiji*, 66, 82, 161, 200, 250–52. Plant 284 had split off from Plant 283 as a separate enterprise in May 1966. Located in Bei-jing, Plant 283 was under the administration of the Seventh Ministry's Second Academy and had been assigned to manufacture data-processing sets for surface-to-air missiles. Plant 284 was merged into Plant 699 in 1979 and was then split off to become a separate unit in 1983.

93. The Seventh Ministry had recommended using Plant 307 for the final as-sembly of the JL-1 missile in 1973. With the end in sight in 1978, the Central Mil-itary Commission approved the remodeling and expansion of the plant for this pur-pose.

Chapter Eight

1. We believe the Chinese also had trouble with solid-propellant ignition but virtually nothing has been published on the subject. An exception is Zhang Jiaxin, 4–8. Zhang references a number of classified papers on the subject, including a paper by Li Fengchun.

2. Unless otherwise noted, this section is based on Lewis and Xue, *China Builds*, 202–3, 209-14 *passim*, 238, 289; Lewis and Hua; Shi Jinkun; and Wang Yongzhi, *Hangtian*, 72, 148–63 *passim*, 182, 200–214 *passim*, 249–50, 287–91 *passim*, 320, 398, 401.

3. The Teller information is from Hansen, 203–5. The Hansen volume also pro-vides short histories of the Polaris W-47 and W-58 warheads. Some information in this section is from Lewis and Hua.

4. Institute 14 had formally been Research Section 4 of Department 1 (Carrier Rocket Overall Design Department). Xie Guang, *Dangdai*, 1:188, 222, 2:511; Wang Yongzhi, *Hangtian*, 244. For more on the early history of warhead devel-opment, see Lewis and Xue, *China Builds*, 207–9.

5. Xie Guang, *Dangdai*, 1:371. The test flight of Batch 01's Yao-7 from the Golf submarine on Oct. 12, 1982, proved the correct design of JL-1's warhead by Institute 14 of the First Academy.

6. The development of the first initiator is described in Lewis and Xue, *China Builds*, 155–60.

7. Zhang Jun, 145–46; Liu Congjun, *Hangtian . . . Yuanshi*, 230, 231.

8. Xue Yu, 14, 15; Zou Jiahua, 74, 271, 549, 556.

9. This paragraph and the next are based on Zhang Jun, 145–46, 147, 148; Liu Congjun, *Hangtian . . . Dashiji*, 165; and Liu Congjun, *Hangtian . . . Yuanshi*, 230, 231.

10. This paragraph and the next are based on Zhong Wen, 42–44; Su Yingxiong, 93–95; and Zou Jiahua, 47, 48, 430, 559–60.

11. Institute 703 comes directly under the Seventh Ministry of Machine Build-ing. Yao Tongbin, a former director of the institute who was killed in the Cultural Revolution, headed teams to test materials for the DF missiles. Zhang Jun, 411, 468; Zhou Xiao. Unless otherwise cited, the remainder of this section is based on Sun Zhenhuan, 137–38; Xie Guang, *Dangdai*, 2:431–32; and Wang Yongzhi,

Hangtian, 72, 87, 106, 119, 137, 206, 224–64 *passim,* 289, 293, 334, 347–48, 349, 402, 405, 428, 450, 466.

12. Plant 211 was originally an aircraft repair plant. In May 1958, the Fifth Academy, predecessor of the Seventh Ministry, took control of the plant from the Fourth Bureau (aviation) of the First Ministry of Machine Building. Bao Keming, 261.

13. The team that developed the coating was headed by Yu Qiao, a specialist on rocket materials at Institute 703. Zhang Jun, 411.

14. The team was formally called the Reentry Warhead Coordinated Task Office. Huang Xu, 511.

15. Institute 701 originally came directly under the Seventh Ministry. In May 1977, the ministry placed it under the administration of the First Academy. For information on this institute, see Zhuang Fenggan, 272, 273; and Ren Xinfa and Wang Xingrang.

16. The successful recovery of two satellites in 1976 and 1978 proved the heat protection system for the DF-5. Jiang Hong, 25; "Guo Jingkun"; Zhang Jun, 310–16; Zou Jiahua, 559.

17. For information on the development of carbon-coated fibers, see Lu Da, 477; Zhu Youdi; and Su Kuoshan et al., "Report on the Efforts."

18. This and the next paragraph are from Chen Bin et al., 101; Xie Guang, *Dangdai,* 1: 141; and Wang Yongzhi, *Hangtian,* 268–69, 275, 283, 285.

19. The commission's 1975 report was entitled "Report on Arrangements for Research and Development on Nuclear-Armed Missiles." In it, the commission advanced the R&D schedules for the JL-1, DF-4, and DF-5 missiles and pledged to deliver the DF-4s and 5s to the Second Artillery Corps by 1977.

20. Deng Xiaoping staged his second political comeback in March 1973. At the second session of the 10th Central Committee in Jan. 1975, he was made vice-chairman of the Central Committee and appointed to the Politburo Standing Committee. *Zhongguo Gongchandang Jianshi,* 354; Party History Research Section, 1981, 199, 203–04.

21. Guo Weicheng and Zhang Shusheng.

22. Su Fangxue, "Report," 5.

23. This paragraph is based on Liu Shaoqiu and Lu Zhen, 5; and Zhang Jun, 60–61, 138.

24. From July 1977 to Dec. 1978, most Party and state affairs were under the joint leadership of Hua Guofeng and Deng Xiaoping. See *Zhonggong Dangshi Dashi,* 220–22; and Party History Research Section, 1981, 216–23.

25. The commission's 1977 report was entitled "Report on the Arrangement of the Research and Development on Strategic Nuclear Missiles and Man-Made Satellites and Their Delivery Systems Before 1980." Unless otherwise cited, the information in this paragraph and the next four is from Zhang Jun, 146; Chen Bin et al., 101; Wang Yongzhi, *Hangtian,* 310; and Liu Congjun, *Hangtian . . . Yuanshi,* 226–27.

26. Based on Han Huaizhi and Tan Jingqiao, 2: 152, 530; and Academy of Military Sciences, *Zhongguo Renmin Jiefangjun Liushi Nian Dashiji,* 700–701. According to a Central Military Commission document, China has deployed only four DF-5 missiles in silos, and all are to be replaced by the year of 2010 by solid-propellant DF-41 ICBMs. Lewis and Hua.

27. *Renmin Ribao* and *Xinhua* Reporters, K11; Zhang Jun, 146.

28. At the third session of the 11th Central Committee, in Dec. 1978, the Party faction headed by Deng Xiaoping prevailed over the members of an allegedly more radical group, including Party leader Hua Guofeng. Party History Research Section, 1981, 222–23.

29. Li Jinting et al., 18. For a discussion of Deng's directive to the nuclear weapons designers, see Lewis and Xue, *China Builds*, 235.

30. In 1975, the State Council created the Eighth General Bureau (four years later the Eighth Ministry) of Machine Building. The ministry was merged into the Seventh Ministry in 1981. For information on the evolution of the Eighth Ministry, see "Eleventh Meeting"; "Resolution of the Standing Committee . . . on Creating the Eighth Ministry"; and "Resolution of the Standing Committee . . . on the Merger."

31. Unless otherwise cited, this paragraph and the next are based on Chen Bin et al., 102; Zhang Jun, 146–47; Liu Congjun, *Hangtian . . . Dashiji*, 161; Liu Congjun, *Hangtian . . . Yuanshi*, 412–16; and Wang Yongzhi, *Hangtian*, 334, 359.

32. This and the next paragraph are based on Qian Xuesen, "Premier Zhou," 290; Chen Bin et al., 103; Zhang Jun, 146–47; Liu Congjun, *Hangtian . . . Dashiji*, 159, 169–70, 188; and Liu Congjun, *Hangtian . . . Yuanshi*, 227.

33. Dai Shizheng, the head of Department 4, was in charge of formulating the JL-1's comprehensive design plan. Later, the Seventh Ministry added to the bureaucratic structure. Song Jian was appointed first deputy chief designer, and Li Xu'e and Wu Mingchang deputy chief designers in Feb. 1980, and Wang Wenchao was made deputy chief designer in May 1982.

34. While technically the head of the Second Academy, Chai Zhi was handicapped by his previous opposition to Zhang Aiping, who had returned to head the Defense Science and Technology Commission. This legacy of factionalism in the Cultural Revolution weakened Chai's influence and made it necessary for Huang Weilu and Song Jian to play the leading role in the JL-1 project.

35. Rocket Engine Test Stand 101 and the manufacture of the JL-1's scale-model rockets there were discussed in Chap. 5. This and the next paragraph are based on Zhang Jun, 146–47; Li Yadan, "Description"; Wang Yongzhi, *Hangtian*, 230–31, 262, 290, 297, 300, 306, 341; and Liu Congjun, *Hangtian . . . Yuanshi*, 228.

36. Plant 307 was originally assigned to manufacture liquid-oxygen recharge vehicles and other ground maintenance equipment for strategic missiles. The Seventh Ministry later assigned it to produce servos for the DF series missiles.

37. In Jan. 1965, Plant 211 was split into five plants (179, 211, 696, 697, and 698), but a decade later, they were all remerged as Plant 211. Wang Yongzhi, *Hangtian*, 8–9, 72, 154, 286–87.

38. The First Academy's Base 062 in Sichuan Province included a rocket assembly center. For information on the base, see Chap. 7, note 80. The Second Bureau of Mechanics and Electricity in Shanghai had built a rocket assembly center at about the same time.

39. This and the next two paragraphs are based on Li Yadan et al., "Description," 47; Li Yadan, "Description"; Zhang Jun, 147–48; Cao Yuhe and Gao Xiangzhu; Liu Congjun, *Hangtian . . . Yuanshi*, 228, 229, 239, 240; Liu Congjun, *Hangtian . . . Dashiji*, 184, 196; and Wang Yongzhi, *Hangtian*, 374.

40. Liu Jiyuan and Sun Jiadong, 259; Bao Keming, 262; Zhang Jun, 147–48.

41. This paragraph and the next three are based on Zhang Jun, 136, 147–48; *Renmin Ribao* and *Xinhua* Reporters, K12; Yang Xuequan; Li Yadan, "Descrip-

tion"; Li Yadan et al., "Description," 47; Liu Congjun, *Hangtian . . . Yuanshi*, 229–39; Liu Congjun, *Hangtian . . . Dashiji*, 177, 179, 183, 187, 192, 199, 240; and Wang Yongzhi, *Hangtian*, 420.

42. In June 1983, Plant 307 shipped Batch 01's Yao-5 to Storage Cave 197.

43. Among the 68 plants and research institutes, 55 worked on the JL-1's solid propulsion.

44. Han Huaizhi and Tan Jingqiao, 2: 96; "Resolution of the Standing Committee . . . on the Creation"; Academy of Military Sciences, *Zhongguo Renmin Jiefangjun Liushi Nian Dashiji*, 717.

45. The remainder of this section is based on Zhang Jun, original draft, Chap. 6: 1, 31; Zhang Jun, 147–48; Yang Xuequan; Liu Congjun, *Hangtian . . . Dashiji*, 184, 187, 194, 195, 196; and Liu Congjun, *Hangtian . . . Yuanshi*, 239–43, 251.

46. After the successful flight test of Batch 01's Yao-7 from the Golf submarine, Yao-8 was flight-tested from a launch tube at Base 25 in May 1983 to verify the JL-1's maximum range. With this success, the engineers dropped the full-range test from the Batch 02 missions. They used Batch 02 only to determine the JL-1's accuracy and the reliability of various on-board components.

47. The Batch 03 missiles were used to finalize the JL-1 design plan. Qian Cansong.

48. Institute 215 was a research body attached to Plant 307.

49. Zhang Jun, 141, 148–50.

50. On the Sino-Soviet accord of Oct. 15, 1957, see also Lewis and Xue, *China Builds*, 62–63, 69–70.

51. Under the Sino-Soviet accord of Oct. 15, 1957, Moscow delivered a surface-to-ship missile (S-2) and a ship-to-ship missile (R-15). The Chinese first code-named the two missiles 542 and 544 but later renamed them HY-1 and SY-1. Liu Congjun, *Hangtian . . . Dashiji*, 9, 25; Liu Congjun, *Hangtian . . . Yuanshi*, 33, 34.

52. Unless otherwise cited, this paragraph is based on Zhang Xinghua et al., 2–3, 6–10, 29; Wang Huique, 402–3; and Shen Shungen, "China's Test," 2.

53. Unless otherwise cited, this paragraph and the next two are based on Jiang Rubiao and Zhang Heng; Yang Guoyu, *Dangdai*, 454–57; *Haijun Shi*, 227–28; Zhang Xinghua et al., 6–14 *passim*, 28, 159–63 *passim*, 196–97; Zou Dayi and Jiang Rubiao; and "Naval Test," 28.

54. In the 1960s and 1970s, the Defense Science and Technology Commission created impact zones in the Xinjiang Uygur Autonomous Region for testing the DF missiles. The three principal locations were Korla and Minfeng (for conventional warheads) and Lop Nur (for nuclear warheads). The headquarters of an impact zone was usually equivalent to the division level of the military. For information on these zones, see Mo Sheng, 18–19; Su Kuoshan and Wu Chuansheng; Zhang Dongfeng and Yan Xinfu; and Su Kuoshan, "Soldiers."

55. Most of China's strategic missiles were flight-tested at Base 20.

56. The locales of the SLBM test range and impact zone are from Zhang Wenxi, 46; and Yang Guoyu, *Dangdai*, 597, 649.

57. The Chinese first coupled photoelectricity to cinetheodolites and then developed a laser range-finder by combining cinetheodolites and laser-ranging devices for tracking and monitoring orbiting satellites and missiles. Song Shilun, *Zhongguo*, 1: 138; Zhang Jun, 379–84.

58. Unless otherwise cited, this paragraph is based on Zhang Xinghua et al., 161–77; and Yang Guoyu, *Dangdai*, 596–97.

59. Created in Jan. 1961 to conduct research on military-related radio electronics, the Tenth Academy was renamed the Radar Bureau in 1982. Liu Yin et al., 139, 652–71 *passim*, 656, 657, 662, 671; Wang Shiguang and Zhang Xuedong, 423; Feng Shizhang, 435–36.

60. Gu Shouren had finished postgraduate study at the Missile Engineering Department of the Naval Academy in Leningrad and returned to China as one of its best radar experts.

61. In 1965, the Fourth Ministry transferred over 1,500 technicians and master workers from the Changjiang Machine-building Plant in Nanjing to Anhui Province to prepare for the construction of the Chang'an Machine-building General Plant. This complex, consisting of one general plant and eight branches, located in Lu'an (headquarters), Yuexi, and Fuyang, was originally assigned to build low-altitude warning radar systems. It now develops civilian radar systems as well. See Liu Yin et al., 580; *Zhongguo Dianzi*, 138; and Chen Ping et al., 94.

62. The department later promoted Gu Shouren to the position of director of the newly created Institute of Measurement and Control (Institute 230). Yang Guoyu, *Dangdai*, 652; Zhang Xinghua et al., 174, 175.

63. Zhang Xinghua et al., 171–73; Su Fangxue, "Dragon," 45–53.

64. Zhang Xinghua et al., 173–77; Liu Yin et al., 153; Yang Guoyu, *Dangdai*, 653.

65. The missile test range's monitoring network is centered in Kelan County, but it has some tracking and monitoring facilities in Wuzhai and Xingxian. Unless otherwise cited, the last part of this section is based on Luo Laiyong, 151; "Long March"; Xu Zhimin, "Successful Launch"; and Wang Yongzhi, *Hangtian*, 219, 298–99.

66. Su Kuoshan, "Nie Rongzhen's Message."

67. The institute, successor to Base 20's Equipment Institute (which was created in 1965), is called the Measurement and Communication Overall Design Institute; it is responsible for designing integrated missile tracking and monitoring systems for missile test ranges. It moved to Luoyang, Henan Province, in the 1970s. Chen Bin et al., 102; Wang Yongzhi, *Hangtian*, 154.

68. The DF-5 was designed to be launched from a hardened silo. For information on the construction of the silo at Base 25, see Li Mingsheng and Xiao Zhou.

69. Xie Guang, *Dangdai*, 1: 99. On the tracking and monitoring system at Base 25, see Guo Fang, 42–47.

70. Qian Wuhuang, 432; Zhi Yin, "Defense," 20. For a brief explanation of measurement and control in missile flight tests, see "Aerospace," 16–17.

71. Wang Daheng, 472.

72. Chinese usually refer to Institute 1010 as Institute 10 of the Tenth Academy (Shiyuan Shisuo). Some research units were later detached from it to concentrate on the development of airborne and shipboard equipment. The institute is still one of the largest research facilities of its kind in China. The rest of this paragraph and the next two are based on Zhi Yin, "Defense," 20; Qian Wuhuang, 432–33; Guo Dong, 2–4; *Zhongguo Dianzi*, 407; and Xie Guang, *Dangdai*, 1: 463–67, 471.

73. Chinese usually refer to Institute 1028 as Institute 28 of the Tenth Academy (Shiyuan Ershibasuo). Liu Xing was later promoted to the directorship of Institute 28. Guo Dong, 5.

74. Over time, various research institutes split off from the Changchun institute as separate organs. Among them were the Xi'an Institute of Optical and Fine Mechanics for developing optical equipment used in nuclear tests, the Shanghai In-

stitute of Optical and Fine Mechanics for developing high-power laser devices for laser fusion, and the Chengdu Institute of Photoelectric Technology for applying photoelectricity to cinetheodolites for tracking and monitoring satellites and ICBMs. Zhang Jingfu, 81; Xiao Guangen; "Birth."

75. In addition to the large-sized cinetheodolite, Project 150 included a timing system (synchronizer), a triggering radar, a program installation, a reading device, and a data-processing control console.

76. Unless otherwise cited, this paragraph is based on Wang Daheng, 471; Zhang Jun, 383–84; Chen Bin et al., 102; and Qian Wuhuang, 433.

77. The photoelectric cinetheodolite can photograph a target as small as a TV set 300km away. Its synchronous filming with a speed of 200 photographs per second can record the collision of two pieces of a missile at these distances. "Birth"; Xie Guang, *Dangdai*, 2: 449.

78. Zou Jiahua, 217, 218, 224; Yang Guoyu, *Dangdai*, 652.

79. Xu Xueyan, 400; Huo Rusu, 3; Yang Fengzhang and Qun Ge, 10; Xu Zhimin, "Description," 3; Xu Zhimin, "China's Oceangoing," 15.

80. Unless otherwise cited, this and the next three paragraphs are based on Li Qi and Nie Li, 393–95; Su Kuoshan, "Birth," 30–31; Chen Youming, "Wise Decision," 17–18; Xu Xueyan, 400; Zhang Ming, "Interview," 4; and Zhou Xiao.

81. Nie's commission submitted the first of these reports, the "Report on the Oceangoing Range Instrumentation Ships," to the Central Military Commission for approval on July 18, hence the code name 718.

82. As a unit directly under the Central Military Commission and the State Council, the Project 718 Leading Group was a higher organ than a ministry.

83. Chen Youming concurrently held the post of director of the Nuclear-Powered Submarine Project Office. Li Zuopeng recommended Liang Jun, chief of staff of the Defense Science and Technology Commission, for director of the Project 718 Office. Zhou Enlai rejected Li's recommendation and made Liang deputy director instead. Liang was arrested in the post–Lin Biao purge, and Li Qi took over his position at the Project 718 Office.

84. Qiu Huizuo was an associate of Lin Biao. In his capacity as deputy chief of the General Staff and head of the PLA General Logistics Department, Qiu concurrently led both the National Defense Industry Leading Group and the Conventional Ordnance Leading Group.

85. Unless otherwise cited, this paragraph and the next are based on Wang Lichun, 508; Xu Zhimin, "Description," 2–3; Su Kuoshan, "Birth," 31, 32; Zhang Ming, "Interview," 4; Xu Xueyan, 400–401; and Li Qi and Nie Li, 394.

86. The next month, Chinese doctors diagnosed Zhou's illness as cancer. Gao Wenqian, 72.

87. Xu Xueyan was chief designer of the oceangoing instrumentation fleet and later became chief engineer at Institute 708. "Honor Roll," 1986; Li Qi and Nie Li, 394; Xu Xueyan, 400, 401; Xu Zhimin, "China's Oceangoing," 15; Xu Zhimin, "Description," 3; Huo Rusu, 3; Xu Wenliang, "Scientific City."

88. Li Qi and Nie Li, 394; Xu Xueyan, 400, 401; Xu Zhimin, "China's Oceangoing," 15; Xu Zhimin, "Description," 3; Huo Rusu, 3.

89. Li Yang, "Visit," 61–64; Wang Lichun, 507; Li Qi and Nie Li, 395. Some sources state that the Jiangnan Shipyard launched the two instrumentation ships in Dec. 1978. We believe the earlier date is correct. See Xu Wenliang, "*Distant Observer*"; Su Kuoshan, "Birth," 32; and Xu Zhimin, "Description," 2.

90. Unless otherwise cited, this paragraph and the next are based on Li Qi and Nie Li, 395; Su Kuoshan, "Birth," 32; Chen Bin et al., 102; Chen Liwei, 441; *Zhongguo Dianzi*, 6, 134, 407; and Wang Shiguang and Zhang Xuedong, 422.

91. As noted earlier, Institute 707 also developed the inertial navigation system for the 09 boats.

92. Liu Yin et al., 165–66; Yu Zhitian and Zhou Dong; "Comrade"; Zhi Yin, "Defense," 18, 22.

93. Guo Dong, 2–3; Su Kuoshan et al., "Report from the Units," 150.

94. Information on the mission of Institute 1028's team of specialists is based on "Honor Roll," 1987; *Zhongguo Dianzi*, 134; and Guo Dong, 2–4.

95. Zheng Qianli, "Close-ups," 260; Li Yang, "Three Victories"; Li Yang, "Technological Transformations"; Su Kuoshan and Li Yang.

96. China's instrumentation fleet consisted of two instrumentation ships (*Distant Observer* Nos. 1 and 2), two survey ships (*Sunflower* Nos. 5 and 10), two salvage vessels (J302, J506), two support ships (X615, X950), and three rescue tugboats (T154, T710, T830). Li Hong, 4; Wang Lichun, 507; Yang Guoyu, *Dangdai*, 639–40; Zhang Jun, 122–24.

97. Zhou Qing; Xu Wenliang, "*Distant Observers*"; Xu Zhimin, "China's Oceangoing," 14.

98. Zou Jiahua, 42, 169; "Military Topography," 2; Wang Youqi, "Officers"; Wang Youqi, "Army Topographers"; Liu Deming and Wang Youqi.

99. Mapping Brigade No. 1 had been set up by the General Staff's Bureau of Topography in 1954. It is currently headquartered in Tianjin. Deng Lifeng, 158; Wang Youqi, "How a Satellite," 65–66; Liao Shenghui et al.; Yi Ying et al.; Wang Youqi, "Heroes." In the late 1980s, over 30 ministry-level departments under the State Council and various provinces had units in charge of topography, and there were more than 270,000 people employed in that enterprise, counting those who manufactured topographic equipment. Zhao Dexin [4], 116, 117; Ni Zhongwen, 330; Yang Jian; "Remarkable Achievements."

100. Liu Ying and Dou Qi; Zhu Jinping; Wang Chuncai, 100; "Military Topography," 2. The Mapping Brigade of the Second Artillery Corps also contributed to the strategic weapons program. Guo Qingsheng and Kang Fashun; Wang Youqi, "China," 44.

101. Unless otherwise cited, this paragraph is based on Ai Ying and You Qi; Wang Chuncai, 81, 83, 84, 102–3; "Military Topography," 2; Liu Luyan; Wang Youqi, "Heroes"; Liao Shenghui et al.; and Wang Youqi, "Army Topographers."

102. Unless otherwise cited, information in this paragraph and the next two is from Li Jinting et al., 18; Zhang Jun, 148–49; Xie Guang, *Dangdai*, 1: 374–75; Li Yadan, "Description"; Liu Xing (2), 36; "Description"; and Liu Congjun, *Hangtian . . . Yuanshi*, 231–34. The quotation is from Li Jinting et al., 18.

103. As a naval unit under Base 23, the impact zone in Inner Mongolia was smaller in scale than other missile impact zones.

104. For information on the JL-1's silo-based launch tubes at Base 25, see Liu Shaoqiu and Lu Zhen, 5.

105. In his capacity as deputy secretary-general of the Central Military Commission, Zhang Aiping remained responsible for Project JL-1 even after the creation of the Commission of Science, Technology, and Industry for National Defense (COSTIND) in July 1982.

106. This paragraph is based on Yang Guoyu, *Dangdai*, 582, 583, 586, 595, 596; Zhang Jun, 149; Liu Xing (2), 36; and Chen Bin et al., 103.

107. Tian Zuocheng was Base 23's commander. Tian Zhenhuan was commander of the measurement corps under the Defense Science and Technology Commission. Unless otherwise cited, the information in this paragraph and the next is from Yang Guoyu, *Dangdai*, 650–51; *Renmin Ribao* and *Xinhua* Reporters, K8, K12; Liu Congjun, *Hangtian . . . Dashiji*, 183; and Liu Congjun, *Hangtian . . . Yuanshi*, 234–35. Xu Junlie's participation in the test is based on "Twenty-three." The quotation is from *Renmin Ribao* and *Xinhua* Reporters, K8.

108. By this time, China had built special transport and loading vehicles for moving large missiles. Xu Zhimin, "Creation."

109. Li Fucai, a graduate of the Harbin Military Engineering Institute, was later made a deputy to the Sixth National People's Congress because of his outstanding contributions to developing the software for the central computer. Unless otherwise cited, the information in this paragraph and the next is from Zhang Xinghua et al., 214–15, 217; *Haijun Shi*, 229–30; Yang Guoyu, *Dangdai*, 652; and *Renmin Ribao* and *Xinhua* Reporters, K10, K11.

110. Zhang Xinghua et al., 182–84; Jiang Rubiao et al., "China's No. 1."

111. From this order, we infer that the Golf had a crew of about 80. Information in the rest of this paragraph is from Shen Shungen, "China's Test," 3; and Zhang Xinghua et al., 181–82, 185.

112. We believe there were two submarine flotillas under the North China Sea Fleet, one (the 12th) operating out of Lüshun, Liaoning Province, and the other (the 22nd) out of Qingdao, Shandong Province. This paragraph is based on Cheng Zhong, 149; Yang Guoyu, *Dangdai*, 652; *Haijun Shi*, 229; Guo Xiangxing and Yi Hai, 80; and *Renmin Ribao* and *Xinhua* Reporters, K7, K8.

113. Shi Zongli had "majored" in SLBMs at the Submarine Institute. Zhu Yida, "Consideration."

114. Yang Guoyu, *Dangdai*, 654; "Announcement."

115. Wang Lichun, 508; Yang Guoyu, *Dangdai*, 651.

116. This and the next paragraph are based on Yang Guoyu, *Dangdai*, 654; *Haijun Shi*, 230; Zhang Xinghua et al., 211–12; and Liu Congjun, *Hangtian . . . Yuanshi*, 236.

117. By 1982, Baoding Radio Factory No. 14 had built a new road-mobile telemetry processing system (code-named YJS-2) for the 9182 test program. Xie Feng et al., 412–13.

118. Unless otherwise cited, the information in this and the next paragraph is from Li Yadan et al., "Description," 47–48; Li Yadan, "Description"; Yang Guoyu, *Dangdai*, 596–97, 654; *Haijun Shi*, 230; Liu Congjun, *Hangtian . . . Dashiji*, 192; and Liu Congjun, *Hangtian . . . Yuanshi*, 236.

119. In Dec. 1968, when the Chinese conducted a full-range flight test of the DF-3 missile from Base 25, Beijing had to depend principally on the base for the result. Zhou Enlai made four phone calls to the base within the first two hours and still could not get any accurate information. Starting in 1978 and continuing into the next decade, the Chinese built a modern command center in Beijing for overseeing strategic weapons tests. Bie Yixun and Su Kuoshan; "Commission."

120. This paragraph and the next two are based on Yang Guoyu, *Dangdai*, 654–65; Zhang Xinghua et al., 212–14; *Renmin Ribao* Reporters; Liu Xing (2), 36–37; *Xinhua* Reporters, K3–K7; *Renmin Ribao* and *Xinhua* Reporters, K7–K12; and Wen Jiaqi, 147.

121. In 1982, Li Guiren had 17 years of submarine service under his belt. In those 17 years, he had reportedly mastered 17 disciplines needed for launching a missile from a submarine. *Renmin Ribao* and *Xinhua* Reporters, K7–K12.

122. Li Yadan et al., "Ode"; Xu Wenliang, *"Distant Observer."*

123. Wang Lichun, 508; Zhu Bin, 8–10. For a photograph of the splashdown, see Yang Guoyu, *Dangdai*, picture No. 99.

124. Reports after the DF-5's flight test in 1980 and the JL-1's in 1988 stressed the recovery of the data capsule. Since no mention of the capsule was made after the JL-1's first test from the Golf submarine, we believe that it was either lost or badly damaged. Unless otherwise cited, information in this paragraph is from *Renmin Ribao* Reporters; *Xinhua* Reporters, K4; Zhang Xinghua et al., 220, 225; and Yang Guoyu, *Dangdai*, 654–55.

125. Yang Guoyu, *Dangdai*, 654–55. Between late July and mid-Oct., Huang had lost more than 24 pounds from overwork. Yang Xuequan; Li Yadan, "Description"; Li Yadan et al., "Description," 47.

126. "Congratulatory Telegram"; "Zhang Aiping."

127. This paragraph and the next are based on Ge Qiguang et al., 16; and Liu Congjun, *Hangtian . . . Yuanshi*, 239, 240.

128. The Chinese did not achieve the precise synchronization of all electronic equipment in their strategic weapons tests until 1990. Yu Shimao.

129. The two 2,000KW long-wave pulse transmitters were built by the Beijing Broadcast Equipment Plant. *Shaanxi*, picture No. 2; Liu Yin et al., 673. For information on the long-wave timing service provided by the Shaanxi Astronomical Observatory, see Li Yang and He Shitian, 58–59; Yuan Chang'an; Dong Lin, 117–22; and "Completion of the Construction."

130. Yu Qingtian and Qian Chengbao.

131. The successful tests of the two DF-21s took place on May 20 and May 31, 1985. This paragraph and the next three are based on Zhang Jun, original draft, Chap. 6: 1, 31; Xie Guang, *Dangdai*, 1: 379–81; Liu Congjun, *Hangtian . . . Yuanshi*, 242–43; and Liu Congjun, *Hangtian . . . Dashiji*, 213, 217, 225, 229.

132. Wan Xiang.

133. Li Yang, "Description."

134. Zhai Huisheng and Su Kuoshan; Li Yadan et al., "Ode"; Su Kuoshan, "Successful Trial"; Xu Wenliang, "Successful Trial."

135. With this and other measures to repair the defects found throughout the test system, the accuracy of tracking and measurement, as well as weather reporting, increased enough that the total number of support vessels assigned to the tests could be reduced. Li Yang and Su Kuoshan; Li Yang, "Technological Transformations"; "Remarkable Accomplishment," 24; Zhai Huisheng; Kou Chengzhen and Li Yang; Zheng Qianli, "Deep Love," 18.

136. Xie Guang, *Dangdai*, 1: 382–83.

137. On the tying up of the nation's communication lines by the strategic weapons tests, see Qian Xuesen, "Premier Zhou," 289.

138. On the looting of military installations in the 1980s, see "Task"; Qiu Mingquan and Zhu Zhenlu; Liu Xinru, "Protect"; "Military Calls"; and "Our Country Will Adopt."

139. Wang Yucai and Song Yunda. For information on the subsequent joint efforts taken by the military and local authorities to tighten security, see "Beijing."

140. The launch of the AsiaSat-1 in April 1990, for example, was impeded when a group of peasants stole five main communication cables at the Xichang Satellite Launch Center (Base 27). Peng Guangfu, the chief culprit, was sentenced to death. "Chief Criminal."

141. Liu Boluo, "Premier Zhou and the CCP," 133; Deng Yingchao; Qian Xuesen, "Premier Zhou," 288–89.

142. In 1987, the military imposed special measures circumscribing the movement of foreign visitors. See, for example, Zhang Zhongpei and Zhang Hua.

143. During the preparations for flight-testing Batch 03, Beijing created the State Bureau for Maintaining Secrecy. Gong Shuangyin. The government later issued the "Law of the People's Republic of China on Guarding State Secrets" and the "PLA Regulations on Maintaining Secrecy," and tightened security in all military units. Deng Buping.

144. This paragraph is based on Qian Xuesen, "Premier Zhou," 291. For a discussion of the organizational changes of the period, see Lewis, Hua, and Xue.

145. Unless otherwise cited, this paragraph and the next are based on Jiang Rubiao et al., "Visit"; Jiang Rubiao, "Sketch," 2; Cheng Wang, intro. to picture 22; and Xi Qixin, 3.

146. Du Yongguo had graduated from the Navigation Department of the Submarine Institute in Qingdao and served as a navigator on a 33-class (Romeo) submarine. Promoted to captain in 1981, he was jumped to commander in Oct. 1988, following the successful JL-1 test. His picture appears on the back cover of *Jianchuan Zhishi*, No. 12, 1988. In the Chinese navy, the captains of a conventional submarine, a nuclear-powered attack submarine, and a nuclear-powered ballistic-missile submarine are of equivalent rank to a battalion commander, a regiment commander, and a deputy division commander, respectively. Based on Min Guoku, 48. On the Submarine Institute and training organs, see Lewis and Xue, *Military Readiness*.

147. Jiang Rubiao et al., "China's No. 1."

148. "China Will Launch."

149. The set of regulations that charges military security units and public security troops with ensuring security during nuclear and missile tests is entitled "Rules on Ensuring Safety and Security in Large-Scale Scientific Tests for National Defense." Jiang Weisen.

150. Unless otherwise cited, information in this paragraph is from Jiang Rubiao, "Sketch," 2; and Zhang Xinghua et al., 207–9.

151. See Jiang Rubiao et al., "Visit"; and Xi Qixin, 3.

152. On the launch date, Sept. 15, see Xie Guang, *Dangdai*, 2: 539; Zou Dayi and Cao Huanrong; and "Our Country Achieves." Unless otherwise cited, information in this paragraph and the next is from Xie Guang, *Dangdai*, 1: 383–84; Zou Dayi and Cao Huanrong; and Jiang Rubiao et al., "Visit."

153. As commander of Base 23, Wang Huique was also in charge of the on-the-spot command post. Huang Caihong, "New Development of the Chinese," 4; "Successful Launch."

154. Qian Cansong. This paragraph is based on Yang Biao and Huang Gangzhou; and Huang Caihong and Cao Guoqiang, "Eyewitness."

155. Li Yang, "Three Victories."

156. "Successful Launch."

157. Jiang Rubiao, "Sketch," 2.

Chapter Nine

1. See, for example, Friedman, Chap. 18.
2. See, for example, Rong Zhi, "Big Powers' Military Strategies," 73.
3. See Lewis and Xue, *China Builds*, esp. Chap. 9.
4. Lewis and Xue, *Military Readiness*.
5. On the traditional aspects of modern Chinese strategy, see Lin Chong-pin; and Tao Hanzhang, *Sun Tzu's Art of War*.
6. Good examples of Mao's writing in this respect are Mao [7]; and Mao [3].
7. Xu Xiangqian, "Heighten Vigilance," 48. Marshal Xu was one of Mao's leading generals and the PRC's first chief of the General Staff.
8. Mao [7], 134.
9. The alleged apostates included at least four of the nation's top military leaders: Peng Dehuai (defense minister, 1954–59), Luo Ruiqing (chief of the General Staff, 1959–65), He Long (vice-chairman of the Central Military Commission, 1959–66), and Lin Biao (defense minister and Mao's heir apparent, 1959–71).
10. Quoted in Tai Ming Cheung, "Trends."
11. See Lewis and Xue, *China Builds*, Chaps. 2, 3.
12. Academy of Military Science, *Zhongguo Renmin Jiefangjun Liushi Nian Dashiji*, 531, 532–33.
13. In Nov. 1955, the three armed services conducted large-scale counter-invasion operations on Liaodong Peninsula in a simulated nuclear environment. The next year, PLA combat units began conducting such combined operations in other regions. Academy of Military Science, *Zhongguo Renmin Jiefangjun Liushi Nian Dashiji*, 553; Zhang Zongxun, 443. In the same year, Chief of the General Staff Su Yu also ordered improvements of defenses against nuclear attack. Han Huaizhi and Tan Jingqiao, 1: 54.
14. Ye Jianying, acting head of the PLA General Department for Training and Supervision, repeatedly called for training troops under "modern conditions." But it was only in Dec. 1959 that he first spoke of a "People's War under modern conditions." Zhang Zongxun, 443; Mo Yang, 7. On the definition of People's War and its impact on strategy and tactics under "modern conditions," see the comments of Nie Rongzhen and Xu Xiangqian in Song Shilun, *Zhongguo*, 2: 876–78.
15. Zhang Jiayu, "Development," 29–30.
16. As late as 1977, for example, we still find the former chief of the General Staff discussing ways to wage a People's War against a superpower in a full-scale conventional war or even a nuclear war. See Su Yu.
17. See, for example, Yang Yong; and "All of Us."
18. Nie Quanlin, 141.
19. For brief information on this combined-forces exercise, see "[PLA Units]."
20. Deng Xiaoping [1], 372.
21. Qin Weidong, "Zhang Aiping," 11; Guo Shouhang, 8, 9; Zhang Qinsheng et al., "Consideration."
22. Deng Xiaoping [3], 249.
23. In 1985, Deng Xiaoping reaffirmed his repeatedly expressed view that China needed a prolonged period of peace to build its economy: "It will be impossible to achieve the four socialist modernizations [of agriculture, industry, national defense, and science and technology] without a peaceful environment. Accordingly, we hope not to go to war for at least 20 years. We even hope not to go

to war for 70 years." "Deng Xiaoping Talks Freely," 9–10. See also "Deng Xiaoping Talks About Preserving," 9; Liu Huinian, "Executive Vice-Chairman," 10; and Tao Bojun, "Some Ideas," 2–3.

24. "Beginning." See also companion articles by Liu Huinian and Xiong Zheng-yan; and Yang Shangkun, "Building."

25. For a typical discussion of the reasons for the reduction of the armed forces, see Zhang Taiheng. On Nov. 7, 1986, Premier Zhao Ziyang further pointed out, "We hope to improve the quality of weapons and equipment and raise their tech-nological standards by reducing the army's numbers." "China Updates."

26. He Zhengwen, 250; Yuan Houchun, 6–7. For events on the eve of and after the enlarged session of the military commission in May–June 1985, see Ai Lingyao, 76. The cut disproportionately hit the officer corps, eliminating 450,000 officers of division commander rank and below as against 550,000 rank and file. Liu Guanxue and Lu Wenqi; Wu Hongye.

27. Pan Shiying, "Historical Understanding."

28. Jiang Cheng and Guo Liyun. On the impact of this and other reforms on the PLA's combat readiness, see Qin Weidong, "Military Reform"; and Tao Bojun, "Understanding," 28.

29. At the same time, Yang appealed for accelerated research on military strat-egy. See Gai Yumin, K21–K22; Li Wei, K4; and "Yang Dezhi's Speech."

30. At this time, he set out a 12-character guiding principle for the CPV: *chijiu zuozhan, jiji fangyu, lunfan canzhan* (wage a protracted war, adopt an active de-fense strategy, and send fresh troops [to Korea] in rotation). That principle re-mained in force through the end of the war. Tan Jingqiao, 436–37; Yang Chengwu, 50; Shi Yan, "My Impressions"; Song Shilun, *Zhongguo*, 1: 631, 2: 1218.

31. Jiang Kejun, 310.

32. Apparently disgruntled by Zhou Enlai's increasing stature in the army, Mao relieved him of his duties as overseer of the military commission's daily affairs in July 1952. Four years later, he removed Zhou from the post of commission vice-chairman. Deng Lifeng, 7, 262; Qi Shengping, 3.

33. Unless otherwise cited, this paragraph is based on Zheng Wenhan, 3.

34. Lei Yuanshen, 226; Zhi Shaozeng, 52; Yan Jingtang, 58.

35. Lin Yunhui et al., 449; Zheng Wenhan, 3; Fu Shangkui, 10.

36. Jiang Kejun, 310. Peng Dehuai emphasized that future wars should be fought on the traditional principles of strategic defensive and operational offen-sives: strategic protracted warfare with quick decisive battles, positional warfare, and mobile warfare. Zhang Zongxun, 444–45.

37. Lin Yunhui et al., 451.

38. Zuo Ying, 8–9.

39. Mao reportedly made this statement in April 1969, at the first session of the Ninth CCP Central Committee. Unless otherwise cited, this paragraph and the next are based on Liao Guoliang et al., 591–92; and Jiang Kejun, 310–11.

40. The Chinese defined "fortifications" as fortified cities, and from studies of Soviet actions in the early phase of the Second World War, were concerned most of all with defending their principal cities. See Lin Boye et al., 240–42.

41. Luo Tongsong and Fan Hao.

42. Mi Zhenyu and Chen Weimin, 93, 96; Zhang Chengang et al., 46, 47, 48.

43. Liao Guoliang et al., 600. Some were less sanguine about the nuclear threat.

Gen. Zhang Zhen, for example, urged his strategists at the National Defense University to conduct research on a full-scale "conventional war under the condition of nuclear deterrence." He considered this the most likely form of the next world war. Unless otherwise cited, this paragraph and the next are based on Zhang Zhen; and *Zhanlüe Xue*, 76–77.

44. Nie Quanlin, 158, 159; Liao Guoliang et al., 600.

45. Liu Jushao, 25; Liu Shengjun and Wang Fengju; Wang Yuxiang et al., 75–78; Zhang Qinsheng et al., "Research," 15–16. For a discussion of the weapon requirements for border wars and medium-scale conventional wars, see Liu Huaqiu, *China*.

46. For Chinese strategists' estimation of future conflicts with Vietnam and India, see Chen Kehou, 109–10; Si Yanwen, "Naval Military"; Tang Fuquan; Wei Chuan, 28; and Xin Si, 26–27. See also Goncharov, "Chinese Concept," 56; and Tai Ming Cheung, "Goodbye," 21.

47. Chen Kehou, 115–17.

48. For a discussion of the types of war in which China might become embroiled, see Long Jize, 139–40.

49. See, for example, Zhang Huairui and Zhu Hengxing, 21–24.

50. In an interview, President Yang Shangkun appeared to belittle the relevance of American military might to his country: "The model [of the Gulf War] is not universal. It cannot, at least, be applied in a country like China, which has a lot of mountains, forests, valleys and rivers. Another characteristic of this war is that the multinational forces faced a very weak enemy." "United States," 44.

51. Quoted in Pan Shiying, "Have a Sober Understanding."

52. See "Strategic Research"; Li Bingyan and Zeng Guangjun; Qi Changming; Zhu Songchun; Xu Jingyue, "Defense"; and Wu Chunqiu, 6.

53. Mao [7], 147, n. 2.

54. The Chinese have reorganized their ground forces in recent years, making the group army (*jituanjun*) the largest independent operational unit in peacetime, and the front army (*fangmianjun*), comprising several group armies, responsible for military affairs at the theater level (i.e., in each of the nation's seven military regions) in war. On the relations between the group and front armies, see Han Yongfa and Yu Guidong.

55. See "International Symposium"; She Shui and Xiao Yue; Xie Guoliang; Huo Yinzhang; Li Bingyan and Sun Jing; and Sun Kaitai.

56. Wu Chunqiu and Dong Lingyun, 471–72.

57. Based on Nie Quanlin, 162.

58. This paragraph is based on Li Jianghe and Hou Aiping, 9, 10.

59. Zhang Qinsheng et al., "Consideration."

60. Wu Chunqiu and Dong Lingyun, 471–72.

61. By the mid-1980s, the navy had pushed the outer limit of China's coastal waters (*jinhai*) to 200nm. Wang Hewen.

62. Yang Guoyu, *Dangdai*, 14; Academy of Military Science, *Zhongguo Renmin Jiefangjun Dashiji*, 303.

63. Yang Guoyu, *Dangdai*, 5, calculates that, from 1840 to 1949, foreign countries invaded China more than 470 times. For a similar calculation, see Li Wen, 23.

64. *Haijun Shi*, 329; Yang Guoyu, *Dangdai*, 39, 683. On Oct. 25, 1949, right after the failure of the Quemoy invasion, the General Staff stated that "without the

coordination of the navy, it was impossible to occupy Jinmen [Quemoy] in the near future." That night, Mao wrote the quoted instruction. Guo Fuwen and Cao Bao-jian, 74.

65. Theoretical Study Group; Yang Guoyu, *Dangdai*, 39, 688.

66. Bai Kemin, 4. We differ with the interpretation of David Muller to the extent that he implies Soviet doctrine dictated China's naval doctrine. He states: "All thinking on the development and employment of naval forces imported from the Soviet Union to China was strictly Young School [of Soviet naval strategy]. . . . And certainly the Chinese were amenable; the Young School of naval force development and employment was made to order for the newly established People's Republic. . . . The components of Chinese maritime strategy in the 1970s were a long and vulnerable coast, a weak economy, a perception of seaborne threat from both Taiwan and the United States, the PLA's land-oriented military tradition, and Soviet Young School naval doctrine." Muller, *China*, 49–50.

67. *Haijun Shi*, 31–32; Yang Guoyu, *Dangdai*, 41–42.

68. Yang Guoyu, *Dangdai*, 40, 689; *Haijun Shi*, 31, 329.

69. Bai Kemin, 4; Yang Guoyu, *Dangdai*, 40, 689, 692–93; *Haijun Shi*, 31, 329.

70. In 1956, the navy's first Party congress resolved that the building of the navy "must accord with the guiding principle that emphasizes the development of the air force and air defense forces and provides for the development of an appropriate-sized navy." Unless otherwise cited, this and the next paragraph are based on *Haijun Shi*, 37, 330–31; and Yang Guoyu, *Dangdai*, 687.

71. Lei Huajian, 26–28; Yu Shifu, 34. This conclusion is echoed in L. Bruce Swanson's analysis of the "seeds of failure" of the naval development of this period. See Swanson, 97–102. For collections of materials on the history of the Chinese navy in the Qing and Republican periods, see Zhang Xia et al.; and Yang Zhiben, *Zhonghua*.

72. This quotation can be found in Yang Guoyu, *Dangdai*, 5, 7–8; and *Haijun Shi*, 8. For Chinese Communist views on the destruction of the North China Sea Fleet in 1894, see Yang Zhiben and Xu Hua; Xu Hua; and Lei Huajian, 28.

73. The information in this and the next paragraph is from Nie Fengzhi et al., 2, 25, 26, 38, 39; *Haijun Shi*, 124–32; and Yang Guoyu, *Dangdai*, 77, 212–14. For other aspects of these decisions concerning the offshore islands, see Lewis and Xue, *China Builds*, Chap. 2. On the increase in the navy budget, see Zhang Han-cheng, 323–24. The 1953 budget was 5.8 times larger than the 1950 budget.

74. *Haijun Shi*, 99–115; Yang Guoyu, *Dangdai*, 12–14; "Life of Comrade Xiao Jinguang," 496; Gao Zhenjia, 347. For a discussion of some aspects of the Nationalist blockade and its consequences, see Lewis and Xue, *China Builds*, 22–27.

75. Tian Zhenhuan, 396; Liu Daosheng, 283. In the battle for Yijiangshan Island and the Dachens in the winter of 1954–55, the navy proved the worth of ambush tactics when it sank the Nationalist escort vessel *Taiping* and the gunboat *Tongting*. On the use of guerrilla tactics at sea in the 1950s and 1960s, see Zhang Yimin; Yang Guoyu, *Dangdai*, 216–18, 380–91; *Haijun Shi*, 128–29, 155–61; and Bai Kemin, 4.

76. One treatment of this "Great Strategy Debate" is in Swanson, 233–36.

77. Proletarian revolutionaries. For a translation of this *Renmin Ribao* article, see *Xinhua*, Sept. 16, 1967, in FBIS: Communist China, Sept. 18, 1967, ccc4–ccc12.

78. By 1974, the Gang of Four had formed a radical faction in the navy under the political commissar, Su Zhenhua, thereby isolating the commander, Xiao Jinguang. Xiao later became a mere figurehead. Xiao Jinguang, *Xiao Jinguang Huiyilu*, 2: 360–63; Xiao Jinguang, "Reminiscences," 14; Zhu Zhongli, *Nanyi*, 147; Zhu Zhongli, *Liming*, 433.

79. Modern Chinese history is filled with debates over maritime-versus-continentalist strategies. See Swanson, 1–2, 83–84, 101–2. Swanson writes: "Chinese naval history over the past millennium has been characterized by two great cultural entities: continental, Confucianist China and maritime China." The theme of his book concerns the "conflict between Chinese continentalism and the maritime spirit."

80. Unless otherwise cited, the information in this paragraph and the next is from Peng Ziqiang, 2, 3; and Yang Guoyu, *Dangdai*, 248–49.

81. On Oct. 3, 1971, Mao appointed Ye Jianying head of the 10-member Administrative Meeting that handled the military commission's daily affairs. The other nine members were Zhang Chunqiao, Xie Fuzhi, Li Xiannian, Li Desheng, Ji Dengkui, Wang Dongxing, Chen Shiqu, Zhang Caiqian, and Liu Xianquan. Academy of Military Science, *Zhongguo Renmin Jiefangjun Liushi Nian Dashiji*, 648–49; Yan Jingtang, 58–59.

82. The approximate maximum range of an ICBM can be calculated by conducting high-low ballistic tests over its partial range and can be estimated from other tests. But full-range tests are required to verify its accuracy, though the gravity corrections for the trajectory to actual targets can only be estimated. Information from an American specialist, 1991.

83. *Xinhua*, March 14, 1977, E1-E2.

84. Yet in May 1975, Mao supported the building of the navy and opposed the radicals on this issue. Lu Qiming, 7; Theoretical Study Group.

85. On the change in China's naval strategy in the 1980s, see Gao Zhenjia, 347; and "Life of Comrade Xiao Jinguang," 496–97.

86. Liu Huaqing, "Build"; *Haijun Shi*, 329; Yang Guoyu, *Dangdai*, 708–9.

87. Wang Ganyi; Yang Guoyu, *Dangdai*, 464, 708–9, 718.

88. Lei Ming; Huang Caihong, "Visit," 2; Du Zhongwei et al., 9.

89. Zhang Huairui and Zhu Hengxing, 21.

90. On the PRC's earlier fears in this regard, see, for example, Theoretical Study Group.

91. Yang Guoyu, *Dangdai*, 679–80. For similar comments, see Xiao Jun, "Chinese Navy," 2.

92. Du Zhongwei et al., 8, 9. For other articles on China's thinking about seapower, see Liu Huaqing, "Build"; Xiao Jun, "Return," esp. 5; Yang Zhiben, "Chinese Nation"; Cai Wenyi; Song Puxuan and Cai Yunhua; and Lei Ming.

93. Jia Wenxian et al., 9.

94. The discussion of the navy's four missions in this and the next paragraph is based on Yang Guoyu, *Dangdai*, 243, 689; Lü Liping; and Bai Kemin, 4.

95. Xiao Jun, "Chinese Navy," 2; Yang Guoyu, *Dangdai*, 523–25.

96. Liu Xinru, "Interview"; Hu Xiaoen and Peng Zhonghuai; Ren Qimin; Jia Wenxian et al. On the navy's mission to protect Chinese territory, see, for example, Shen Changjing and Xiao Jun, 4–5; Kan Shiying and He Delai; Sheng Geng; and Zhang Nan.

97. For information on this Sino-Vietnamese sea battle, see Huang Caihong

and Guo Diancheng; Zhang Ze'nan, "Guards," 2–3; Wei Chuan, 28; and Xiao Jun, "Return," 4–5. On Chinese concerns about Vietnam's geographical advantage in the South China Sea, see Yang Zhiben, "Chinese Nation"; Xin Si, 27; Wei Chuan; Ling Yu, "Secretly Build"; and Song Lijun, 16.

98. Song Puxuan and Cai Yunhua; "Threat." The latter is a translation of an article by U.S. Adm. Ronald J. Hays. The journal in which it appears, *Xiandai Junshi*, is a monthly sponsored by COSTIND.

99. On the improvement of Sino-Vietnamese relations, see Wang Rongjiu and Yang Mu; and Wang Rongjiu.

100. For instance, whereas the Spratlys are about 1,150km, 1,480km, and 1,700km, respectively, from the naval bases at Yulin, in Hainan Province, and at Zhanjiang and Guangzhou, in Guangdong Province, Vietnam's two key naval bases, Cam Ranh Bay and Da Nang, are just 500km and 900km away. Xiao Jun, "Key Projects," 3, 4; "Mainland China Has Raised"; Xin Si, 27; Yang Zhiben, "Chinese Nation"; Wei Chuan.

101. Zhang Ze'nan, "New Developments," 2.

102. Capable of firing the C-601 antiship missile, the H-6D (B-6D) has a maximum combat radius of 1,800km. For detailed information, see Yu Fei; and Zhang Heping and Zhang Guorong. The closest landing fields for the H-6D are in Guangdong and Hainan provinces.

103. Based on Xin Si, 27; Wei Chuan; Ling Yu, "Secretly Build"; and Song Lijun, 16.

104. The medium-range DF-25 is a two-stage, solid-propellant, surface-to-surface ballistic missile for tactical operations. It uses inertial guidance. The missile is designed to be stored in semi-hardened launch sites and can be trucked to launch sites far from its storage areas. The Ministry of Aerospace Industry has assigned the First and Fourth academies to the DF-25 program. Although the DF-21/JL-1's maximum range is almost the same, it only has a payload of 600kg, too small to destroy the enemy strongpoints on the Nansha Islands; hence, the need for a missile with a payload of 2,000kg. Unless otherwise cited, the information in the rest of this paragraph is from Lewis and Hua. On the possible conventional use of strategic missiles, see Lu Haozhong et al., 291–92; and Wang Zhenping.

105. The navy now has over 100 military ports, over 10,000 containers, and several large-scale storage facilities with which to provide oceangoing logistic support. Huang Caihong, "Tonnage"; Zhang Ze'nan, "New Developments," 3. On *Dongyun 615*, one of the first of a new class of supply ships, see Zhang Ze'nan, "Dongyun," 32–33.

106. "Chinese Navy." The head of the Naval Logistics Department stated that the navy could "guarantee the supply of fuel, water, staple foods, and other foodstuffs, as well as materials and equipment when we send a squadron to the Pacific Ocean or the Indian Ocean." "Our Navy."

107. See, for example, Xue Jianhua.

108. The quotes in this paragraph can be found in Lu Keng, *Hu Yaobang*, 15–18; and Lu Keng, "Visit," 6–7.

109. Muller, "Chinese Blockade," is one of the most authoritative articles on this subject. See also He Zhenming.

110. Guo Xiangxing, "Interview," 6. See also Xu Shiming, 73.

111. Some of these exercises were meant to train PLA combat units in a nuclear environment. Lü Liping; Yang Guoyu, *Dangdai*, 101–2, 273–74, 472–76; *Haijun*

Shi, 335. Both the Guangzhou and the Shenyang military region conducted several large exercises testing quick-reaction capabilities in anti-landing and anti-air operations in the late 1980s. Zhu Dacheng and He Delai; Li Zhichen and Hong Heping.

112. The Chinese have paid particular attention to articles by Soviet writers on the Red Army's campaign in Manchuria at the end of the Second World War. See Vasilevsky.

113. Zhang Huairui and Zhu Hengxing. For similar proposals to cope with surprise attacks against China's coastal areas, see Jia Wenxian et al., 9; Liu Huaqing, "Build"; and Chai Limin.

114. Xiao Jun, "Key Projects," 3. On the emphasis on China's economic development along the coast, see Chen Xiaoxing, 39–41.

115. See, for example, Wang Hewen; Shen Shungen, "Visits," 2; and Bai Kemin, 4.

116. Based on Tang Fuquan; Huang Caihong, "Visit," 2; Xiao Jun, "Key Projects," 3, 4; and Bai Kemin, 4. The change from a coastal defense to an offshore defense strategy reflects the resolution of the long-standing debate on whether greater importance should be attached to fighting the enemy at sea or repulsing his landing operations. See Fan Zhongyi; Song Puxuan and Cai Yunhua; Lei Huajian, 28; and Yu Shifu.

117. Xiao Jun, "Key Projects," 2–4; Bai Kemin, 4.

118. Shen Shungen, "Oceangoing Capability"; Shen Shungen, "Visits," 2, 3.

119. Each navy base (see Chap. 5, note 136) can order combat assignments and thereby determine the actual defense perimeter. The navy from the late 1980s began carrying out a 12-character operational guideline for control of the total defense perimeter: *kuaisu fanying, guangfan jidong, zhengti zuozhan* (quick reaction in case of need, maneuver swiftly in vast sea areas, and conduct combined operations by various arms). See, for example, Chen Fangyou and Chai Limin.

120. On the priorities for naval spending through the year 2000, see Xiao Jun, "Description"; Wang Hewen; Xiao Jun, "Key Projects," 3, 4; and Bai Kemin. See also Liu Huaqing, "Key," 17. Adm. Liu Huaqing, vice-chairman of the Central Military Commission, is currently responsible for the commission's daily affairs.

121. Du Zhongwei et al., 9. See also Chen Shoukang.

Chapter Ten

1. Liu Huaqiu, "Sun Zi's Art of War," 75; Ma Lütian et al., 11. The translation is ours; for another translation, see Tao Hanzhang, *Sun Tzu's Art of War*, 99.

2. Song Shilun, "Military Science," 17; Zhang Jiayu, "Development," 25.

3. Mao [4], 181. Most of Zhu De's important writings on People's War are found in his *Selected Works*. See esp. 141–90.

4. In the 1950s, Mao was paying ever more attention to the nuclear "gun." On Jan. 15, 1955, Mao said: "Sooner or later, we would have had to pay attention to it [atomic bomb]. Now, it is time for us to pay attention to it." With these words, he launched the bomb project. Li Jue et al., 14, 21; Qian Sanqiang.

5. Mao [5], 288.

6. Zhang Jiayu, "On the Nuclear," 2; Zhang Jinxi and Wang Xiancun, 4.

7. *Nie Rongzhen Huiyilu*, 814.

8. China has not relied heavily on nuclear weapons for its defense and does not consider them the main basis for its deterrent strategy. See, for example, Chen

Chongbei et al., 214–16; Rong Zhi, "Big Powers' Military Strategies," 73; and Nie Quanlin, 196–201.

9. Wang Shouyun, 26–27; Zhang Jinxi and Wang Xiancun, 4; Shi Yan, "Creation," 48; Quan Yanchi, *Zhongguo*, 20.

10. Mao reportedly gave first priority to keeping the nuclear arsenal small and effective. Shi Yan, "Creation," 48.

11. See Zhang Jinxi and Wang Xiancun, 4. Unless otherwise cited, this discussion of Mao's principles for building China's nuclear arsenal is based largely on the most important official statements on nuclear weapons: "Statement" [Oct. 16, 1964]; "Press Communiqué on Our Country's Successful Test"; and "Press Communiqué on the Successful Detonation." For a discussion of the most famous of Mao's quotes, see Lewis and Xue, *China Builds*, 66–69.

12. For the statement of the Chinese government, see *Break*.

13. China's public statements have tended to blur the nature of its second-strike policy. For example, when Sino-Soviet border conflicts were escalating in 1969, Beijing stated: "If a handful of war maniacs dare to . . . make a surprise attack on China's strategic places, . . . Chinese people will . . . resort to a revolutionary war to eliminate the aggressive war." "Statement" [Oct. 7, 1969].

14. Guo Hualun, "Study," 13. China did not develop low-yield weapons and nuclear-armed tactical missiles (such as the DF-15/M-9) until the late 1980s. By the 1970s, it had retrofitted several aircraft (H-6, H-5, and Q-5) for delivering nuclear warheads in theater operations. Duan Zijun, *Dangdai*, 170, 175, 186. For a discussion of China's tactical missile program, see Lewis and Hua.

15. Based on Li Jue et al., 59–64, 275–91.

16. Based on Wang Shouyun, 26–27; Ma Lütian et al., 11; Zhang Jiayu, "On the Nuclear," 7; and Chen Chongbei et al., 214. For a Western work with the same perspective, see Kemp.

17. On the "small but inclusive" principle as Mao's guideline for China's strategic weapons program, see, for example, Deng Sanrui, 167.

18. Shi Yan, "Creation," 48; Zhang Jinxi and Wang Xiancun, 5.

19. Zhang Qinsheng et al., "Consideration"; Zhang Jinxi and Wang Xiancun, 4.

20. Based on Zhang Jiayu, "On the Nuclear," 7. As the author states, Mao and his colleagues held that only when China possessed nuclear weapons would it be able to pursue the no-first-use policy and have the right to advance a proposal on its own initiative for banning and destroying the existing stockpiles of nuclear weapons. For a similar interpretation, see Xiao Jun, "Chinese Navy," 3. As early as Dec. 1964, Zhou Enlai pointed out, "We should have sophisticated [weapons]. Only when we possess strategic missiles and nuclear weapons will we not have to use missiles and nuclear weapons. If we don't have missiles, imperialism will surely use missiles." Zhang Jiayu, "On the Nuclear," 7. On the use of "minimal means" to stage a nuclear counterattack, see *Nie Rongzhen Huiyilu*, 814.

21. Based on Su Yu. Gen. Su stated that when both sides had nuclear weapons, only the side whose industries and population were highly concentrated was truly vulnerable. "Our economic construction," he concluded, "cannot therefore be destroyed by nuclear weapons." See also Rong Zhi, "Big Powers' Military Strategies," 73; and Nie Quanlin, 197.

22. Quoted in Xia Zhengnan, 111.

23. "Our Country Has Built a Relatively Integrated Defense"; "China's Stra-

tegic Missile"; "Our Army's Strategic Missile," p. 3; Xiao Xingbo. Xiao's book is the most authoritative work on civil defense and massive population evacuation from a Chinese perspective.

24. Lewis and Xue, *China Builds*, 214.

25. Chen Dechun and Shi Zhibao; Han Yongfa and Yu Guidong; Shi Yan, "Creation," 49; Ma Lütian et al., 11; Zhang Jinxi and Wang Xiancun, 5.

26. Nie Quanlin, 199. At a 1986 Central Military Commission meeting, Yang Shangkun explicitly referred to the concept of "our army's limited strategic deterrent forces." *Ibid.*, 194, 200. On China's strategy of "limited nuclear deterrence," see also Chen Chongbei et al., 214–15. Other strategists would rather define China's current nuclear strategy as *youxian he baofu* (limited nuclear retaliation). See Zhang Jianzhi, K29-K33; and Ma Lütian et al., 11. We choose to use "limited nuclear deterrence."

27. Li Fumin and Li Dunsong, 51; Ma Lütian et al., 11; Shi Yan, "Creation," 48; Zhang Jinxi and Wang Xiancun, 5.

28. Nie Quanlin, 194. Zhang Aiping made this statement in Dec. 1986 at an enlarged meeting of the Central Military Commission. Li Jianghe and Hou Aiping, 9.

29. On uncertainty, see Zhang Jianzhi. The Chinese closely guard the information on their strategic weapons programs in part to reinforce the uncertainty that they deem essential to deterrence.

30. For example, China deployed the DF series missiles (DF-2, DF-2A, DF-3, DF-3A, DF-4, DF-5, DF-21, DF-21A) with different ranges, and recently developed short- and medium-range missiles, such as the M-9/DF-15, M-18, M-11/DF-11, and DF-25.

31. Chen Chongbei et al., 214; Nie Quanlin, 205–6; Shi Yan, "Creation," 48. Only the chairman of the Central Military Commission has the power to order a launch of nuclear weapons; presumably such a decision would come only after the senior leaders had reached a consensus on their use. Guo Qingsheng, "China," 24.

32. Based on Li Jue et al., 59–64, 275–91.

33. On the capabilities of China's military aircraft (H-6, H-5, and Q-5) to deliver gravity nuclear bombs, see "Q-5"; Yu Fei, 42–43; and Duan Zijun, *Dangdai*, 170, 175, 186.

34. Though most Chinese strategists hold that China now has a viable triad (see, for example, Nie Quanlin, 205–6), a few (like Chen Chongbei et al., 215; and Zheng He, 19) do not consider the bomber a true leg of a survivable triad.

35. See Lewis and Hua; and Nie Quanlin, 189, 190. The quote can be found in Nie Quanlin, 190.

36. China tested a neutron bomb on Dec. 19, 1984. Xie Guang, *Dangdai*, 1: 223, 274; Gao Chao, "Cherish." Gao Chao was former deputy director of the Chinese Academy of Engineering Physics, successor of the Northwest Nuclear Weapons Research and Design Academy (Ninth Academy). Gao Chao, "Experiences," 220; Jiao Huibiao.

37. Stober; "Chinese Communists Achieve."

38. The DF-15/M-9 is a single-stage, solid-propellant, surface-to-surface tactical missile. (M-9 is its code name within the M-family of missiles for sale abroad). Nine meters in length, it uses inertial guidance and can be fitted for either a conventional or a nuclear warhead. The missile is stored in semi-hardened launch sites and can be trucked by eight-wheelers to launch sites far from its storage areas. It

has been part of the Second Artillery Corps's arsenal since 1990. Lewis, Hua, and Xue; "China Shows."

39. Based on Xing Qiuheng, 281; and Zhang Aiping, 76.

40. See, for example, Yang Heng, 159; and Rong Zhi, "Big Powers' Military Strategies," 73.

41. By 1978, all the DF-2 and DF-2A (range-extended DF-2) had been retired from first-line service. Unless otherwise cited, the information in this paragraph is from Lewis and Xue, *China Builds*, 212–14; Academy of Military Science, *Zhongguo Renmin Jiefangjun Liushi Nian Dashiji*, 612, 633; and Wang Yongzhi, *Hangtian*, 169, 243, 272, 345, 382.

42. The DF-3, DF-4, and DF-5 missiles use storable fuel. The DF-3 and DF-4 use unsymmetrical dimethylhydrazine (UDMH) and a liquid oxidizer (AK-27), nitric acid and nitrogen tetroxide; the DF-5 uses UDMH and an oxidizer of 100% nitrogen tetroxide. Lewis and Xue, "Strategic Weapons," 550, 551. The DF-3 and DF-4 have response times of one hour, 50 minutes, and two and a half hours, respectively. The response time for the DF-5 is less.

43. By 1988, the land-based version of the JL-1 missile, the 1,700km DF-21, had entered first-line service. The solid-propellant DF-31, a land-based version of the JL-2, and DF-41 missiles are both under development. They will have maximum ranges of 8,000km and 12,000km, respectively. Wang Yongzhi is the chief designer. Wang Yongzhi, *Hangtian*, 506; Lewis and Hua; Zhong Yi, 6.

44. This paragraph is based on Du Zhongwei et al., 9; Rong Zhi, "Big Powers' Military Strategies," 73; Xiao Jun, "Chinese Navy," 2–3; Xiao Jun, "Key Projects," 4; and Zhu Yida, "Combat Use," 48.

45. Yang Heng, deputy commander of the Second Artillery Corps, has openly expressed his concerns about the penetrability of China's strategic missiles. See Yang Heng, 159.

46. Chen Chongbei et al., 215; Guo Qingsheng, "Young Strategic Missile Troops," 17. Unless otherwise cited, this paragraph is based on Guo Qingsheng, "Visit," 98–99; Guo Qingsheng, "China," 25; Zhang Jinxi and Wang Xiancun, 5; Gu Boliang; Guo Qingsheng, "Second Artillery Corps"; Guo Qingsheng and Gu Boliang; Li Fumin and Li Dunsong, 51; Yao Yanjin, 28; and Wang Yongzhi, *Hangtian*, 285, 327.

47. Most of the caves for the DF-3s and 4s were built by the engineering regiments of the Second Artillery Corps. These regiments are responsible for constructing launch sites, command posts, and dormitories for combat units. Yin Weixing, 18; Guo Qingsheng and Zhang Jiajun.

48. See, for example, Du Zhongwei et al., 9; Rong Zhi, "Big Powers' Military Strategies," 73; and Shen Lijiang, "Commander," 2. In 1990, the Second Artillery Corps maintained four DF-5s in camouflaged hardened silos on continuous alert; it also maintained a number of fake silos to deceive enemy reconnaissance satellites. Lewis and Hua.

49. Each cave housing a missile is connected to several closeby launch sites. At the order to fire, a launch-unit commander has the authority to select which site to use and must take into account the missile's vulnerability en route. The commander is trained to use "guerrilla tactics" for moving the DF-3, DF-3A, DF-21, and DF-21A missiles. The size of the DF-4 and the fixed location of the DF-5 make such tactics inappropriate for those two missiles. Despite advances in the rapid launching of the mobile DF-21 and DF-21A missiles over the earlier liquid-fueled missiles,

some problems remain. For example, the large number of vehicles needed to convoy the missiles to the launch site—five equipment vehicles plus the missile transporter—increases the risk of detection.

50. Most of the information in the rest of this section is from an untitled and undated copy of an article by Chen Youming in *Haijun Zhuangbei* [Naval Equipment].

51. Xiao Jun, "Chinese Navy," 2. The commander of the nuclear submarine corps made this same point in a speech in the first half of 1989; see "Strengthening (1)."

52. The JL-1 is estimated to have about twice the probability of pre-launch survivability and penetrability as the DF-21 and the DF-21A. Based on Ni Huocai and Li Fangchun, 28; Yi Da, 57; and Du Zhongwei et al., 9.

53. For similar points of view on equating an intermediate-range SLBM with an ICBM, see Xiao Jun, "Chinese Navy," 3.

54. Most of China's mobile land-based missiles are targeted at the former Soviet Union. But the SLBMs are regarded as a deterrent against both the nuclear superpowers.

55. On the stages of dependence, interdependence, and independence that characterized the evolution of China's nuclear weapons program, see Lewis and Xue, *China Builds*, 219–26.

56. On the emergence of politically relevant policy networks in the Cultural Revolution, see Lewis, *Political Networks*.

57. See Deng Xiaoping [9], 29; Deng [2], 39, 40; and Deng [4], 43, 45.

58. Liu Xianfu and Li Jiang, 141.

59. The Chinese pinyin for this ancient saying is *daoqiang ru ku, ma fang nanshan. Nanshan* is an abbreviation for *Zhongnanshan* (Zhongnan Mountain). Loosely translated, the saying means "shift from a wartime to a peacetime mentality."

References Cited

References Cited

Chinese romanizations are not provided for newspaper or journal articles. English names are given in brackets for all journals and newspapers except the most frequently cited ones:

Guangming Ribao [Bright Daily]
Guofang Daxue Xuebao [National Defense University Gazette]
Hangkong Zhishi [Aerospace Knowledge]
Hangtian [Spaceflight]
Jianchuan Zhishi [Naval and Merchant Ships Knowledge]
Jiefangjun Bao [Liberation Army Daily]
Junshi Lishi [Military History]
Junshi Shijie [Military World] (Hong Kong)
Junshi Shilin [Military History Circles]
Liaowang [Outlook]
Renmin Ribao [People's Daily]
Shijie Ribao [World Journal] (New York)
Xiandai Junshi [Conmilit] (Hong Kong)

Unless otherwise stated, all Chinese-language journals and newspapers are published in Beijing. Two abbreviations are used in this list:

FBIS   *Foreign Broadcast Information Service*
HGYZW   *Nie Li and Huai Guomo, chief eds., Huigu yu Zhanwang*

Academy of Military Science. *Zhongguo Renmin Jiefangjun Dashiji (1927–1982)* [Chronicle of Major Events of the Chinese People's Liberation Army (1927–1982)]. Beijing, 1983.
———. *Zhongguo Renmin Jiefangjun Liushi Nian Dashiji (1927–1987)* [Chronicle of Major Events of the Chinese People's Liberation Army over the Past 60 Years (1927–1987)]. Beijing, 1988.
"Administrative Expenditure Are a Heavy Financial Burden," *Shijie Ribao*, March 12, 1991.
"Adopt a Correct Attitude Toward Intellectuals," *Guangming Ribao*, Jan. 7, 1981.
"Aerospace Terminologies," *Hangtian*, No. 6, 1989.

Ai Lingyao. "Eight Campaigns to Simplify and Reorganize the Chinese Army," *Junshi Shijie*, No. 1, 1990.

Ai Ying and You Qi. "Chairman of the Central Military Commission Deng Xiaoping Confers the Title 'Heroic Mapping Brigade' on Mapping Brigade No. 1 of the General Staff," *Jiefangjun Bao*, April 1, 1989.

Alexandrov, A. P., et al. "The Atomic Icebreaker 'Lenin,'" *Proceedings of the Second United Nations International Conference on the Peaceful Uses of Atomic Energy*. Geneva, 1958, Vol. 8, Part 1.

"All of Us Should Concern Ourselves with Strategic Research," *Jiefangjun Bao*, May 7, 1986.

"Announcement of the *Xinhua* News Agency," *Renmin Ribao*, Oct. 2, 1982."An Annual Increase of Chinese Defense Budget by Ten Percent in the 1990s," *Shijie Ribao*, March 7, 1991.

"Appointments of Ministers of Three Ministries of Machine Building by President Liu Shaoqi," *Renmin Ribao*, Sept. 14, 1960.

Arkhipov, Ivan. Untitled comment on Soviet-Chinese relations, in *USSR-China in the Changing World*. Moscow, 1989.

"Attach Importance to the Construction of Frontier Defense and Coastal Defense, and Concern Ourselves About the Weal and Woe of the Soldiers Who Are Garrisoning the Frontiers," *Jiefangjun Bao*, April 8, 1988.

Bai Hande. "The Military Application and Development of Glass-Reinforced Plastics," *Bingqi Zhishi* [Ordnance Knowledge], No. 4, 1989.

Bai Kemin. "Some Ideas on the Developmental Direction of Our Country's Navy," *Jianchuan Zhishi*, No. 12, 1988.

Bao Keming. "Break a Path of Our Own," in HGYZW.

Barnett, A. Doak. *Cadres, Bureaucracy, and Political Power in Communist China.* New York, 1967.

"The Beginning of a New Phase for the Modern Construction of the People's Liberation Army," *Renmin Ribao*, July 31, 1984.

"Beijing Issues an Order to Strengthen Protection of Military Installations," *Guoji Ribao* [International Daily News] (Los Angeles), Oct. 7, 1991.

Bi Shiguan. "Missile Guidance Systems (1)," *Jianchuan Zhishi*, No. 6, 1986.

———. "Missile Guidance Systems: Their Basic Composition, Functions, and Work Process," *Jianchuan Zhishi*, No. 8, 1986.

Bie Yixun and Su Kuoshan. "The Commission of Science, Technology, and Industry for National Defense Builds a Modern Command Center," *Jiefangjun Bao*, May 29, 1988.

"The Birth of the Home-Made New-Type Photoelectric Theodolite Which Can Take Photographs of Small Objects 300km Away," *Renmin Ribao*, overseas ed., June 10, 1987.

Blake, Bernade, ed. *Jane's Weapon Systems, 1987–88*. London, 1987.

Boffa, Giuseppe. *Inside the Khrushchev Era*. New York, 1959.

Break the Nuclear Monopoly, Eliminate Nuclear Weapons. Beijing, 1965."A Brief Introduction to *Selected Works of He Long on Military Affairs*," *Jiefangjun Bao*, April 28, 1989.

"The Bright Light Illuminating the Sea . . . ," *Xinhua*, Oct. 15, 1977, in FBIS: *China*, Oct. 17, 1977.

Brown, George. *United States Military Posture for FY1977*. Washington, D.C., 1976.

Bukalov, V. N., and A. A. Narusbaev. *Proektirovanie Atomnykh Podvodnykh Lo-dok* [Atomic-Powered Submarine Design]. Leningrad, 1964.

Cai Wenyi. "View National Defense from the Angle of Resources Crisis," *Jiefang-jun Bao*, Nov. 18, 1988.

Cao Yuhe and Gao Xiangzhu. "The Successful Promotion of Quality [in Electronic Components] by Adopting 'Seven Special Measures,'" in HGYZW.

Cao Zhang et al. "The Whole Story of the Plot of the 'Gang of Four' to Stage an Armed Revolt in Shanghai," *Gongren Ribao* [Workers' Daily], Dec. 13, 1980.

Chai Limin. "The Trend of 'Integrated Operations' [of the Three Armed Services] in Future Sea Battles," *Guofang Daxue Xuebao*, No. 2, 1986.

Chang Gong. "Missile Flight Control Systems," 2 parts, *Hangkong Zhishi*, Nos. 6, 7, 1975.

Chen Baoshan. "Anhui and Shanghai Remake 'Minor Third-Line' Enterprises," *Renmin Ribao*, March 10, 1987.

Chen Bin et al. "The 'Three Key Projects' Continue the Efforts in Scaling New Heights in Defense Science and Technology After the 'Missile and Nuclear Bomb Projects,'" in HGYZW.

Chen Chongbei et al. *Weishe Zhanlüe* [Strategy of Deterrence]. Beijing, 1989.

Chen Chu, chief ed. *Chuanti Hanjie Bianxing* [The Deformation of a Ship's Hull in Welding]. Beijing, 1985.

Chen Dechun and Shi Zhibao. "Our Country Has Made Breakthroughs in Theoretical Studies on Nuclear Strategy," *Jiefangjun Bao*, Nov. 21, 1987.

Chen Fangyou and Chai Limin. "A Study on Basic Thinking of the Naval Operational Art," *Guofang Daxue Xuebao*, No. 11, 1987.

Chen Fucai. "A Brief Biography of Luo Shunchu," *Fujian Dangshi Yuekan* [Fujian Party's History Monthly], No. 8, 1988.

Chen He and Yang Zhibin. "Some Ideas on the Industrial Mobilization System of Our Country," *Guofang Daxue Xuebao*, No. 10, 1987.

Chen Kehou, chief ed. *Zhanzheng Heping yu Guofang* [War, Peace, and National Defense]. Beijing, 1989.

Chen Liwei. "My Experiences in Developing Computation for Military Purpose," in HGYZW.

Chen Ming and Zhou Zongmin. "Our Country Is Making Modern Combat Ships," *Renmin Ribao*, overseas ed., Aug. 2, 1987.

Chen Mingxian et al. *Xin Zhongguo Sishi Nian Yanjiu* [Studies on the 40 Years of the New China]. Beijing, 1989.

Chen Ping et al., chief eds. *Xin Zhongguo de Jiben Jianshe Guofang Gongye Juan* [Capital Construction in the New China—Volume on the National Defense Industry]. Beijing, 1987.

Chen Rulong, chief ed. *Dangdai Zhongguo Caizheng* [Contemporary China's Finance]. Beijing, 1988, Vols. 1, 2.

Chen Shiqu. "Memories of the Construction of the Missile and Atomic Bomb Test Bases," *Junshi Shilin*, No. 5, 1989.

Chen Shoukang. "The Formation and Development of Naval Strategy," *Jiefangjun Bao*, Nov. 17, 1989.

Chen Siyi and Gu Mainan. "China's Defense Industry Confronts a Historical Turning Point," *Liaowang*, overseas ed., Feb. 10, 1986.

Chen Wanjun and Li Kewen. "I Have Devoted All My Life to Torpedoes," *Jiefang-jun Bao*, March 22, 1991.

Chen Weijun. "Jiang Zemin and Li Peng Support Generals' Request for a Large Increase in the Military Budget in Preparation for Any Contingency," *Guang-jiaojing* [Wide-Angle Lens] (Hong Kong), No. 2, 1991.

Chen Xiang'an. "Xu Xing Talks About Defense Construction in Response to Reporters' Questions," *Renmin Ribao*, April 5, 1987.

Chen Xiaoxing. "The Requirements Placed by Coastal Economic Development on Naval Building," *Junshi Jingji Yanjiu* [Military Economic Research], No. 7, 1989.

Chen Xiaoyu, ed. *Qianting he Qianshuiqi Jiegou de Dizhou Pilao* [Cyclic Fatigue of the Structures of Submarines and Submersible Boats]. Beijing, 1990.

Chen Xingxin. "Electronic Components for Military Use and the Modernization of Weapons and Equipment," in HGYZW.

Chen Xiuxian. "Science and Technology in the Service of Power," *Tien-hsia* [Under Heaven] (Taipei), June 1, 1989.

Chen Xueren. "The Significance of Coordinating the Solution of Key Problems and the Management of Problem-Solving," *Kexue yu Kexue Jishu Guanli* [Science and the Management of Science and Technology], No. 6, 1984.

Chen Xuewei. "Debates on the Guiding Principle for Economic Construction in the 1950s," *Dangshi Wenhui* [Collection on Party History], No. 2, 1989.

———. "On Economic Construction During the Ten-Year 'Cultural Revolution,'" in Tan Zongji et al., *Shinian hou de Pingshuo Wenhua Degeming Shi Lunji* [Comments After Ten Years: A Collection of Essays on the 'Cultural Revolution']. Beijing, 1987.

Chen Youming. "The Concern of Zhou Enlai and Other Veteran Revolutionaries for the Nuclear-Powered Submarine Project," 2 parts, *Junshi Shilin*, Nos. 3, 4, 1988.

———. "A New Shipping Line," *Jiefangjun Bao*, July 11, 1988.

———. "Wise Decision, Arduous Task," *Haijun Zhuangbei* [Naval Equipment], No. 4, 1989.

Chen Zhiqiang. "The Combination of Military and Civilian Production over the Past Nine Years," *Liaowang*, March 14, 1988.

Cheng Wang, chief ed. *Dangdai Zhongguo de Chuanbo Gongye* [Contemporary China's Shipbuilding Industry]. Beijing, 1992.

Cheng Zhenzhong. "The Ship Hydrodynamic Laboratory Is Accepted as a Formal Member of the International Ship Pool Conference," *Guangming Ribao*, June 29, 1987.

Cheng Zhong. *Haiyang zai Zhaohuan* [Our Mission on the Ocean]. Nanning, 1990.

Cheng Zihua. "My Experiences in Shortening the Battle Line of Capital Construction in the 1960s," *Dangshi Wenhui* [Collection on Party History], No. 3, 1990.

Cheng Zihua and Lü Zhengcao. "Reminiscences on Comrade Sun Zhiyuan," *Renmin Ribao*, Oct. 27, 1985.

Cheung, Tai Ming. "Goodbye People's War: PLA Unveils New Strategy to Counter Soviet Invasion," *Far Eastern Economic Review*, Dec. 1, 1989.

———. "Trends in the Research of Chinese Military Strategy," *Survival*, May/June 1987.

"Chief Criminal of a Bandit Executed for Stealing Cables," *Shijie Ribao*, June 14, 1991.

"China Shows Its Latest Weaponry," *Xiandai Junshi*, No. 2, 1987.

"China Updates Weapons and Equipment for Self-Defense," *Renmin Ribao*, overseas ed., Nov. 8, 1986.

"China Will Launch Rockets Toward the Pacific Ocean," *Renmin Ribao*, overseas ed., Sept. 8, 1988.

"China's Defense Budget Rises by 20 Percent After the June 4 Incident," *Xingdao Ribao* [Sing Tao Daily] (Hong Kong), March 3 and 4, 1990.

"China's Strategic Missile Troops Will Use an Automatic System for Operational Command After Ten Years of Efforts," *Renmin Ribao*, overseas ed., May 5, 1988.

"Chinese Communist Nuclear Submarines Once Navigated the Taiwan Strait Underwater," *Shijie Ribao*, May 8, 1989.

"Chinese Communists Achieve Success in Their Neutron Bomb Test Detonation," *Shijie Ribao*, Nov. 9, 1988.

"Chinese Communists Are Test-Launching a New Type of Torpedo in the Taiwan Strait," *Shijie Ribao*, Feb. 15, 1990.

"Chinese Communists Own 130 Submarines," *Shijie Ribao*, Oct. 11, 1989.

"The Chinese Navy Has Extended Its Training to Oceangoing Operations," *Renmin Ribao*, overseas ed., Dec. 6, 1987.

Chu Jiakang. "[What Will Happen] After the Destruction of the Shipboard Nuclear Power Plant?" *Jianchuan Zhishi*, No. 6, 1986.

Cihai [A Sea of Words (Dictionary)]. Shanghai, 1980.

"Circular of the Central Committee of the Chinese Communist Party," in *CCP Documents of the Great Proletarian Cultural Revolution, 1966–1967*. Hong Kong, 1968.

Clemow, J. *Missile Guidance*. London, 1962.

"Comment of the CCP Central Committee on the Transmission of the Report of the Work Group of the Central Committee Concerning the Problem of Lo Jui-ch'ing's Mistakes," in *CCP Documents of the Great Proletarian Cultural Revolution, 1966–1967*. Hong Kong, 1968.

"The Commission of Science, Technology, and Industry for National Defense Builds a Modern Command Center," *Renmin Ribao*, overseas ed., May 30, 1988.

"The Completion of the Construction of a Long-Wave Timing Center at the Shaanxi Astronomical Observatory," *Renmin Ribao*, Dec. 17, 1983.

"The Completion of a Long-Distance Radio Navigation System," *Renmin Ribao*, overseas ed., Aug. 20, 1990.

"Comrade Ci Yungui, a Famous Computation Scientist, Died of an Illness," *Jiefangjun Bao*, Aug. 25, 1990.

Cong Jin. *1949–1989 Nian de Zhongguo Quzhe Fazhan de Suiyue* [Years of Tortuous Development: China from 1949 to 1989]. Zhengzhou, 1989, Vol. 2.

"The Congratulatory Telegram on the Successful Launch of a Carrier Rocket at Sea," *Renmin Ribao*, Oct. 17, 1982.

"Correctly Handle Contradictions with Two Different Natures, Hold Fast to the General Orientation of the Struggle," *Renmin Ribao*, June 25, 1967.

"The Cradle of Chinese Modern Rockets: The Carrier Rocket Technology Academy," *Hangtian*, No. 3, 1989.

Cui Chengwu and Zhang Quncheng. "A Visit to Base 067 of the Ministry of Aerospace Industry (1)," *Wenhui Bao* [Encounter Daily] (Hong Kong), April 8, 1990.

Cui Xiaonan and Chen Wanjun. "The Birth of the New 'China Sturgeon' Torpedo," *Jiefangjun Bao*, Oct. 25, 1990.

Cui Xiaonan and Zheng Shuyan. "A Torpedo Expert," *Jiefangjun Bao*, March 17, 1991.

Da Ying. "A Description of the Hardships General Luo Ruiqing Suffered," in Zhou Ming, chief ed., *Lishi zai Zheli Chensi* [History Stops Here Deep in Contemplation]. Beijing, 1986, Vol. 1.

Dai Lan. "A Look at the Past and Future Application of Glass-Reinforced Plastics in China," *Renmin Ribao*, overseas ed., July 27, 1990.

Dalu Zaochuan Gongye Gaikuang [A General Introduction to the Shipbuilding Industry in Mainland China]. Taipei, 1968.

Dalu Zaochuan Gongye Xianshi [A Survey of the Shipbuilding Industry in Mainland China]. Taipei, 1969.

Dao Yin. "The Advancing and Shaping of the Guideline 'Readjustment, Consolidation, Reinforcement, and Improvement,'" *Dangshi Wenhui* [Collection on Party History], No. 3, 1990.

Davies, A. C. *The Science and Practice of Welding*. Cambridge, Eng., 1984, 2 vols.

Davis, Vincent. *The Politics of Innovation: Patterns in Navy Cases*. Denver, 1967.

Deng Buping. "At the All-Army Conference on Maintaining Secrecy, Yang Baibing Stresses Maintaining Secrecy Is Saving Lives; Maintaining Secrecy Is Ensuring Victories," *Jiefangjun Bao*, May 18, 1991.

Deng Huaxu et al. "A Visit to the Marine Corps of the Chinese People's Liberation Army," *Renmin Ribao*, overseas ed., Aug. 2, 1988.

Deng Lifeng, ed. *Xin Zhongguo Junshi Huodong Jishi (1949–1959)* [The True Records of New China's Military Affairs (1949–1959)]. Beijing, 1989.

Deng Sanrui. "Thinking About Ways to Compel the Enemy to Yield Without Resorting to Force," in Yang Dezhi et al., *Guofang Fazhan Zhanlüe Sikao* [Thinking on National Defense Military Strategies]. Beijing, 1987.

Deng Xiaoping (the following works are all reprinted in *Selected Works of Deng Xiaoping [1975–1982]*. Beijing, 1984)

[1]. "Build Powerful, Modern, and Regularized Revolutionary Armed Forces" [Sept. 19, 1981].

[2]. "On Consolidating National Defense Enterprises" [Aug. 3, 1975].

[3]. "Simplify Troops, Raise Combat Capability" [March 12, 1980].

[4]. "Some Comments on Industrial Development" [Aug. 18, 1975].

[5]. "Some Comments on Work in Science and Education" [Aug. 8, 1977].

[6]. "Some Problems Outstanding in the Iron and Steel Industry" [May 29, 1975].

[7]. "Speech at the Opening Ceremony of the National Conference on Science" [March 18, 1978].

[8]. "Speech at a Plenary Meeting of the Military Commission of the Central Committee of the CPC" [Dec. 28, 1977].

[9]. "The Task of Consolidating the Army" [July 14, 1977].

"Deng Xiaoping Talks About the Situation at Home and Abroad," *Liaowang*, Sept. 16, 1985.

"Deng Xiaoping Talks About Preserving World Peace," *Liaowang*, Feb. 4, 1985.

"Deng Xiaoping Talks Freely About the Situation at Home and Abroad," *Liaowang*, Sept. 16, 1985.

Deng Xiucheng and Zhou Zhiwu. "The Maiden Voyage of a Submarine," *Renmin Ribao*, overseas ed., Nov. 19, 1985.

Deng Yingchao. "A Communist Party Member Who Observed Rigorous Security Discipline," *Renmin Ribao*, June 30, 1982.

"A Description of Huang Weilu, an Expert on Missiles," *Dagong Bao* [Impartial Daily] (Hong Kong), Oct. 21, 1982.

Dian Dian. *Feifan de Niandai* [Unusual Years]. Beijing, 1987.

———. "Smile—For Dear Father," in Zhou Ming, chief ed., *Lishi zai Zheli Chensi* [History Stops Here Deep in Contemplation]. Beijing, 1986, Vol. 1.

Dianzi Gongye Jishu Cidian [Dictionary of Electronics Industrial Technology]. Beijing, 1980, Vols. 1, 2.

Ding Shu. *Renhuo Da Yuejin yu Da Jihuang* [Man-Made Calamities: The Great Leap Forward and the Widespread Famine]. Hong Kong, 1991.

Dong Baocun. "The Commander of the Beijing Garrison in the Years of Turmoil," *Yanhuang Zisun* [The Chinese], No. 1, 1988.

———. *Yang Yu Fu Shijian Zhenxiang* [The Truth About the Incident Involving Yang (Chengwu), Yu (Lijin), and Fu (Chongbi)]. Beijing, 1988.

Dong Kegong et al. "Comrade Nie Rongzhen with the Intellectuals," *Guangming Ribao*, Oct. 4, 1982.

Dong Lin. "Memorable Nights," in *Huainian Zhou Enlai* [Cherish the Memory of Zhou Enlai]. Beijing, 1986.

Dong Shitang. "A Pearl on the Banks of Lake Tai," in HGYZW.

Donnithorne, Audrey. *China's Economic System*. New York, 1967.

Du Chunshi. "A Description of Uranium Metallurgist Zhang Peilin," in *He Kexuejia de Zuji* [The Footprints Left by the Nuclear Scientists]. Beijing, 1989.

Du Zhiying, ed. *Jianchuan Xiaoci* [Demagnetization of Warships and Boats]. Beijing, 1983.

Du Zhongwei et al. "The Sea, the Navy, and the New Technological Revolution: An Interview with Naval Commander Liu Huaqing," *Liaowang*, Aug. 13, 1984.

Duan Junyi et al. "Comrade Zhao Erlu, a Prominent Organizer of the Construction of Our Country's Defense Industry," *Renmin Ribao*, Jan. 13, 1982.

Duan Zijun. "Premier Zhou's Great Concern for the Aviation Industry," *Hangkong Zhishi*, No. 4, 1988.

———. "The Principal Founder of the New China's Aviation Industry," in *Bujin de Sinian* [Boundless Recollections]. Beijing, 1987.

———, chief ed. *Dangdai Zhongguo de Hangkong Gongye* [Contemporary China's Aviation Industry]. Beijing, 1988.

"The Eighth Central Committee of the Communist Party of China Holds Its Ninth Plenum," *Renmin Ribao*, Jan. 21, 1961.

"The Eleventh Meeting of the Standing Committee of the National People's Congress Adopts Environmental Protection Law and Several Resolutions," *Renmin Ribao*, Sept. 14, 1979.

Engelhardt, John. "The Chinese on Submarine Combat Survivability," *Submarine Review*, Oct. 1988.

"Evolution of the Commission of Science, Technology, and Industry for National Defense," *Jiefangjun Bao*, Oct. 24, 1988.

"The Exchange of Ammunition Technologies Between the Zhengzhou Machinery and Electronics Institute and SNIABPD," *Xiandai Junshi*, No. 7, 1987.

Fan Gui. "A Group of Enterprises in the Third-Line Regions Open over 1,000 Companies in the Coastal Areas," *Renmin Ribao*, overseas ed., Nov. 7, 1987.

Fan Jun. "Our Country Is Readjusting the Distribution of the Third-Line Enterprises," *Renmin Ribao*, overseas ed., Nov. 21, 1985.

Fan Shouxing. "Further Understanding of the Year 1957," *Dangshi Yanjiu yu Jiaoxue* [Study and Teaching of the Party's History] (Fuzhou), No. 4, 1988.

Fan Zhongyi. "The Strategic Thought on Coastal Defense in *Chouhai Tubian*," *Junshi Shilin*, No. 4, 1986.

Fang Ren. "Our Country Has Built Its First Pulse Reactor," *Jiefangjun Bao*, Aug. 15, 1990.

"Farewell Ceremony for Zhou Xihan's Remains Held in Beijing," *Jiefangjun Bao*, Dec. 6, 1988.

Feng Chongzhe and Huang Jianyi. "Gyroscopes and Their Bearings (1)," *Jianchuan Zhishi*, No. 8, 1987.

Feng Shizhang. "The Development of Radar Systems and Automatic Command System in Retrospect," in HGYZW.

Fiebig R. "Untersuchungen zur Dynamik des Reaktors des Kernenergieschiffes OTTO HAHN, II. Tiel," *Atomkernenergie (ATKE)*, 24 (1974), No. 2.

"The First Submarine of the People's Navy," *Jiefangjun Bao*, Nov. 26, 1990.

"Foreign Minister Qian Qichen's Speech at a Press Conference," *Renmin Ribao*, overseas ed., March 28, 1991.

Fourth Session of the Sixth National People's Congress (April 1986). Beijing, 1986.

Friedman, Lawrence. *The Evolution of Nuclear Strategy*. 2d ed. London, 1991.

Fu Shangkui. "An Exploration into the Development of Our Country's Active Defense Thinking in Peacetime," *Junshi Shilin*, No. 4, 1991.

Fukuyama, Francis. "Nuclear Shadowboxing: Soviet Intervention Threats in the Middle East," *Orbis*, 25, No. 3 (Fall 1981).

Gai Yumin. "Yang Dezhi at Lecture on Defense Modernization," *Xinhua*, March 1, 1986, in FBIS: China, March 3, 1986.

Gan Guanshi and Xiao Xiaoqin. "A Survey of the Causes of the 'Great Leap Forward' and People's Commune Campaigns," *Dangshi Yanjiu yu Jiaoxue* [Study and Teaching of the Party's History] (Fuzhou), No. 1, 1990.

Gao Chao. "Cherish the Memory of Comrade [Deng] Jiaxian," *Guangming Ribao*, Aug. 30, 1987.

———. "The Experiences and Lessons in Organizing and Administering the Nuclear Weapons Program," in HGYZW.

Gao Keren and Yu Huijie, chief eds. *Daodan Jishu Cidian* [Dictionary of Missile Technology]. Beijing, 1984.

Gao Mingkun, chief ed. *Daodan Fashe Zhuangzhi Gouzao* [The Structure of the Missile Launch System]. Beijing, 1985.

Gao Wenqian. "A Description of Comrade Zhou Enlai When He Was Hospitalized for Critical Illness," in Zhou Ming, chief ed., *Lishi Zai Zheli Chensi* [History Stops Here Deep in Contemplation] (Beijing, 1986), Vol. 1.

Gao Xinqing. "A Description of Huang Weilu, Chief Designer of a Carrier Rocket," *Renmin Ribao*, overseas ed., Sept. 26, 1989.

Gao Zhenjia. "Infinite Pains Taken in the Construction of the People's Navy," in Yang Shangkun et al., *Yidai Yuanrong* [A Supreme Commander]. Beijing, 1991.

Ge Qiguang et al. *Zai Weilai de Zhanchang shang Shuimian he Shuixia Zhanchang*

[Future Battlefields: The Battlefields On and Under the Sea]. Beijing, 1989, Vol. 4.

"A Glossary of Space Terminology," 2 parts, *Hangtian*, No. 3, 1989, No. 2, 1990.

Goldman, Merle. *Literary Dissent in Communist China*. Cambridge, Mass., 1967.

———. "Party Policies Toward the Intellectuals: The Unique Blooming and Contending of 1961–2," Chap. 8, in John W. Lewis, ed., *Party Leadership and Revolutionary Power in China*. London, 1970.

Goncharov Sergei. "The Chinese Concept of National Security," in *New Approaches to Security in the Asian-Pacific Region*. Stanford, Calif., 1990.

———. "From Alliance Through Enmity to Good Neighborliness," *Literaturnaia Gazeta* [Literary Gazette], Oct. 4, 1989. Chinese translation in *Cankao Ziliao* [Reference Materials], Oct. 30, 1989.

Goncharov Sergei, John W. Lewis, and Xue Litai. *Uncertain Partners: Stalin, Mao, and the Korean War*. Stanford, Calif., 1993.

Gong Shuangyin. "The Creation of the State Bureau for Maintaining Secrecy," *Dagong Bao* [Impartial Daily] (Hong Kong), Sept. 9, 1988.

Great Britain, Department of Industry. *Second Report on the Nuclear Ship Study*. London, 1975.

———, Department of Trade and Industry. *Report on the Nuclear Ship Study*. London, 1971.

"Great Contributions Made by 14 Middle-Aged Experts on Science and Technology," *Renmin Ribao*, overseas ed., Aug. 3, 1987.

Gromyko, Andrei. *Memoirs*. New York, 1989.

———. *Pamyatnoye* [Memoirs]. Moscow, 1988, Vol. 2.

Gu Boliang. "Sidelights on the Test Exercise of a Combat Unit Under the Strategic Missile Troops," *Jiefangjun Bao*, Dec. 1, 1987.

Gu Mainan. "His Course of Life From a Little 8th Route Armyman to a Scientist," *Liaowang*, Jan. 5, 1987.

Gu Mu. "Reminiscences on Esteemed Premier Zhou (2)," *Renmin Ribao*, overseas ed., March 2, 1989.

Gu Weilun. "The Integrated Inertial/GPS Navigation System," *Xiandai Junshi*, No. 8, 1987.

Gu Yu. "How to Tackle the Organization of Key Scientific and Technical Problems," *Liaowang*, July 20, 1982.

———. "Reminiscences About the Initial Development of Our Country's Defense Scientific Research," in HGYZW.

Guan Shan. *Deng Xiaoping Jiangxi Mengnan Ji* [The Tragic Years of Deng Xiaoping in Jiangxi]. Hong Kong, 1990.

Gunston, Bill. *Rockets & Missiles*. London, 1979.

Guo Binwei and Tan Zongji. *Zhonghua Renmin Gongheguo Jianshi* [A Summary History of the People's Republic of China]. Beijing, 1988.

Guo Dong. "His Departure . . . ," *Zuoping yu Zhengming* [Works and Contentions], No. 1, 1988.

Guo Fang. "The Composition of the Tracking System of the Long March No. 4 Carrier Rocket," *Zhongguo Hangtian* [Chinese Spaceflight], No. 9, 1991.

Guo Fuwen and Cao Baojian. "Advance Toward the Pacific Ocean," *Hainan Jishi* [Record of Actual Events (Hainan)] (Haikou), No. 7, 1989.

Guo Hualun [Warren Kuo]. "A Study of Mao Zedong's Military Thought," in Zhou

Ziqiang, ed., *Gongfei Junshi Wenti Lunji* [A Collection of Essays on Chinese Communist Military Issues]. Taipei, 1974.

————. *Zhonggong Mingci Shuyu Cidian* [A Comprehensive Glossary of Chinese Communist Terminology]. Taipei, 1978.

"Guo Jingkun: A Newly Elected Member of the Chemical Department of the Chinese Academy of Sciences," *Renmin Ribao*, overseas ed., Jan. 22, 1992.

Guo Qingsheng. "China Has a Nuclear Counterattack Capability—A Visit to China's Strategic Missile Units," *Liaowang*, April 22, 1985.

————. "The Second Artillery Corps Gains a 100% Success Rate in Flight-Testing Missiles," *Jiefangjun Bao*, Dec. 28, 1990.

————. "A Visit to Li Xuge, Commander of the Second Artillery Corps," in *Junwei Jinxingqu—Renmin Jiefangjun Xiandaihua Jianshe* [Military Marches—The Modern Construction of the People's Liberation Army]. Beijing, 1987.

————. "Young Strategic Missile Troops," *Liaowang*, July 13, 1987.

Guo Qingsheng and Gu Boliang. "The Second Artillery Corps Has Preliminarily Formed an Energetic Training System," *Jiefangjun Bao*, May 21, 1988.

Guo Qingsheng and Kang Fashun. "The Birth of a New System for Topographic and Astronomical Measurement," *Jiefangjun Bao*, Jan. 28, 1991.

Guo Qingsheng and Zhang Jiajun. "The Second Artillery Corps Confers the Title 'Advanced Regiment for Defense Construction' on an Engineering Regiment for Completing Its Tasks in Three Consecutive Years," *Jiefangjun Bao*, April 24, 1987.

Guo Shouhang. *Deng Xiaoping Guofang Xiandaihua Sixiang Yanjiu* [A Study of Deng Xiaoping's Thinking on Modern Defense]. Beijing, 1989.

Guo Tiejun. "Technology on Colored Glazed Sand Coating Developed by the Fourth Institute of the First Academy of the Ministry of Nuclear Industry Is in Great Demand," *Jingji Ribao* [Economic Daily], May 30, 1985.

Guo Weicheng and Zhang Shusheng. "The Past and Future of Defense Modernization—An Interview with Minister of Defense Zhang Aiping," *Renmin Ribao*, Oct. 3, 1984.

Guo Xiangxing. "An Interview with Vice-Admiral Zhang Lianzhong, Commander of the Chinese Navy," *Xiandai Junshi*, No. 7, 1991.

————. "Outstanding Contributions of a Certain Naval Representative Section to the Nuclear-Powered Submarine Project," *Jiefangjun Bao*, Dec. 17, 1990.

————. "A Think Tank of the Modern Chinese Navy," *Jiefangjun Bao*, May 27, 1991.

————. "A Visit to the China Naval Research Center," *Junshi Shijie*, No. 2, 1989.

Guo Xiangxing and Yi Hai. "The Construction of the 'Great Wall Under the Water,'" *Junshi Shijie*, No. 1, 1989.

Guo Xiangxing et al. "A Description of Li Honghai, Head of the Mechanics and Electricity Department of a Certain Nuclear-Powered Submarine," *Jiefangjun Bao*, May 27, 1991.

Haijun Shi [The History of the (Chinese) Navy]. Beijing, 1989.

Halperin, Morton. *The 1958 Taiwan Straits Crisis: A Documented History*. Rand Memo RM-4900-ISA. Santa Monica, Calif., 1966.

Han Hong. "We Have Built a Large-Scale Long-Distance Radio Navigation System," *Renmin Ribao*, overseas ed., Feb. 10, 1992.

Han Huaizhi, chief ed. *Dangdai Zhongguo Minbing* [Contemporary China's Militia]. Beijing, 1989.

Han Huaizhi and Tan Jingqiao, chief eds. *Dangdai Zhongguo Jundui de Junshi Gongzuo* [Military Affairs of the Contemporary Chinese Army]. Beijing, 1989, Vols. 1, 2.

Han Nianlong, chief ed. *Dangdai Zhongguo Waijiao* [Contemporary China's Foreign Affairs]. Beijing, 1987.

Han Xilin and Li Nanqing. "Reminiscences on the Great Leap Forward That Occurred Thirty Years Ago," *Tianfu Xinlun* [Sichuan Forum] (Chengdu), No. 1, 1989.

Han Yongfa and Yu Guidong. "The Shenyang Military Region Command Strengthens Theoretical Study on Defensive Warfare Under Nuclear Conditions," *Jiefangjun Bao*, Aug. 22, 1987.

Hansen, Chuck. *US Nuclear Weapons: The Secret History*. New York, 1988.

He Chunchao, chief ed. *Guoji Guanxi Shi* [History of International Relations]. Wuhan, 1984, Vol. 2.

He Di. "The Taiwan Straits Crisis and the Formulation of Chinese Policy on Jinmen [Quemoy] and Mazu," *Meiguo Yanjiu* [American Studies], No. 3, 1988.

He Jun. "My Opinion on the Factors That Generated the 'Great Leap Forward' Campaign," *Zhongguo Renmin Jingguan Daxue Xuebao Zheshe Ban* [Bulletin of the Chinese People's Police Officer University (Philosophy and Social Sciences Edition)], No. 4, 1989.

He Li, ed. *Lin Biao Jiazu Jishi* [A Record of Events in Lin Biao's Family]. Beijing, 1989.

He Long. *He Long Junshi Wenxuan* [Selected Military Writings of He Long]. Beijing, 1989.

He Long Nianpu [A Chronicle of He Long's Life]. Beijing, 1988.

He Ping. "Wang Dezhao Talks About the Development of Acoustics in China," *Liaowang*, overseas ed., June 16, 1986.

He Xiaolu. "A Marshal and a Diplomat (2)," *Kunlun* [Kunlun], No. 4, 1984.

He Zhenming. "Inside Information on the Promotion of Liu Huaqing by Deng [Xiaoping]," *Zhengming* [Contend] (Hong Kong), No. 12, 1989.

He Zhengwen. "On the Eve of and After the Reduction of Troops by One Million," in Yang Guoyu et al., eds., *Ershiba Nian Jian—Cong Shi Zhengwei dao Zong Shuji* [28 Years—From Division Political Commissar to General Secretary]. Beijing, 1989.

Hewlett, Richard G., and Francis Duncan, *Nuclear Navy: 1946–1962*. Chicago, 1974.

History Team of the Naval Research Institute. "A Look Back at the People's Navy on Its 40th Anniversary," *Junshi Lishi*, No. 5, 1989.

Hong Liu. "The Trial Implementation of a New Policy Allowing Officers' Wives to Live with Their Husbands While Keeping Their Original Jobs Without Pay," *Jiefangjun Bao*, Oct. 5, 1988.

Hong Shikun and Li Renli. "Jiujiang Shipbuilding Industry Has Manifested Its Technological Superiority," *Renmin Ribao*, overseas ed., April 13, 1988.

"Honor Roll of Exemplary Intellectuals," *Guangming Ribao*, Nov. 5, 1986, Feb. 5, 1987.

Hou Jiayin. "Accelerating the Readjustment of the Enterprises in the Third-Line Regions," *Renmin Ribao*, overseas ed., April 22, 1987.

Houldcroft, Peter, and John Robert. *Welding and Cutting: A Guide to Fusion Welding and Associated Cutting Processes*. New York, 1989.

Howe, Jonathan. *Multicrises: Sea Power and Global Politics in the Missile Age.* Cambridge, Mass., 1971.

Hu Chunhua. "A Visit to Xu Zuoren, First Captain of Our Country's Nuclear Missile Submarine," *Bingqi Zhishi* [Ordnance Knowledge], No. 3, 1989.

Hu Guoping. "A Historical Survey of the Issue of Our Country's 'Overheated' Economic Construction," *Fujian Dangshi Yuekan* [Fujian Party's History Monthly], No. 8, 1989.

Hu Hongbo. "They Have a Common Name: Nuclear-Powered Submarine—A Description of the Communist Party Members of a Military Representative Section of the Navy," *Jiefangjun Bao*, April 4, 1991.

Hu Maozi. "The Present Condition and Development of the Shipbuilding Technology," *Jianchuan Zhishi*, No. 12, 1989.

Hu Nianqiu. "Fulfill the Task of Producing Military Supplies and Military Hardware," *Jiefangjun Bao*, Feb. 28, 1989.

Hu Sheng. *Zhongguo Gongchandang de Qishi Nian* [The 70 Years of the Chinese Communist Party]. Beijing, 1991.

Hu Shihong. "A Description of General Zhang Aiping, Front Commander in Chief," in Nie Fengzhi et al., *Sanjun Huige Zhan Donghai* [A Campaign by the Three Armed Services in the East China Sea]. Beijing, 1985.

———. "The National Defense Scientists and Technicians' Visit to Marshal Nie Rongzhen," *Liaowang*, Nov. 5, 1984.

Hu Xiaoen and Peng Zhonghuai. "'Strengthening Frontier Defenses' Should Be the Main Content of [Our] Military Strategy," *Jiefangjun Bao*, Jan. 22, 1988.

Hu Zhanfan and Peng Baowu. "A Description of the Submariners' Life," in *Junwei Jinxingqu—Renmin Jiefangjun Xiandaihua Jianshe* [Military Marches—The Modern Construction of the People's Liberation Army]. Beijing, 1987.

Huang Caihong. "The Chinese Submarine Corps Ranks Among the World's Most Advanced," *Liaowang*, overseas ed., June 22, 1987.

———. "The First Successful Oceangoing Navigation of Our Country's Nuclear-Powered Submarine," *Renmin Ribao*, overseas ed., Jan. 1, 1987.

———. "The New Development of China's Navy," *Liaowang*, overseas ed., Dec. 22, 1986.

———. "The New Development of Chinese Naval Missiles—An Interview with Commander of the Naval Missile Test Base Wang Huique," *Liaowang*, overseas ed., Nov. 14, 1988.

———. "Our Country's Submarine Units Are Expanding in Leaps and Bounds," *Liaowang*, June 8, 1987.

———. "The Tonnage of Our Naval Service Ships Is Nearly Thrice That of Ten Years Ago," *Renmin Ribao*, overseas ed., May 6, 1987.

———. "A Visit to Vice-Admiral Zhang Xusan, Deputy Naval Commander and Chief of Naval Staff," *Jianchuan Zhishi*, No. 4, 1989.

Huang Caihong and Cao Guoqiang. "Eyewitness to the Underwater Launch of a Rocket from a Nuclear-Powered Submarine," *Dagong Bao* [Impartial Daily] (Hong Kong), Sept. 29, 1988.

———. "For the Birth of China's Nuclear-Powered Submarine (1, 2)," *Renmin Ribao*, overseas ed., Sept. 28 and 29, 1988.

Huang Caihong and Guo Diancheng. "The Truth About the Sino-Vietnamese Armed Conflicts on the Nansha Islands," *Renmin Ribao*, April 1, 1988.

Huang Chaoxing. "The Town That First Meets the Changjiang River" (including the text for an accompanying picture), *Renmin Ribao*, overseas ed., Nov. 15, 1989.

Huang Shanhu. "The U.S. Plan for Communicating with Submarines by Extremely Low Frequency Radio," *Xiandai Junshi*, No. 6, 1987.

Huang Shengtian. "Zhang Aiping Right After the Creation of the East China People's Navy," *Dajiang Nanbei* [On Both Sides of the Changjiang River], No. 3, 1990.

Huang Weilu. "Quality Is the Life of Astronautic Products," in HGYZW.

Huang Xiaohui. "The 'Air Bladders' of a Submarine," *Jianchuan Zhishi*, No. 10, 1987.

Huang Xu. "The Construction of the China Aerodynamics Research and Development Center," in HGYZW.

Huang Xuhua. "On the Overall Design Plan for the Nuclear-Powered Submarine," in HGYZW.

Hudson, George E. "Soviet Naval Doctrine, 1953–72," in Michael MccGwire, ed., *Soviet Naval Developments: Capability and Context*. New York, 1973.

Huiyi He Long [Reminiscences on He Long]. Shanghai, 1984, Vol. 2.

Huo Rusu. "Forty Years of New China's Shipbuilding Industry," *Jianchuan Zhishi*, No. 10, 1989.

Huo Yinzhang. "Ancient Military Strategist: Sun Bin," *Junshi Shilin*, No. 2, 1986.

"If Nie Rongzhen Doesn't Surrender, He Will Be Exterminated," in *Survey of China Mainland Press*, Aug. 16, 1968, No. 4240.

"An Increase of Chinese Military Budget by 12 Percent," *Shijie Ribao*, March 25, 1991.

"The Increasing Output Value of the Military Industrial Enterprises in Sichuan Province," *Renmin Ribao*, overseas ed., Jan. 3, 1990.

"Institute 707's Degenerate Party Committee Disbanded by the Tianjin Municipal Party Committee," *Renmin Ribao*, May 14, 1984.

"International Symposium on 'Sun Zi's Art of War' Will Be Held Next Year in Linyi, Shandong," *Shijie Ribao*, April 24, 1991.

"An Introduction to the 10 New Ministries and Commissions Established by the State Council," *Renmin Ribao*, overseas ed., March 29, 1988.

Ji Bing. "Readjust the Structure of the Defense Industry and Create a Dual Military-Civilian Industrial System," *Guofang Daxue Xuebao*, No. 2, 1991.

Ji Xichen. "Disturbances Around Diaoyutai," in Yu Gong, ed., *Lin Biao Shijian Zhenxiang* [The Truth About the Lin Biao Incident]. Beijing, 1988.

Ji Yanglin. "Our Country Has Built a Long-Distance Navigation System," *Jiefangjun Bao*, Aug. 19, 1990.

Jia Wenxian et al. "On the Specific Laws Concerning Future Local Conflicts That Will Involve Our Country," *Guofang Daxue Xuebao*, No. 11, 1987.

Jia Yuping and Sun Yongan. "A Commander of a Nuclear-Powered Submarine," *Liaowang*, July 22, 1991.

Jiang Cheng and Guo Liyun. "On the Readjustment of Our Army's Cadres [Policy]," *Jiefangjun Bao*, Feb. 2, 1988.

Jiang Chengwei. "Review of the Development of Our Country's Explosive and Powder Industry over the Past 40 Years," in HGYZW.

Jiang Fuyi. "A Historical Survey of the Political System of the People's Republic of China," *Shixue Yuekan* [History Science Monthly], No. 5, 1989.

Jiang Hong. "Mao Zedong on the Yuelushan Mountain in 1974 and 1975," *Mao*

Zedong Sixiang Yanjiu [Studies on Mao Zedong's Thought] (Chengdu), No. 3, 1989.

Jiang Jun. "The Military Satellites of Various Hues (1)," *Bingqi Zhishi* [Ordnance Knowledge], No. 6, 1988.

Jiang Kejun. "On the Features of the Past Shifts in Our Army's Strategic Guiding Principles," in Shao Chengye, chief ed., *Huigu Zhanwang Tantao* [Retrospect, Prospect, and Exploration]. Chengdu, 1987.

Jiang Lin. "The Development of Defense Science and Technology Needs an Appropriate Policy," *Jiefangjun Bao*, April 7, 1988.

Jiang Ming and Xu Sen. "[An Introduction to] the Naval Engineering Institute," *Bingqi Zhishi* [Ordnance Knowledge], No. 6, 1988.

Jiang Rubiao. "Head of the Naval Communications Department Wang Dongshan Talks About Naval Communications," *Jiefangjun Bao*, March 2, 1989.

———. "The Progressive Renewal of Naval Communication Equipment," *Jiefangjun Bao*, March 25, 1989.

———. "A Sketch of the Launch of a Carrier Rocket from a Nuclear-Powered Submarine," *Jianchuan Zhishi*, No. 12, 1988.

Jiang Rubiao and Deng Haiming. "Each of the Navy's Fleets Creates a Combat Ship Training Center," *Jiefangjun Bao*, Aug. 6, 1988.

Jiang Rubiao and Xiang Xin. "A Description of Li Honghai, a Model Naval Technical Officer," *Renmin Ribao*, overseas ed., Sept. 9, 1991.

Jiang Rubiao and Yang Jianmin. "The Navy Confers Professional Posts on Technical Officers on Fighting Ships," *Jiefangjun Bao*, Aug. 28, 1988.

Jiang Rubiao and Zhang Heng. "The Navy Has Constructed a Modern Comprehensive Naval Test Base," *Jiefangjun Bao*, Oct. 21, 1988.

Jiang Rubiao and Zhang Ming. "Messages from the 'Dragon Palace,'" *Jiefangjun Bao*, April 7, 1988.

———. "A Visit to a Naval Long-Wave Radio Station," *Junshi Shijie*, No. 1, 1988.

Jiang Rubiao et al. "China's No. 1 Submarine Repairing Team," *Jiefangjun Bao*, Sept. 11, 1991.

———. "A Visit to a Nuclear Missile Submarine," *Jiefangjun Bao*, Sept. 28, 1988.

Jiang Siyi. *Zhanlüexing de Da Zhuanbian* [A Major Change in Strategy]. Beijing, 1987.

Jiang Weisen. "The Conference on Ensuring Safety and Security in National Defense Tests," *Jiefangjun Bao*, Nov. 30, 1989.

Jiang Zemin. "Attach Great Importance to the Vigorous Development of Science and Technology," *Zijing* [Bauhinia] (Hong Kong), No. 8, 1991.

Jiao Huibiao. "An Unknown Scientific City—Mianyang," *Dagong Bao* [Impartial Daily] (Hong Kong), Nov. 27, 1988.

Jiao Xinguang. "A Scientific Strong Woman," *Jiefangjun Bao*, June 28, 1991.

Jiao Yong. "Premier Zhou Enlai's Concern for the Space Cause," *Hangtian*, No. 2, 1988.

Jiao Yulin. "Microelectronics and Precision-Guided Munitions," *Xiandaihua* [Modernization], No. 3, 1984.

Jin Chunming et al., eds. *Wenge Shiqi Guaishi Guaiyu* [Unusual Events and Terminologies During the Cultural Revolution]. Beijing, 1988.

Jin Chuntian. "Visits to the Veteran Revolutionaries Xiao Jinguang, Wang Shoudao, Li Jingquan, and Wu Xiuquan," *Fujian Dangshi Yuekan* [Fujian Party's History Monthly], No. 5, 1988.

Jin Chunxiang. "Bring into Full Play the Local Authorities' Role in Promoting the Development of the Defense Science and Industry," in HGYZW.

Jin Tao. "The Navy's First Imported Submarine," *Jianchuan Zhishi*, No. 7, 1989.

Jin Zhude et al. *Guofang Jingji Lun* [On the Defense Economy]. Beijing, 1987.

Kan Shiying and He Delai. "The China Sea Is Calling Us," *Jiefangjun Bao*, Dec. 20, 1988.

Ke Bitian. "Rocket Engines—Solid and Solid-Liquid Rocket Engines (2)," *Hangkong Zhishi*, No. 10, 1975.

Kemp, Geoffrey. *Nuclear Forces for Medium Powers*. International Institute for Strategic Studies, Adelphi Papers 106 and 107. London, 1974.

Kennan, George. "Introduction," in Veljko Micunovic, *Moscow Diary*. Tr. David Floyd. Garden City, N. Y., 1980.

Khrushchev, Nikita. *Khrushchev Remembers*. Tr. and ed. Strobe Talbott. Boston, Mass., 1970.

———. *Khrushchev Remembers: The Last Testament*. Tr. and ed. Strobe Talbott. Boston, Mass., 1974.

Kou Chengzhen and Li Yang. "The Tracking and Control Performance of *Distant Observer* Nos. 1 and 2 Greatly Enhanced After Overhaul and Technical Innovations," *Jiefangjun Bao*, Dec. 10, 1987.

Lai Jinlie. "Take the Road of Hard Work in Constructing an Ordnance Industry with Chinese Characteristics," in HGYZW.

Lank S. W., and O. H. Oakley. "Application of Nuclear Power to Icebreakers," *Society of Naval Architects and Marine Engineers Transactions*, Vol. 67, 1959.

"A Last-Ditch Struggle of the Jiang Qing Clique Before Its Destruction," in Lin Riqing, ed., *Wenge shi Shangceng Lingdao Juezhan Jingguo Zhengxiang* [The Truth of the Giants' Struggles at the Top in the Cultural Revolution]. Hong Kong, 1982.

Lei Huajian. "On Historical Lessons from Old China's Coastal Defense Strategy," *Guofang Daxue Xuebao*, No. 6, 1989.

Lei Ming. "Maritime Thinking and State Security," *Jiefangjun Bao*, Aug. 26, 1988.

Lei Xinlong. "Remarkable Success Achieved in Our Country's Coordinated Efforts to Manufacture Military Hardware," *Jiefangjun Bao*, Feb. 26, 1989.

Lei Xun. "Arduous Struggle, Courageous Exploration, and Great Plan," in HGYZW.

Lei Yuanshen. "The Evolution of the Central Military Commission," *Zhonggong Dangshi Ziliao* [Materials on CCP History]. Beijing, 1990, Vol. 34.

Lewis, John W. *Political Networks and the Chinese Policy Process*. Stanford, Calif., 1986.

———. "Revolutionary Struggle and the Second Generation in Communist China," *China Quarterly*, No. 21 (Jan.–March 1965).

Lewis, John W., and Hua Di. "China's Ballistic Missile Programs: Technologies, Strategies, Goals," *International Security*, 17, No. 2 (Fall 1992).

Lewis, John W., Hua Di, and Xue Litai. "Beijing's Defense Establishment: Solving the Arms-Export Enigma," *International Security*, 15, No. 4 (Spring 1991).

Lewis, John W., and Xue Litai. *China Builds the Bomb*. Stanford, Calif., 1988.

———. "Chinese Strategic Weapons and the Plutonium Option," *Critical Technologies Newsletter* (Los Alamos), April/May 1988.

———. *Military Readiness and the Training of China's Sailors*. Stanford, Calif., 1989.

————. "Strategic Weapons and Chinese Power: The Formative Years," *China Quarterly*, Dec. 1987.

Li Bingyan and Sun Jing. "Lay Stress on Tactics: The Character of theAncient Oriental Art of War," *Jiefangjun Bao*, April 21, 1989.

Li Bingyan and Zeng Guangjun. "Our Army's Strategic Studies Become Active," *Jiefangjun Bao*, May 10, 1986.

Li Derun. "Deng Xiaoping Warmly Meets with Middle-Aged Scientists and Engineers," *Jiefangjun Bao*, July 25, 1987.

Li Fengchun. "The Theory of Ignition of Solid Rocket Propellants." Unpublished report, 1984.

Li Fumin and Li Dunsong. "A Brief Account of the Growth and Development of Our Country's Strategic Missile Troops," *Junshi Shilin*, No. 5, 1988.

Li Hong. "What I Saw and Heard from the Oceangoing Instrumentation Fleet," *Jiefangjun Wenyi* [Literature and Art of the Liberation Army], No. 7, 1980.

Li Huaixing. "The Three Fair Circles of Defense Economy," *Jiefangjun Bao*, Feb. 25, 1988.

Li Jianghe and Hou Aiping. "What We Think About Our Country's Defense Developmental Strategy," *Junshi Shilin*, No. 5, 1987.

Li Jie. "Panorama of Modern Submarines," *Junshi Shilin*, No. 3, 1989.

————. "The Various Means to Conceal Submarines," *Xiandai Junshi*, No. 7, 1991.

Li Jinting et al. "Spaceflight Chief Engineer," *Liaowang*, Oct. 20, 1982.

Li Jue et al., chief eds. *Dangdai Zhongguo de He Gongye* [Contemporary China's Nuclear Industry]. Beijing, 1987.

Li Ke and Hao Shengzhang. *Wenhua Dageming zhong de Renmin Jiefangjun* [The People's Liberation Army in the Great Cultural Revolution]. Beijing, 1989.

Li Maoju. "The Lishan Microelectronics Institute Is Developing New Products," *Renmin Ribao*, overseas ed., Aug. 18, 1988.

Li Maoqin. "For Those First-Generation Submariners Who Devoted Themselves to the Development of the Chinese Navy," *Jianchuan Zhishi*, No. 4, 1989.

Li Min et al. "Bombard Nie Rongzhen and Completely Take the Lid Off Class Struggle in the Defense Science and Technology Commission's Organs," in *Survey of China Mainland Press*, Aug. 12, 1968, No. 4236.

Li Mingsheng and Xiao Zhou. "Commander of the Xichang Satellite [Launch Center]," *Renmin Ribao*, overseas ed., Sept. 17, 1990.

Li Nanling and Cheng Jian. "The Third-Line Enterprises Become Full of Vitality in Readjustment," *Renmin Ribao*, Dec. 8, 1990.

Li Peng. "Report on the Outline of the Ten-Year Programme and of the Eighth Five-Year Plan for National Economic and Social Development" [March 25, 1991], *Beijing Review*, April 15–21, 1991.

Li Pu and Shen Rong. "He Is My Good Teacher—General Xiao Ke Talks About Marshal Liu [Bocheng]," *Liaowang*, Nov. 10, 1986.

Li Qi and Nie Li. "The Construction of the '718' Oceangoing Instrumentation Fleet," in HGYZW.

Li Rui. "Lessons from the Lushan Plenum," *Dangxiao Luntan* [Party School Forum], No. 3, 1989.

————. *Lushan Huiyi Shilu* [A True Record of the Lushan Plenum]. Beijing, 1989.

————. "Why Did Peng Dehuai Write [Mao Zedong] the Letter?" *Xinhua Wenzhai* [New China Digest], No. 4, 1989.

Li Runshan. "Nuclear Radiation and Protective Measures on a Nuclear-Powered Submarine," *Xinhua Wenzhai* [New China Digest], No. 9, 1987.

Li Wei. "Yang Dezhi Describes First Phase of Streamlining and Reorganization of the Chinese Army as Having Basically Come to an End," *Zhongguo Xinwen She*, March 26, 1986, in FBIS: China, March 27, 1986.

Li Wen. "A Brief Report on the Big Powers' Invasion of Our Country's Ports," *Hanghai* [Navigation], No. 4, 1980.

Li Xiangqian. "Divergent Views on the Economic Adjustment of 1962," *Zhonggong Dangshi Yanjiu* [Studies on CCP History], No. 6, 1988.

Li Xianying. "The Navy Submarine Institute Promotes Scientific Research for Enhancing Fighting Capacity," *Jiefangjun Bao*, May 27, 1989.

Li Xiguang. "The Birth of [Our Country's] First Production Line for [Special] Tiny Aluminum Spheres," *Renmin Ribao*, overseas ed., June 27, 1990.

Li Xiuqing. "The Enormous Role Played by Our Country's Satellites," *Renmin Ribao*, overseas ed., April 22, 1991.

Li Xueyin. "Inadequate Military Budgets and the Defense Modernization That Cannot Be Slowed Down," *Jiefangjun Bao*, Nov. 30, 1987.

Li Xueyin and Guo Xiangxing. "Great Successes Achieved by the Naval Research Center," *Renmin Ribao*, Jan. 29, 1988.

———. "The Naval Research Center Undertakes Research Works on Almost All Naval Weapons and Equipment," *Jiefangjun Bao*, Jan. 25, 1988.

Li Xueyin and Zhang Heng. "We Are Perfecting Our Sea Range Day by Day," *Jiefangjun Bao*, Aug. 28, 1987.

Li Yadan. "A Description of Professor Huang Weilu, Chief Designer of Our Country's Submarine-Launched Missile," *Jiefangjun Bao*, May 12, 1987.

———. "The Man who Deals with Explosives," *Junshi Shijie*, No. 1, 1989.

———. "Open a New Prospect in Readjustment and Reform," *Jiefangjun Bao*, Nov. 28, 1988.

———. "What We Saw at the Military Industrial Enterprises in Shaanxi (1)," *Jiefangjun Bao*, May 26, 1988.

Li Yadan et al. "A Description of Huang Weilu, Chief Designer of China's Submarine-Launched Missile," *Junshi Shijie*, No. 1, 1988.

———. "Ode to the 'Spirit of *Distant Observer*,'" *Jiefangjun Bao*, Oct. 12, 1989.

Li Yang. "A Description of Bian Qifen, an Engineer on a Radar Transmitter," *Jiefangjun Bao*, Sept. 1, 1988.

———. "Technological Transformations of the *Distant Observer* Instrumentation Ships Approved as Acceptable," *Jiefangjun Bao*, May 20, 1989.

———. "The Three Victories Scored by the *Distant Observer* Instrumentation Ships in 1988," *Jiefangjun Bao*, Jan. 5, 1989.

———. "A Visit to the Chinese Oceangoing Astronautic Measurement Base," *Junshi Shijie*, No. 2, 1990.

Li Yang and He Shitian. "A Visit to the Synchronous Timing Center of the *Distant Observer* Instrumentation Ship," *Junshi Shijie*, No. 2, 1990.

Li Yang and Su Kuoshan. "The 'Eyes' of the Marine Scientific City," *Jiefangjun Bao*, July 13, 1989.

Li Yimin. *Li Yimin Huiyilu* [Memoirs of Li Yimin]. Beijing, 1986.

Li Yiwei. "The Development of Polyurethane Propellants," *Xiandai Bingqi* [Modern Weaponry], No. 3, 1986.

———. "The Evolution of Composite Propellant and Its Adhesive," *Xiandai Bingqi* [Modern Weaponry], No. 12, 1986.

Li Yongzeng and Li Shuzhong. "A Historic Turning Point for Construction in China's Third-Line Region," *Liaowang*, overseas ed., June 30, 1986.

Li Yueran. *Waijiao Wutai shang de Xin Zhongguo Lingxiu* [Leaders of the New China on the Diplomatic Scene]. Beijing, 1989.

Li Yuliang and Qi Sanping. "49 Military Schools Will Recruit New Students from Local High Schools," *Jiefangjun Bao*, May 1, 1989.

Li Yunsheng. "The Development of and Prospects for Our Army's Communication Equipment," in HGYZW.

Li Zhichen and Hong Heping. "The Air Force Is Conducting Air Defense Exercises in a Nuclear Environment," *Jiefangjun Bao*, Oct. 30, 1990.

Li Zhongshi and He Wannan. "'Urgent Delivery of Guns' and 'Secret Production of Guns,'" *Jiefang Ribao* [Liberation Daily] (Shanghai), Dec. 17, 1980.

Liao Guoliang et al. *Mao Zedong Junshi Sixiang Fazhan Shi* [The Development of Mao Zedong's Military Thinking]. Beijing, 1991.

Liao-Shen Zhanyi [The Liaoxi-Shenyang Campaign]. Beijing, 1988.

Liao Shenghui et al. "A Description of the 'Heroic Mapping Brigade' (1)," *Jiefangjun Bao*, Nov. 26, 1989.

"The Life of Comrade Xiao Jinguang," in Yang Shangkun et al., *Yidai Yuanrong* [A Supreme Commander]. Beijing, 1991.

Lin Biao. "Long Live the Victory of People's War," *Peking Review*, No. 36 (Sept. 3, 1965).

Lin Boye et al. *Mao Zedong Junshi Bianzhengfa Sixiang Xintan* [An Exploration of Mao Zedong's Dialectical Thinking on Military Affairs]. Beijing, 1987.

Lin Chong-pin. *China's Nuclear Weapons Strategy: Tradition Within Evolution.* Lexington, Mass., 1988.

Lin Shen. "The Application of Compressed Air to Missile Technologies," *Bingqi Zhishi* [Ordnance Knowledge], No. 3, 1985.

Lin Tianyi. "From the Beginning to the End of the 1959 Lushan Plenum," *Fujian Dangshi Yuekan* [Fujian Party's History Monthly], No. 2, 1989.

Lin Xi and Ji Yin. "Information and Enlightenment from Visits to the Enterprises in the Third-Line Region," *Renmin Ribao*, overseas ed., June 8, 1987.

Lin Yingguang and Wu Qingyu. "Forty Years of the Chinese Navy," *Junshi Shijie*, No. 2, 1989.

Lin Yunhui et al. *1949–1989 Nian de Zhongguo Kaige Xingjin de Shiqi* [China's Triumphant March from 1949 to 1989]. Zhengzhou, 1989.

Linden, Carl A. *Khrushchev and the Soviet Leadership, 1957–1964.* Baltimore, 1966.

Ling Xiang. "The Underwater Killer: Nuclear-Powered Submarines," *Junshi Shilin*, No. 5, 1988.

Ling Xiang and Gu Han. "The Nuclear Wolves in the Dragon Palace," *Zhongguo Minbing* [Chinese Militia], No. 4, 1989.

Ling Yu. "The Chinese Navy's New Types of Light Surface Combatants," *Guangjiaojing* [Wide-Angle Lens] (Hong Kong), No. 10, 1990.

———. "Secretly Build an Aircraft Carrier: The Future Trend of the Chinese Communist Navy," *Guangjiaojing* [Wide-Angle Lens] (Hong Kong), No. 12, 1989.

———. "The Strength of the Chinese Communist Submarine Fleet," *Guangjiaojing* [Wide-Angle Lens] (Hong Kong), Oct. 16, 1989.

Liu Boluo. "Premier Zhou and the CCP Central Special Commission," in HGYZW.

———. "Premier Zhou Devoted All His Energies to Our Country's Sophisticated Scientific and Technological Cause," in *Bujin de Sinian* [Boundless Recollections]. Beijing, 1987.

———. "A True Record of the Development of China's Sophisticated Science and Technology," *Junshi Shijie*, No. 1, 1989.

Liu Chang'an et al. "The Birth of New InGaAs Integrated Circuits," *Renmin Ribao*, overseas ed., Jan. 4, 1991.

Liu Chen. "The Development of Our Country's Satellite Communications," *Hangtian*, No. 1, 1991.

Liu Congjun, chief ed. *Hangtian Gongye Bu Dier Yanjiuyuan Dashiji* [A Chronicle of Major Events of the Second Academy of the Ministry of Aerospace Industry]. Beijing, 1987.

———. *Hangtian Gongye Bu Dier Yanjiuyuan Yuanshi* [The History of the Second Academy of the Ministry of Aerospace Industry]. Beijing, 1987.

Liu Daosheng. "Boundless Recollections," in Yang Shangkun et al., *Yidai Yuanrong* [A Supreme Commander]. Beijing, 1991.

Liu Deming and Wang Youqi. "The Creation of Our Country's First Topographic Data Bank," *Jiefangjun Bao*, Oct. 17, 1990.

Liu Dengrong et al., eds. *Bingqi Cidian* [A Dictionary of Ordnance]. Beijing, 1987.

Liu Fangyu. "On the Optimization of Industrial Distribution," *Qiusuo* [Seek Truth] (Changsha), No. 3, 1990.

Liu Guanxue and Lu Wenqi. "450,000 Officers Now Work and Live in Contentment," *Renmin Ribao*, overseas ed., July 29, 1987.

Liu Guohua. "The Ocean's Echo," *Jiefangjun Bao*, Feb. 7, 1987.

Liu Huaqing. "Build a Powerful Navy, Develop Our Country's Marine Cause," *Renmin Ribao*, Nov. 24, 1984.

———. "The Key to Building a Powerful, Modern Navy Lies in Qualified Personnel," *Hongqi* [Red Flag], No. 2, 1986.

"Liu Huaqing Speaks on China's Naval Submarine Force," *Zhongguo Xinwen She* [China News Agency], Sept. 26, 1985, in FBIS: China, Oct. 1, 1985.

Liu Huaqiu. *China and the Neutron Bomb*. Stanford, Calif., 1988.

———. "'Sun Zi's Art of War' and Modern Nuclear Deterrence," *Xiandai Junshi*, No. 2, 1991.

Liu Huinian. "Executive Vice-Chairman of the Central Military Commission Yang Shangkun Talks About How to Reform the Military System and Streamline and Reorganize the Army," *Liaowang*, July 8, 1985.

———. "Vital Strategic Decision-Making," *Liaowang*, July 8, 1985.

Liu Huinian and Xiong Zhengyan. "The Liberation Army Composed Mainly of a New Generation of Educated Soldiers," *Renmin Ribao*, Aug. 1, 1984.

Liu Huinian and Yi Jianru. "An Interview with Head of the PLA General Staff Yang Dezhi," *Liaowang*, July 29, 1985.

Liu Jianghai. "Great Achievements in Our Country's Research on Inertial Technology," *Jiefangjun Bao*, May 20, 1989.

Liu Jie. "Victory of the Socialist Road in the Development of Science and Technology with Chinese Characteristics—In Commemoration of the 30th Anniversary of the Founding of the Nuclear Industry," *Renmin Ribao*, Nov. 1, 1985.

Liu Jingzhi. "A Description of Huang Xuhua, Chief Designer of the Nuclear-Powered Missile Submarine," *Junshi Shijie*, No. 7, 1989.

Liu Jiyuan and Sun Jiadong. "The Scientific Management of Space Engineering," in HGYZW.

Liu Jizeng and Mao Lei, chief eds. *Zhongguo Gongchandang Lingdao Gongzuo Shigao* [Evolution of the Work-Styles of the CCP Leadership (Draft)]. Beijing, 1988.

Liu Jushao. "At Recent Top-Level PLA Meeting, Zhao Ziyang Urges Vigilance Against Partial War," *Wenhui Bao* [Encounter Daily] (Hong Kong), May 11, 1988, in FBIS: China, May 11, 1988.

Liu Kun. "Prospect for the Development of Torpedoes Up to the Year 2000," *Jianchuan Zhishi*, No. 6, 1987.

Liu Luyan. "Topography: The Vanguard of Economic Construction," *Renmin Ribao*, overseas ed., Nov. 29, 1986.

Liu Shaoqiu and Lu Zhen. "China's First SLBM," *Hangtian*, No. 2, 1989.

Liu Shengdong and Zhang Weixing. "A Description of the Party Branch of the 11th Crew of a Certain Naval Base," *Jiefangjun Bao*, July 3, 1991.

Liu Shengjun and Wang Fengju. "A Symposium Held in Chengdu to Discuss [How to Strengthen] Logistic Support for Local Wars," *Renmin Ribao*, May 24, 1988.

Liu Shuqing and Zhang Jifu. "A Loud Crash of Thunder—Report on the Detonation of Our Country's First Atomic Bomb," in *Mimi Licheng* [A Secret Course]. Beijing, 1985.

Liu Xianfu and Li Jiang. "Mao Zedong's Philosophical Thought and Defense Modernization," *Mao Zedong Sixiang Yanjiu* [Studies on Mao Zedong's Thought] (Chengdu), No. 4, 1990.

Liu Xiao. *Chushi Sulian Banian* [Eight Years in the Soviet Union as Ambassador]. Beijing, 1986.

———. "A Mission to the Soviet Union (4–6)," *Shijie Zhishi* [World Knowledge], Nos. 14, 16, 18, 1987.

Liu Xing. "The 'Trilogy' in the Development of a Solid Missile (1–2)," *Junshi Shijie*, Nos. 1, 2, 1989.

Liu Xinru. "An Interview with Zhang Xusan, Deputy to the National People's Congress and Deputy Commander of the Navy," *Jiefangjun Bao*, March 26, 1989.

———. "Protect Military Installations and Safeguard National Defense," *Jiefangjun Bao*, Dec. 21, 1989.

Liu Xiyao. "On the Eve of and After My Appointment as Premier Zhou's Liaison Man," in *Bujin de Sinian* [Boundless Recollections]. Beijing, 1987.

Liu Yin et al., chief eds. *Dangdai Zhongguo de Dianzi Gongye* [Contemporary China's Electronics Industry]. Beijing, 1987.

Liu Ying. "The Years of Adversity: Recollections of [Zhang] Wentian (1)," *Liaowang*, Aug. 12, 1985.

Liu Ying and Dou Qi. "The Naming Ceremony of the 'Heroic Mapping Brigade' Held in Beijing," *Jiefangjun Bao*, April 15, 1989.

Liu Youguang. "The Initial Ideological Work in Our Country's Space Cause," in HGYZW.

Liu Youguang and Zhang Jun. "The Path of Development for Our Country's Space Cause," in HGYZW.

Lockheed Missiles and Space Company. *A History of the FBM System*. Sunnyvale, Calif., 1989.

Long Jize. "Thinking and Experiments in Military Strategy," in *Guoji Xingshi yu Guofang Zhanlüe* [International Situation and Defense Strategy]. Beijing, 1987.

"The Long March No. 4 and the Taiyuan [Satellite Launch] Center," *Dagong Bao* [Impartial Daily] (Hong Kong), Sept. 9, 1988.

Lu Da. "Studies on Metallurgical Materials Have Served the National Defense for Forty Years," in HGYZW.

Lu Dadong. "Bring into Full Play the Role of the Military Industrial Network in the Third-Line Region by Attaching Importance to Readjustment and [Technological] Transformation," in HGYZW.

Lu Haozhong et al. "Predictions on the Military Situation in the Asian-Pacific Region in the Early 21st Century and Its Impact on the Construction of Our Country's Strategic Nuclear Forces," in *YaTai de Xuanwo* [Eddies in the Asian and Pacific Region]. Beijing, 1989.

Lu Jianxun. "A Look at the Past and Future of the Warship Scientific and Research Program," in HGYZW.

Lu Keng. *Hu Yaobang Fangwen Ji* [An Interview with Hu Yaobang]. New York, 1985.

———. "A Visit with Hu Yaobang," *Pai Shing* [People] (Hong Kong), June 1, 1985.

Lü Liping. "Unusual Courage and Resourcefulness, Brilliant Feats [of Ye Jianying]," *Guangming Ribao*, Nov. 9, 1986.

Lu Peifa and Liu Gang. "What We Saw at the Third-Line Enterprises in Sichuan," *Renmin Ribao*, overseas ed., July 9, 1987.

Lu Qiming. *Dahai de Jiaoao Renmin Haijun Jishi zhi Yi* [The Pride of the Ocean: Descriptions of the People's Navy]. Beijing, 1983.

Lu Tianyi. "The Development of Defense Science and Technology in Restraint," *Jiefangjun Bao*, April 1, 1989.

Lu Yingjie. "Zhou Enlai and China's Nuclear-Powered Submarine," *Junshi Shijie*, No. 3, 1988.

Luo Chuanli and Shao Fuling. "A Look to the Past and Future of the Deep-Water Torpedo System," *Xiandai Junshi*, No. 8, 1990.

Luo Laiyong. "People in the Rocket City—A Sketch of China's Limited-Range ICBM Test City," *Kunlun* [Kunlun], No. 1, 1986.

Luo Ronghuan Yuanshuai [Marshal Luo Ronghuan]. Beijing, 1987.

Luo Ruiqing. *Commemorate the Victory over Fascism! Carry the Struggle Against U.S. Imperialism Through to the End!* [May 10, 1965]. Beijing, 1965.

———. *The People Defeated Japanese Fascism and They Can Certainly Defeat U.S. Imperialism Too* [Sept. 2, 1965]. Beijing, 1965.

Luo Tongsong and Fan Hao. "An Interview with Wang Chenghan, Political Commissar of the Academy of Military Science," *Renmin Ribao*, July 30, 1988.

Ma Hong, chief ed. *Dangdai Zhongguo Jingji* [Contemporary China's Economy]. Beijing, 1987.

Ma Lu et al. *Guofang Buzhang Fuchen Ji* [The Rise and Fall of the Defense Minister]. Beijing, 1989.

Ma Lütian et al. "Some Ideas on the Role and Significance of Deterrent Strategy," *Guofang Daxue Xuebao*, No. 10, 1987.

Ma Qibin et al. *Zhongguo Gongchandang Shizheng Sishi Nian (1949–1989)* [40 Years of the CCP in Power (1949–1989)]. Beijing, 1989.

Ma Yunfei. "Liu Shaoqi and the Readjustment of the National Economy in the 1960s," *Zhonggong Dangshi Yanjiu* [Studies on CCP History], No. 5, 1988.

MacFarquhar, Roderick. *The Hundred Flowers*. New York, 1960.

MacKenzie, Donald. *Inventing Accuracy: A Historical Sociology of Nuclear Missile Guidance.* Cambridge, Mass., 1990.

"Mainland China Creates the China State Electronics Corporation to Upgrade Military Science and Technology," *Shijie Ribao,* June 8, 1991.

"Mainland China Has Raised the Power of Its Strategic Missile Corps," *Zhongbao* [Central Daily News] (New York), May 7, 1988.

Mao Rongfang, "A Description of Liu Xing, Deputy Chief Engineer at the Chinese Ship Science Research Center," *Guangming Ribao,* Jan. 25, 1988.

Mao Zedong [Mao Tsetung] (all Chinese works published in Beijing unless otherwise noted)

[1]. "Analysis of the Classes in Chinese Society" [March 1926], in *Selected Readings from the Works of Mao Tse-tung.* 1967.

[2]. "Mao Tse-tung's Speeches at the CCP Chengtu Conference" [March 10, 1958], in *Issues and Studies* (Taipei), Nov. 1973.

[3]. "On Protracted War" [May 1938], in *Selected Military Writings of Mao Tse-tung.* 1966.

[4]. "On Some Important Problems of the Party's Present Policy" [Jan. 18, 1948], in *Selected Works of Mao Tse-tung.* 1961, Vol. 4.

[5]. "On the Ten Major Relationships" [April 25, 1956], in *Selected Works of Mao Tsetung.* 1977, Vol. 5.

[6]. "The Order of the Chairman of the People's Republic of China," *Renmin Ribao,* Feb. 12, 1958.

[7]. "Problems of Strategy in China's Revolutionary War" [Dec. 1936], in *Selected Military Writings of Mao Tse-tung.* 1966.

[8]. "Speech at the Group Leaders Forum of the Enlarged Conference of the Military Affairs Commission [Central Military Commission]" [June 28, 1958], in *Chinese Law and Government,* 1, No. 4 (Winter 1968/69).

[9]. "Speech at the Sixth Plenum of the Eighth Central Committee" [Dec. 19, 1958], in *Miscellany of Mao Tse-tung Thought (1949–1968),* JPRS 61269-1, Feb. 20, 1974.

[10]. "Speech at the Supreme State Conference" [Jan. 28, 1958], in *Chinese Law and Government,* 1, No. 4 (Winter 1968/69).

[11]. "Speeches at the Second Session of the Eighth Party Congress" [May 8–23, 1958], in *Miscellany of Mao Tse-tung Thought (1949–1968),* JPRS 61269-1, Feb. 20, 1974.

[12]. "Talk of 22 March," in Stuart Schram, ed., *Chairman Mao Talks to the People; Talks and Letters: 1956–1971.* New York, 1974.

[13]. "Talk on Putting Military Affairs Work into Full Effect and Cultivating Successors to the Revolution," in *Miscellany of Mao Tse-tung Thought (1949–1968),* JPRS 61269-2 (Feb. 20, 1974).

[14]. "Talk on the Third Five-Year Plan," in *Miscellany of Mao Tse-tung Thought (1949–1968),* JPRS 61269-2, Feb. 20, 1974.

[15]. "Talks at the Nanning Conference" [Jan. 11–12, 1958], in *Miscellany of Mao Tse-tung Thought (1949–1968),* JPRS 61269-2 (Feb. 20, 1974).

MccGwire, Michael. "Current Soviet Warship Construction," in Michael MccGwire, ed., *Soviet Naval Developments: Capability and Context.* New York, 1973.

Mi Zhenyu and Chen Weimin. "The Determination of Military Strategic Goals Is a Question of the First Importance in Studying the Strategy for Defense Development," in *Guoji Xingshi yu Guofang Zhanlüe* [International Situation and Defense Strategy]. Beijing, 1987.

Micunovic, Veljko. *Moscow Diary.* Tr. David Floyd. Garden City, N. Y., 1980.

Miles, Wyndham D. "The Polaris," in Eugene M. Emme, ed., *The History of Rocket Technology: Essays on Research, Development, and Utility.* Detroit, Mich., 1964.

"The Military Calls for Punishment of the Criminals Who Destroyed Military Installations," *Renmin Ribao*, overseas ed., Feb. 18, 1989.

"Military Snub," *Far Eastern Economic Review*, Oct. 18, 1990.

"Military Topography Is Indispensable for Developing Space Technology," *Hangkong Zhishi*, No. 5, 1988.

Min Guoku. "The Eddy Left by a Nuclear-Powered Submarine in the Deep Sea," *Kunlun* [Kunlun], No. 3, 1984.

Min Li. "On the Eve of and After the Mao Zedong–Stalin Talks in Moscow," in Min Li et al., *Mao Zedong Sidalin Mosike Huiwu Qianhou* [On the Eve of and After the Mao Zedong-Stalin Talks in Moscow]. Chengdu, 1989.

Mo Sheng. "An Impact Zone in South Xinjiang," *Hangtian*, No. 6, 1990.

Mo Yang. "Comrade Ye Jianying's Great Contributions to the Army-Wide Training System and the Work of All the Army's Institutes and Schools," *Guofang Daxue Xuebao*, No. 4, 1986.

Monan Sui Duo Xin Wu Xia [He Was Still Loyal Although He Endured Untold Sufferings]. Beijing, 1978.

Moore, John. *The Soviet Navy Today.* New York, 1976.

———, ed. *Jane's Fighting Ships, 1985–86.* London, 1985.

———. *Jane's Warsaw Pact Warships Handbook.* London, 1986.

Mu Pinghe. "The Superguide at Sea," *Hanghai* [Navigation], No. 6, 1980.

Muller, David G., Jr. *China as a Maritime Power.* Boulder, Colo., 1983.

———. "A Chinese Blockade of Taiwan," *U.S. Naval Institute Proceedings*, Sept. 1984.

Murphey, Rhoads. "The Treaty Ports and China's Modernization," in Mark Elvin and G. William Skinner, eds., *The Chinese City Between Two Worlds.* Stanford, Calif., 1974.

"Name List of Appointments Approved by the 17th Meeting of the Central People's Government Council," *Xin Hua Yuebao* [New China Monthly], Sept. 25, 1952.

Naughton, Barry. "Industrial Policy During the Cultural Revolution: Military Preparation, Decentralization, and Leaps Forward," in William Joseph, Christine Wong, and David Zweig, eds., *New Perspectives on the Cultural Revolution.* Cambridge, Mass., 1991.

———. "The Third Front: Defence Industrialisation in the Chinese Interior," *China Quarterly*, Sept. 1988.

"The Naval Test Base of Our Country," *Jianchuan Zhishi*, No. 1, 1989.

"Navy Factories Are Being Transformed from Production Type into Management Type," *Renmin Ribao*, overseas ed., Dec. 30, 1986.

Needham, Joseph. *Science and Civilization in China.* London, 1986, Vol. 7.

"A New Breakthrough in Our Country's Underwater Launching Technologies," *Jianchuan Zhishi*, No. 11, 1992.

New China News Agency Reporters. "Beloved Premier Zhou, Sailors Dearly Cherish the Memory of You!" in *Renmin de Hao Zongli Zhou Enlai Tongzhi Yong-*

yuan Huo zai Women Xingzhong [The People's Good Premier: Comrade Zhou Will Live Forever in Our Hearts]. Shanghai, 1978, Vol. 3.

Newman, David B. *Space Vehicle Electronics*. Princeton, N. J., 1964.

Ni Huocai and Li Fangchun. "How Are Missiles Launched from a Submerged Submarine?" *Jianchuan Zhishi*, No. 1, 1988.

Ni Zhongwen, chief ed. *Zhonghua Renmin Gongheguo Jianguo Shi Shouce* [Manual on China's History After the Founding of the People's Republic]. Beijing, 1989.

Nie Fengzhi et al. *Sanjun Huige Zhan Donghai* [The Three Armed Services' Campaign in the East China Sea]. Beijing, 1985.

Nie Li and Huai Guomo, chief eds., *Huigu yu Zhanwang* [Retrospect and Prospect: 40 Years of Defense Technology and Industry in the New China]. Beijing, 1989.

Nie Quanlin, chief ed. *Guoji Huanjing yu Weilai Guofang* [The International Environment and Future National Defense]. Beijing, 1989.

Nie Rongzhen. *Inside the Red Star: The Memoirs of Marshal Nie Rongzhen*. Beijing, 1988.

———. *Nie Rongzhen Huiyilu* [Memoirs of Nie Rongzhen]. Beijing, 1986, Vol. 3.

———. "On the Science and Technology Front," in HGYZW.

Nie Rongzhen Nianpu [A Chronicle of Nie Rongzhen's Life]. Beijing, 1989.

Nie Rongzhen Yuanshuai [Marshal Nie Rongzhen]. Beijing, 1989.

Niu Guohua. "The Bohai Yard Achieves Success in Dual Military-Civilian Production," *Jiefangjun Bao*, Feb. 1, 1991.

Nye, Joseph S., Jr. "U.S.-Soviet Cooperation in a Nonproliferation Regime," in Alexander L. George et al., eds., *U.S.-Soviet Security Cooperation: Achievements, Failures, Lessons*. New York, 1988.

"On the Struggle of Proletarian Revolutionaries to Seize Powers," *Renmin Ribao*, Jan. 31, 1967.

"Order of the President of the PRC (No. 2)," *Renmin Ribao*, overseas ed., March 30, 1993.

"Order of the President of the PRC (No. 19)," *Renmin Ribao*, Sept. 21, 1984.

"Our Army's Strategic Missile Troops Are Fully Equipped," *Hangkong Zhishi*, No. 7, 1987.

"Our Country Achieves Success in Launching Missiles Underwater," *Renmin Ribao*, overseas ed., Sept. 28, 1988.

"Our Country Has Built a Relatively Integrated Defense Engineering System," *Renmin Ribao*, overseas ed., Feb. 2, 1987.

"Our Country Has Built Its First Long-Distance Radio Navigation System," *Jianchuan Zhishi*, No. 12, 1990.

"Our Country Will Adopt Legal Means to Protect Military Installations Classified by Three Grades," *Renmin Ribao*, overseas ed., Dec. 21, 1989.

"Our Country's First Warship Demagnetization Laboratory at the Naval Engineering Institute," *Jianchuan Zhishi*, No. 3, 1990.

"Our Navy Has the Capacity for Oceangoing Logistics and Supply," *Renmin Ribao*, overseas ed., June 8, 1987.

Pan Shiying. "Have a Sober Understanding of the Principal Contradiction in Army Building," *Jiefangjun Bao*, Sept. 11, 1987.

———. "A Historical Understanding of the Laws of Managing the Army," *Jiefangjun Bao*, Jan. 8, 1988.

Pan Xianjue. "My Experience in the Initial Research on Rockets for the New China," *Hangtian*, No. 4, 1989.

Pang Xianzhi. "Mao Zedong and His Secretary Tian Jiaying," in Dong Bian et al., eds., *Mao Zedong he Tade Mishu Tian Jiaying* [Mao Zedong and His Secretary Tian Jiaying]. Beijing, 1989.

Party History Research Section of the Central Committee of the CCP. *Zhonggong Dangshi Dashi Nianbiao* [Chronological Table of Major Events in CCP History]. Beijing, 1981; revised, 1987.

Pei Di. "On the 1958 Chengdu Conference," *Zhonggong Dangshi Yanjiu* [Studies on CCP History], No. 5, 1988.

Pei Duan. "The Chinese Navy and the Naval Research Institute." Unpublished speech, 1988.

Peng Cheng. "[A Profile of] Luo Ruiqing," *Xinghuo Liaoyuan* [A Single Spark Can Start a Prairie Fire], No. 5, 1985.

Peng Cheng and Wang Fang. *Lushan 1959* [Lushan (Plenum), 1959]. Beijing, 1989.

———. "Mao's Last Decision Made Beside the Swimming Pool at His Residence," in Chen Zaidao et al., *Zhongguo Zhengju Beiwanglu* [Memoranda of China's Political Scenes]. Beijing, 1989.

Peng Dehuai. *Memoirs of a Chinese Marshal*. Beijing, 1984.

———. "Why Did I Write the Letter to Chairman Mao?" *Xinhua Wenzhai* [New China Digest], No. 11, 1990.

Peng Jichao et al. "The Motherland Won't Forget," *Shenjian* [Magical Sword], No. 6, 1988.

Peng Jieqing. *Hangtian Qing* [His Spaceflight Passion]. Beijing, 1993.

Peng Min, chief ed. *Dangdai Zhongguo de Jiben Jianshe* [Contemporary China's Capital Construction]. Beijing, 1989, Vol. 1.

Peng Shilu. "Recall Premier Zhou's Concern for the Nuclear-Powered Submarine Project," *Shenjian* [Magical Sword], No. 1, 1988.

Peng Shilu and Zhao Renkai. "A Few Words About Our Participation in the Research and Development on Our Country's Nuclear-Powered Submarine," in HGYZW.

Peng Ziqiang. "The Birth of Our Country's Sixth Comprehensive Spaceflight Measuring Fleet," *Shenjian* [Magical Sword], No. 6, 1986.

Pethybridge, Roger. *A Key to Soviet Politics: The Crisis of the Anti-Party Group*. New York, 1962.

Phoenix. "The Potential of the Nuclear Submarine," *Submarine Review*, Oct. 1984.

"[PLA Units Under] the Beijing Command and the Air Force Conducted a Military Exercise," *Renmin Ribao*, Sept. 27, 1981.

Pocock, Rowland F. *Nuclear Ship Propulsion*. London, 1970.

Pollack, Jonathan. "Perception and Process in China Foreign Policy: The Quemoy Decision," Ph.D. diss., Univ. of Michigan, 1976.

"Press Communiqué on Our Country's Successful Test of a Nuclear-Armed Missile" [Oct. 27, 1966], *Renmin Ribao*, Oct. 28, 1966.

"Press Communiqué on the Successful Detonation of Our Country's First Hydrogen Bomb" [June 17, 1967], *Renmin Ribao*, June 18, 1967.

Proletarian Revolutionaries of the PLA General Staff. "A Thorough Criticism of Luo Ruiqing's Bourgeois and Revisionist Military Thinking," *Renmin Ribao*, Sept. 16, 1967, in FBIS: Communist China, Sept. 18, 1967.

Puckett, Allen E., and Simon Ramo, eds. *Guided Missile Engineering*. New York, 1959.

"Q-5 Attack Fighters Constitute One of the Mainstays of Mainland China's Air Force," *Guoji Ribao* [International Daily News] (Los Angeles), May 13, 1991.

Qi Changming. "Strengthen Strategic Studies, Deepen Military Reform," *Jiefangjun Bao*, May 8, 1988.

Qi Miyun. "The Shift of the Guiding Principles in Army Construction as Judged by [the Decrease in] Military Funds," *Junshi Shilin*, No. 4, 1987.

Qi Shengping. "A Description of Marshal Liu Bocheng, the Prime Mover of the Military Academy [in Nanjing]," *Xinghuo Liaoyuan* [A Single Spark Can Start a Prairie Fire], No. 2, 1985.

Qian Cansong. "A Description of Liu Yongli, Assistant Meteorological Engineer on the Instrumentation Ship *Distant Observer* No. 1," *Jiefangjun Bao*, Aug. 2, 1990.

Qian Junrui. *Qian Junrui Xuanji* [Selected Works of Qian Junrui]. Taiyuan, 1986.

Qian Sanqiang. "Cherish the Memory of Premier Zhou's Concern for Our Country's Scientific and Technological Undertakings and His Instructions to Scientific and Technical Personnel," *Renmin Ribao*, March 10, 1979.

Qian Wuhuang. "The Self-Reliant Development of Our Country's Wireless Monitor and Control Systems for [Test-Launching] Missiles and Satellites," in HGYZW.

Qian Xuesen. "Organization and Management Work in Science and Technology," *Hongqi* [Red Flag], No. 22 (Nov. 19, 1963).

———. "Premier Zhou Assigned Me to Develop Missiles," in *Bujin de Sinian* [Boundless Recollections]. Beijing, 1987.

Qiao Tianfu. "National Treasures of China," *Jiefangjun Bao*, April 26, 1990.

Qiao Yimin and Liu Qi. "On the Damage and Historical Lessons of Being Impatient for Success and Pursuing Unrealistic Purity," *Mao Zedong Sixiang Yanjiu* [Studies on Mao Zedong's Thought] (Chengdu), No. 1, 1989.

Qin Weidong. "Military Reform Achieved Great Success," *Renmin Ribao*, overseas ed., June 25, 1987.

———. "Zhang Aiping Talks About Modern Construction in an Army Under Reform," *Liaowang*, July 27, 1987.

Qiu Mingquan and Zhu Zhenlu. "Xinjiang Takes Vigorous Measures to Punish the Criminals Who Destroyed Military Installations," *Jiefangjun Bao*, Sept. 16, 1989.

Quan Yanchi. *Zhongguo Zuida Baohuangpai* [China's Number One Royalist]. Hong Kong, 1991.

———. *Zouxia Shentan de Mao Zedong* [Everyday Life of Mao Zedong]. Beijing, 1989.

Quan Zong. "A Large-Scale Aviation Industrial Base Hidden in Remote Mountains," *Liaowang*, overseas ed., June 30, 1986.

Qun Ren. "The Development of Solid Propellants," *Hangkong Zhishi*, No. 9, 1977.

"The Rapid Development of Our Country's Microelectronics Industry," *Renmin Ribao*, overseas ed., April 11, 1986.

"Remarkable Achievements with the Carrying Out of a License System in the Topographic Industry," *Renmin Ribao*, overseas ed., April 22, 1988.

"Remarkable Accomplishment of Tasks by *Distant Observer* Ships," *Jianchuan Zhishi*, No. 8, 1990.

Ren Qimin. "Some Ideas on Coastal and Border Defense During Peacetime," *Guofang Daxue Xuebao*, No. 6, 1989.

Ren Tao and Guo Xiangxing. "An Interview with State Councillor and Defense Minister Zhang Aiping," *Renmin Ribao*, overseas ed., Aug. 1, 1987.

Ren Xinfa and Wang Xingrang. "A Visit to Cui Erjie, an Expert on Astronautic Aerodynamics," *Jingji Ribao* [Economics Daily], Jan. 13, 1987.

Ren Xinmin. "A Look to the Past and Future of Our Country's Space Cause," in HGYZW.

Renmin Ribao Reporters. "Eyewitness to the Launch of a Missile from a Submerged Submarine," *Renmin Ribao*, Oct. 17, 1982.

Renmin Ribao and *Xinhua* Reporters. "A Sudden Clap of Thunder Shakes the Sea and Sky—Notes on the Underwater Launching of a Missile from a Submarine of Our Country," in FBIS: China, Oct. 18, 1982.

"Report on the Problem of Lo Jui-ch'ing's Mistakes," in Ying-mao Kau, ed., *The People's Liberation Army and China's Nation-Building*. White Plains, N. Y., 1973. Also translated in *Chinese Law and Government*, 4, No. 3–4 (Fall-Winter 1971–72).

Research Section on Logistics History, Logistics Academy. "A Review of the Buildup of Our Army's Logistics After the Founding of the Republic," *Junshi Lishi*, No. 5, 1989.

"The Resolution of the Standing Committee of the National People's Congress on Creating the Eighth Ministry of Machine Building, the Ministry of Justice, and the Ministry of Geology, and on Appointments and Removals," *Renmin Ribao*, Sept. 14, 1979.

"The Resolution of the Standing Committee of the National People's Congress on the Creation of the Commission of Science, Technology, and Industry for National Defense," *Renmin Ribao*, Aug. 24, 1982.

"The Resolution of the Standing Committee of the National People's Congress on the Merger of the Eighth Ministry of Machine Building into the Seventh Ministry of Machine Building," *Renmin Ribao*, Sept. 11, 1981.

"The Resolution on the Adjustment of the Organizations Under the State Council," *Xin Hua Banyuekan* [New China Semimonthly], March 10, 1958.

"The Riddle of Research and Development on China's Atomic Bomb, Hydrogen Bomb, and Nuclear-Powered Submarine," *Liaowang*, overseas ed., June 15, 1987.

Rixin Yueyi de Mao he Dun [(The Performance of Modern) Spears and Shields Change Day After Day]. Guangzhou, 1981.

"Rocket Fragments Fell on Cuba," *New York Times*, Dec. 2, 1960.

Rong Zhi. "The Big Powers' Military Strategies and Our Countermeasures by the End of This Century," in *Guoji Xingshi yu Guofang Zhanlüe* [The International Situation and Defense Strategy]. Beijing, 1987.

―――. "On Postwar Soviet Foreign Policies," in *Guoji Zhengzhi Jiang zuo (Xubian)* [Lectures on International Politics]. Beijing, 1987, Vol. 2.

Run Bei. "A Description of Admiral Xiao Jinguang, the First Commander of the Chinese Navy," *Jianchuan Zhishi*, No. 5, 1989.

Sapolsky, Harvey M. *The Polaris System Development: Bureaucratic and Programmatic Success in Government*. Cambridge, Mass., 1972.

Schurmann, Franz. *Ideology and Organization in Communist China.* New, enlarged ed. Berkeley, 1970.

Shaanxi Sishi Nian (1949–1989) [Forty Years of Shaanxi Province (1949–1989)]. Beijing, 1989.

Shao Dingrong and Gu Weilun. "The Integrated Satellite/Omega Navigation System," *Xiandai Junshi,* No. 9, 1987.

Sharpe, Richard, ed. *Jane's Fighting Ships (1989–90).* London, 1989.

She Shui and Xiao Yue. "Selection of Papers Submitted to China's First International Symposium on 'Sun Zi's Art of War,'" *Junshi Shilin,* No. 5, 1989.

Shen Changjing and Xiao Jun. "Nansha: What We Were Told," *Jianchuan Zhishi,* No. 2, 1988.

Shen Hongyuan. "At Which Depth Should Weapons Be Launched from a Submarine?" *Jianchuan Zhishi,* No. 5, 1988.

———. "Ignition Underwater or After Clearing the Surface?" *Jianchuan Zhishi,* No. 5, 1987.

———. "On Whether the SLBM Is a Launch-and-Leave Missile," *Jianchuan Zhishi,* No. 3, 1987.

———. "On Which Parts [of a Surface Warship or a Submarine] Should the Sonar Systems Be Installed?" *Jianchuan Zhishi,* No. 6, 1988.

———. "The Self [Generated] Noise of a Submarine," *Jianchuan Zhishi,* No. 9, 1988.

———. "Single Hull and Double Hull," *Jianchuan Zhishi,* No. 3, 1988.

———. "The Structural Design of Modern Submarines," *Xiandai Junshi,* No. 5, 1988.

———. "What Measures Should Be Adopted After High-Pressure Air Is Used Up?" *Jianchuan Zhishi,* No. 9, 1987.

———. "Why Were Running Water Holes [*liushui kong*] Opened on Submarines' Upper Parts?" *Jianchuan Zhishi,* No. 7, 1988.

———. "Will the Submarine's Conning Tower Disappear?" *Jianchuan Zhishi,* No. 7, 1987.

Shen Lijiang. "Commander of the Navy Liu Huaqing Speaks on the Chinese Navy Submarine Corps," *Jianchuan Zhishi,* No. 12, 1985.

———. "U.S. Chief of Naval Operations Visits China's Nuclear-Powered Submarine," *Jianchuan Zhishi,* No. 1, 1989.

———. "A Visit to a Campsite of the Chinese Marine Corps," *Jianchuan Zhishi,* No. 8, 1987.

Shen Rongjun, chief ed. *Zhongguo Guofang Keji* [China Defense Research and Development]. Beijing, 1988.

Shen Shungen. "China's Test Range for Naval Weapons and Equipment," *Jianchuan Zhishi,* No. 9, 1989.

———. "A Description of the Rapidly Developing Chinese Navy Submarine Corps," *Renmin Ribao,* overseas ed., June 18, 1987.

———. "Oceangoing Capability Is an Important Sign of the Fighting Capacity at Sea—A Visit to the Commander of the People's Navy Zhang Lianzhong," *Renmin Ribao,* Aug. 1, 1988.

———. "Our Country's Submarine Force Has Become the Backbone of the Navy's Combat Capability," *Jiefangjun Bao,* Aug. 28, 1989.

———. "Prizes Awarded for the Results of 103 Items of Scientific and Technological Work at the Naval Research Center," *Jiefangjun Bao,* July 22, 1988.

————. "Visits to the Commander of the Navy and the Heads of Two Navy Head-quarters Departments," *Jianchuan Zhishi*, No. 8, 1988.

Shen Shungen and Wu Yundian. "The Cradle of Submariners," *Jiefangjun Bao*, May 9, 1989.

Shen Shungen and Zhang Ze'nan. "The New Look of the Modern People's Navy," in *Junwei Jinxingqu—Renmin Jiefangjun Xiandaihua Jianshe* [Military Marches—The Modern Construction of the People's Liberation Army]. Beijing, 1987.

Sheng Geng. "Everywhere in Nansha Is Stamped with the Brand of China," *Jiefang-jun Bao*, Aug. 26, 1988.

Shi Changxue. "The Naval Engineering Institute Has Built Our Country's First Warship Demagnetization Laboratory," *Jiefangjun Bao*, Dec. 21, 1989.

Shi Changxue and Xia Hongqing. "What We Saw and Heard at the Naval Engineering Institute's Warship Demagnetization Laboratory," *Jiefangjun Bao*, Oct. 3, 1989.

Shi Changxue et al. "The Naval Engineering Institute Gave Priority to the Requirements of Combat Units in Teaching and Scientific Research," *Jiefangjun Bao*, Nov. 12, 1990.

Shi Dongbing. "The Initial Opposition—Peng Zhen on the Eve of the Cultural Revolution," *Dangshi Wenhui* [Collection on Party History], No. 4, 1988.

Shi Gong. "The Satellite Navigation Receiver on the Freighter *Songlin*," *Hanghai* [Navigation], No. 2, 1979.

Shi Jinkun. "The Situation and Prospects of Preventing Nuclear Proliferation in the World," *International Strategic Studies* (Beijing), No. 2, 1993.

Shi Qingsheng. "On the Crash-Speed Economic Developmental Strategy and the Hasty Transition [from Socialism to Communism] in the 1950s," *Zhejiang Xuekan* [Zhejiang Learned Journal] (Hangzhou), No. 4, 1989.

Shi Wenting et al. "Reform Is the Only Path for Realizing the Modernization of Our Army," *Jiefangjun Bao*, Sept. 18, 1987.

Shi Xiaoyan. "The Persecution of Comrade Xiao Jinguang by Wang Ming's Line," in *Geming Shi Ziliao* [Materials on Revolutionary History]. Beijing, 1981, Vol. 2.

Shi Yan. "The Creation and Development of the Second Artillery Corps," *Junshi Shilin*, No. 6, 1989.

————. "My Impressions of Du Ping's Memoir 'At the CPV's Headquarters,'" *Renmin Ribao*, July 19, 1990.

Shi Yingfu. *Mimi Chubing Yare Conglin YuanYue KangMei Jishi* [Secret Jungle Warfare: Records on Aiding Vietnam and Resisting America]. Beijing, 1990.

"The Shipbuilding Capacity of the Dalian Shipyard Is Number One in Mainland China," *Shijie Ribao*, Nov. 17, 1990.

Shu Deqi and Li Chunfang. "A Monument in the Deep Ocean," *Kunlun* [Kunlun], No. 1, 1992.

Shu Deqi and Ling Xiang. "The Birth of China's Nuclear-Powered Submarines (1, 6, 7)," *Zhongguo Junzhuanmin Bao* [China Defense Conversion Newspaper], Aug. 11, Sept. 15, 22, 1992.

Si Yanwen. "Naval Military Academic Research Plays an Increasingly Dynamic Role," *Jiefangjun Bao*, Sept. 21, 1989.

————. "A New Torpedo Successfully Developed by Senior Cadre Wang Dianju and Other Comrades," *Jiefangjun Bao*, July 29, 1988.

"Song Jian Appointed State Councillor," *Renmin Ribao*, overseas ed., April 13, 1986.

"Song Jian on Science and Technology Reform," Beijing International Service, Aug. 13, 1985, in FBIS: China, Aug. 19, 1985.

Song Ke. "An Organizational Introduction to the Central Military Commission Before the War to Resist Japan," *Dangshi Yanjiu* [Studies on the Party's History], No. 4, 1981.

Song Lijun. "The Chinese Communists Are Speeding up the Building of Military Aircraft and Aircraft Carriers," *Guangjiaojing* [Wide-Angle Lens] (Hong Kong), No. 5, 1988.

Song Puxuan and Cai Yunhua. "The Ocean: The Hot Spot of Military Struggles in the New Period," *Jiefangjun Bao*, Aug. 26, 1988.

Song Renqiong. "A Few Words Written Before the Publication of 'Continuation of Xiao Jinguang's Memoirs,'" *Jiefangjun Bao*, Jan. 31, 1989.

Song Shilun. "The Illustrious Name and Outstanding Achievement of Comrade Su Yu Will Shine Through the Ages," in *Yidai Mingjiang Huiyi Su Yu Tongzhi* [A Famous General: Reminiscences on Comrade Su Yu]. Shanghai, 1986.

——. "Military Science," in Song Shilun, chief ed., *Zhongguo Dabaike Quanshu Junshi* [Chinese Encyclopedia (of Military Affairs)]. Beijing, 1989, Vol. 1.

——, chief ed. *Zhongguo Dabaike Quanshu Junshi* [Chinese Encyclopedia (of Military Affairs)]. Beijing, 1989, Vols. 1, 2.

"Stable Implementation of the Readjustment of the Enterprises in China's Third-Line Regions," *Renmin Ribao*, overseas ed., Oct. 4, 1988.

State Statistical Bureau, comp. *Statistical Yearbook of China, 1981*. Hong Kong, 1982.

"Statement of the Government of the People's Republic of China" [Oct. 16, 1964], *Renmin Ribao*, Oct. 17, 1964.

"Statement of the Government of the People's Republic of China" [Oct. 7, 1969], *Renmin Ribao*, Oct. 8, 1969.

Stephenson, Michael, and John Weal. *Nuclear Dictionary*. London, 1985.

Stober, Dan. "Chinese Neutron Bomb May Have Local Origin," *San Jose Mercury*, Nov. 21, 1990.

Stolper, Thomas. *China, Taiwan, and the Offshore Islands*. Armonk, N. Y., 1985.

"Strategic Research Is a Key Link in the Successful Realization of the Strategic Change [in the Guiding Principles for Our Army-Building]," *Jiefangjun Bao*, May 16, 1986.

"A Strategic Shift of the Guiding Ideology for Our Country's Defense Construction," *Zhongguo Minbing* [Chinese Militia], No. 1, 1987.

"The Strengthening of the Power of Chinese Nuclear-Powered Submarine Group (1–3)," *Zhongbao* [Central Daily News] (New York), May 13, 15, 16, 1989.

Su Donghai. "Twelve Important Meetings During the Period of the Great Leap Forward," in Party History Research Section of the Chinese Revolutionary Museum, ed., *Dangshi Yanjiu Ziliao* [Research Materials on Party History]. Chengdu, 1982, Vol. 3.

Su Fangxue. "The Dragon Flies After Casting Off the Yoke [of Blind Worship of Everything Foreign]," *Jiefangjun Wenyi* [Literature and Art of the Liberation Army], No. 2, 1984.

——. "National Spirit: Professor Wang Ganchang, an Outstanding Chinese," *Zhongguo Zuojia* [Chinese Writers], No. 2, 1990.

————. "Report from the Ocean," *Jiefangjun Wenyi* [Literature and Art of the Liberation Army], No. 12, 1982.

Su Kuoshan. "The Birth of the *Distant Observer* Instrumentation Ships," *Xin Guancha* [New Observation], No. 17, 1988.

————. "Nie Rongzhen's Message of Congratulation to a Certain Rocket Test Base," *Renmin Ribao*, overseas ed., April 27, 1987.

————. "The Soldiers Who Search for Missiles in the 'Sea of Death,'" *Jiefangjun Bao*, Sept. 8, 1988.

————. "The Successful Trial Operation of Our Country's Sea-based Satellite Communication Ground Station," *Renmin Ribao*, overseas ed., May 20, 1988.

Su Kuoshan and Li Yang. "The Oceangoing Instrumentation Fleet's Base Increases Its Ratio of Duty Officers," *Jiefangjun Bao*, April 26, 1989.

Su Kuoshan and Wu Chuansheng. "From a Soldier to a Commander," *Jiefangjun Bao*, Feb. 16, 1989.

Su Kuoshan et al. "The Report from the Units Dealing with Defense Scientific Research and Testing," in *Junwei Jinxingqu—Renmin Jiefangjun Xiandaihua Jianshe* [Military Marches—The Modern Construction of the People's Liberation Army]. Beijing, 1987.

————. "A Report on the Efforts of the Scientific and Research Personnel of the National Defense Science and Technology University in Scaling Heights in Science and Technology," *Jiefangjun Bao*, April 21, 1990.

Su Wenming, ed. *China's Army—Ready for Modernization*. Beijing, 1985.

Su Yingxiong. "Advanced Composites," *Mingbao Yuekan* [Ming Pao Monthly] (Hong Kong), No. 4, 1991.

Su Yu. "Great Victory of Chairman Mao's Guideline for War," *Renmin Ribao*, Aug. 6, 1977.

"The Successful Launch of a Missile from a Chinese-Built Nuclear-Powered Submarine," *Wenhui Bao* [Encounter] (Hong Kong), Sept. 28, 1988.

Sun Jilian. "Some Words Spoken on Behalf of the Units on Ready Alert and the Combat Units in Full-Time Training," *Jiefangjun Bao*, June 6, 1988.

Sun Junren, chief ed. *Zhongguo Dabaike Quanshu Dianzixue yu Jisuanji* [Chinese Encyclopedia: Electronics and Computers]. Beijing, 1986, Vols. 1, 2.

Sun Kaitai. "The Military Thinking of Wu Qi," *Hunan Shifan Daxue Shehui Kexue Xuebao* [Hunan Normal University Social Science Journal] (Changsha), No. 2, 1986.

Sun Minqiang. "Our Country Manufactures the Integrated Circuits Urgently Needed by High-Technologies," *Renmin Ribao*, overseas ed., Dec. 24, 1986.

Sun Yinnan et al. "All for the Development of the Motherland's Space Undertaking—On Missile Expert Huang Weilu," *Xinhua*, Oct. 20, 1982, in FBIS: China, Oct. 26, 1982.

Sun Zhenhuan. *Zhongguo Guofang Jingji Jianshe* [The Construction of China's Defense Economy]. Beijing, 1991.

"The Surface Warships of the Nationalist Navy Placed Under Threat by the Chinese Communists' Test Launches of a New Torpedo in the Taiwan Strait," *Shijie Ribao*, Feb. 15, 1990.

Sutton, George P. *Rocket Propulsion Elements: An Introduction to the Engineering of Rockets*. 5th ed. New York, 1986.

Swanson, L. Bruce., Jr. *Eighth Voyage of the Dragon: A History of China's Quest for Seapower*. Annapolis, Md., 1982.

Tan Jingqiao, chief ed. *KangMei YuanChao Zhanzheng* [The War to Resist America and Aid Korea]. Beijing, 1990.

Tang Fuquan. "Recognition of Our Country's Maritime Strategy," *Jiefangjun Bao*, Sept. 15, 1989.

Tang Yunchang. "The Future of Torpedes," *Bingqi Zhishi* [Ordnance Knowledge], No. 2, 1984.

Tang Zhongfan. "The American 'Trident 1' SLBM," *Jianchuan Zhishi*, No. 2, 1989.

Tao Bojun. "Some Ideas on Comrade Deng Xiaoping's Contributions to Military Affairs in the New Period," *Junshi Shilin*, No. 5, 1987.

———. "Understanding Comrade Deng Xiaoping's Statements on [Our] Army's Military Works in the New Period," in Shao Chengye, chief ed., *Huigu Zhanwang Tantao* [Retrospect, Prospect, and Exploration]. Chengdu, 1987.

Tao Hanzhang. *Sun Tzu's Art of War: The Modern Chinese Interpretation.* New York, 1987.

Tao Tao. "Developing New Chemical Materials in the Science, Technology, and Industry for National Defense," in HGYZW.

"A Task of Great Urgency to Punish the Criminals Who Seriously Destroyed Military Installations," *Jiefangjun Bao*, Feb. 17, 1989.

Temple, Robert. *The Genius of China: 3,000 Years of Science, Discovery and Invention.* Intro. by Joseph Needham. New York, 1986.

Theoretical Group of the National Defense Industry Office. "The Strategic Guiding Principle for Strengthening Defense Construction," *Guangming Ribao*, Jan. 20, 1977.

Theoretical Study Group of the Navy. "Hold High the Banner of Chairman Mao, Build a Powerful Navy," *Renmin Ribao*, June 24, 1977.

"The Threat from Cam Ranh Bay," *Xiandai Junshi*, No. 3, 1988.

"This Year the Chinese Army Begins Enforcing a New Regulation," *Renmin Ribao*, overseas ed., July 12, 1987.

Tian Zhenhuan. "Comrade Xiao Jinguang at the Naval Academy," in Yang Shangkun et al., *Yidai Yuanrong* [A Supreme Commander]. Beijing, 1991.

Tong Zhipeng. "Forty Years of Military Communication Technology," in HGYZW.

Turetsky, Mikhail. *The Introduction of Missile Systems into the Soviet Navy (1945–1962).* Falls Church, Va., 1983.

"Twenty-three Key Results in Science and Technology Win the State's Top-Class Award for Progress in Science and Technology," *Renmin Ribao*, overseas ed., May 16, 1986.

United Nations. *Proceedings of the Second United Nations International Conference on the Peaceful Uses of Atomic Energy.* Sept. 1–13, 1958. Geneva, 1958, Vol. 8.1.

United States, Defense Intelligence Agency. *Ballistic Missile Guidance and Control—USSR and China.* DST-1000S-294-81. Washington, D.C., May 1981.

———, ———. *Ballistic Missile Payloads (Current and Projected)—USSR and China.* DST-1000S-520-80. Washington, D.C., 1980.

———, Department of the Air Force. *Guided Missiles Fundamentals.* AFM 527-31. Washington, D.C., 1972.

———, ———. *Space Systems Current and Projected—China.* DST-1400S-237-80. Washington, D.C., 1980.

————, Department of the Navy. *Polaris Management: Fleet Ballistic Missile Program.* Washington, D.C., 1961.

"The United States Also Sells Weapons," *U.S. News & World Report*, May 27, 1991.

Vasilevsky, A. "Rout of the Kwantung Army," *Soviet Military Review*, No. 8, 1980, supplement.

Wan Xiang. "The 'Magic Men' Who Handle Distillation Plants on the Pacific Ocean," *Jiefangjun Bao*, June 2, 1988.

Wan Yuan and Liu Yonghua, "Outstanding Scientific Achievements by 100,000 Communist Party Members on the Military Industrial Front in the Southwest," *Jiefangjun Bao*, June 21, 1991.

Wang Caiyao. "Dust and Gyroscopes," *Hangkong Zhishi*, No. 4, 1977.

Wang Chengxuan. "A Technical Breakthrough in Hydraulic Servo Drives for Control Rods," *Renmin Ribao*, overseas ed., July 18, 1992.

Wang Chuliang. "Why Did Li Hongzhang Choose Lüshun to Create a Naval Base?" *Junshi Lishi*, No. 2, 1989.

Wang Chuncai. "On the Top of the Earth," in *Laizi Zongcanmoubu de Baogao* [Reports from the General Staff]. Beijing, 1987.

Wang Daheng. "Optics Research Will Have a Great Future," in HGYZW.

Wang Ding. "Doctor Zeng Zhaoqi Talks About He Long," in Hua Lin, ed., *Mao Zedong he Tade Zhanyou Men* [Mao Zedong and His Comrades-in-Arms]. Beijing, 1990.

————. "Marshal He Long and His Doctor," *Yanhuang Zisun* [The Chinese], No. 4, 1988.

Wang Dinglie, chief ed. *Dangdai Zhongguo Kongjun* [Contemporary China's Air Force]. Beijing, 1989.

Wang Ganyi. "Strategy for Navy's Development Is Outlined," *China Daily*, April 11, 1987.

Wang Hewen. "New Discussion on 'Coastal Waters' and 'Local Mastery of the Sea,'" *Jiefangjun Bao*, April 11, 1986.

Wang Huilin ed. *Xiandai Bingqi Daguan* [Magnificent Spectacle of Modern Weapons]. Beijing, 1987.

Wang Huique. "Commander Xiao Concerned Himself with the Construction of Our [Naval] Test Range," in Yang Shangkun et al., *Yidai Yuanrong* [A Supreme Commander]. Beijing, 1991.

Wang Jianying. "Main Leaders of All Previous Central Military Commissions and Central Revolutionary Military Commissions," *Xinghuo Liaoyuan* [A Single Spark Can Start a Prairie Fire], No. 2, 1985.

Wang Jinhe. "Over 100 Types of Radar Applied to Various Fields," *Renmin Ribao*, overseas ed., Nov. 5, 1986.

Wang Jinzhong. "Nuclear-Powered Submarines: A Crystallization of Modern Science and Technology," *Kexue Shiyan* [Scientific Experiments], No. 9, 1984.

Wang Lichun. "A Description of the Birth and Development of the *Distant Observer* Oceangoing Instrumentation Ships," in HGYZW.

Wang Lihua and Zhang Jiade. "A Look Back on the History of Logistics in Scientific and Research Tests," in HGYZW.

Wang Linchen. "Ejection Technology of Ballistic Missiles," *Bingqi Zhishi* [Ordnance Knowledge], No. 2, 1986.

————. "Nuclear-Powered Submarines and Guided Missiles," *Bingqi Zhishi* [Ordnance Knowledge], No. 4, 1984.

Wang Nianyi. "Mao Zedong's Appraisal of the Situation When He Unleashed the Cultural Revolution," in Xiao Yanzhong, chief ed., *Wannian Mao Zedong* [The Late Years of Mao Zedong]. Beijing, 1989.

————. *1949–1989 Nian de Zhongguo Da Dongluan de Niandai* [China from 1949 to 1989: A Period of Turmoil]. Zhengzhou, 1988.

Wang Rongjiu. "The Foreign Ministers of China and Vietnam Are Holding Negotiations," *Renmin Ribao*, overseas ed., Feb. 15, 1992.

Wang Rongjiu and Yang Mu. "The Foreign Ministers of China and Vietnam Hold That the Implementation of the Results of the Sino-Vietnamese Summit Has Gone Smoothly," *Renmin Ribao*, overseas ed., Feb. 15, 1992.

Wang Rongsheng. "Revitalize the Shipbuilding Industry to Serve the Modern Construction of Naval Equipment," in HGYZW.

Wang Shangrong. "Cherish the Memory of Comrade He Long, Who Performed Outstanding Feats," *Renmin Ribao*, June 8, 1979.

Wang Shiguang and Zhang Xuedong. "Develop Military Electronics to Promote Defense Modernization," in HGYZW.

Wang Shihui and Ying Mingyang. "The Design of a Hardened Computer System Is Accepted," *Jiefangjun Bao*, Nov. 30, 1988.

Wang Shouyun. "The Defense Economy—A Realistic Question for Study," *Baike Zhishi* [Encyclopedic Knowledge], No. 10, 1984.

Wang Yamin. "Pondering the Construction of Our Army's Weapons and Equipment," *Guofang Daxue Xuebao*, No. 7, 1987.

Wang Yaping. "A Strategic Decision of Historic Significance," in *Dangshi Yanjiu* [Studies on the Party's History], No. 6, 1986.

Wang Yongzhi. "The Success and Prospect of Our Country's Missiles," *Renmin Ribao*, overseas ed., May 29, 1990.

————, chief ed. *Hangtian Gongye Bu Diyi Yanjiuyuan Dashiji 1957–1987* [A Chronicle of Major Events of the First Academy of the Ministry of Aerospace Industry (1957–1987)]. Beijing, 1987.

Wang Youqi. "Army Topographers Determine the Launch Direction of a Missile," *Jiefangjun Bao*, June, 23, 1988.

————. "China Gained Important Achievements in Building the Nationwide Satellite Doppler Network," *Junshi Shijie*, No. 3, 1988.

————. "Heroes Who Deal with Astronomical Geodesy," *Jiefangjun Bao*, Aug. 27, 1987.

————. "How a Satellite Was Sent into a Predetermined Orbit," *Junshi Shijie*, No. 3, 1988.

————. "The Officers and Soldiers Who Are Roaming the Seas of Data," *Jiefangjun Bao*, April 10, 1989.

Wang Yu, chief ed. *Zhonggong Dangshi Jianbian* [Concise History of the CCP]. Beijing, 1988.

Wang Yucai and Song Yunda. "The Setting Up of Police Substations at Military Warehouses in Three Provinces in the Northeast," *Jiefangjun Bao*, Oct. 21, 1987.

Wang Yuxiang et al. "The Guiding Role of Mao Zedong's Military Thinking for Local Wars," *Mao Zedong Sixiang Yanjiu* [Studies on Mao Zedong's Thought] (Chengdu), No. 3, 1988.

Wang Zhanyi, chief ed. *Dangdai Zhongguo de Shuiyun Shiye* [Contemporary China's Waterborne Transportation]. Beijing, 1989.

Wang Zhe and Liu Wencai. "Our Shipbuilding Industry Has Participated in International Competition and Made Considerable Progress," *Guangming Ribao*, March 21, 1988.

Wang Zhenping. "The Requirement for the Construction of the Second Artillery Corps Determined by the Development of the Military Situation in the Asian-Pacific Region," in *YaTai de Xuanwo* [Eddies in the Asian and Pacific Region]. Beijing, 1989.

Wang Zhenxian. "The Defense Minister's Stick," in *Shenjian Zhulian Qu* [The Casting of a Magical Sword]. Beijing, 1987.

Wei Chuan. "Contemplation After the March 14 Sea Battle," *Haiyang Shijie* [Marine World], No. 3, 1989.

Wen Guang. "Qiu Huizuo Talks About His 16-Year Life as a Prisoner," *Jingbao Yuekan* [The Mirror] (Hong Kong), No. 8, 1988.

Wen Jiaqi. *Yinjian Shenwei* [The Magical Power of Rockets]. Nanning, 1990.

Wen Xing. "Chinese Rockets and Rocket Control Experts," *Chongqing Ribao*, July 21, 1986.

Wu Baokun and Yuan Youqing. "The Application of Microcomputers (2, 3)," *Hangkong Zhishi*, Nos. 3, 5, 1978.

Wu Bin. *Lin Biao An Zhong An* [A Case Within the Case of Lin Biao]. Hong Kong, 1989.

Wu Chunqiu. *Zhanlüe Yanjiu yu Xiandai Guofang* [Strategic Studies and Modern Defense]. Shanghai, 1988.

Wu Chunqiu and Dong Lingyun. "Defense Strategy," in *Zhanzheng yu Zhanlüe Lilun Jicui* [The Essence of Theories on War and Strategy]. Beijing, 1989. Excerpts of a special report of 1986.

Wu Hongye. "The Realization of the One-Million Man Cut in the Armed Forces," *Renmin Ribao*, Aug. 5, 1987.

Wu Lengxi. "Recall Comrade Liu Shaoqi's Working Style in the 7,000-Man Conference [in January 1962]," in Dong Bian et al., eds., *Mao Zedong he Tade Mishu Tian Jiaying* [Mao Zedong and His Secretary Tian Jiaying]. Beijing, 1989.

Wu Min. "On Integrated Navigation Systems," *Jianchuan Zhishi*, No. 12, 1988.

Wu Ming. "A Description of Zhang Peilin: Our Country's Uranium Metallurgist," *Renmin Ribao*, April 19, 1990.

Wu Qungan. "The Contributions of Zhou Enlai in the Period of National Economy Readjustment," *Dangshi Yanjiu yu Jiaoxue* [Study and Teaching of the Party's History] (Fuzhou), No. 4, 1988.

Wu Wenzheng, chief ed. *Daodan Yinlun* [An Introduction to Missiles]. Beijing, 1990.

Wu Yirong and Xiao Min. "A Description of the Unleashing of 'Fierce Tigers' from the Mountains," *Renmin Ribao*, overseas ed., Dec. 4, 1989.

Wu Yundian and Shu Jianping. "A Sketch of the Chinese Navy's Submarine Institute," *Liaowang*, overseas ed., June 1, 1987.

Wu Yundian and Tang Xun. "The Navy Submarine Institute Strengthens Discipline Starting with Ideological Education," *Jiefangjun Bao*, Sept. 30, 1987.

Wu Yuwen. "A Review of the Two Radical Economic Campaigns After the Founding of the Republic," *Shixue Yuekan* [History Science Monthly], No. 1, 1990.

Wudunn, Sheryl. "China to Raise Arms Spending Again," *New York Times*, March 27, 1991.

Xi Qixin. "A Sudden Clap of Thunder in the Deep Sea," *Hangtian*, No. 1, 1989.

Xi Qixin and Liu Jingzhi. "A New Type Missile Submarine," *Guangming Ribao*, July 28, 1987.

Xia Yinshan. "The Development of Modern Technology to Reduce Submarine Noise," *Xiandai Junshi*, No. 9, 1990.

Xia Yuansheng. "Develop Our Country's Sophisticated Science and Technology on Self-Reliance," *Mao Zedong Sixiang Yanjiu* [Studies on Mao Zedong's Thought] (Chengdu), No. 2, 1990.

Xia Zhengnan. "On the Political Essence of War and the Atomic Age," *Mao Zedong Sixiang Yanjiu* [Studies on Mao Zedong's Thought] (Chengdu), No. 2, 1990.

Xiang Bing and Zhao Mingliang. "What We Saw at the Third-Line Enterprises in the Hanzhong Area," *Renmin Ribao*, Oct. 11, 1987.

Xiang Dong. "A Sudden Clap of Thunder," *Shenjian* [Magical Sword], No. 4, 1988.

Xiao Guangen. "The Entry of Our Research on Laser Nuclear Fusion into the World's Advanced Rank," *Renmin Ribao*, overseas ed., June 28, 1987.

Xiao Hao. "The Modernization of the Means for Training Chinese Troops," *Renmin Ribao*, overseas ed., July 30, 1987.

Xiao Heng. "A Description of Analytical Chemist Chen Guozhen," in *He Kexuejia de Zuji* [The Footprints Left by the Nuclear Scientists]. Beijing, 1989.

Xiao Jinguang. "Mourn Comrade Su Yu," in *Yidai Mingjiang Huiyi Su Yu Tongzhi* [A Famous General: Reminiscences on Comrade Su Yu]. Beijing, 1986.

———. "Reminiscences on Comrade Wang Jiaxiang," in *Huiyi Wang Jiaxiang* [Reminiscences on Wang Jiaxiang]. Beijing, 1985.

———. *Xiao Jinguang Huiyilu* [Memoirs of Xiao Jinguang]. Beijing, 1988, Vol. 2.

Xiao Jun. "The Chinese Navy and Its Nuclear Force at Sea—An Interview with Wang Huique, Commander of a Naval Base," *Jianchuan Zhishi*, No. 1, 1989.

———. "Combat Ships of the Chinese Navy from the 1950s to the 1980s," *Jianchuan Zhishi*, No. 4, 1988.

———. "A Description of the Research and Development on Tactical Software at the Dalian Warship Institute," *Jianchuan Zhishi*, No. 11, 1989.

———. "Key Projects and Balance—Rear Admiral Lin Zhiye's Ideas on the Guidelines for the Construction of the Chinese Navy," *Jianchuan Zhishi*, No. 11, 1989.

———. "Return from the Nansha Islands," *Jianchuan Zhishi*, No. 6, 1988.

Xiao Ke. "Zhou Enlai and the Regular and Modern Construction of Our Army," *Jiefangjun Bao*, March 4, 1988.

Xiao Li. "China's Shipbuilding Industry Is a New Force Suddenly Coming to the Fore," *Liaowang*, overseas ed., March 9, 1987.

Xiao Min. "On the Structural Readjustment of the Third-Line Industries," *Jingji Ribao* [Economic Daily], July 14, 1989.

Xiao Xingbo, *He Zhanzheng yu Renfang* [Nuclear War and Civil Defense]. Beijing, 1989.

Xie Chu. "World Aeronautics and Astronautics Chronology," 2 parts, *Hangkong Zhishi* (Serial Nos. 44, 51), No. 8, 1987, No. 3, 1988.

Xie Feng et al., chief eds. *Dangdai Zhongguo de Hebei* [Contemporary China's Hebei (Province)]. Beijing, 1990, Vol. 1.

Xie Guang. "The Science, Technology, and Industry for National Defense Are Uninterruptedly Advancing Along with the Deepening Reform," in HGYZW.

————, chief ed. *Dangdai Zhongguo de Guofang Keji Shiye* [Contemporary China's Defense Science and Technology Cause]. Beijing, 1992, Vols. 1, 2.

Xie Guangbin and Huang Zong. "The First Arms Exhibition in Kunming," *Junshi Shijie*, No. 3, 1989.

Xie Guoliang. "Studies on the Thought of 'Sun Zi,'" 5 parts, *Junshi Shilin*, Nos. 1–5, 1986.

Xin Si. "When Can China Possess an Aircraft Carrier?" *Haiyang Shijie* [Marine World], No. 3, 1989.

Xinhua. March 14, 1977, in FBIS: People's Republic of China, March 16, 1977.

Xinhua Reporters. "Breaking Through the Blue Waves, Soaring into the Azure Skies," in FBIS: China, Oct. 18, 1982.

Xing Qiuheng. "Develop Our Country's Solid Rocket Program on [the Basis of] Self-Reliance," in HGYZW.

Xiong Huayuan. "The Course of Putting Forward a Guiding Principle for Economic Construction That Avoids Both Conservatism and Rash Advance," *Dangshi Yanjiu yu Jiaoxue* [Study and Teaching of the Party's History] (Fuzhou), No. 2, 1988.

Xiong Lei. "An Unusual Experience Concerning the 'September 13' Incident," *Xin Guancha* [New Observation], No. 18, 1986.

Xu Bo. "The Completion of Our Country's First Nuclear Reactor Using Depleted Fuel," *Renmin Ribao*, overseas ed., Aug. 8, 1991.

————. "The Operation of [China's] First Pulse Reactor," *Renmin Ribao*, overseas ed., June 21, 1991.

Xu Haofeng, chief ed. *Dangdai Zhongguo de Biaozhunhua* [Contemporary China's Standardization]. Beijing, 1986, Vol. 2.

Xu Hua. "The North China Sea Fleet: Modern China's Biggest Fleet," *Jianchuan Zhishi*, No. 9, 1988.

Xu Jiling. "The Successful Development of a Shipborne Phased Scanning Three-Dimensional Radar," *Renmin Ribao*, overseas ed., Dec. 16, 1987.

Xu Jingyue. "Defense Strategic Research Is Now in the Ascendant," *Renmin Ribao*, overseas ed., July 26, 1987.

————. "The Development of a New Structure for Chinese Special Troops," *Liaowang*, overseas ed., June 8, 1987.

————. "The Formation of a New Structure for the PLA Armed Services," *Renmin Ribao*, overseas ed., July 22, 1987.

Xu Liangchen. "Talk About Reform Proceeding from the Rational Division of Missions and All-Round Development of Communications and Transportation," *Renmin Ribao*, overseas ed., Feb. 17, 1987.

Xu Shiming. "My Point of View on Chinese Naval Strategy," *Junshi Shijie*, No. 2, 1990.

Xu Simin. "An Investigative Tour of Dalian," *Jingbao Yuekan* [The Mirror] (Hong Kong), No. 9, 1987.

Xu Wenliang. "*Distant Observer* Achieves Success in the Pacific Ocean," *Jiefangjun Bao*, March 23, 1988.

————. "The Scientific City at Sea," *Jiefangjun Bao*, April 21, 1988.

———. "The Successful Trial Operation of Our Country's First Sea-Based Satellite Communication Ground Station," *Jiefangjun Bao*, March 13, 1988.

Xu Xiangqian. "Heighten Vigilance, Be Ready to Fight," *Hongqi* [Red Flag], No. 8, 1978.

———. *Lishi de Huigu* [A Look Back at History]. Beijing 1987.

Xu Xing. "The Practice and Thinking of Putting Together the Military and Civilian Missions of the Defense Science and Industry in Shaanxi," in HGYZW.

Xu Xueyan. "Recalling the Design Work for Three Types of Ships Attached to the Oceangoing Instrumentation Fleet," in HGYZW.

Xu Yan'an. "The Dalian Yard Ranks Among the World's Most Advanced Yards," *Renmin Ribao*, overseas ed., Aug. 31, 1989.

Xu Yuandong et al. *Zhongguo Gongchandang Lishi Jianghua Xubian* [A Guide to CCP History]. Beijing, 1988, Vol. 2.

Xu Zhimin. "China's Oceangoing Instrumentation Fleet Ranks Among the World's Most Advanced," *Liaowang*, overseas ed., Sept. 12, 1988.

———. "The Creation of a Transport and Support System for Defense Scientific Research Experiments," *Jiefangjun Bao*, April 1, 1989.

———. "A Description of Our Country's First Oceangoing Instrumentation Fleet," *Hangtian*, No. 6, 1988.

———. "The Successful Launch of Our Country's Meteorological Satellite 'Wind and Cloud No. 1,'" *Renmin Ribao*, overseas ed., Sept. 8, 1988.

Xue Hanjun, chief ed. *Heneng Dongli Zhuangzhi* [Nuclear Power Plants]. Beijing, 1990.

Xue Jianhua. "President Yang Shangkun Solumnly Declares: Taiwan Is China's Territory Since Ancient Times and China Will by No Means Tolerate Any Move to Split Her Territory," *Renmin Ribao*, overseas ed., Oct. 10, 1991.

Xue Muqiao et al. "The Stabilization and Readjustment of Prices in the First Half of the 1960s," *Jingji Yanjiu* [Economic Studies], No. 3, 1985.

Xue Yu. "The Separation of the Two Stages of a Multistage Missile," *Hangkong Zhishi*, No. 1, 1975.

Yan Fangming. "A Review of Third-Line Construction," *Dangshi Yanjiu* [Studies on the Party's History], No. 4, 1987.

Yan Jingtang. "A Brief Introduction to the Evolution of the Central Military Commission," *Dangshi Yanjiu* [Studies on the Party's History], No. 2, 1983.

Yang Biao. "The Success of the State-Run Changzhou Machinery Plant in Building Military Products," *Jiefangjun Bao*, Dec. 6, 1990.

Yang Biao and Huang Gangzhou. "The Successful Underwater Launch of Missiles from [One of] Our Country's Nuclear-Powered Submarines," *Jiefangjun Bao*, Sept. 28, 1988.

Yang Bo. "A Good Teacher and a Helpful Friend," in Dong Bian et al., eds., *Mao Zedong he Tade Mishu Tian Jiaying* [Mao Zedong and His Secretary Tian Jiaying]. Beijing, 1989.

Yang Chengwu. "A Call on Chairman Mao," *Dangshi Yanjiu yu Jiaoxue* [Study and Teaching of the Party's History] (Fuzhou), No. 5, 1990.

"Yang Dezhi's Speech at the Fourth Session of the Sixth National People's Congress," *Renmin Ribao*, March 27, 1986.

Yang Fengzhang and Qun Ge. "The Oceangoing Instrumentation Ship: A Special Military Auxiliary," *Jianchuan Zhishi*, No. 3, 1987.

Yang Guoyu. "Reminiscences on the Concerns of Premier Zhou Enlai and Several Marshals for Missile Research and Development," *Liaowang*, April 20, 1983.
————, chief ed. *Dangdai Zhongguo Haijun* [Contemporary China's Navy]. Beijing, 1987.
Yang Han and Wei Naiwen. "A Look at the History of the Research and Development on the Ejection System of the Underwater-to-Surface Missile," in HGYZW.
Yang Heng. "The Development of Our Country's Strategic Nuclear Weapons and Equipment," in HGYZW.
Yang Jian. "The Topographic Industry Creates a Team in Charge of Scientific and Technological Coordination," *Guangming Ribao*, Oct. 19, 1987.
Yang Jianming. "The First Spaceflight Port," in *Shenjian Zhulian Qu* [The Casting of a Magical Sword]. Beijing, 1987.
Yang Jizhu. "The Total Value of Industrial Output of Liaoning Province Increased Almost 100 Times over the Past 40 Years," *Renmin Ribao*, overseas ed., Sept. 12, 1989.
Yang Jun. "Achievements in Simulators for Educational Purposes at the Navy Submarine Institute," *Jiefangjun Bao*, Feb. 14, 1989.
Yang Jun and Lu Wu. "Sidelights on the Second Summer Camp of the Naval Institutes and Schools," *Jiefangjun Bao*, Oct. 20, 1987.
Yang Minqing. "Description of Wang Youwei," *Jiefangjun Bao*, Jan. 2, 1989.
Yang Shangkun. "Building Chinese-Style Modernized Armed Forces," *Hongqi* [Red Flag], No. 15, 1984.
————. "A Speech Delivered at the 60th Anniversary Celebrations of the PLA," *Renmin Ribao*, overseas ed., Aug. 1, 1987.
Yang Shaoqiao and Zhao Fasheng. "Zhou Enlai and Our Country's Grain Work," in *Bujin de Sinian* [Boundless Recollections]. Beijing, 1987.
Yang Shi'e. "Hydroacoustic Equipment Changing Day After Day," *Jianchuan Zhishi*, No. 1, 1985.
Yang Weiyuan. "The Navy Has Successfully Developed Our Country's First Multipurpose Testing Instrument for Satellite Navigators," *Jiefangjun Bao*, Sept. 20, 1988.
————. "Promotion of the Navy's Ship Repair Capabilities," *Jiefangjun Bao*, March 9, 1989.
Yang Xuequan. "A Description of Huang Weilu, Chief Designer of a New-Type Solid Missile and a National Advanced Worker," *Jiefangjun Bao*, Sept. 23, 1989.
Yang Yong. "We Must Liquidate the 'Leftist' Ideological Influence on Military Affairs," *Jiefangjun Bao*, March 22, 1983.
Yang Zhiben. "The Chinese Nation Needs Marine Rights," *Jiefangjun Bao*, March 17, 1989.
————, chief ed. *Zhonghua Minguo Haijun Shiliao* [Historical Materials on the Navy of the Republic of China]. Beijing, 1986.
Yang Zhiben and Xu Hua. "On Ding Ruchang's Mistakes in Commanding Sea Battles," *Jindai Shi Yanjiu* [Contemporary History Studies], No. 1, 1988.
Yao Yanjin. "Zhou Enlai's Great Contributions to Our Army Building," 2 parts, *Guofang Daxue Xuebao*, Nos. 8, 9, 1987.
Ye Yonglie. "Miscellaneous Recollections of the Cultural Revolution," *Xin Guancha* [New Observation], No. 9, 1988.

Yi Da. "The King of Strategic Weapons: The Nuclear-Powered Ballistic-Missile Submarine," *Junshi Shijie*, No. 3, 1990.

Yi Jianru. "Strengthening Research on the Defense Economy," *Liaowang*, March 4, 1985.

Yi Shaolin, ed. *Chuanbo Zuli* [The Wave Resistance of Ships]. Beijing, 1985.

Yi Xuan. "A Method to Protect the Hull of a Ship from Corrosion," *Jianchuan Zhishi*, No. 2, 1985.

Yi Ying et al. "Report from Mapping Brigade No. 1 of the General Staff," *Jiefangjun Bao*, March 20, 1988.

Yin Weixing. "The Weight That Shapes a Global Balance," *Zhongguo Qingnian* [China Youth], No. 1–2, 1987.

Ying Zhe. "Talk About the Precision of Inertial Instruments," *Hangkong Zhishi*, No. 3, 1977.

Yu Baotang. "Contemplating the 'Great Leap Forward' in 1958," *Huadong Shifan Daxue Xuebao* [East China Teachers' University Journal], No. 4, 1989.

Yu Fei. "B-6/B-6D [H-6/H-6D]—China's Medium-Range Bombers," *Xiandai Junshi*, No. 10, 1987.

Yu Gong, ed. *Lin Biao Shijian Zhenxiang* [The Truth About the Lin Biao Incident]. Beijing, 1988.

Yu Nan. "Probing into the Rise and Fall of the Lin Biao Clique," in Tan Zongji et al., *Shinian hou de Pingshuo Wenhua Degeming Shi Lunji* [Comments After Ten Years: A Collection of Essays on the 'Cultural Revolution']. Beijing, 1987.

Yu Qingtian. "The Commission of Science, Technology, and Industry for National Defense Is Implementing Two Circulars of the State Council and the Central Military Commission," *Jingji Ribao* [Economic Daily], July 6, 1984.

Yu Qingtian and Qian Chengbao. "A Description of Yang Qingzeng, Deputy Chief Engineer of the Taiyuan Satellite Launch Center," *Jiefangjun Bao*, Oct. 20, 1988.

Yu Qiuli. "The Great Contributions of Premier Zhou Enlai to Stabilizing the Economy in the 'Cultural Revolution,'" *Renmin Ribao*, Jan. 11, 1990.

Yu Shifu. "Some Ideas on Modern China's Coastal Defense Strategy," *Junshi Lishi*, No. 6, 1989.

Yu Shimao. "A Description of Yu Jinglong, an Engineer at the Taiyuan Satellite Launch Center," *Jiefangjun Bao*, Nov. 15, 1990.

Yu Youhua. "Submarine's Source of Information—Sonar," *Jianchuan Zhishi*, No. 4, 1990.

Yu Zhengdao and Lei Xinlong. "A New Stride in Defense Conversion," *Jiefangjun Bao*, Dec. 16, 1990.

Yu Zhibin. "The Latest Development of Western Conventional Submarines (1)," *Jianchuan Zhishi*, No. 2, 1990.

Yu Zhitian and Zhou Dong. "The Development of China's Electronics Industry," *Jiefangjun Bao*, Sept. 2, 1989.

Yuan Chang'an. "The Scientific City in Our Country's West," *Renmin Ribao*, overseas ed., July 25, 1991.

Yuan Houchun. "Cut Armed Forces by One Million," *Kunlun* [Kunlun], No. 2, 1987.

Yuan Jiaxin. "Pondering the Strategic Shift of the Guiding Ideology for Our Army's Construction," *Junshi Shilin*, No. 4, 1987.

Yuan Wei, ed. *Zhongguo Renmin Jiefangjun Wuda Yezhan Budui Fazhan Shilüe*

[A Concise History of the Development of the Five Field Armies of the Chinese People's Liberation Army]. Beijing, 1987.

Zhai Huisheng. "Our Country's Instrumentation Fleet Returns to Base," *Guangming Ribao*, March 20, 1988.

Zhai Huisheng and Su Kuoshan. "A Description of the Crew Members of the Oceangoing Instrumentation Ships *Distant Observer* Nos. 1 and 2," *Guangming Ribao*, May 2, 1988.

Zhang Aiping. "A Look to the Past and Future," in HGYZW.

"Zhang Aiping on the Modernization of Strategic Weapons," *Jiefangjun Bao*, Oct. 18, 1982.

Zhang Chengang et al. "A Tentative Study on Some Questions About the Strategy for Building Our Peacetime Army," *Weilai yu Fazhan* [Future and Development], No. 3, 1987.

Zhang Chunting. "China Displays Its Weapons, Equipment, and Technologies for the First Time," *Liaowang*, Oct. 20, 1986.

———. "Jiang Shengjie, a Chinese Expert on Nuclear Energy," *Liaowang*, overseas ed., July 20, 1987.

Zhang Dongfeng and Yan Xinfu. "The Missile Search Company in the Gobi Desert," *Jiefangjun Bao*, Jan. 19, 1989.

Zhang Hancheng. "Cherish the Memory of the Founder [of Our Navy]," in Yang Shangkun et al., *Yidai Yuanrong* [A Supreme Commander]. Beijing, 1991.

Zhang Heping. "Rocket Expert Wang Yongzhi Talks About His Understanding of Jiang Zemin's Speech," *Renmin Ribao*, overseas ed., May 21, 1990.

Zhang Heping and Zhang Guorong. "Our Naval Air Force Is Equipped with New Weapons and Equipment," *Renmin Ribao*, overseas ed., Jan. 13, 1987.

Zhang Hongru et al., chief eds. *Zhonghua Renmin Gongheguo Dashidian (1949–1988)* [A Glossary of Major Issues in the People's Republic of China (1949–1988)]. Beijing, 1989.

Zhang Huairui and Zhu Hengxing. "Resist the Enemy's Surprise Attacks on Our Country's Coastal Areas by Employing the Integrated Combat Capabilities of the Army, the Navy, and the Air Force," *Guofang Daxue Xuebao*, No. 7, 1987.

Zhang Jianzhi. "Views on Medium-Sized Nuclear Powers' Nuclear Strategy," *Jiefangjun Bao*, March 20, 1987, in FBIS: China, April 1, 1987.

Zhang Jiaxin. "New Mechanism for Solid Propellant Ignition," *Yuhang Xuebao* [Journal of the Chinese Society of Astronautics], No. 3 (July), 1990. Tr. in *Science and Technology: China*, JPRS-CST-90-029, Nov. 26, 1990.

Zhang Jiayu. "The Development of the Concept of People's War," *Mao Zedong Sixiang Yanjiu* [Studies on Mao Zedong's Thought] (Chengdu), No. 3, 1983.

———. "On the Nuclear Strategic Thought of Mao Zedong and Zhou Enlai," *Junshi Lishi Yanjiu* [Military History Studies]. Undated reprint.

———. "A Tentative Study of the Nuclear Strategic Thinking of Mao Zedong and Zhou Enlai," *Junshi Lishi Yanjiu* [Studies on Military History]. Undated reprint.

Zhang Jingfu. "The Chinese Academy of Sciences and Defense Science and Technology," in HGYZW.

Zhang Jinke and Zhou Wenbin. "Reminiscences on the Struggle of the Underground Party in Munitions Plant 70 in Beiping," in *Beiping Dixiadang Douzheng Shiliao* [Historical Data on the Struggle of the Underground Party in Beiping]. Beijing, 1988.

Zhang Jinqing. "The Exploitation of High-Tech Industries in Shijiazhuang," *Renmin Ribao*, overseas ed., Feb. 26, 1991.

Zhang Jinxi and Wang Xiancun. "Mao Zedong's Military Thought and Our Country's Nuclear Strategic Theory," *Junshi Zhishi* [Military Knowledge], No. 5, 1988.

Zhang Jun, chief ed. *Dangdai Zhongguo de Hangtian Shiye* [Contemporary China's Space Cause]. Beijing, 1986. Original draft "Dangdai Zhongguo de Hangtian Shiye Shugao," 1985. All citations are to the published version unless otherwise noted.

Zhang Ming. "An Interview with Chen Youming, Former Head of the Naval Equipment and Technology Department," *Jianchuan Zhishi*, No. 3, 1989.

———. "The Navy Takes Measures to Induce Officers to Stay On," *Jiefangjun Bao*, June 29, 1987.

Zhang Ming and Shen Shungen. "An Interview with Director of the China Warship Research and Design Academy Lu Jianxun," *Jiefangjun Bao*, April 20, 1989.

Zhang Minjie and Lan Gongjue. "The Development of the New China's Shipbuilding Industry," *Junshi Shilin*, No. 3, 1991.

Zhang Nan. "Historical Facts Cannot Be Altered," *Jiefangjun Bao*, Aug. 30, 1988.

Zhang Pan. "Speech on Our Country's Economic Situation and Strategy," *Xuebao* [Learned Journal] (Institute for International Technical Economy, Beijing), No. 1, 1987.

Zhang Ping. "Submarine Fleet Leads Chinese Naval Force," *China Daily*, Sept. 28, 1989.

Zhang Pingli. "A Major Technological Breakthrough in Our Shipbuilding Industry," *Renmin Ribao*, overseas ed., Jan. 17, 1987.

Zhang Qinsheng and Zhang Chunting. "Reform and Opening [to the Outside World] Have Caused Thoroughgoing Changes in the Chinese Army," *Liaowang*, overseas ed., April 21, 1986.

Zhang Qinsheng et al. "A Consideration of the Strategy for the Development of National Defense," *Jiefangjun Bao*, March 21, 1986.

———. "Research on and Exploration of the Theory of Localized War," *Liaowang*, overseas ed., Sept. 15, 1986.

Zhang Taiheng. "Integrate Picked Regular Troops with Powerful Reserve Forces," *Jiefangjun Bao*, June 5, 1987.

Zhang Tuosheng. "Deng Xiaoping and the 1975 Overall Shakeup," in *Zhonggong Dangshi Fengyun Lu* [Records of the Main Events in CCP History]. Beijing, 1990.

Zhang Wei and Jun Qi. *Xiao Jinguang Dajiang* [Fleet Admiral Xiao Jinguang]. Zhengzhou, 1987.

Zhang Wenxi. "The Finalization of the Design of the T2-1 Mine-Monitoring Display," *Junshi Shijie*, No. 3, 1988.

Zhang Xia et al., eds. *Qingmo Haijun Shiliao* [Historical Materials on the Navy of the Late Qing Dynasty]. Beijing, 1982.

Zhang Xinghua et al. *Shenmi de Shiming Zhongguo Haifang Daodan Shiyanchang Fazhan Jishi* [A Mysterious Mission: A Description of the Development of China's Naval Missile Test Range]. Beijing, 1988.

Zhang Xinxin. "Probing the Mystery of the Chinese Navy's Submarine Institute," in FBIS: China, Sept. 4, 1986.

Zhang Xiuying. "An Exploration into the International Origin of the 1958 'Left'

Rash Advance," *Shixue Yuekan* [Historical Studies Monthly] (Zhengzhou), No. 4, 1989.

Zhang Yimin. "Advance Along the Course Charted by Chairman Mao, Build the Strongest People's Navy in the World," *Renmin Ribao*, Dec. 7, 1967.

Zhang Yining. "A Survey of Defense Construction in Peacetime," *Jiefangjun Bao*, Jan. 31, 1989.

Zhang Yuanping. "The Successful Trial Voyage of a Submarine in the Changjiang River," *Jiefangjun Bao*, Sept. 16, 1987.

Zhang Yunsheng. *Maojiawan Jishi Lin Biao Mishu Huiyilu* [What I Saw and Heard in Maojiawan: The Memoirs of a Secretary of Lin Biao]. Beijing, 1988.

Zhang Ze'nan. "'*Dongyun 615*'—China's Oceangoing Fuel/Water Supply Ship," *Junshi Shijie*, No. 1, 1990.

———. "Guards on the Nansha—A Visit to the Chinese Sailors Who First Ascended the Atolls [of the Nansha Islands]," *Jianchuan Zhishi*, No. 10, 1988.

———. "New Developments in the Modern Construction of the Chinese Navy," *Jianchuan Zhishi*, No. 8, 1987.

Zhang Zhaozhong. "Modern Communication with Submarines," *Junshi Shijie*, No. 3, 1989.

Zhang Zhen. "Several Questions About the Development of Operational Arts for Our Army," *Guofang Daxue Xuebao*, No. 2, 1986.

Zhang Zhongpei and Zhang Hua. "The Gansu Military District Ensures Military Installations Closely Sealed in Receiving Foreign Guests," *Jiefangjun Bao*, May 4, 1987.

Zhang Zongxun. *Zhang Zongxun Huiyilu* [Memoirs of Zhang Zongxun]. Beijing, 1990.

Zhanlüe Xue [Strategy]. Beijing, 1982.

Zhao Dexin, chief ed. (the following collections were all published in Zhengzhou; the first appeared in 1988, and the others in 1989)

[1]. *Zhonghua Renmin Gongheguo Jingji Shi (1949–1966)* [The Economic History of the People's Republic of China (1949–1966)].

[2]. *Zhonghua Renmin Gongheguo Jingji Shi (1967–1984)* [The Economic History of the People's Republic of China (1967–1984)].

[3]. *Zhonghua Renmin Gongheguo Jingji Zhuanti Dashiji (1949–1966)* [Specialized Chronology on the Economy of the People's Republic of China (1949–1966)].

[4]. *Zhonghua Renmin Gongheguo Jingji Zhuanti Dashiji (1967–1984)* [Specialized Chronology on the Economy of the People's Republic of China (1967–1984)].

Zhao Jianhua. "Our Country's Largest Wave-Water Tank," *Hanghai* [Navigation], No. 2, 1980.

Zhao Linsen. "How Mao Zedong Misunderstood Peng Dehuai's Opinions at the Lushan Plenum," *Dangshi Wenhui* [Collection on Party History], No. 1, 1988.

Zhao Shaokui. "Why Can a Missile Hit Its Target Accurately?" *Hangtian*, No. 2, 1990.

Zheng Chiying. "Motherland, I Dedicate Myself to You," *Jiefangjun Wenyi* [Literature and Art of the Liberation Army], No. 7, 1984.

Zheng Hantao and Li Ruhong. "A Look Back on 40 Years of Defense Industry," in HGYZW.

Zheng He. "Underwater-to-Surface Missiles," *Bingqi Zhishi* [Ordnance Knowledge], No. 3, 1989.

Zheng He and Long Yunhe. "A Successful Flight Test of a Missile from a Submerged Chinese-Made Nuclear-Powered Submarine," *Junshi Shijie*, No. 3, 1988.

Zheng Ming et al. "Modern Naval Technology (3)," *Jianchuan Zhishi*, No. 12, 1990.

Zheng Qianli. "Close-ups of *Distant Observer* Instrumentation Ships," in *Shenjian Zhulian Qu* [The Casting of a Magical Sword]. Beijing, 1987.

———. "Deep Love," *Shenjian* [Magical Sword], No. 2, 1988.

Zheng Shuyan and Xu Wenliang. "A Description of the Guizhou Astronautics Industry Corporation," *Jiefangjun Bao*, Aug. 3, 1989.

Zheng Wenhan. "Chief Peng's Great Contributions to the Building of Our Army in the 1950s," *Junshi Lishi*, No. 6, 1988.

Zhi Shaozeng. "Essentials of the Evolution of the Central Military Commission," *Junshi Lishi*, No. 6, 1989.

Zhi Yin. "A Chronicle of China's Weapons Technology," *Junshi Shijie*, No. 2, 1990.

———. "Defense Electronic Technology in China," *Junshi Shijie*, No. 1, 1990.

———. "Inside Stories About China's Nuclear-Powered Submarines," *Junshi Shijie*, No. 6, 1989.

Zhong Wen. "Ablative Materials of Rockets and Missiles," *Hangkong Zhishi*, No. 3, 1976.

Zhong Xie, ed. *Qianting Jichu Zhishi* [Basic Knowledge of Submarines]. Beijing, 1985.

Zhong Yi. "A Brief Introduction to Chinese Space Scientists," *Hangtian*, No. 5, 1988.

Zhonggong Dangshi Yanjiu Lunwenxuan [Selected Research Papers on CCP History]. Beijing, 1984, Vol. 2.

Zhongguo Dianzi Gongye Qishiye Minglu [List of Chinese Electronics Industrial Enterprises]. Beijing, 1985.

Zhongguo Gongchandang Jianshi Jiangyi [Teaching Materials on a Summary History of the CCP]. Guangzhou, 1985.

Zhongguo Qiye Gaikuang [A Directory of Chinese Enterprises]. Beijing, 1988, Vol. 4.

Zhongguo Renmin Jiefangjun Fazhan Xulie (1927–1949) [The Evolution of the Battle Order of the Chinese People's Liberation Army (1927–1949)]. Beijing, 1985.

Zhongguo Renmin Jiefangjun Jiangshuai Minglu [Biographic Dictionary of the Generals and Marshals of the PLA]. Beijing, 1986, Vol. 1.

Zhongguo Shenzhen Jishu Jiaoyihui Huikan [China Shenzhen Technology Fair Bulletin]. Shenzhen, 1986.

Zhou Enlai. "The Implementation of the First Five-Year Plan and the Basic Tasks of the Second Five-Year Plan" [Sept. 16, 1956], in *Zhou Enlai Xuanji* [Selected Works of Zhou Enlai] (Beijing, 1984), Vol. 2.

Zhou Guoquan et al. *Wang Ming Pingzhuan* [A Critical Biography of Wang Ming]. Hefei, 1989.

Zhou Jiading. "Zhou Enlai's Outstanding Contributions to the New China's National Defense Program," *Guofang Daxue Xuebao*, No. 5, 1988.

Zhou Qing. "What I Saw and Heard from the Oceangoing Instrumentation Ships," *Renmin Ribao*, overseas ed., Feb. 22, 1986.

Zhou Xiao. "Chinese Space Scientists," *Renmin Ribao*, Aug. 16, 1985.

Zhou Zhenhua. "A Historic Evaluation of the Distribution of Productive Forces After the Founding of the Republic," *Mao Zedong Sixiang Yanjiu* [Studies on Mao Zedong's Thought] (Chengdu), No. 4, 1990.

Zhu Bin. "Revelations on China's Naval Air Force," *Jianchuan Zhishi*, No. 12, 1990.

Zhu Bin and Chen Ming. "Successful Development of the Training Mine That Surfaces as a Whole," *Jiefangjun Bao*, Dec. 22, 1987.

Zhu Dacheng and He Delai. "A Combined-Forces Exercise Conducted by the Three Armed Services of the Guangzhou Military Region," *Jiefangjun Bao*, Nov. 8, 1988.

Zhu De. *Selected Works of Zhu De*. Beijing, 1986.

Zhu Guangya. "Around the Explosion of Our Country's First Atomic Bomb," in *Bujin de Sinian* [Boundless Recollections]. Beijing, 1987.

Zhu Jianhong. "A Description of the New China's Shipbuilding Industry," *Renmin Ribao*, overseas ed., Oct. 4, 1989.

Zhu Jinping. "The General Staff Circulates a Notice Commending 'Mapping Brigade No. 1,'" *Jiefangjun Bao*, June 22, 1988.

Zhu Jizhong and Cai Chuandao. "The Everlasting Military Spirit: Luo Ruiqing and Guo Xingfu," *Zhongshan* [Zhong Mountain] (Nanjing), No. 1, 1990.

Zhu Lemin. "The Successful Navigation of the Submarine Depends on Its Able Designers," *Renmin Ribao*, overseas ed., Dec. 1, 1985.

Zhu Songchun. "Chinese Scholars Are Probing into the Developmental Strategy for National Defense for the Year 2,000," *Liaowang*, overseas ed., July 21, 1986.

Zhu Yida. "The Combat Use of Nuclear Submarines," *Junshi Shijie*, No. 3, 1990.

———. "Consideration of the 'Saddle-Back' Road," *Jiefangjun Bao*, Jan. 12, 1988.

———. "An Important Link in Bringing Up Commanding Officers from the Ranks of Exemplary Sailors," *Jiefangjun Bao*, Jan. 9, 1990.

Zhu Youdi. "The Formation of a Chemical Defense Industry Network," *Jiefangjun Bao*, Dec. 7, 1990.

Zhu Zhongli. *Liming yu Wanxia* [Dawn and Sunset]. Beijing, 1986.

———. *Nanyi Wangque de Zuotian Wang Jiaxiang Xiaozhuan* [The Unforgettable Yesterday: Profile of Wang Jiaxiang]. Xiamen, 1987.

Zhuang Fenggan. "Our Country's Aerodynamics Program," in HGYZW.

Zou Dayi and Cao Huanrong. "Eyewitness to the Launch of a Missile from a Submerged Submarine of Our Country," *Renmin Ribao*, overseas ed., Sept. 28, 1988.

Zou Dayi and Jiang Rubiao. "The Great Success Achieved by the Naval Test Base over the Past Three Decades," *Renmin Ribao*, overseas ed., Oct. 20, 1988.

Zou Jiahua, chief ed. *Zhongguo Dabaike Quanshu Hangkong Hangtian* [Chinese Encyclopedia: Aeronautics and Astronautics]. Beijing, 1985.

Zu Wei. "An Illustrious but Unknown Course of Life," *Wenhui Yuekan* [Encounter Monthly] (Shanghai), No. 6, 1987.

Zu Wei and Lin Pukai, "A Description of Reactor Engineering Specialist Peng Shilu," in *He Kexuejia de Zuji* [The Footprints Left by the Nuclear Scientists]. Beijing, 1989.

Zuo Yang. "Rockets and Powders," *Hangkong Zhishi* [Aerospace Knowledge], No. 6, 1977.

Zuo Ying. "Cherish the Memory of Comrade Liu Peishan," *Fujian Dangshi Yuekan* [Fujian Party's History Monthly], No. 7, 1987.

Index

Library of Congress Cataloging-in-Publication Data

Lewis, John Wilson, 1930–
    China's strategic seapower : the politics of force modernization
in the nuclear age / John Wilson Lewis and Xue Litai.
        p.   cm. — (Studies in international security and arms
control)
    Includes bibliographical references (p.   ) and index.
    ISBN 0-8047-2303-6 (alk. paper)
    1. Sea-power—China—History. 2. Nuclear submarines—China—
History. 3. Fleet ballistic missile weapons systems—China—
History. 4. China—History—1976– . I. Xue, Litai, 1947– .
II. Title. III. Series.
VA633.L48   1994
359.9'3834—dc20   94-11688
                                                         CIP

  ⊗ This book is printed on acid-free paper.